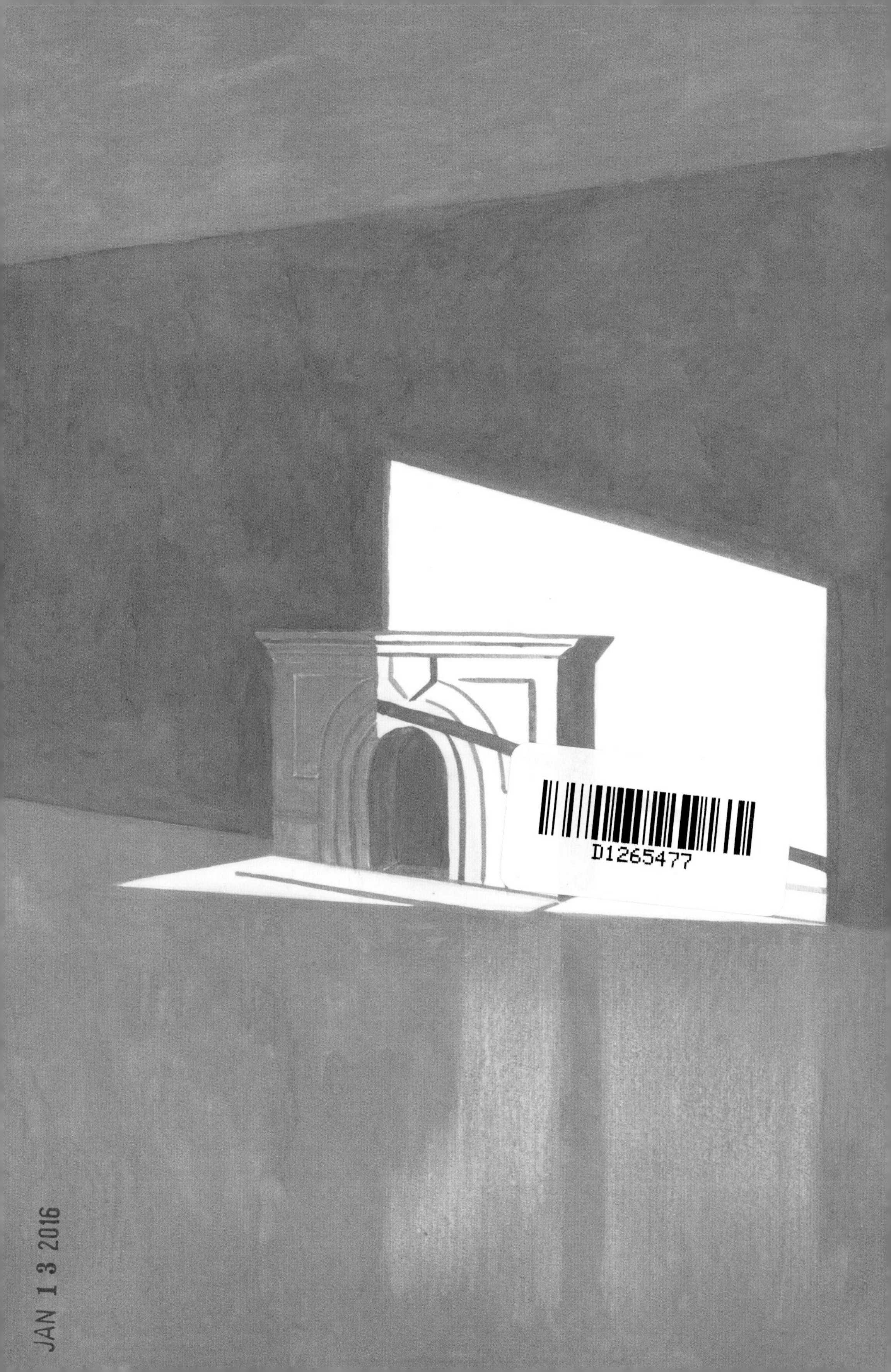

HERE

RICHARD MCGUIRE

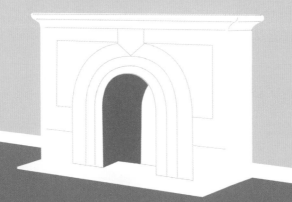

Pantheon Books

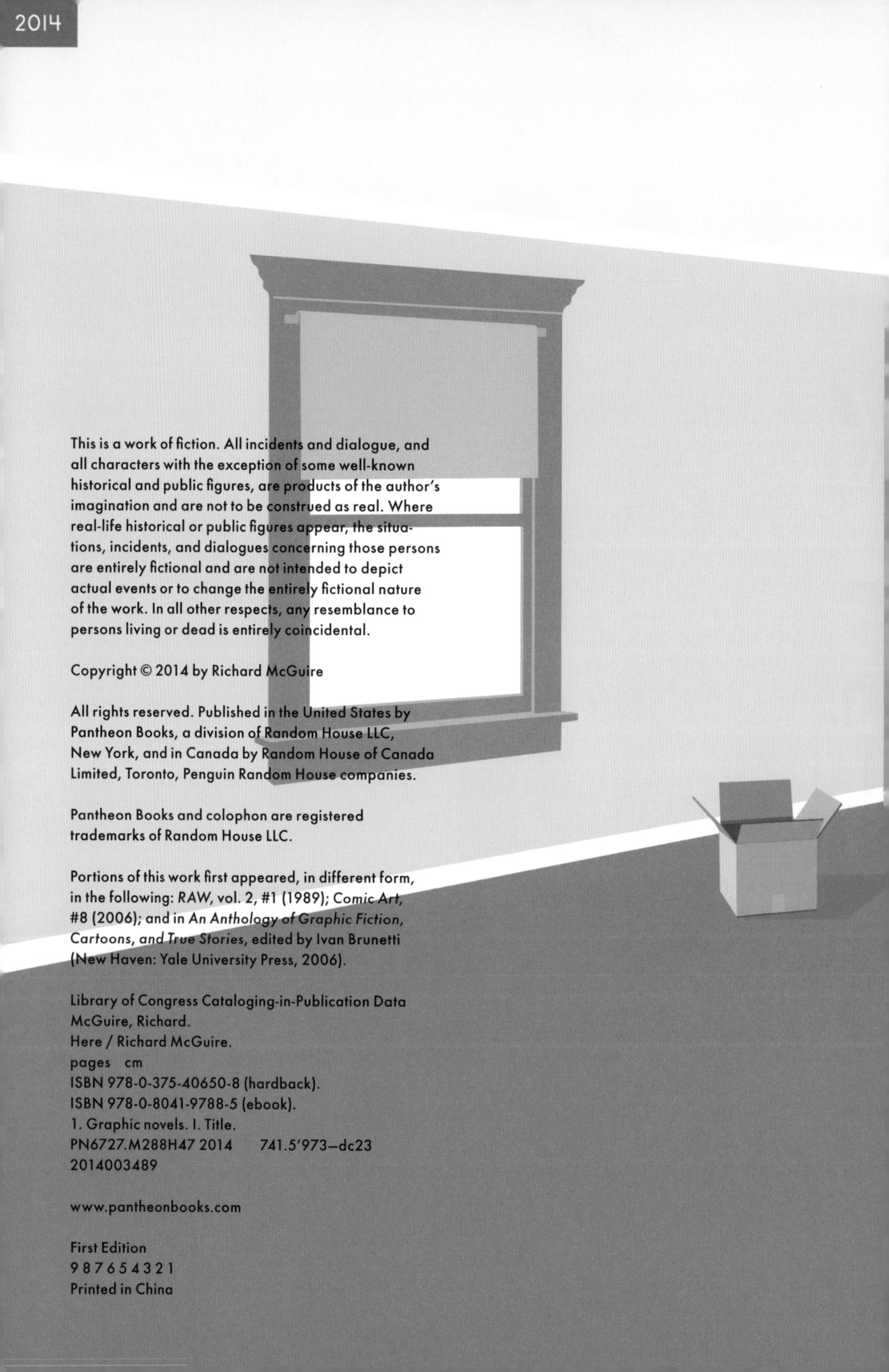
2014

Pantheon Books and colophon are registered trademarks of Random House LLC.

Portions of this work first appeared, in different form, in the following: *RAW*, vol. 2, #1 (1989); *Comic Art*, #8 (2006); and in *An Anthology of Graphic Fiction, Cartoons, and True Stories*, edited by Ivan Brunetti (New Haven: Yale University Press, 2006).

Library of Congress Cataloging-in-Publication Data
McGuire, Richard.
Here / Richard McGuire.
pages cm
ISBN 978-0-375-40650-8 (hardback).
ISBN 978-0-8041-9788-5 (ebook).
1. Graphic novels. I. Title.
PN6727.M288H47 2014 741.5'973—dc23
2014003489

www.pantheonbooks.com

First Edition
9 8 7 6 5 4 3 2 1
Printed in China

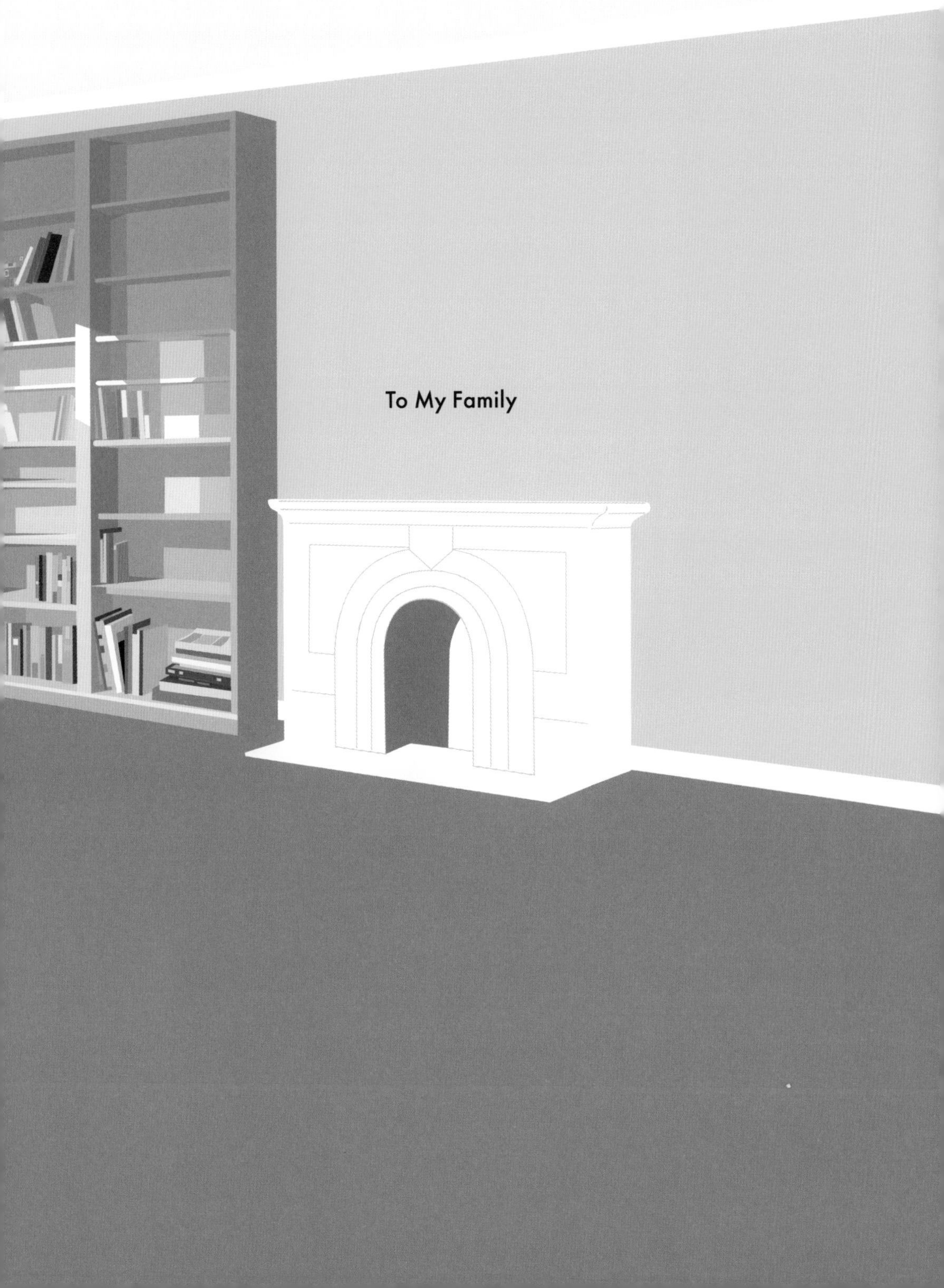

To My Family

1957

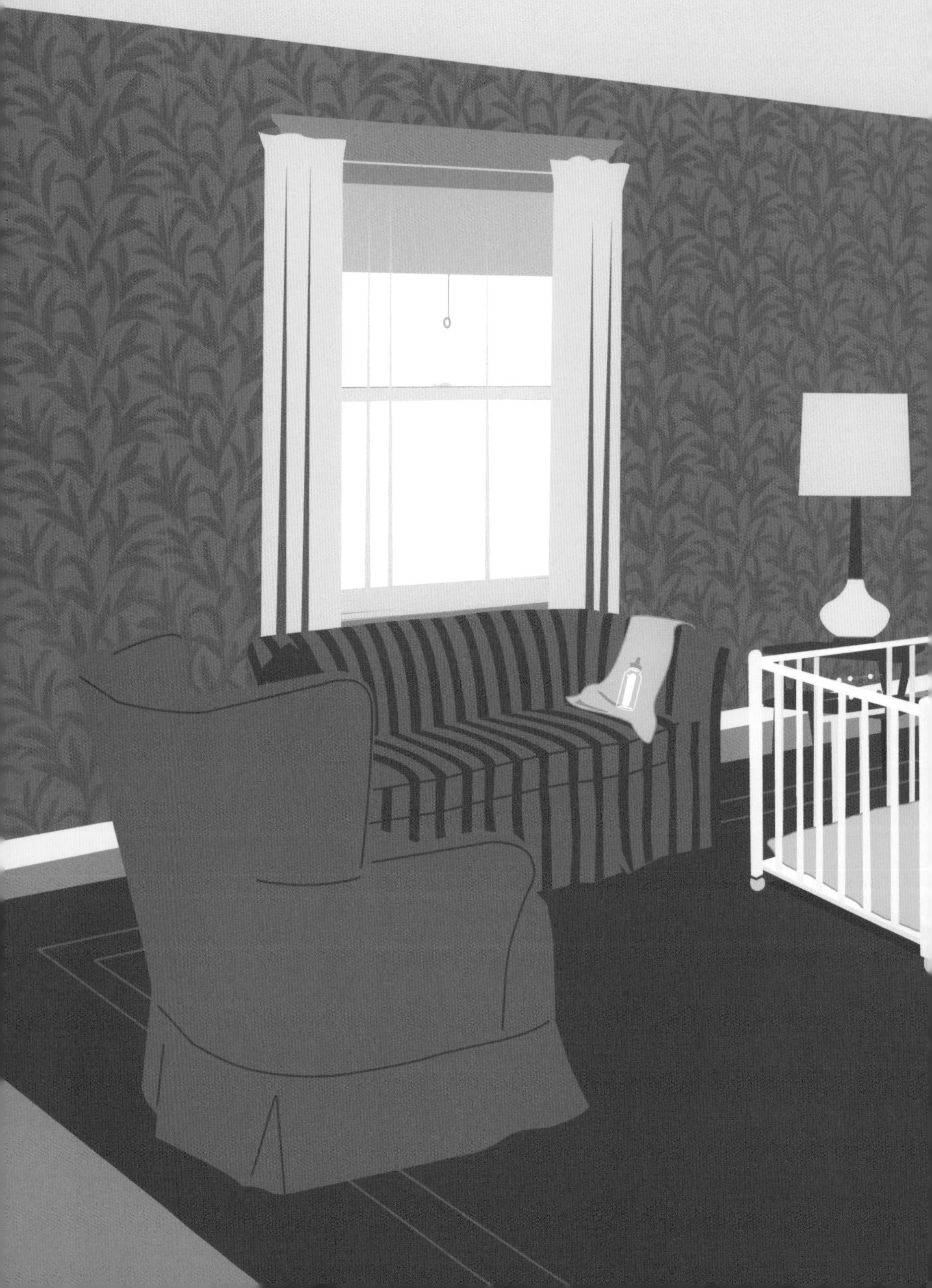

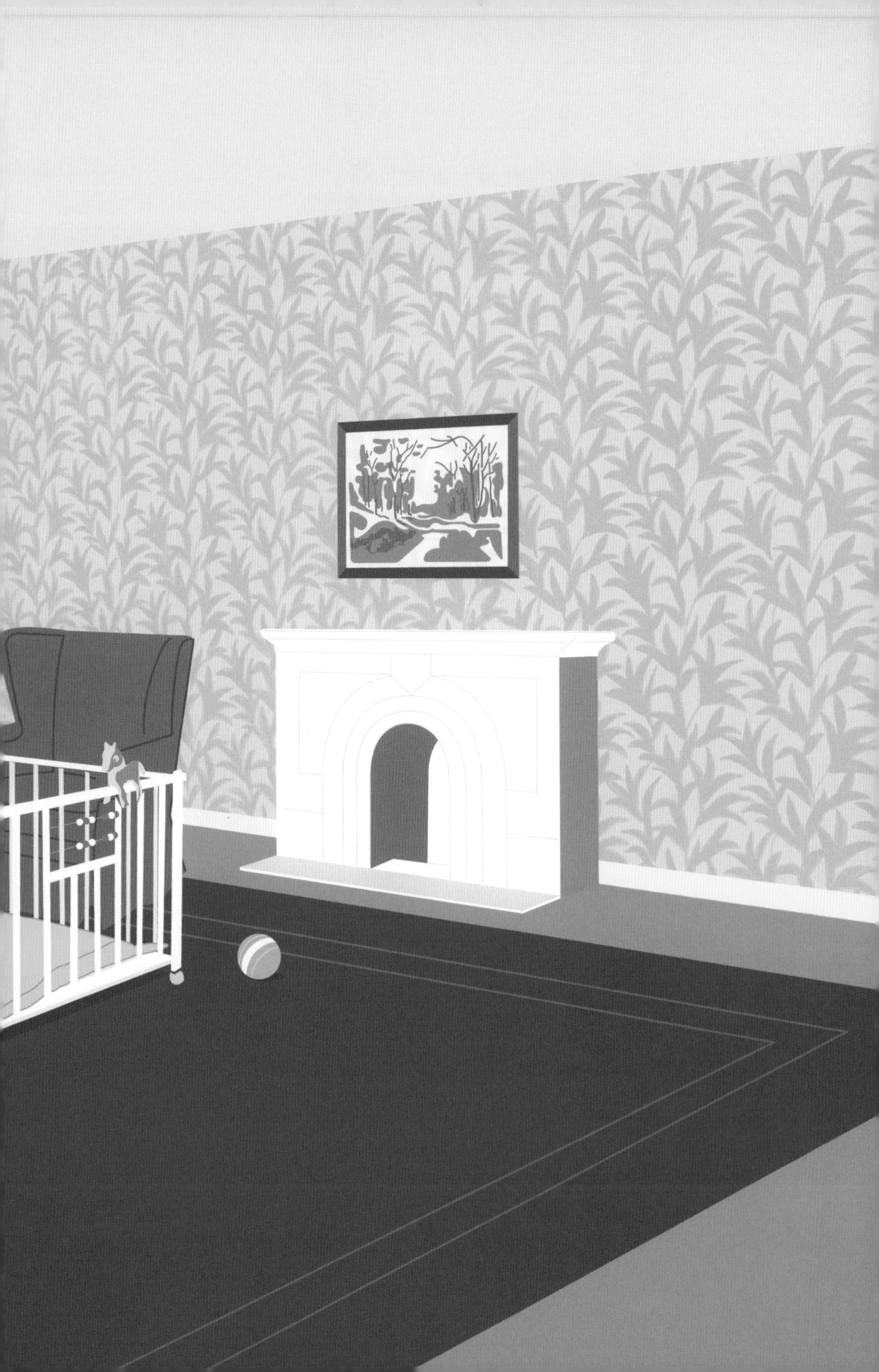

1942

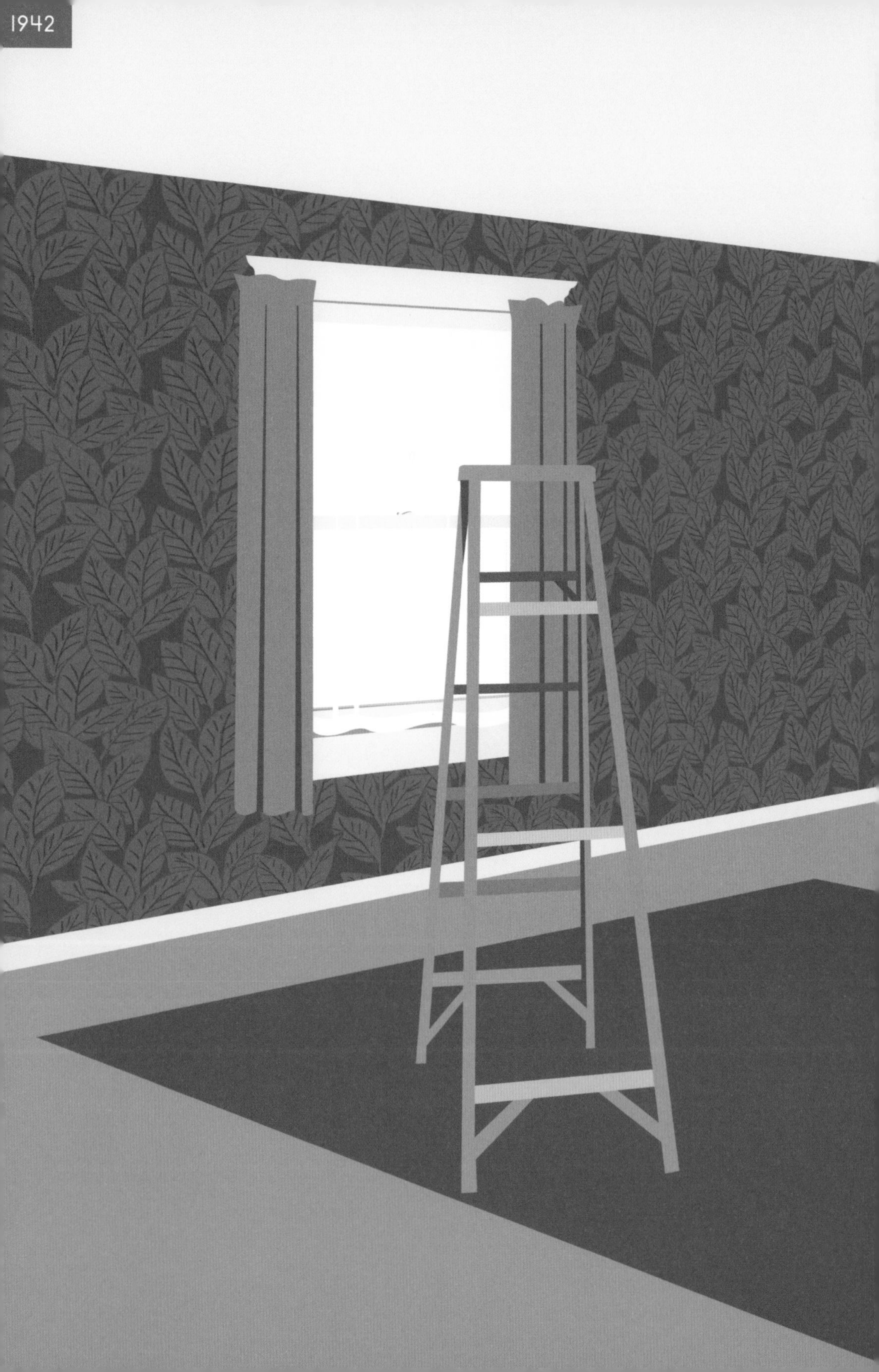

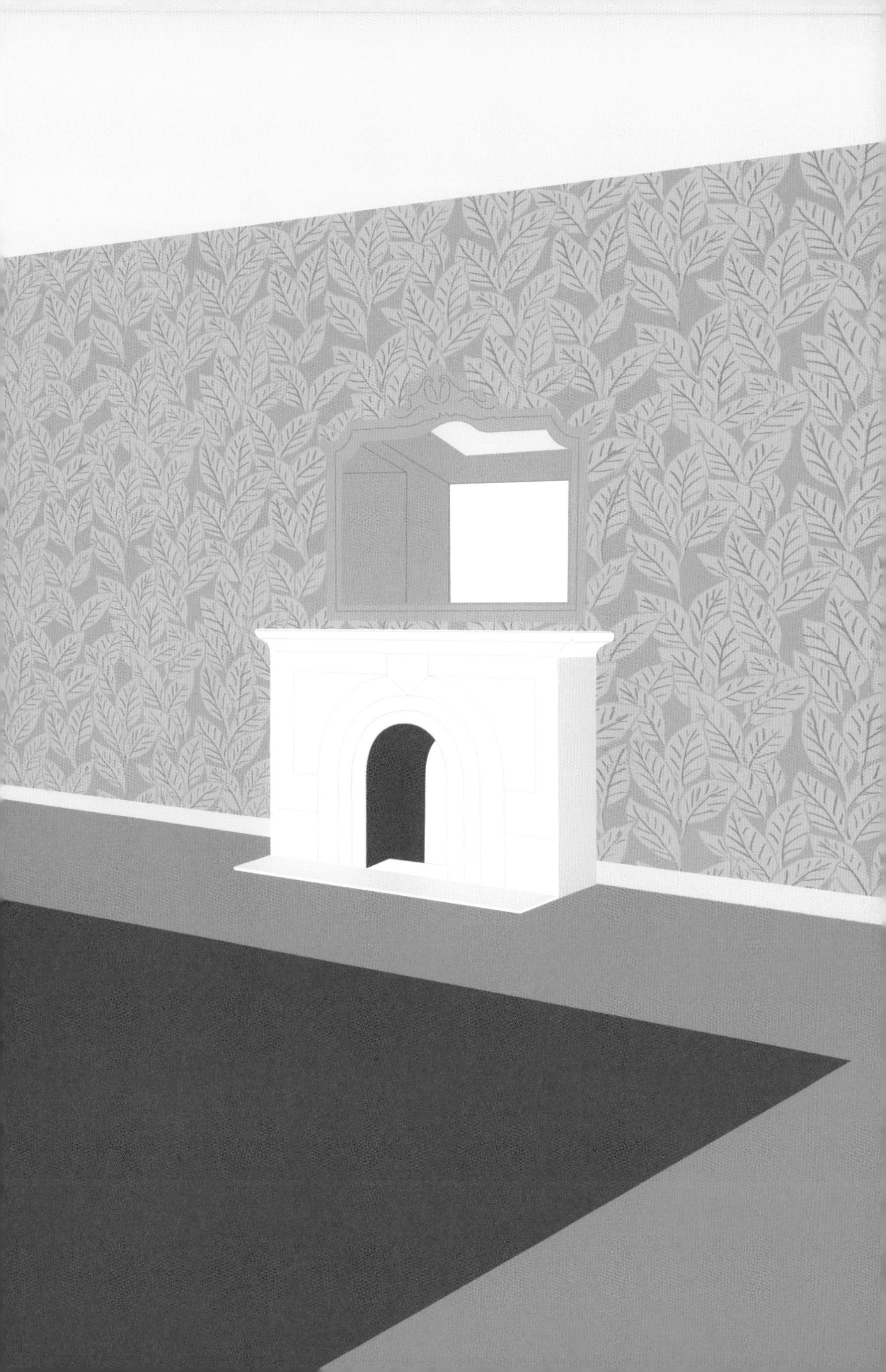

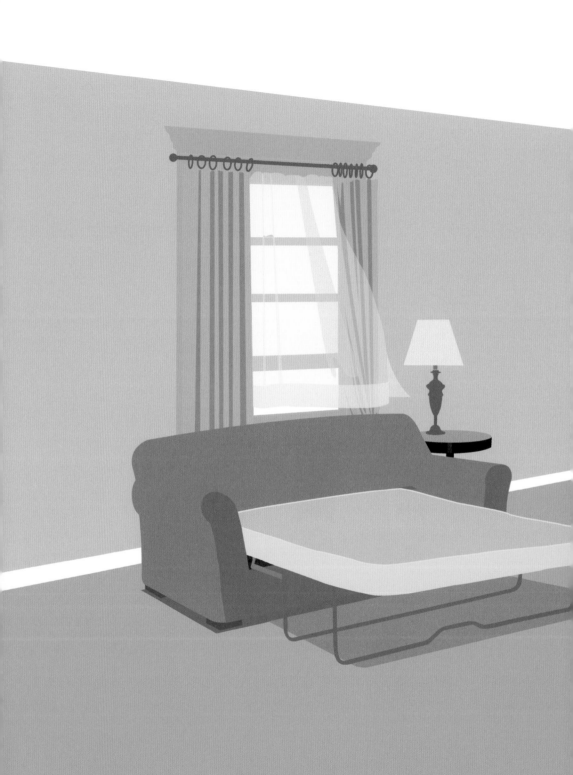

1957

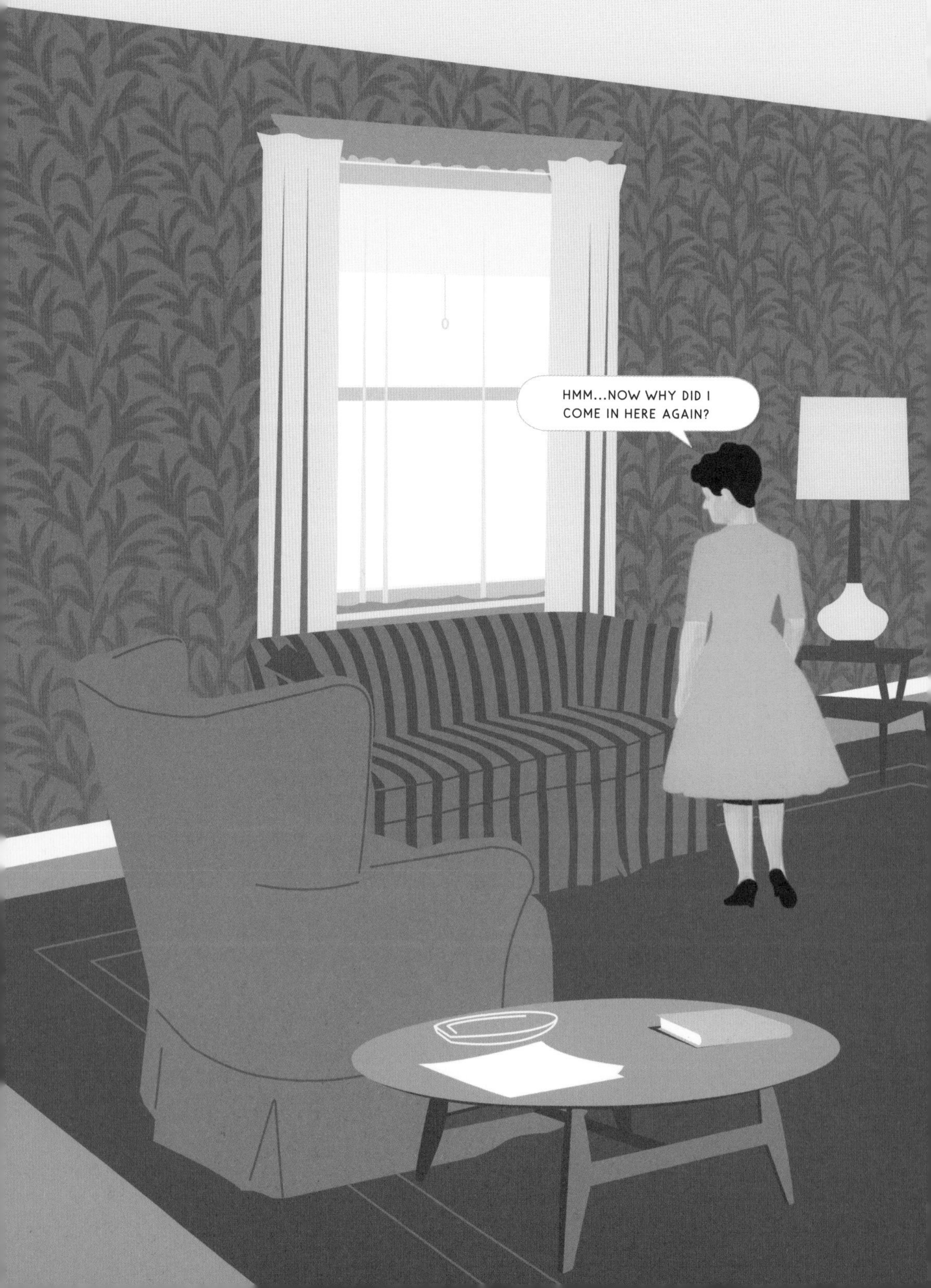
HMM...NOW WHY DID I COME IN HERE AGAIN?

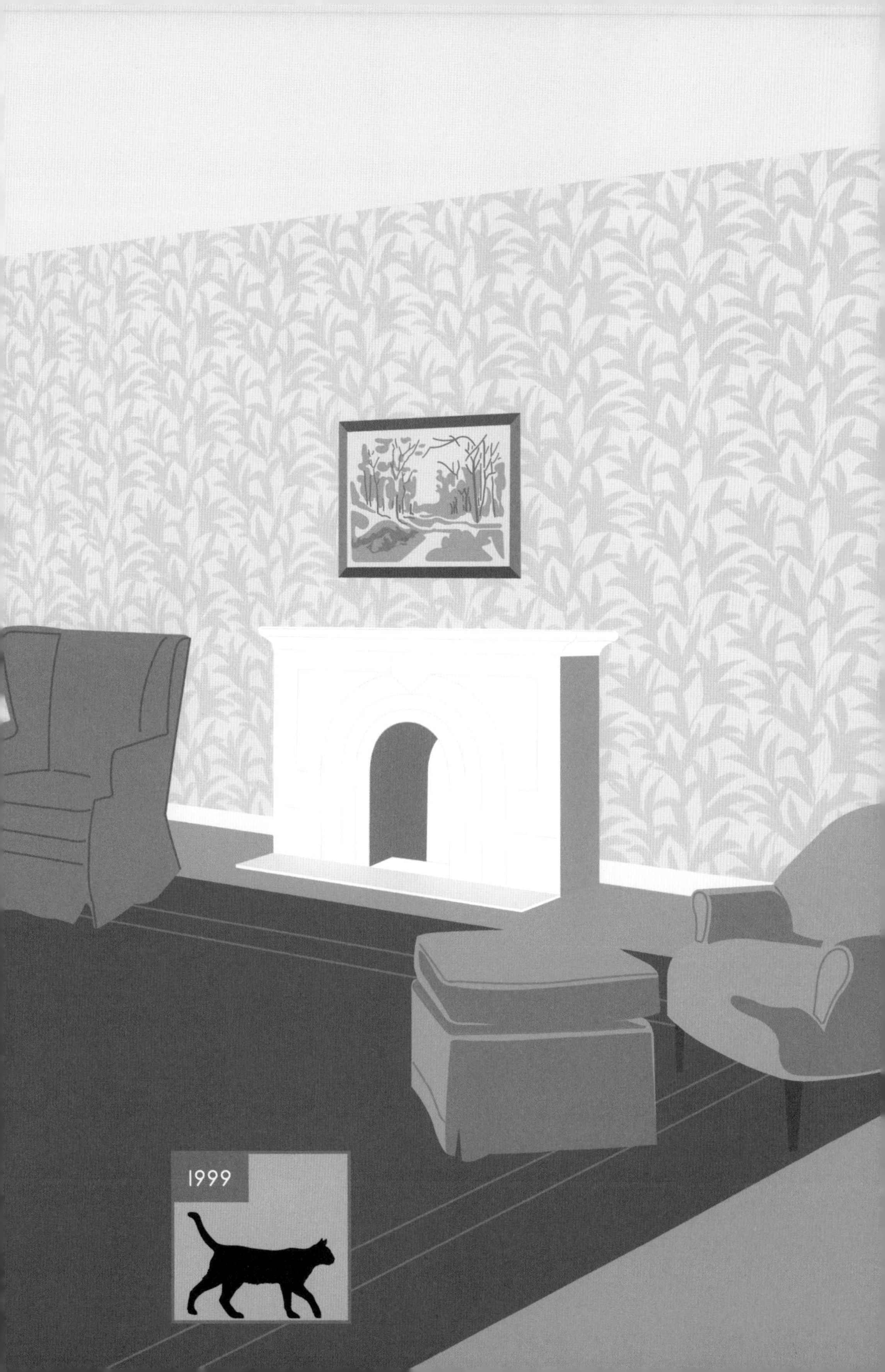
1999

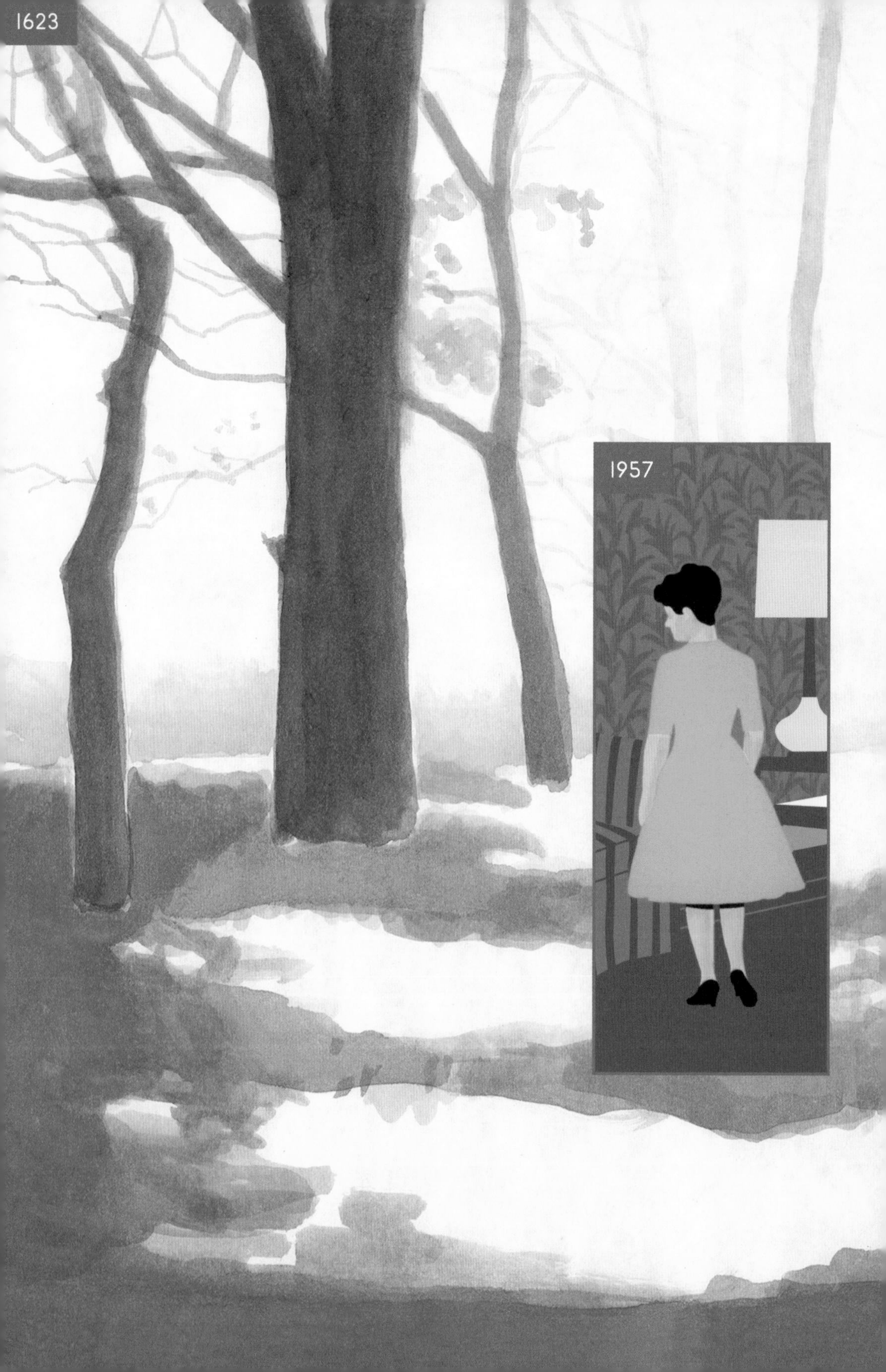
1623
1957

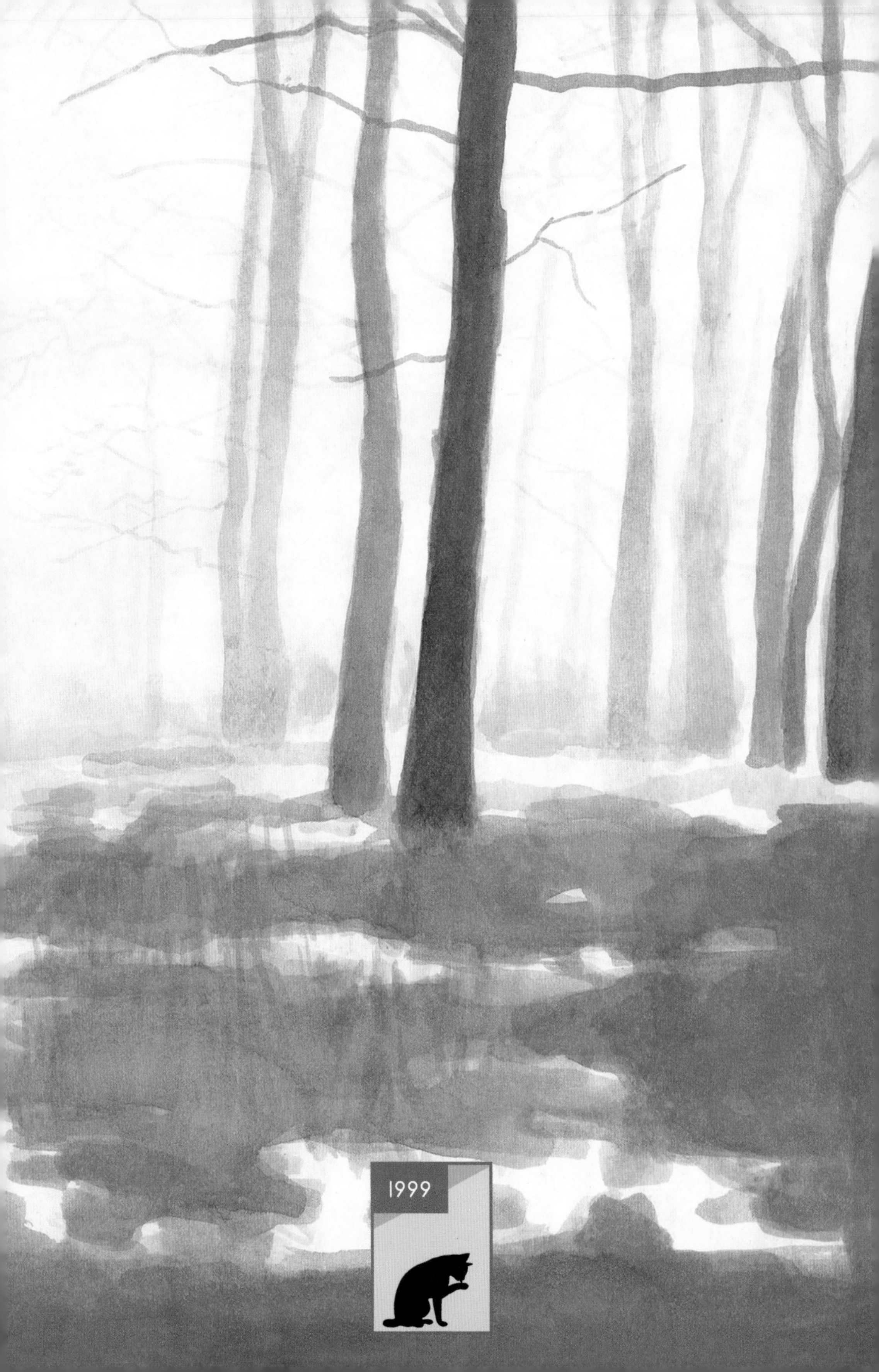

1999

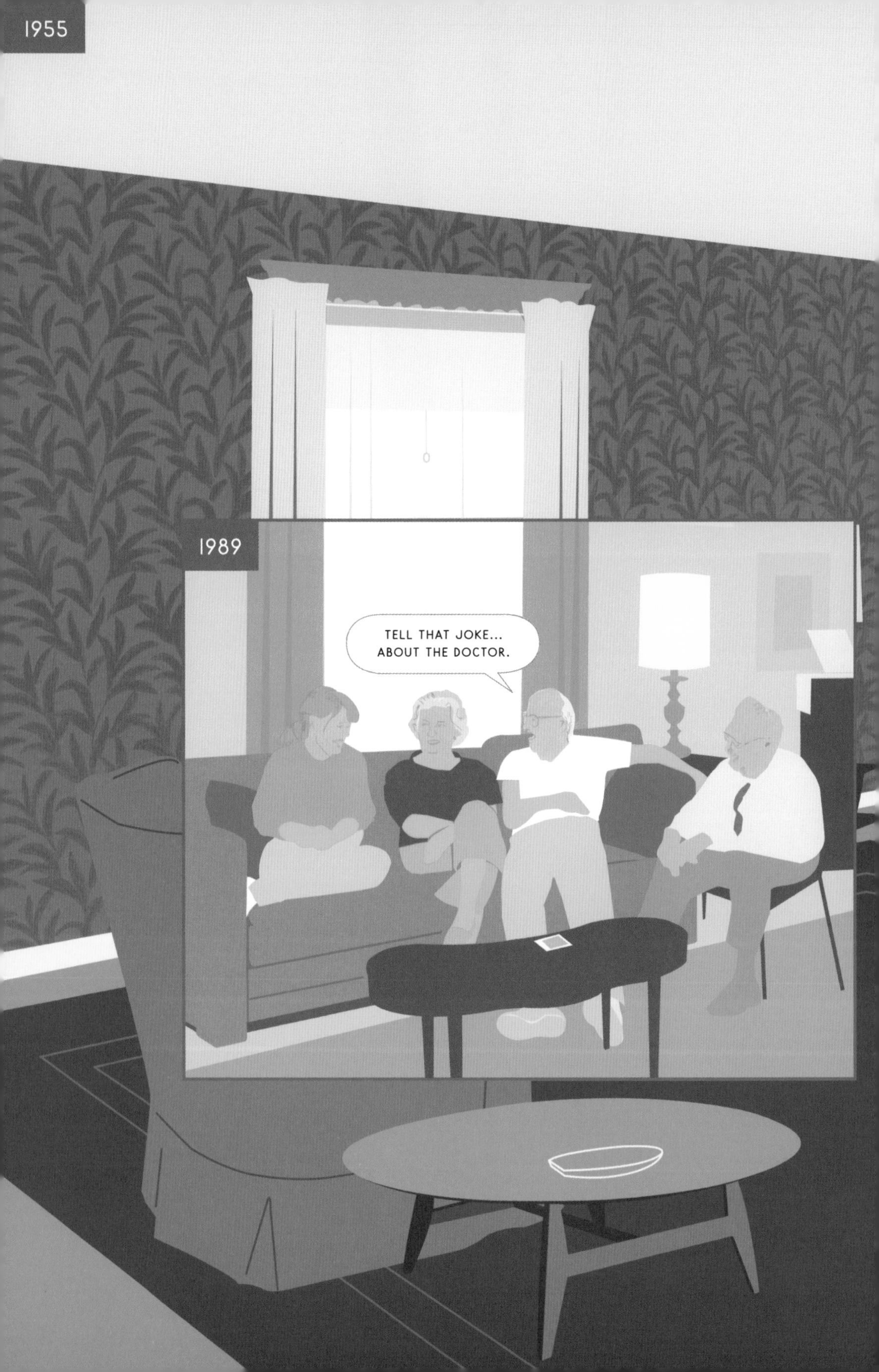
1955
1989
TELL THAT JOKE...
ABOUT THE DOCTOR.

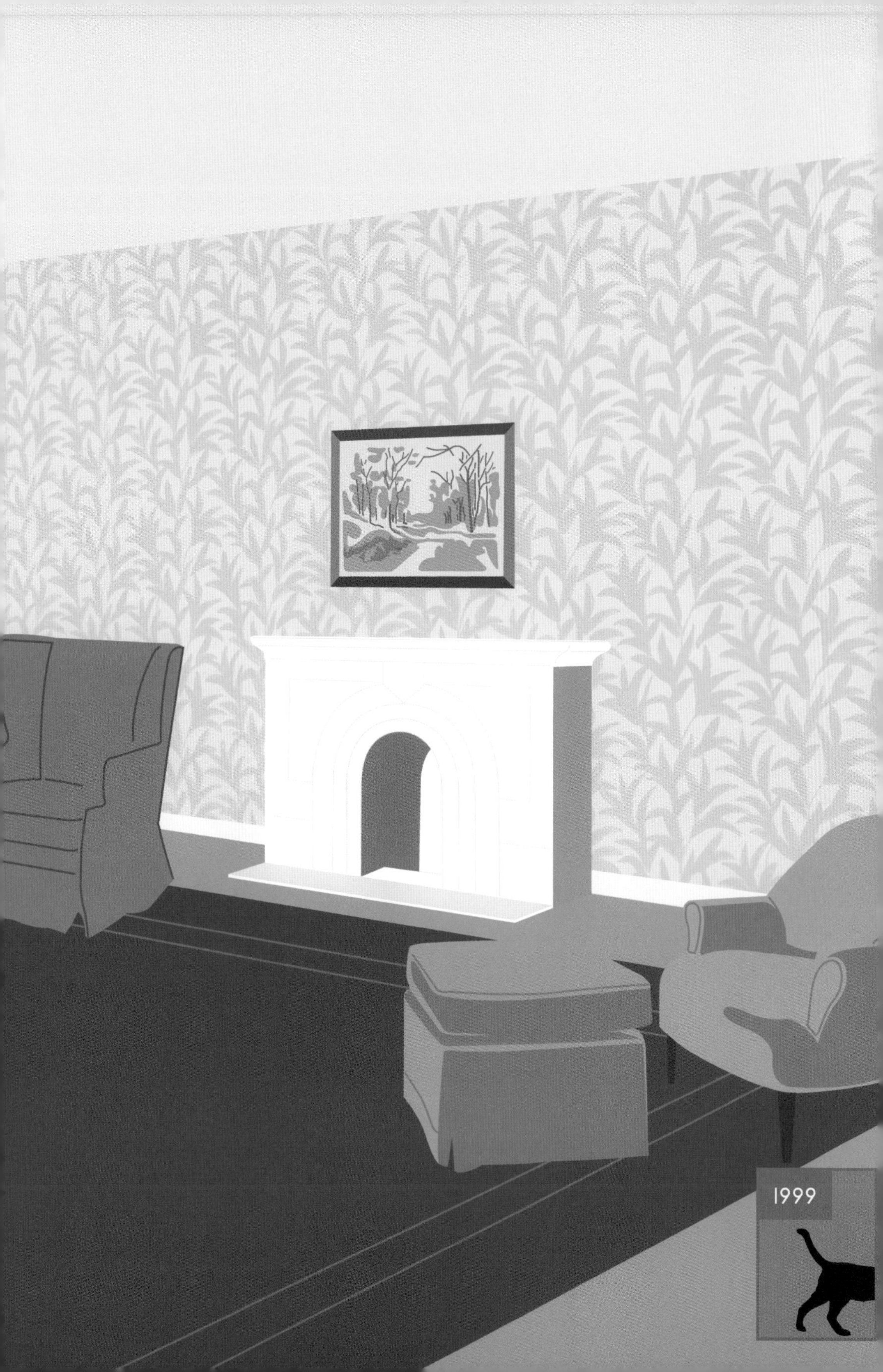
1999

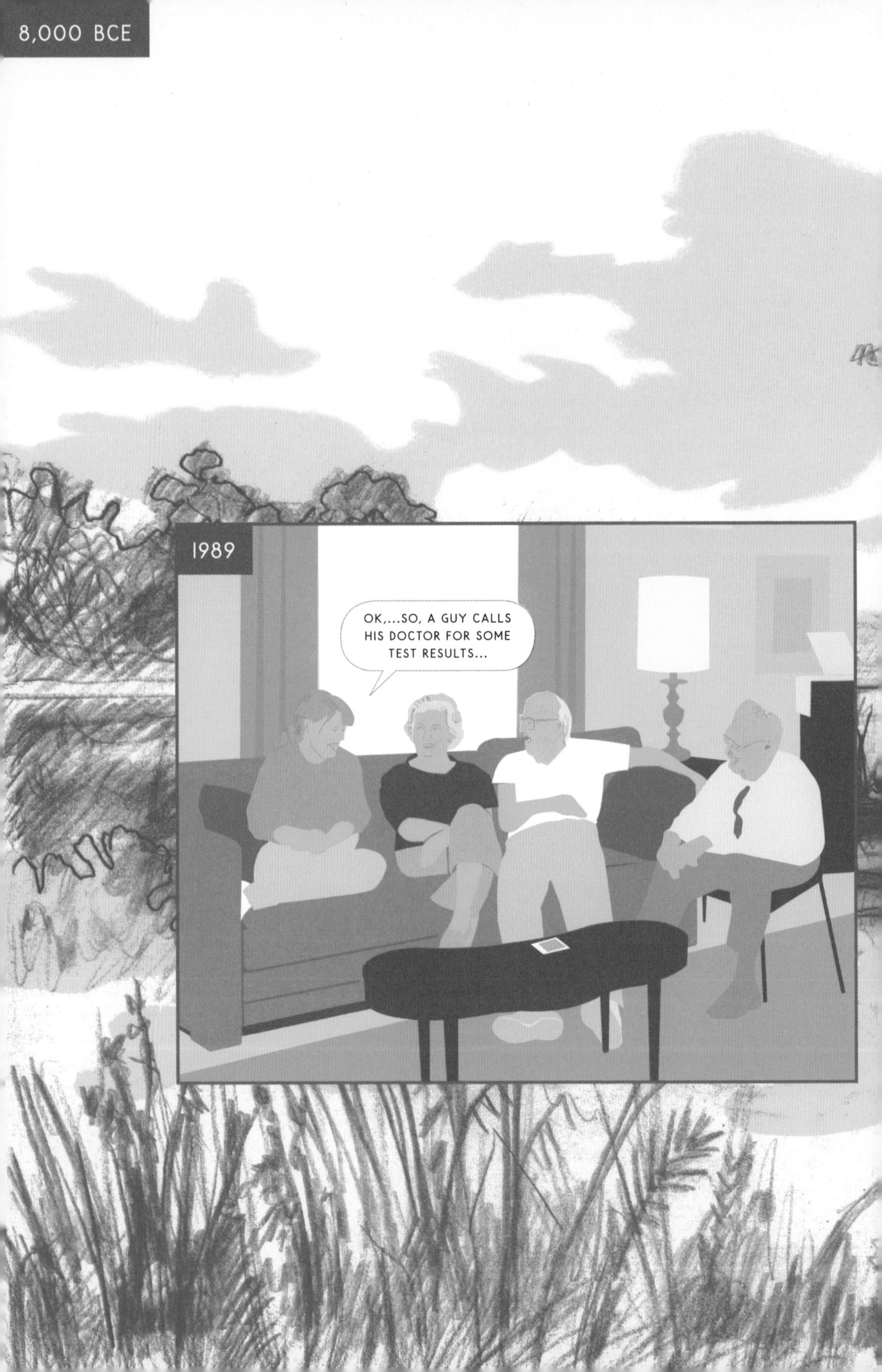
8,000 BCE
1989
OK,...SO, A GUY CALLS HIS DOCTOR FOR SOME TEST RESULTS...

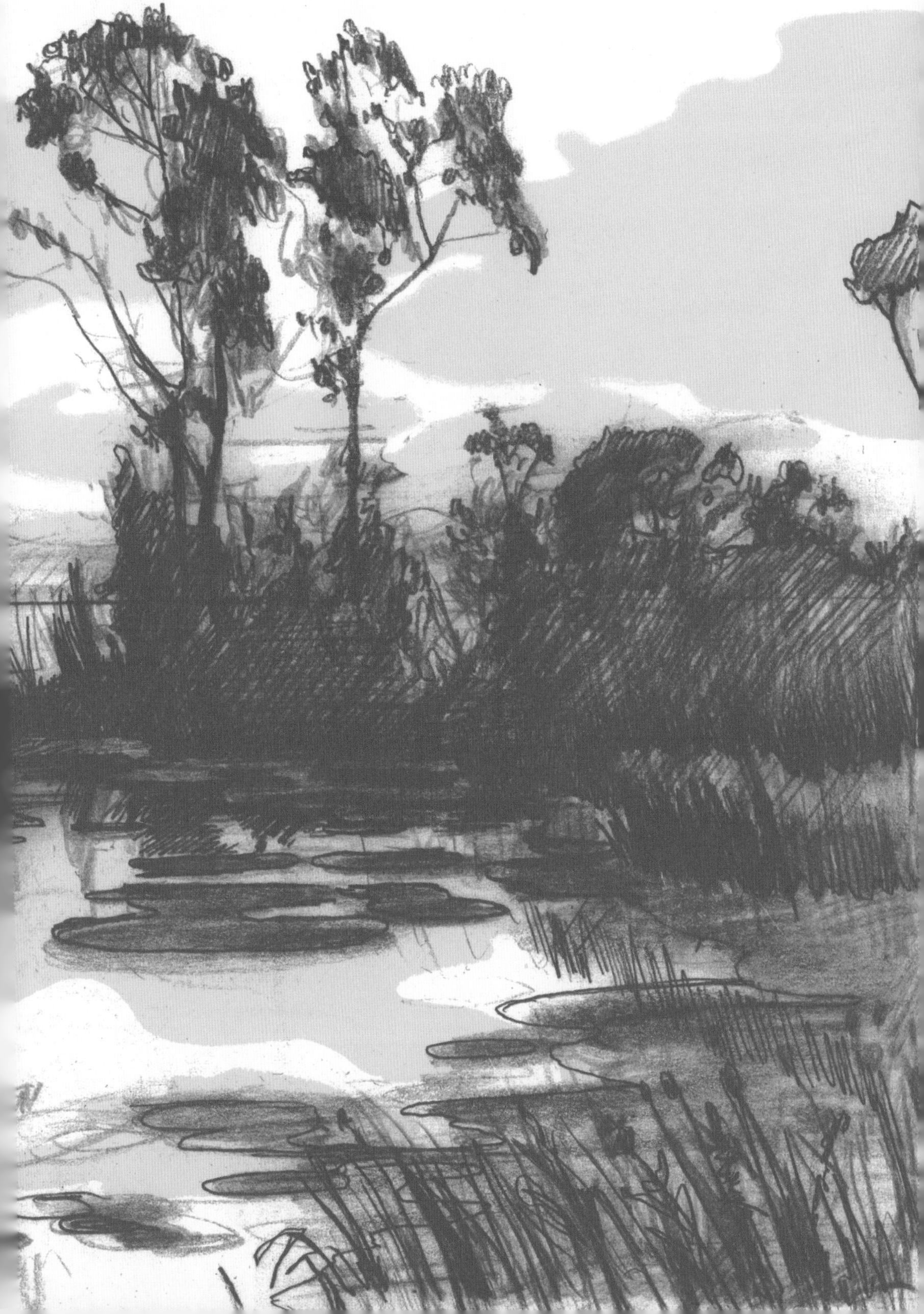

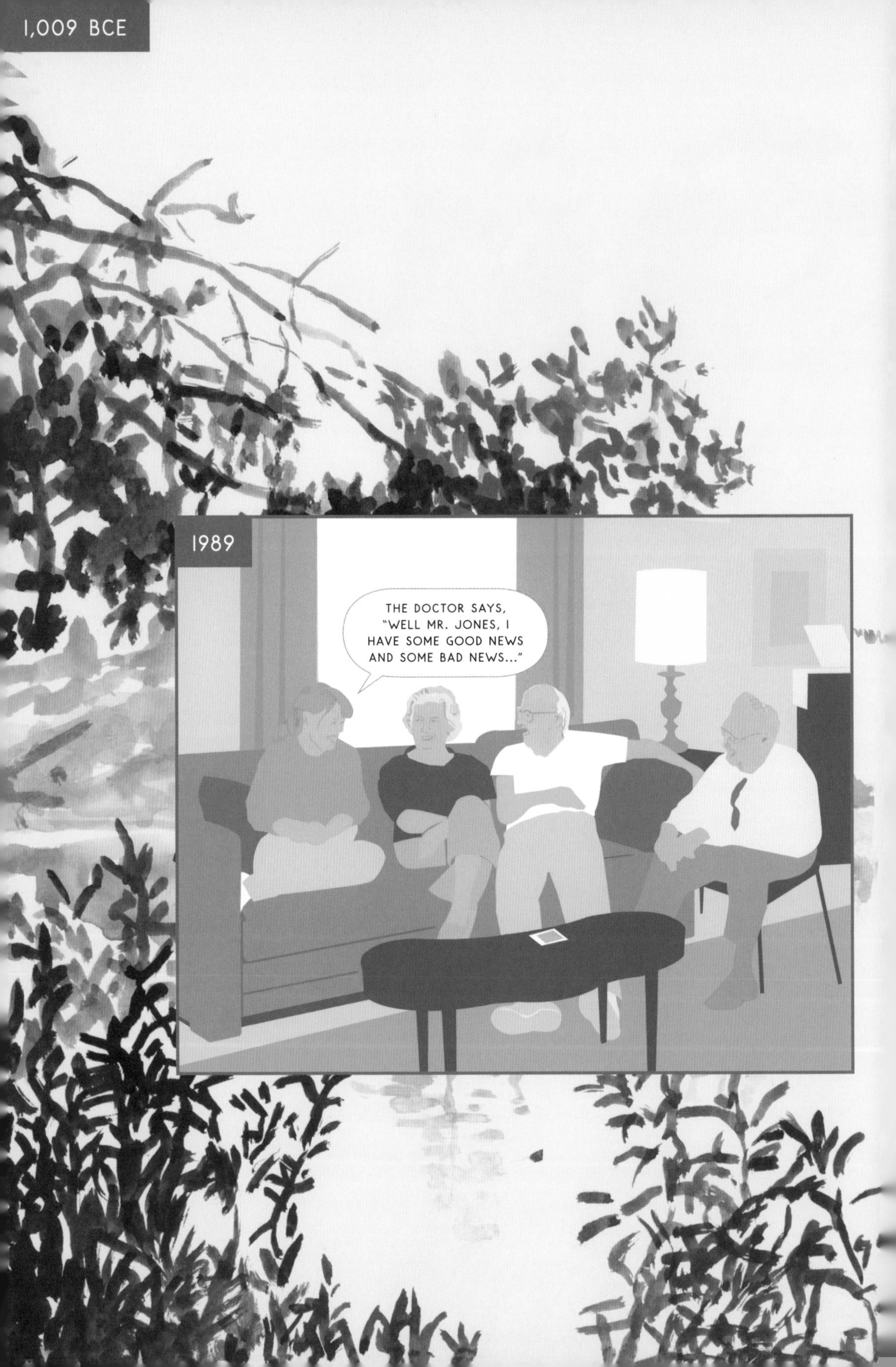
1,009 BCE
1989
THE DOCTOR SAYS, "WELL MR. JONES, I HAVE SOME GOOD NEWS AND SOME BAD NEWS..."

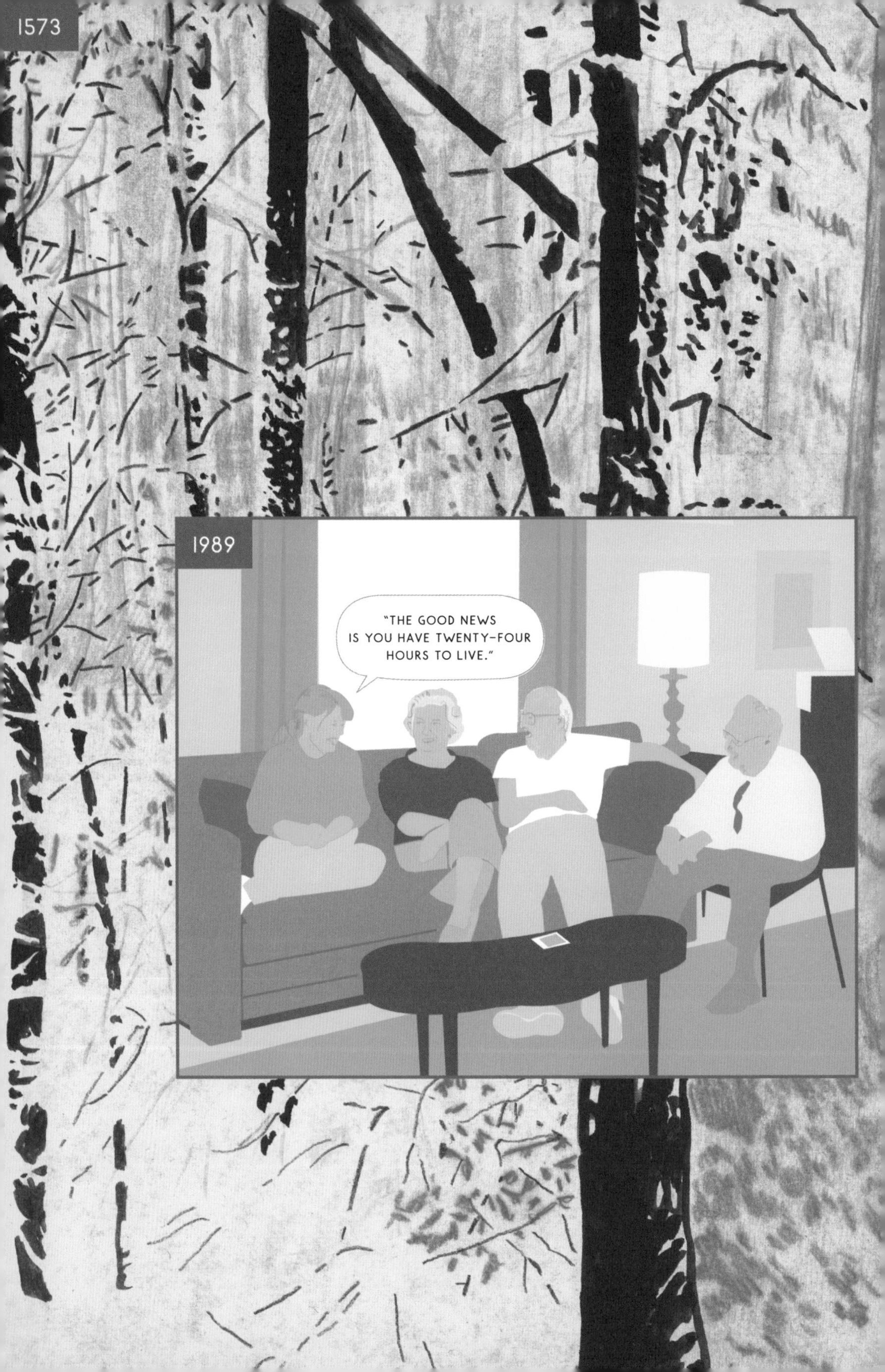
1573
1989
"THE GOOD NEWS IS YOU HAVE TWENTY-FOUR HOURS TO LIVE."

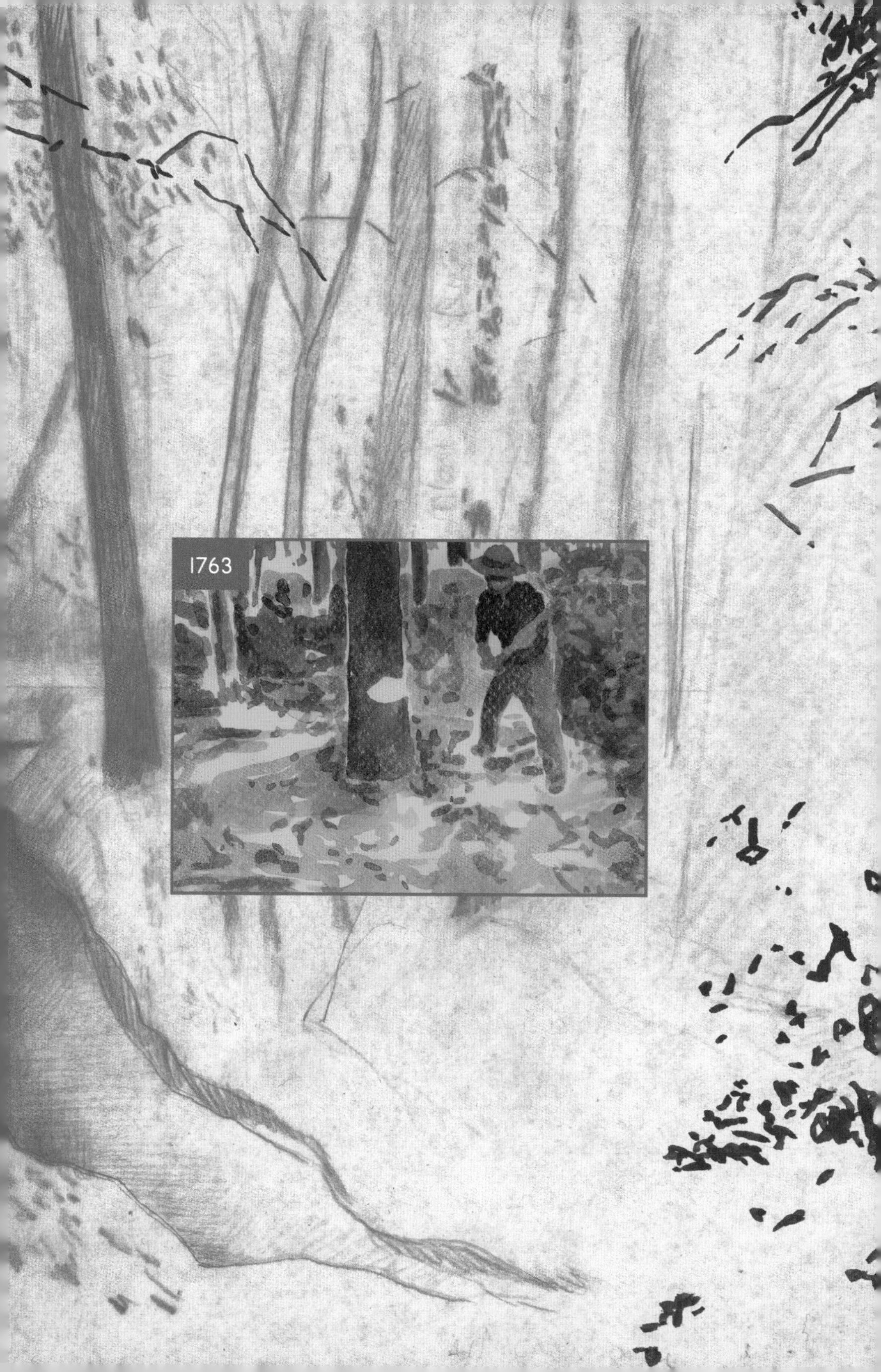
1763

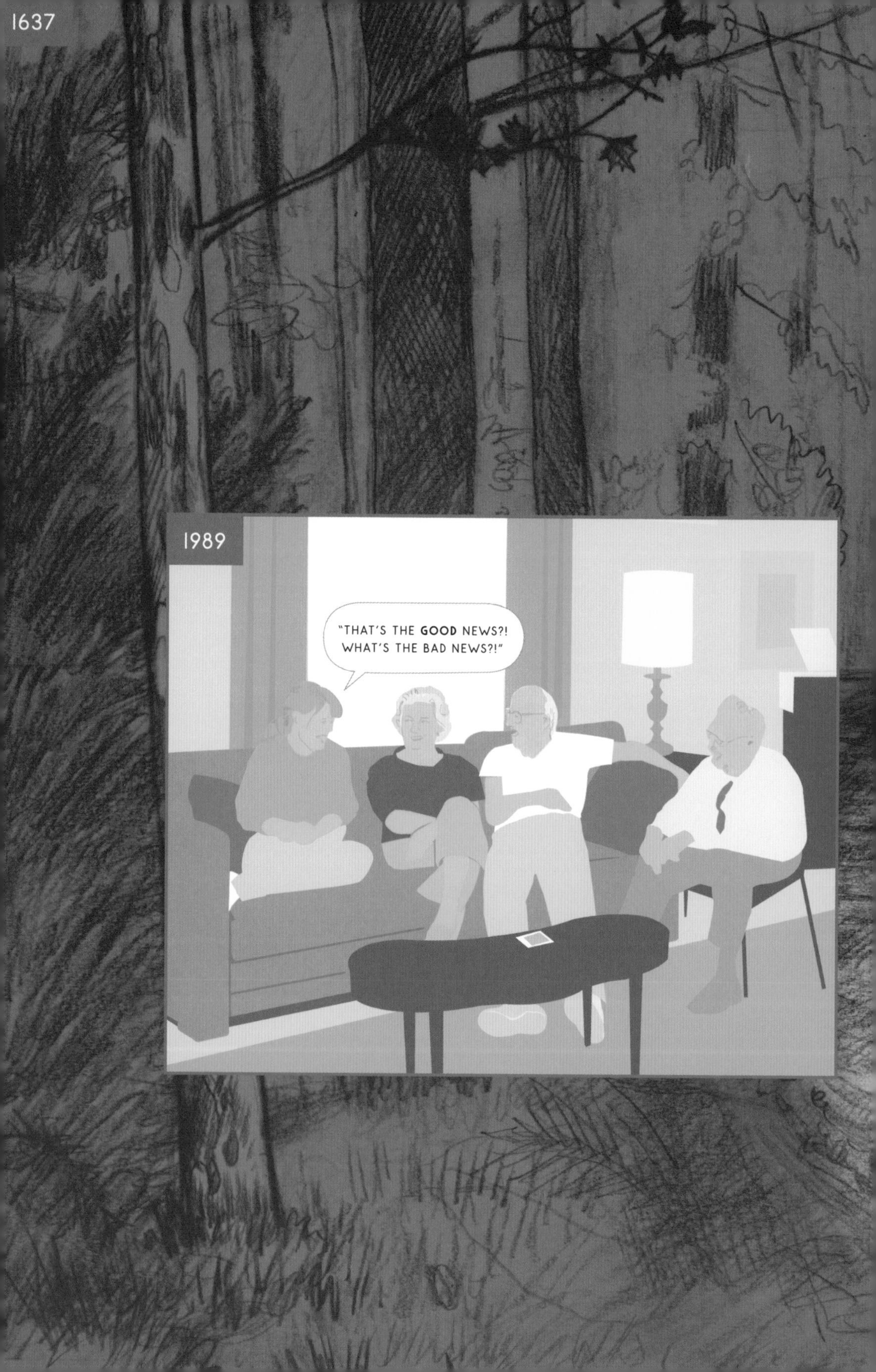
1637
1989
"THAT'S THE GOOD NEWS?!
WHAT'S THE BAD NEWS?!"

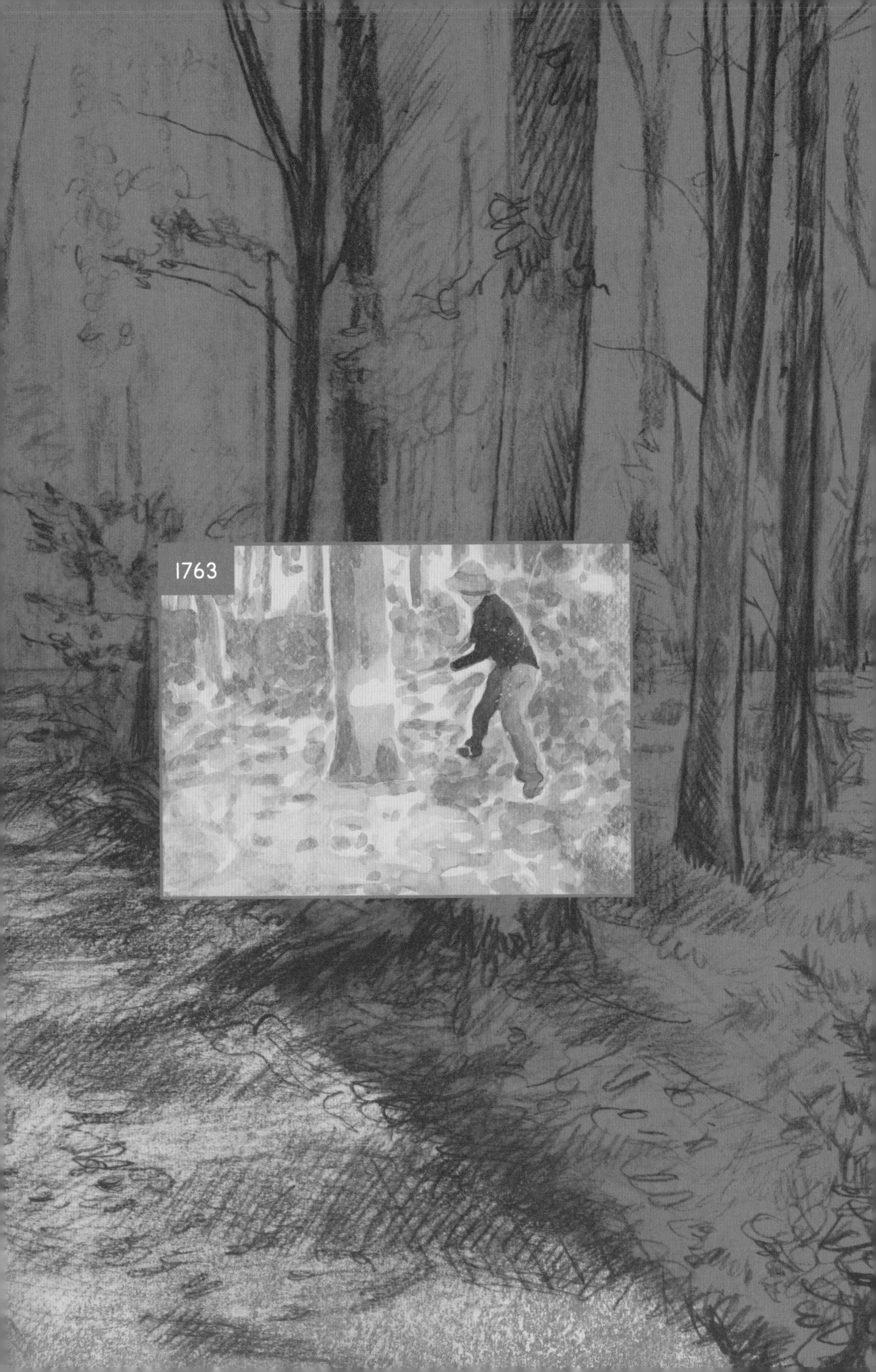
1763

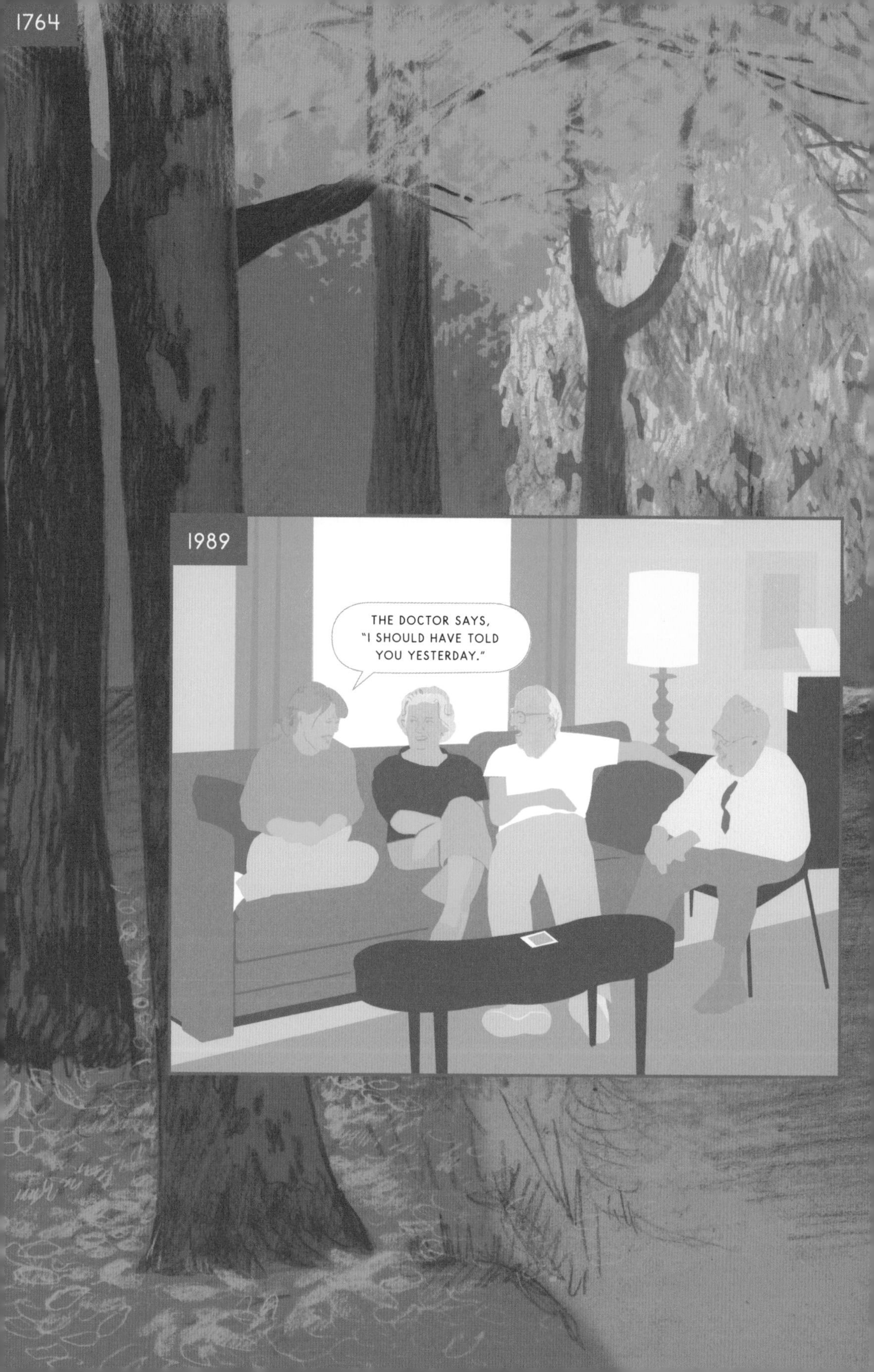
1764
1989
THE DOCTOR SAYS, "I SHOULD HAVE TOLD YOU YESTERDAY."

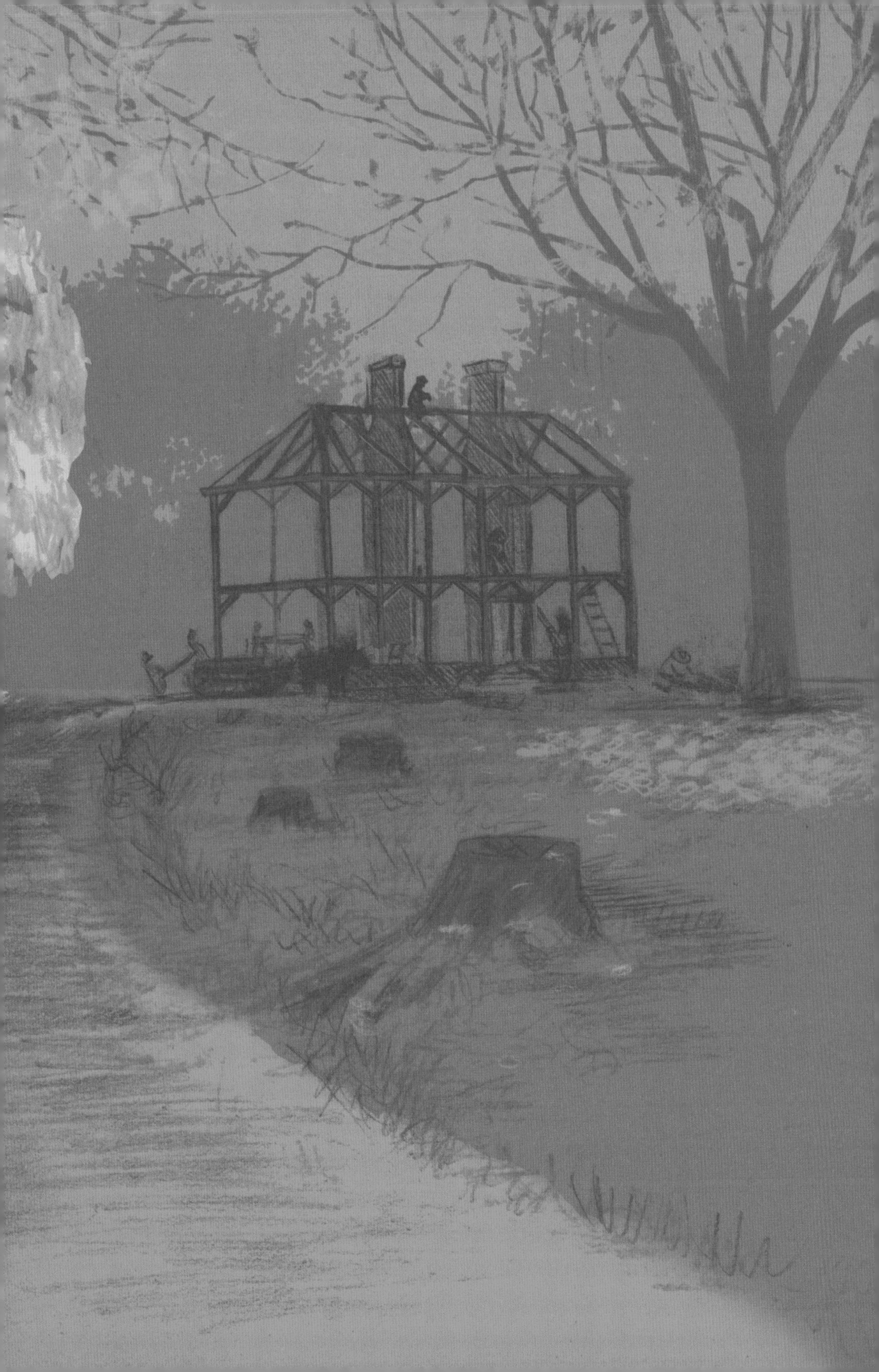

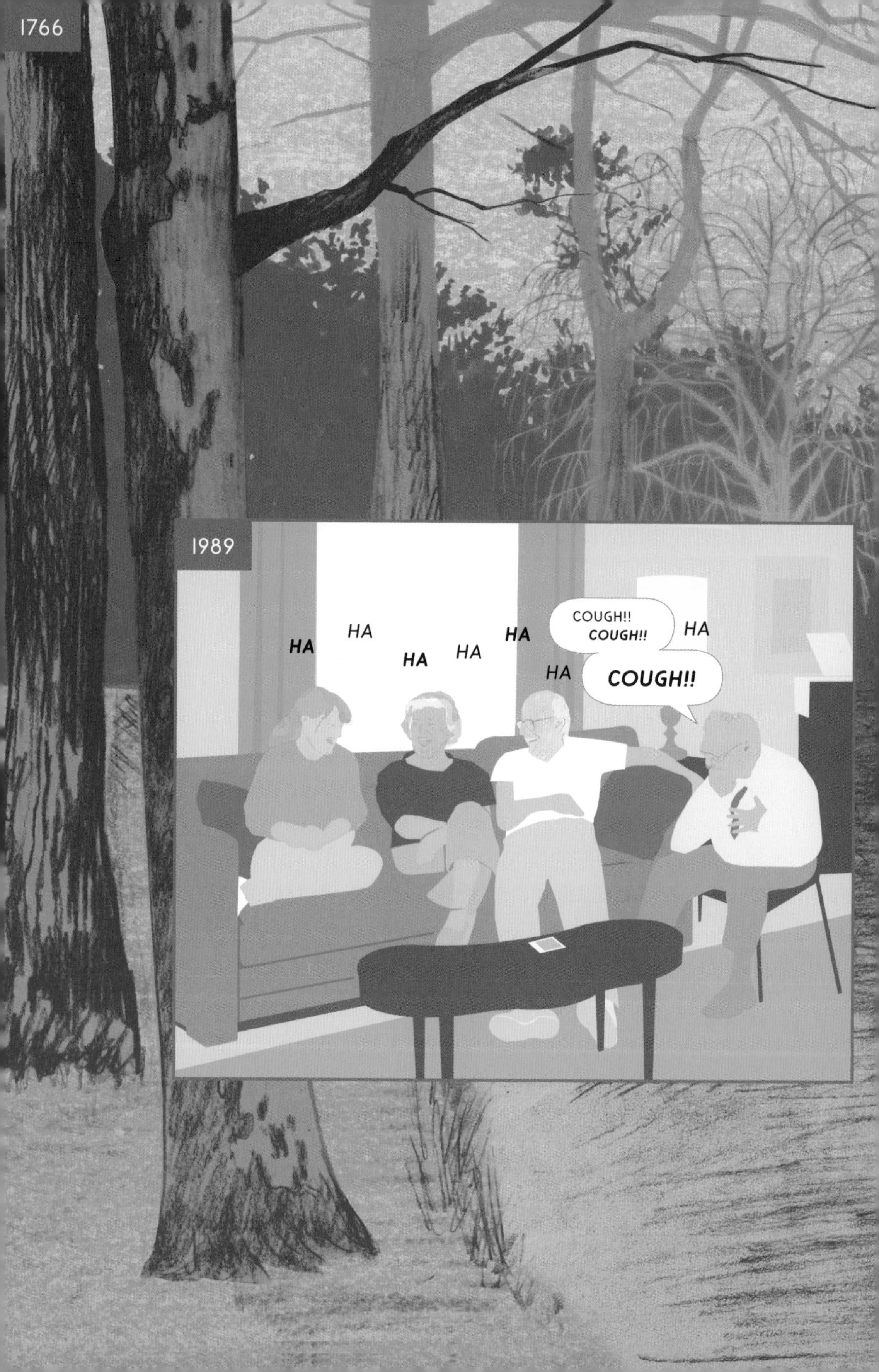
1766
1989
HA
HA
HA
HA
HA
HA
COUGH!!
COUGH!!
HA
COUGH!!

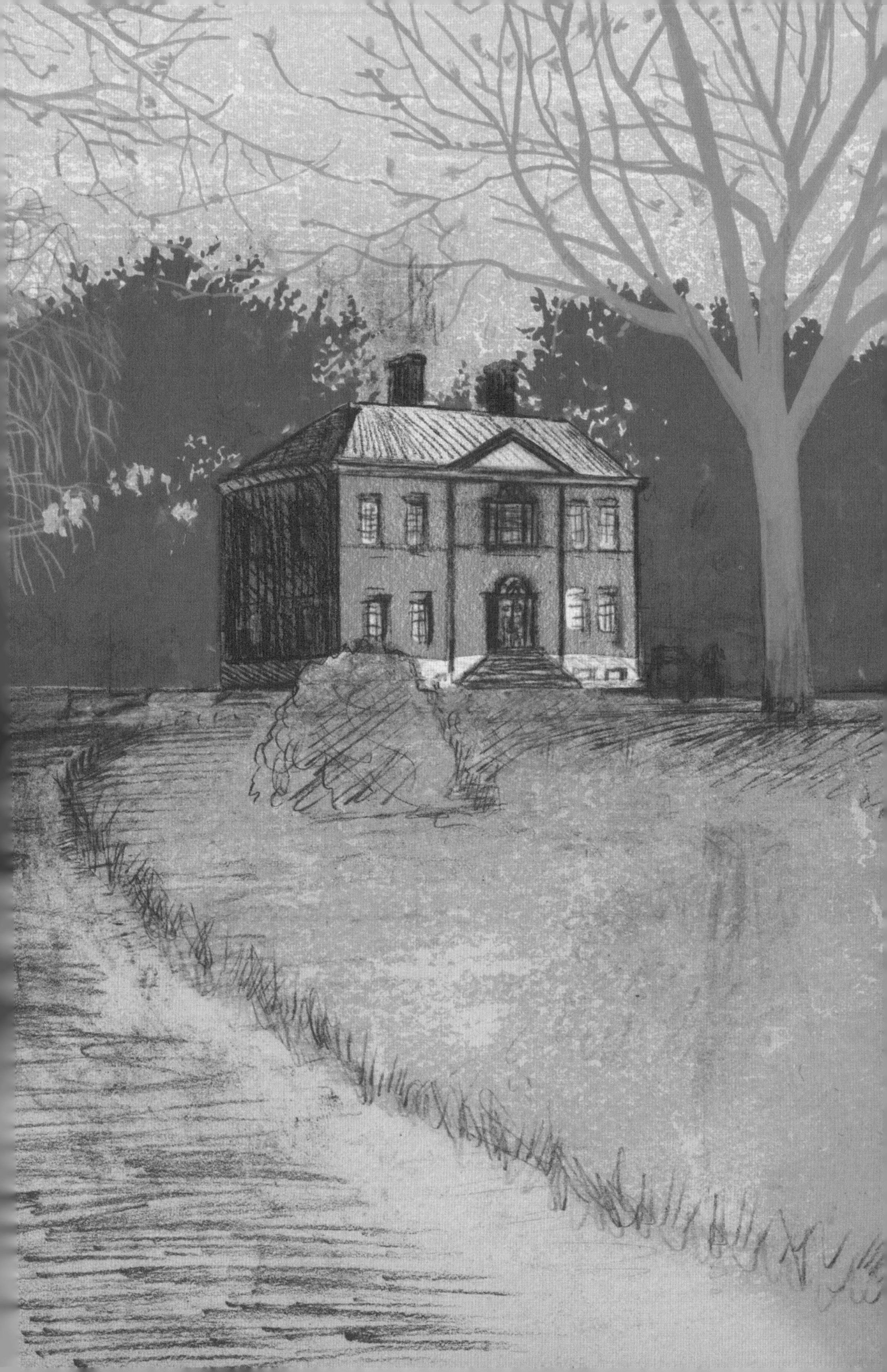

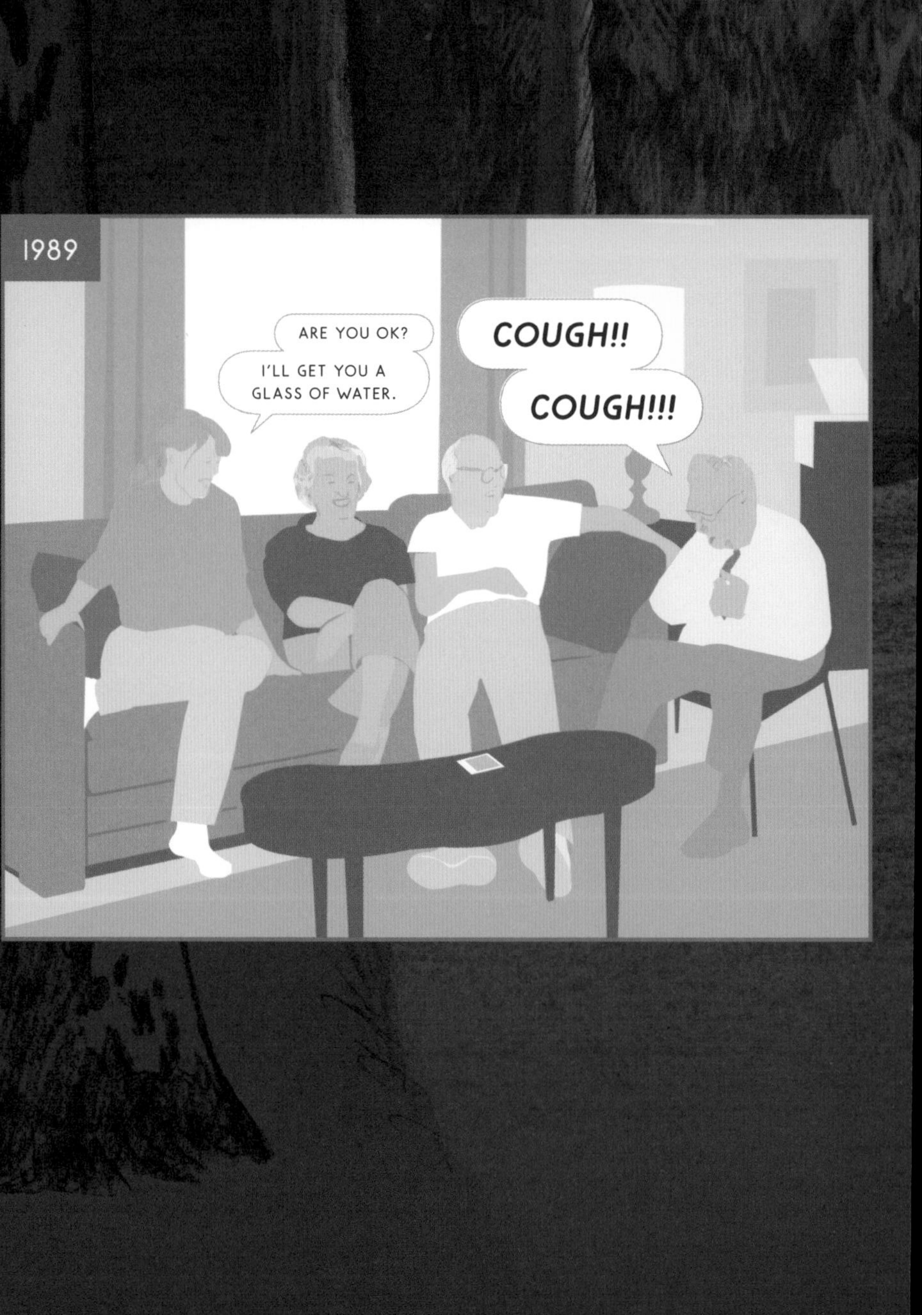
1989
ARE YOU OK?
I'LL GET YOU A GLASS OF WATER.
COUGH!!
COUGH!!!

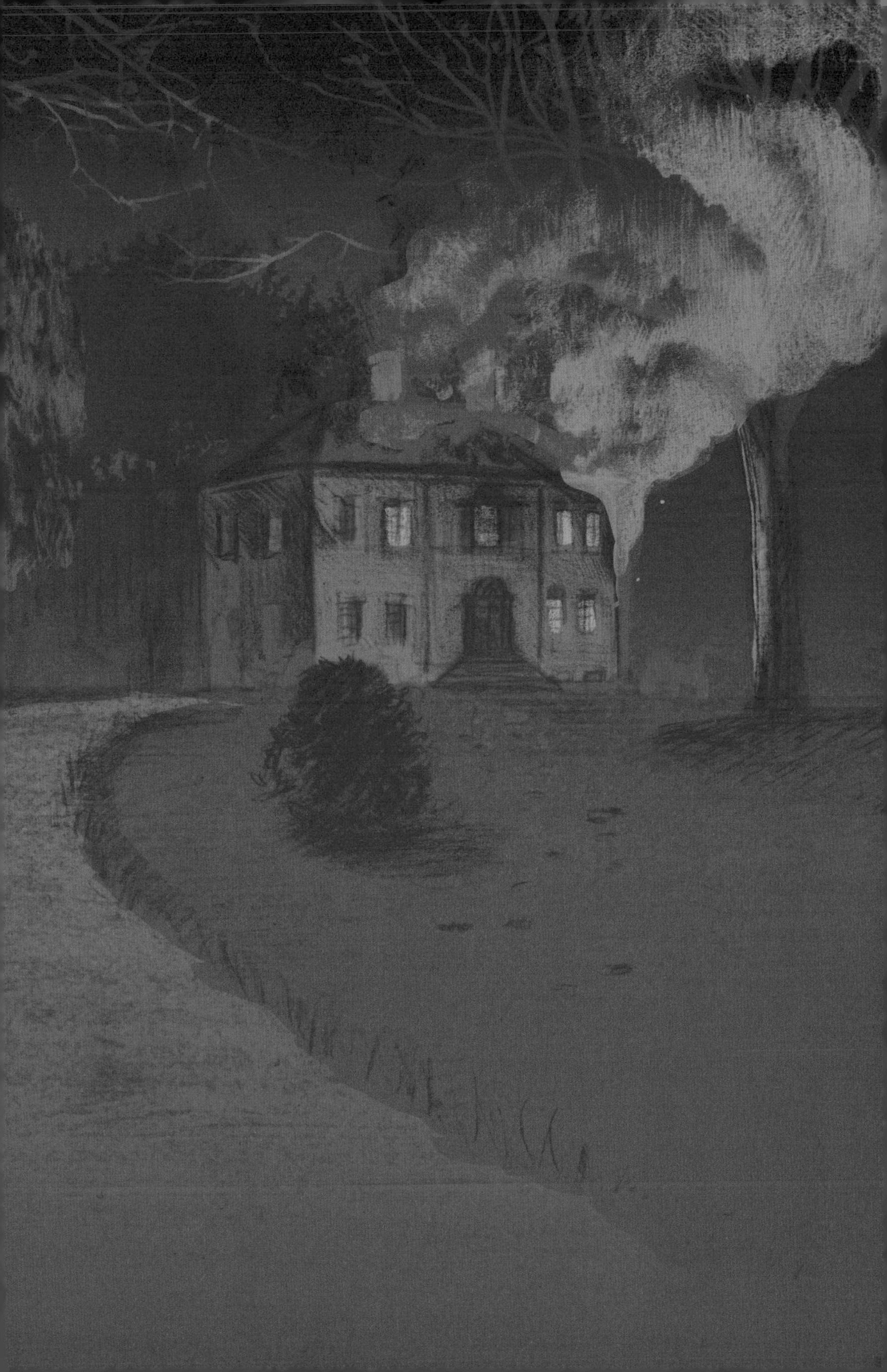

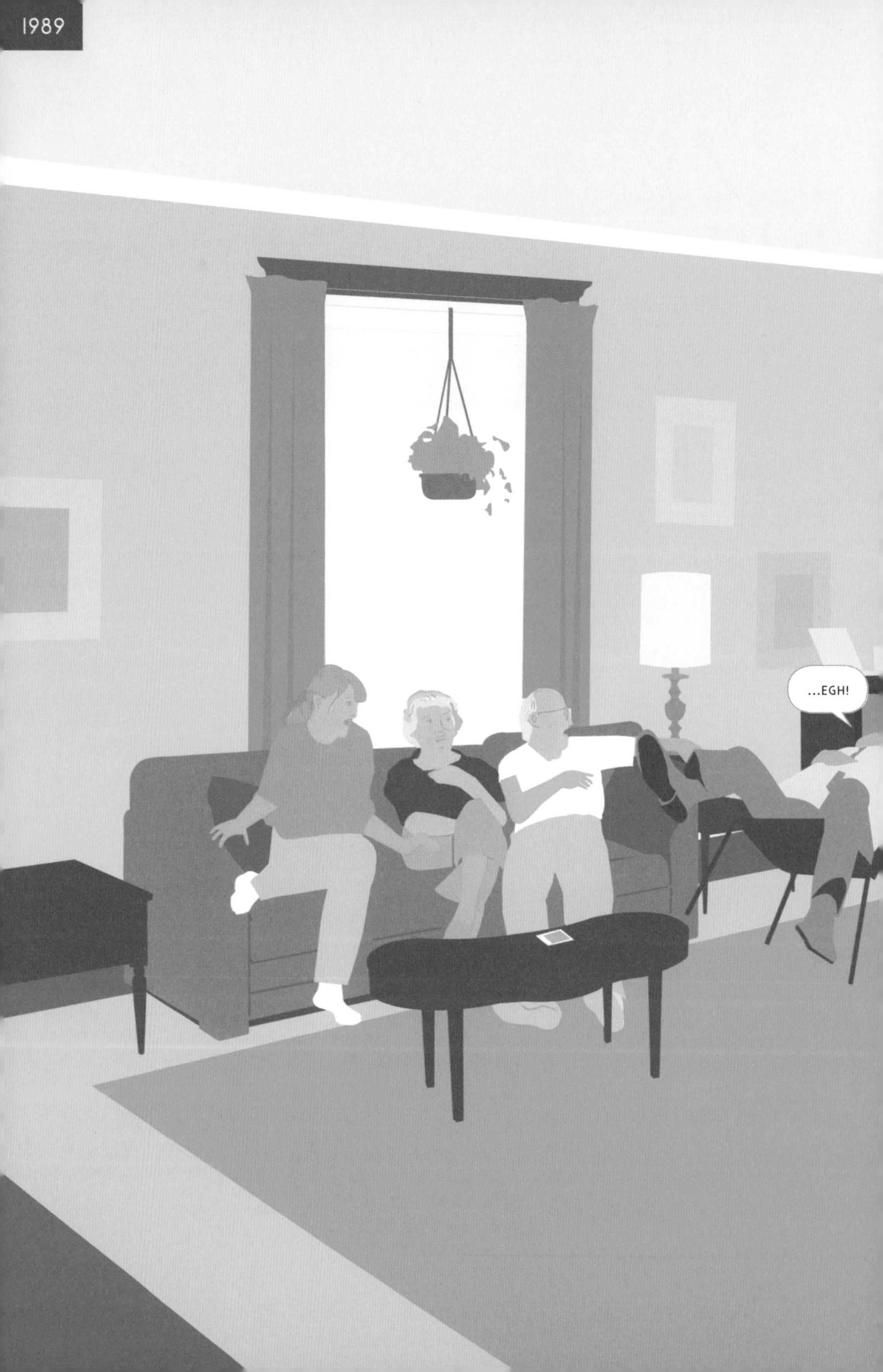
1989
...EGH!

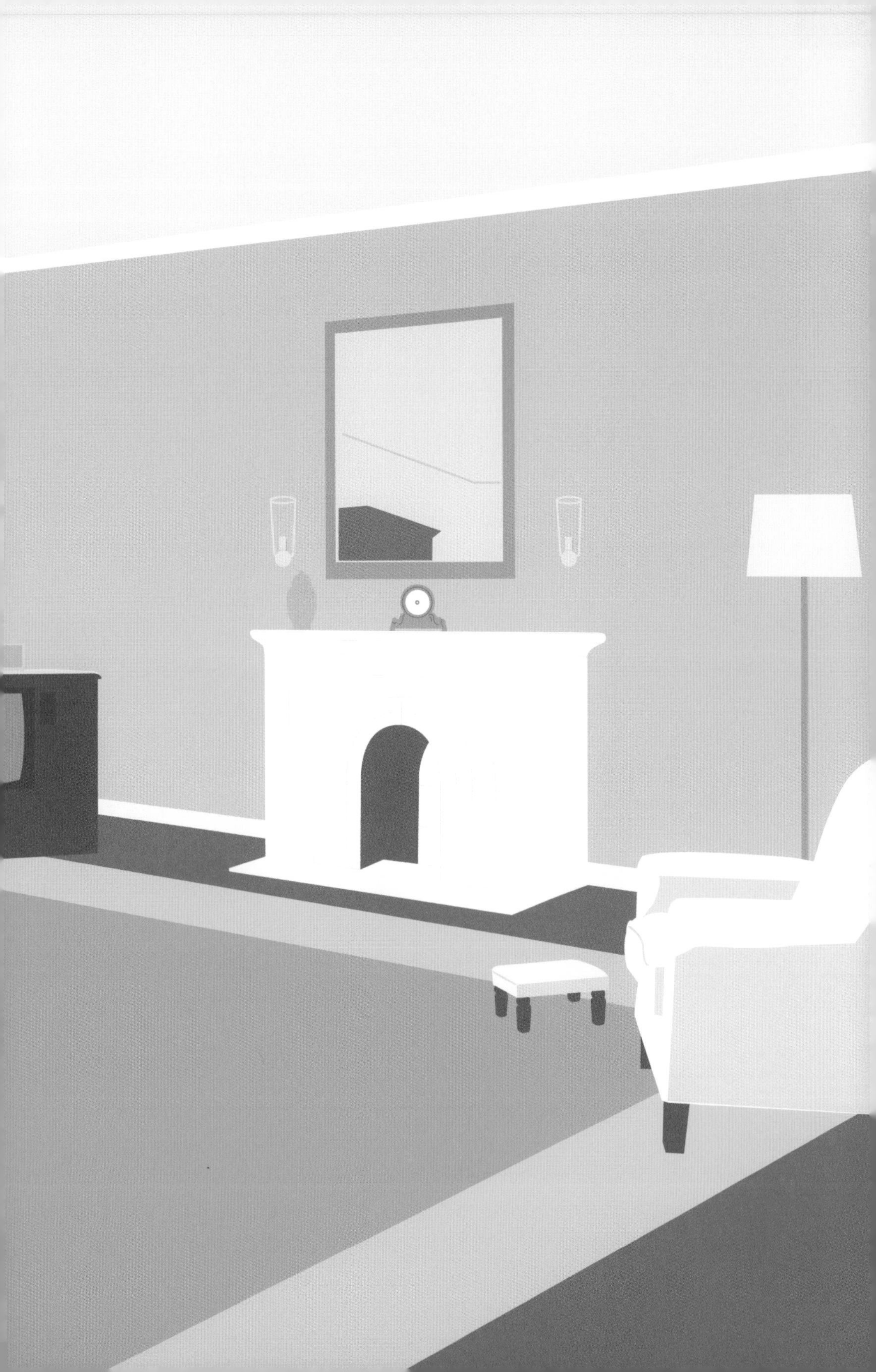

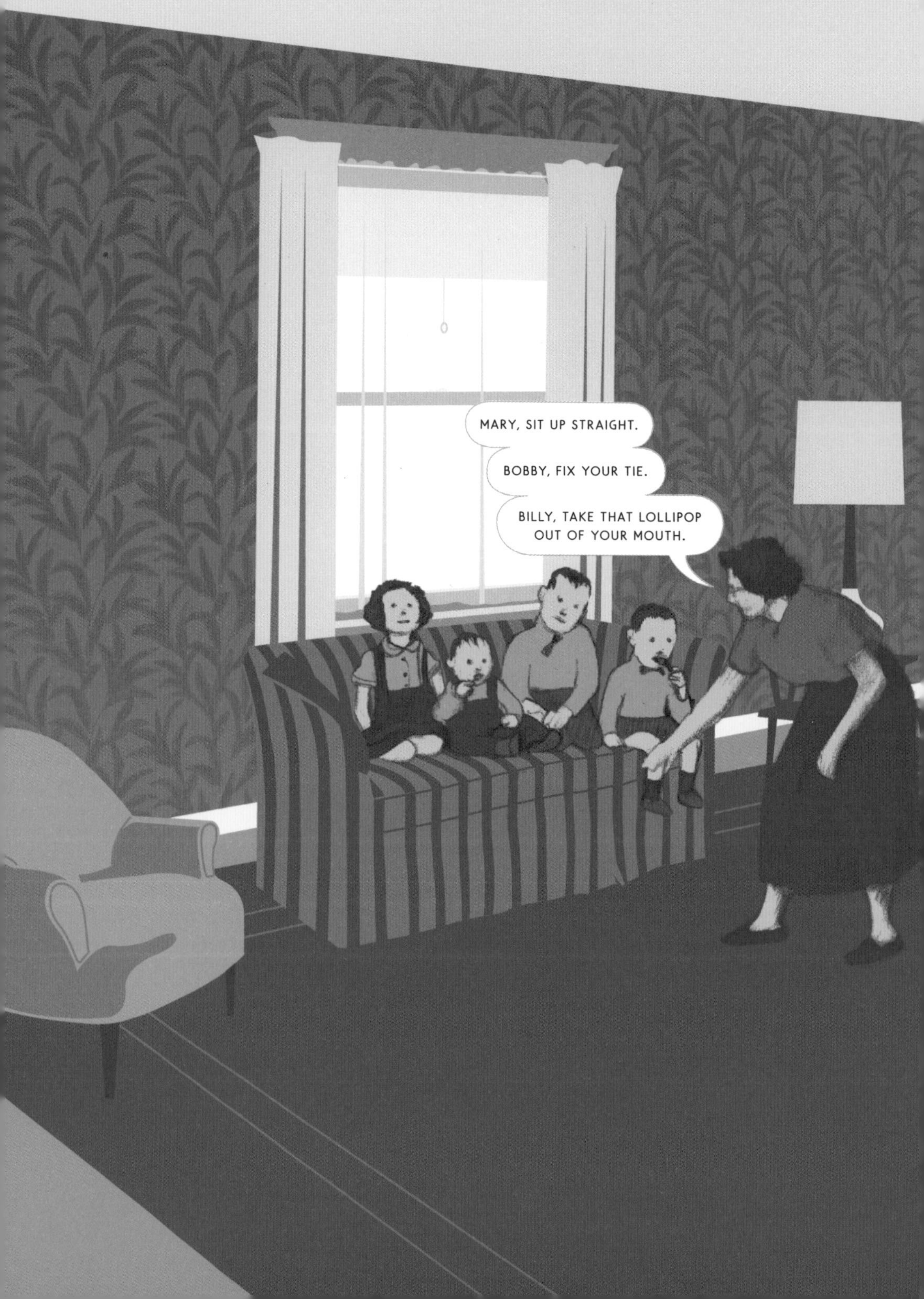
MARY, SIT UP STRAIGHT.
BOBBY, FIX YOUR TIE.
BILLY, TAKE THAT LOLLIPOP OUT OF YOUR MOUTH.

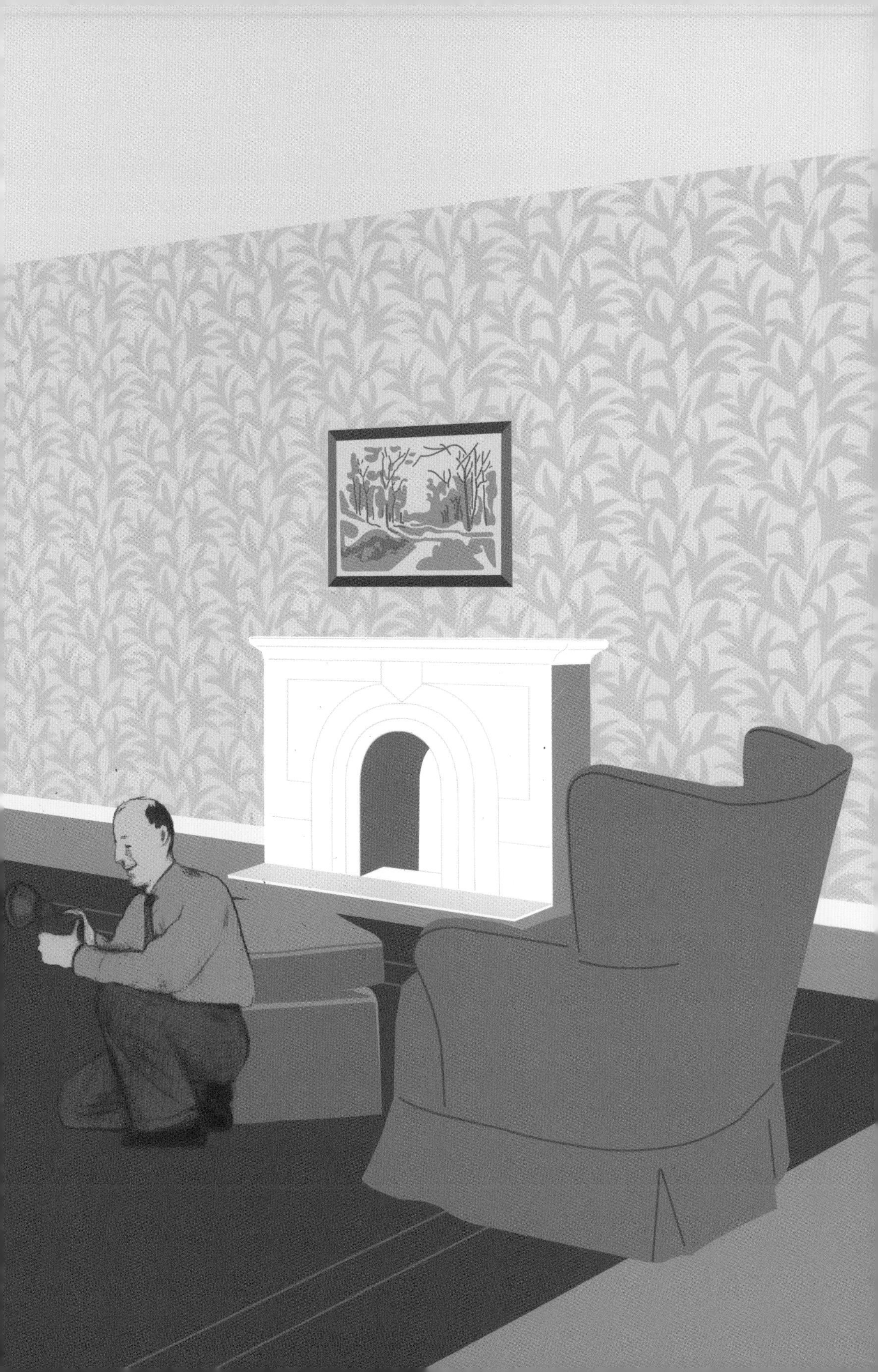

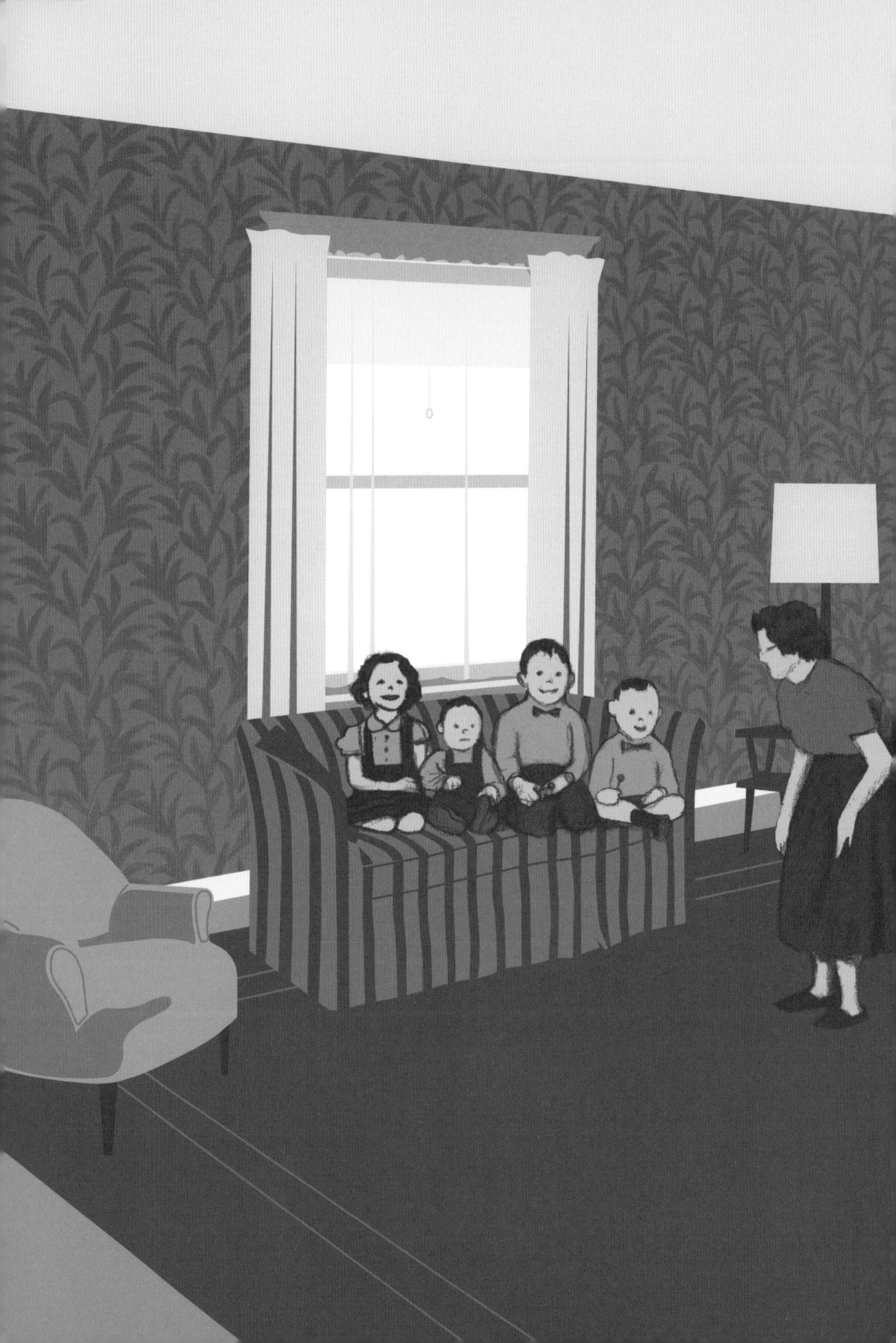

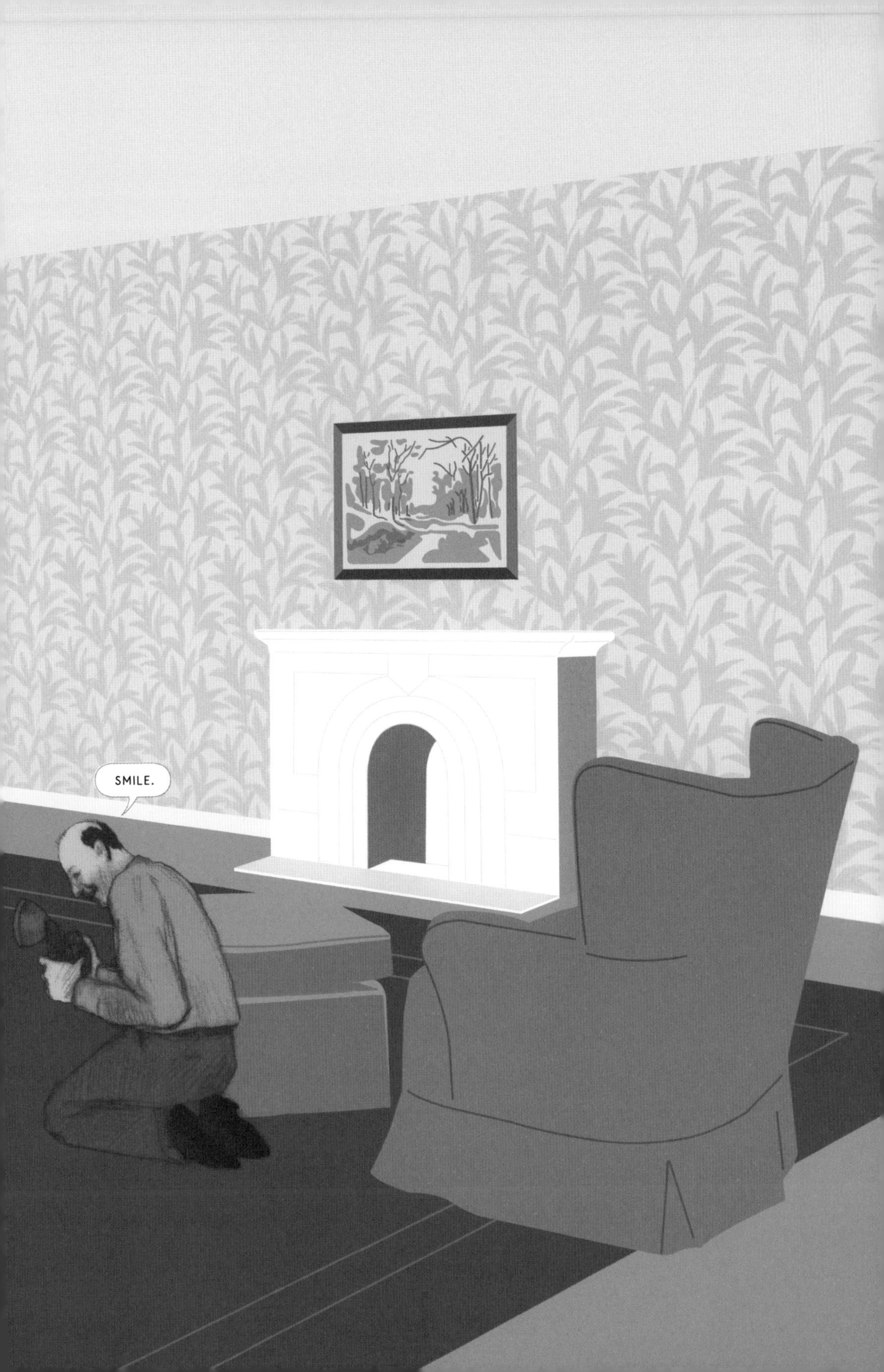
SMILE.

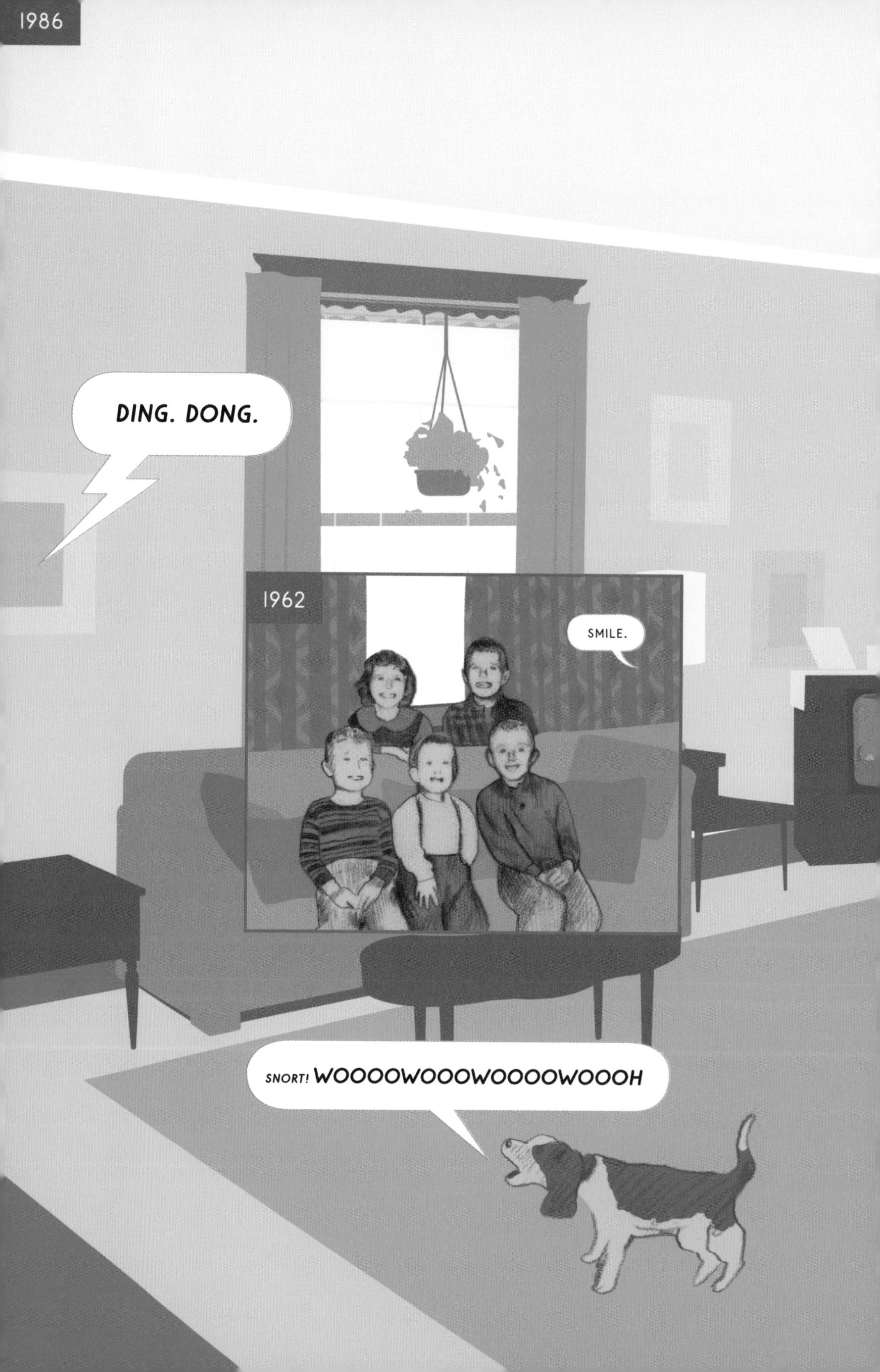
1986
DING. DONG.
1962
SMILE.
SNORT! WOOOOWOOOWOOOOWOOOH

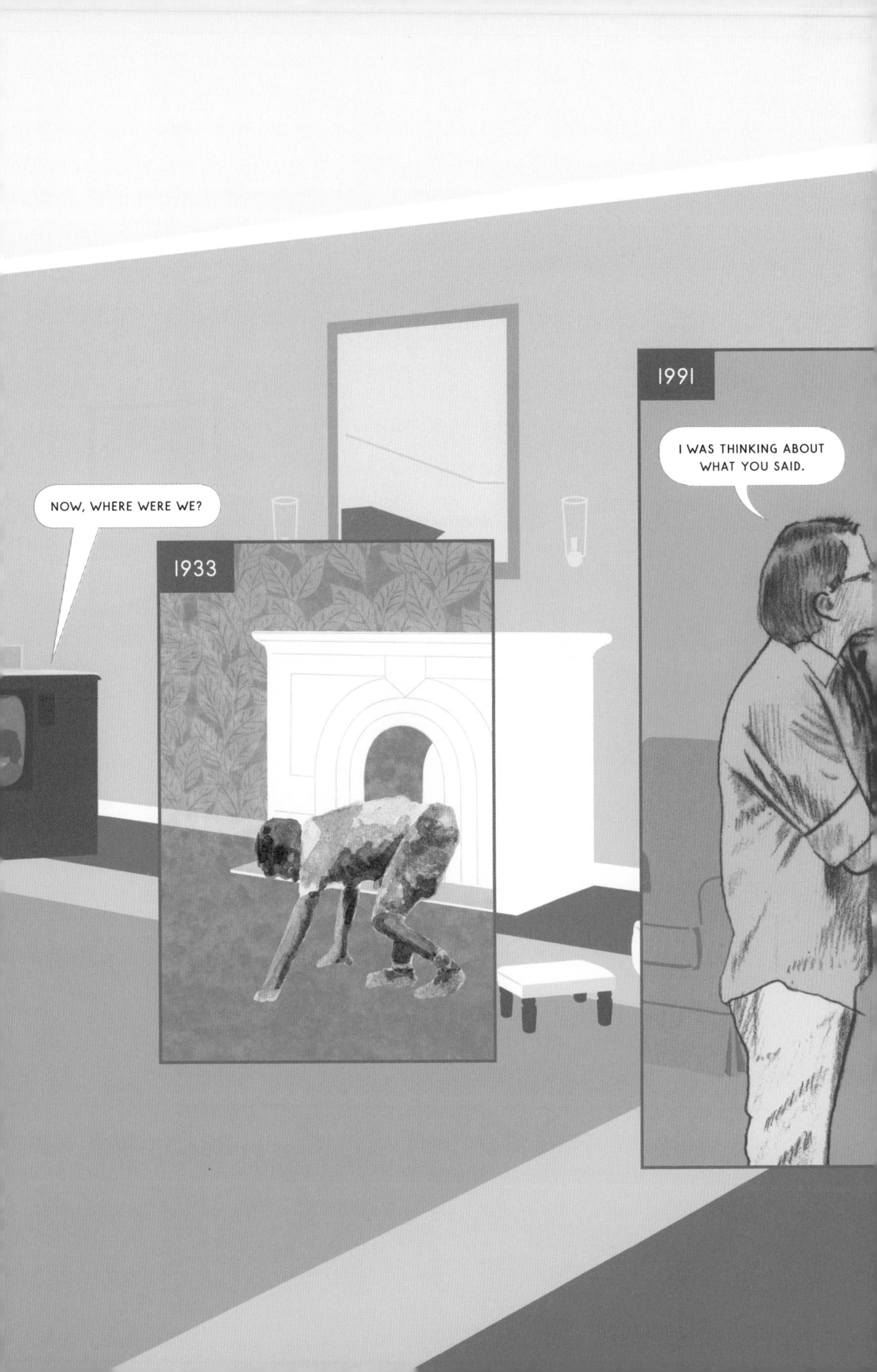
NOW, WHERE WERE WE?
1933
1991
I WAS THINKING ABOUT WHAT YOU SAID.

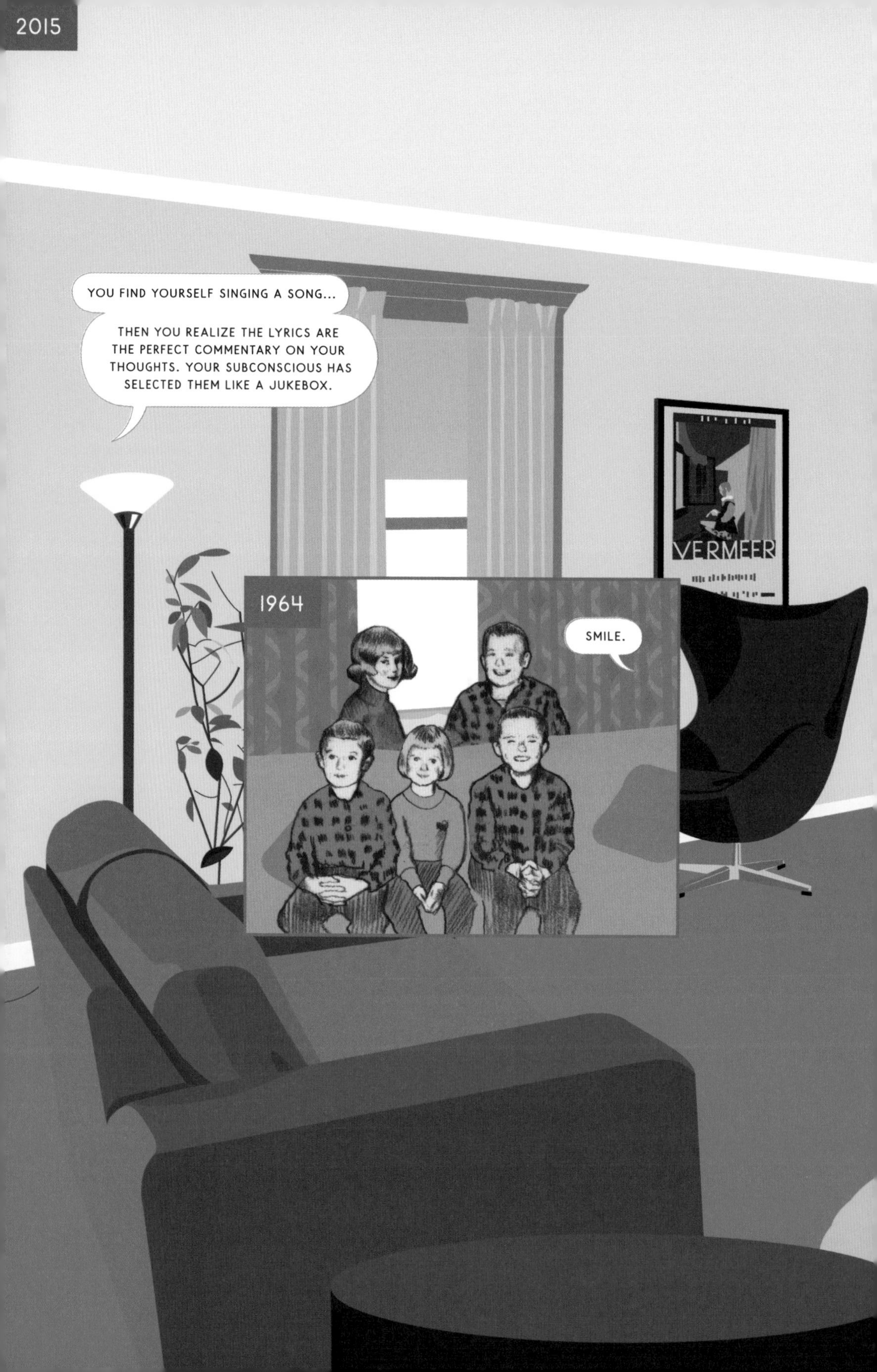
2015
YOU FIND YOURSELF SINGING A SONG...
THEN YOU REALIZE THE LYRICS ARE THE PERFECT COMMENTARY ON YOUR THOUGHTS. YOUR SUBCONSCIOUS HAS SELECTED THEM LIKE A JUKEBOX.
VERMEER
1964
SMILE.

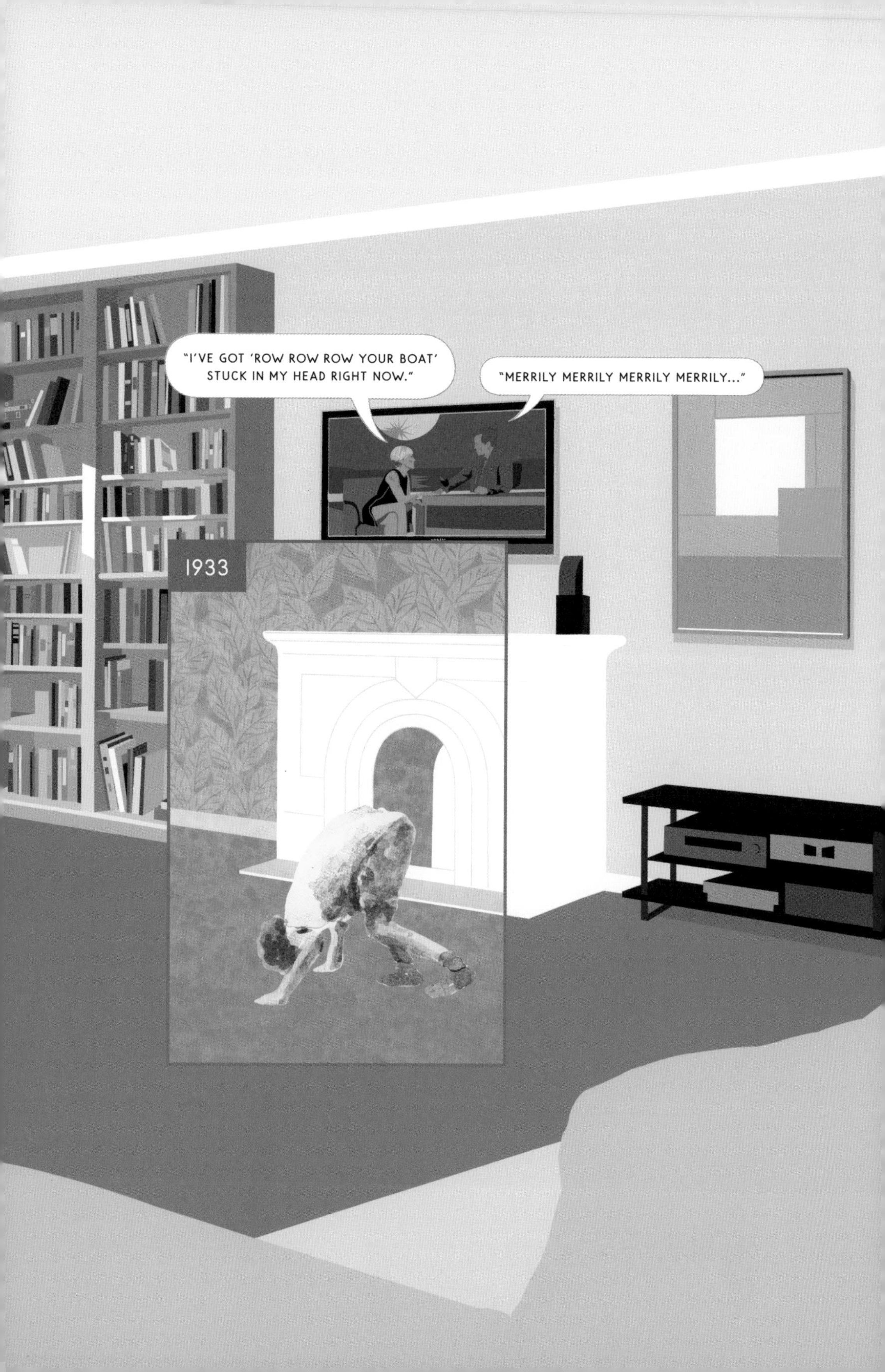
"I'VE GOT 'ROW ROW ROW YOUR BOAT' STUCK IN MY HEAD RIGHT NOW."
"MERRILY MERRILY MERRILY MERRILY..."
1933

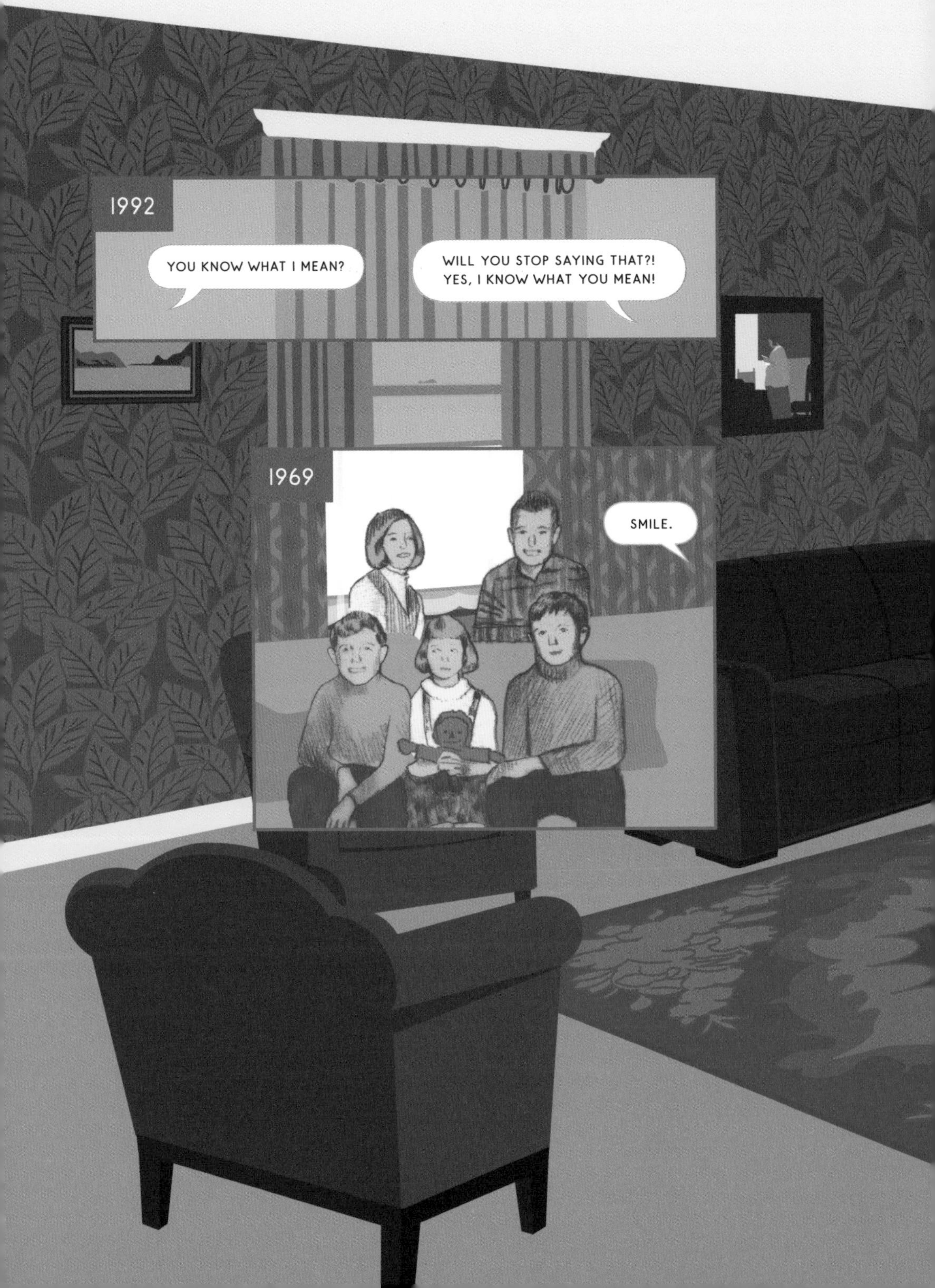
1992
YOU KNOW WHAT I MEAN?
WILL YOU STOP SAYING THAT?! YES, I KNOW WHAT YOU MEAN!
1969
SMILE.

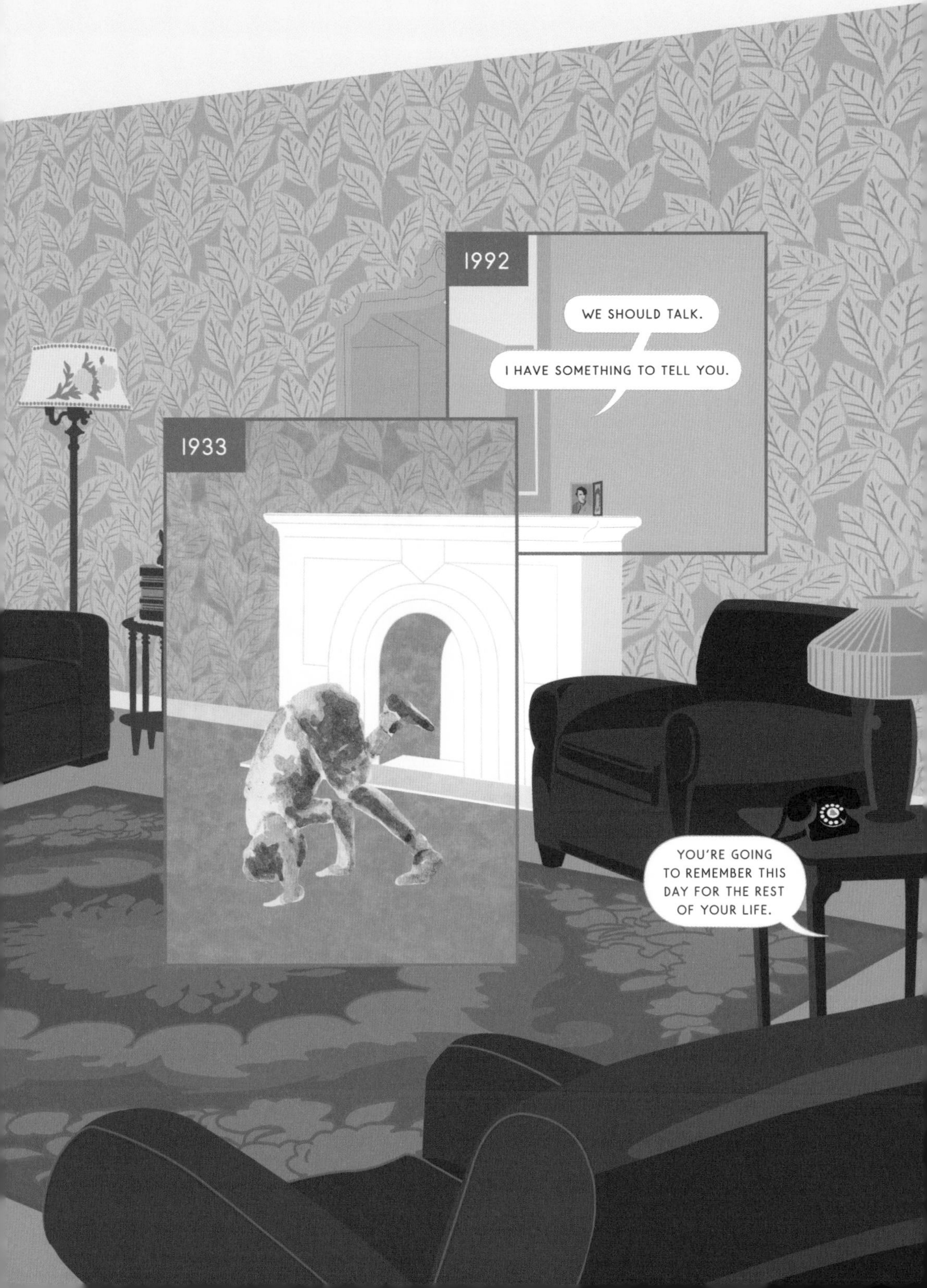
1992
WE SHOULD TALK.
I HAVE SOMETHING TO TELL YOU.
1933
YOU'RE GOING TO REMEMBER THIS DAY FOR THE REST OF YOUR LIFE.

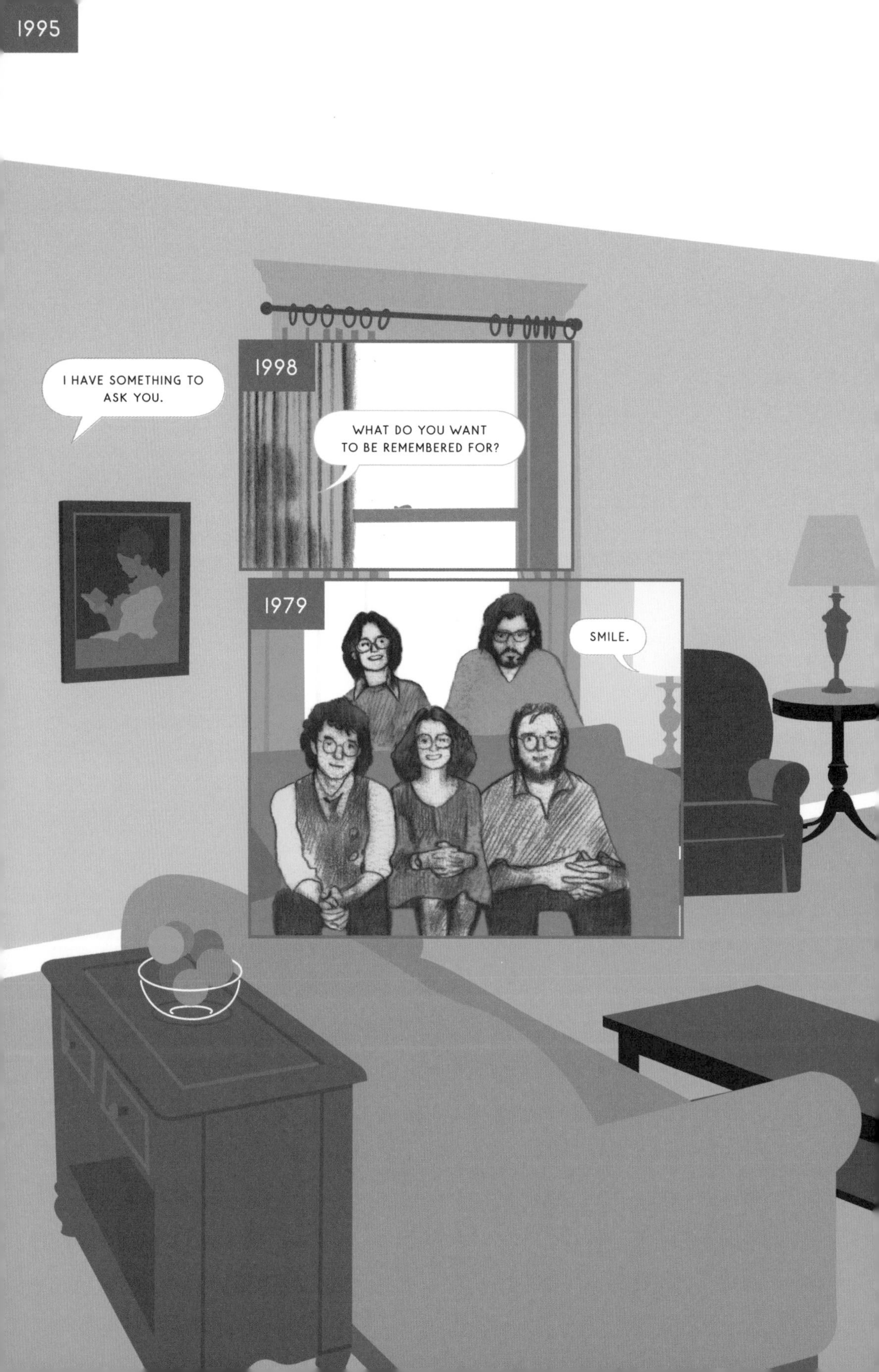
1995
I HAVE SOMETHING TO ASK YOU.
1998
WHAT DO YOU WANT TO BE REMEMBERED FOR?
1979
SMILE.

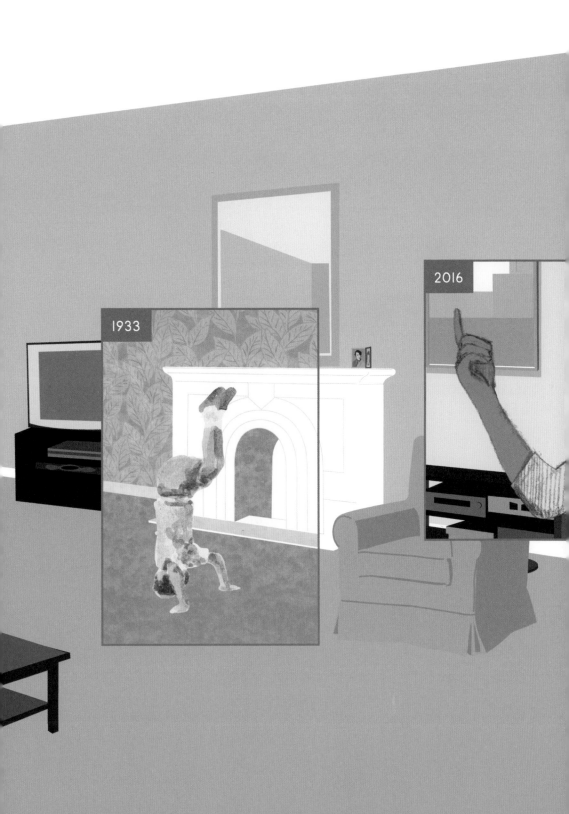

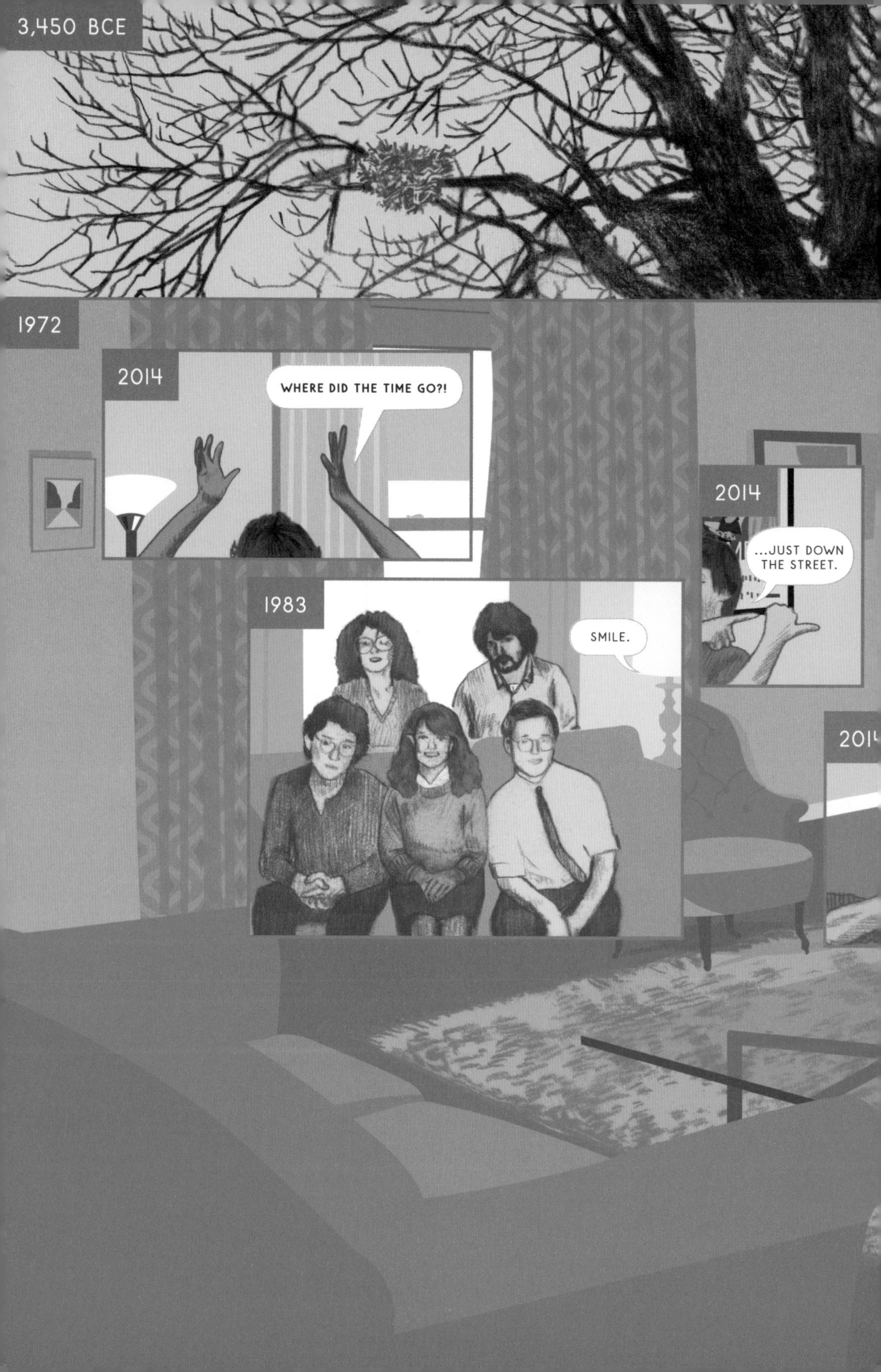
3,450 BCE
1972
2014
WHERE DID THE TIME GO?!
2014
...JUST DOWN THE STREET.
1983
SMILE.

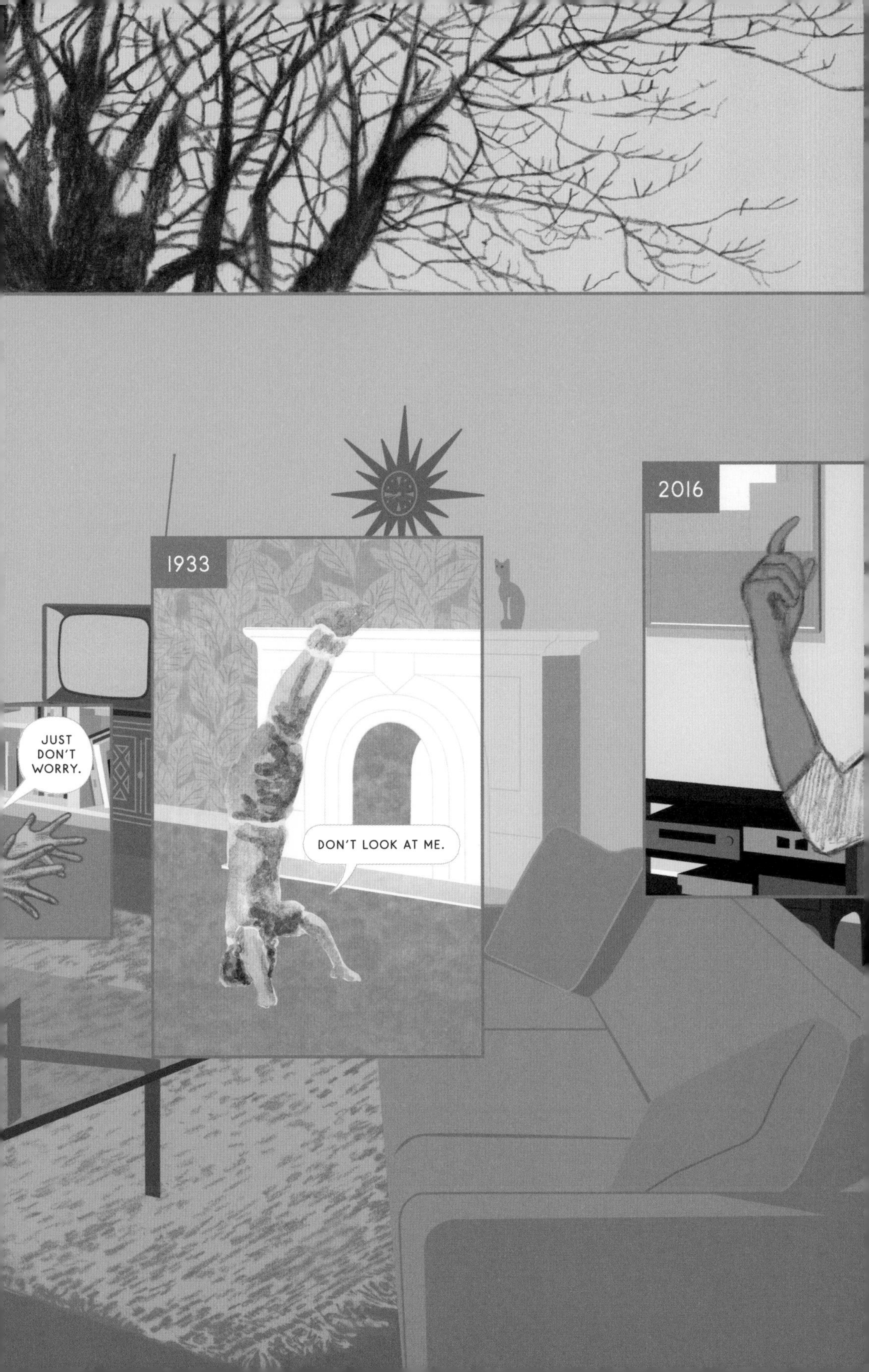
1933
2016
JUST DON'T WORRY.
DON'T LOOK AT ME.

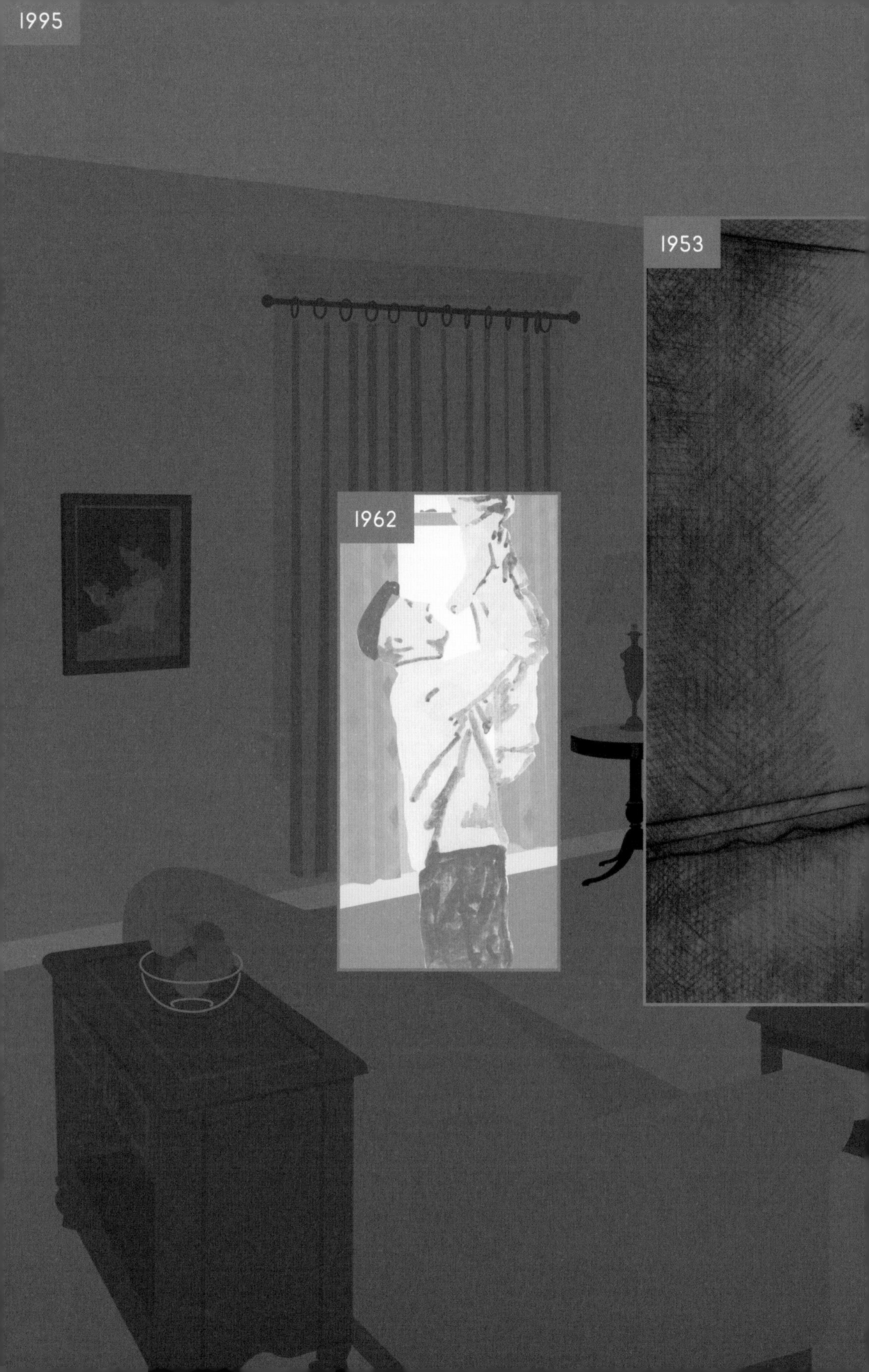
1995
1953
1962

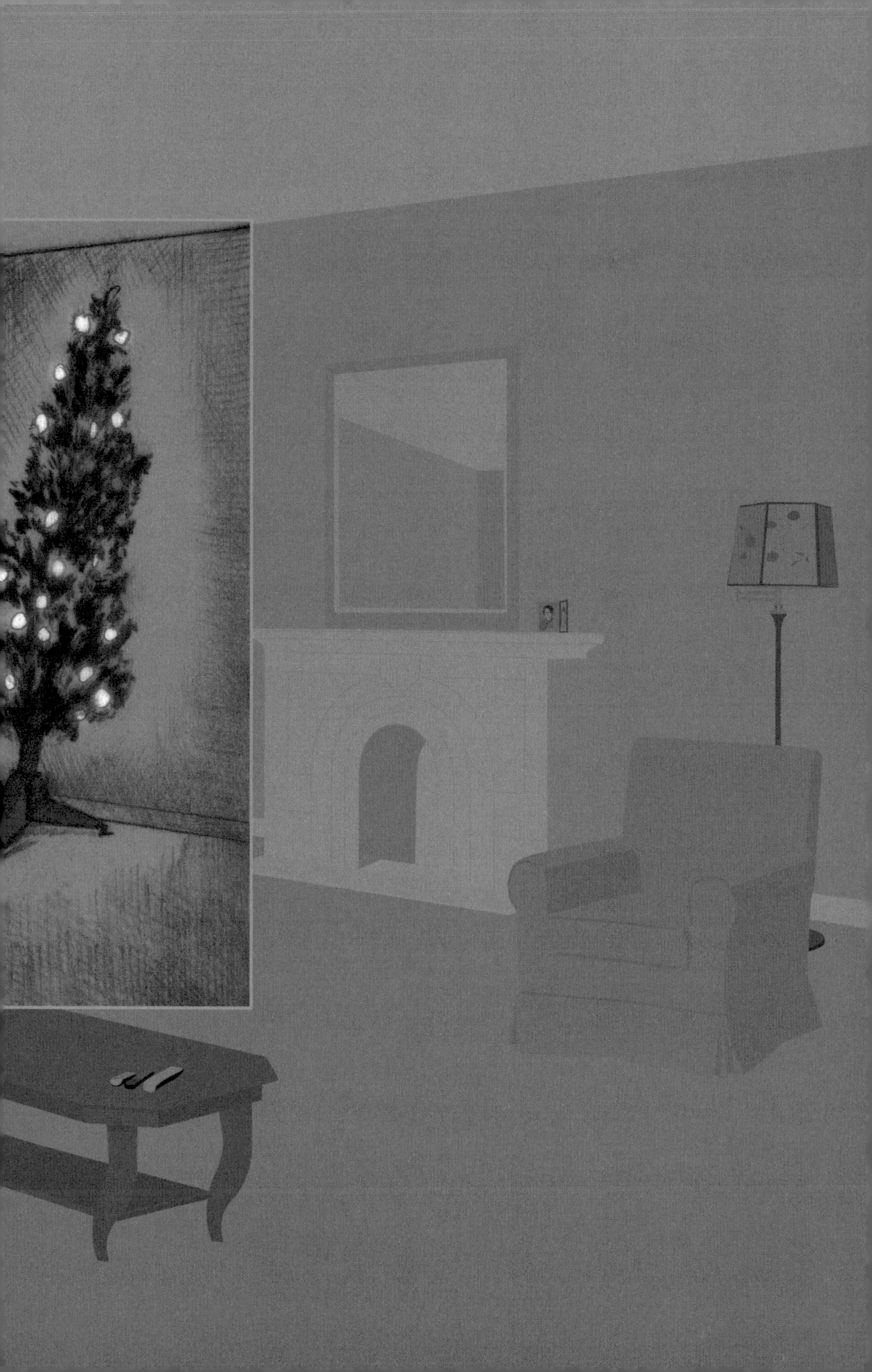

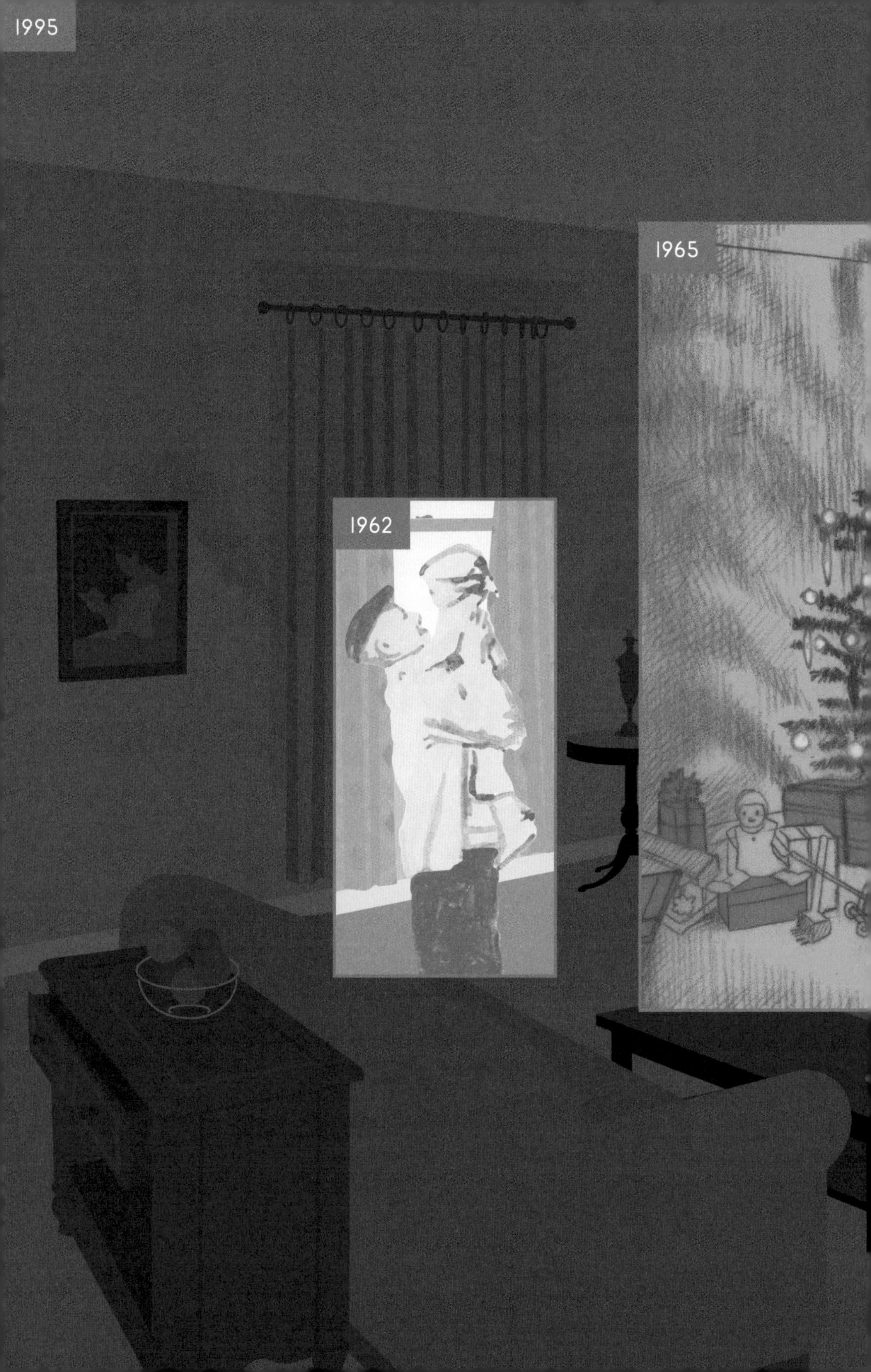
1995
1962
1965

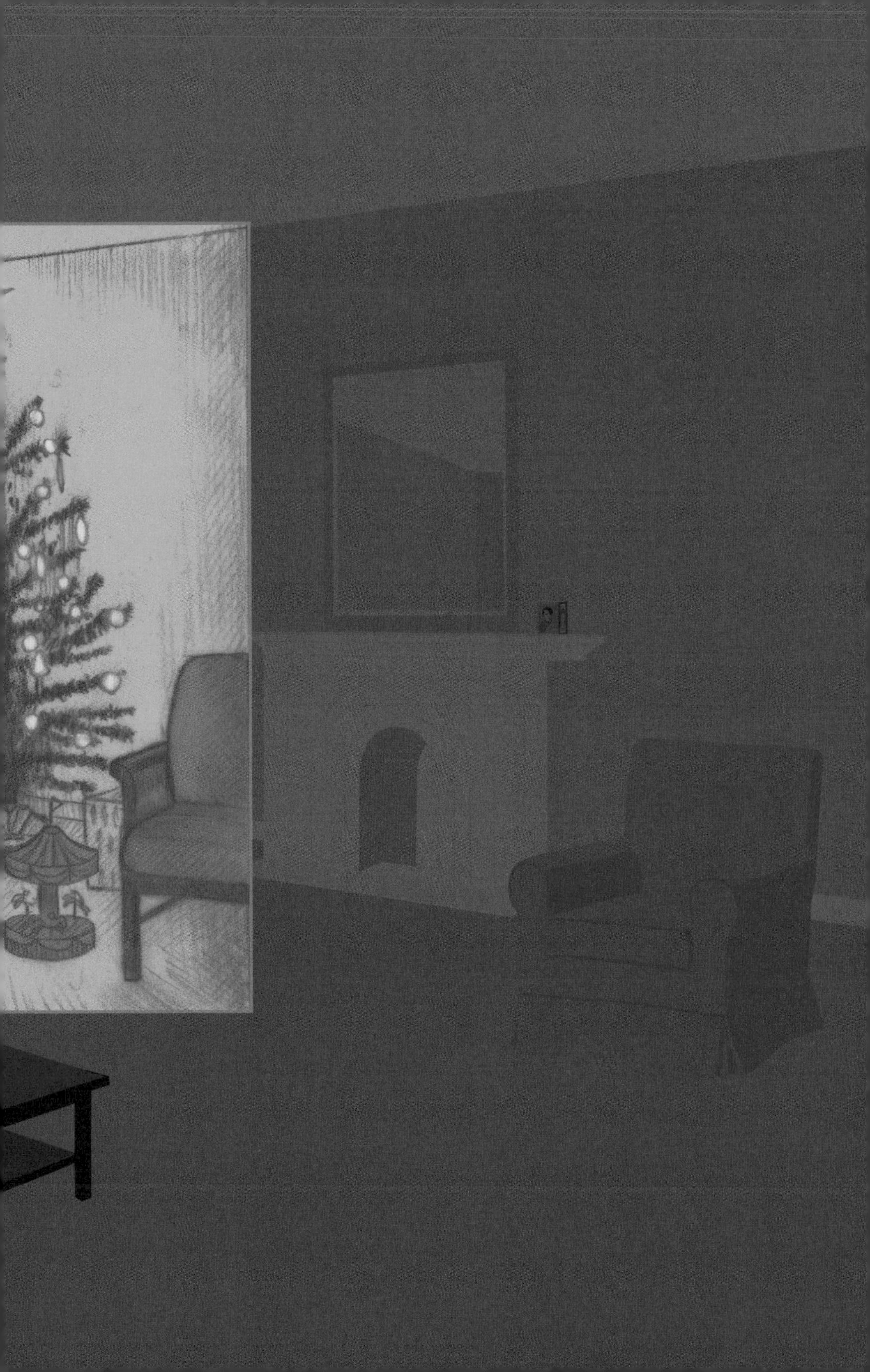

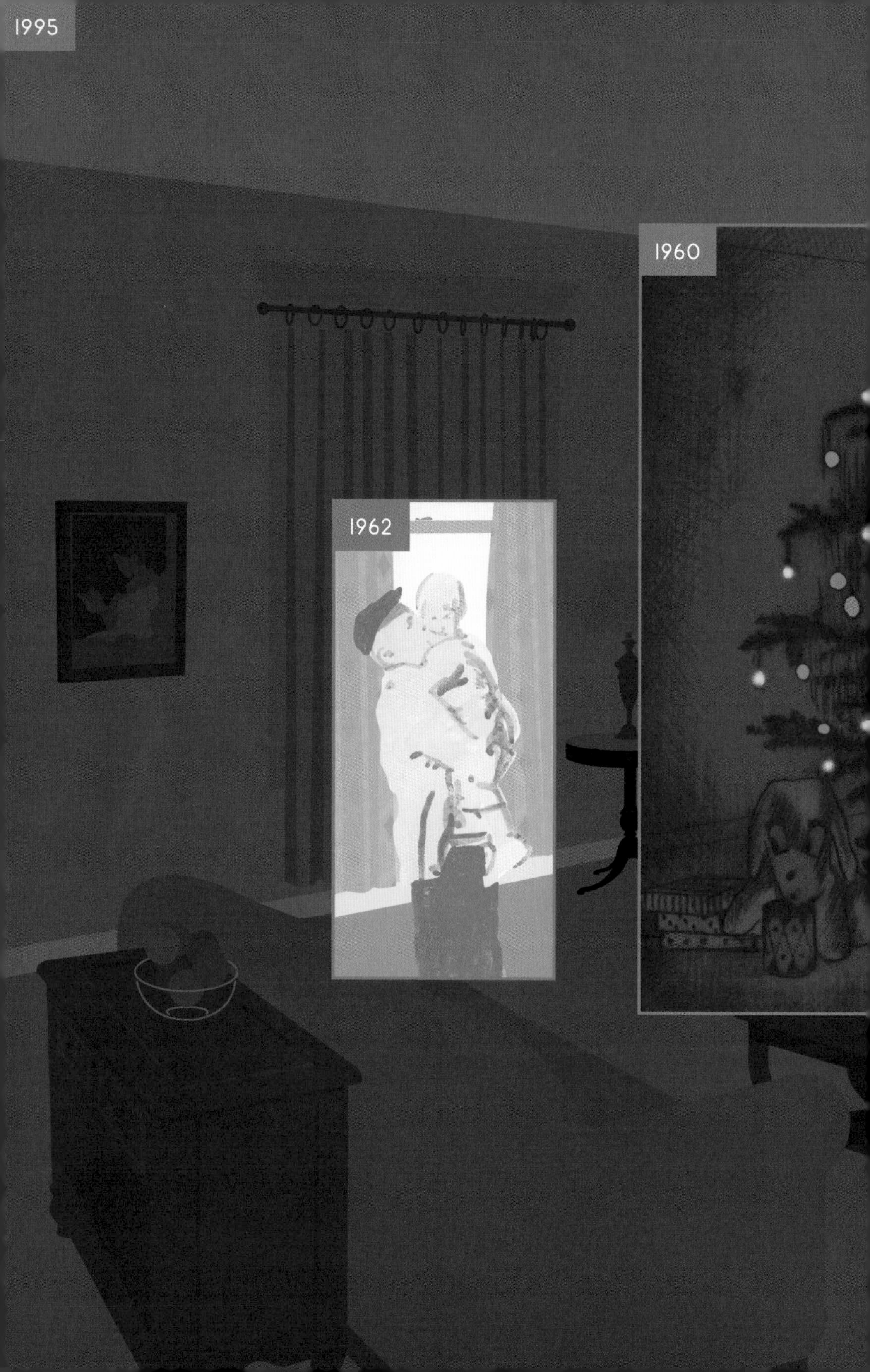
1995
1960
1962

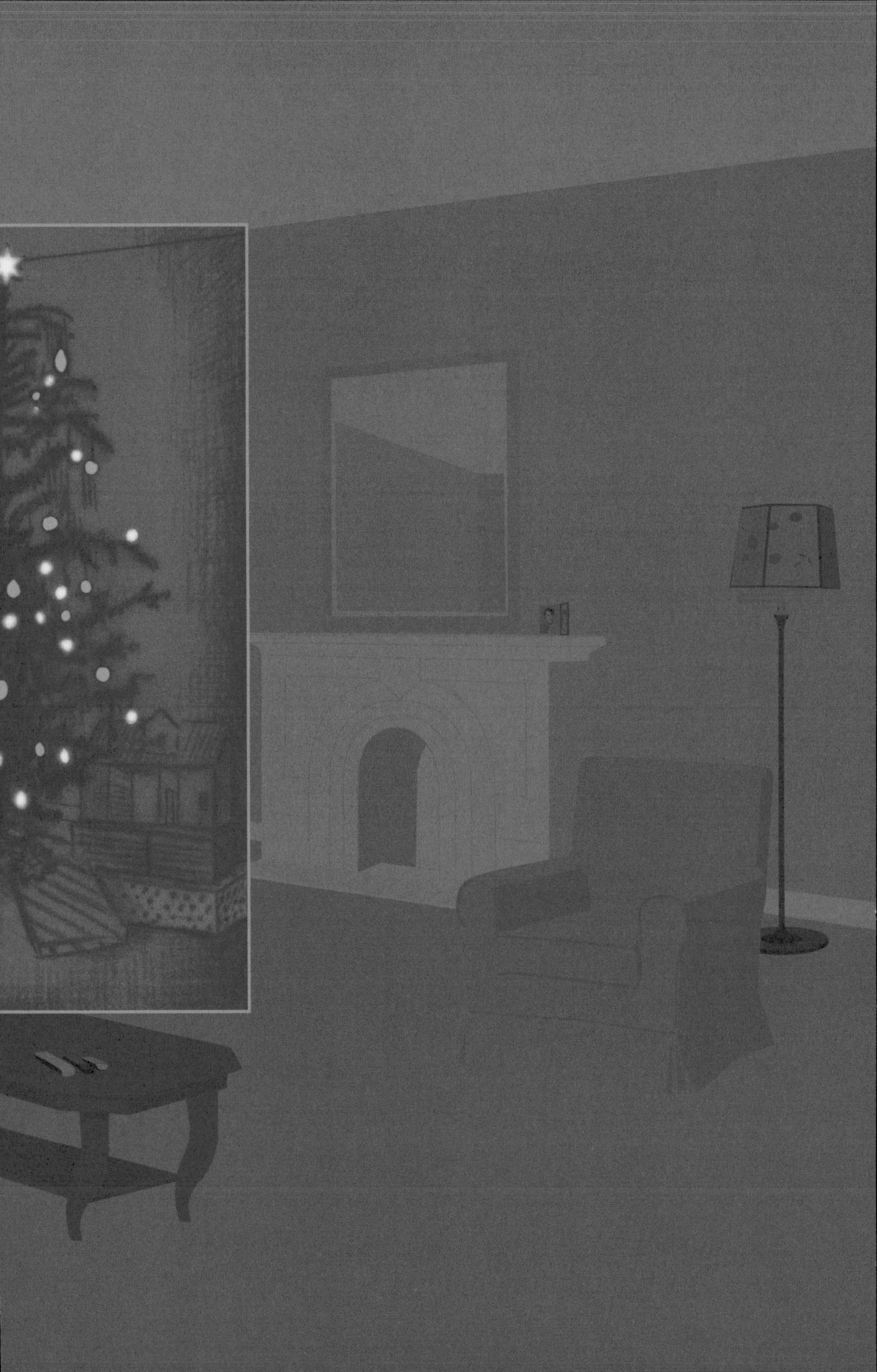

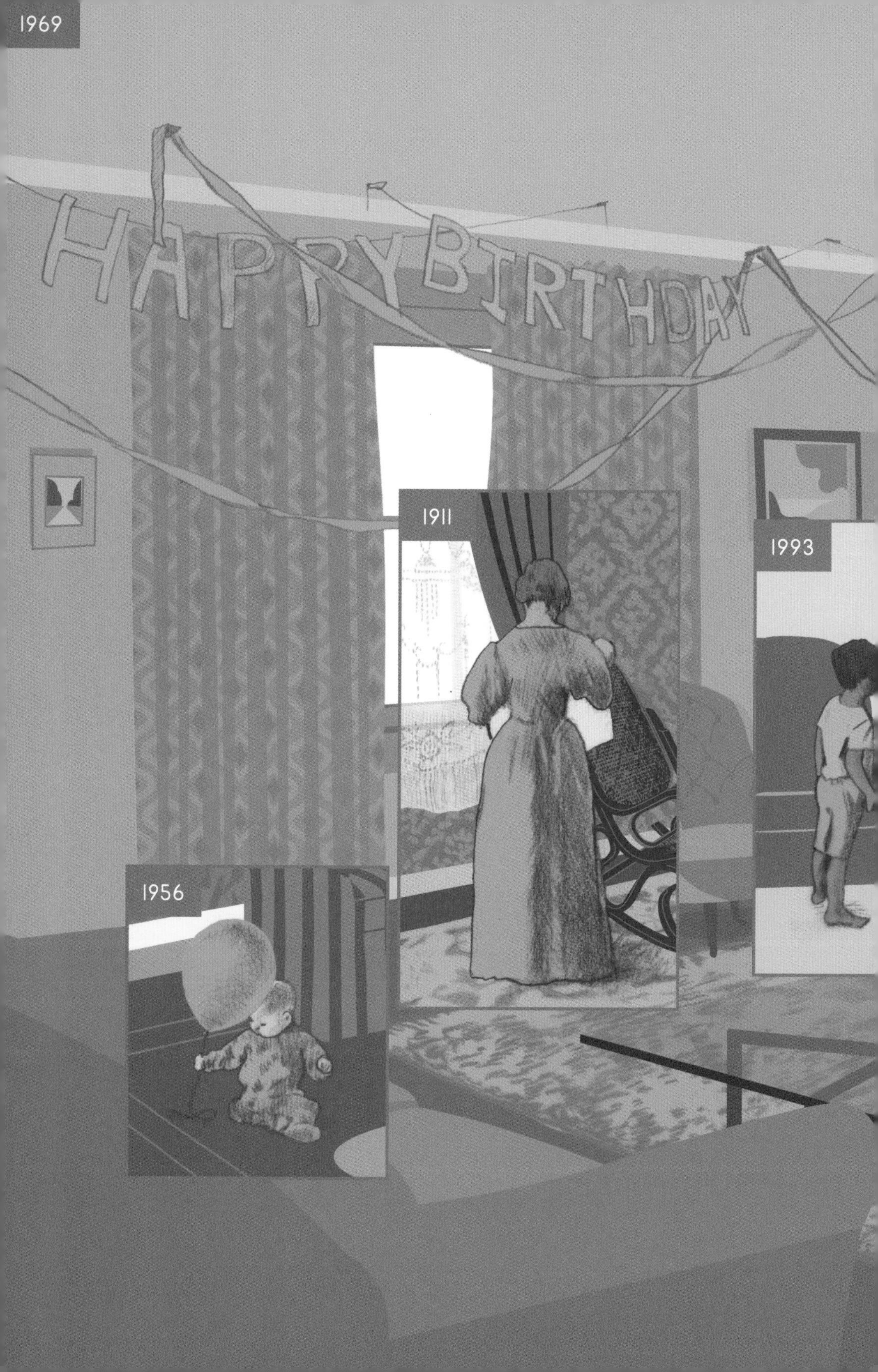
1969
HAPPY BIRTHDAY
1911
1993
1956

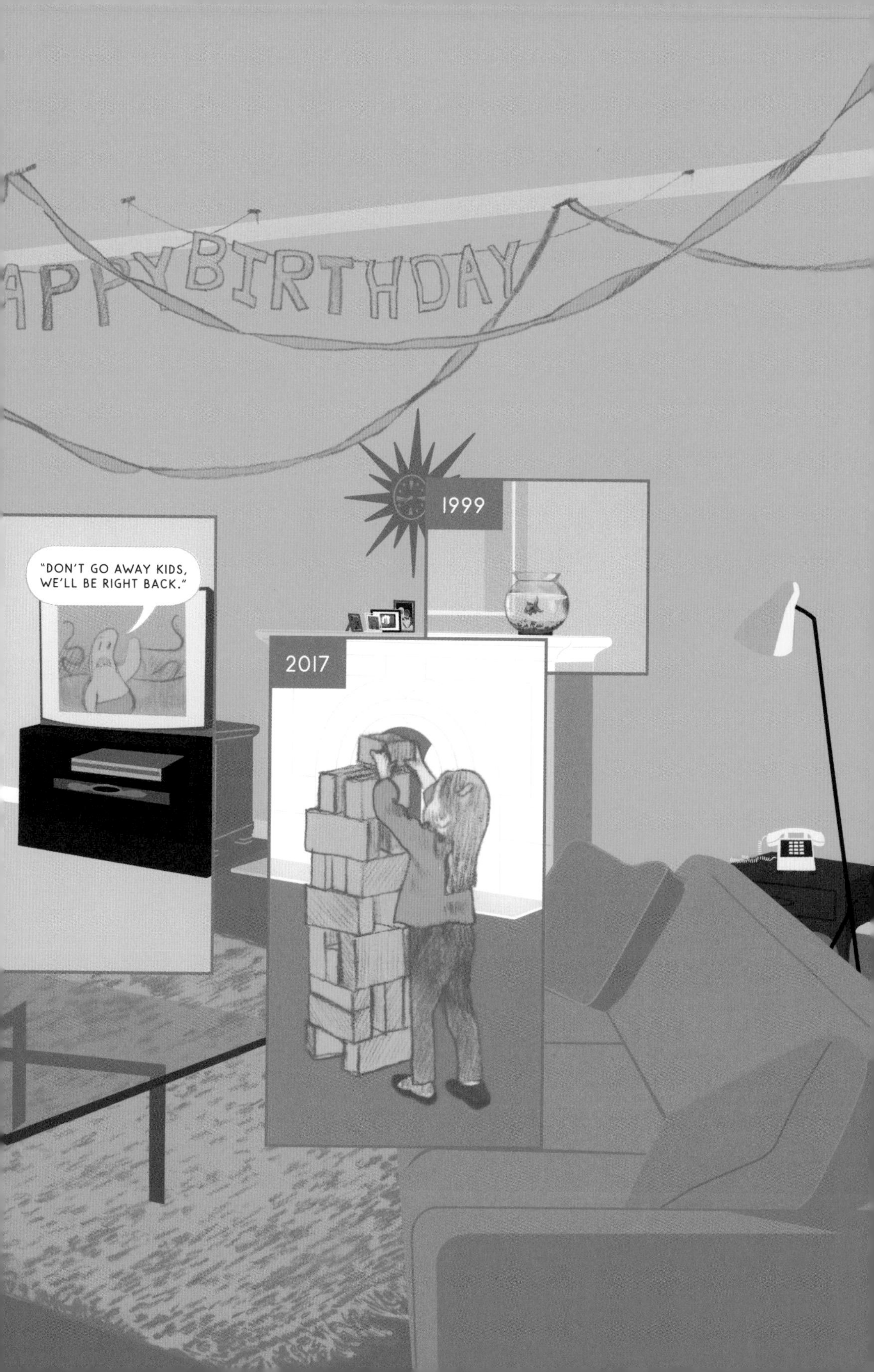

APPY BIRTHDAY
1999
"DON'T GO AWAY KIDS, WE'LL BE RIGHT BACK."
2017

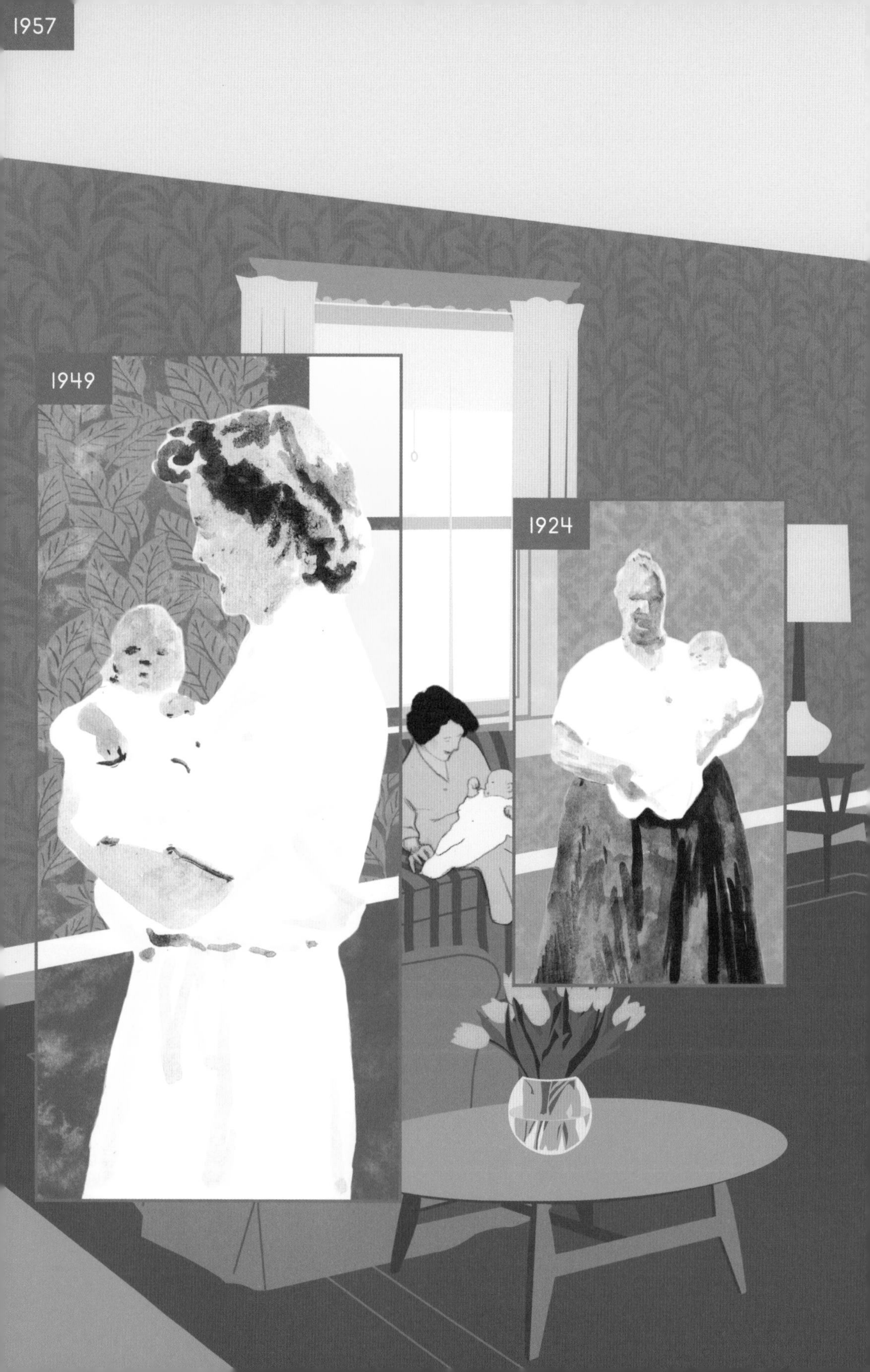
1957
1949
1924

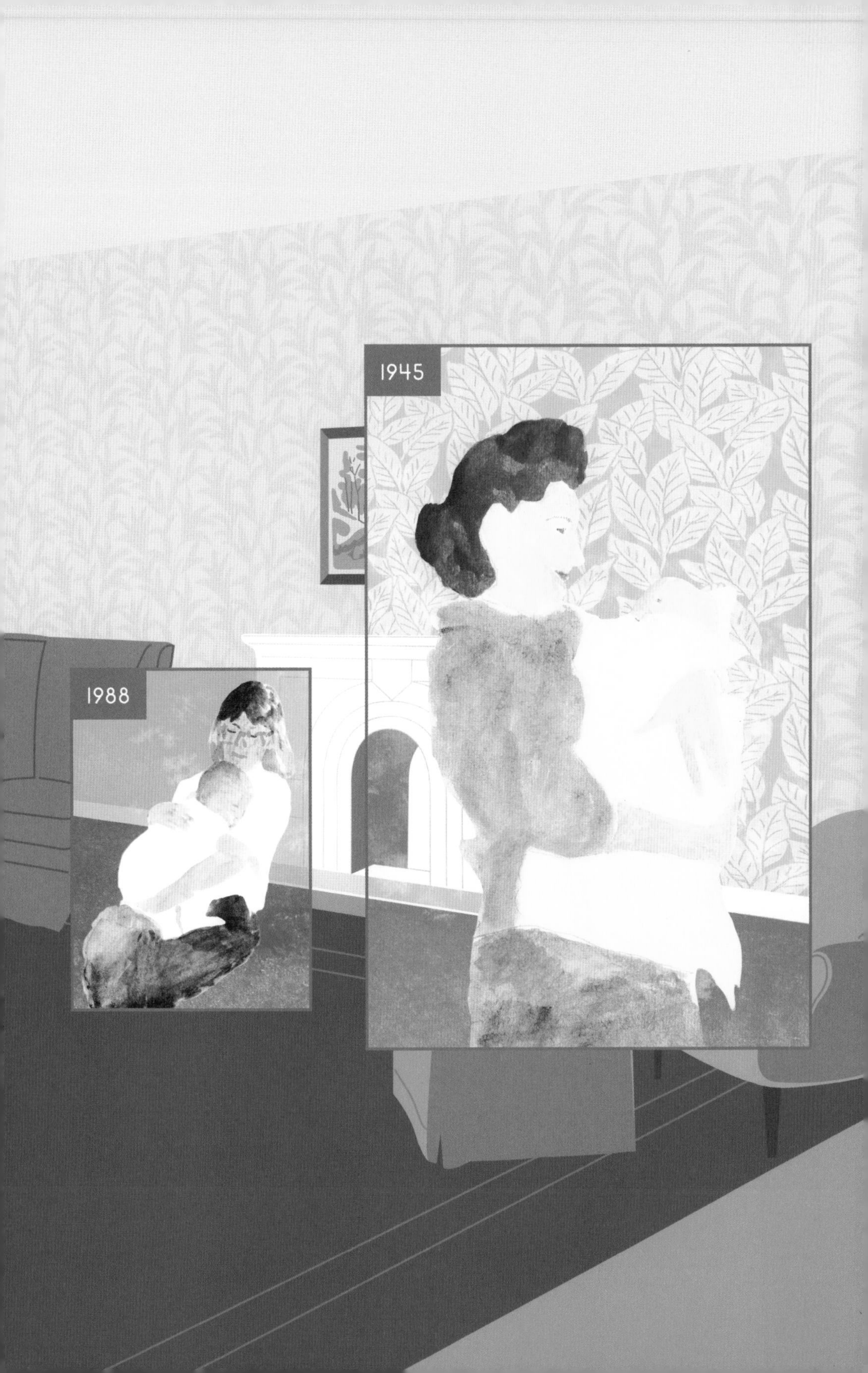
1945
1988

1986

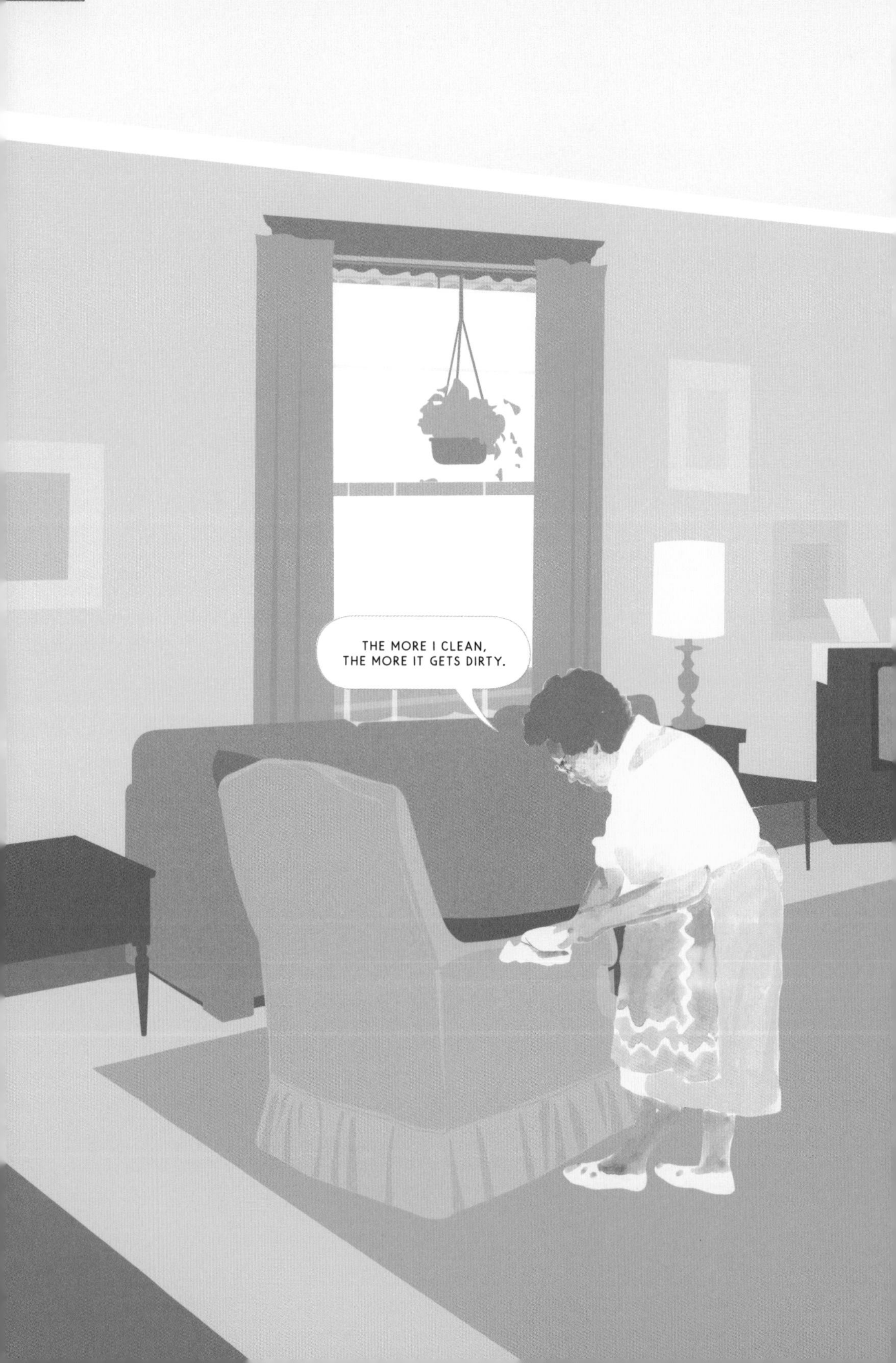

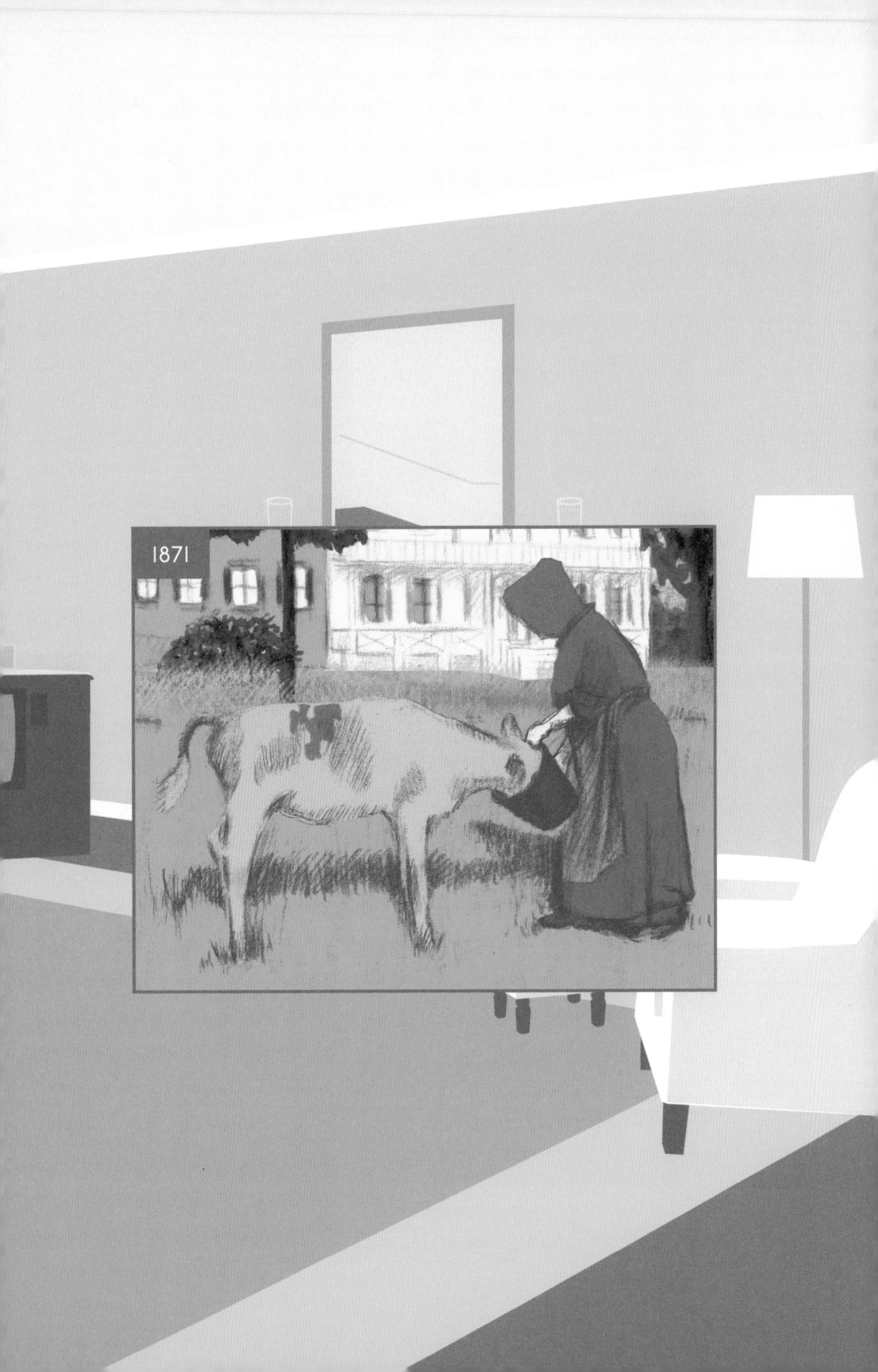
1871

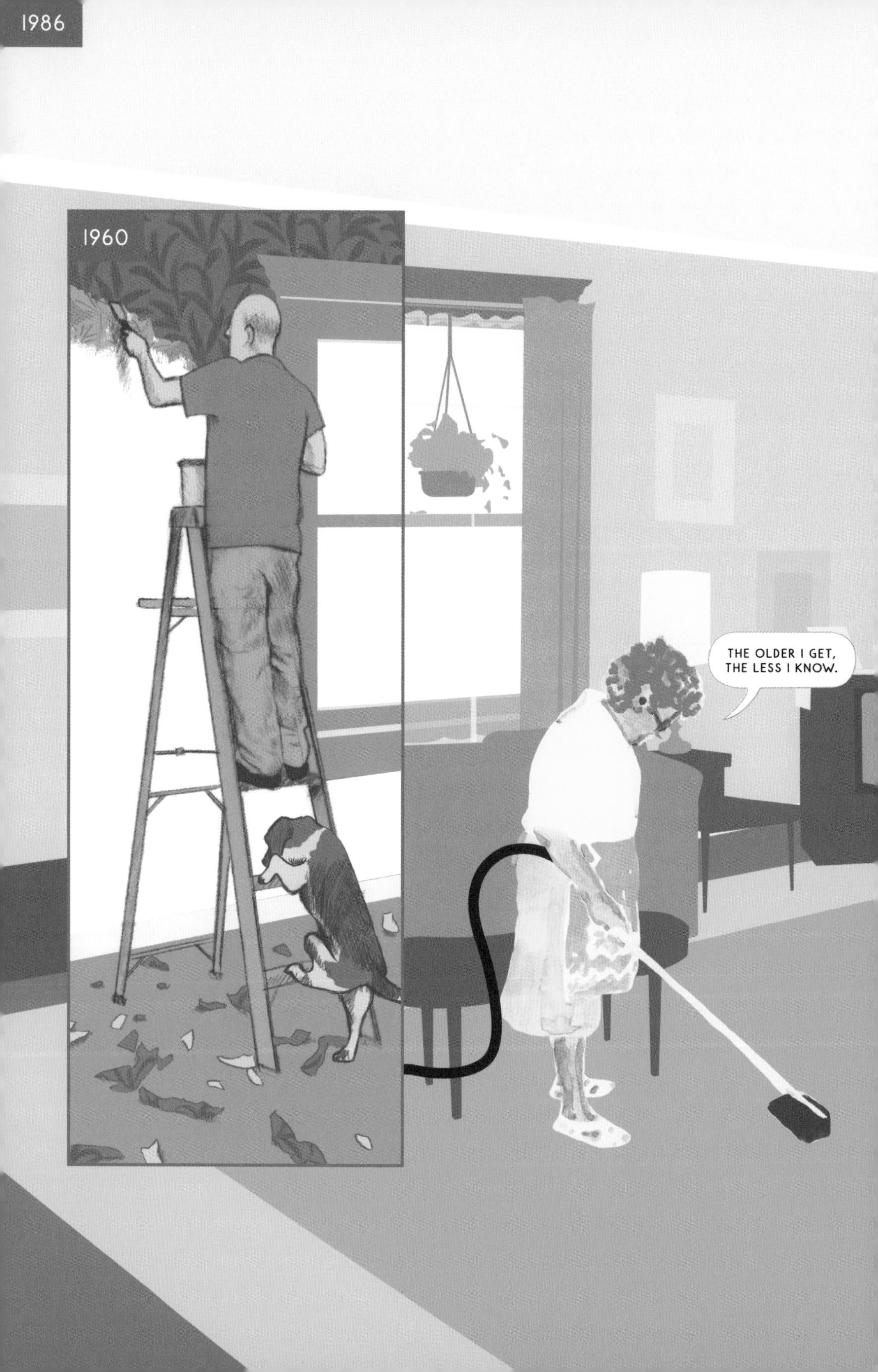
1986
1960
THE OLDER I GET, THE LESS I KNOW.

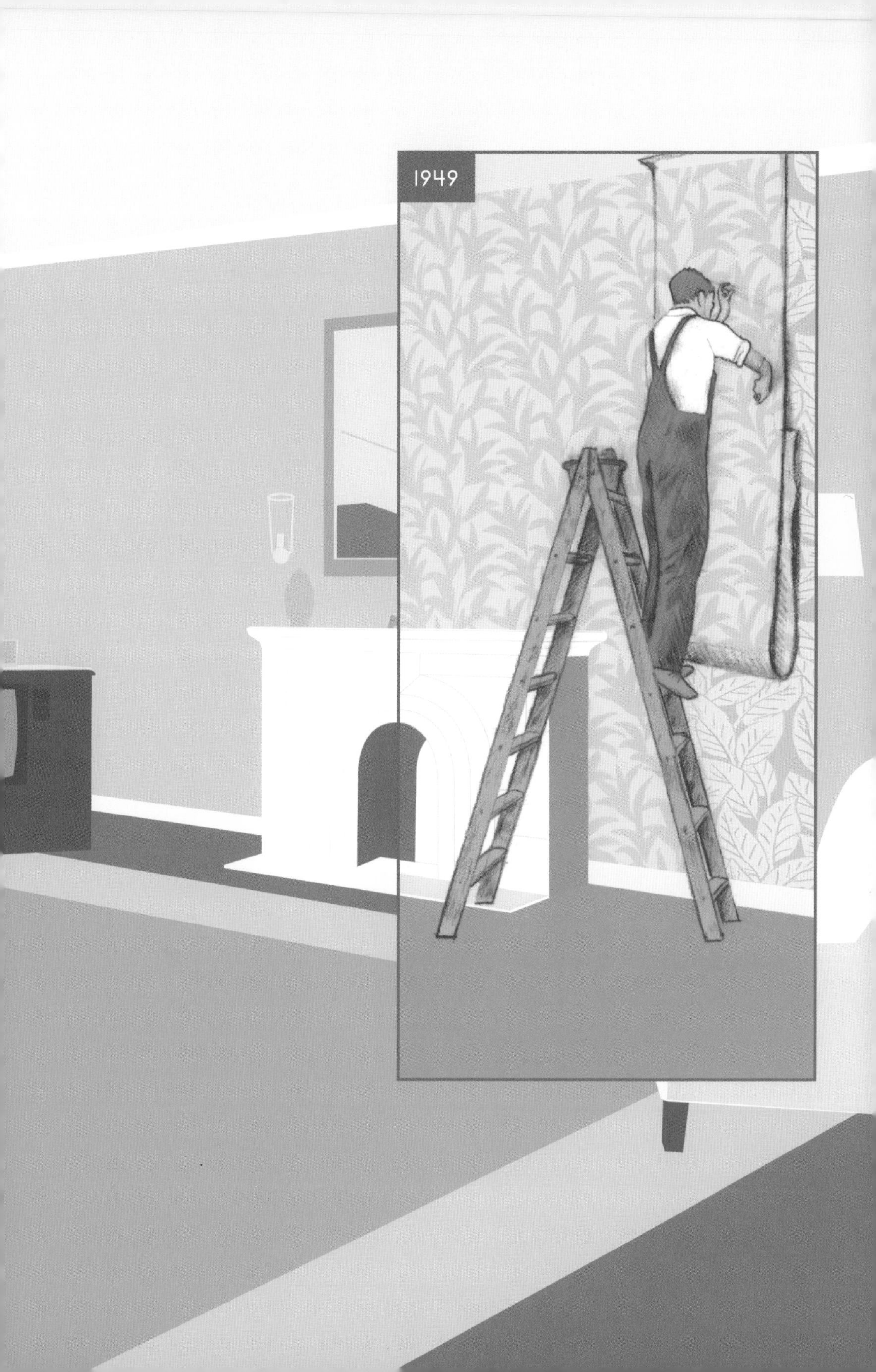
1949

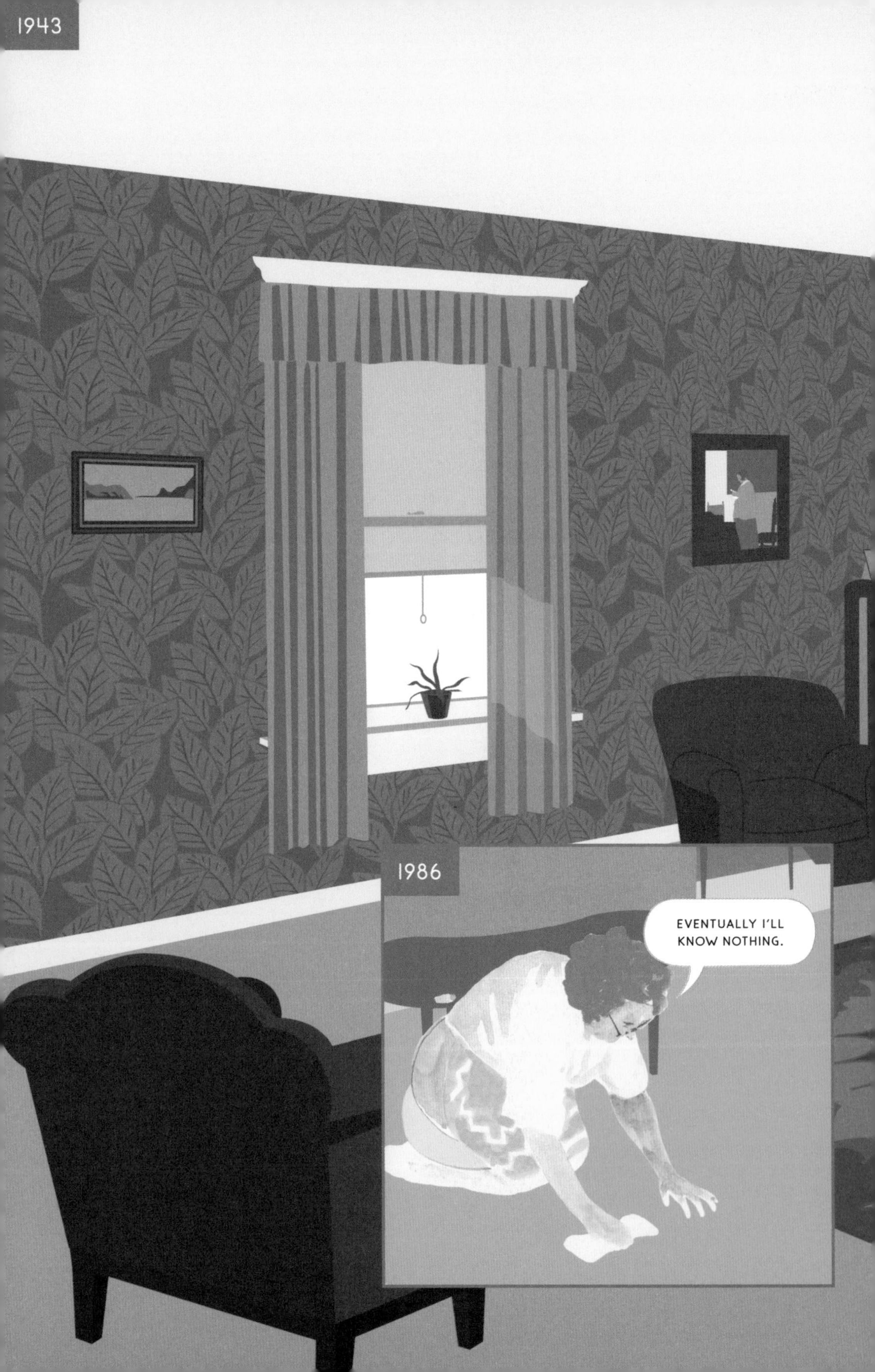
1943
1986
EVENTUALLY I'LL KNOW NOTHING.

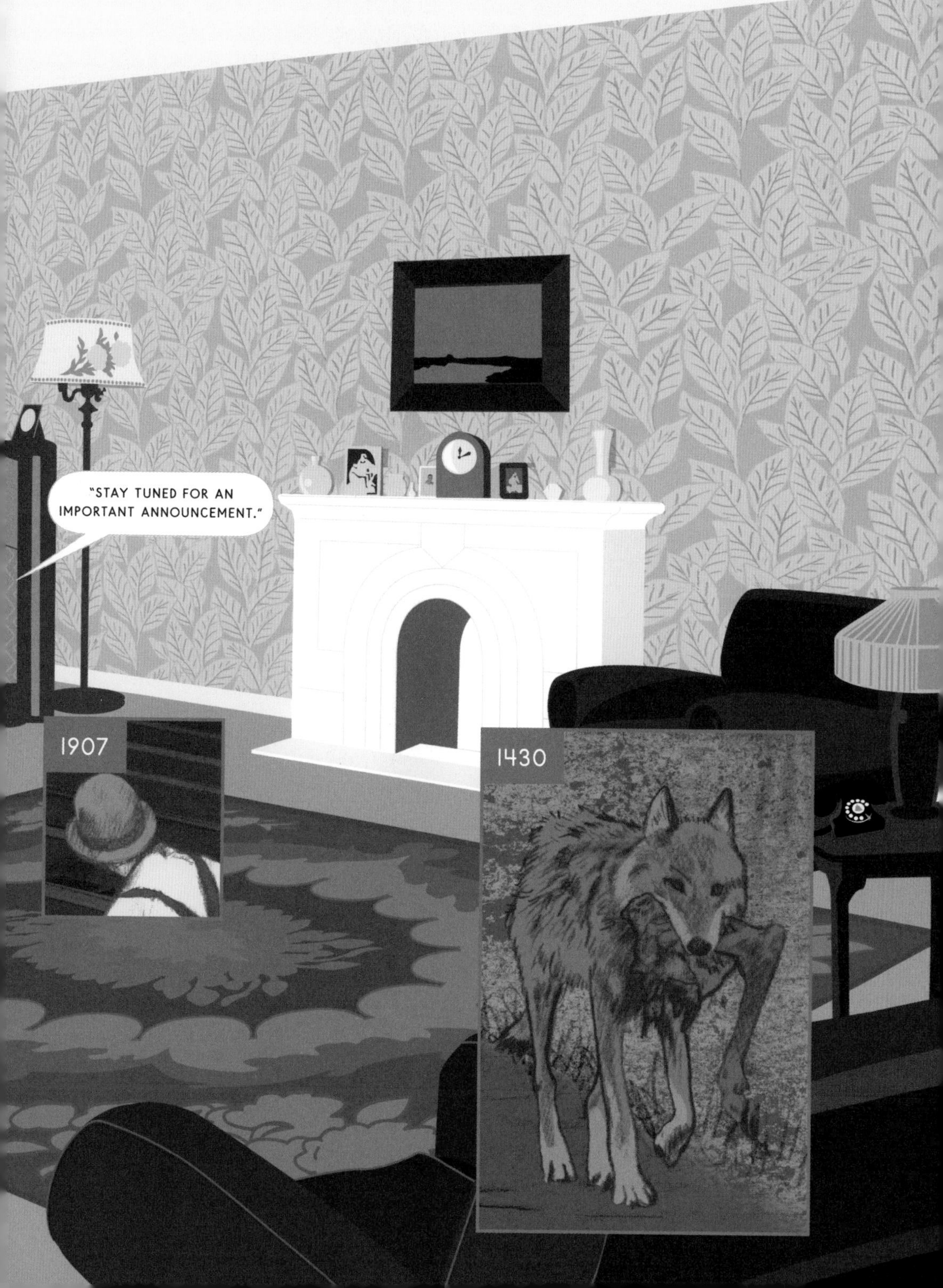
"STAY TUNED FOR AN IMPORTANT ANNOUNCEMENT."
1907
1430

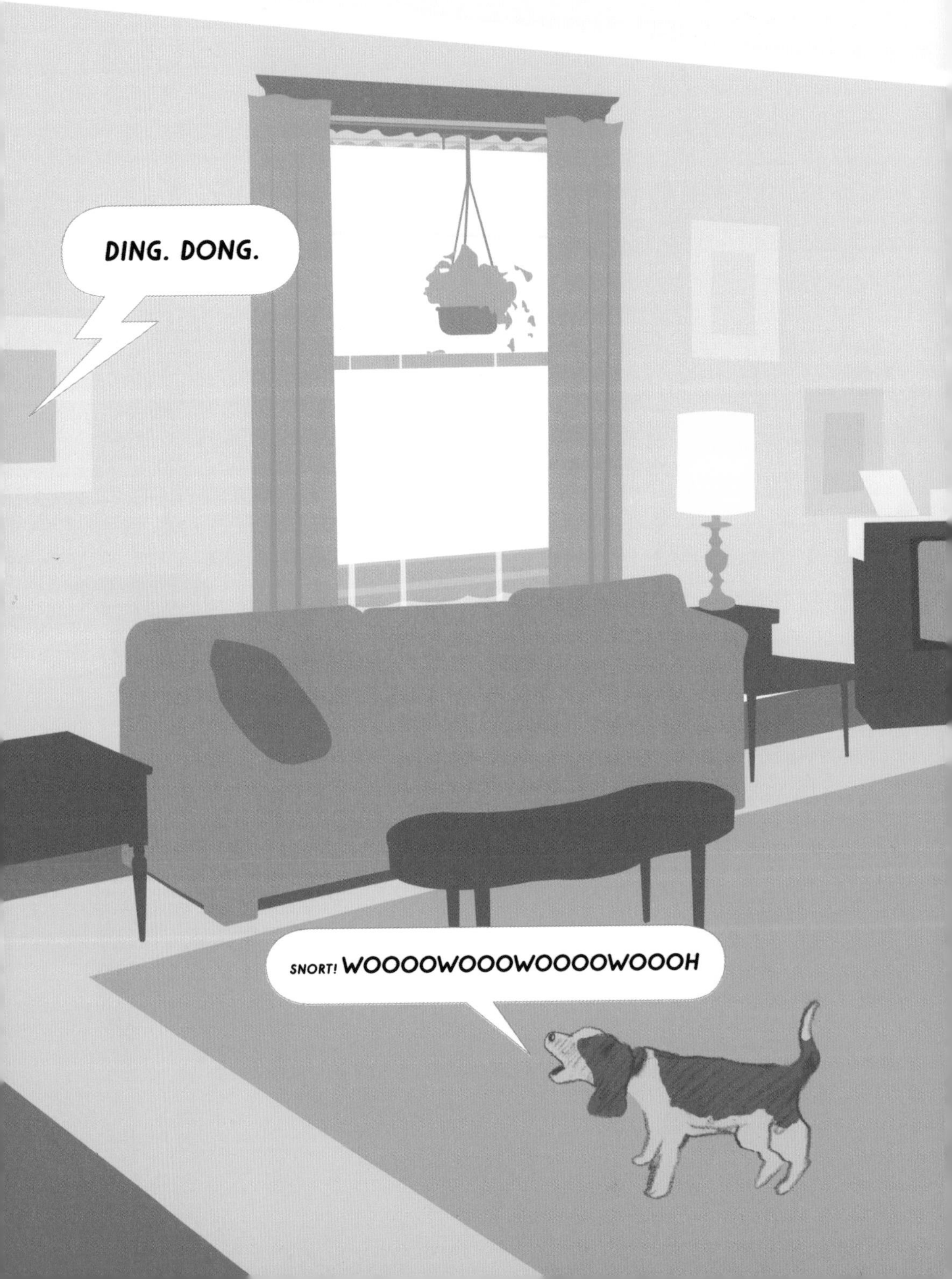
DING. DONG.
SNORT! WOOOOWOOOWOOOOWOOOH

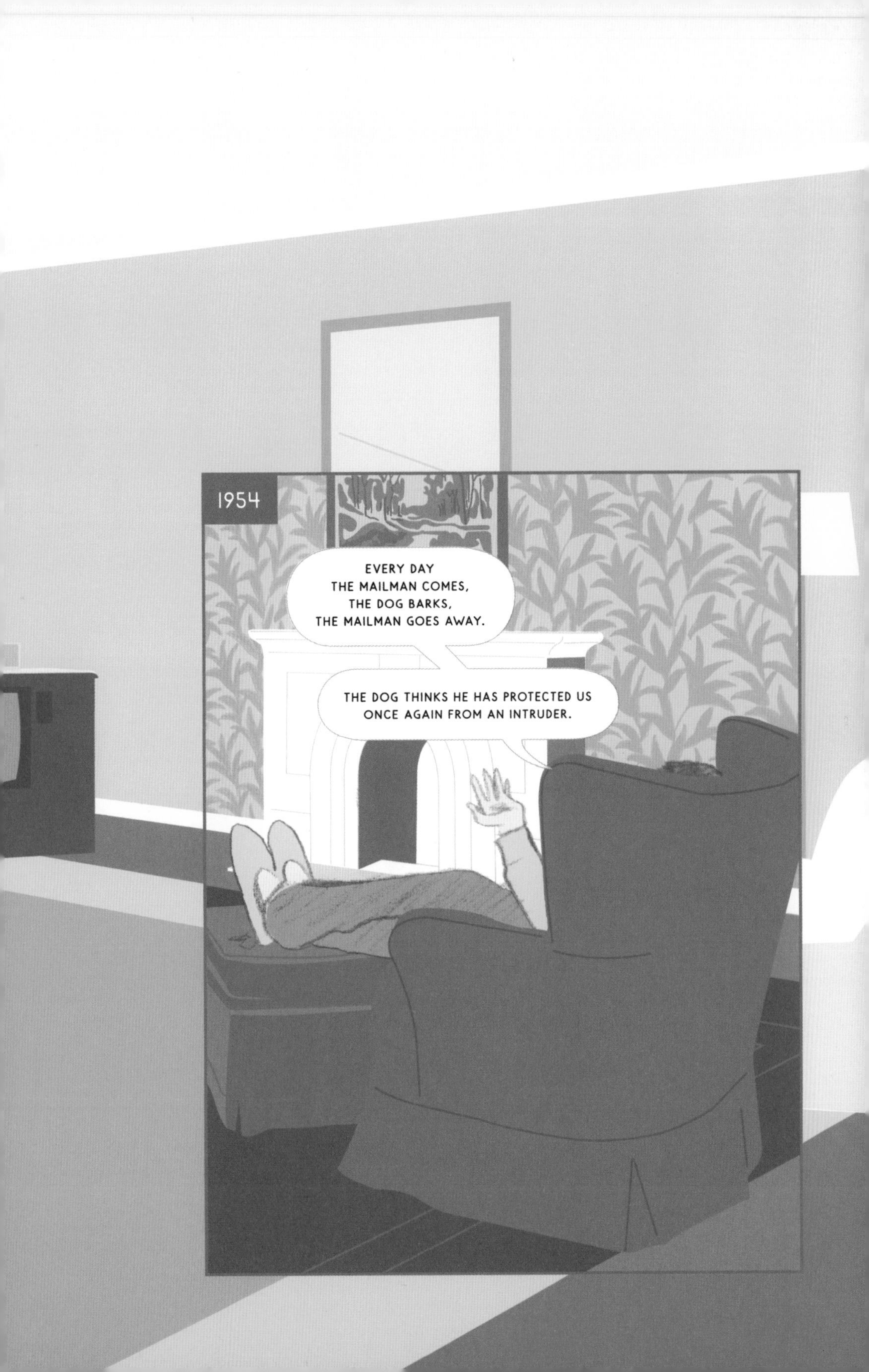
1954
EVERY DAY THE MAILMAN COMES, THE DOG BARKS, THE MAILMAN GOES AWAY.
THE DOG THINKS HE HAS PROTECTED US ONCE AGAIN FROM AN INTRUDER.

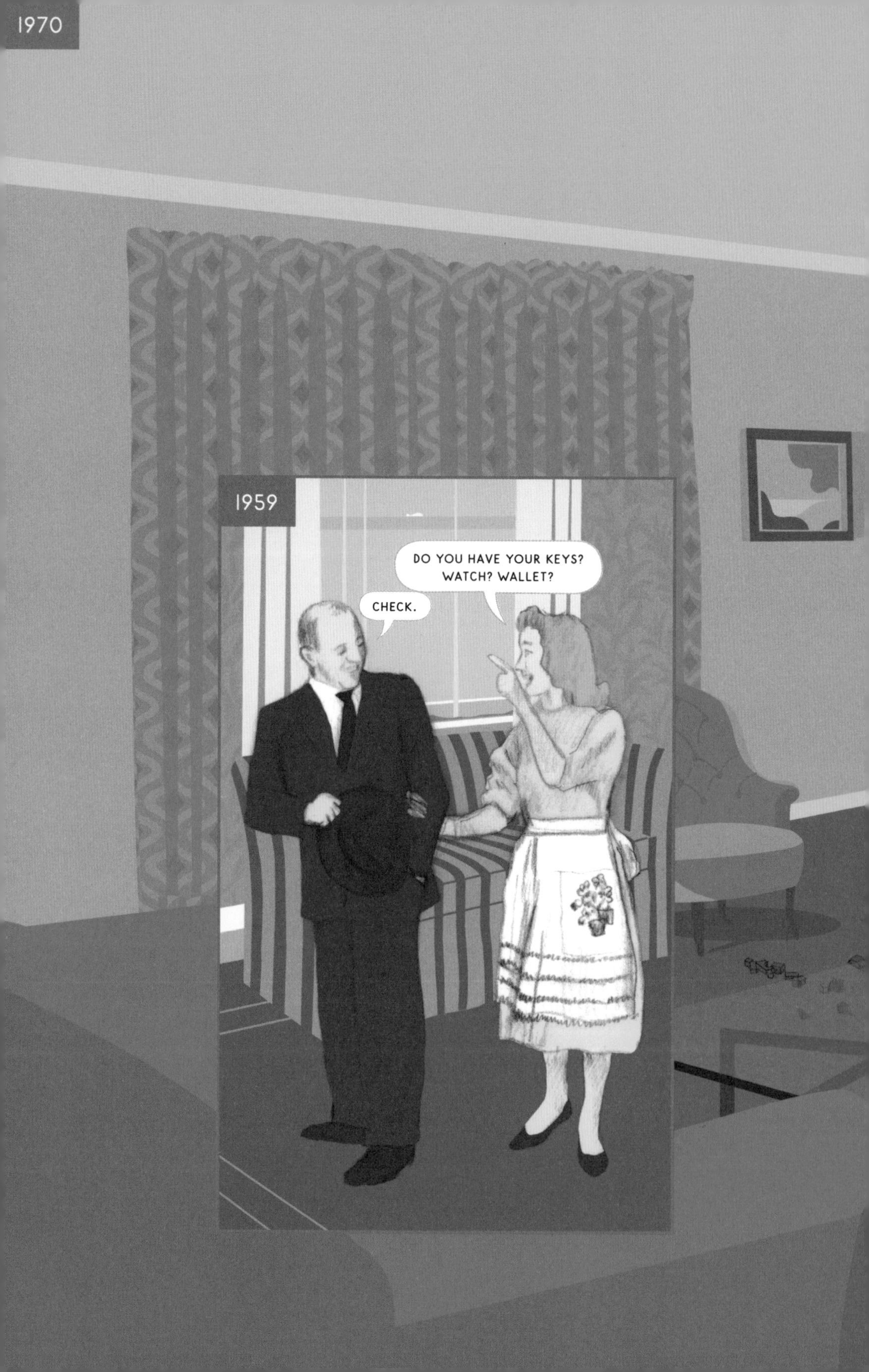
1970
1959
DO YOU HAVE YOUR KEYS? WATCH? WALLET?
CHECK.

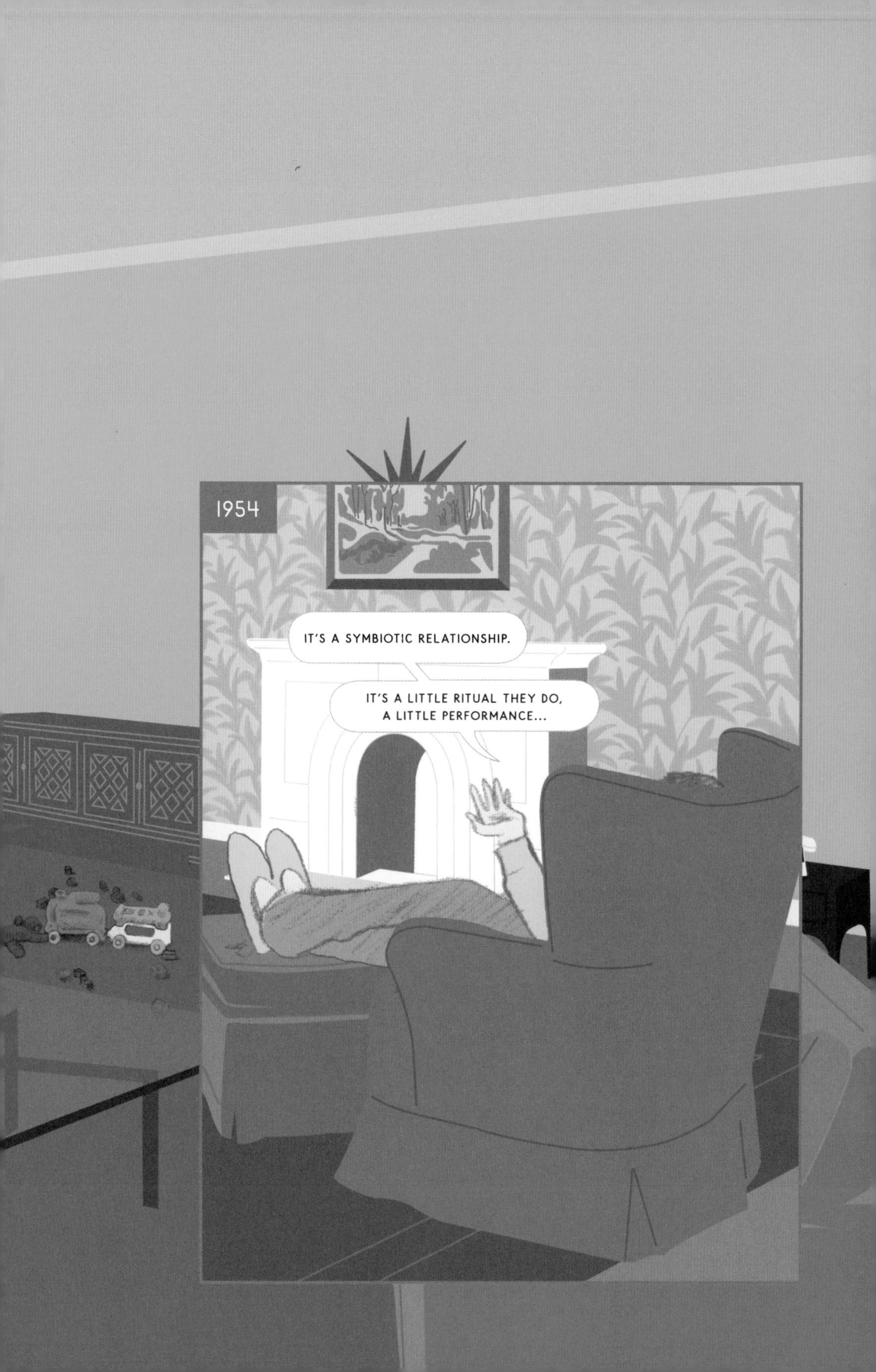
1954
IT'S A SYMBIOTIC RELATIONSHIP.
IT'S A LITTLE RITUAL THEY DO,
A LITTLE PERFORMANCE...

1953

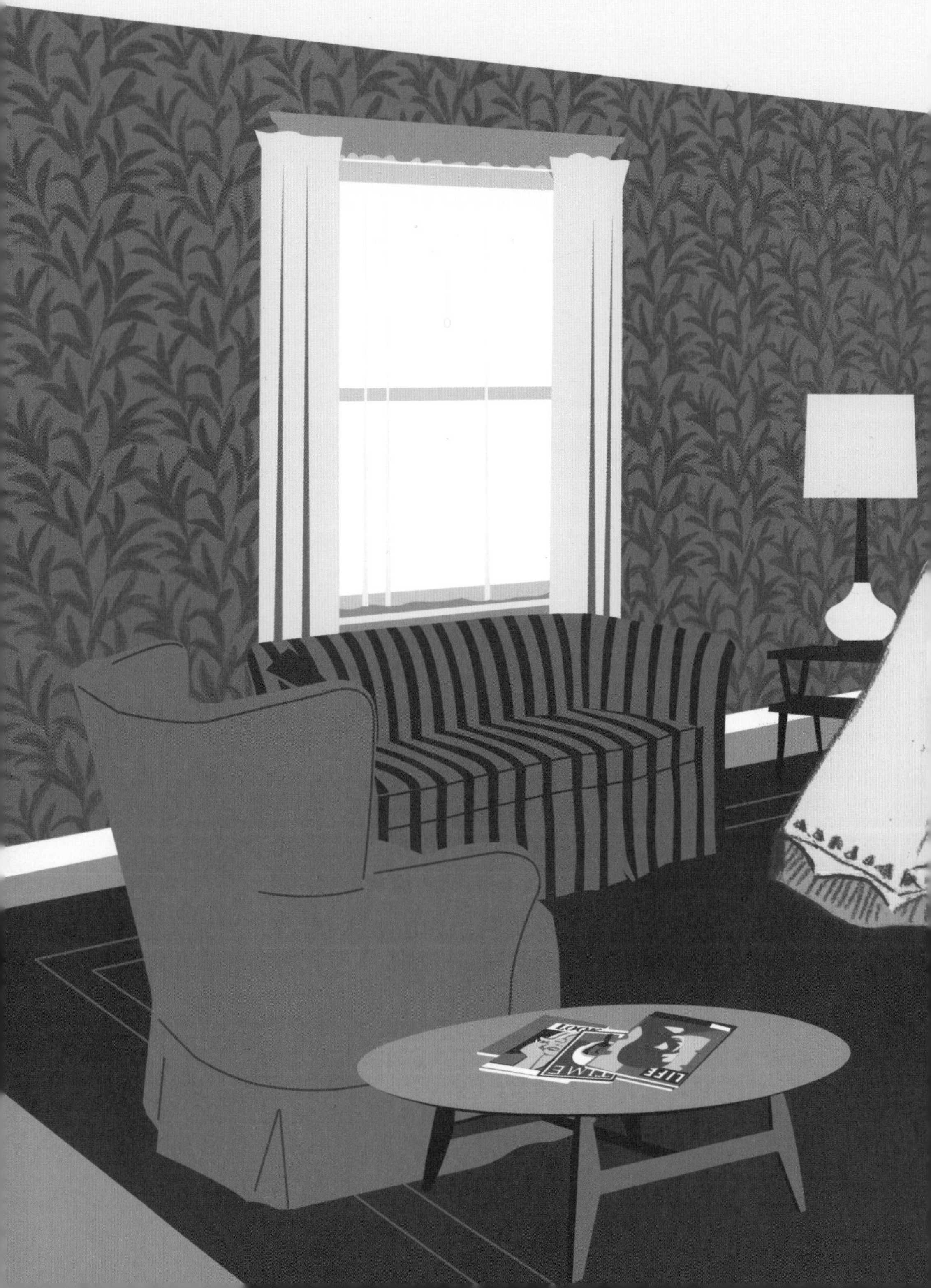
TIME
LIFE

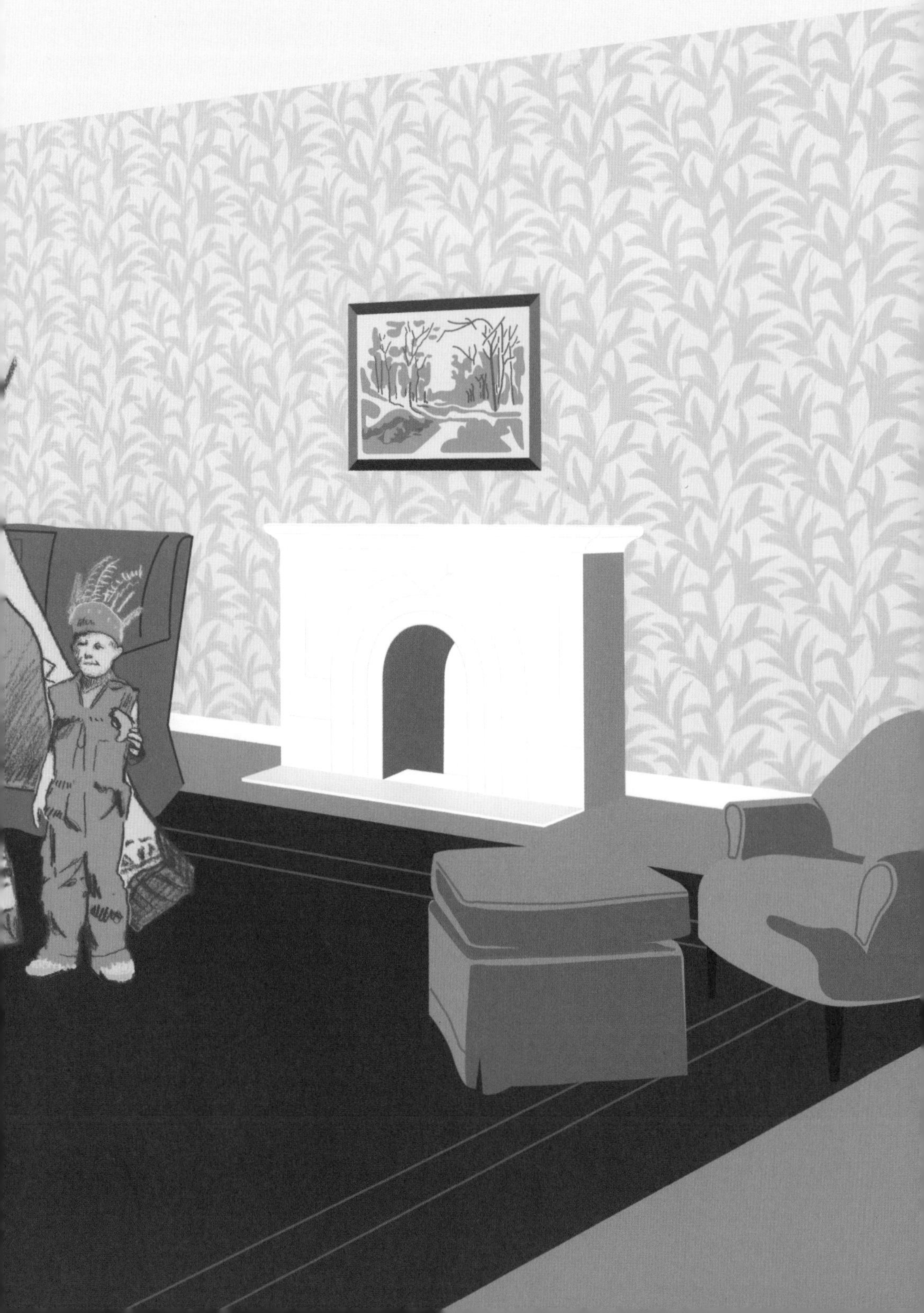

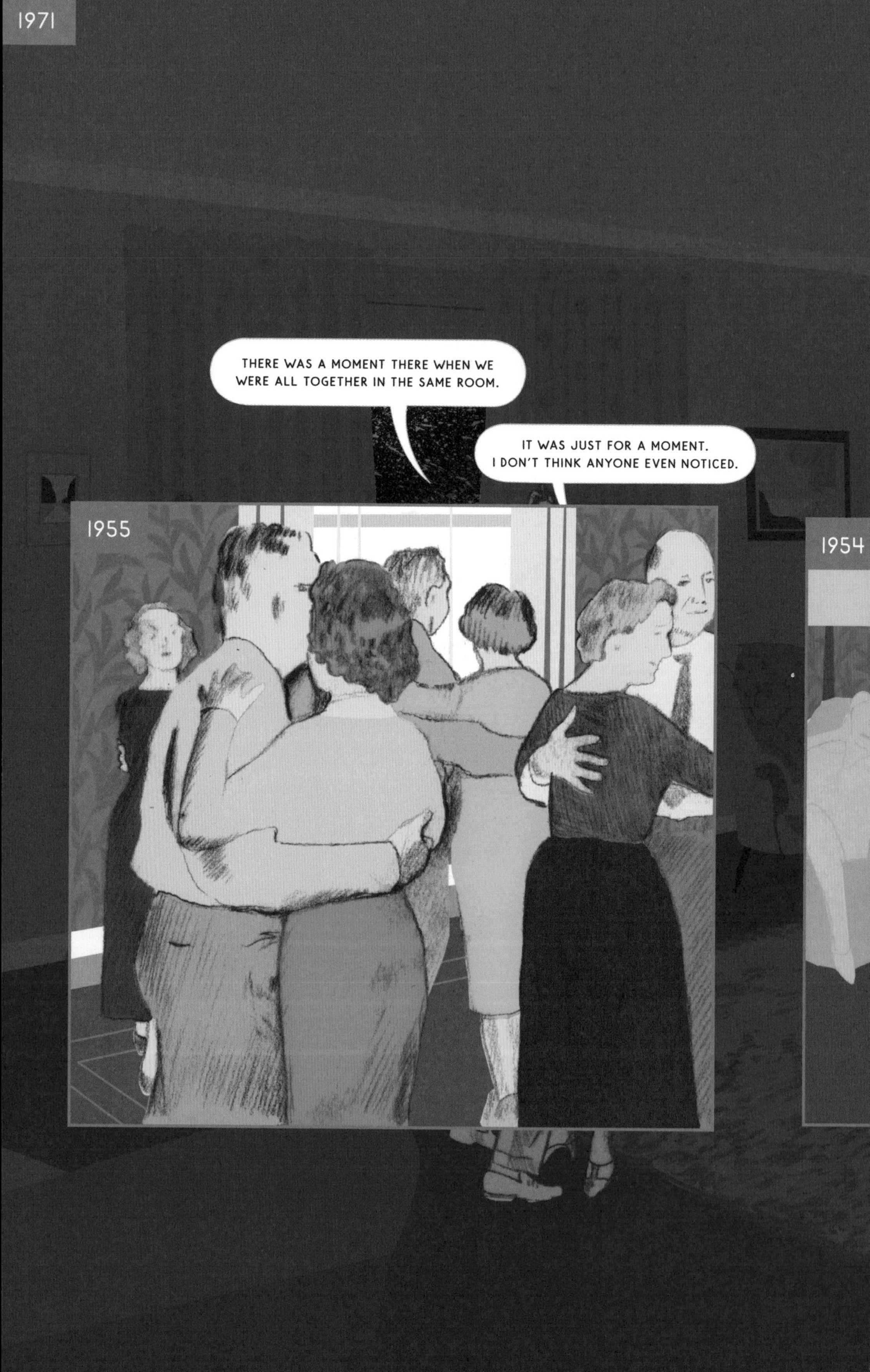
1971
THERE WAS A MOMENT THERE WHEN WE WERE ALL TOGETHER IN THE SAME ROOM.
IT WAS JUST FOR A MOMENT. I DON'T THINK ANYONE EVEN NOTICED.
1955
1954

I SHOULD GO.
A SKELETON WALKS INTO A BAR.
HE ORDERS A BEER AND A MOP.

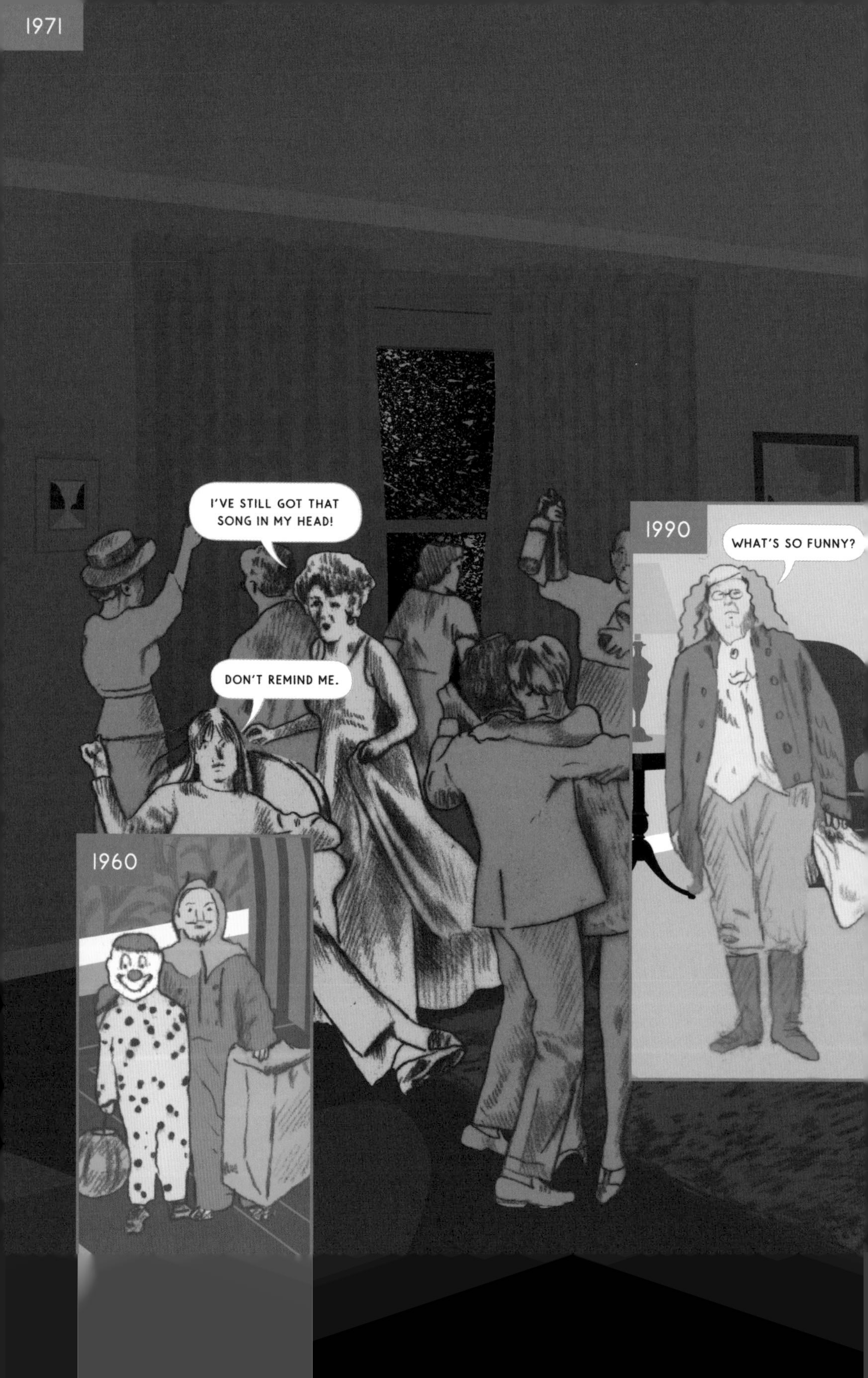
1971
I'VE STILL GOT THAT SONG IN MY HEAD!
DON'T REMIND ME.
1990
WHAT'S SO FUNNY?
1960

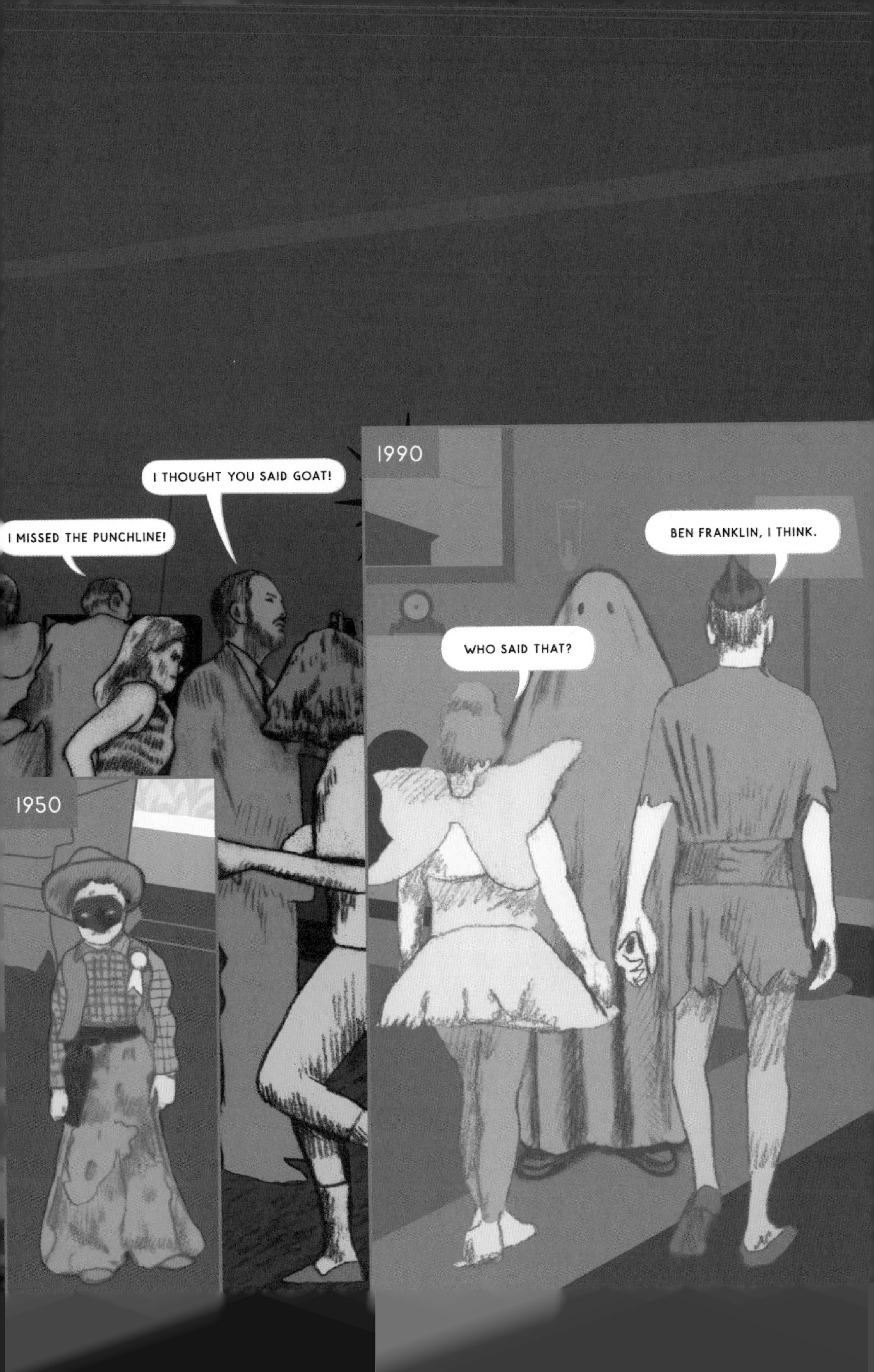
1950
I MISSED THE PUNCHLINE!
I THOUGHT YOU SAID GOAT!
1990
WHO SAID THAT?
BEN FRANKLIN, I THINK.

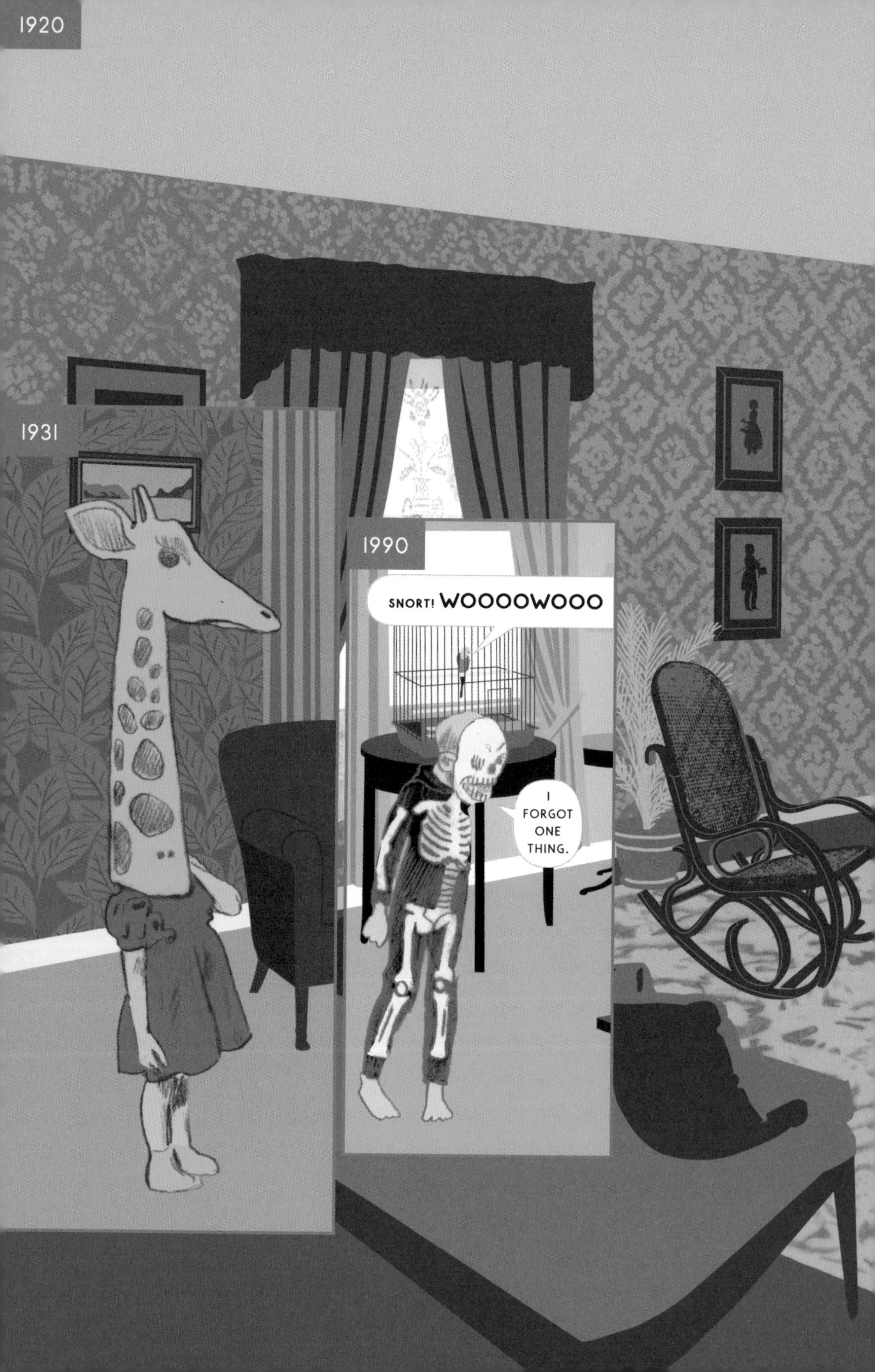
1920
1931
1990
SNORT! WOOOOWOOO
I FORGOT ONE THING.

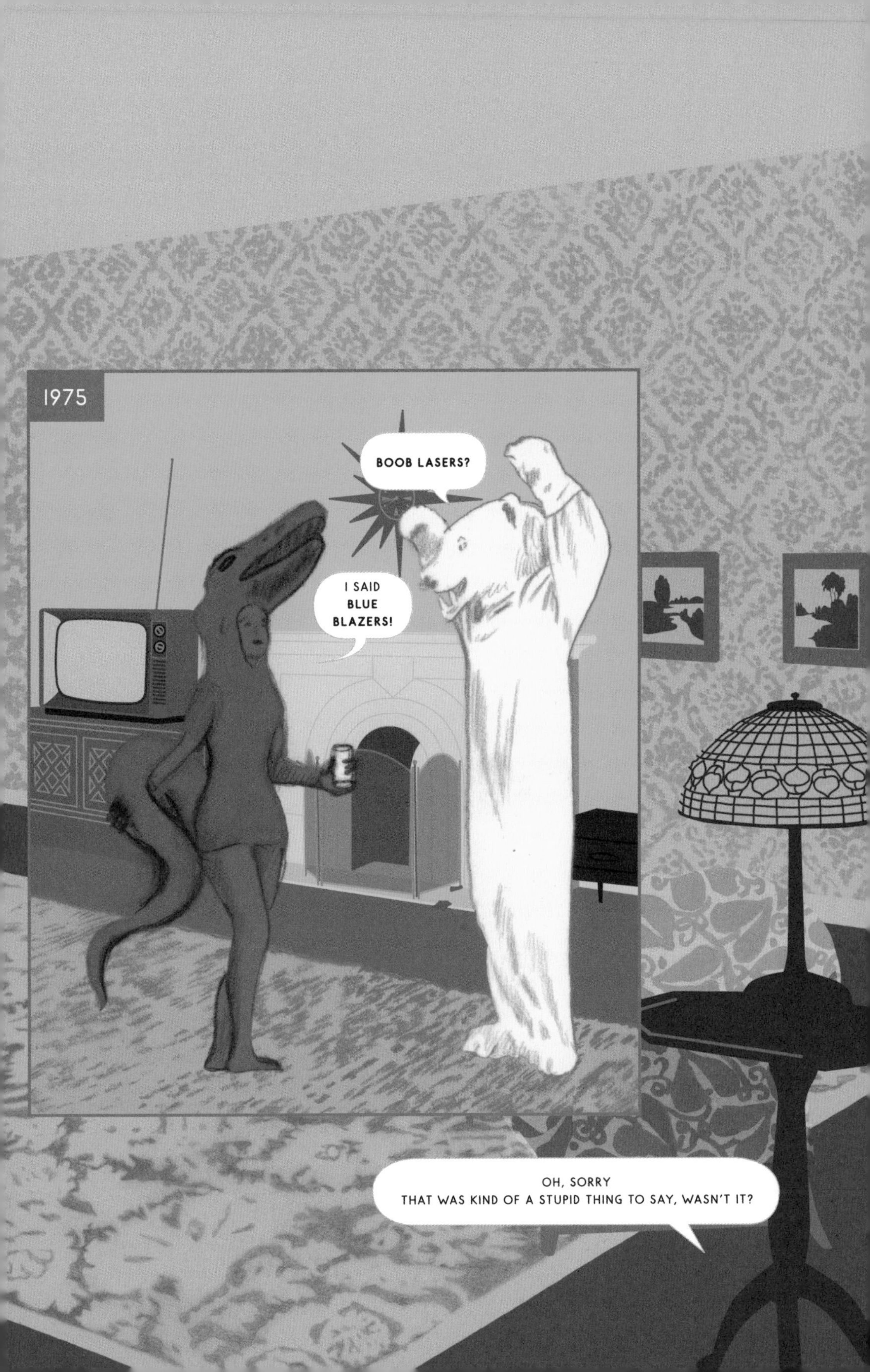

1975
BOOB LASERS?
I SAID BLUE BLAZERS!
OH, SORRY
THAT WAS KIND OF A STUPID THING TO SAY, WASN'T IT?

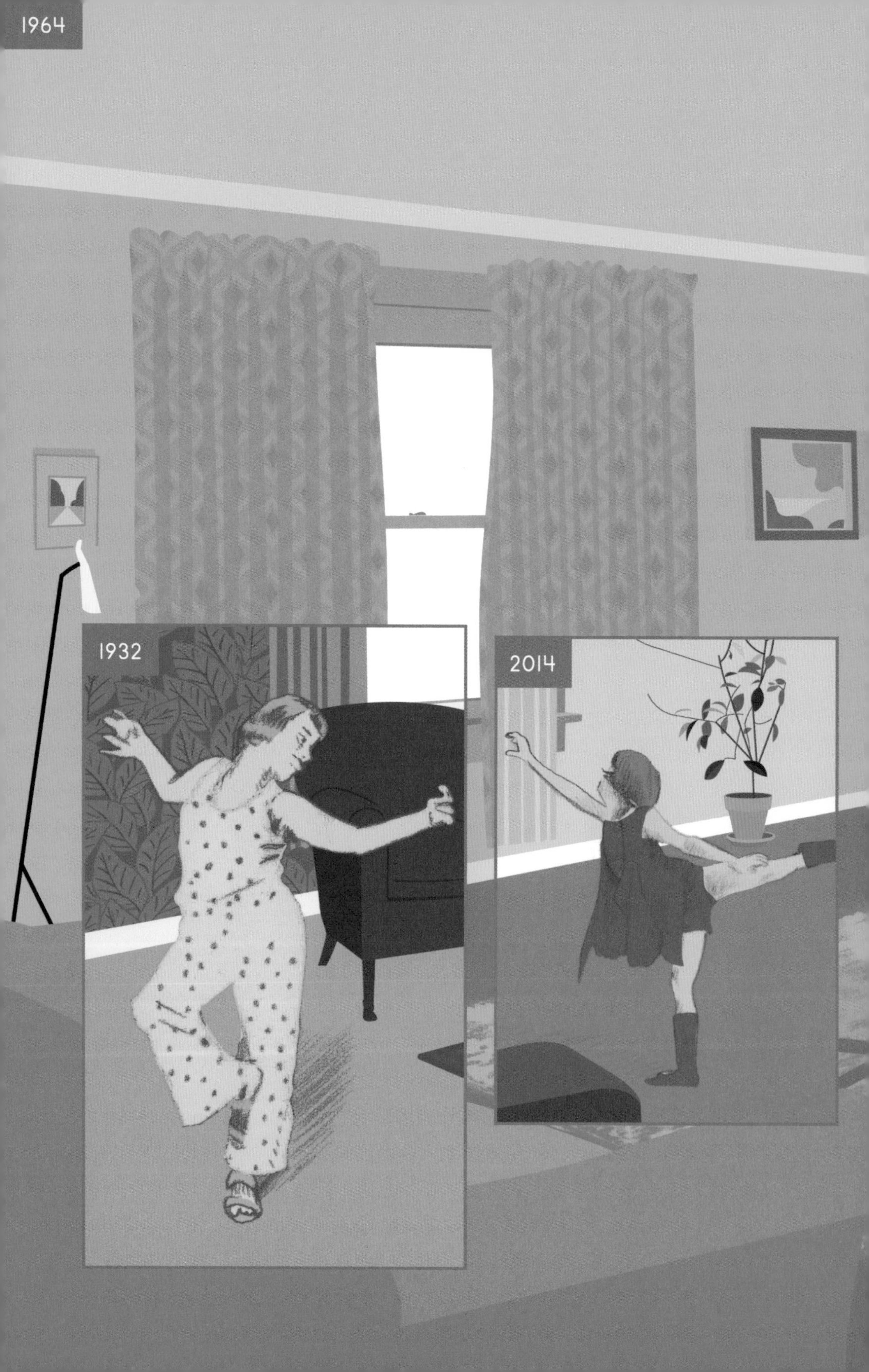
1964
1932
2014

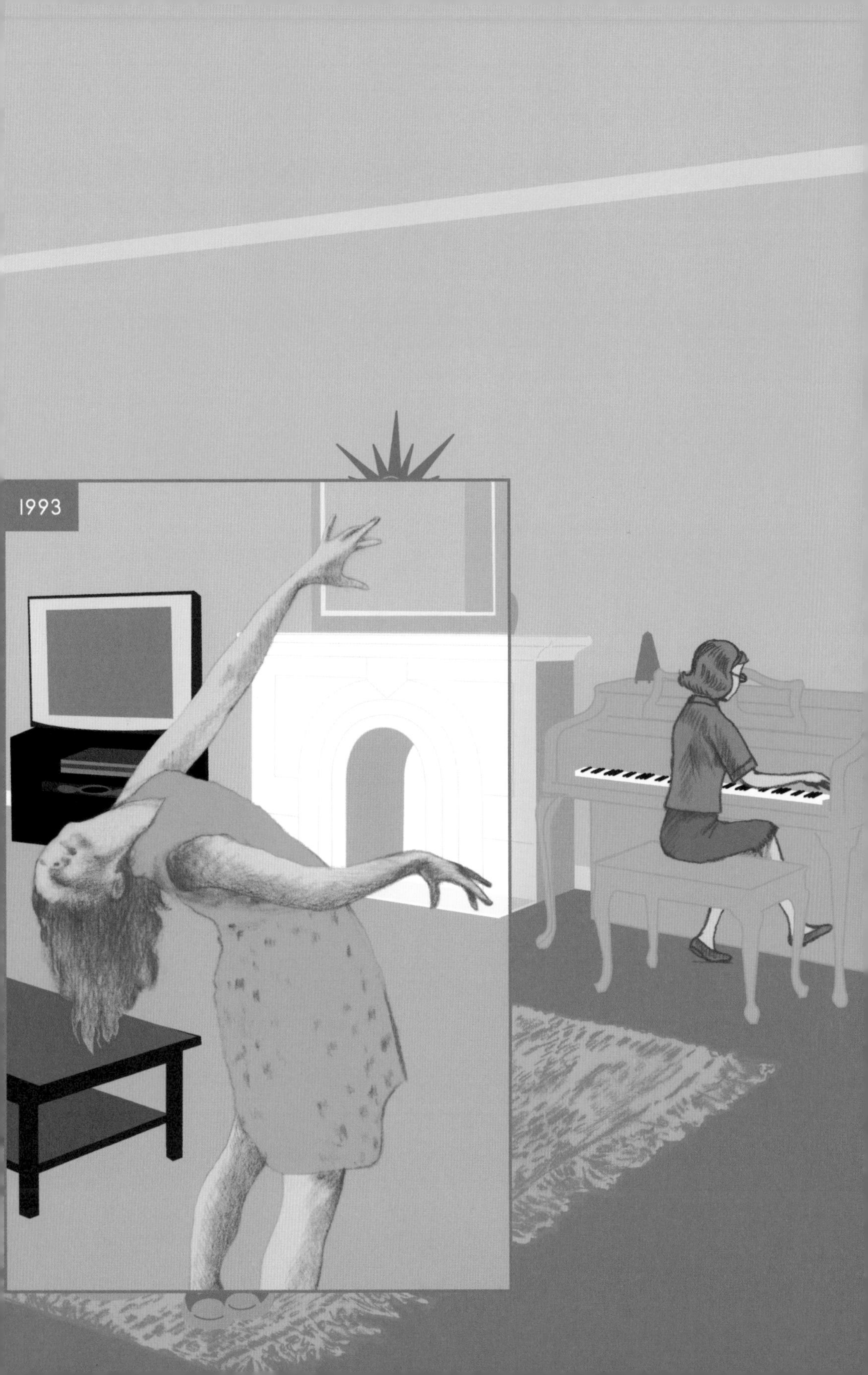
1993

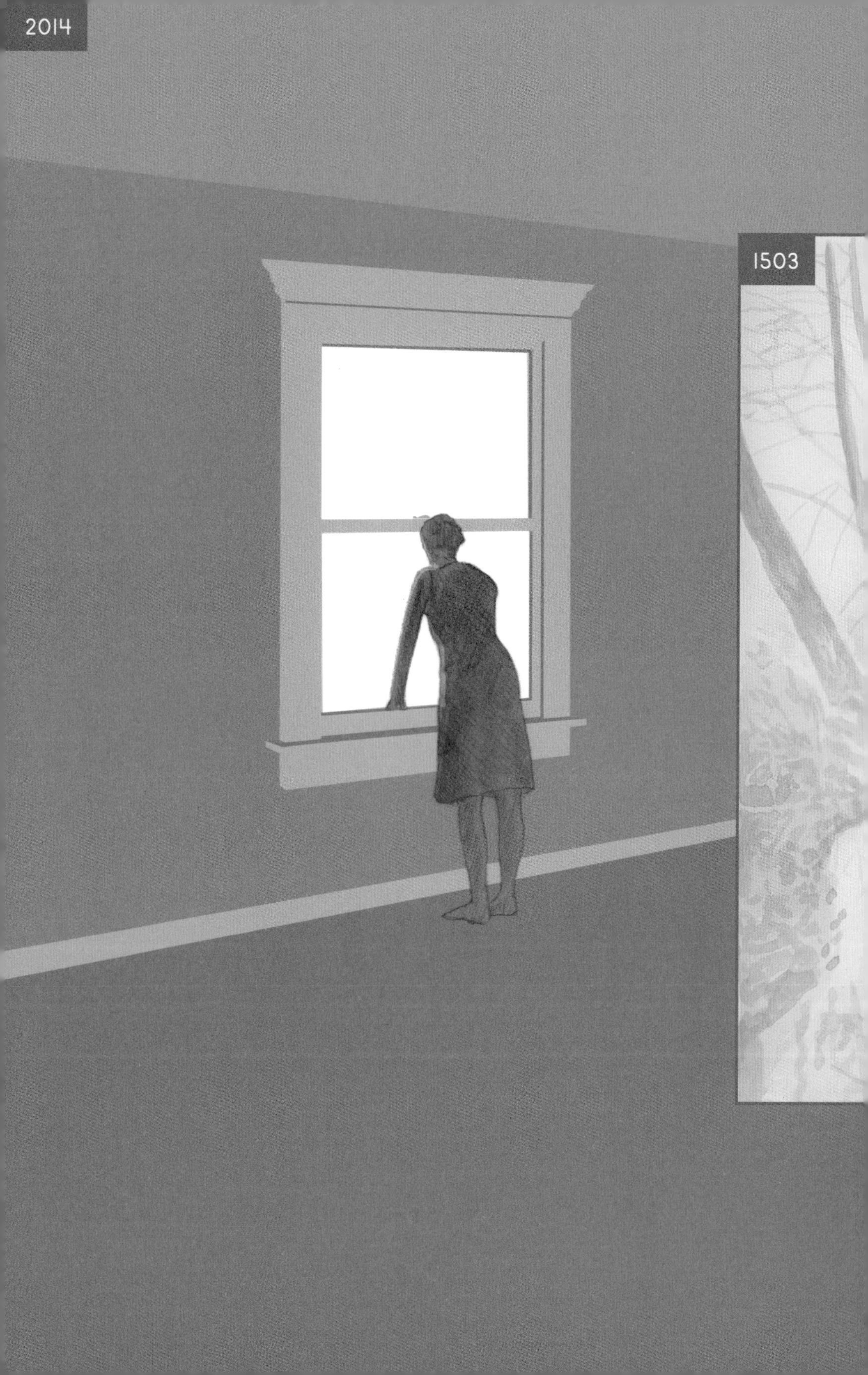
2014
1503

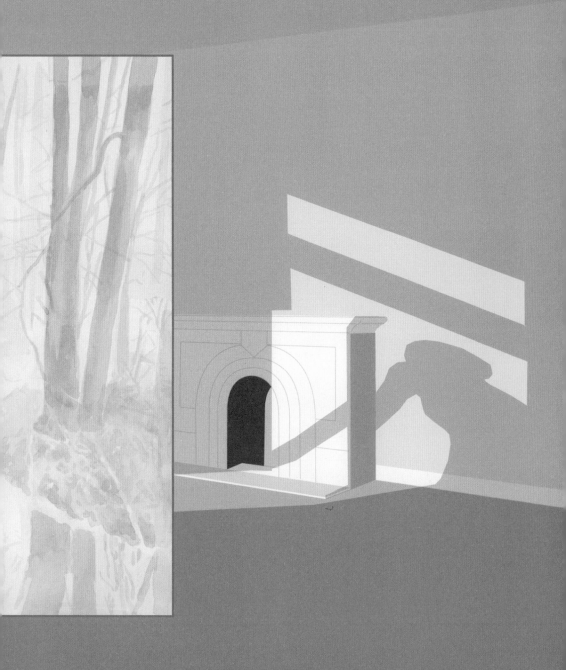

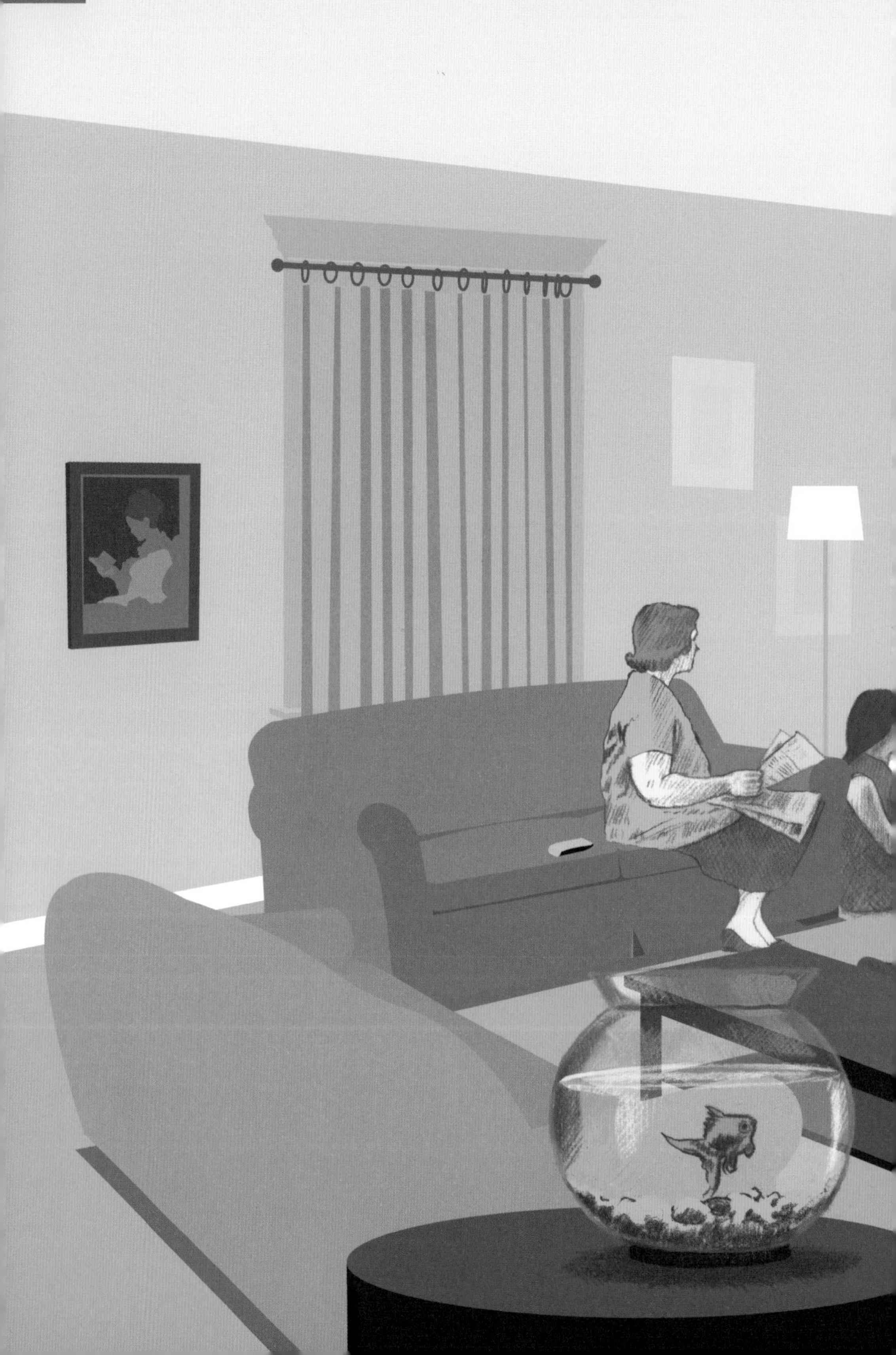

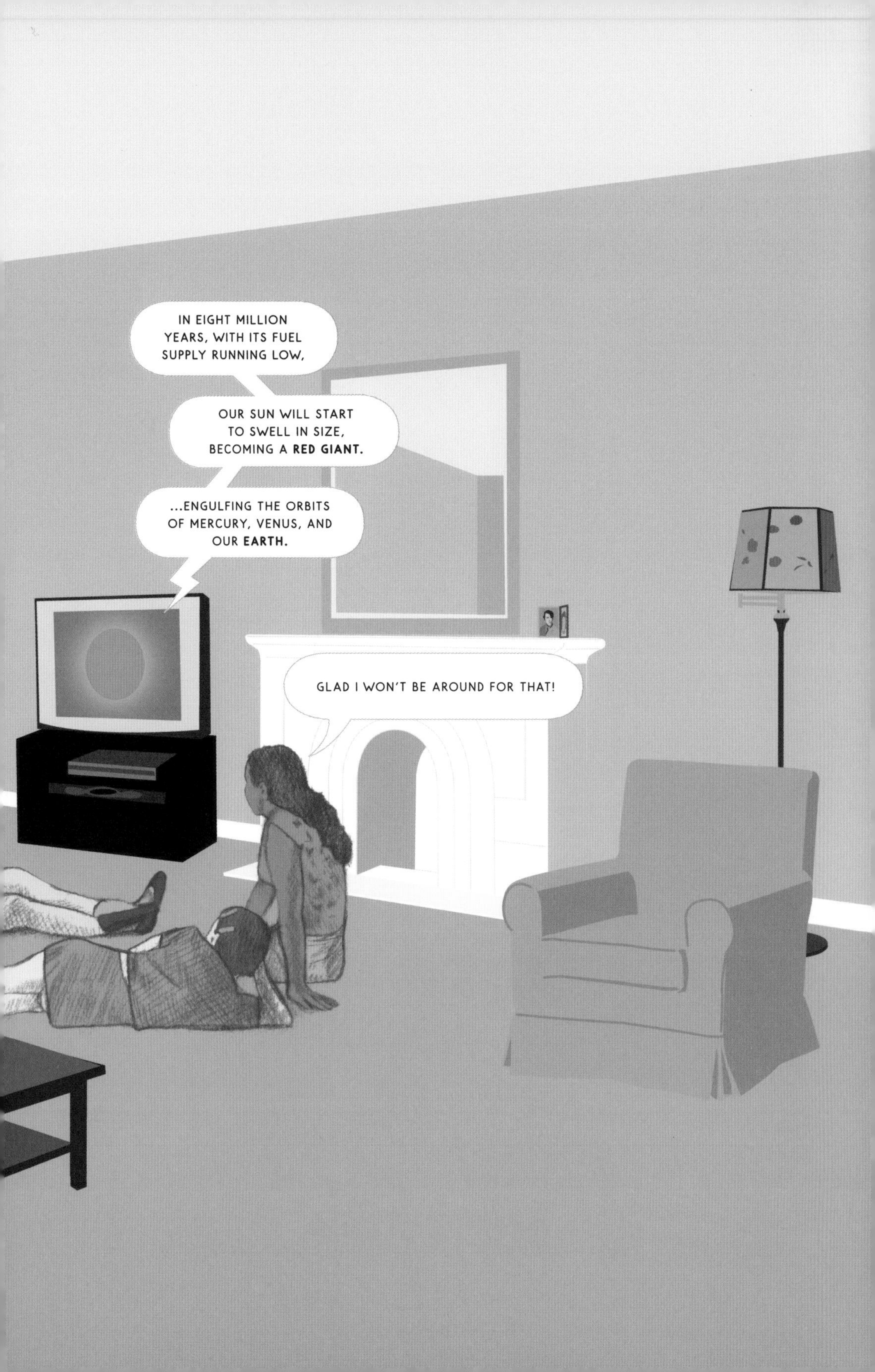
IN EIGHT MILLION YEARS, WITH ITS FUEL SUPPLY RUNNING LOW,
OUR SUN WILL START TO SWELL IN SIZE, BECOMING A **RED GIANT.**
...ENGULFING THE ORBITS OF MERCURY, VENUS, AND OUR **EARTH.**
GLAD I WON'T BE AROUND FOR THAT!

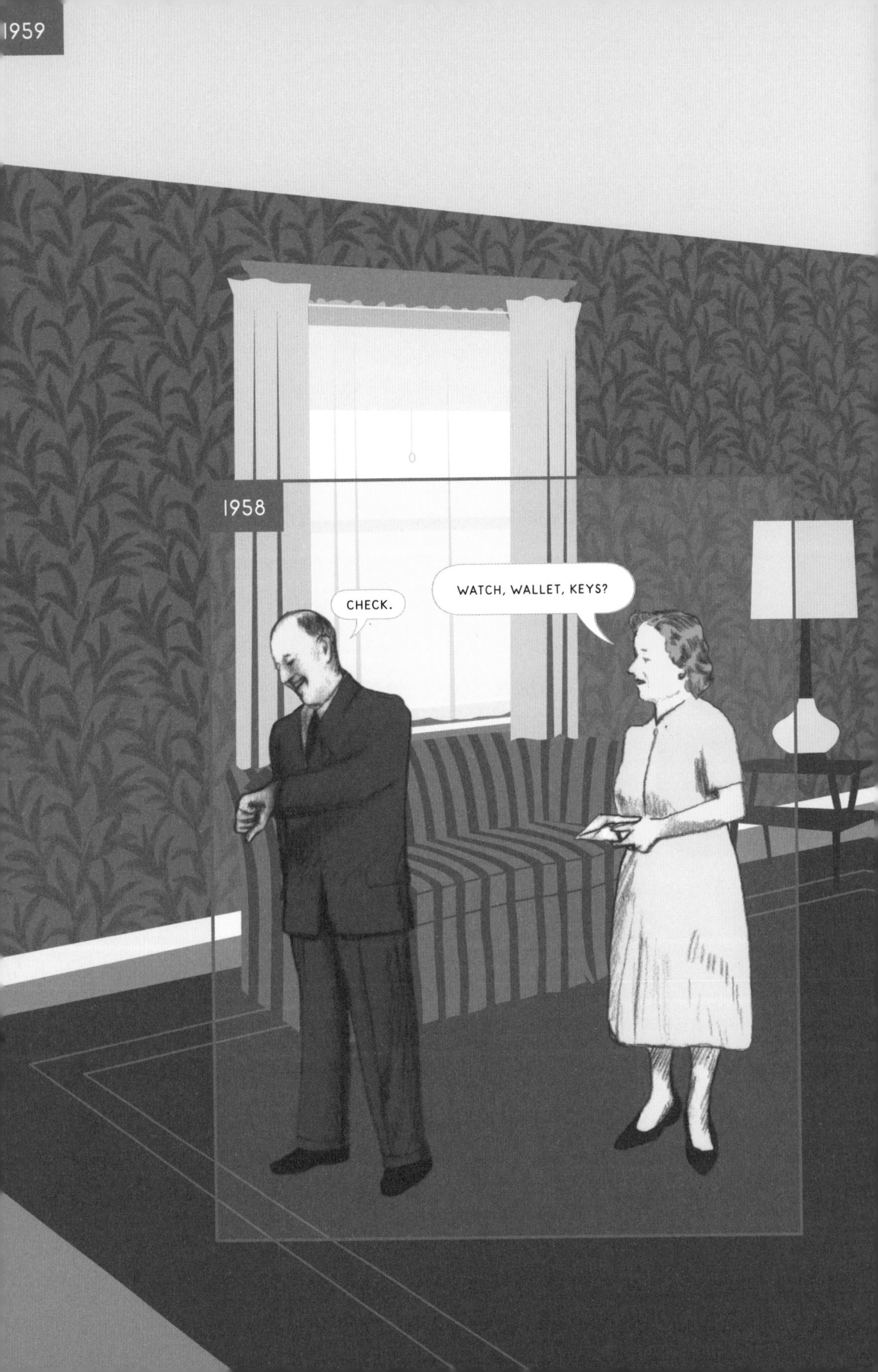
1959
1958
CHECK.
WATCH, WALLET, KEYS?

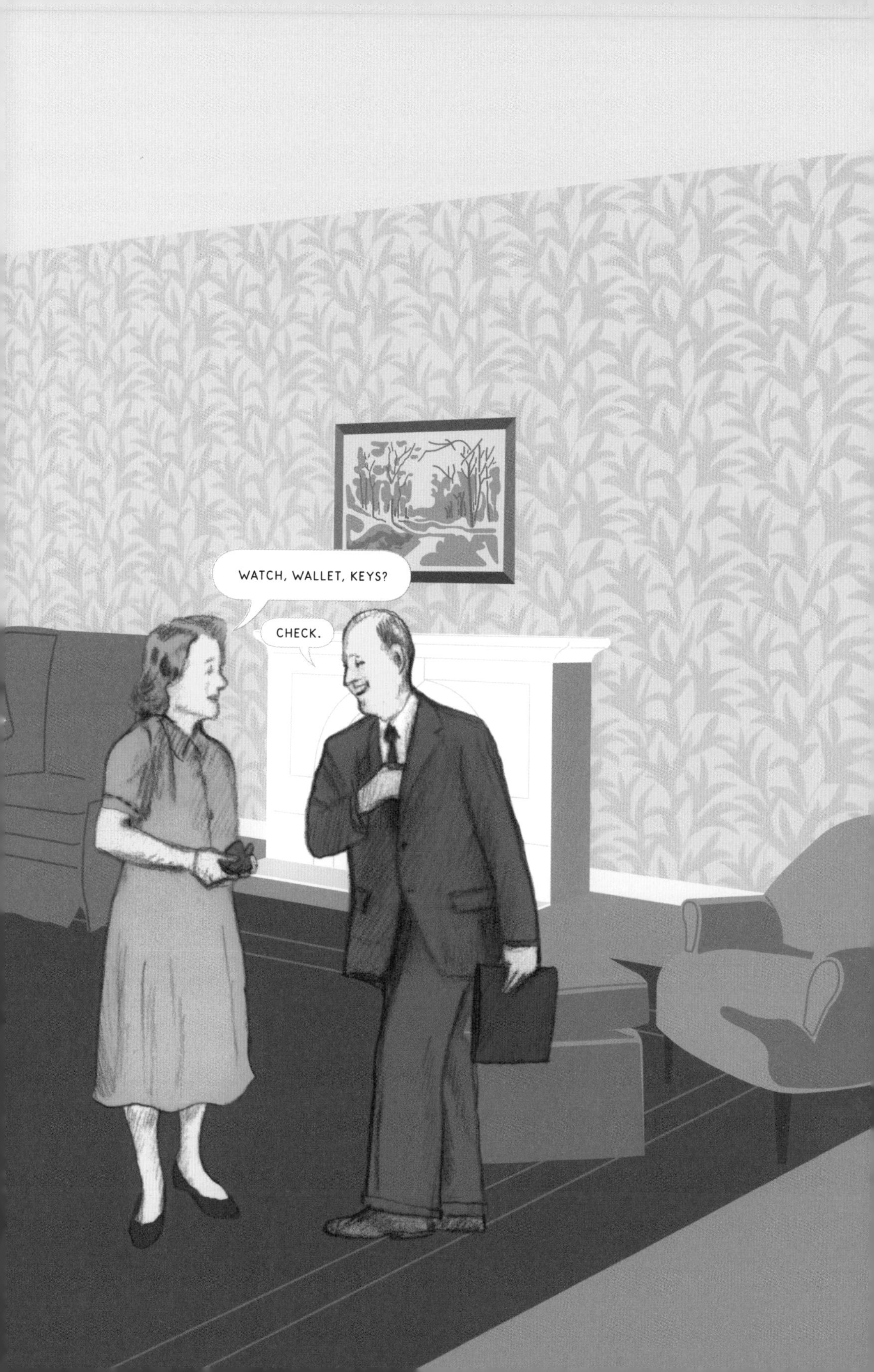
WATCH, WALLET, KEYS?
CHECK.

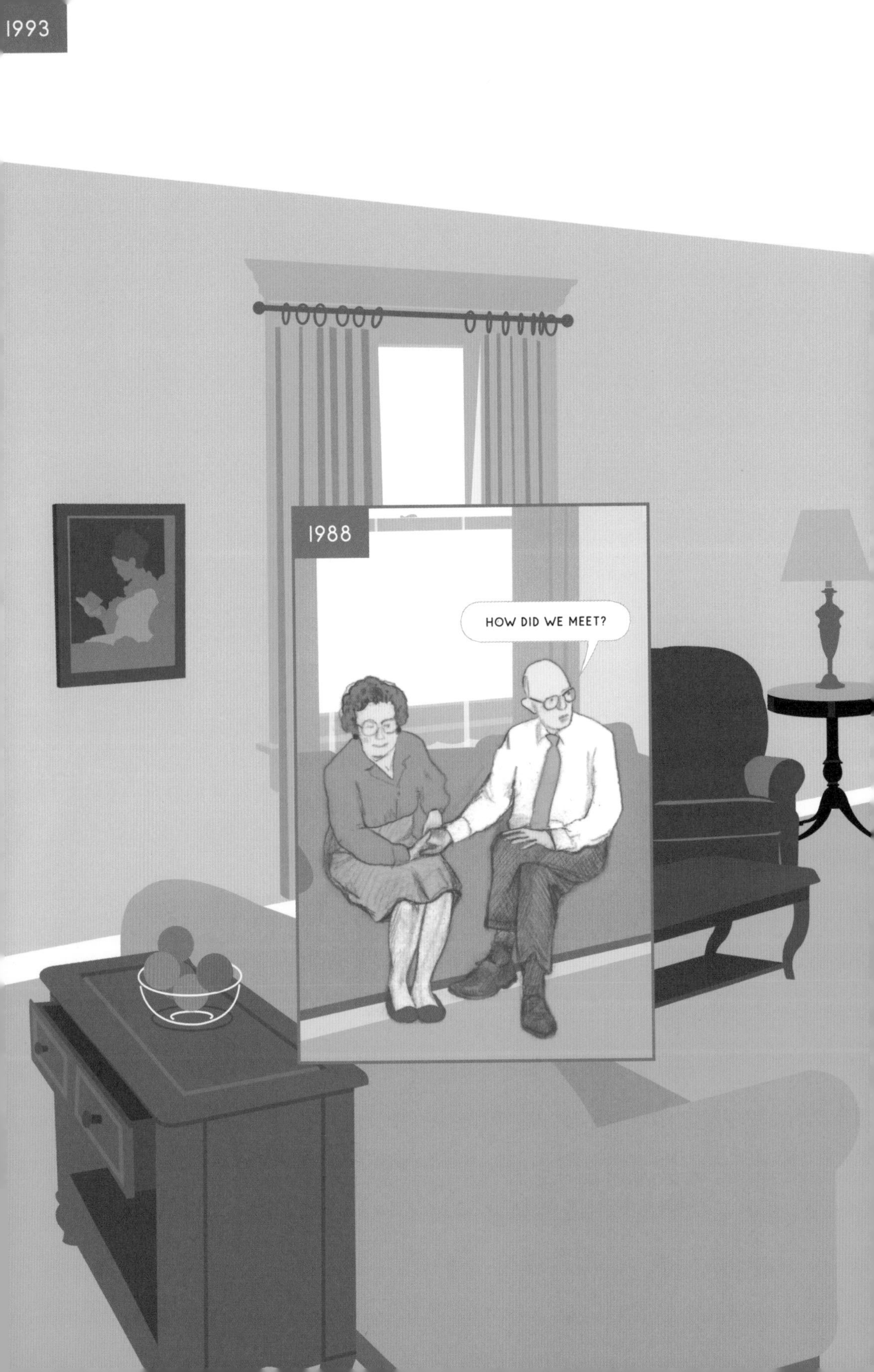
1993
1988
HOW DID WE MEET?

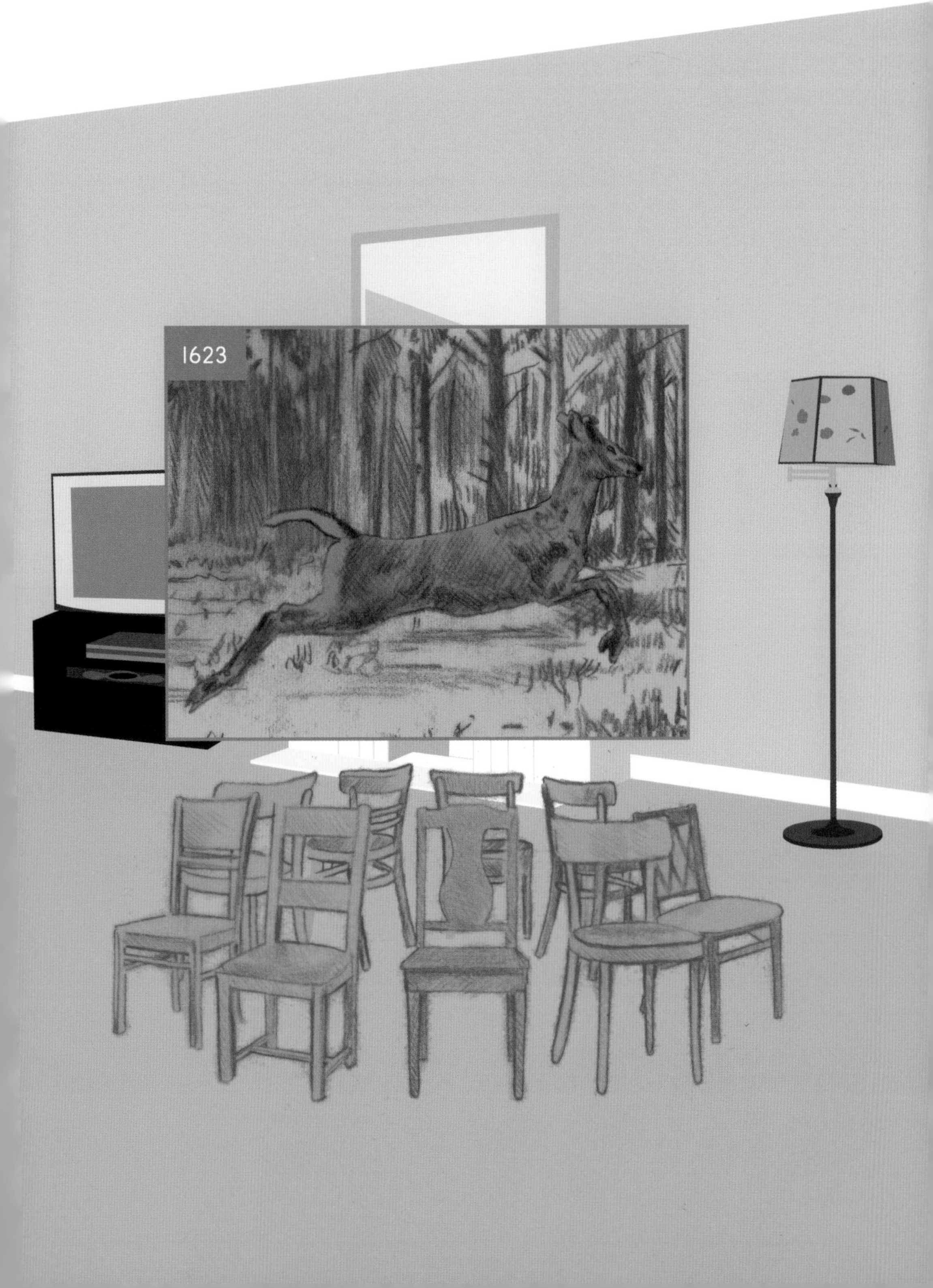
1623

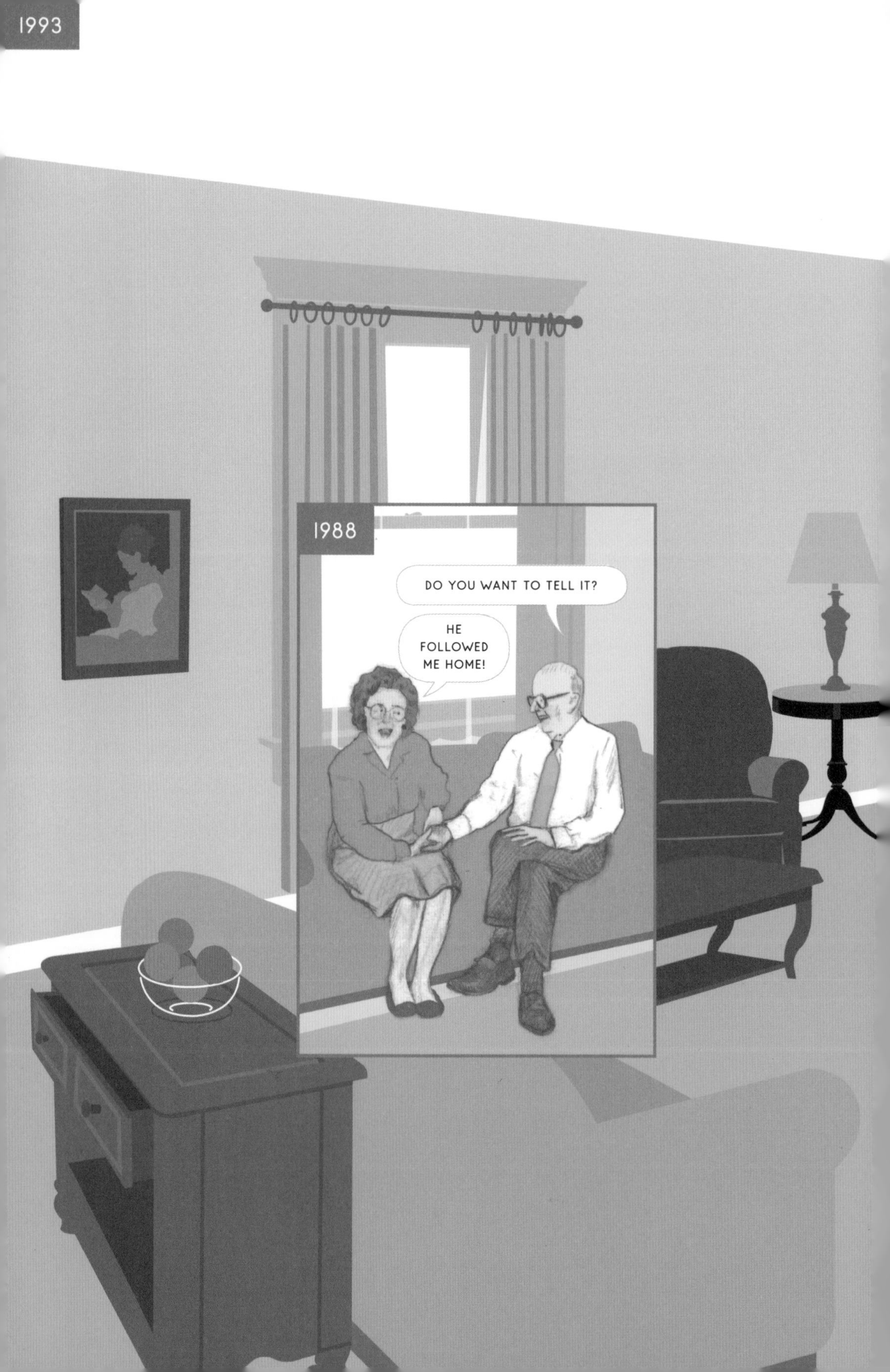
1993
1988
DO YOU WANT TO TELL IT?
HE FOLLOWED ME HOME!

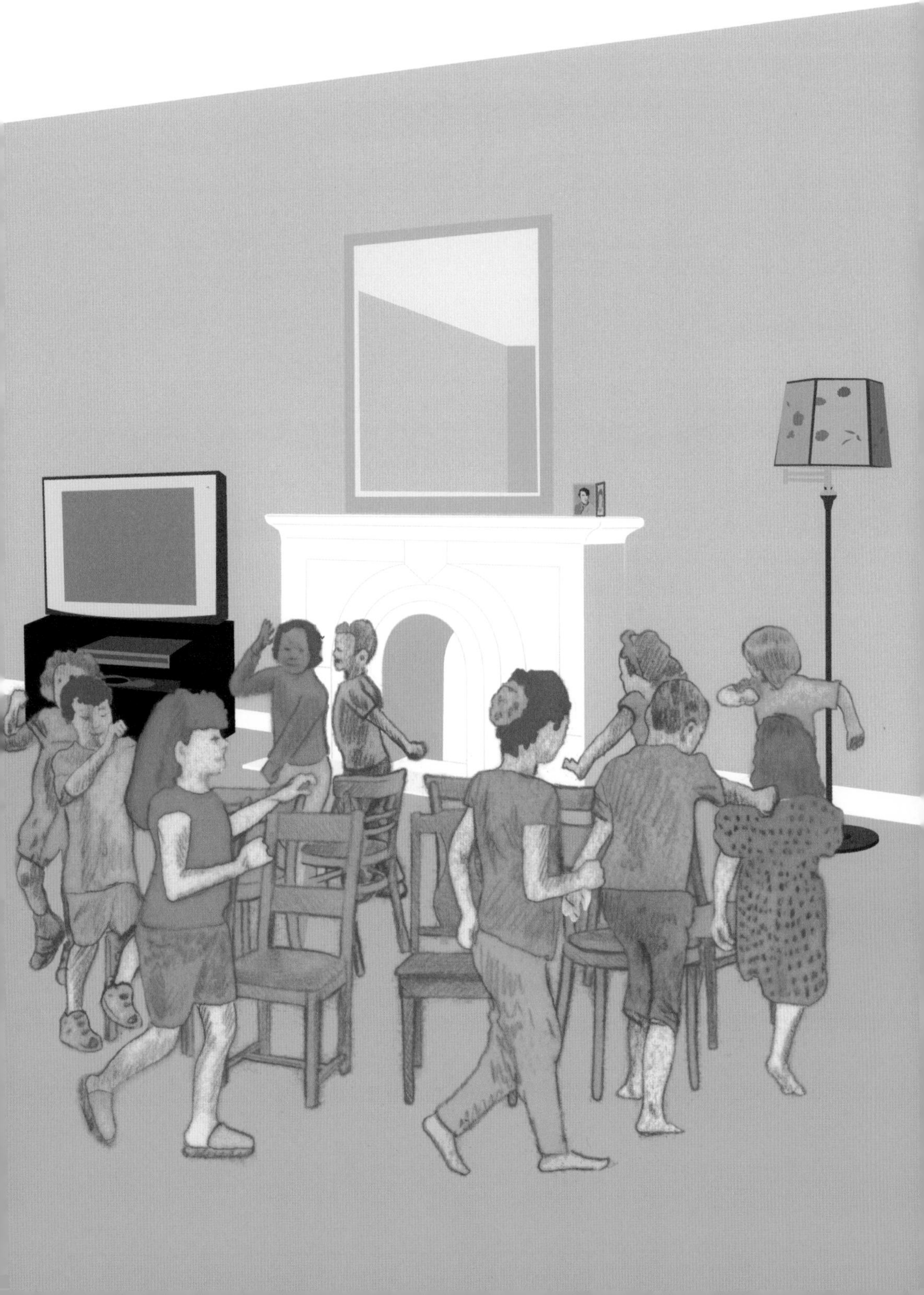

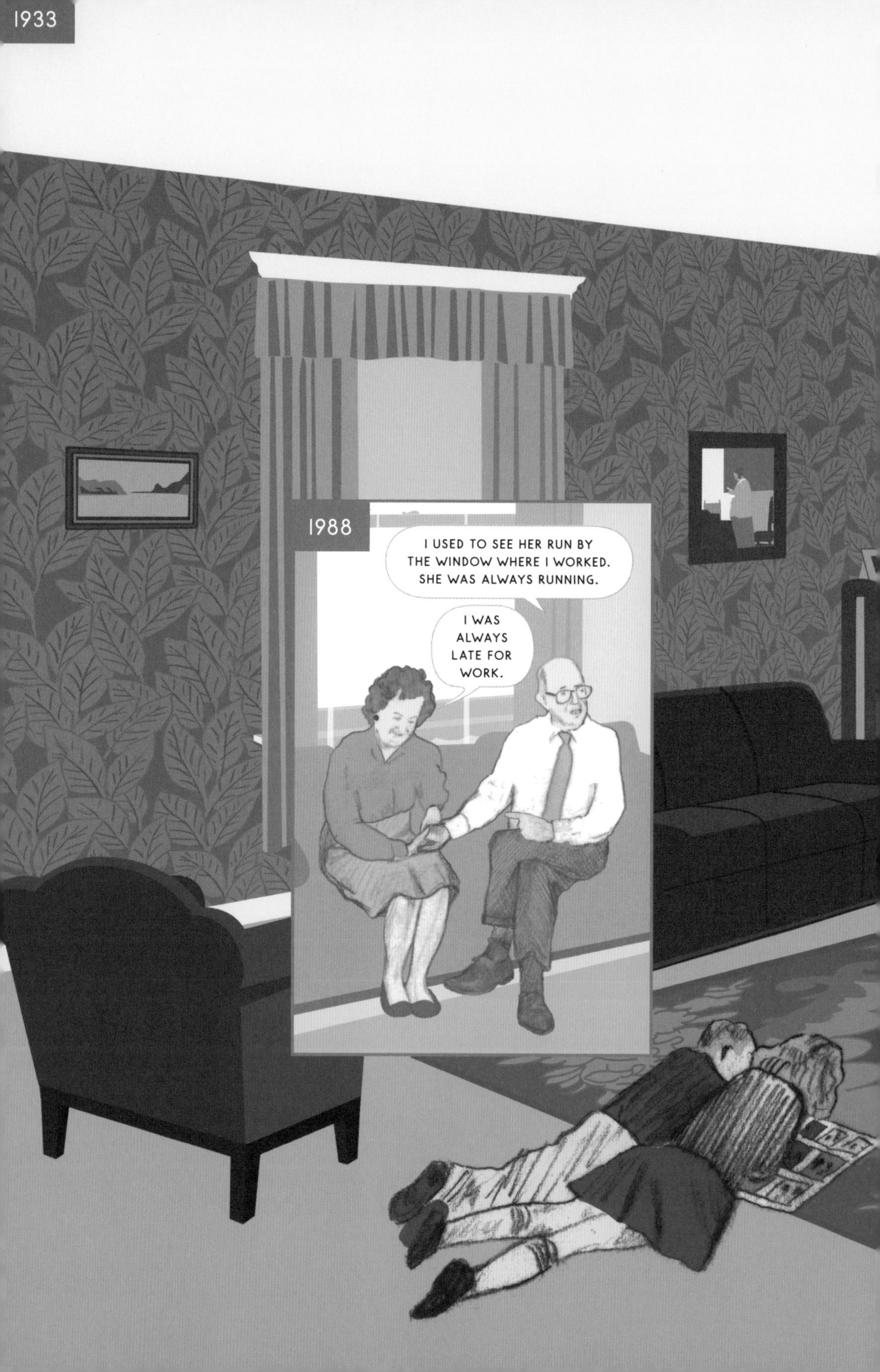
1933
1988
I USED TO SEE HER RUN BY THE WINDOW WHERE I WORKED. SHE WAS ALWAYS RUNNING.
I WAS ALWAYS LATE FOR WORK.

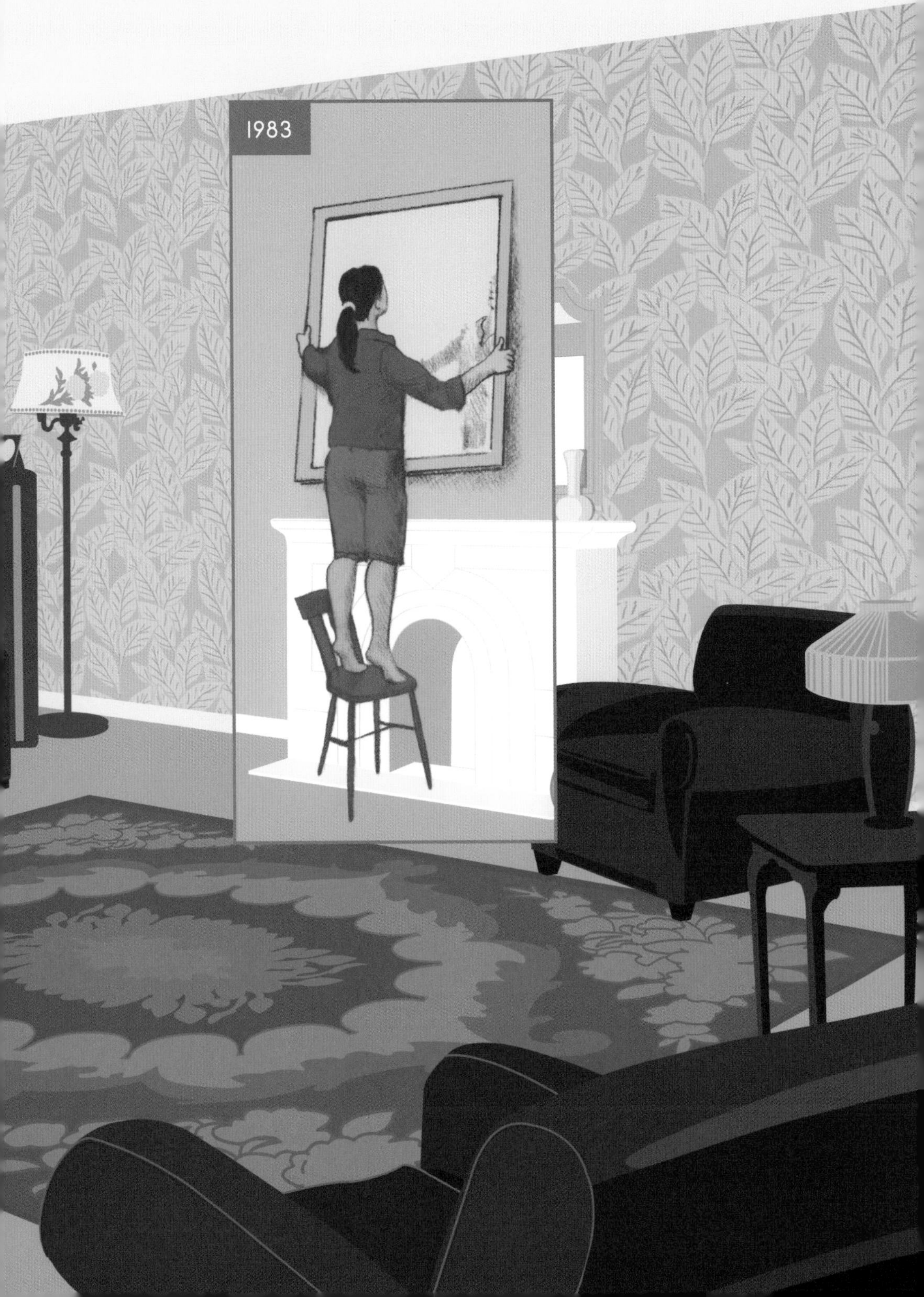
1983

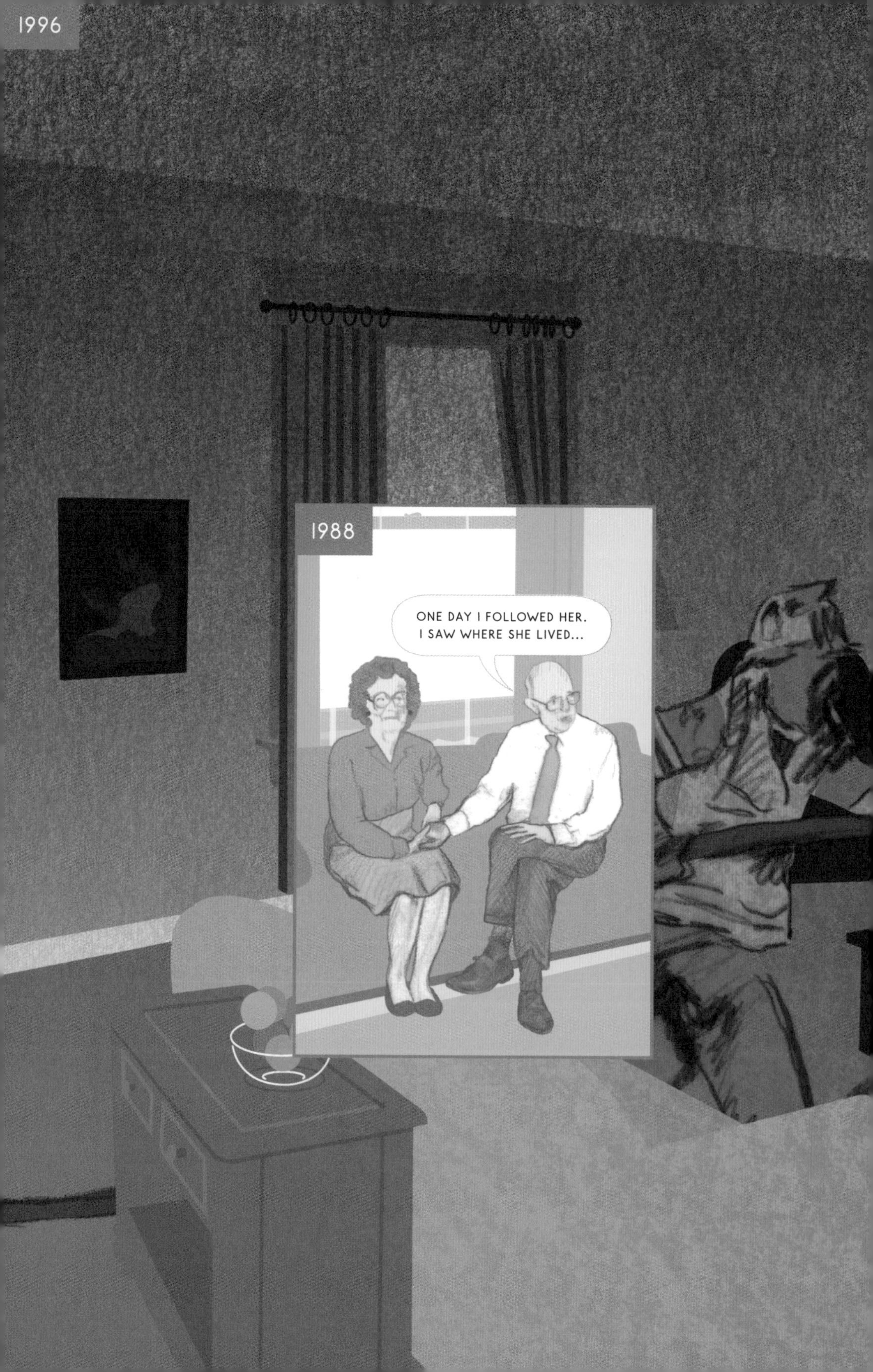
1996
1988
ONE DAY I FOLLOWED HER.
I SAW WHERE SHE LIVED...

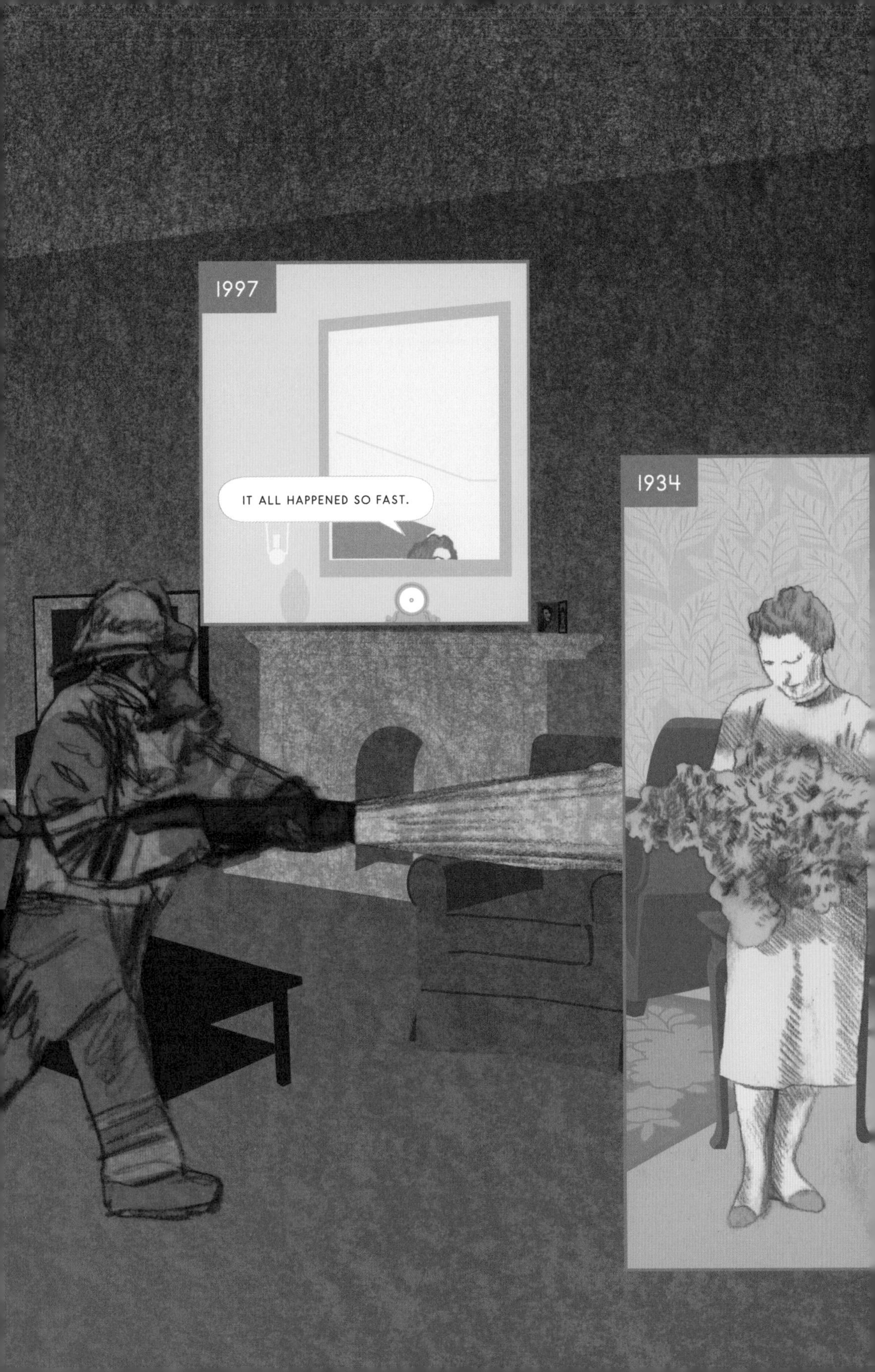
1997
IT ALL HAPPENED SO FAST.
1934

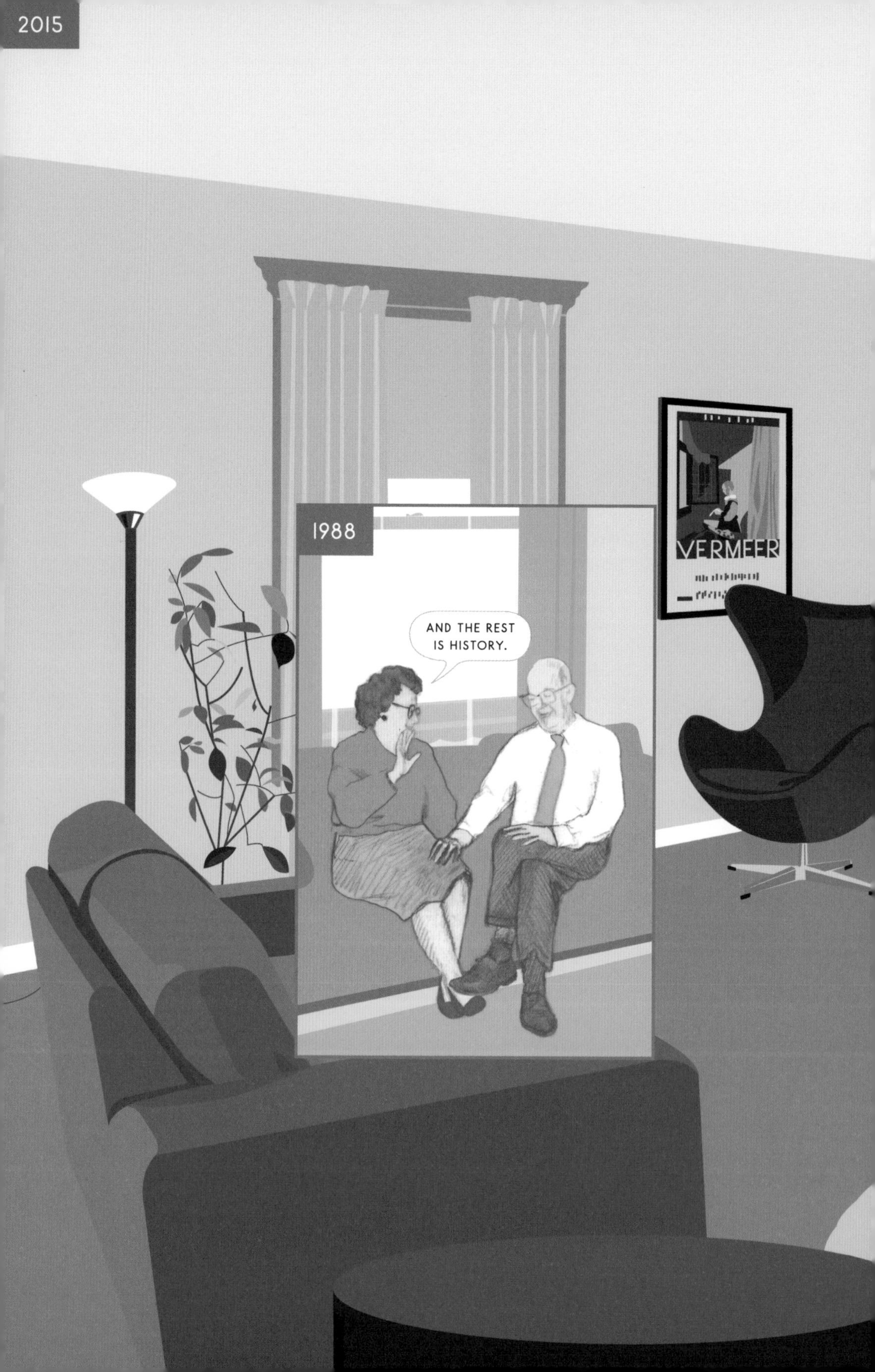
2015
1988
AND THE REST IS HISTORY.
VERMEER

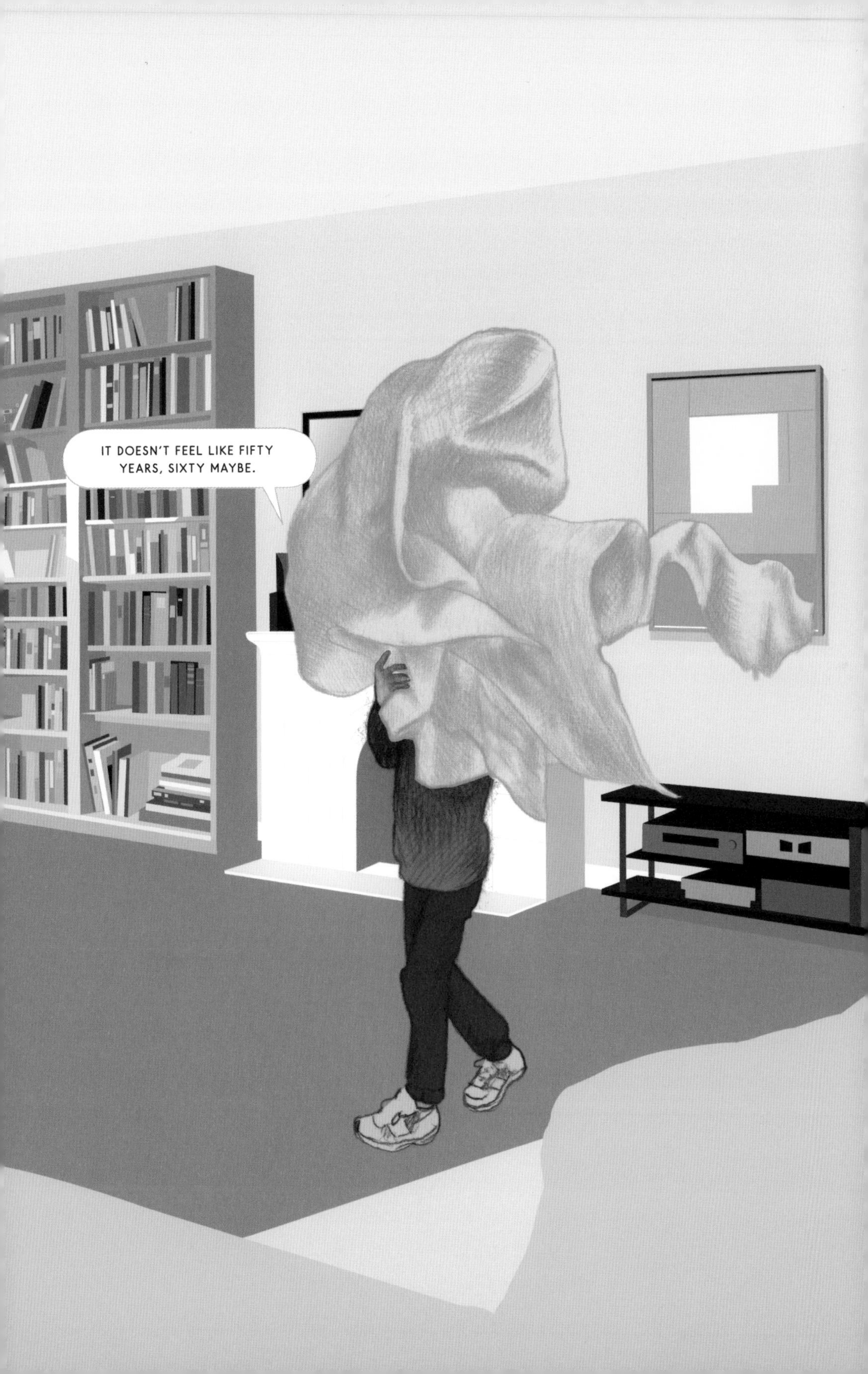
IT DOESN'T FEEL LIKE FIFTY YEARS, SIXTY MAYBE.

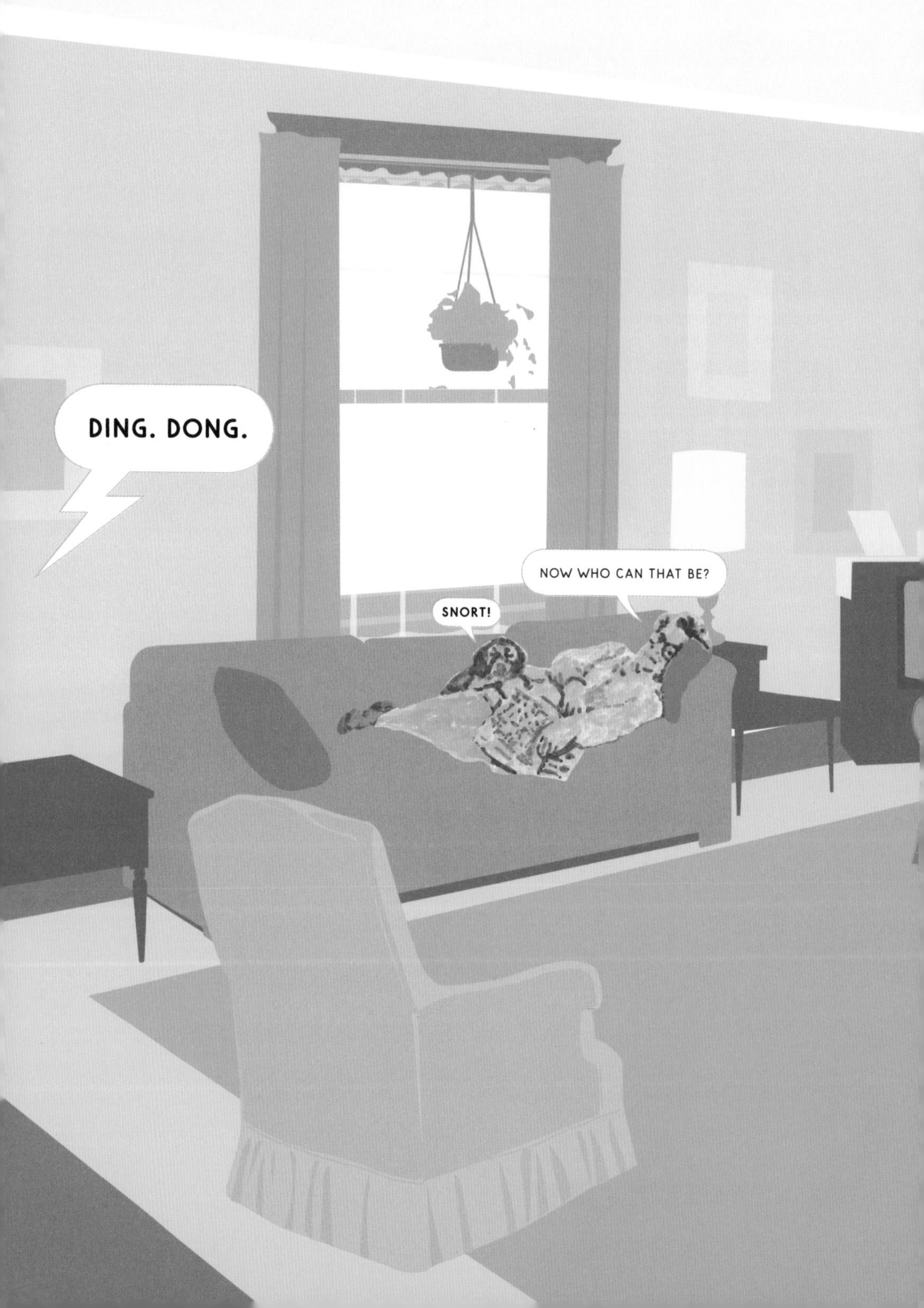
DING. DONG.
NOW WHO CAN THAT BE?
SNORT!

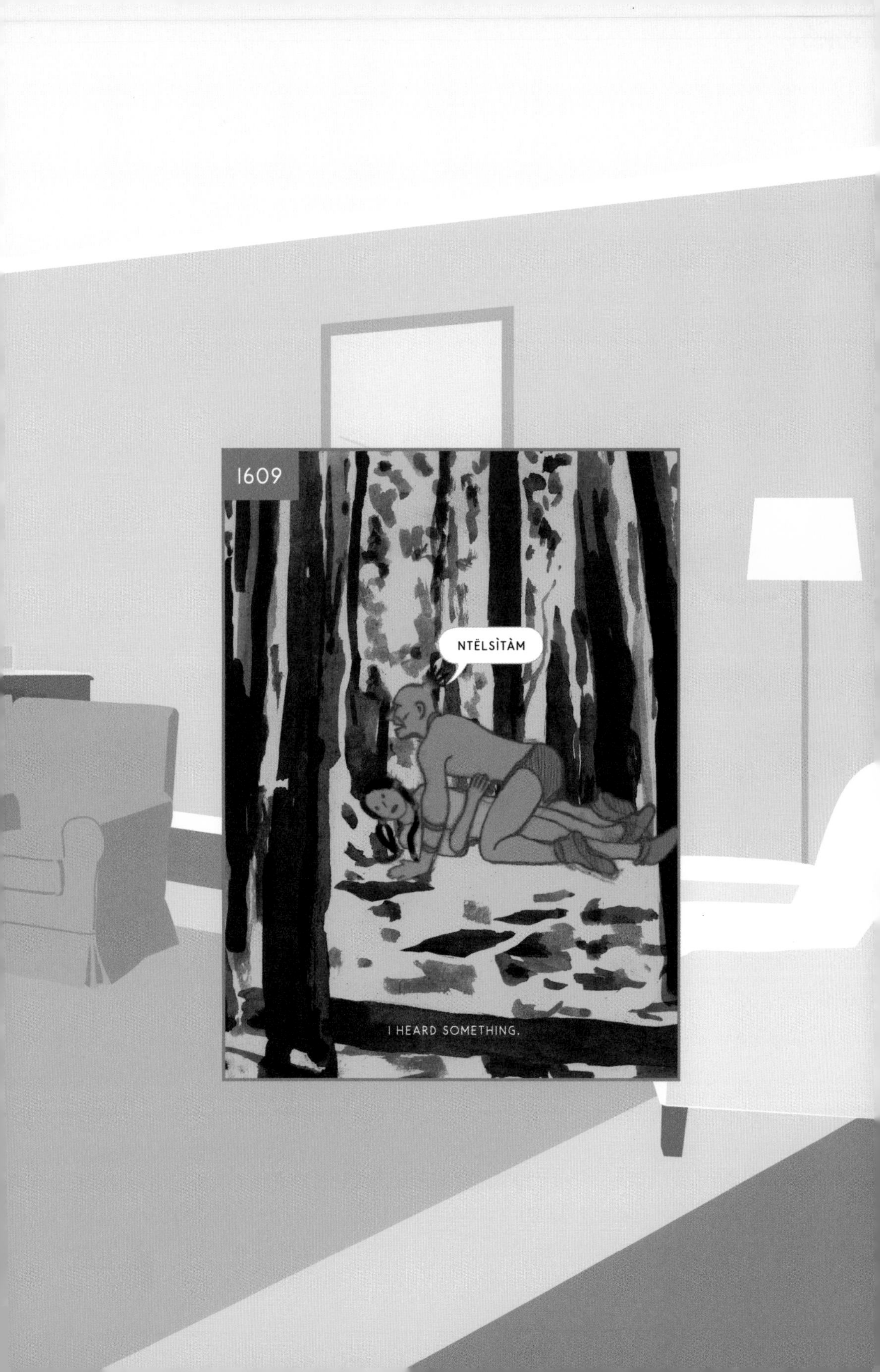
1609
NTËLSÌTÀM
I HEARD SOMETHING.

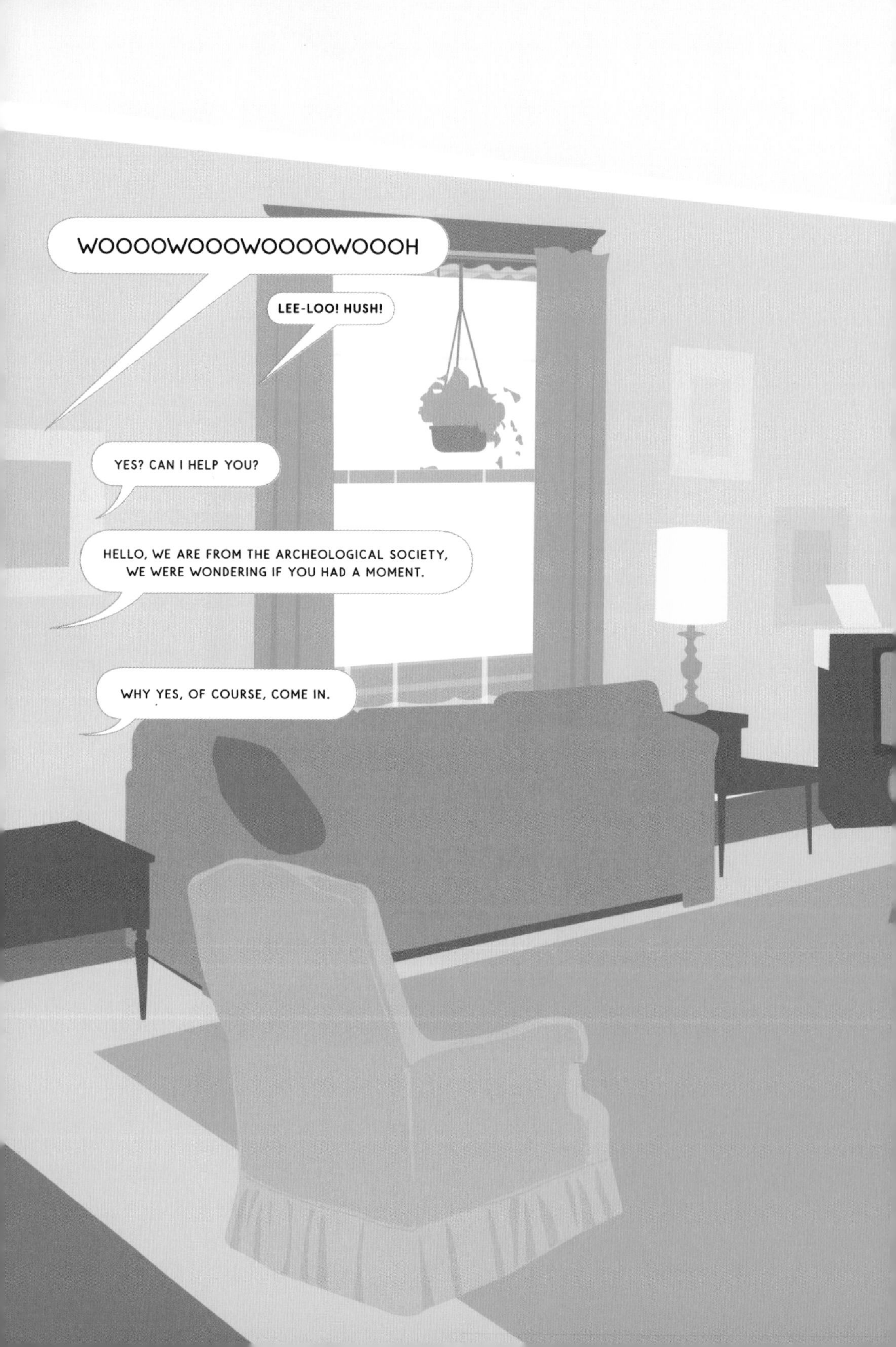
WOOOOWOOOWOOOOWOOOH
LEE-LOO! HUSH!
YES? CAN I HELP YOU?
HELLO, WE ARE FROM THE ARCHEOLOGICAL SOCIETY, WE WERE WONDERING IF YOU HAD A MOMENT.
WHY YES, OF COURSE, COME IN.

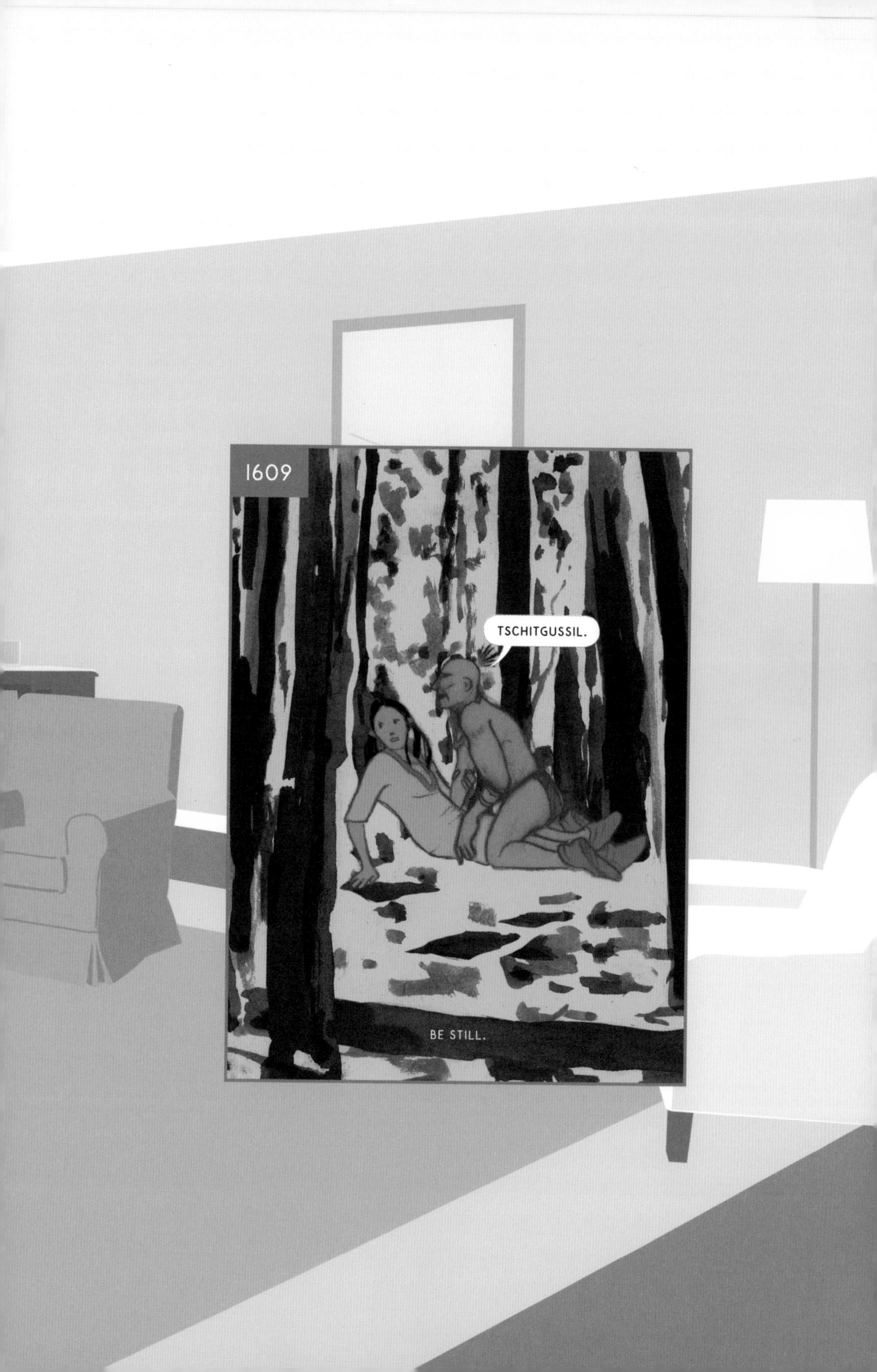
1609
TSCHITGUSSIL.
BE STILL.

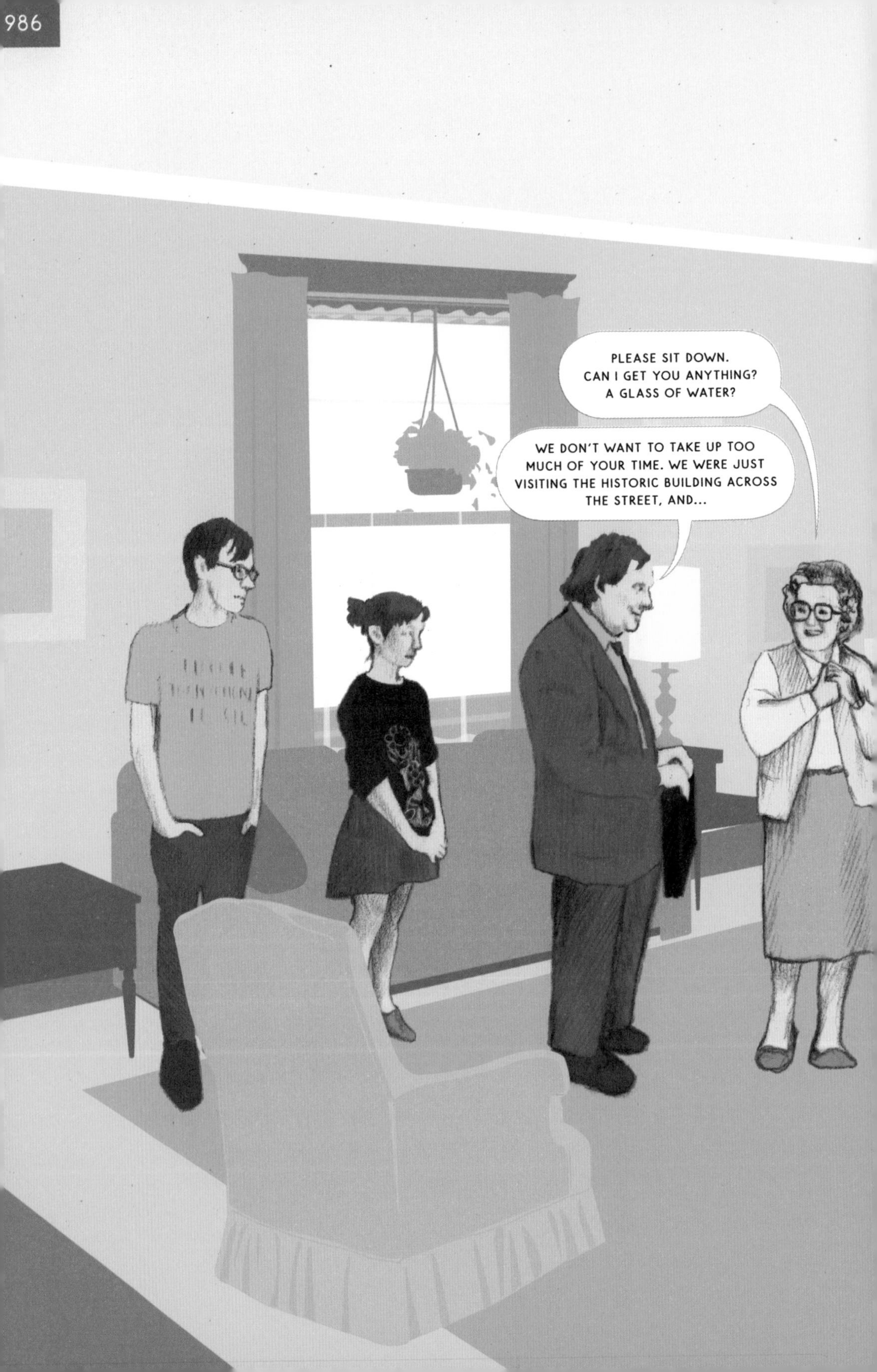
986
PLEASE SIT DOWN. CAN I GET YOU ANYTHING? A GLASS OF WATER?
WE DON'T WANT TO TAKE UP TOO MUCH OF YOUR TIME. WE WERE JUST VISITING THE HISTORIC BUILDING ACROSS THE STREET, AND...

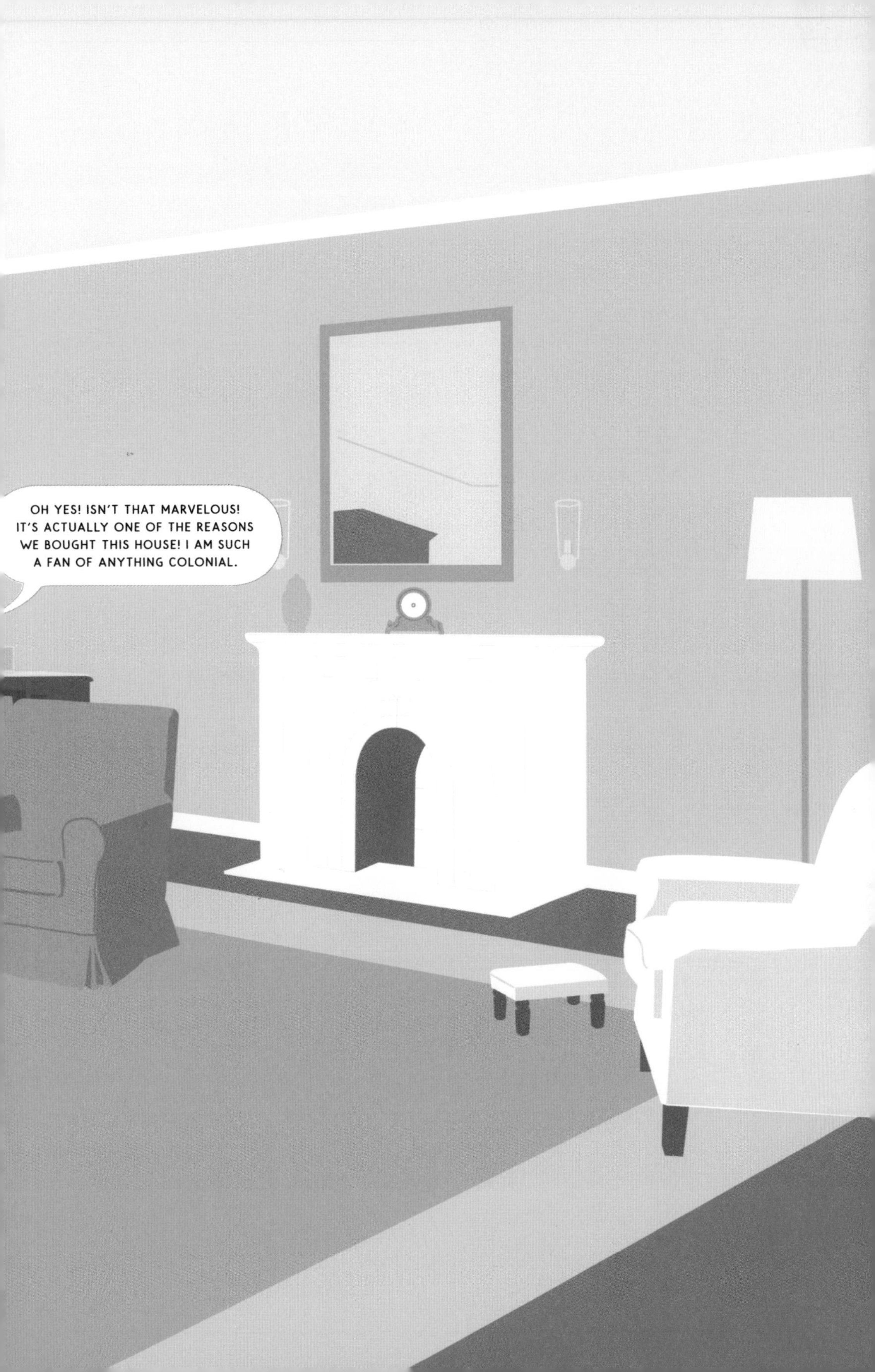
OH YES! ISN'T THAT MARVELOUS! IT'S ACTUALLY ONE OF THE REASONS WE BOUGHT THIS HOUSE! I AM SUCH A FAN OF ANYTHING COLONIAL.

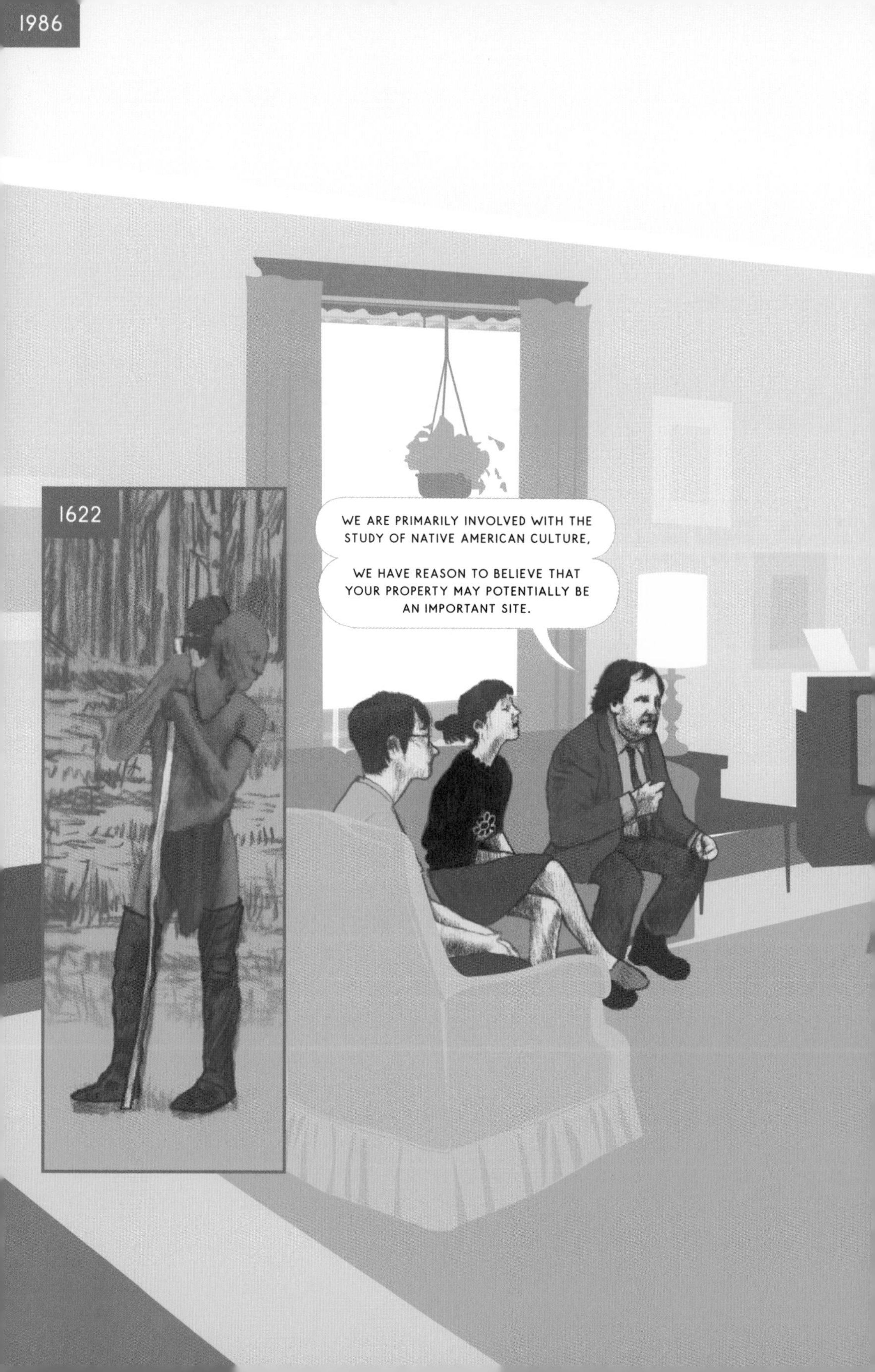
1986
1622
WE ARE PRIMARILY INVOLVED WITH THE STUDY OF NATIVE AMERICAN CULTURE,
WE HAVE REASON TO BELIEVE THAT YOUR PROPERTY MAY POTENTIALLY BE AN IMPORTANT SITE.

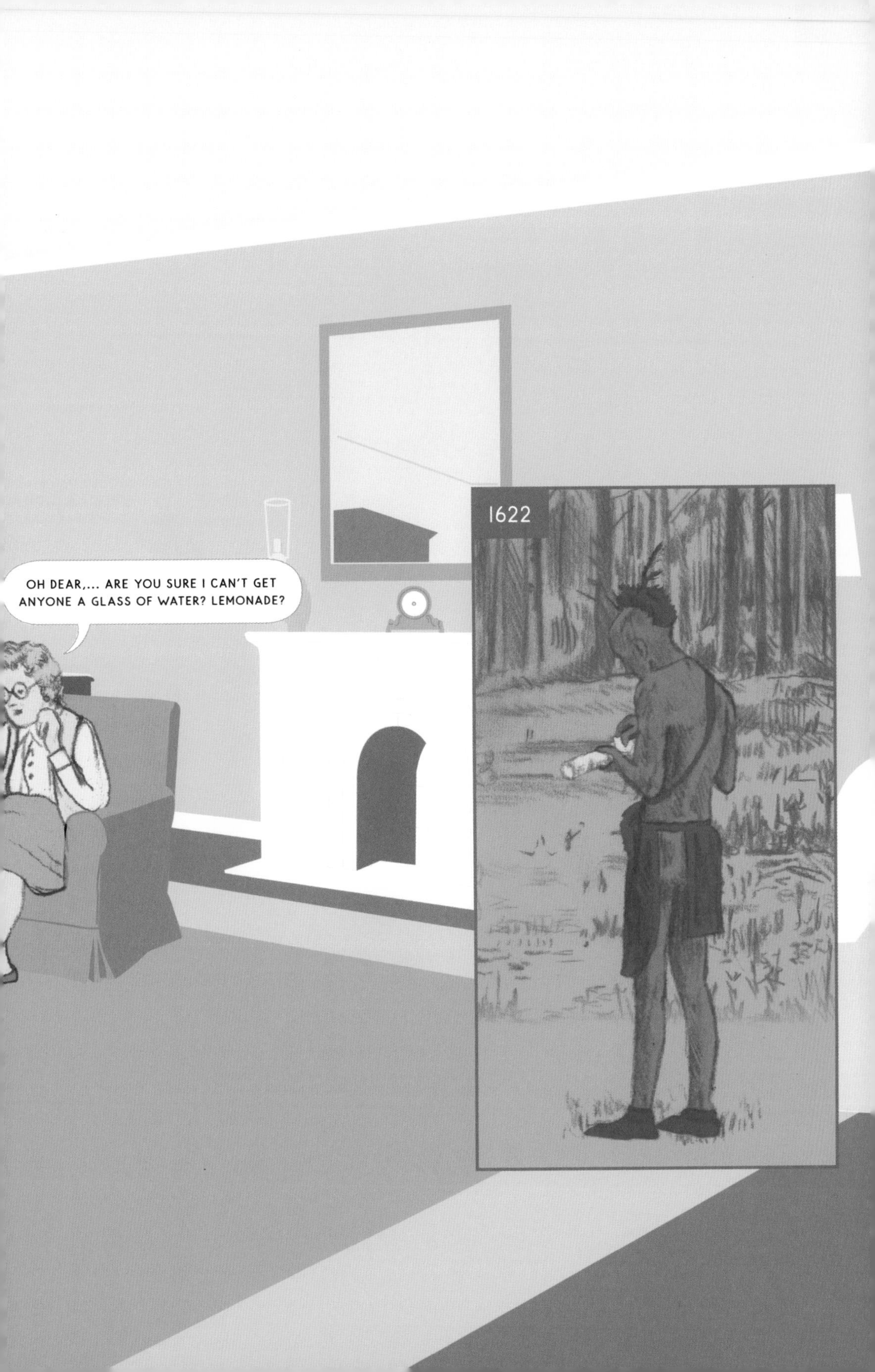
OH DEAR,... ARE YOU SURE I CAN'T GET ANYONE A GLASS OF WATER? LEMONADE?
1622

1986

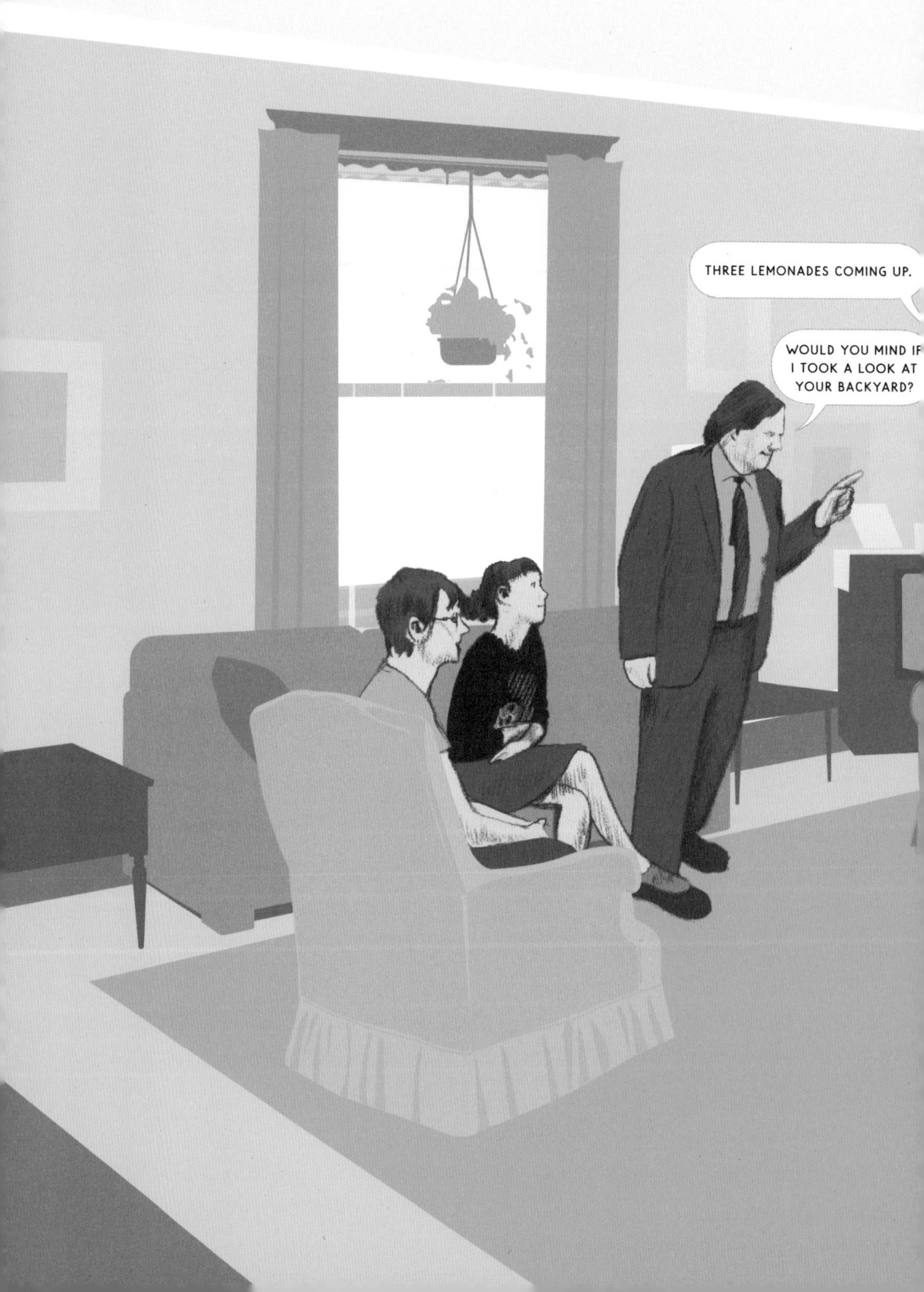
THREE LEMONADES COMING UP.
WOULD YOU MIND IF I TOOK A LOOK AT YOUR BACKYARD?

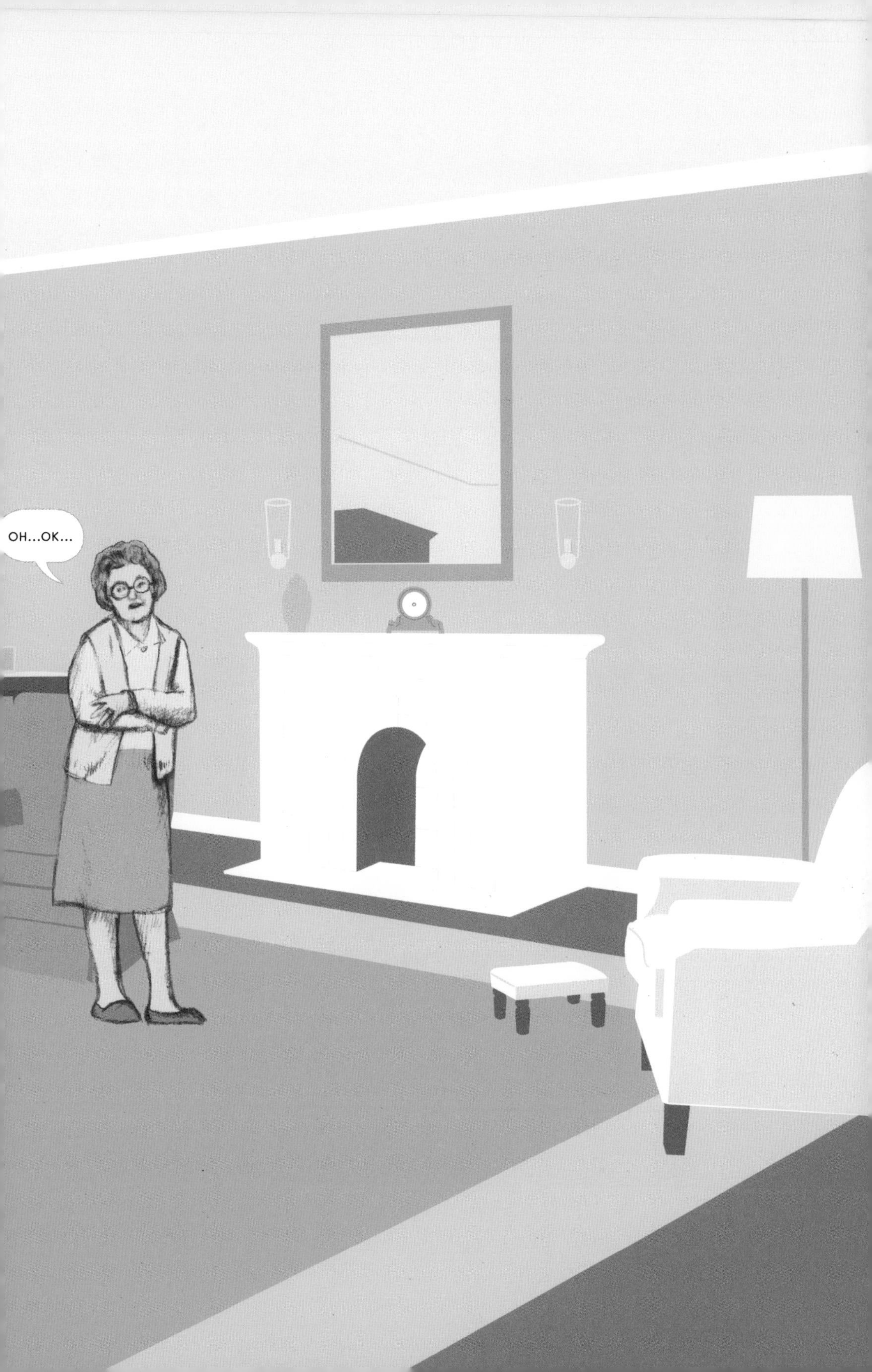
OH...OK...

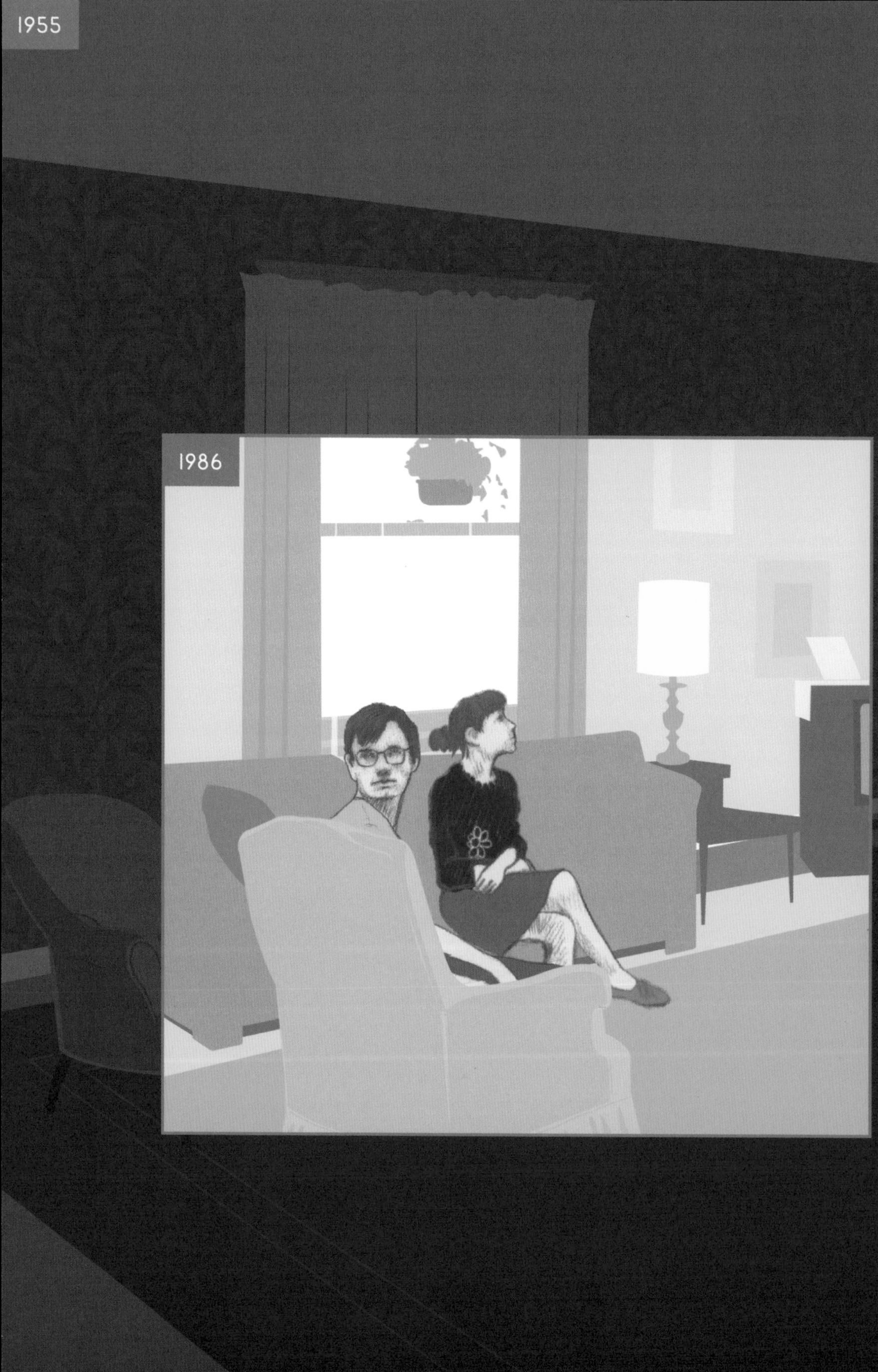
1955
1986

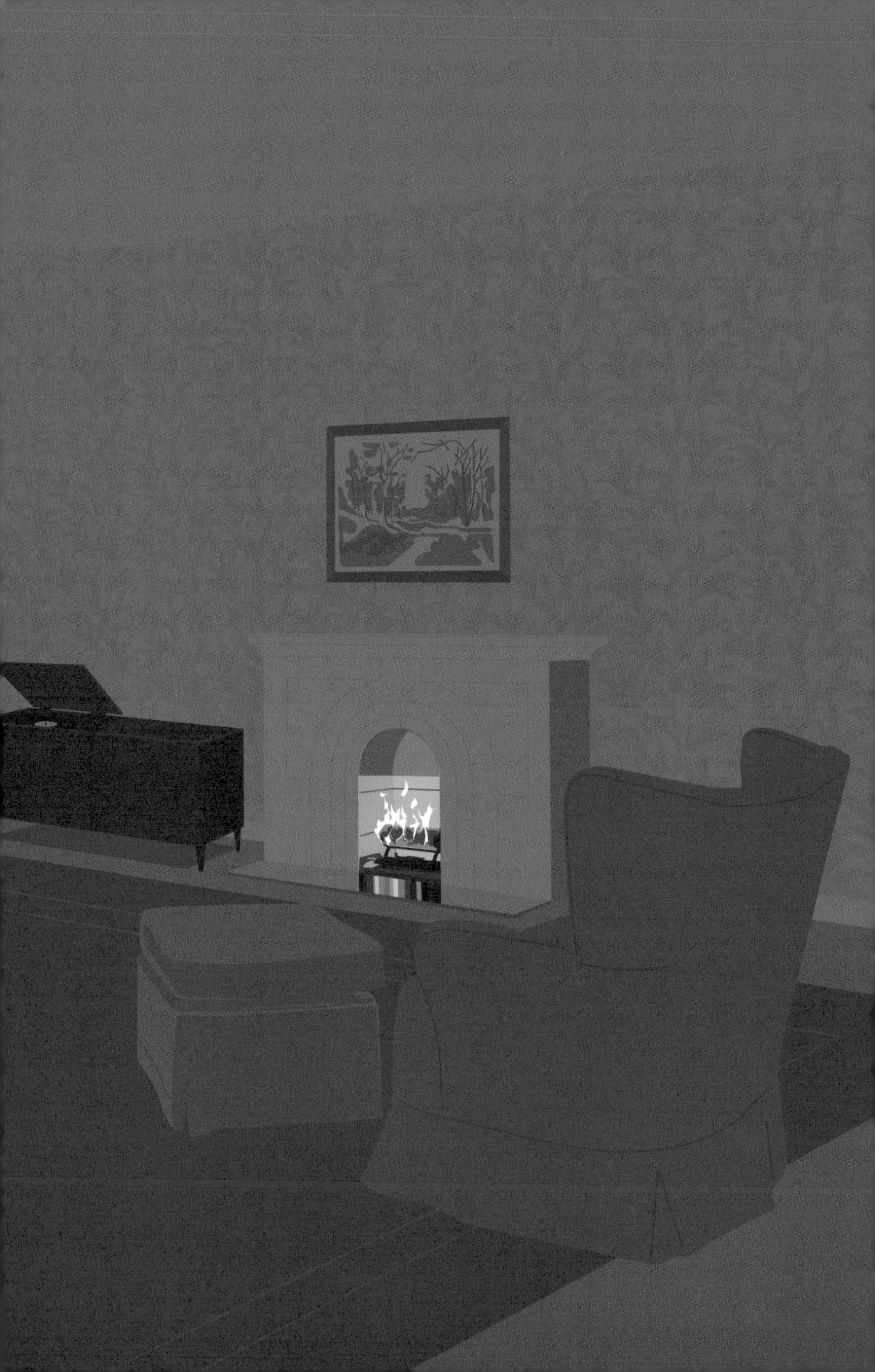

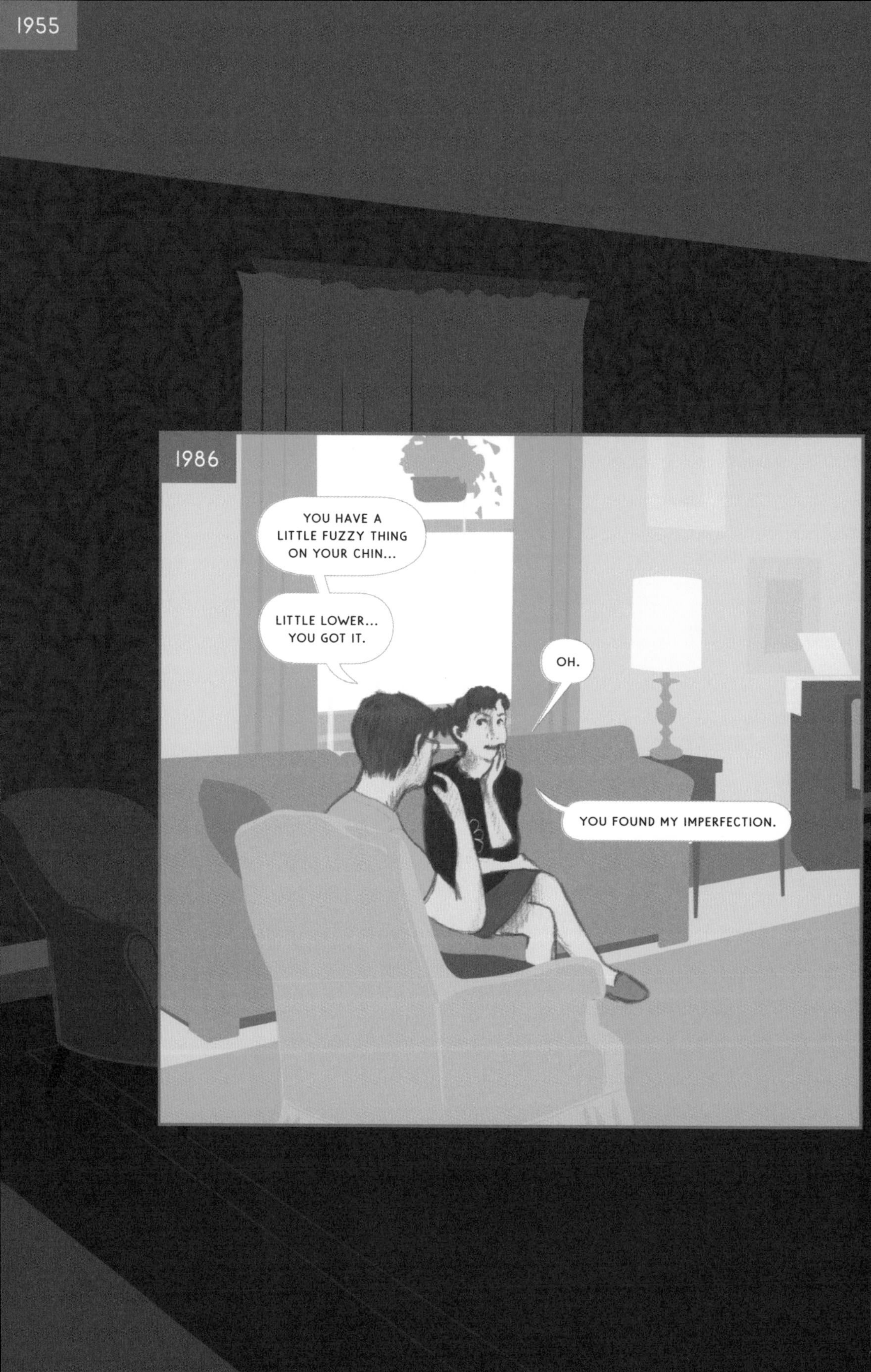
1955
1986
YOU HAVE A LITTLE FUZZY THING ON YOUR CHIN...
LITTLE LOWER... YOU GOT IT.
OH.
YOU FOUND MY IMPERFECTION.

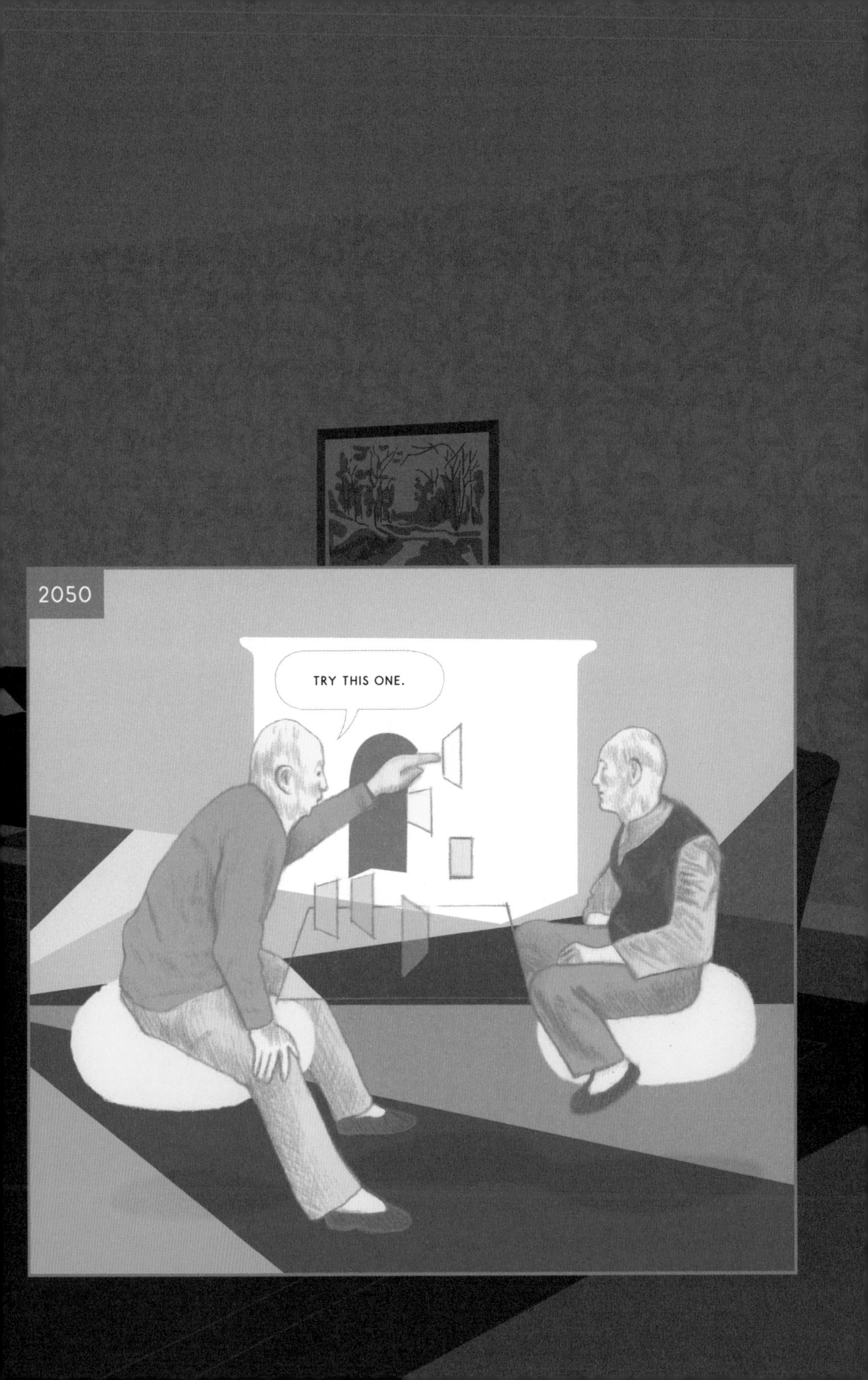
2050
TRY THIS ONE.

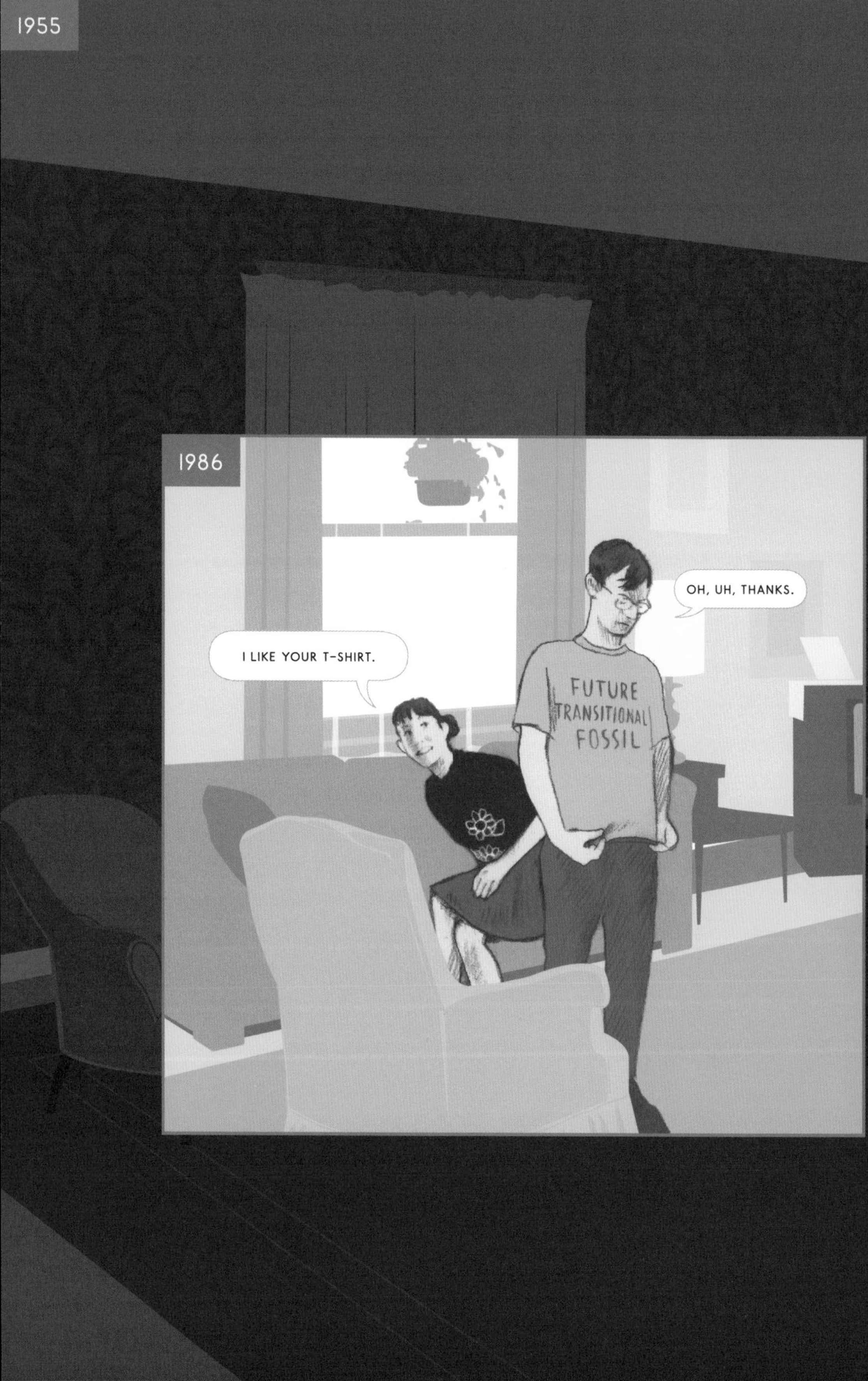
1955
1986
I LIKE YOUR T-SHIRT.
OH, UH, THANKS.
FUTURE TRANSITIONAL FOSSIL

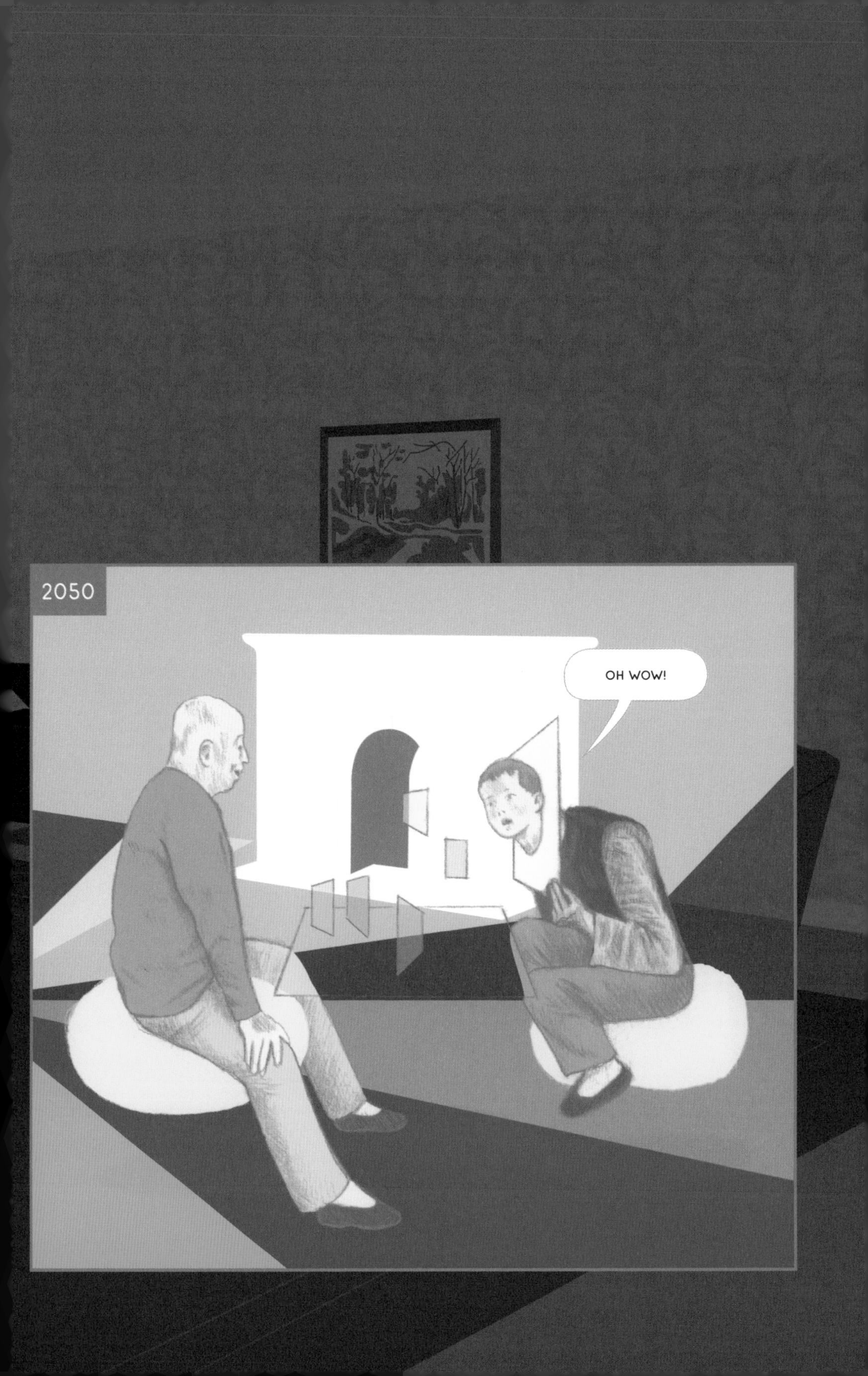
2050
OH WOW!

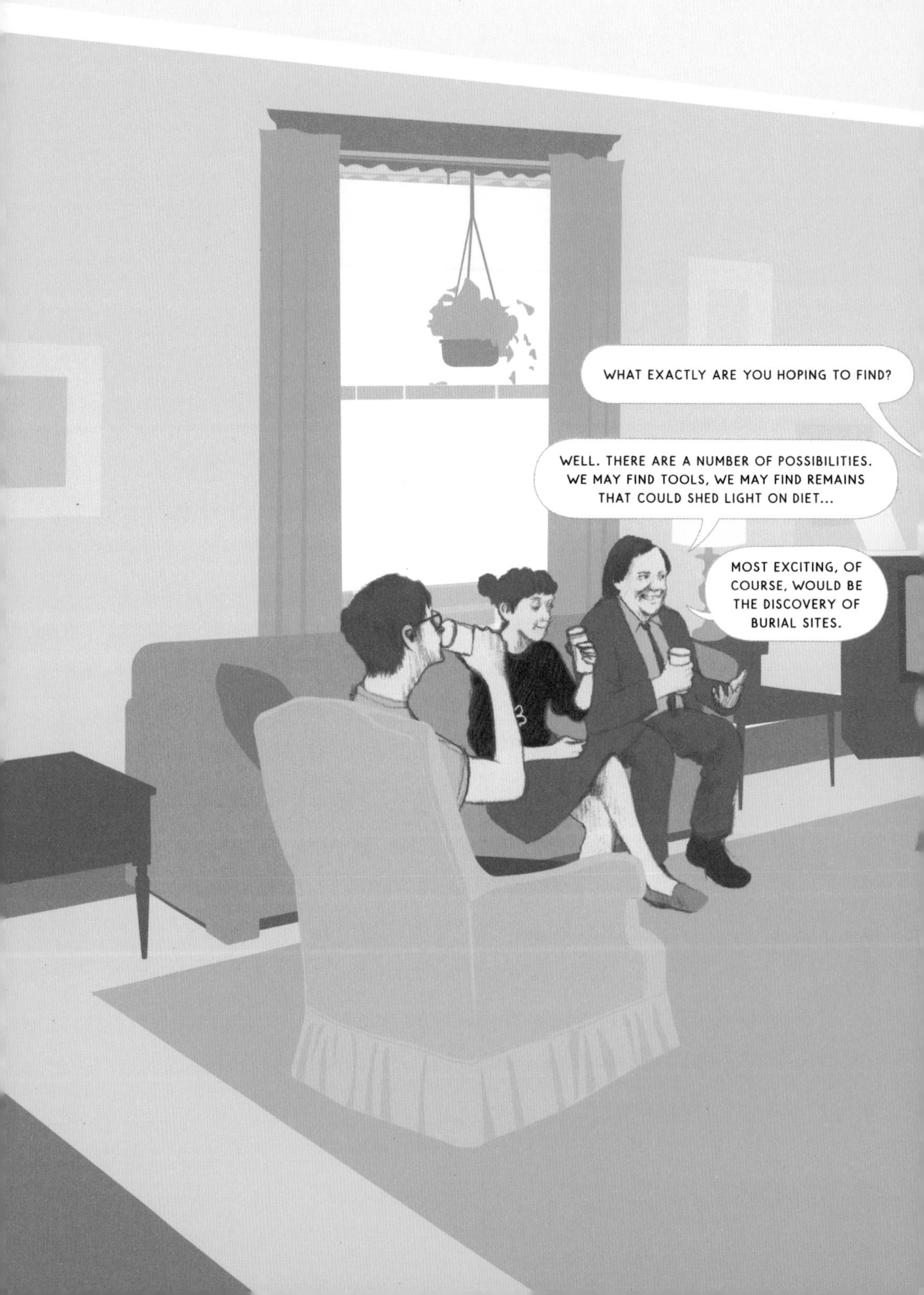
WHAT EXACTLY ARE YOU HOPING TO FIND?
WELL. THERE ARE A NUMBER OF POSSIBILITIES. WE MAY FIND TOOLS, WE MAY FIND REMAINS THAT COULD SHED LIGHT ON DIET...
MOST EXCITING, OF COURSE, WOULD BE THE DISCOVERY OF BURIAL SITES.

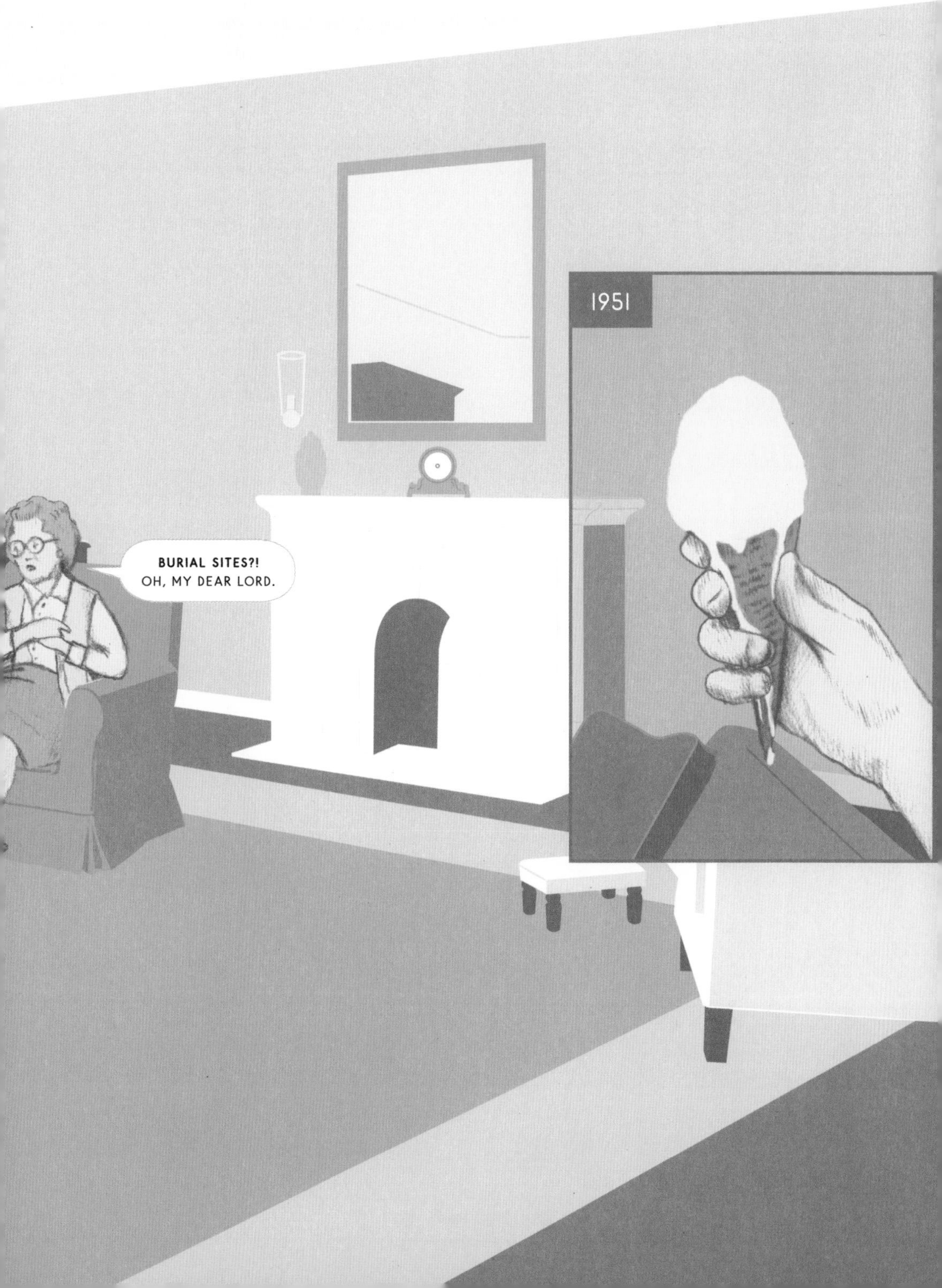
BURIAL SITES?!
OH, MY DEAR LORD.
1951

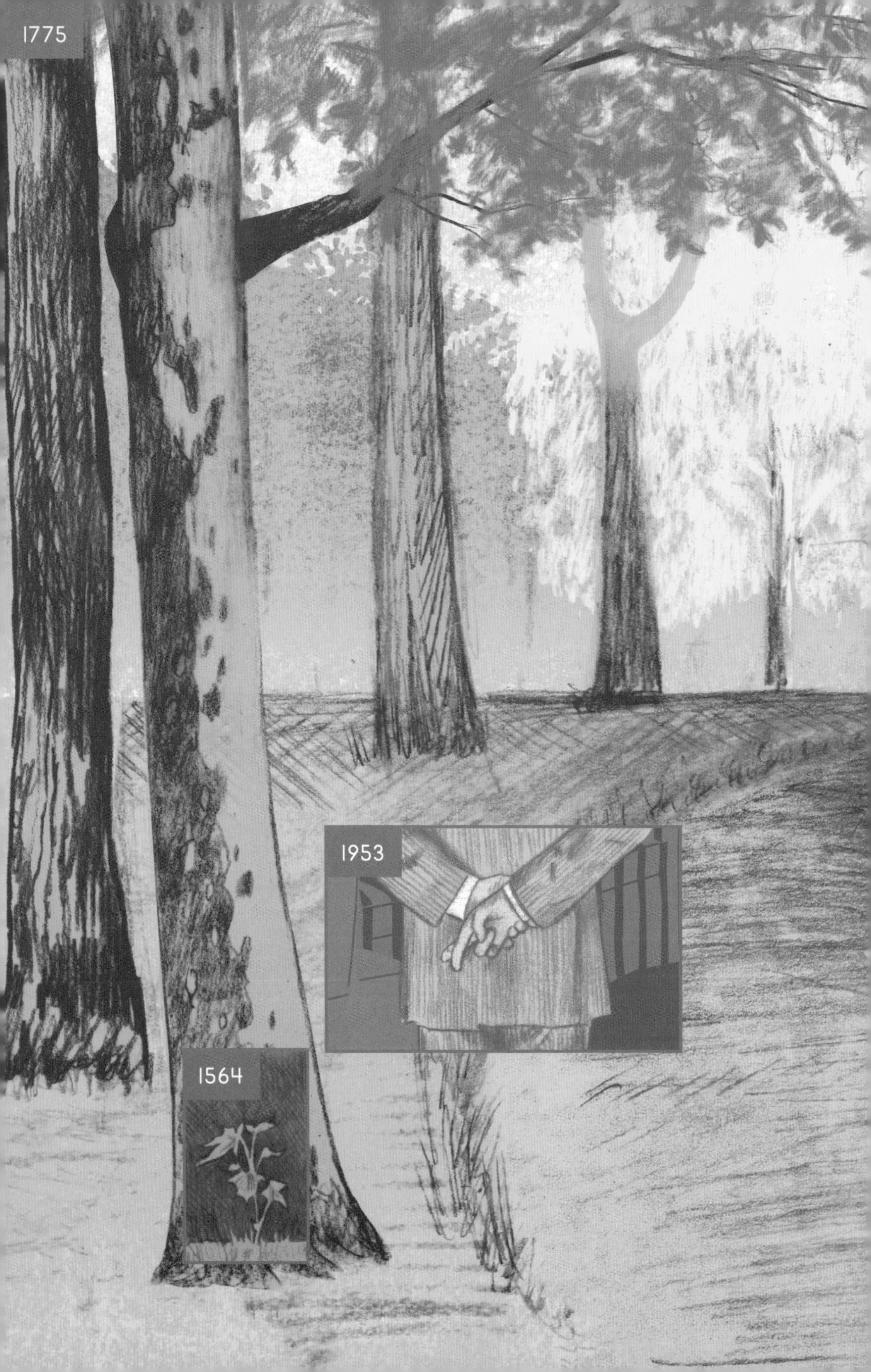
1775
1953
1564

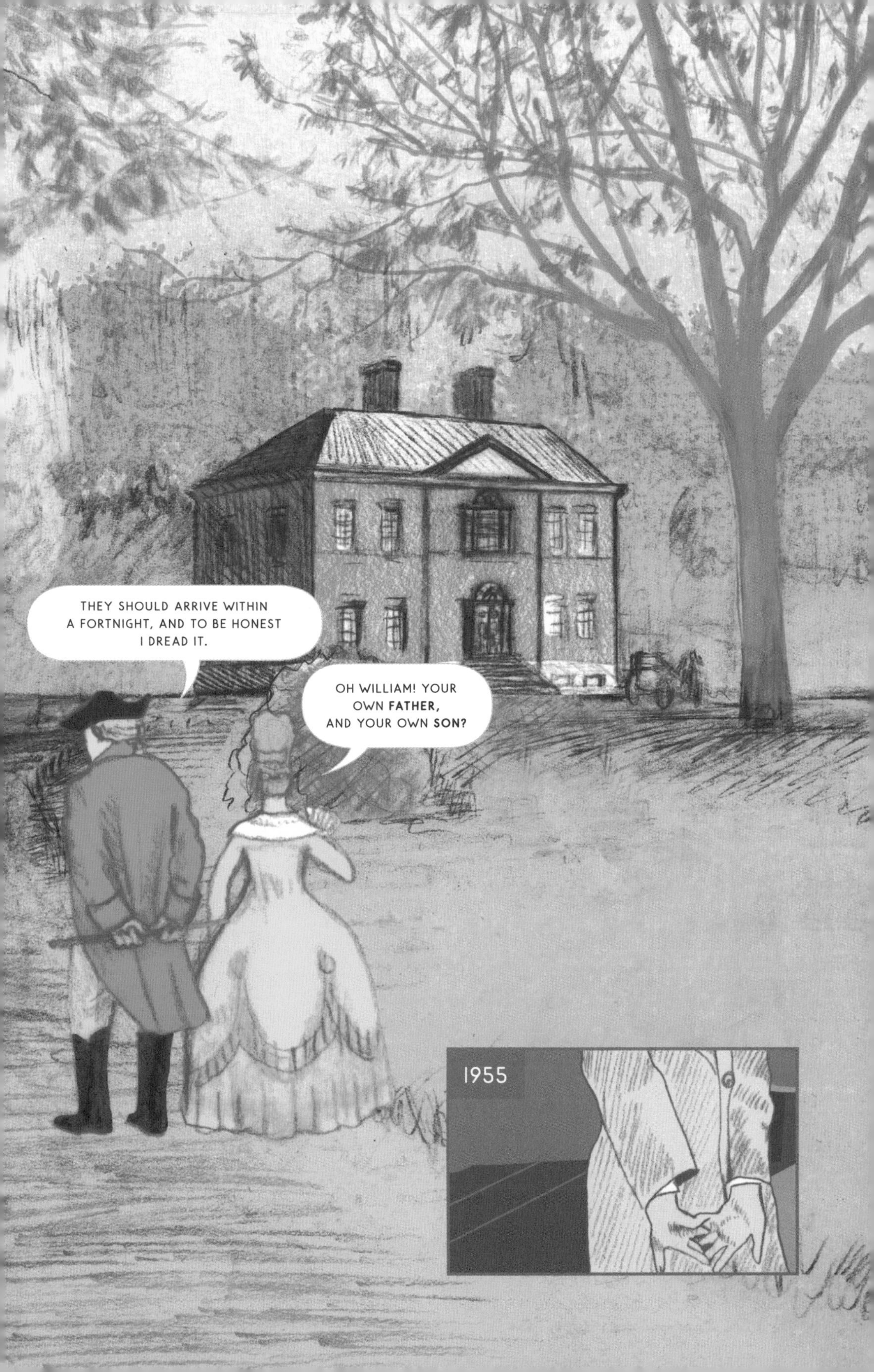
THEY SHOULD ARRIVE WITHIN A FORTNIGHT, AND TO BE HONEST I DREAD IT.
OH WILLIAM! YOUR OWN FATHER, AND YOUR OWN SON?
1955

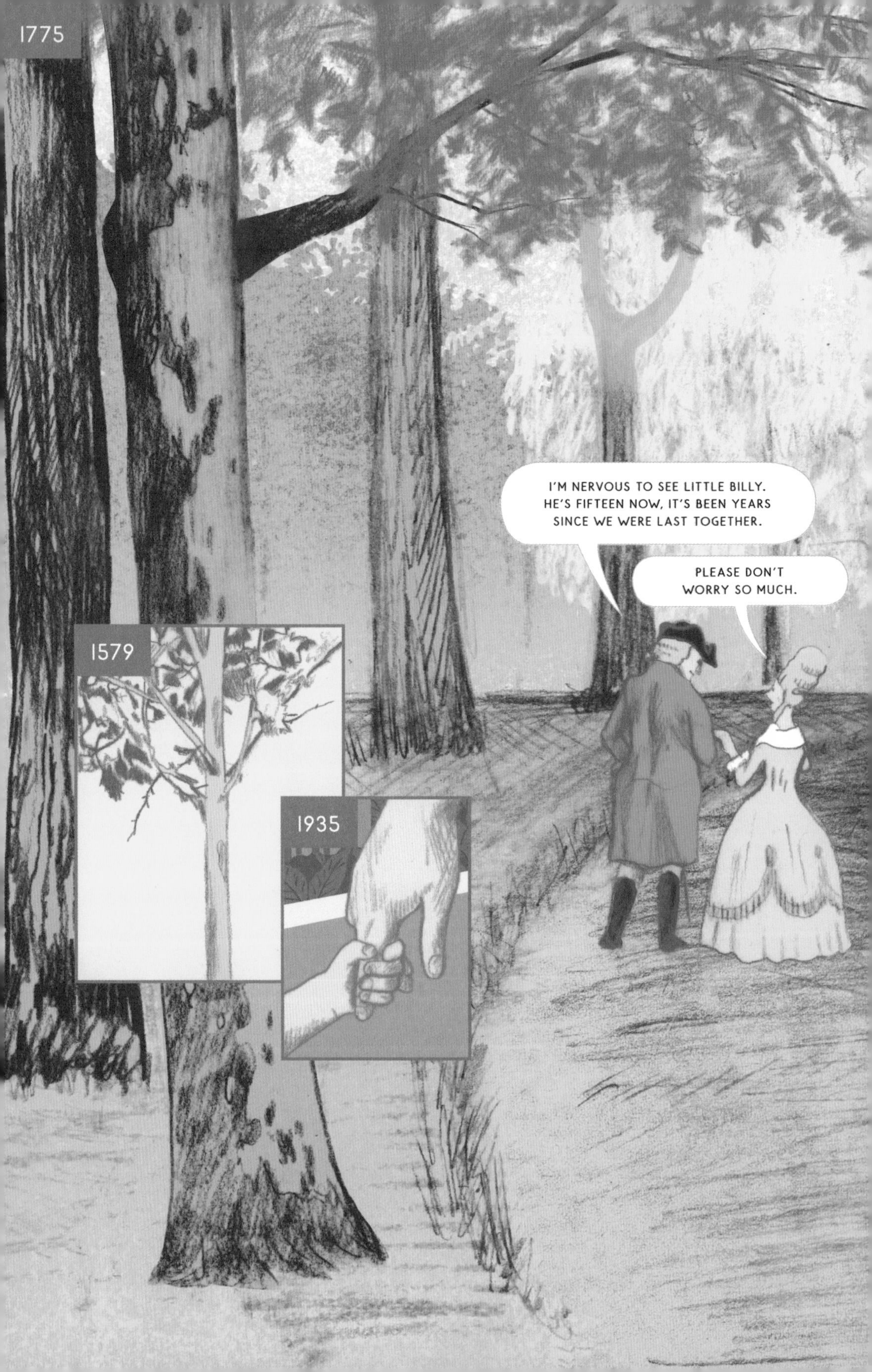
1775
I'M NERVOUS TO SEE LITTLE BILLY. HE'S FIFTEEN NOW, IT'S BEEN YEARS SINCE WE WERE LAST TOGETHER.
PLEASE DON'T WORRY SO MUCH.
1579
1935

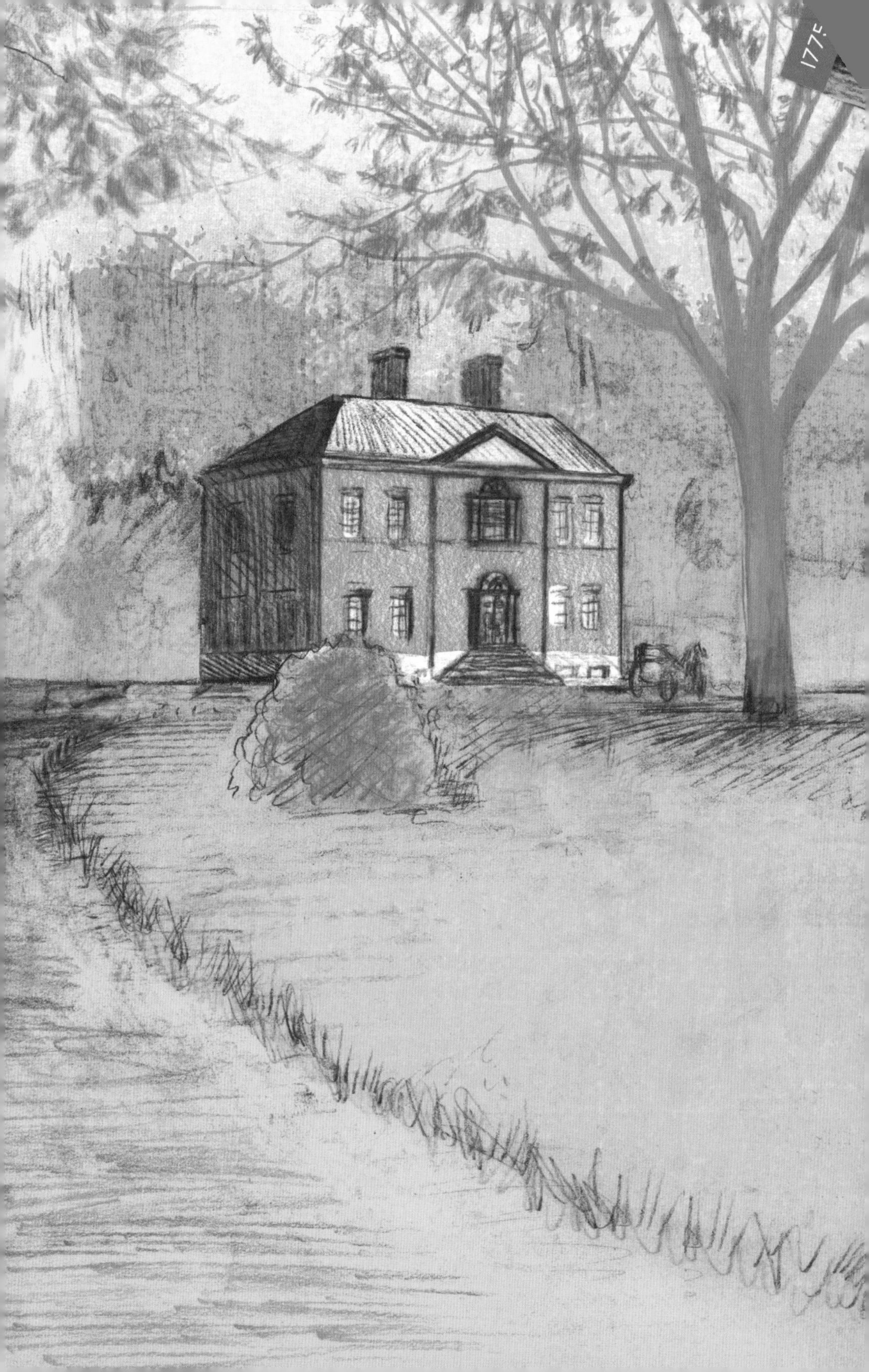

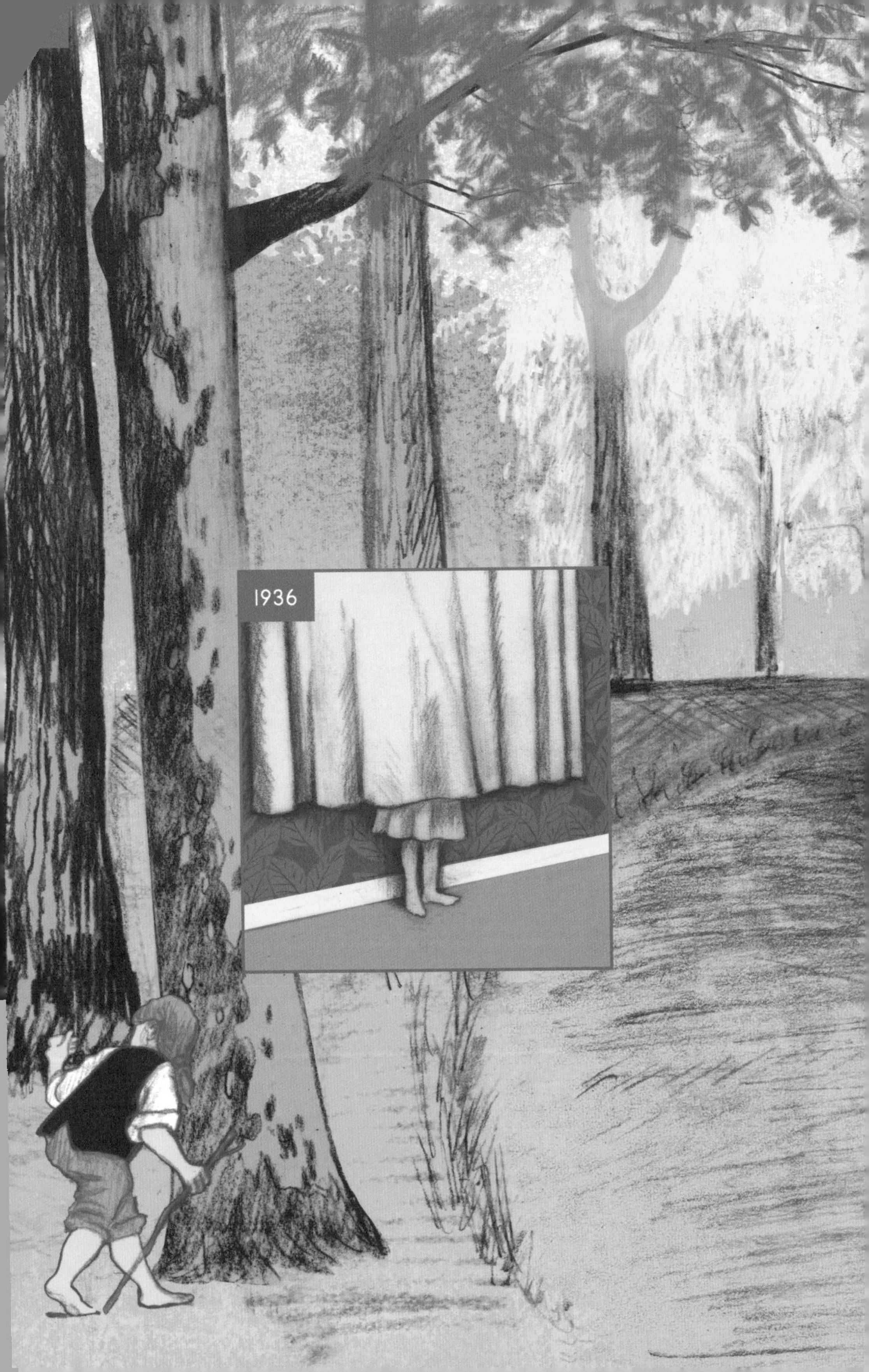
1936

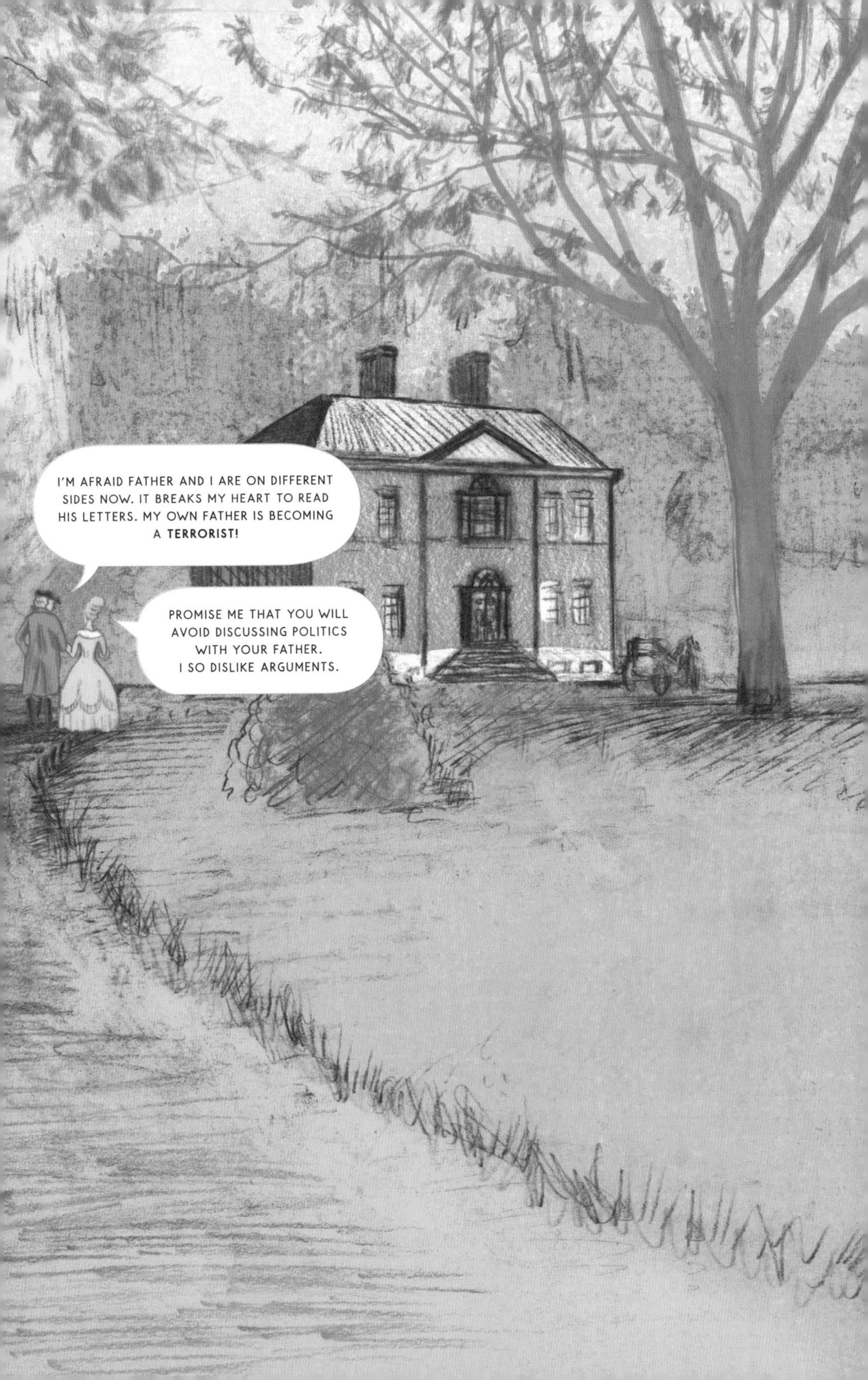
I'M AFRAID FATHER AND I ARE ON DIFFERENT SIDES NOW. IT BREAKS MY HEART TO READ HIS LETTERS. MY OWN FATHER IS BECOMING A **TERRORIST!**
PROMISE ME THAT YOU WILL AVOID DISCUSSING POLITICS WITH YOUR FATHER. I SO DISLIKE ARGUMENTS.

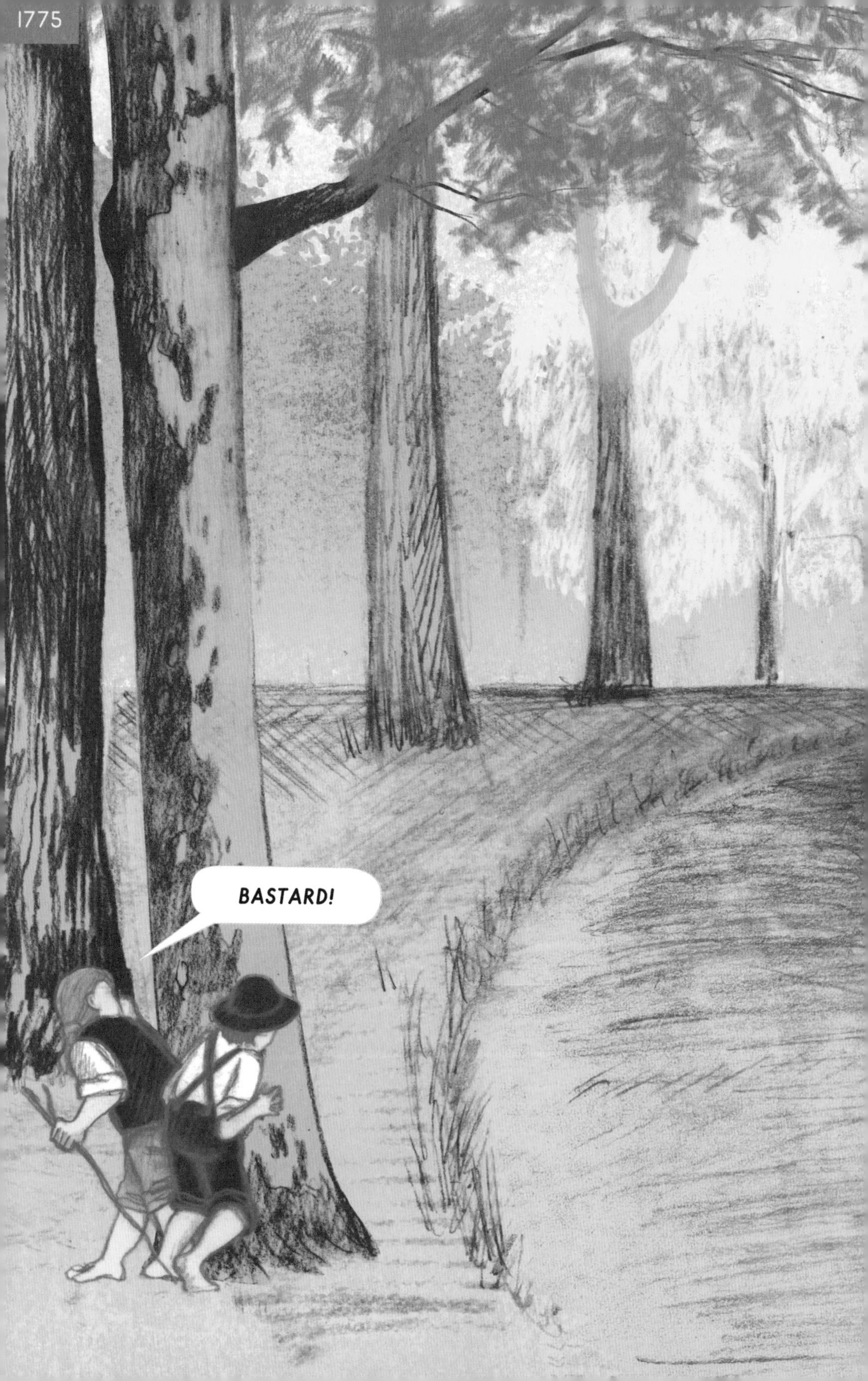
BASTARD!

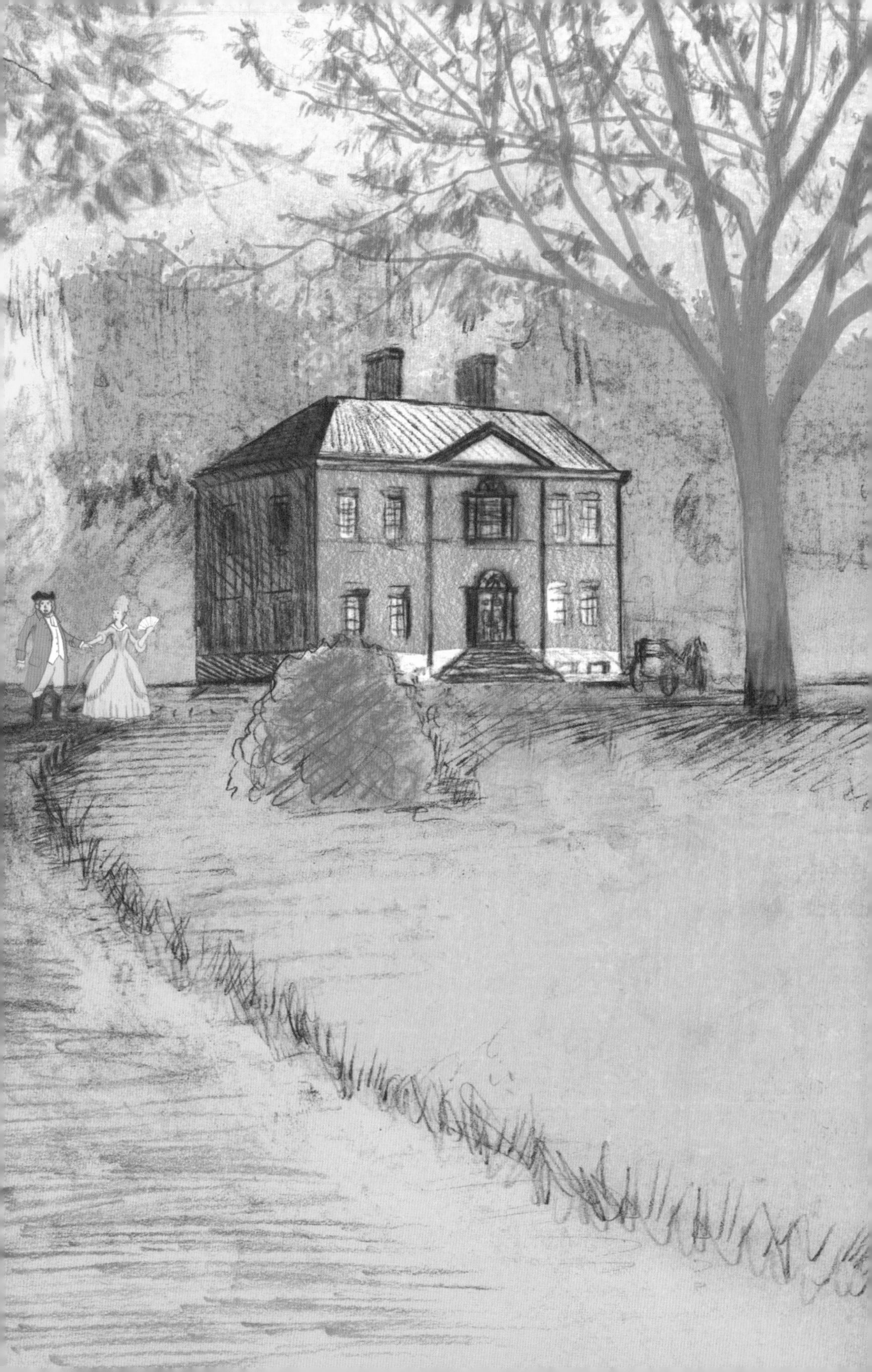

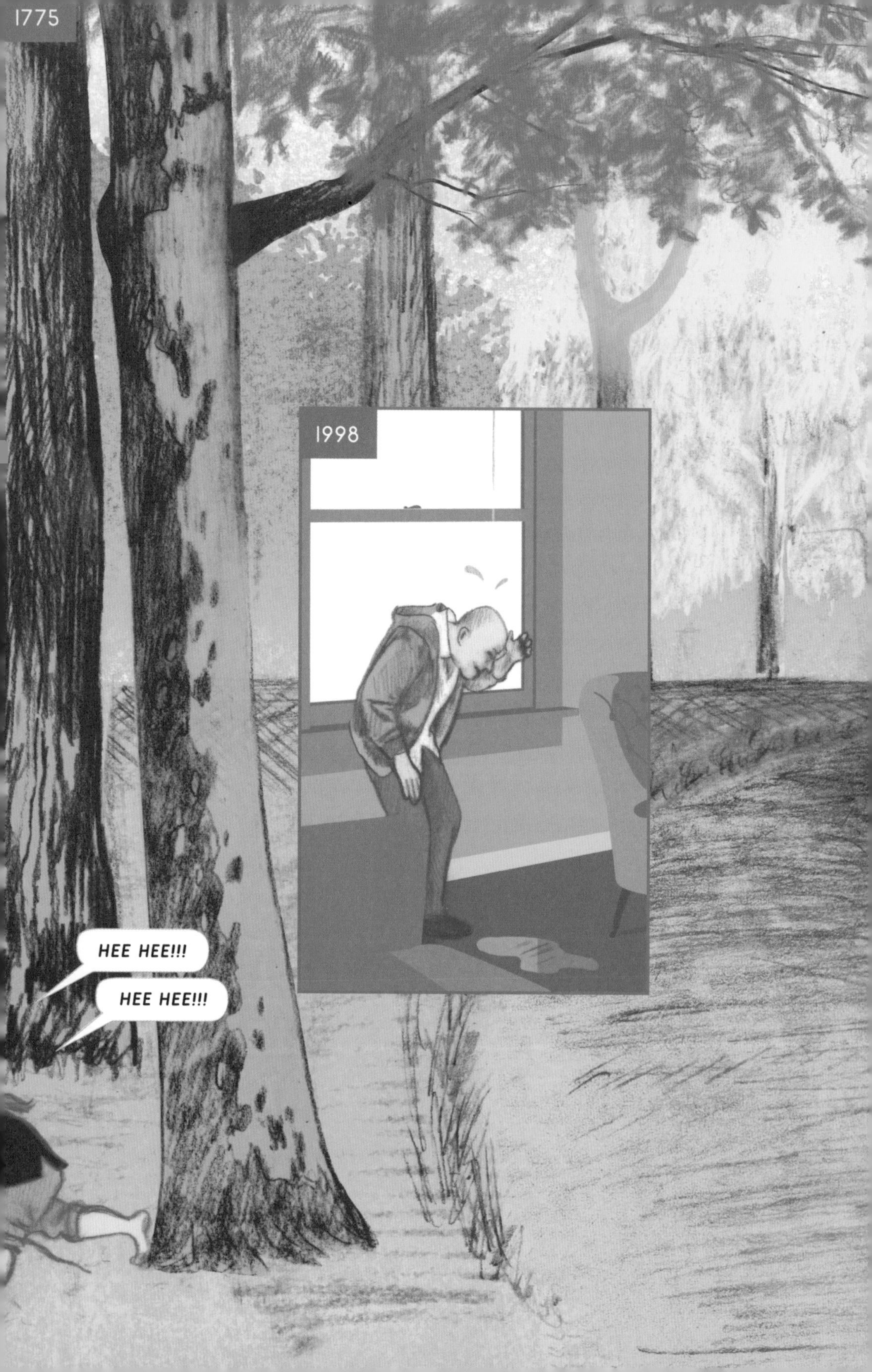
1775
1998
HEE HEE!!!
HEE HEE!!!

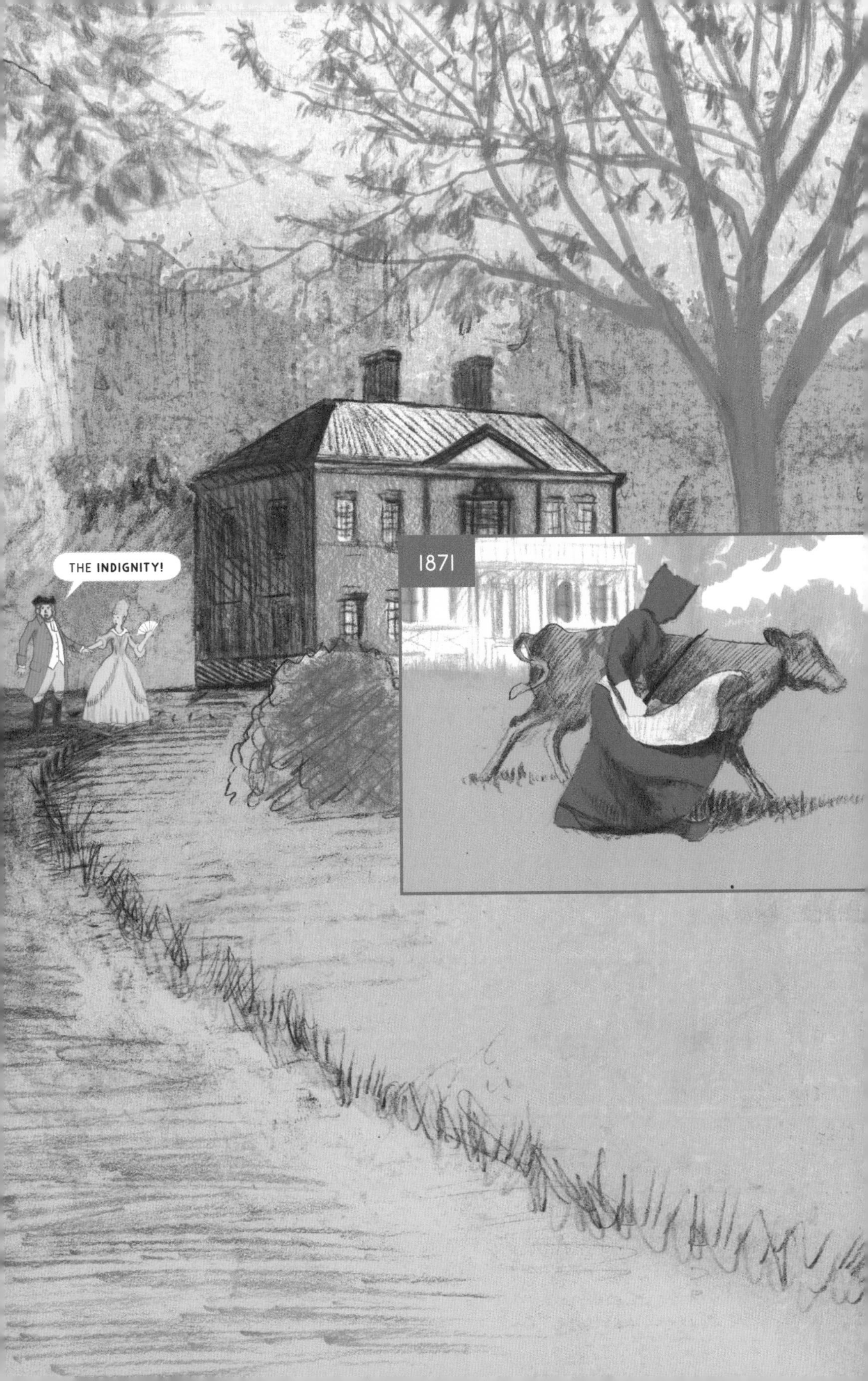
THE **INDIGNITY!**
1871

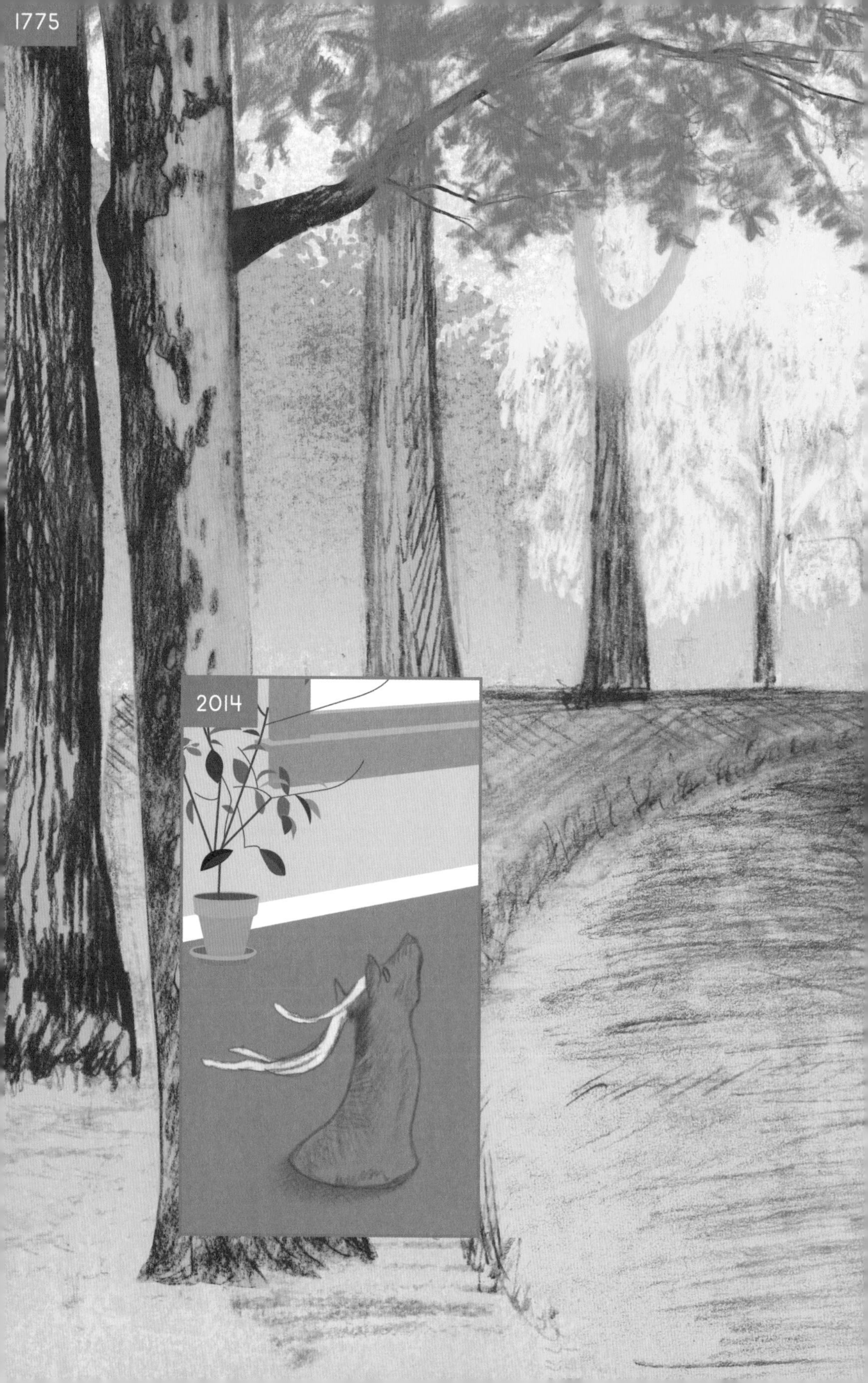
1775
2014

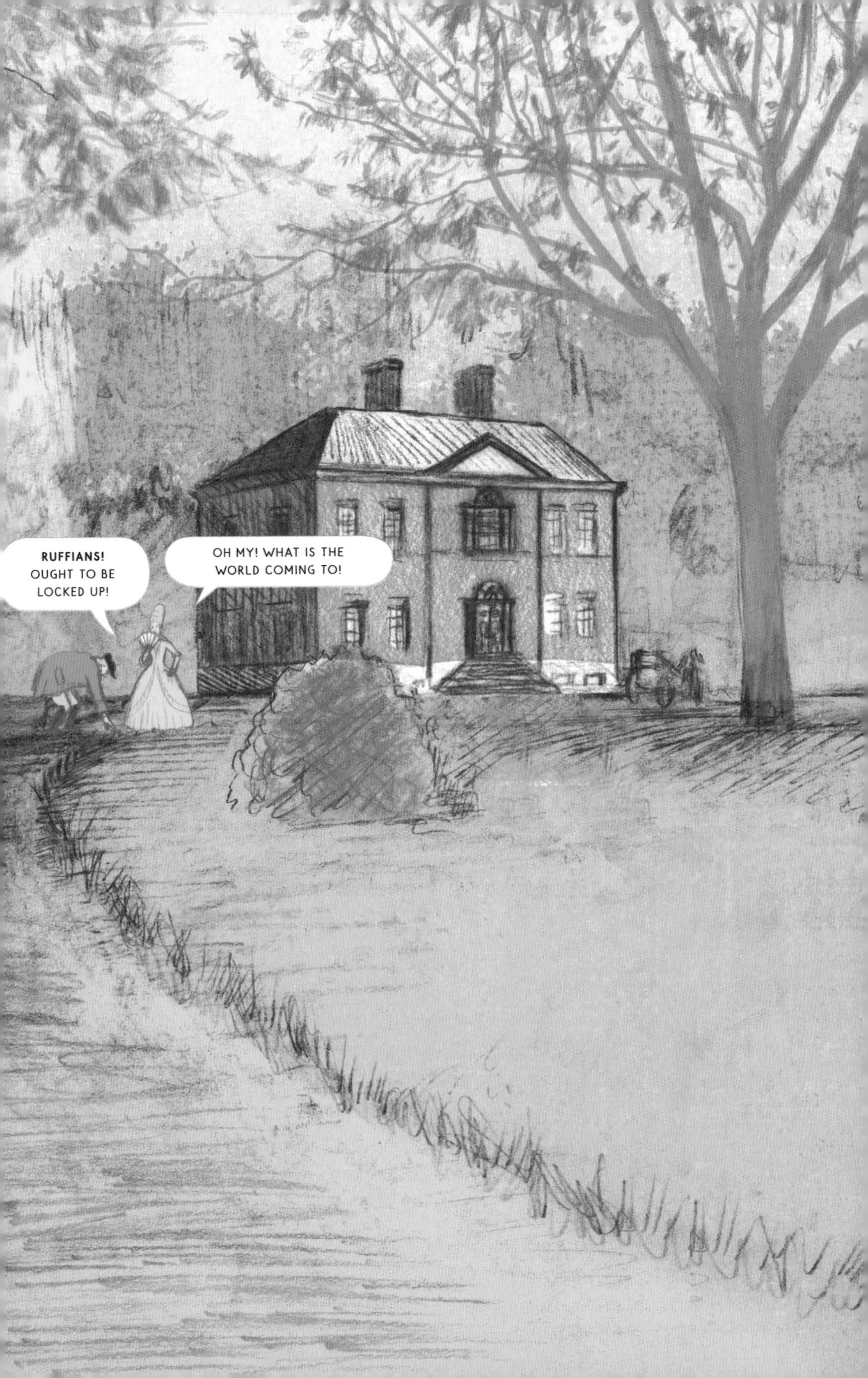
RUFFIANS! OUGHT TO BE LOCKED UP!
OH MY! WHAT IS THE WORLD COMING TO!

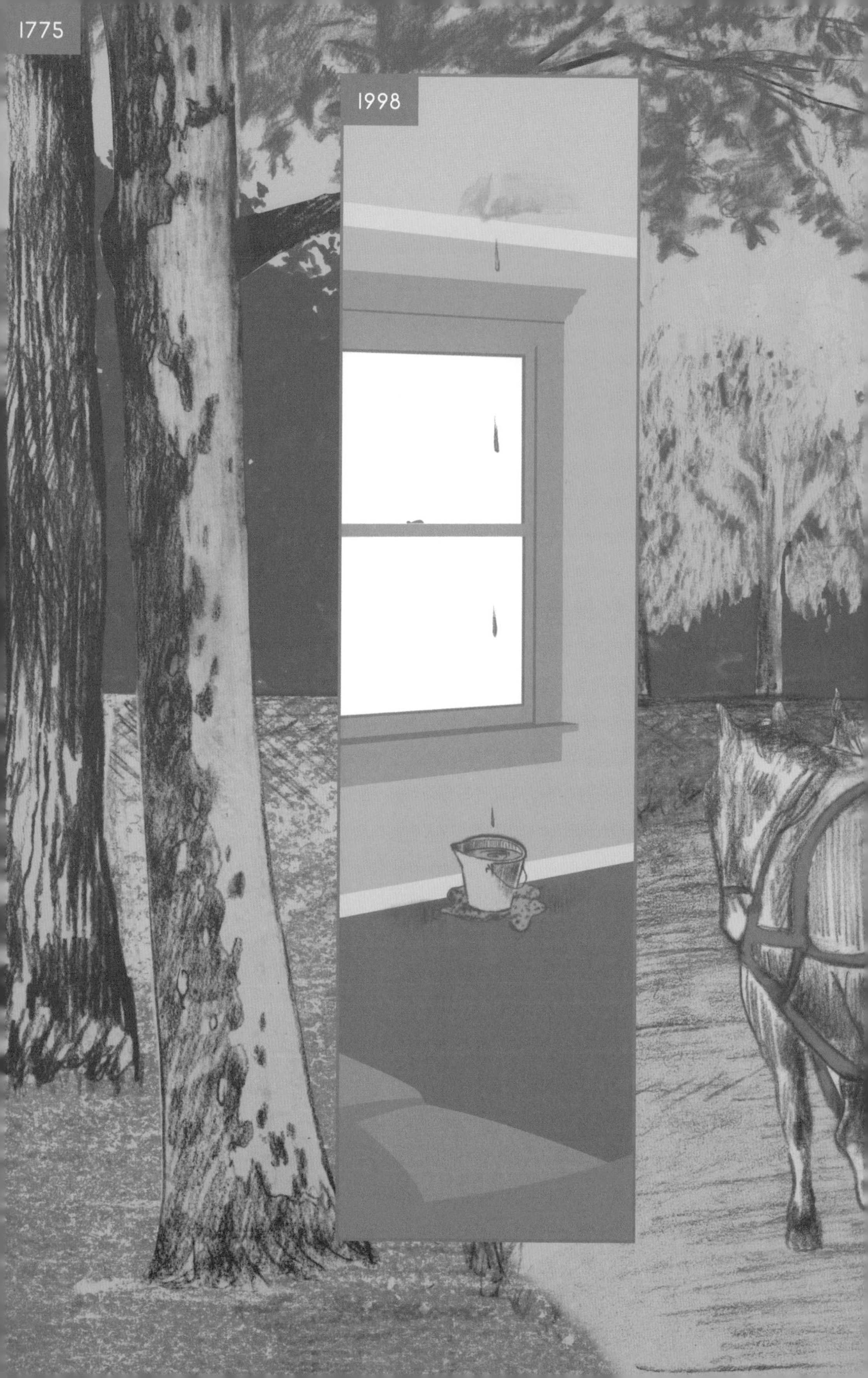
1775
1998

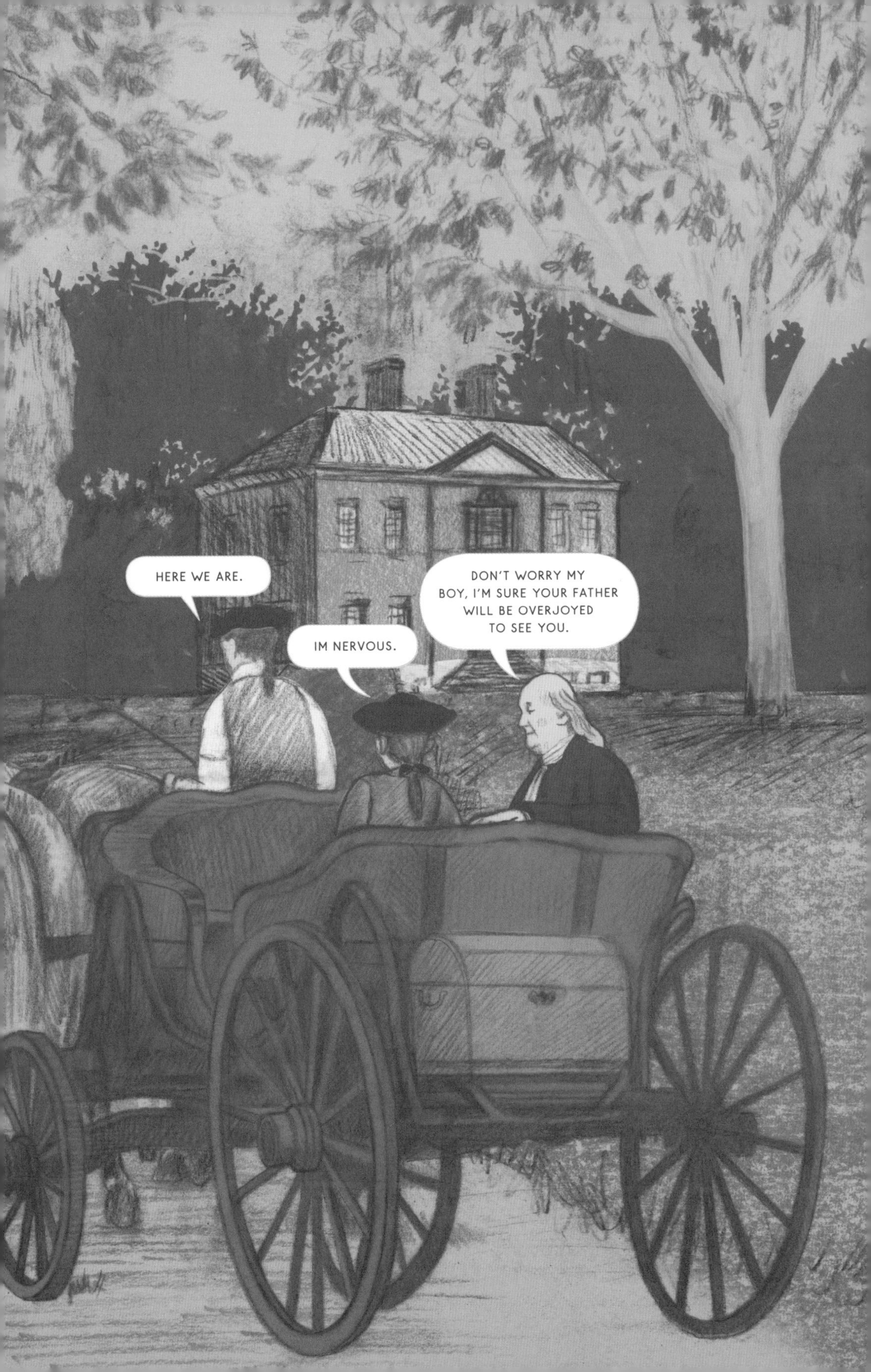
HERE WE ARE.
IM NERVOUS.
DON'T WORRY MY BOY, I'M SURE YOUR FATHER WILL BE OVERJOYED TO SEE YOU.

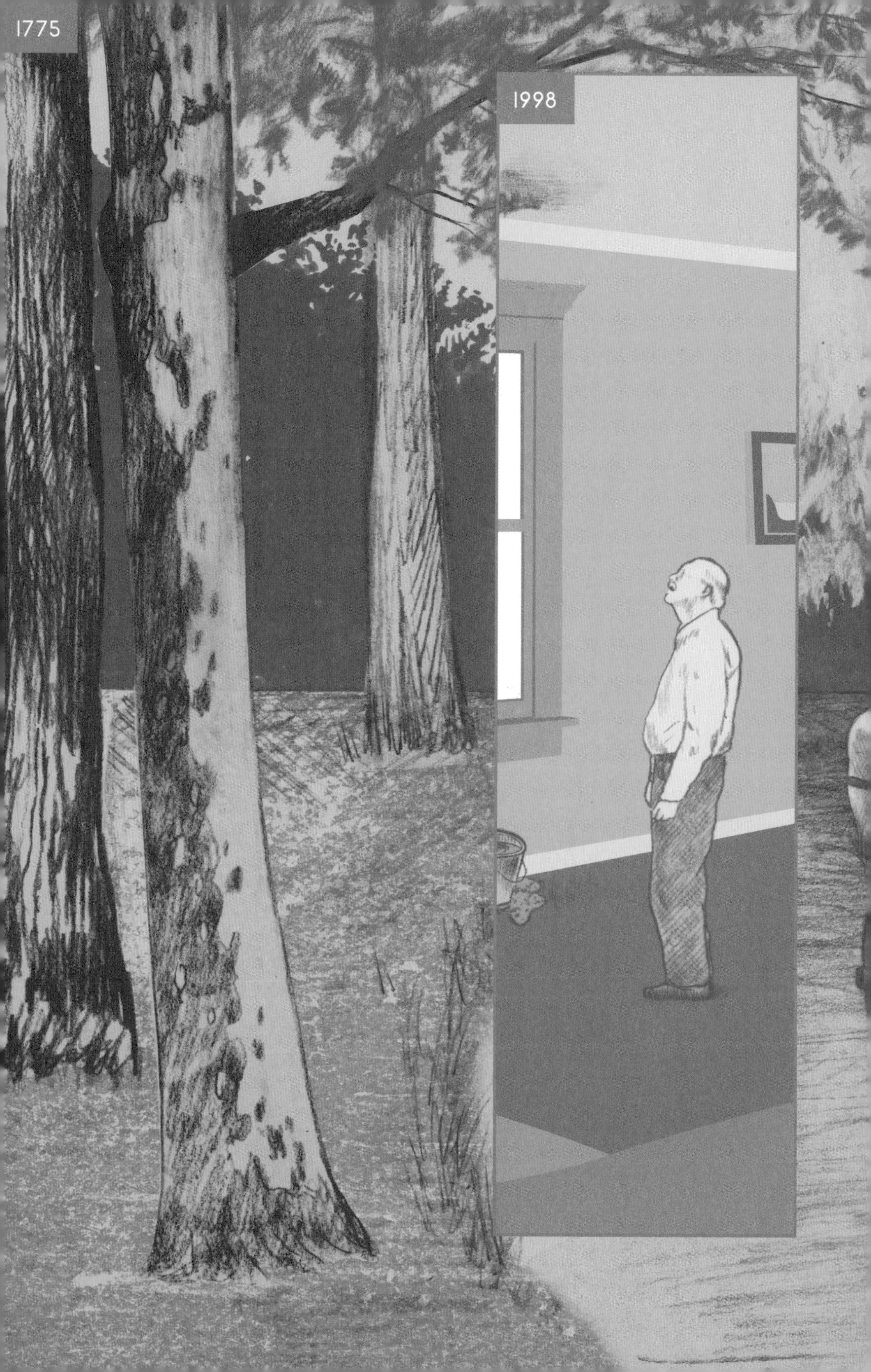
1775
1998

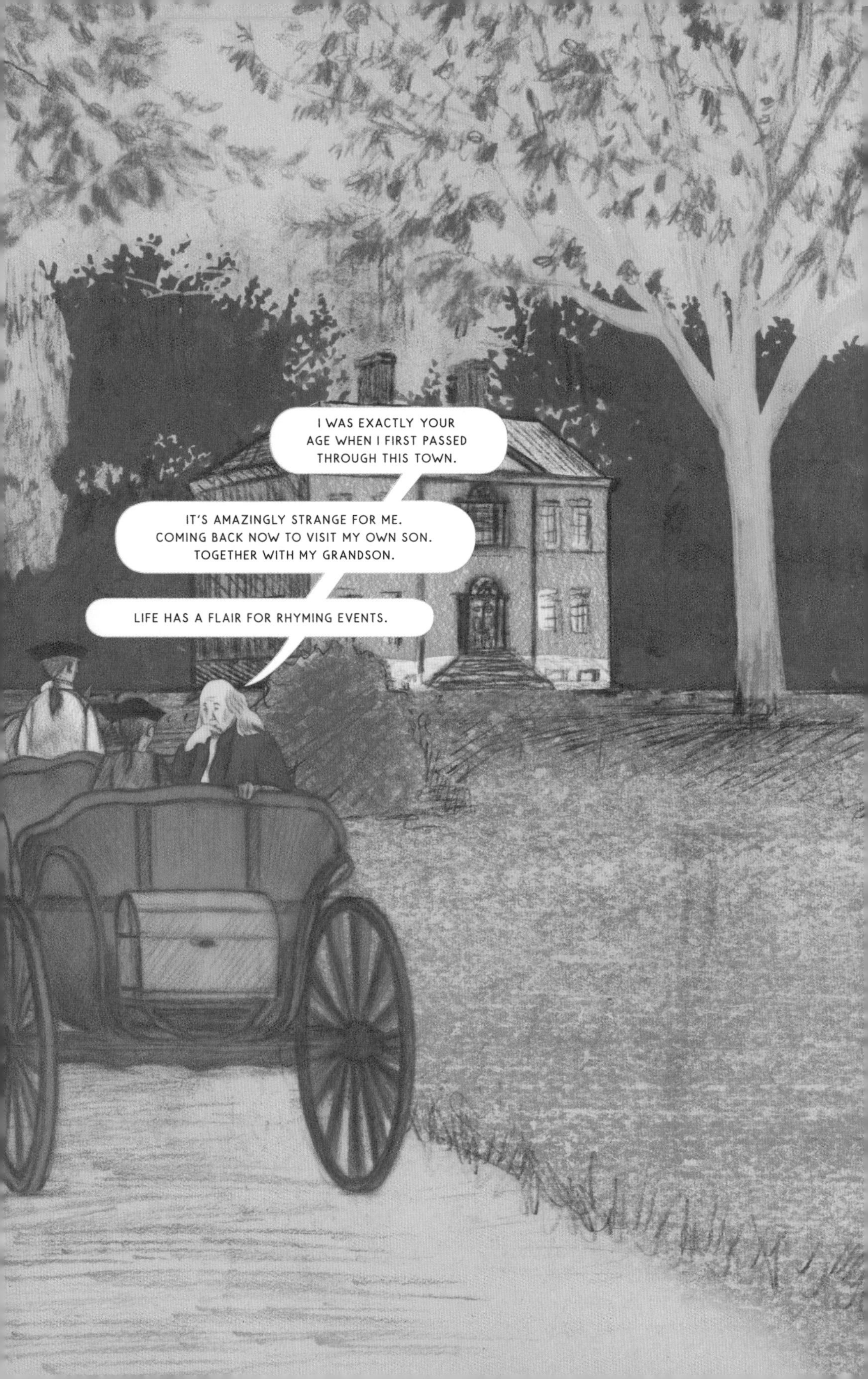
I WAS EXACTLY YOUR AGE WHEN I FIRST PASSED THROUGH THIS TOWN.
IT'S AMAZINGLY STRANGE FOR ME. COMING BACK NOW TO VISIT MY OWN SON. TOGETHER WITH MY GRANDSON.
LIFE HAS A FLAIR FOR RHYMING EVENTS.

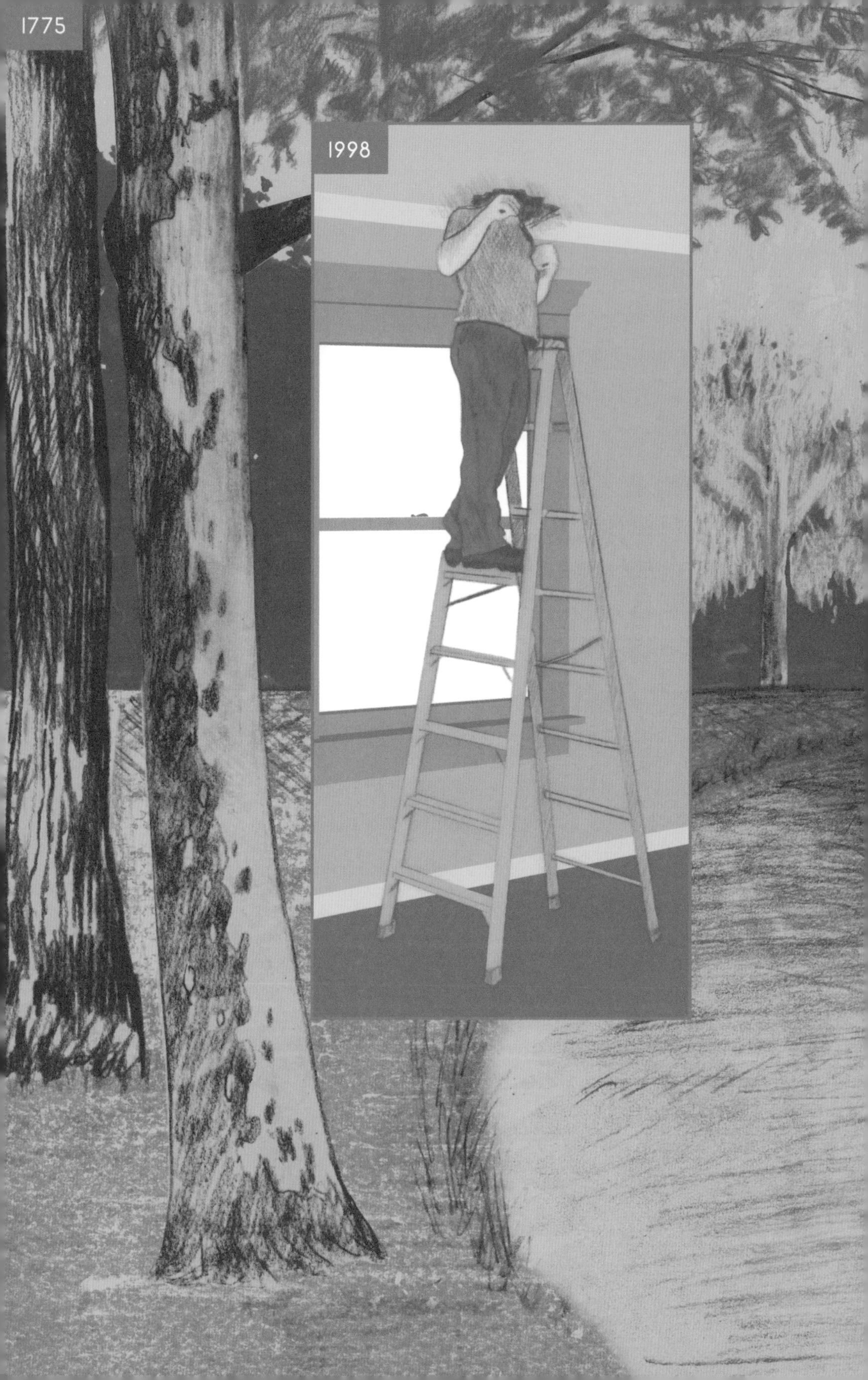
1775
1998

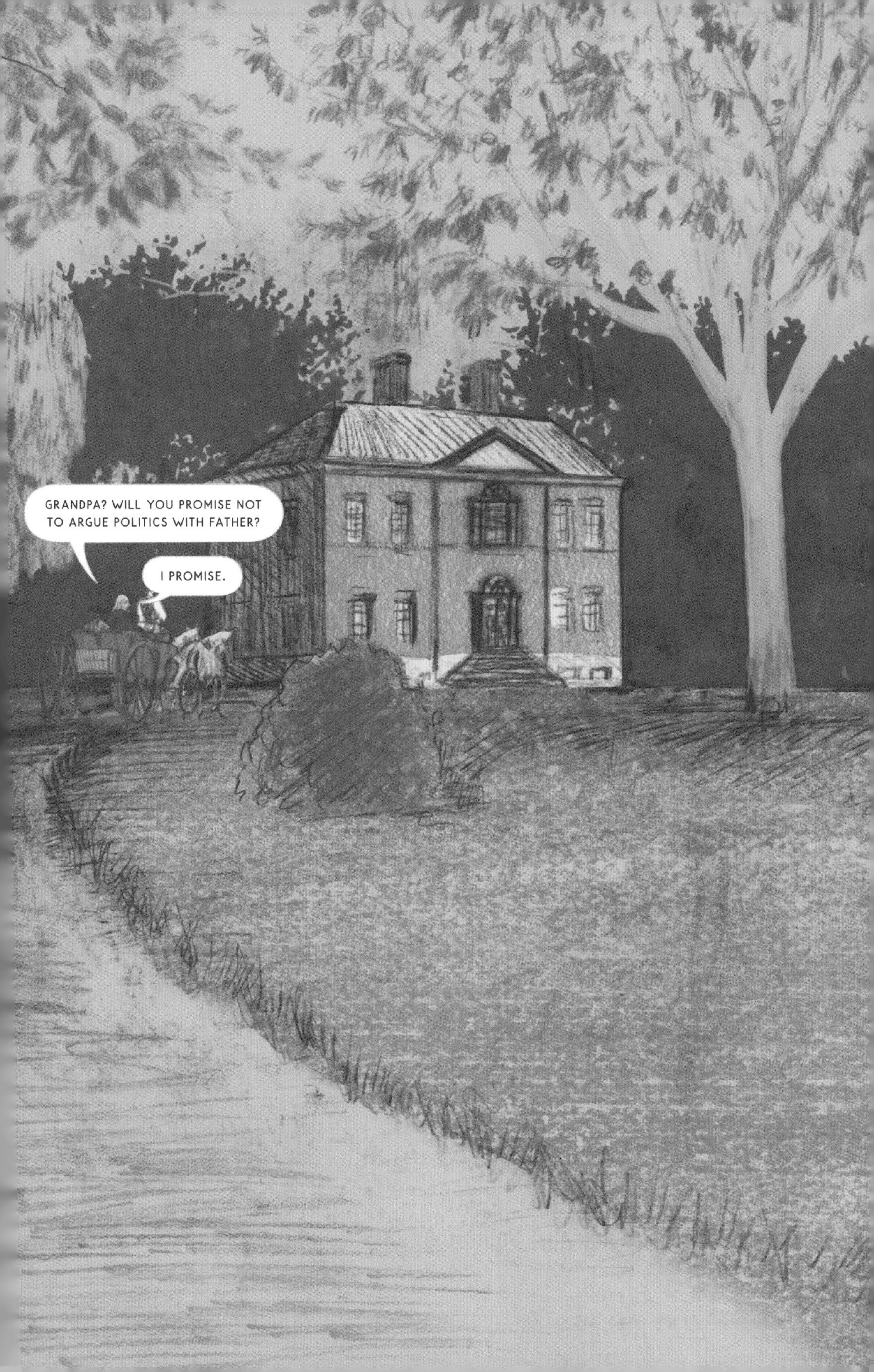
GRANDPA? WILL YOU PROMISE NOT TO ARGUE POLITICS WITH FATHER?
I PROMISE.

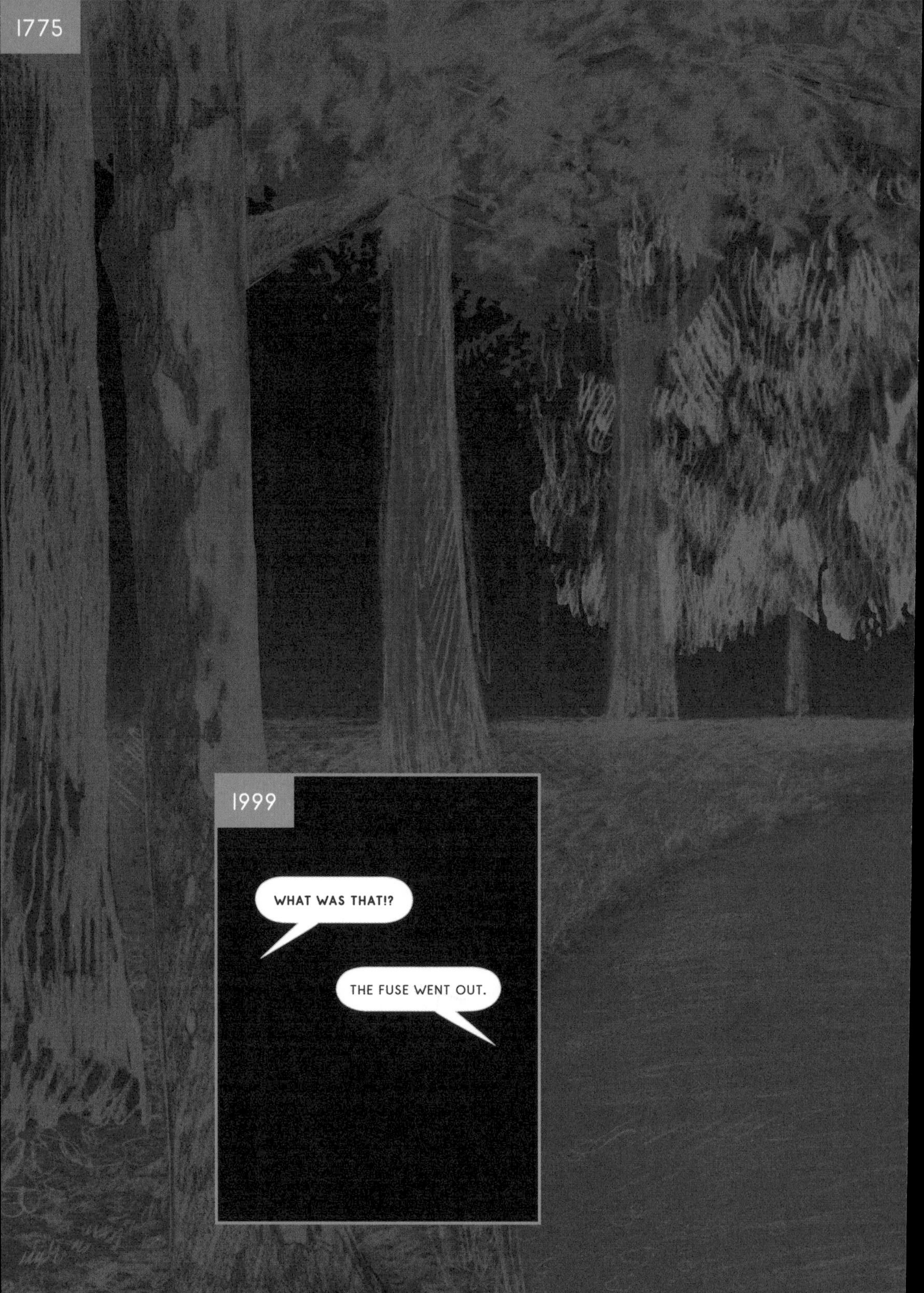
1775
1999
WHAT WAS THAT!?
THE FUSE WENT OUT.

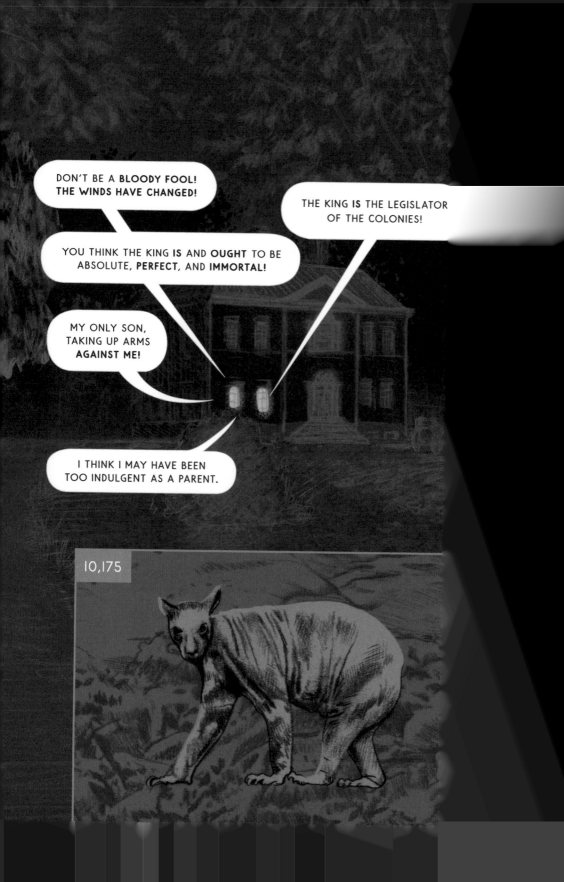

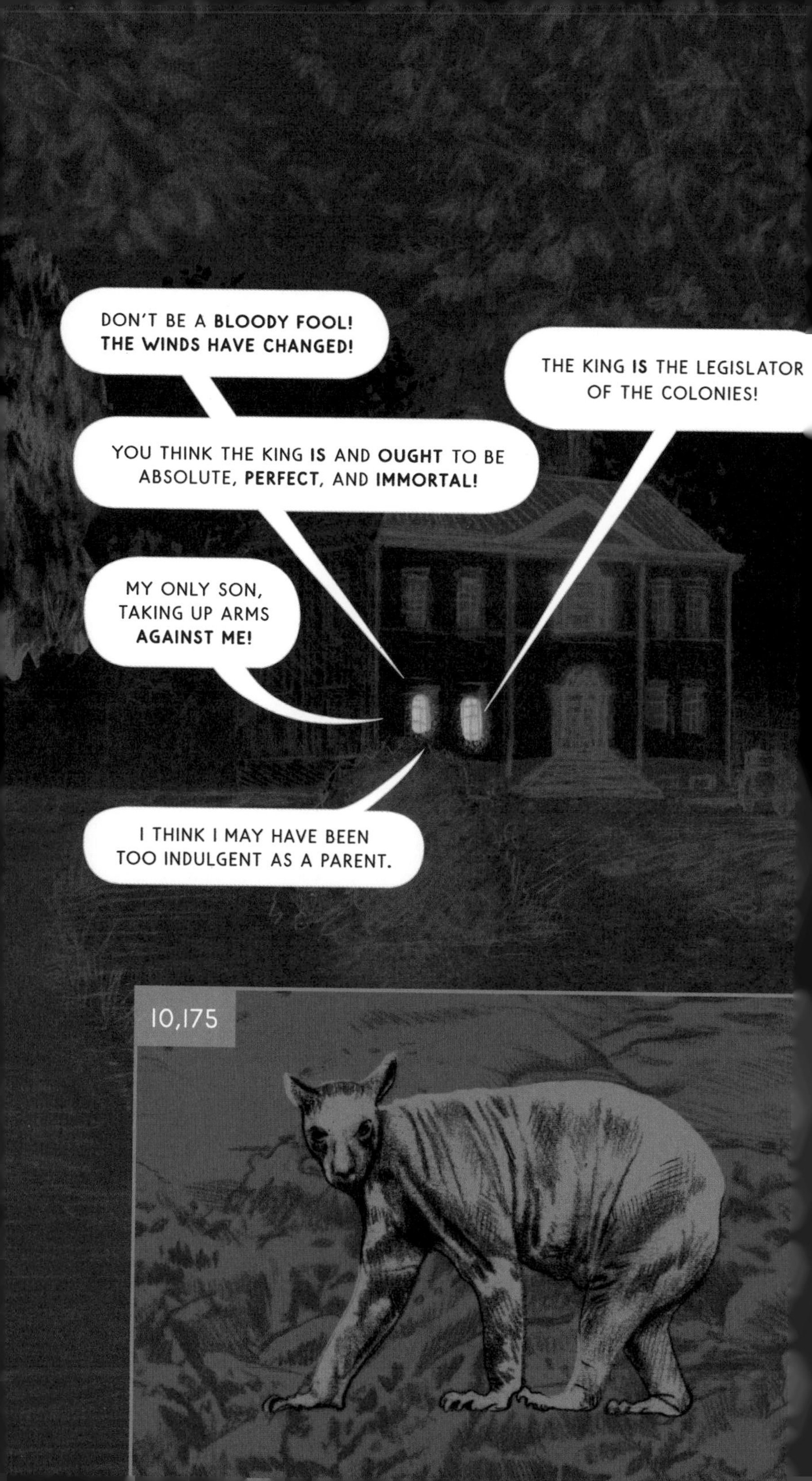
DON'T BE A BLOODY FOOL! THE WINDS HAVE CHANGED!
THE KING IS THE LEGISLATOR OF THE COLONIES!
YOU THINK THE KING IS AND OUGHT TO BE ABSOLUTE, PERFECT, AND IMMORTAL!
MY ONLY SON, TAKING UP ARMS AGAINST ME!
I THINK I MAY HAVE BEEN TOO INDULGENT AS A PARENT.
10,175

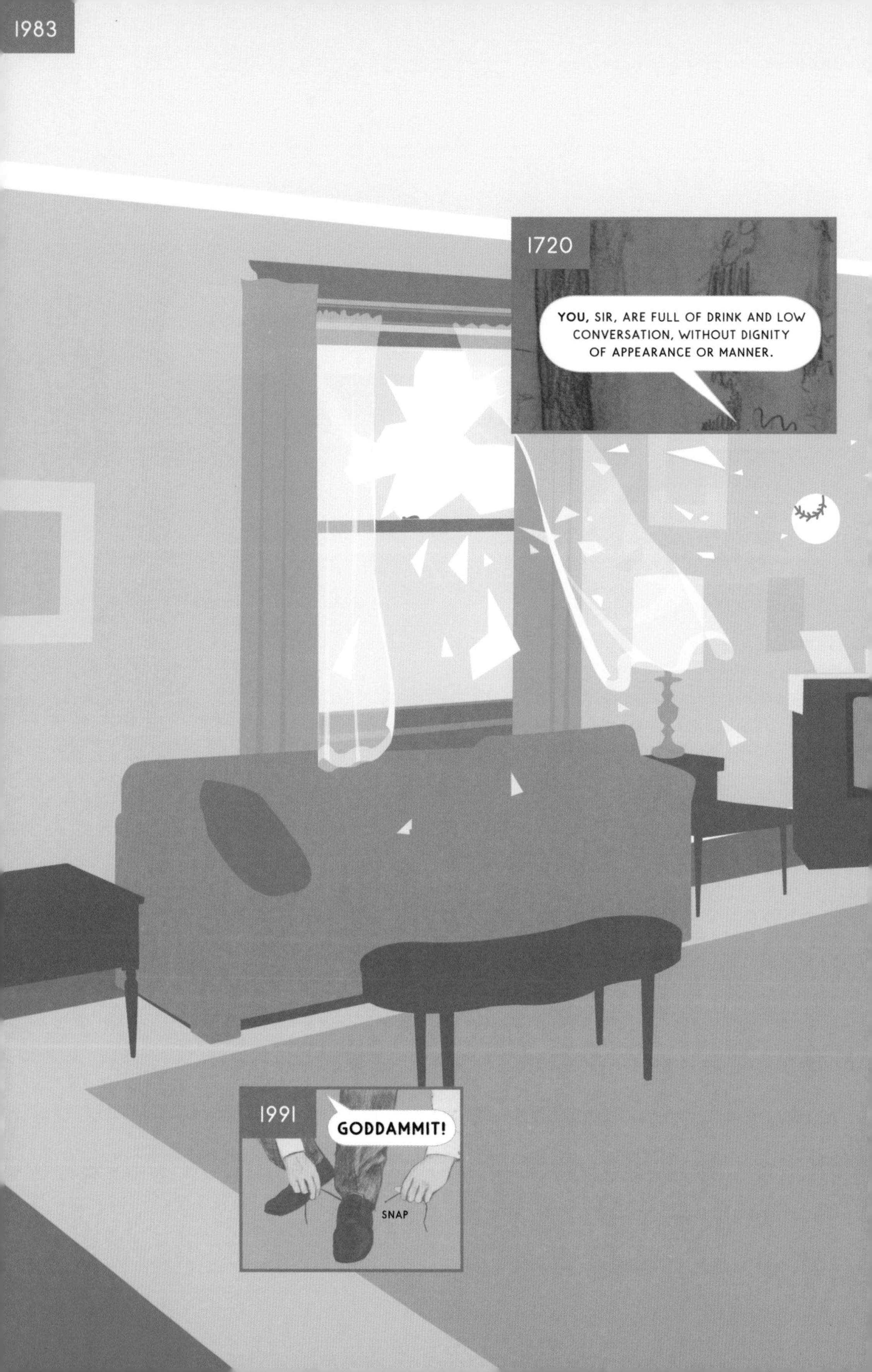
1983
1720
YOU, SIR, ARE FULL OF DRINK AND LOW CONVERSATION, WITHOUT DIGNITY OF APPEARANCE OR MANNER.
1991
GODDAMMIT!
SNAP

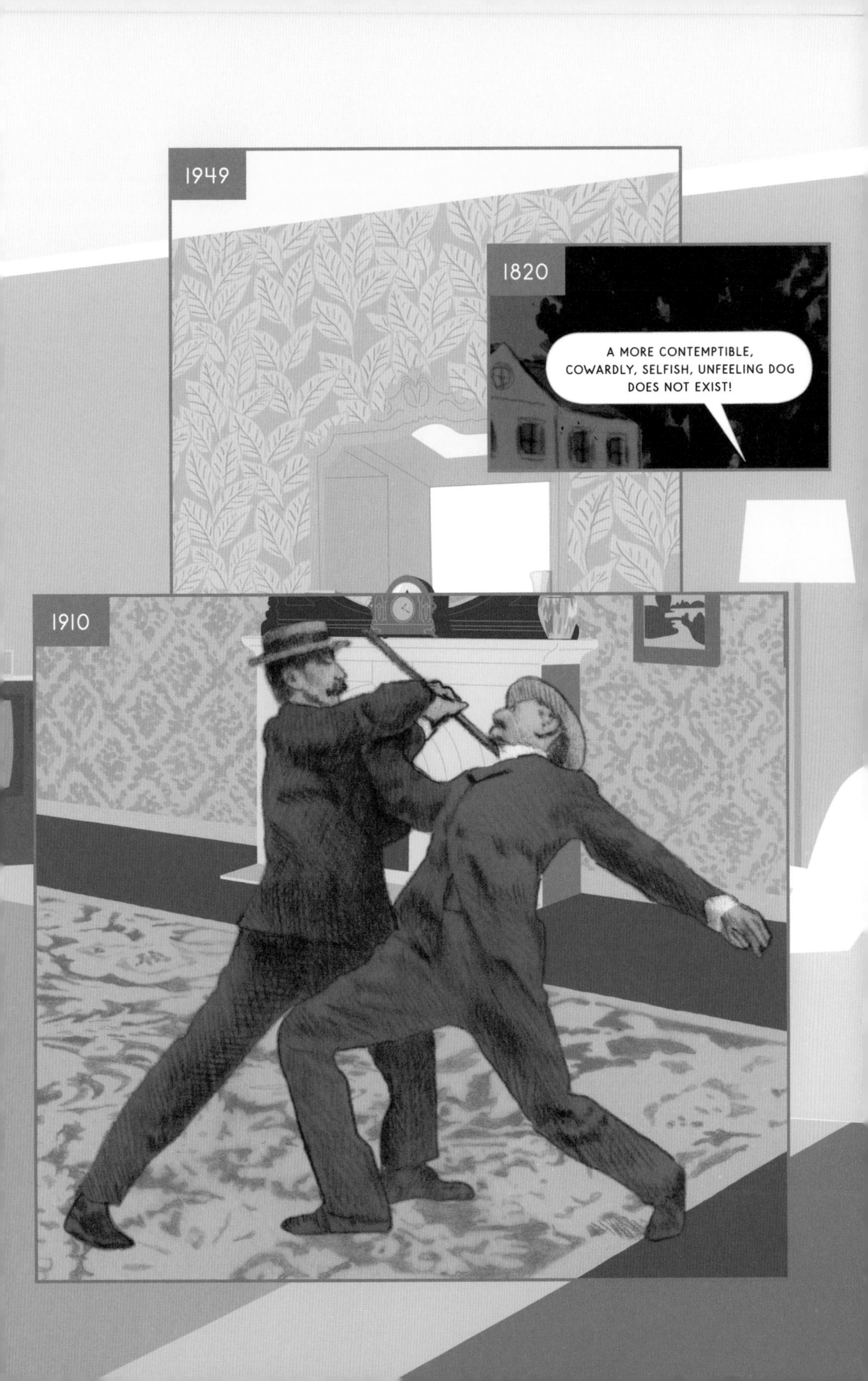
1949
1820
A MORE CONTEMPTIBLE, COWARDLY, SELFISH, UNFEELING DOG DOES NOT EXIST!
1910

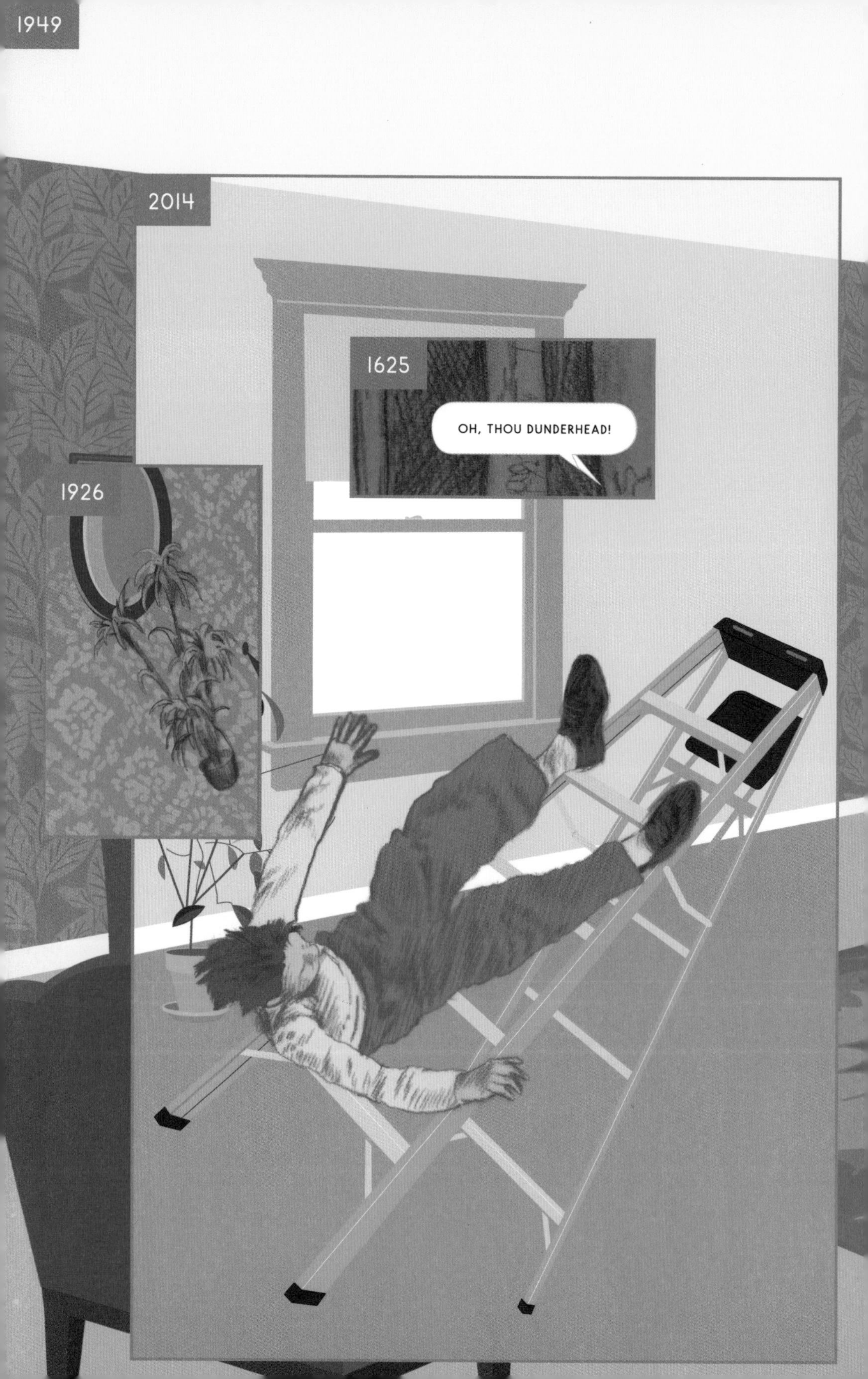
1949
2014
1625
OH, THOU DUNDERHEAD!
1926

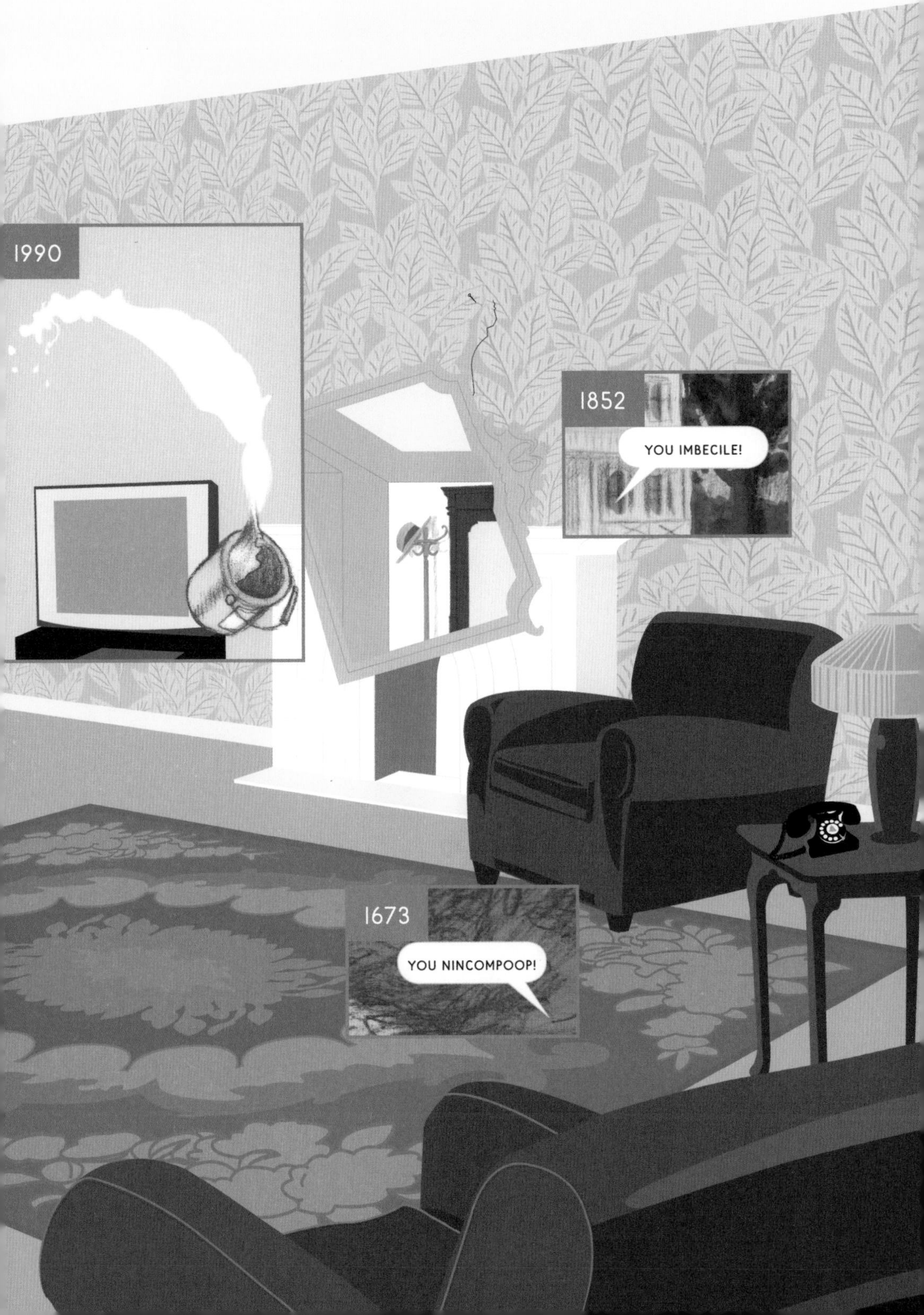
1990
1852
YOU IMBECILE!
1673
YOU NINCOMPOOP!

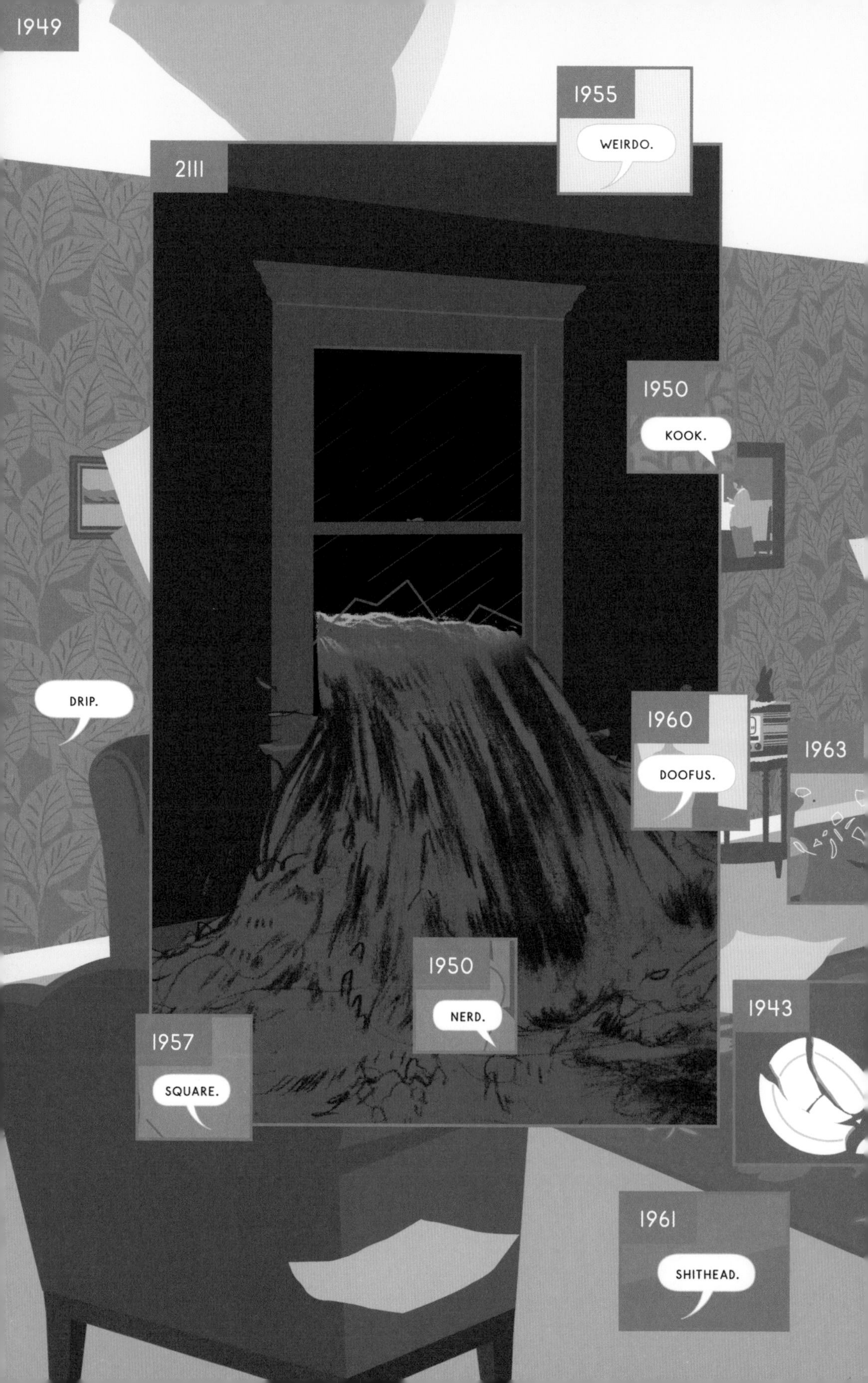
1949
1955
WEIRDO.
2111
1950
KOOK.
DRIP.
1960
DOOFUS.
1963
1950
NERD.
1943
1957
SQUARE.
1961
SHITHEAD.

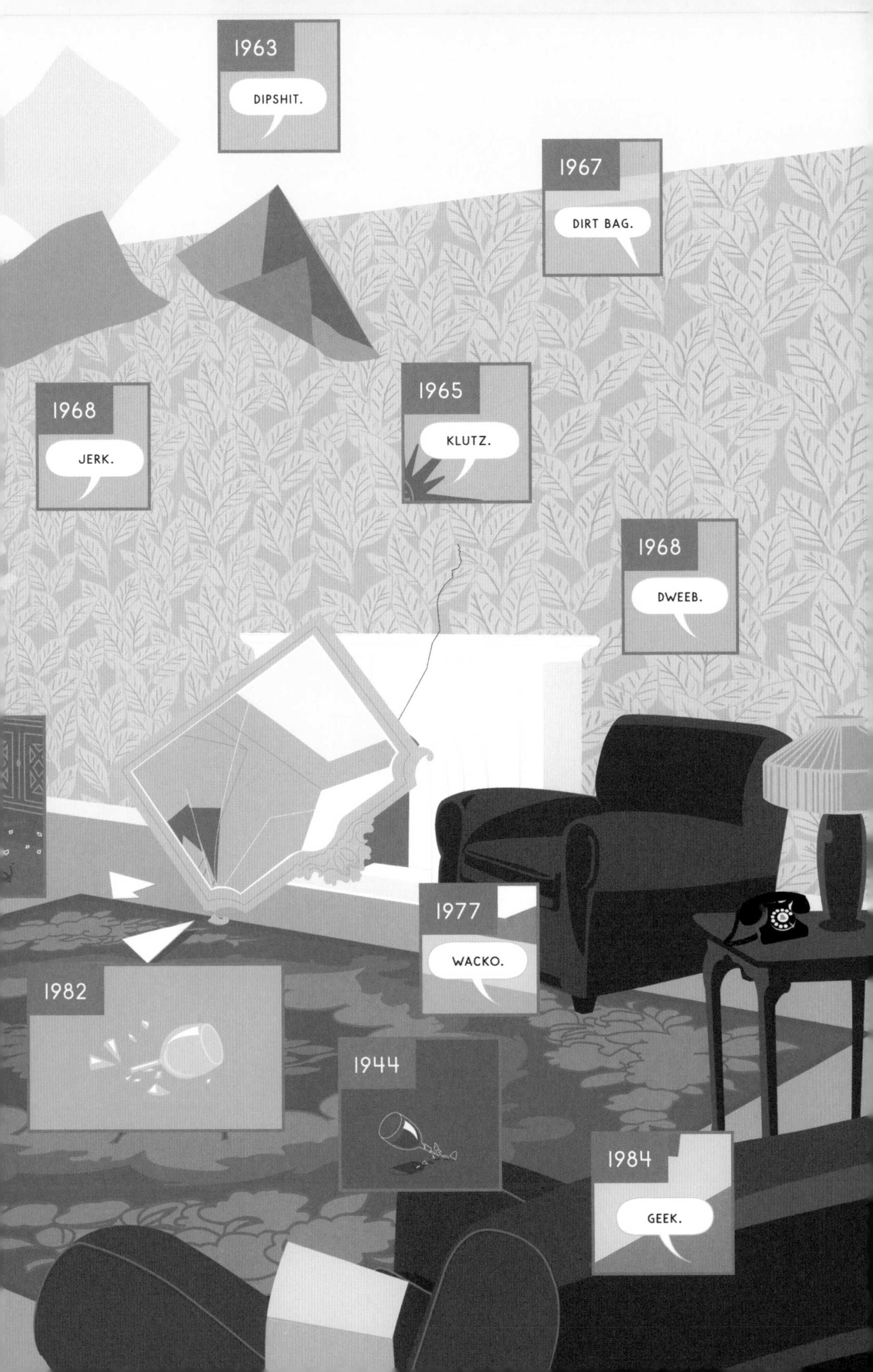
1963
DIPSHIT.
1967
DIRT BAG.
1968
JERK.
1965
KLUTZ.
1968
DWEEB.
1977
WACKO.
1982
1944
1984
GEEK.

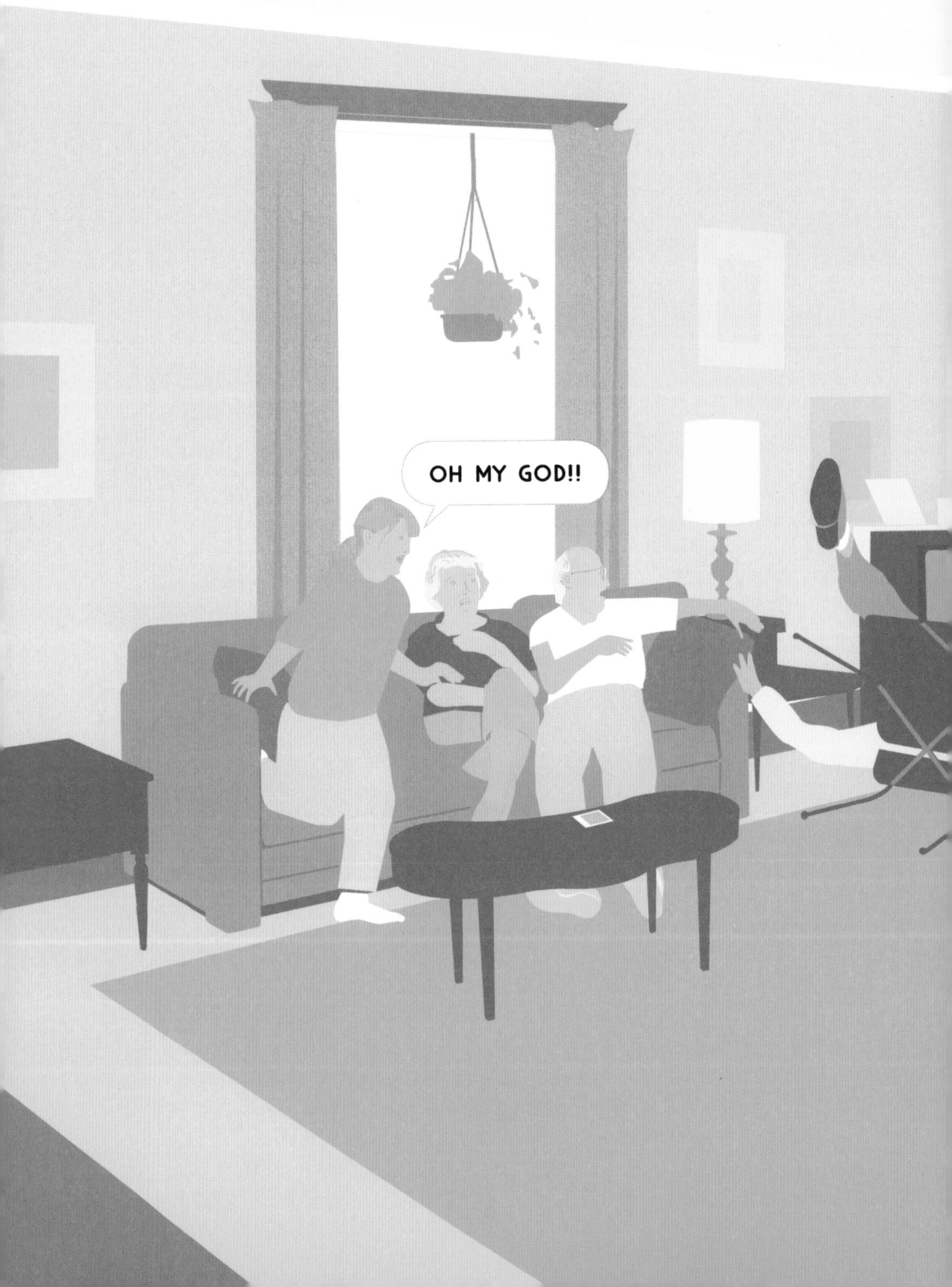
OH MY GOD!!

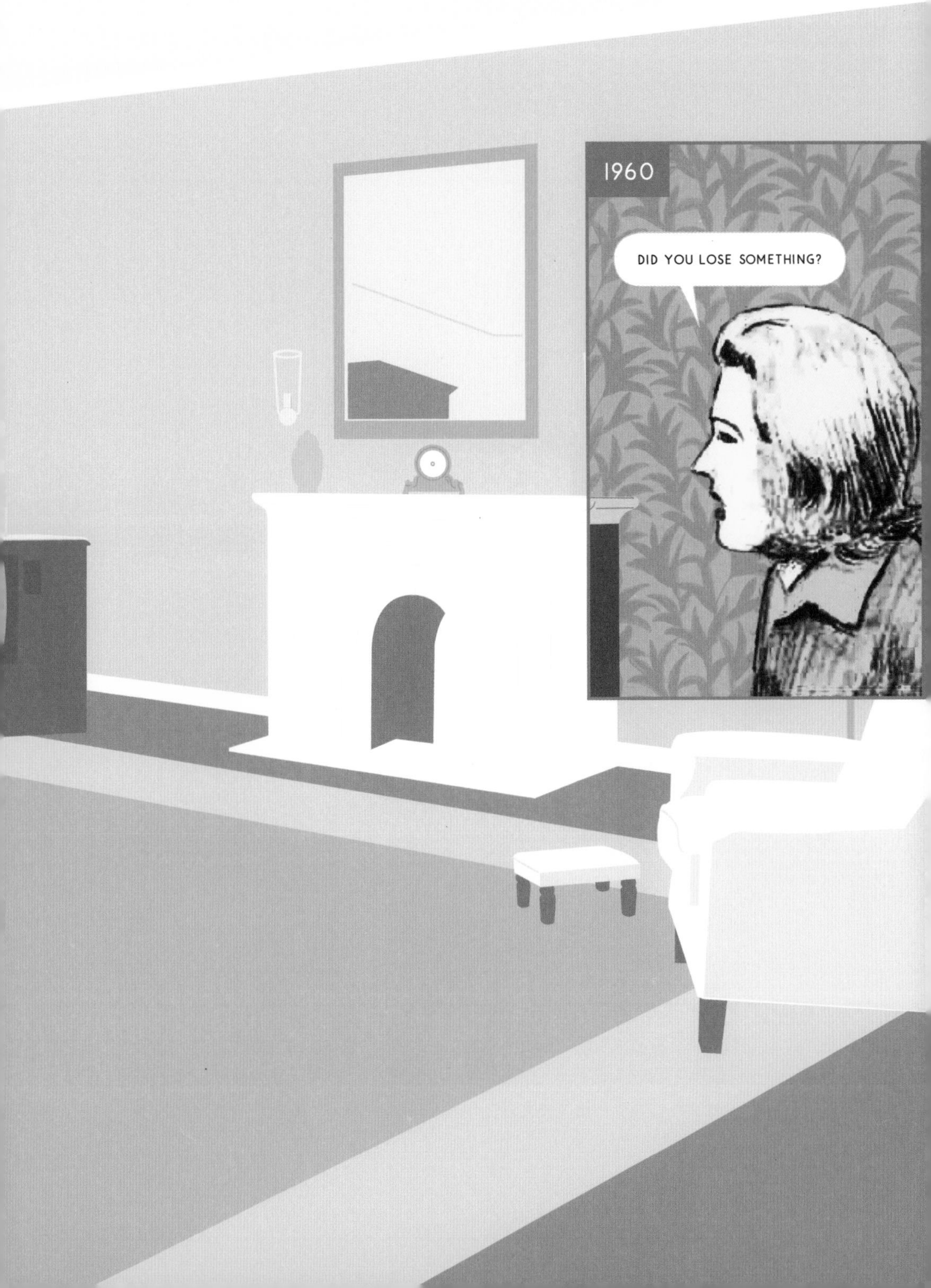
1960
DID YOU LOSE SOMETHING?

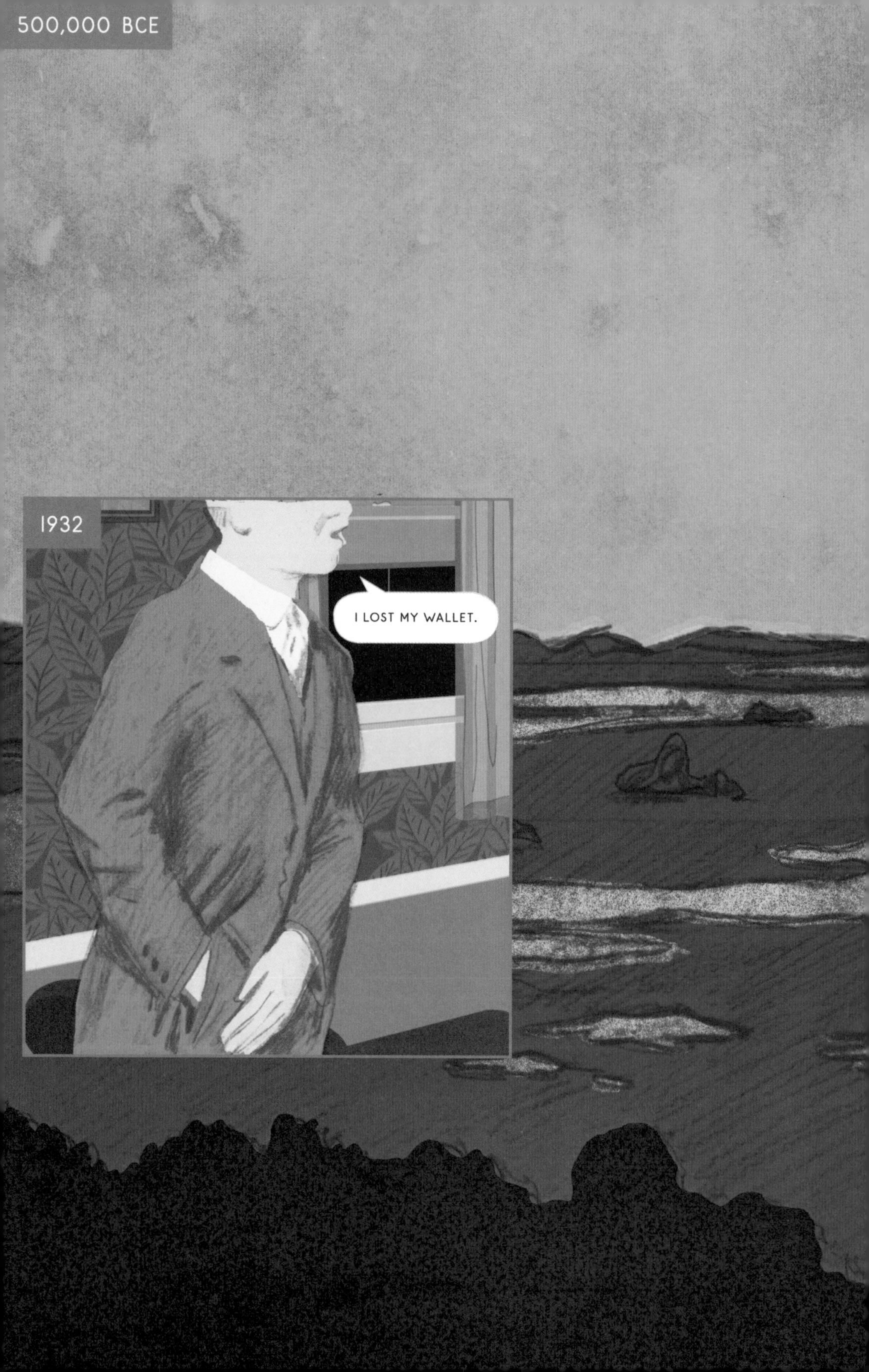
500,000 BCE
1932
I LOST MY WALLET.

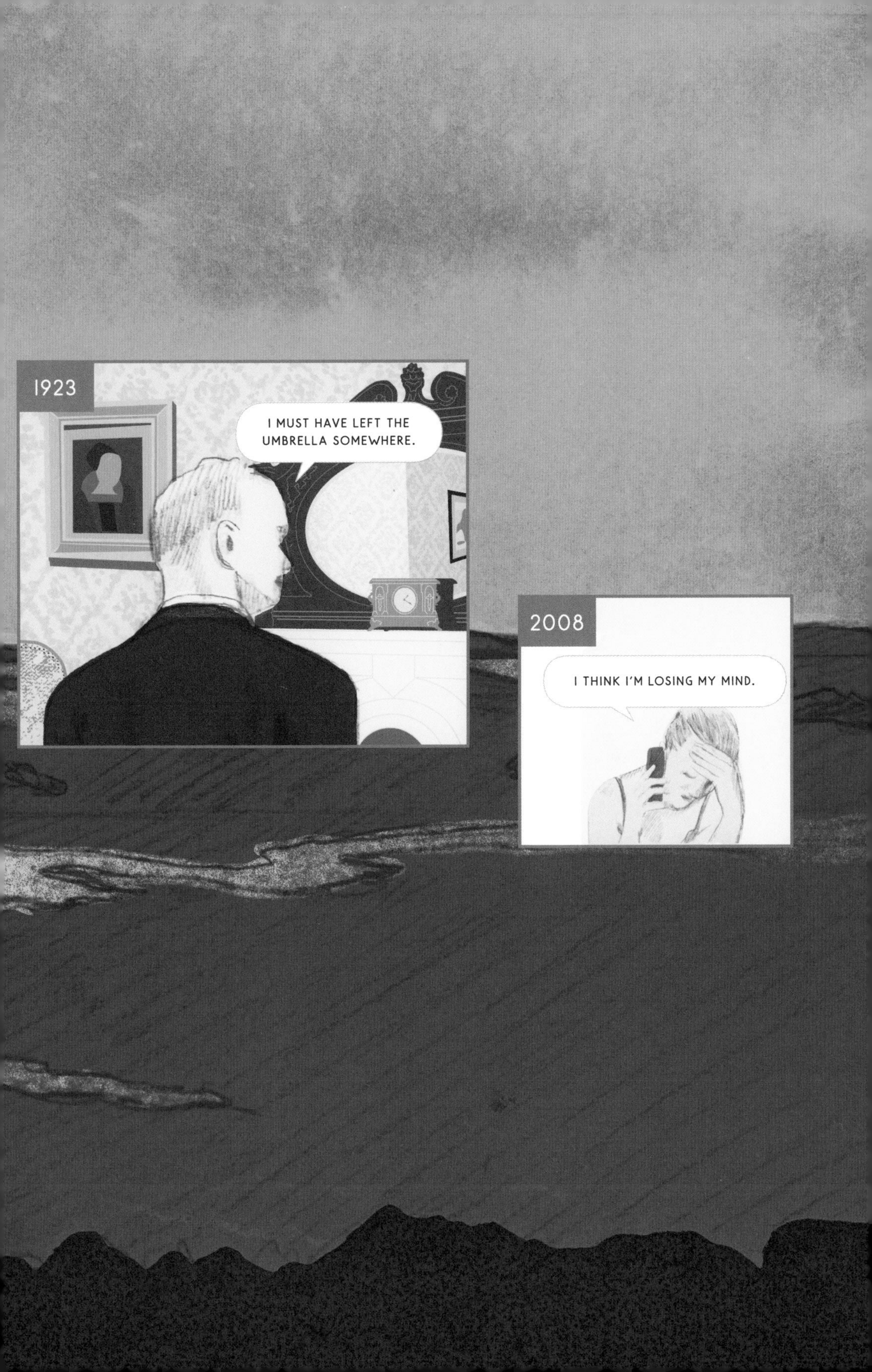
1923
I MUST HAVE LEFT THE UMBRELLA SOMEWHERE.
2008
I THINK I'M LOSING MY MIND.

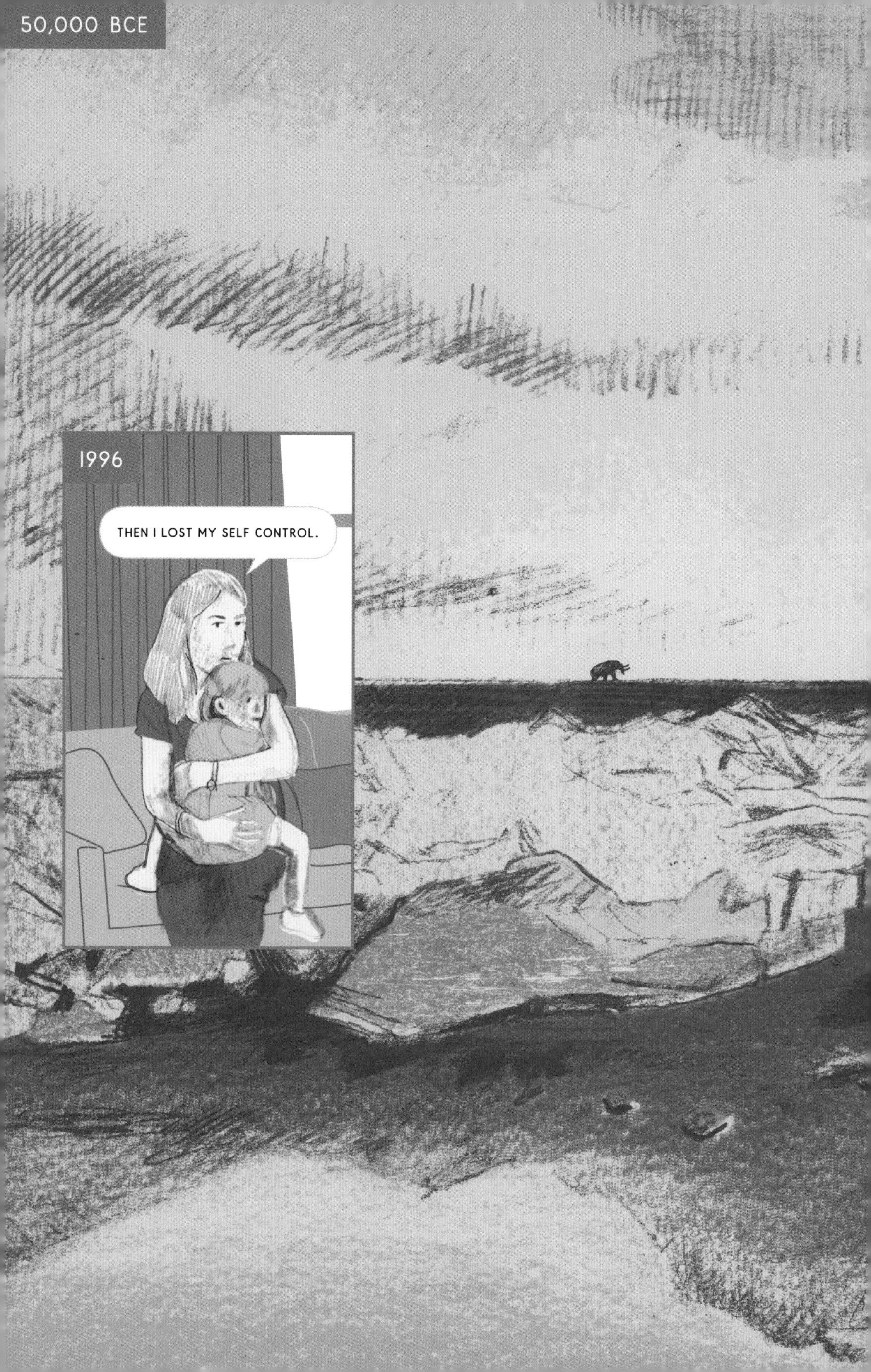
50,000 BCE
1996
THEN I LOST MY SELF CONTROL.

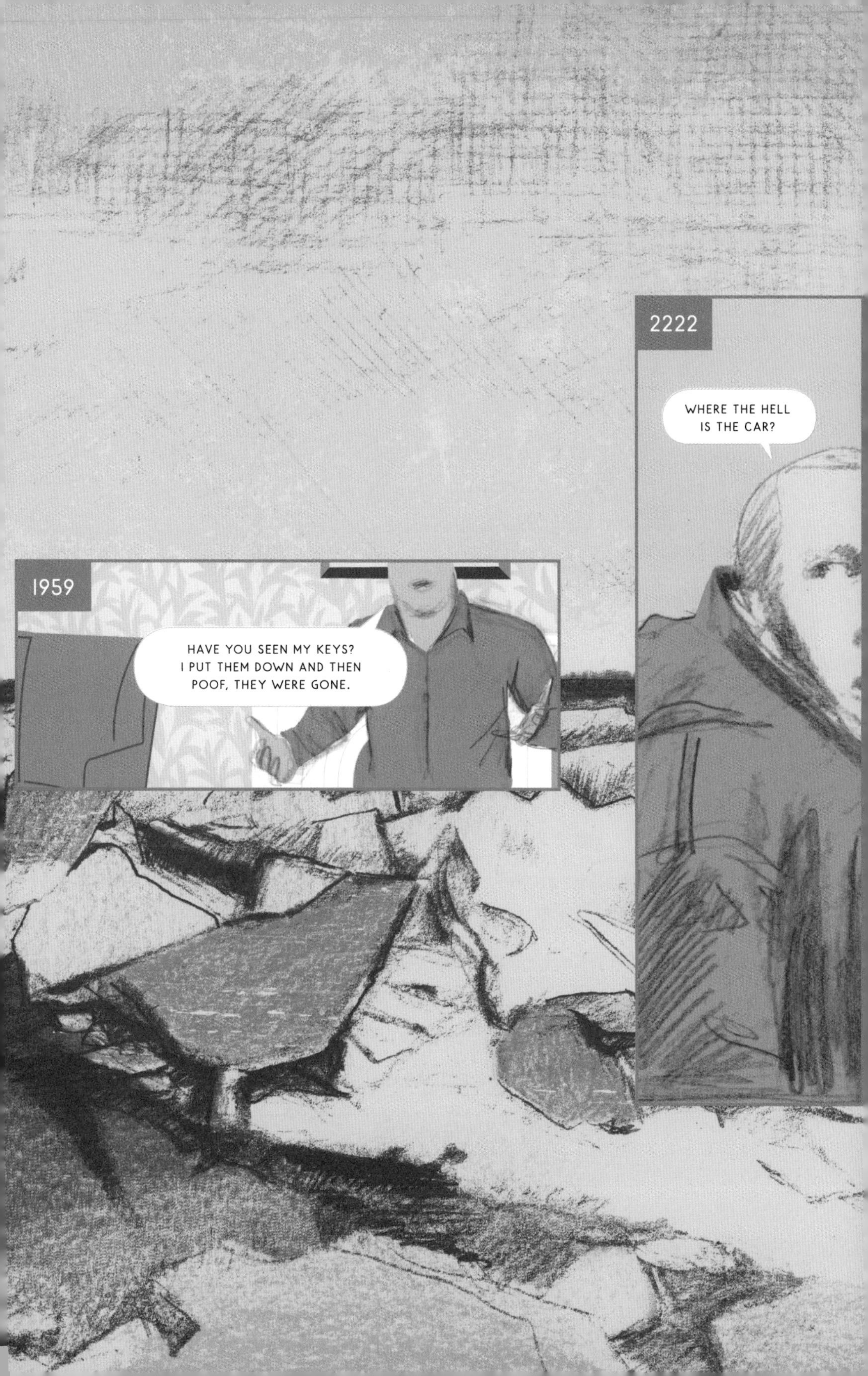
2222
WHERE THE HELL IS THE CAR?
1959
HAVE YOU SEEN MY KEYS? I PUT THEM DOWN AND THEN POOF, THEY WERE GONE.

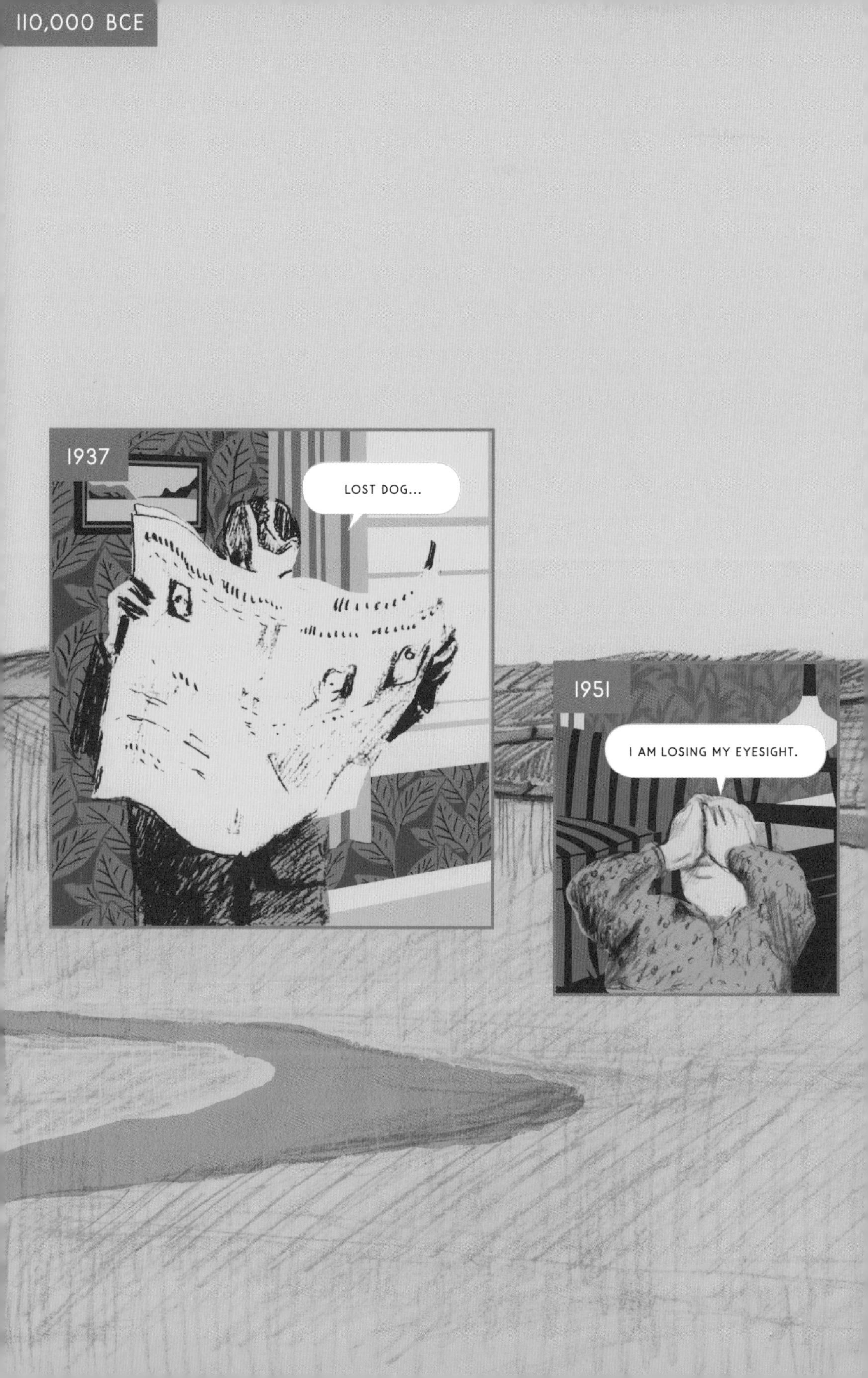
110,000 BCE
1937
LOST DOG...
1951
I AM LOSING MY EYESIGHT.

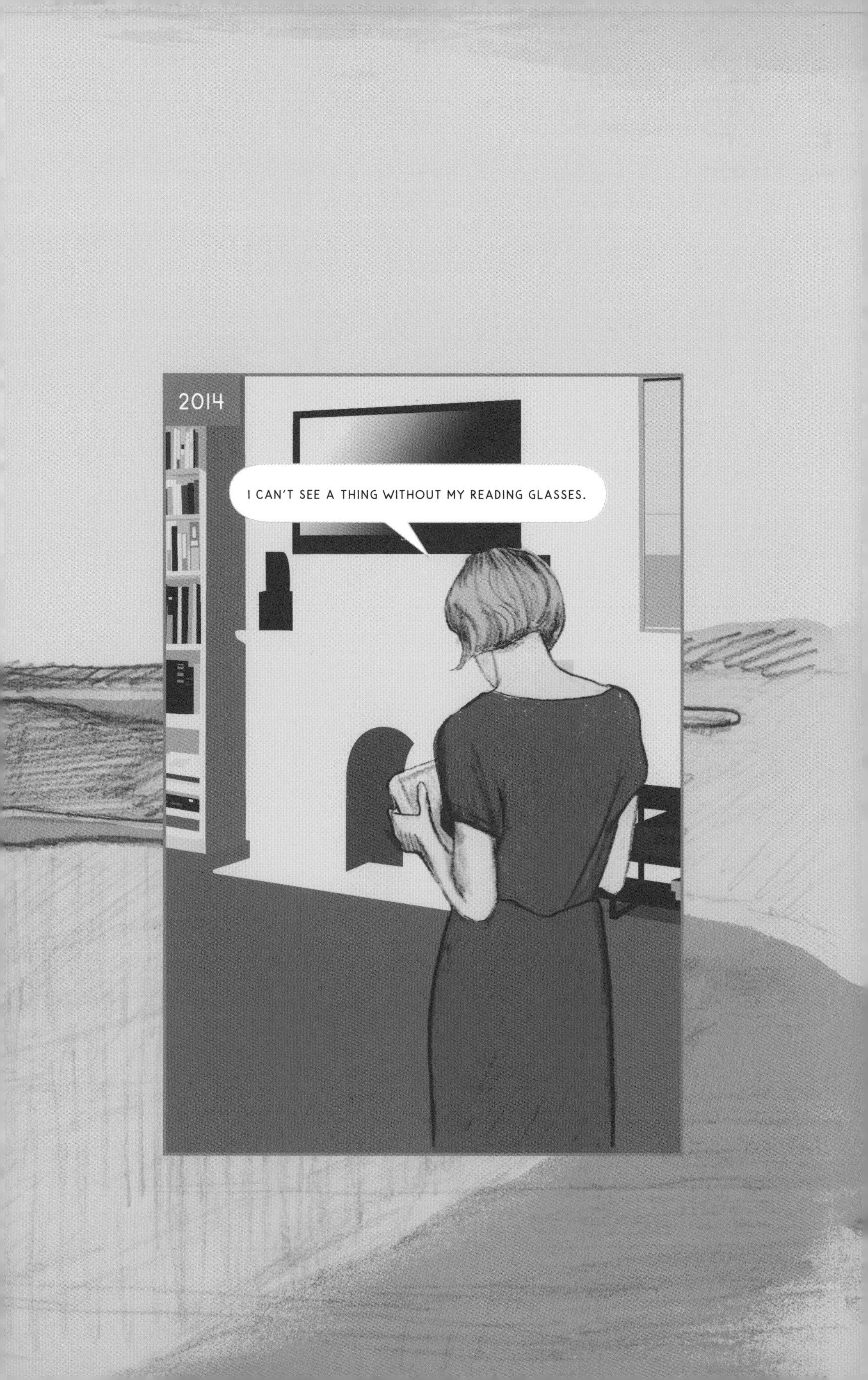
2014
I CAN'T SEE A THING WITHOUT MY READING GLASSES.

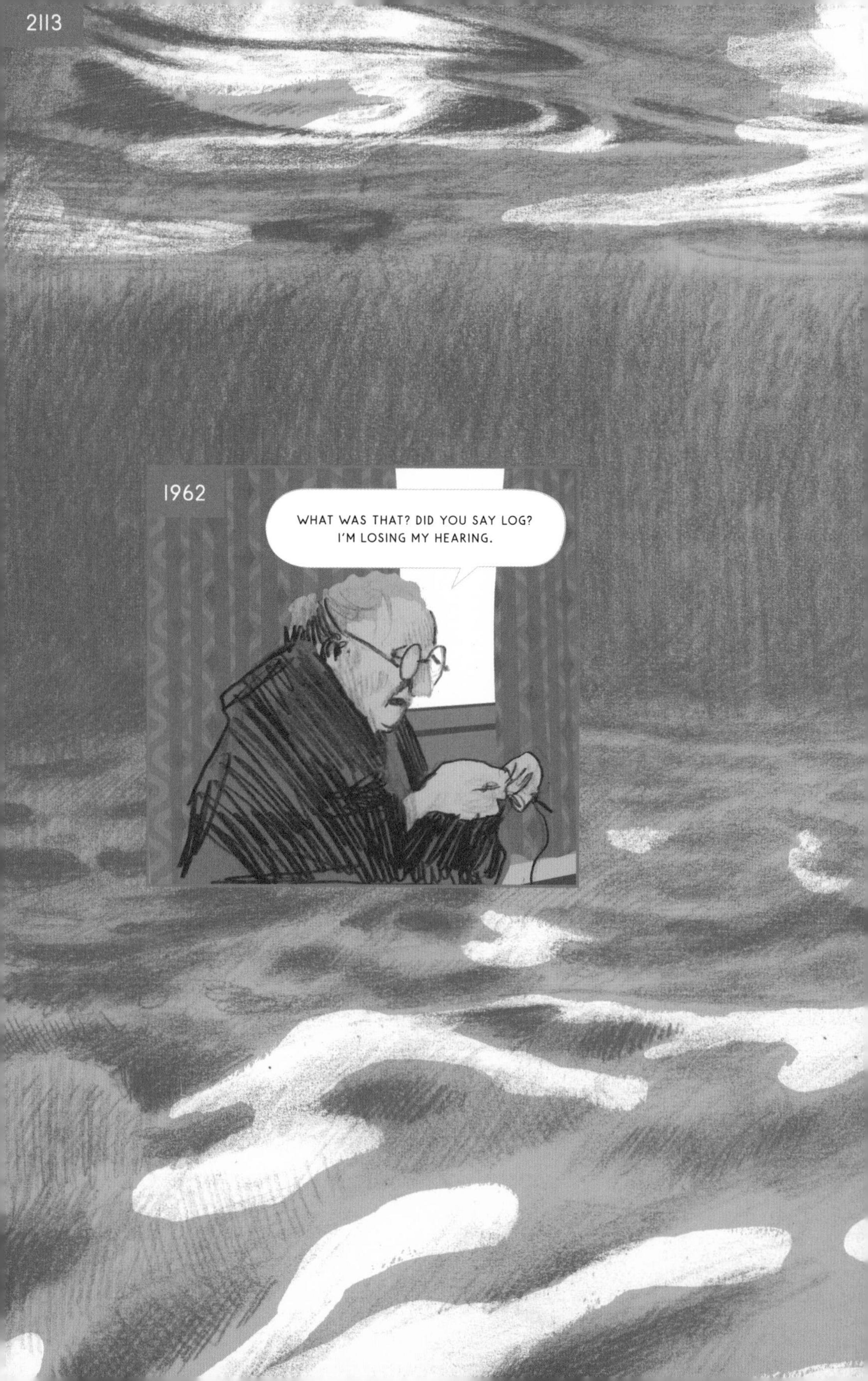
2113
1962
WHAT WAS THAT? DID YOU SAY LOG?
I'M LOSING MY HEARING.

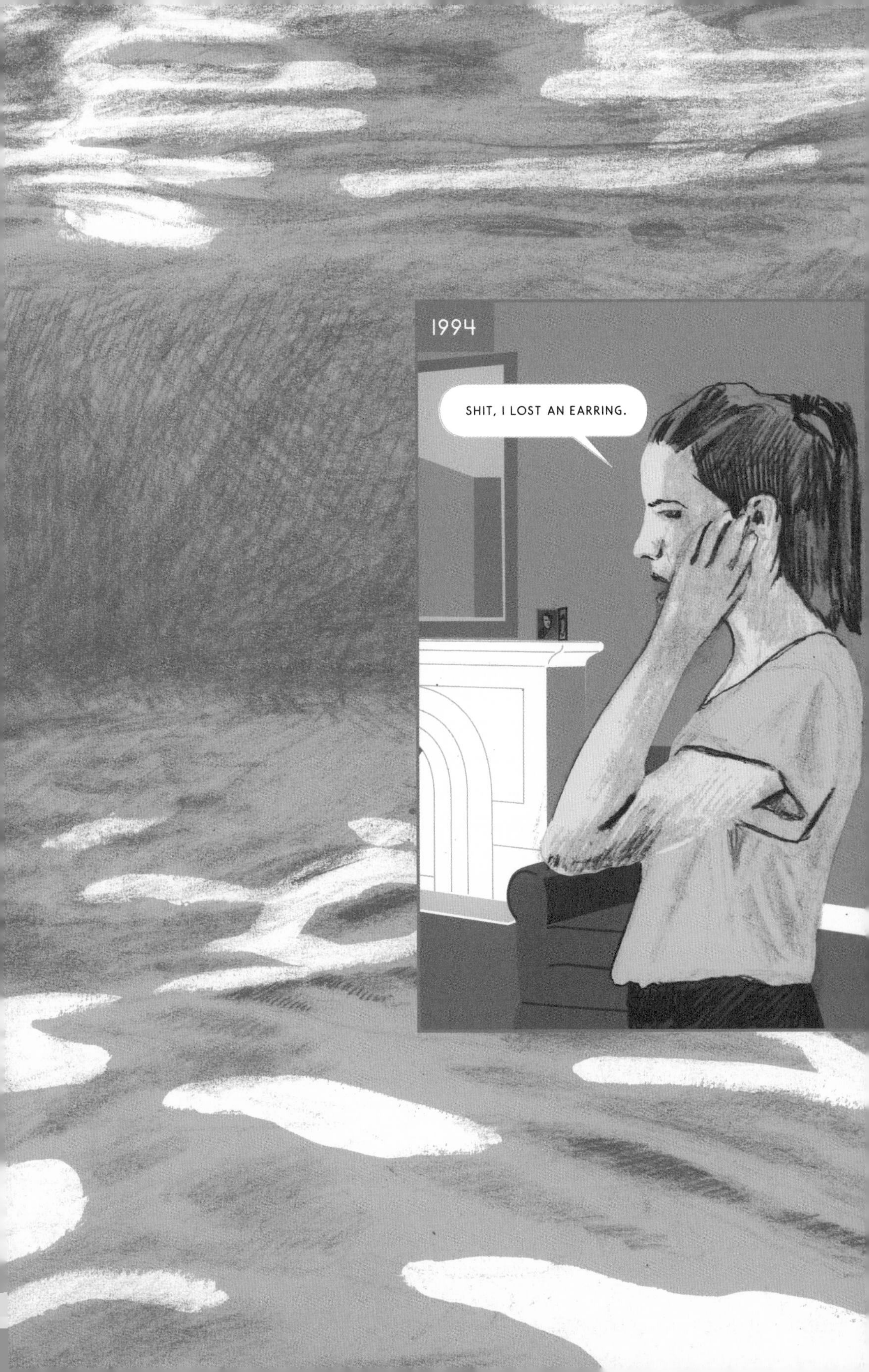
1994
SHIT, I LOST AN EARRING.

1,000,000 BCE

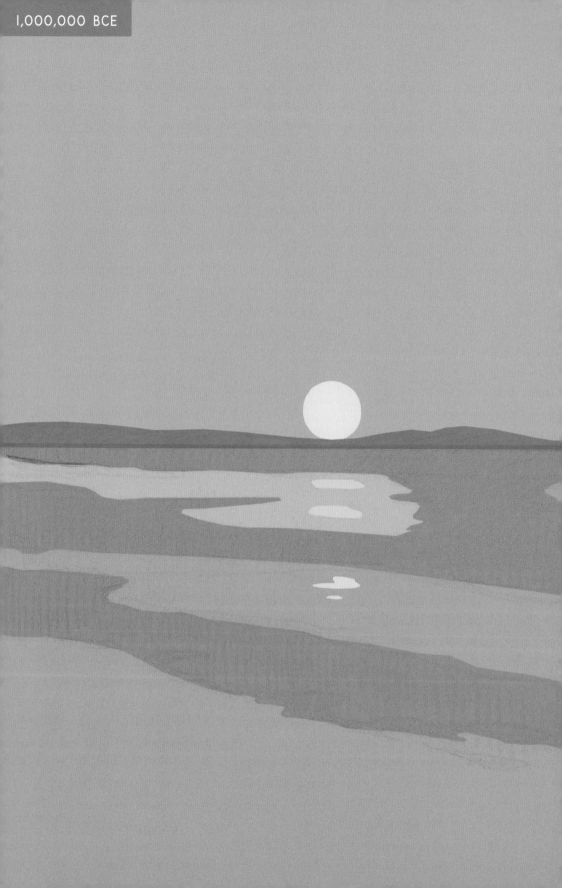

3,000,000,000 BCE

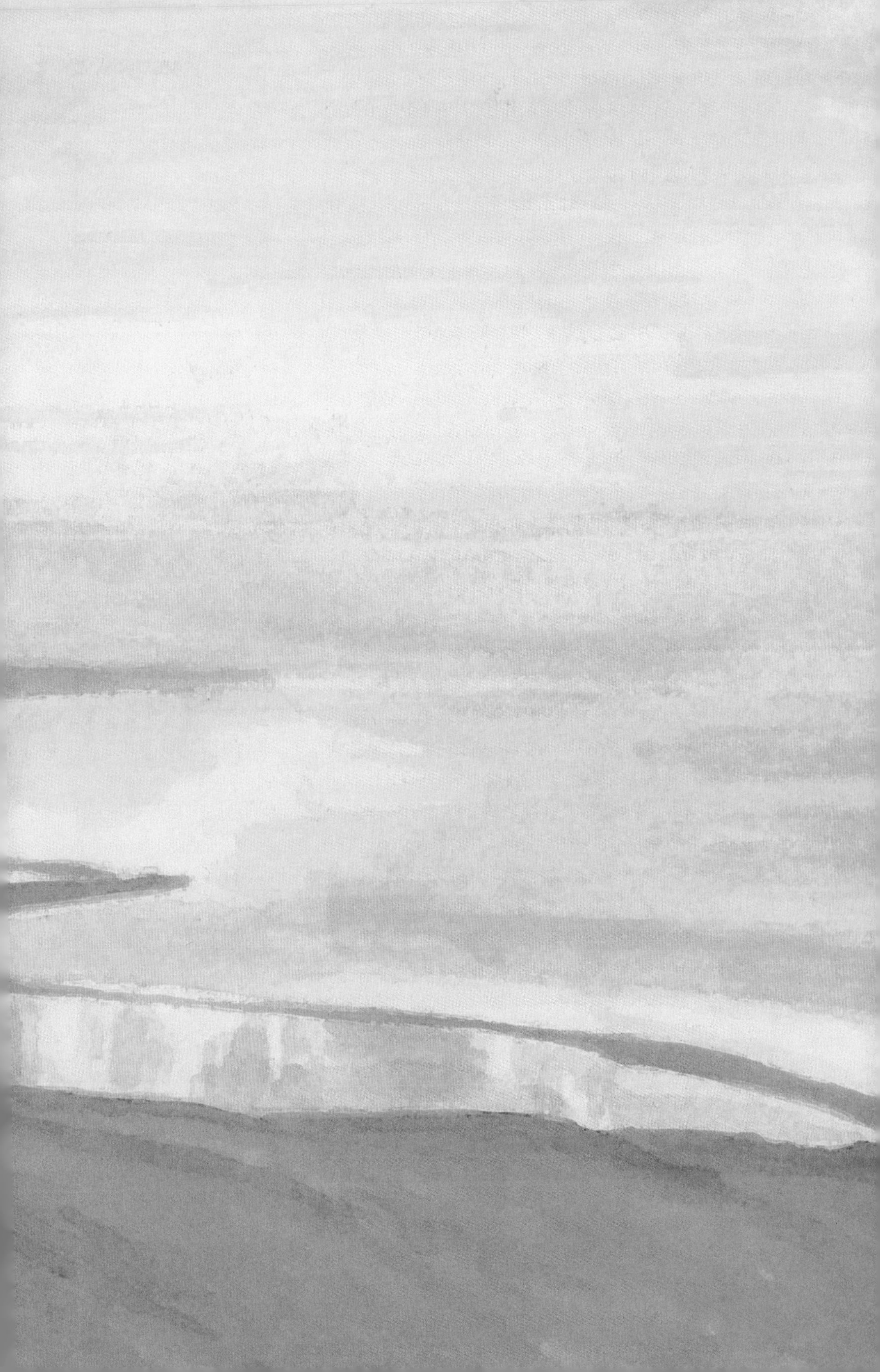

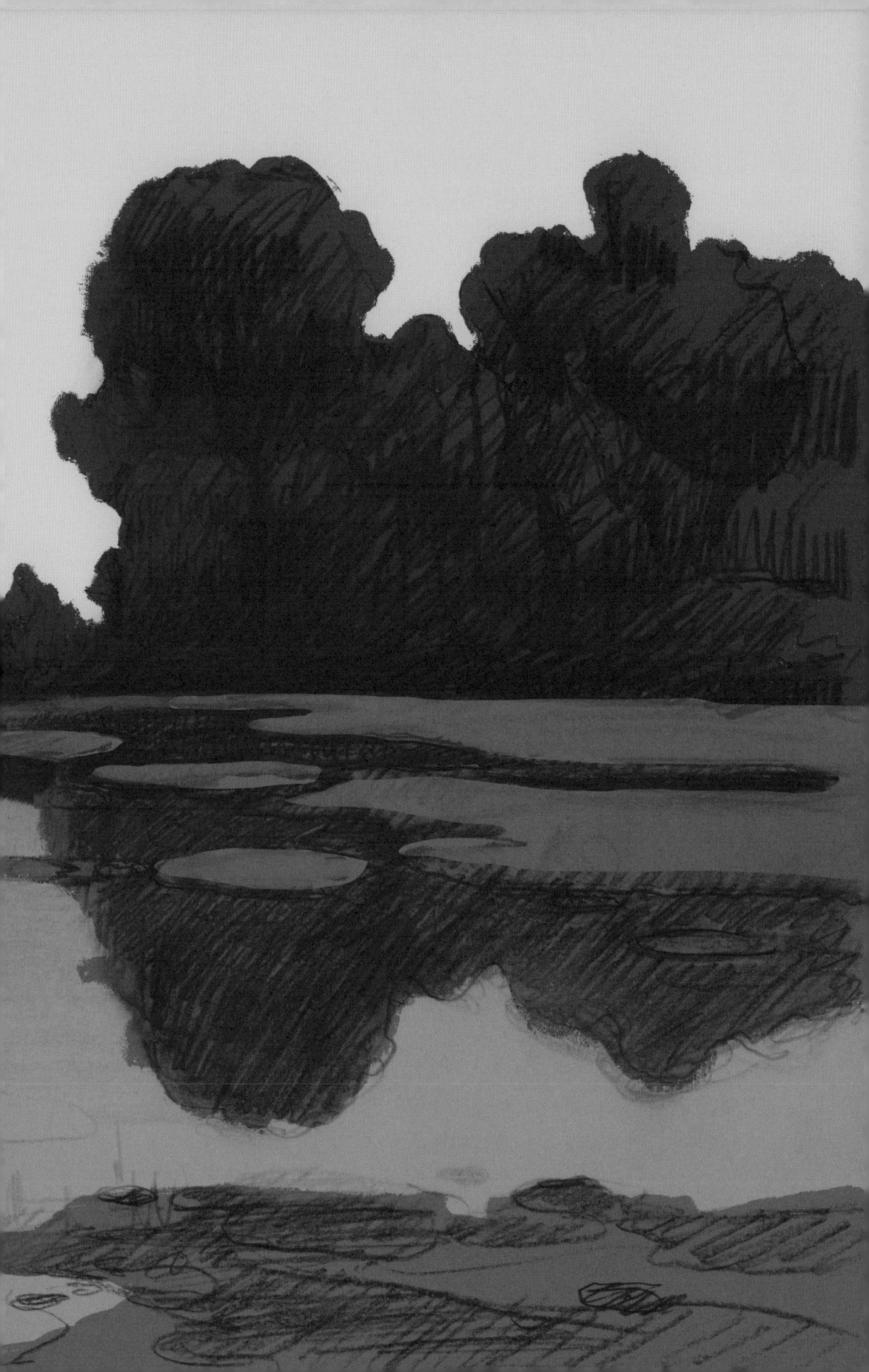

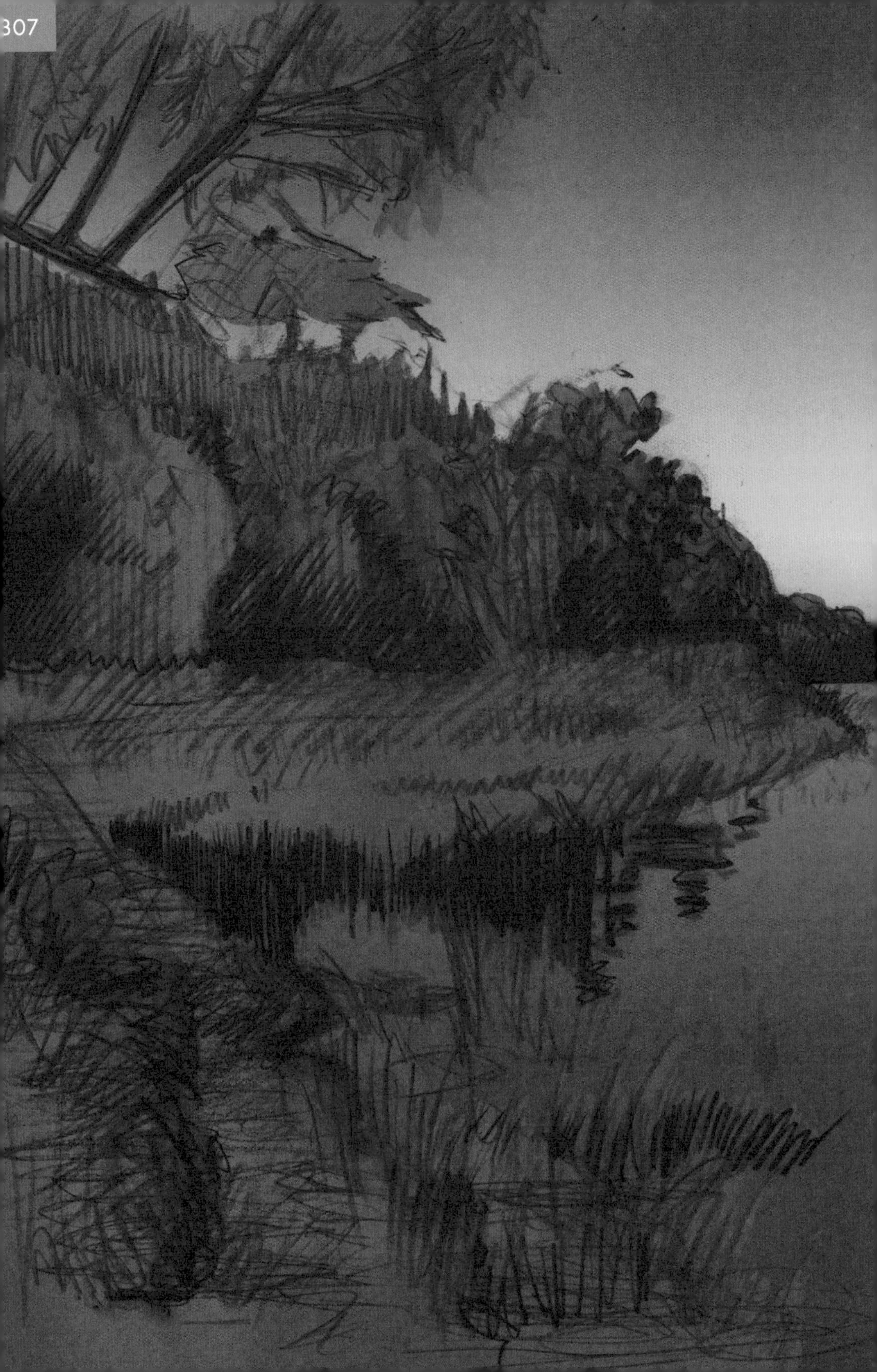

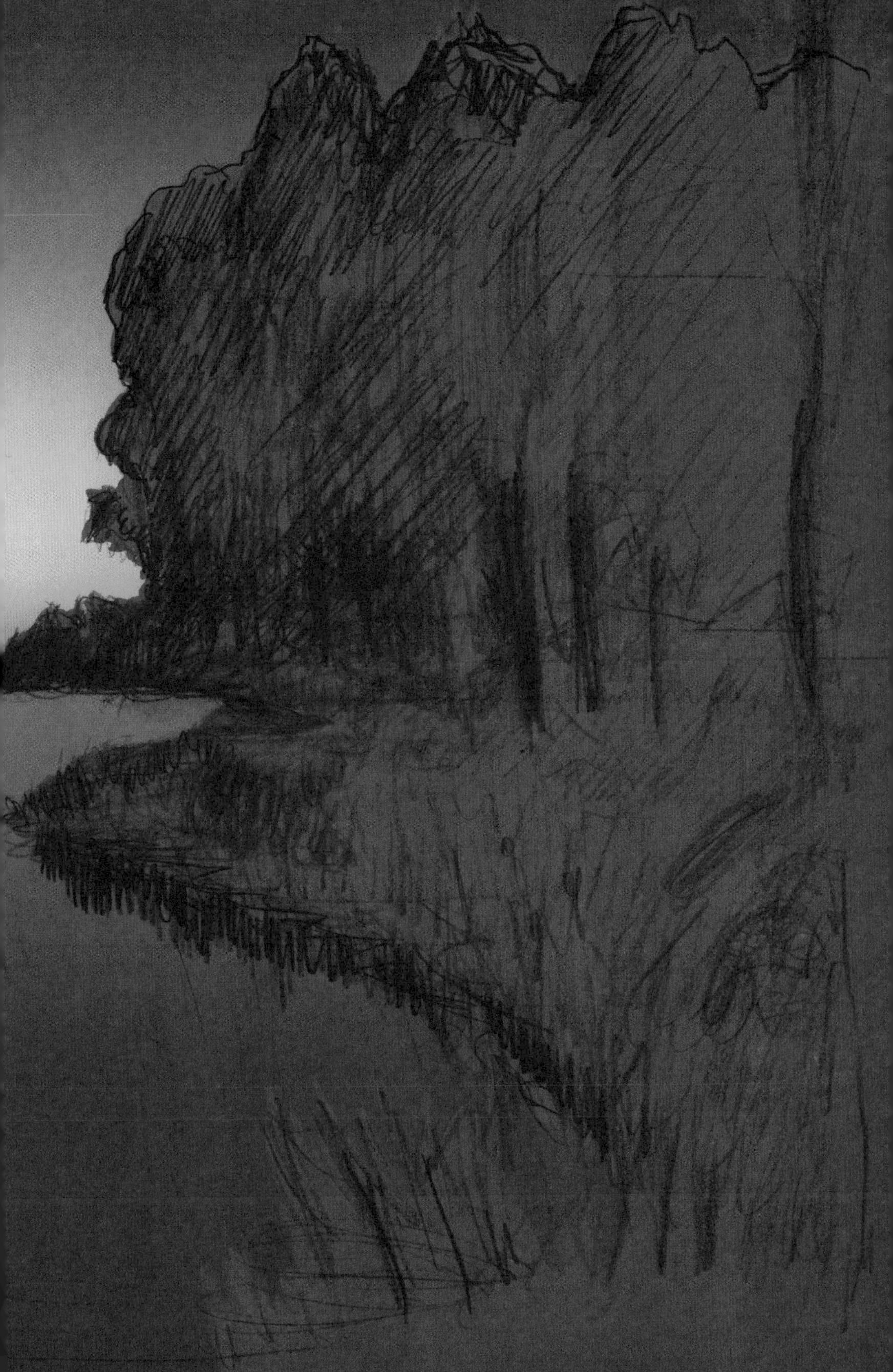

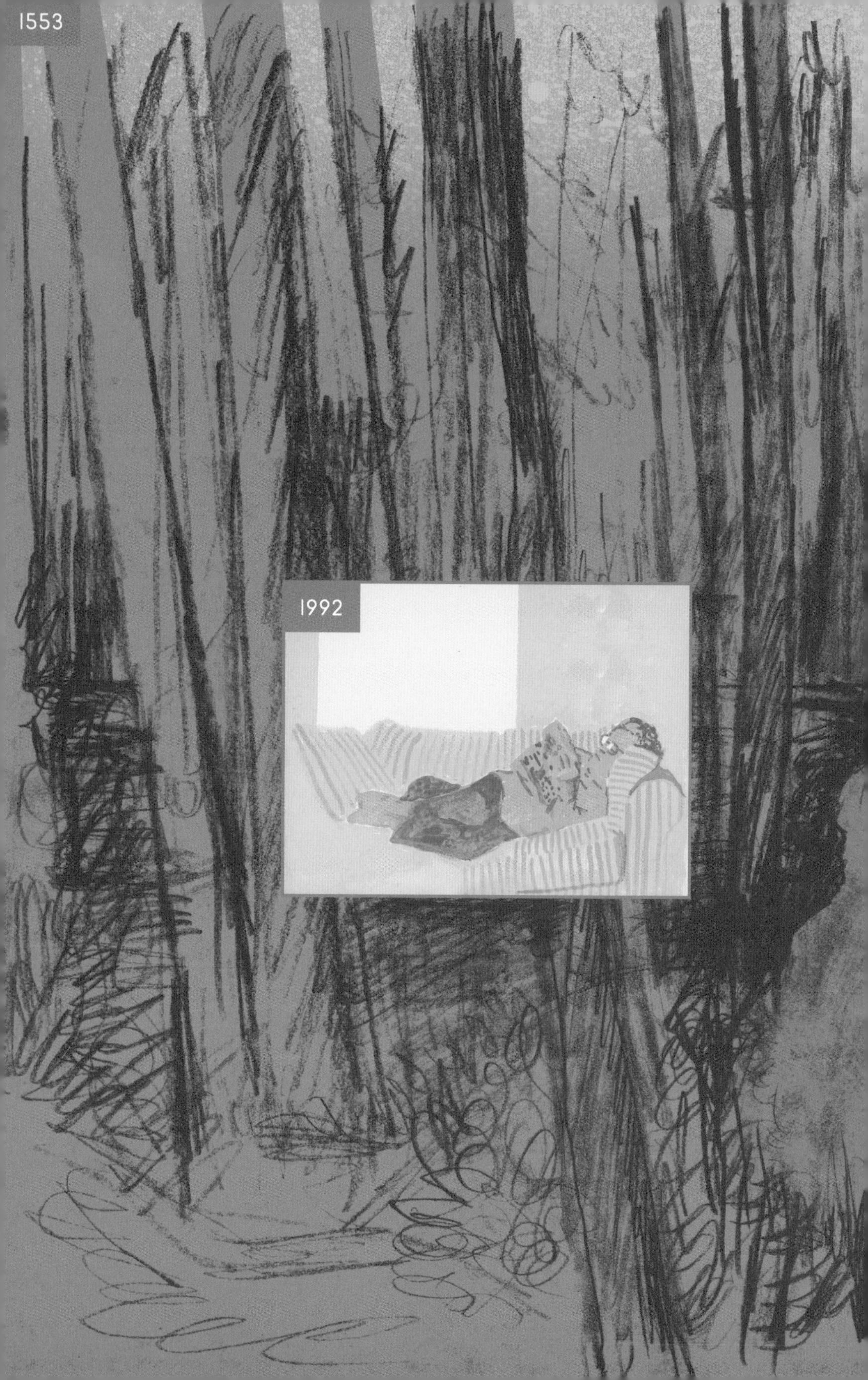
1553
1992

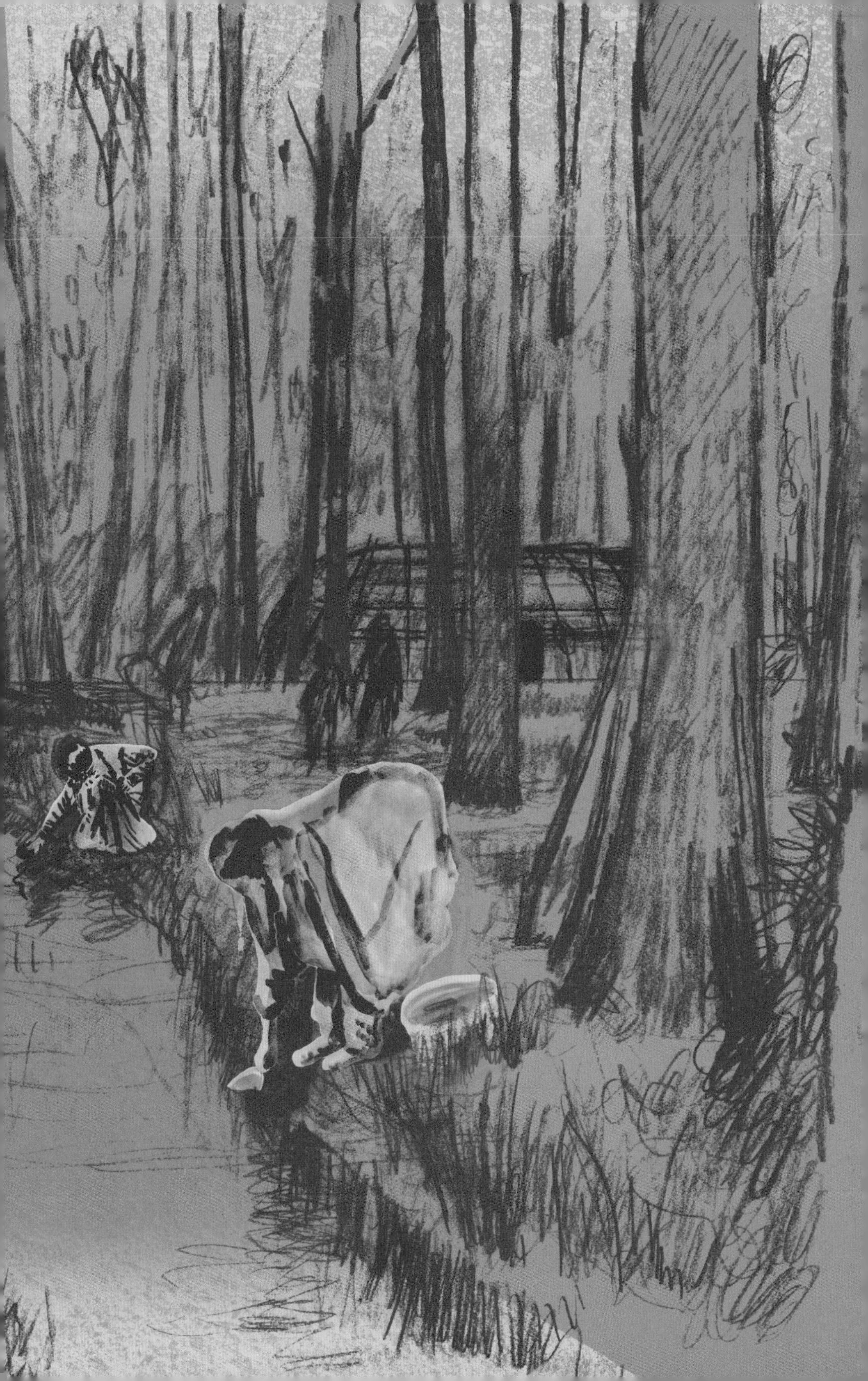

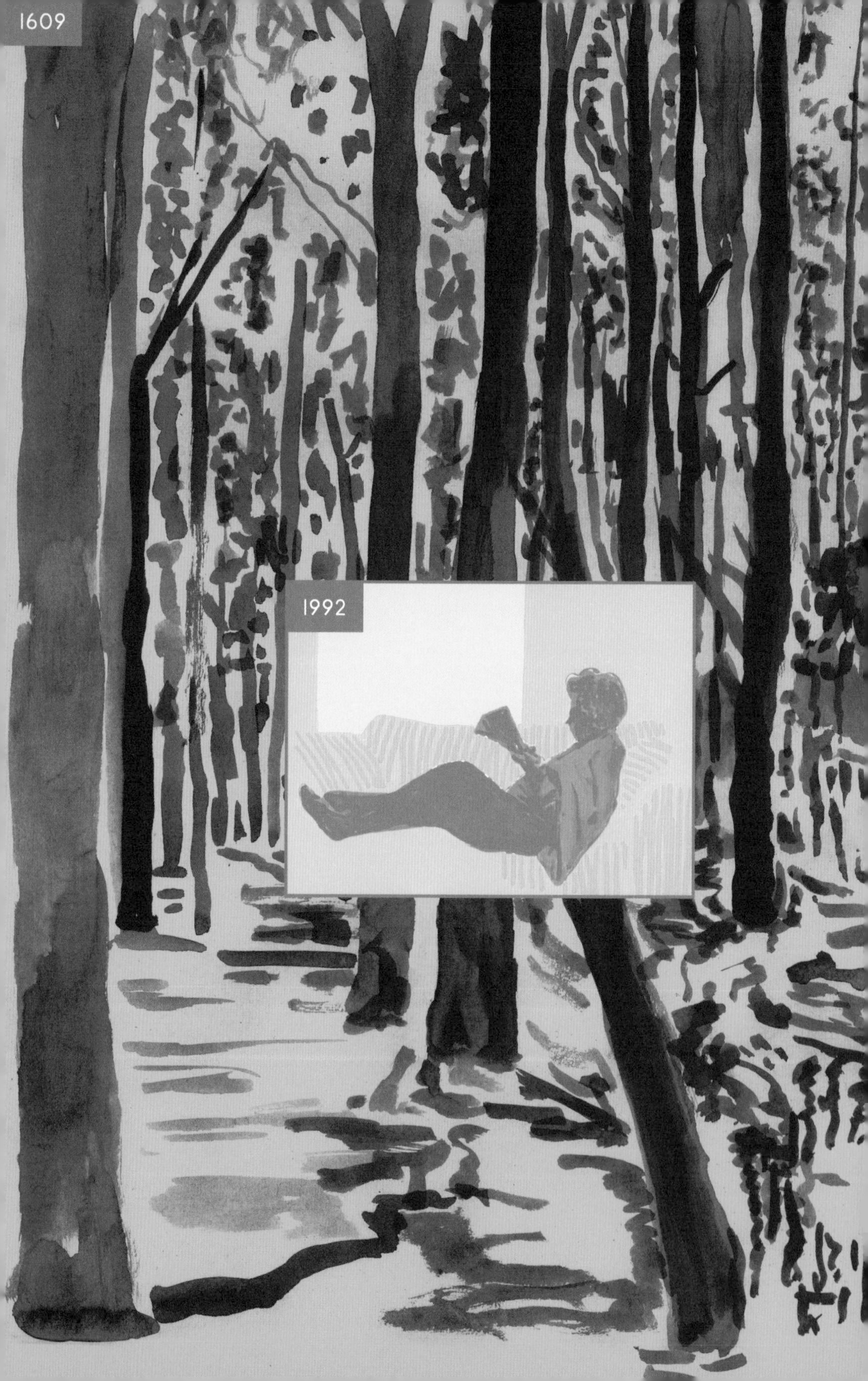
1609
1992

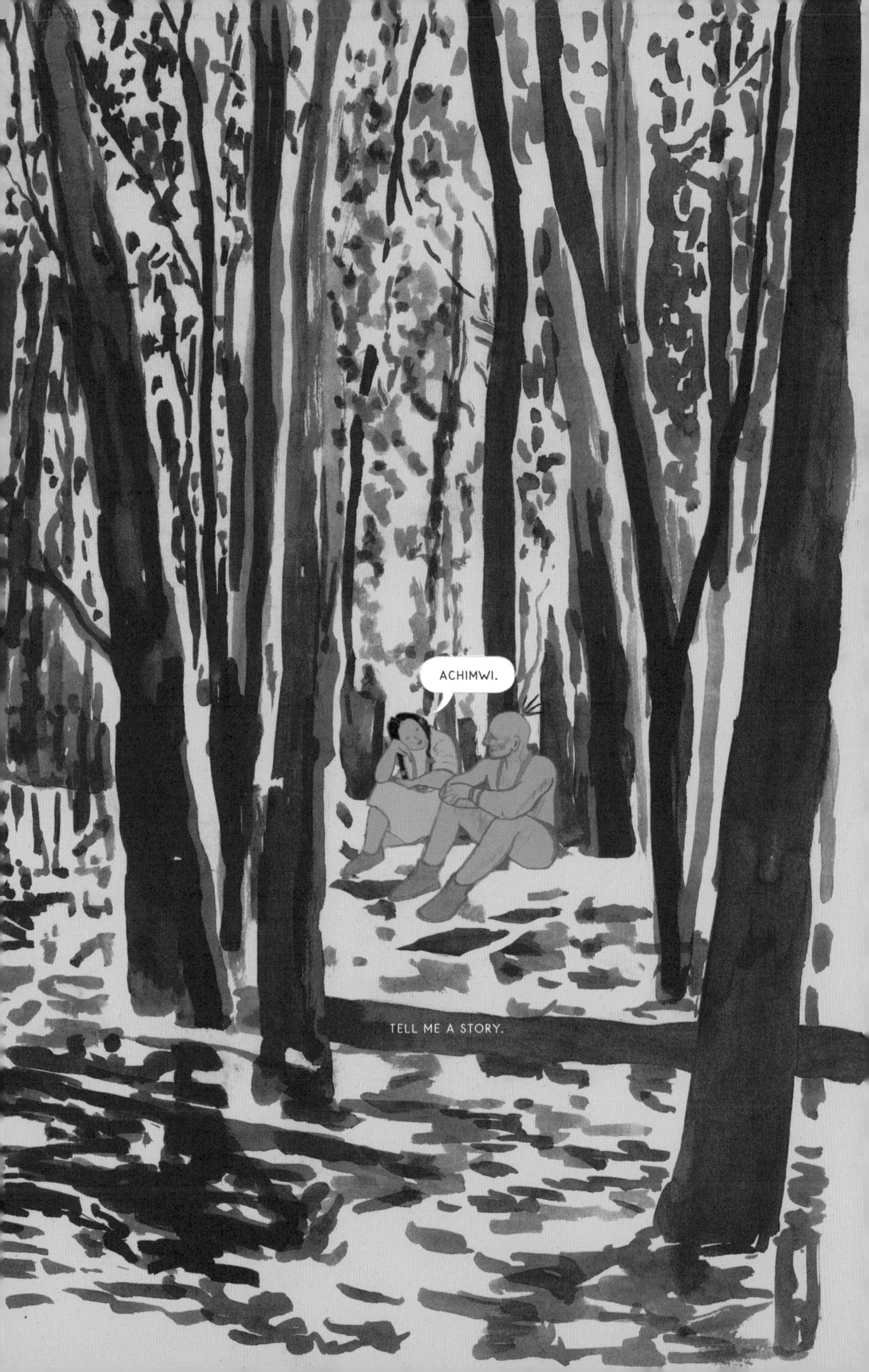
ACHIMWI.
TELL ME A STORY.

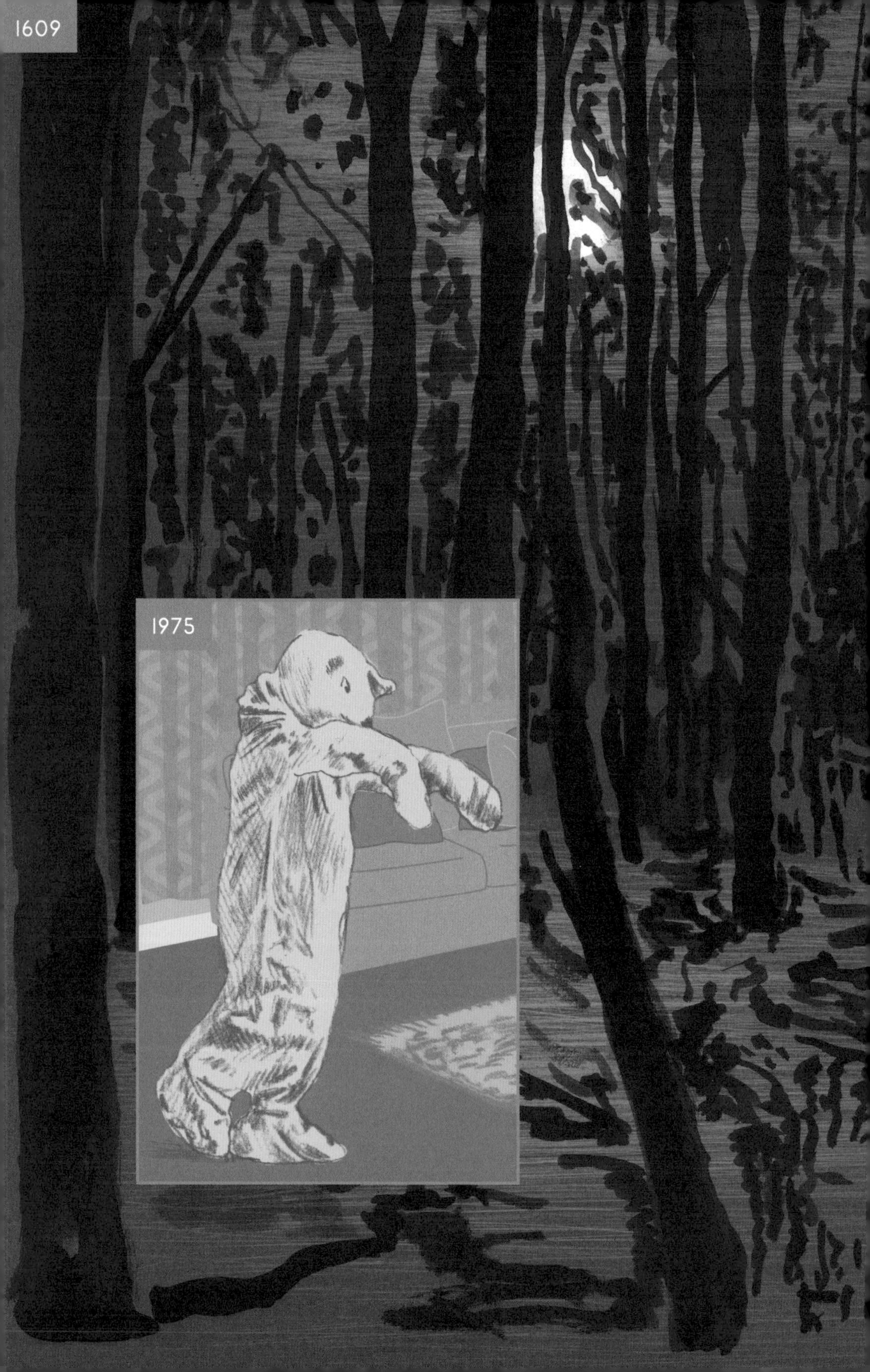
1609
1975

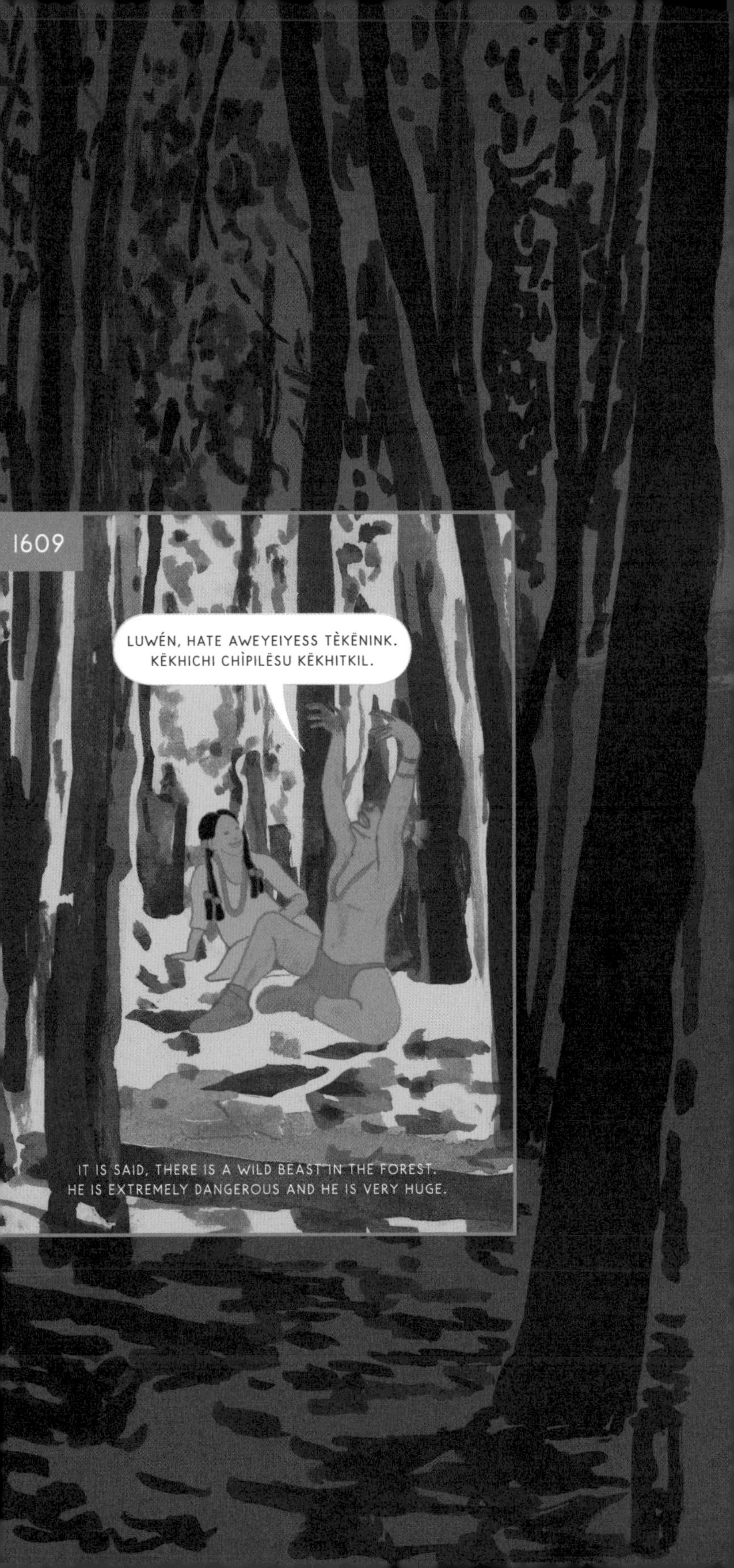
1609
LUWÉN, HATE AWEYEIYESS TÈKËNINK. KËKHICHI CHÌPILËSU KËKHITKIL.
IT IS SAID, THERE IS A WILD BEAST IN THE FOREST. HE IS EXTREMELY DANGEROUS AND HE IS VERY HUGE.

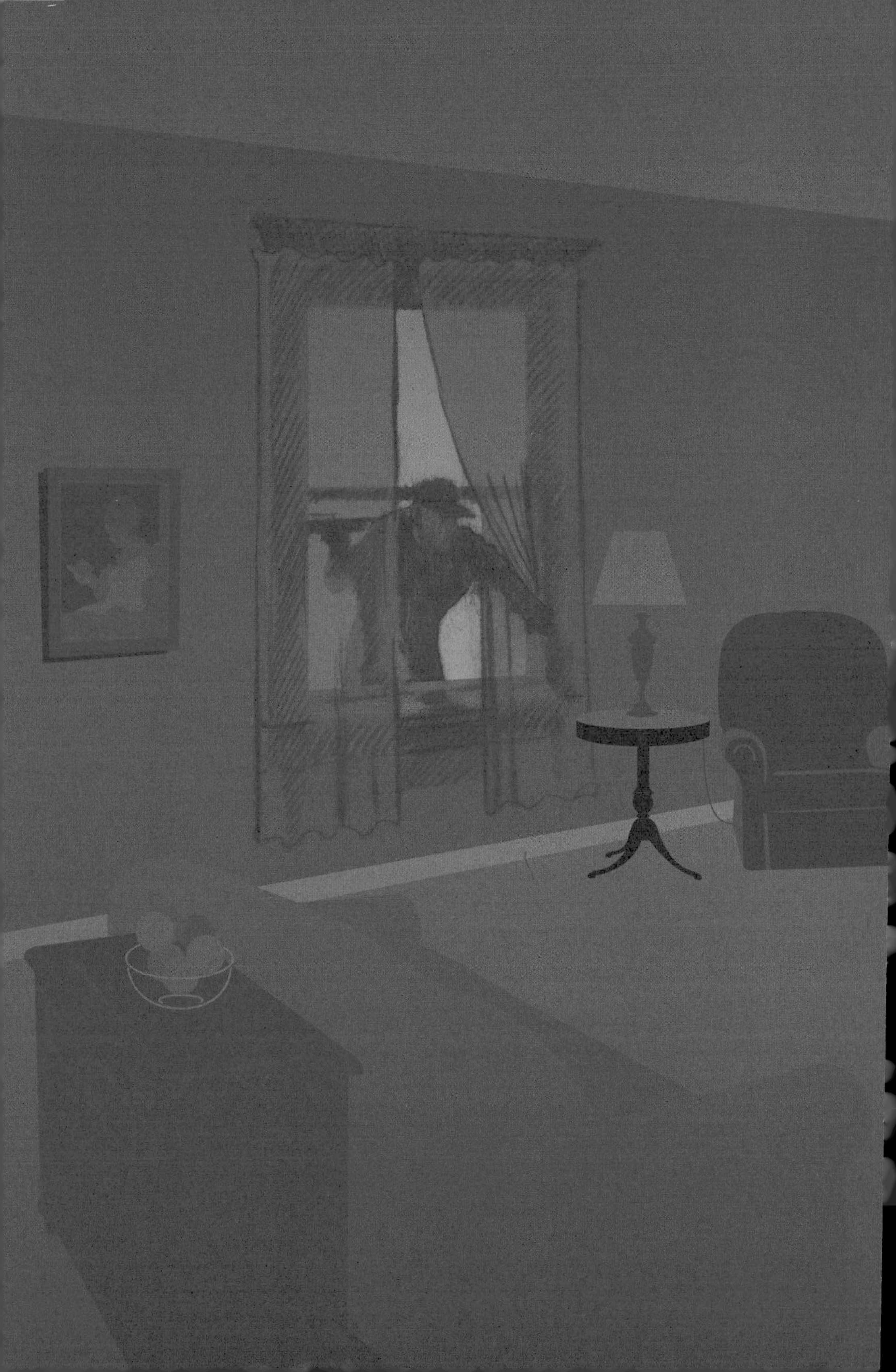

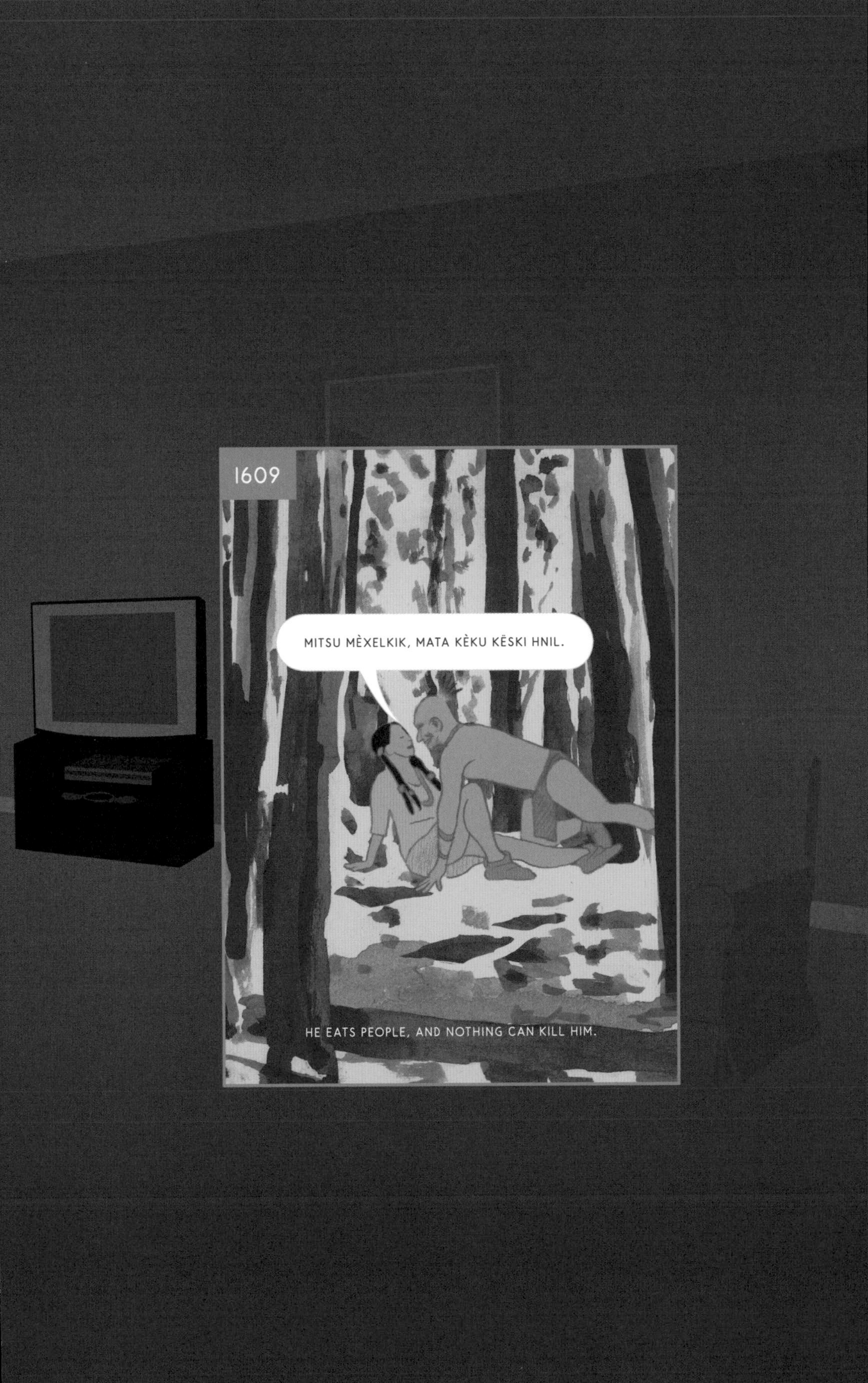
1609
MITSU MÈXELKIK, MATA KÈKU KĒSKI HNIL.
HE EATS PEOPLE, AND NOTHING CAN KILL HIM.

1998

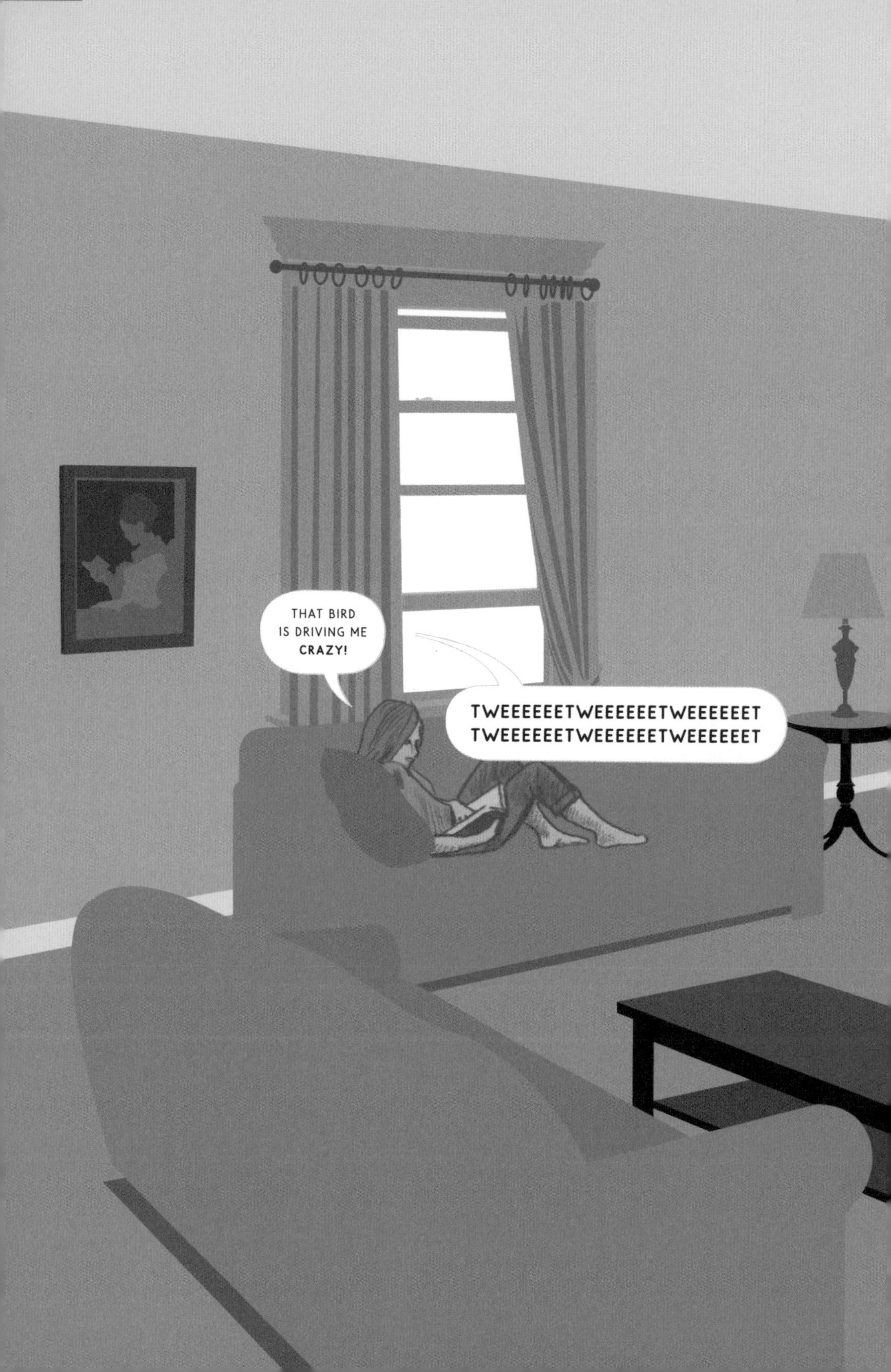
THAT BIRD IS DRIVING ME CRAZY!
TWEEEEEEETWEEEEEEETWEEEEEET TWEEEEEEETWEEEEEEETWEEEEEET

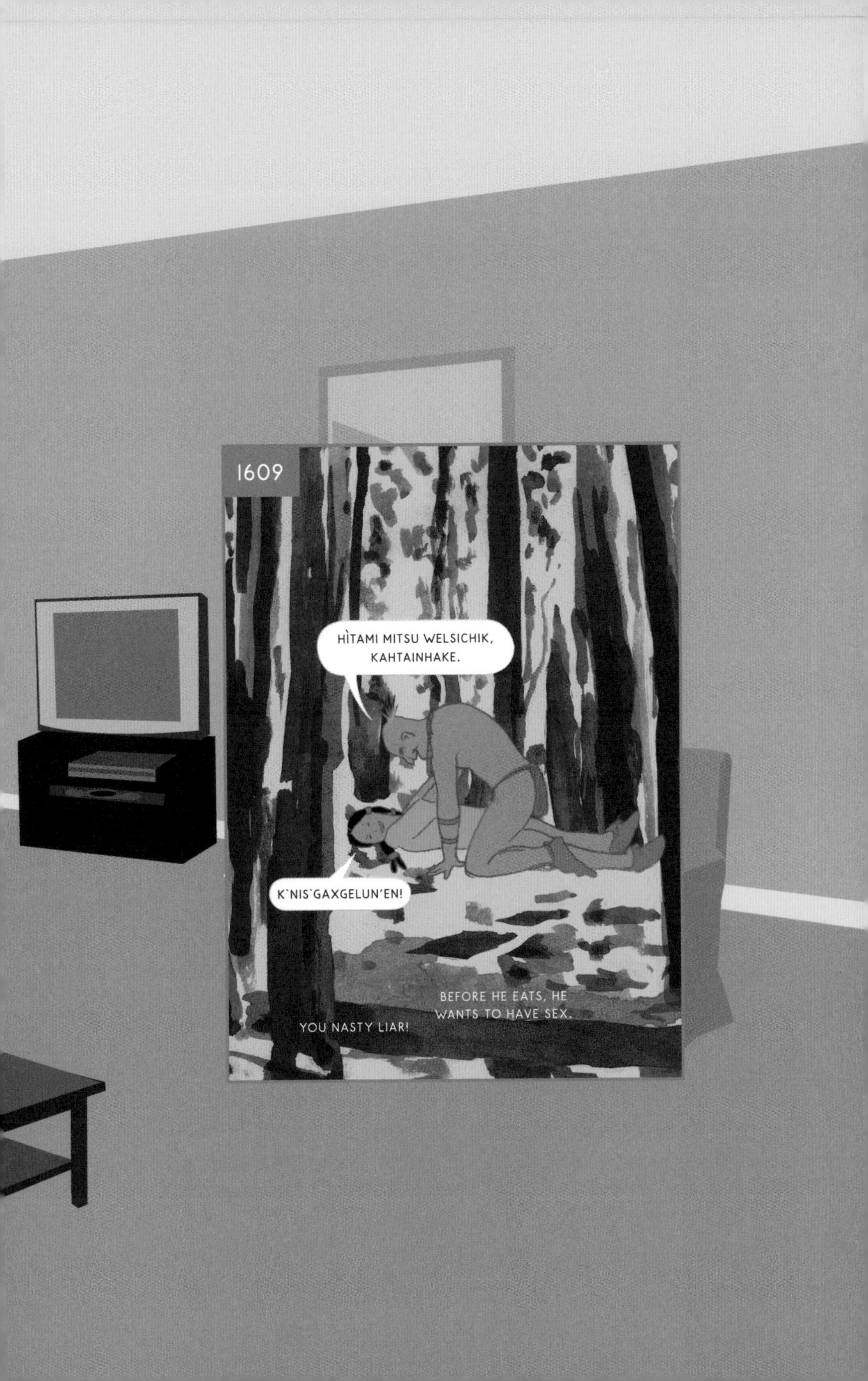
1609
HÌTAMI MITSU WELSICHIK, KAHTAINHAKE.
K`NIS`GAXGELUN'EN!
BEFORE HE EATS, HE WANTS TO HAVE SEX.
YOU NASTY LIAR!

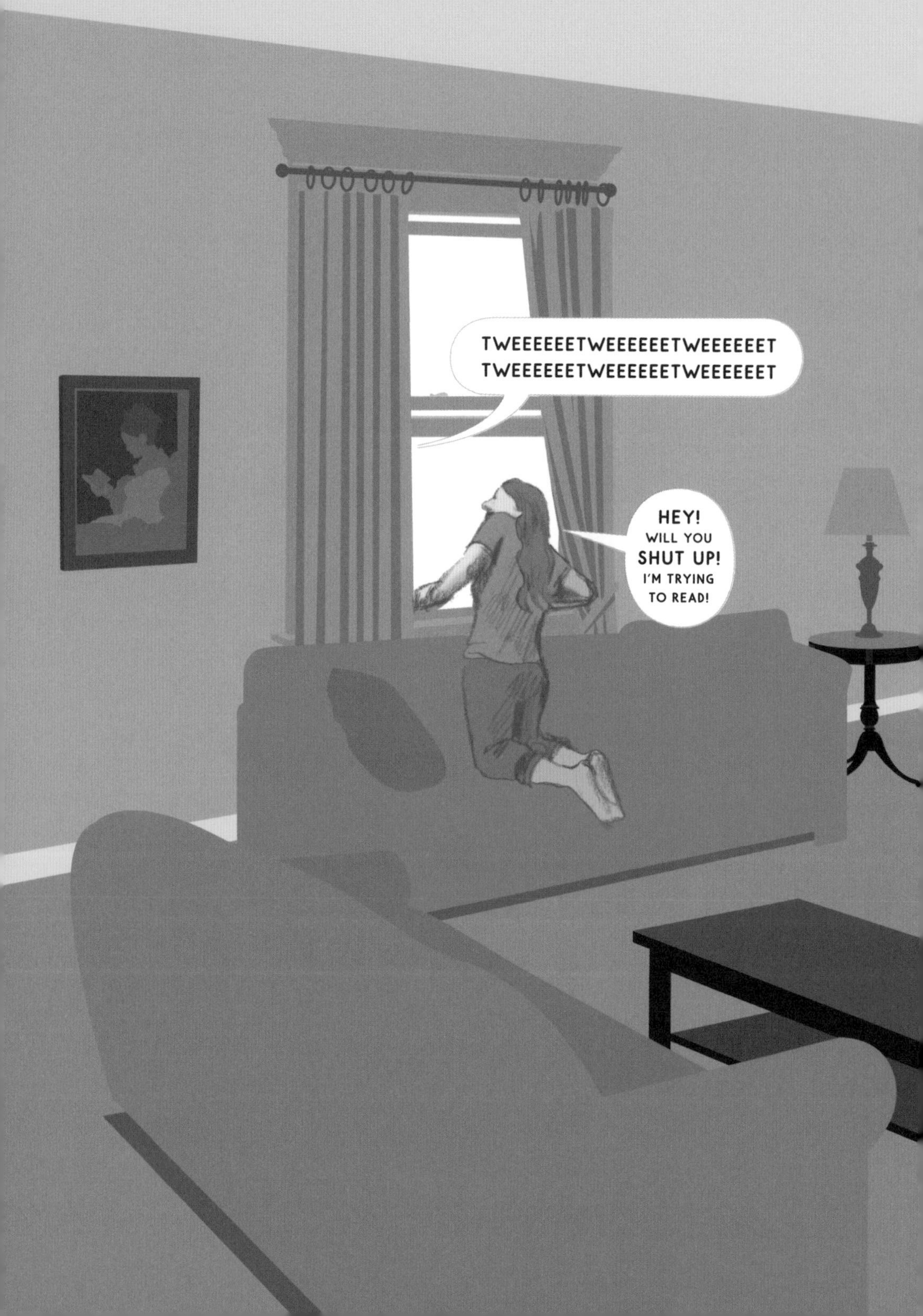
TWEEEEEETWEEEEEETWEEEEEET
TWEEEEEETWEEEEEETWEEEEEET
HEY! WILL YOU SHUT UP! I'M TRYING TO READ!

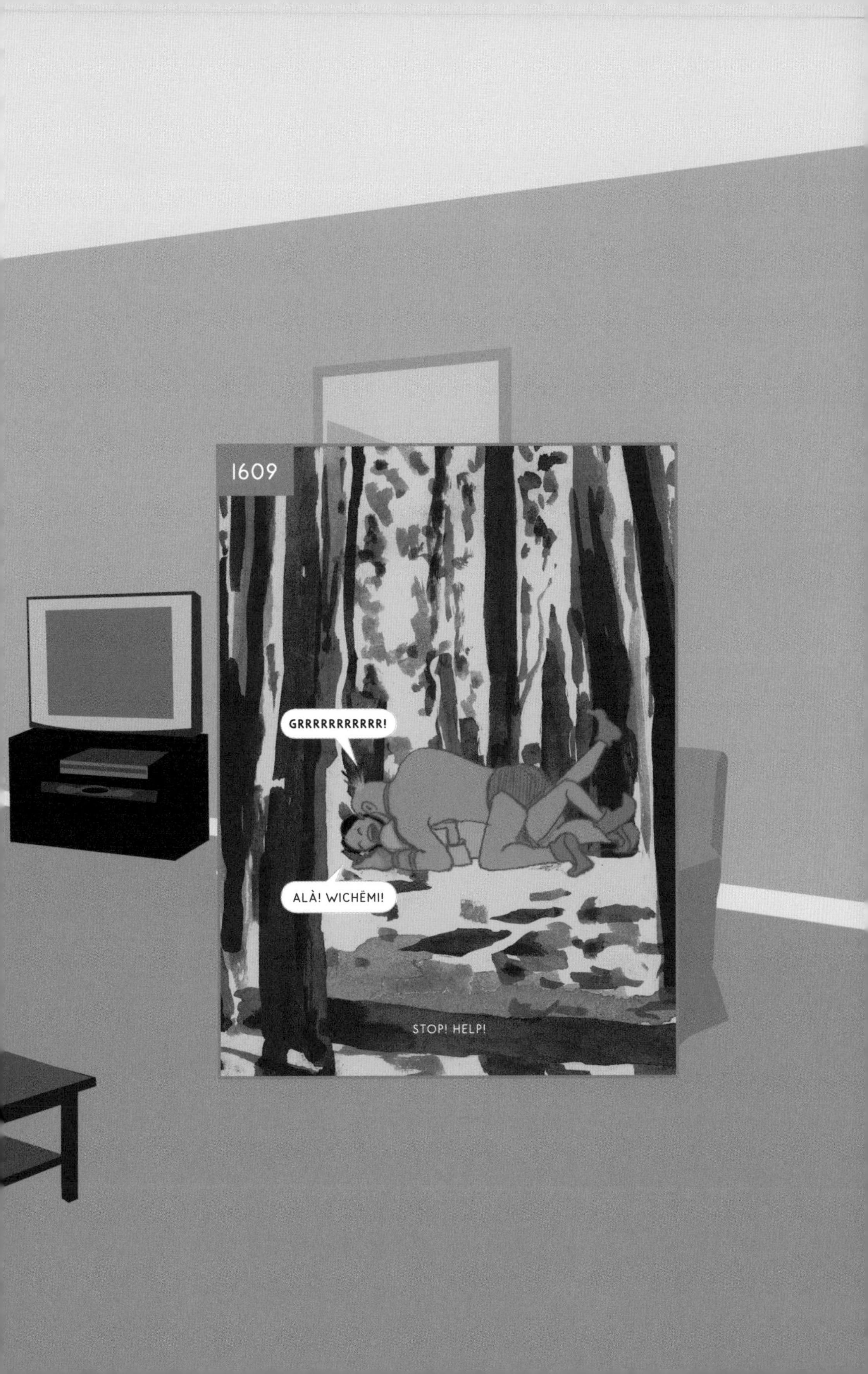
1609
GRRRRRRRRRRR!
ALÀ! WICHËMI!
STOP! HELP!

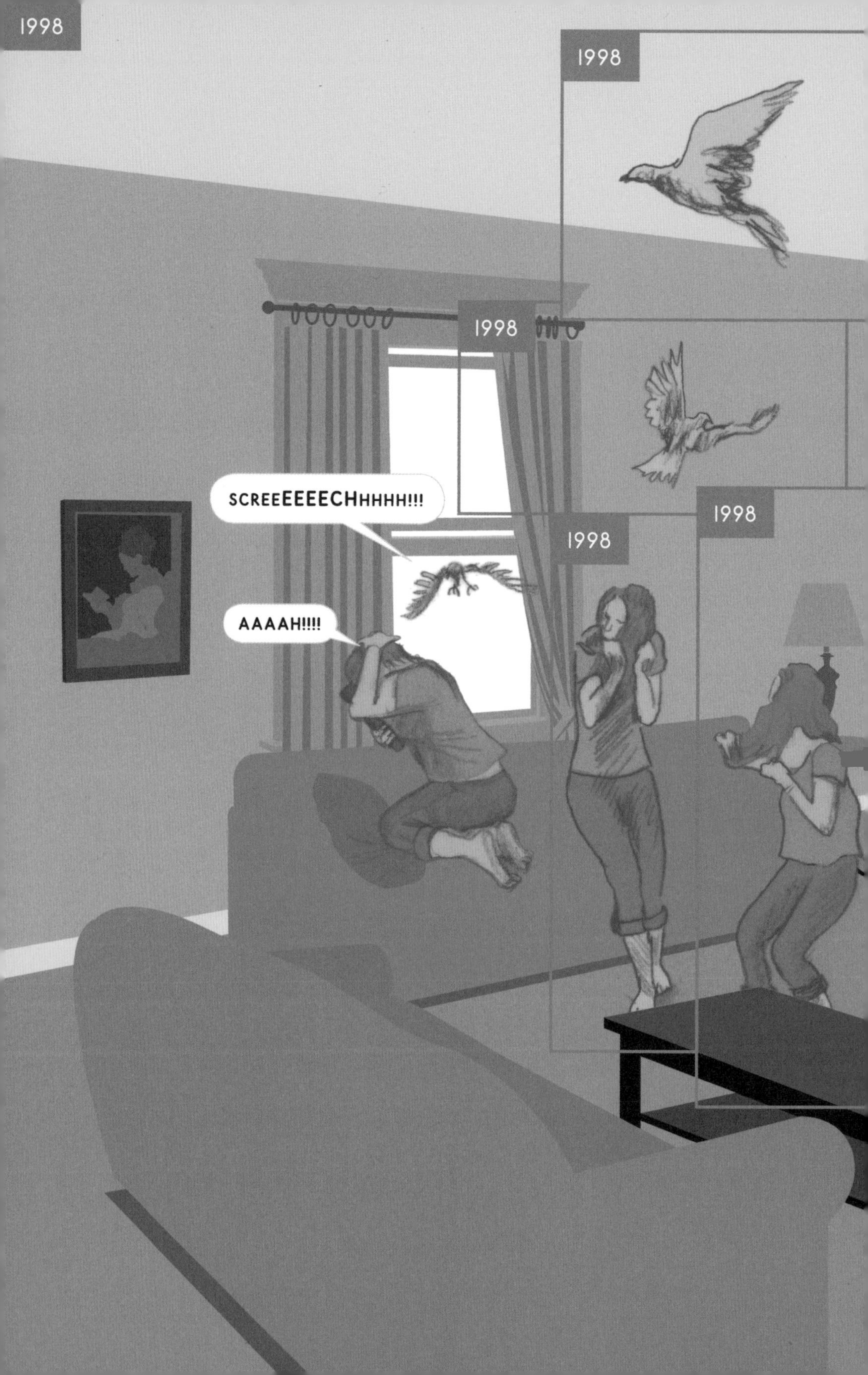
1998
1998
1998
SCREEEEEECHHHHH!!!
AAAAH!!!!
1998
1998

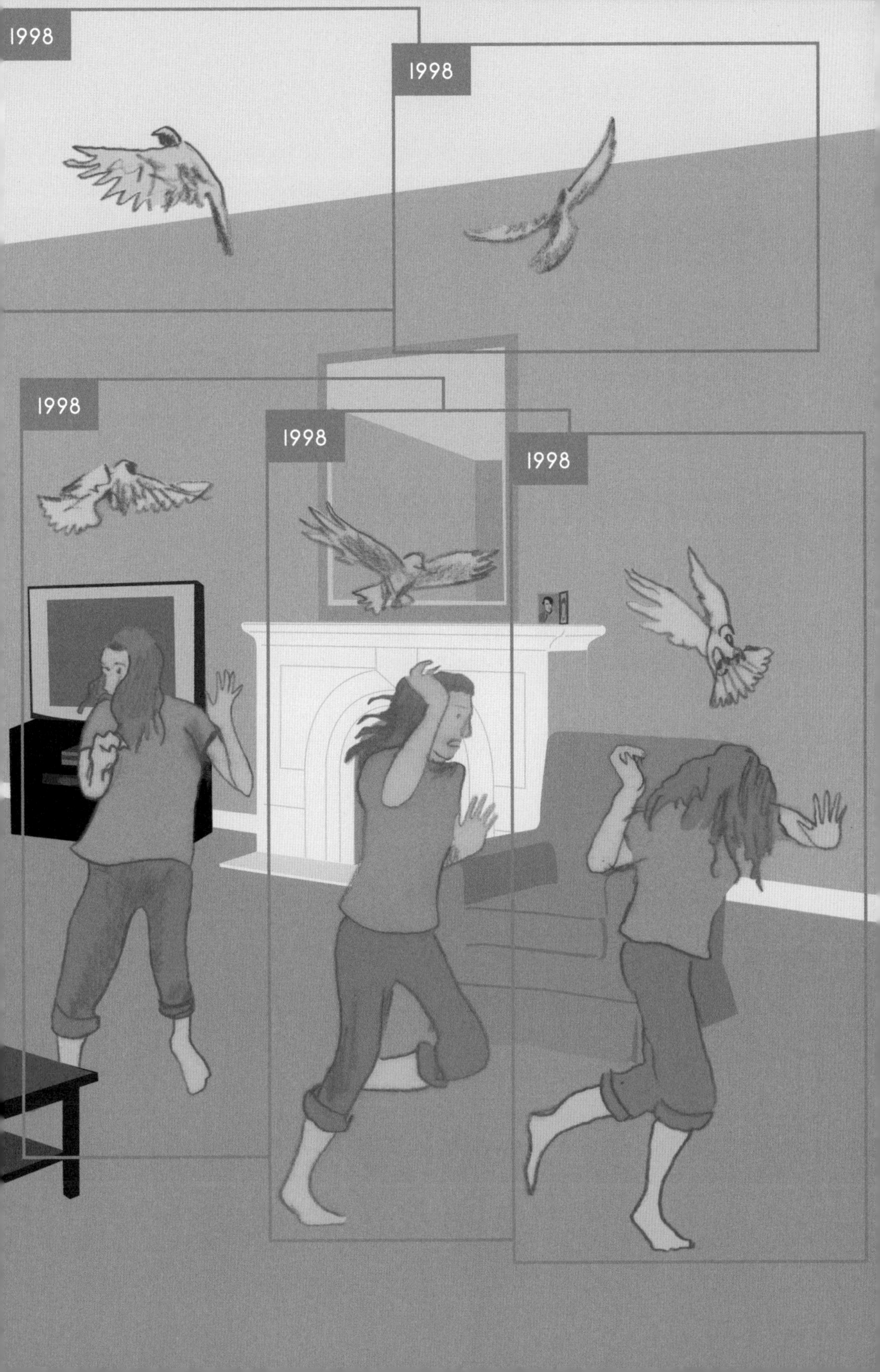
1998
1998
1998
1998
1998

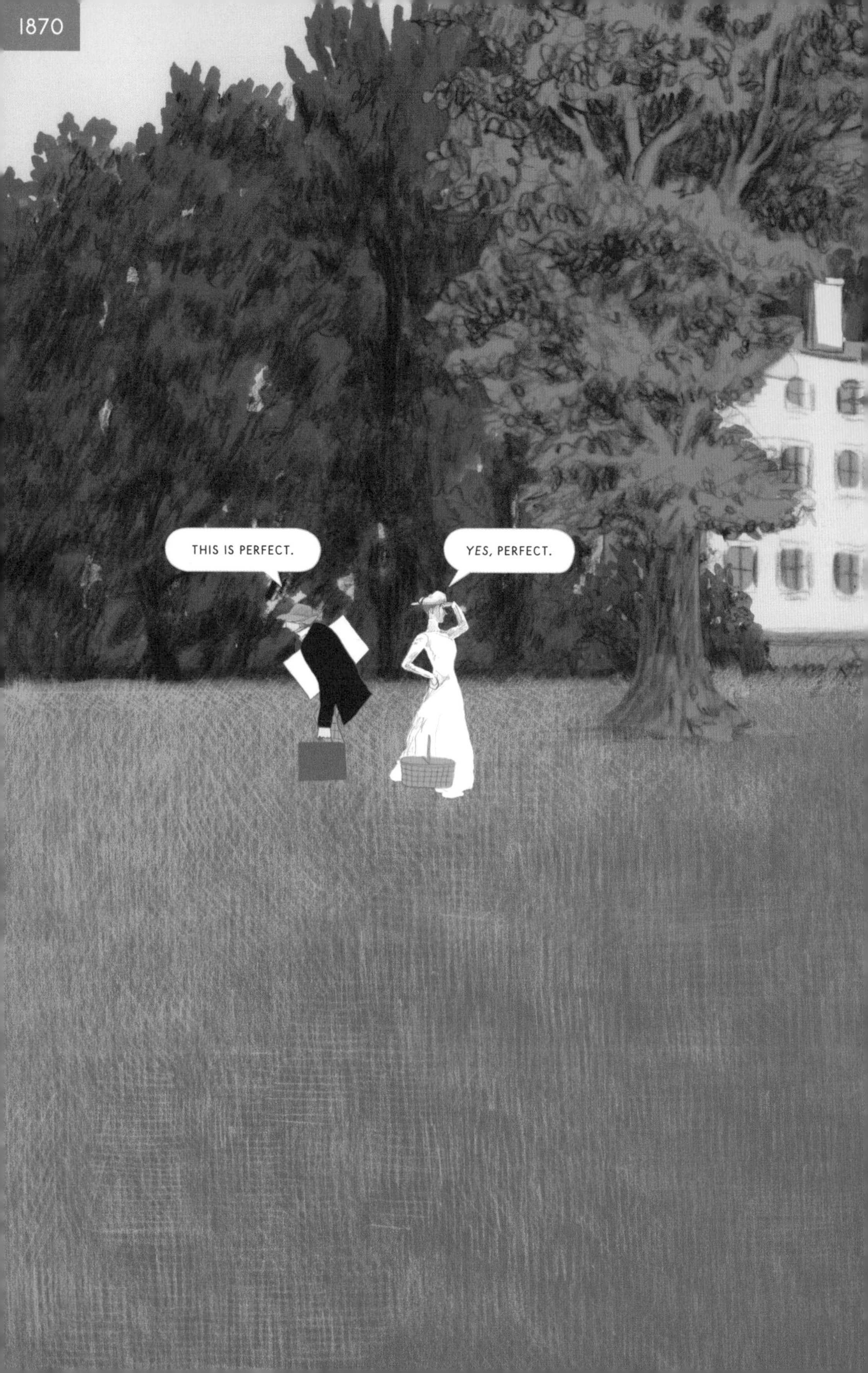
1870
THIS IS PERFECT.
YES, PERFECT.

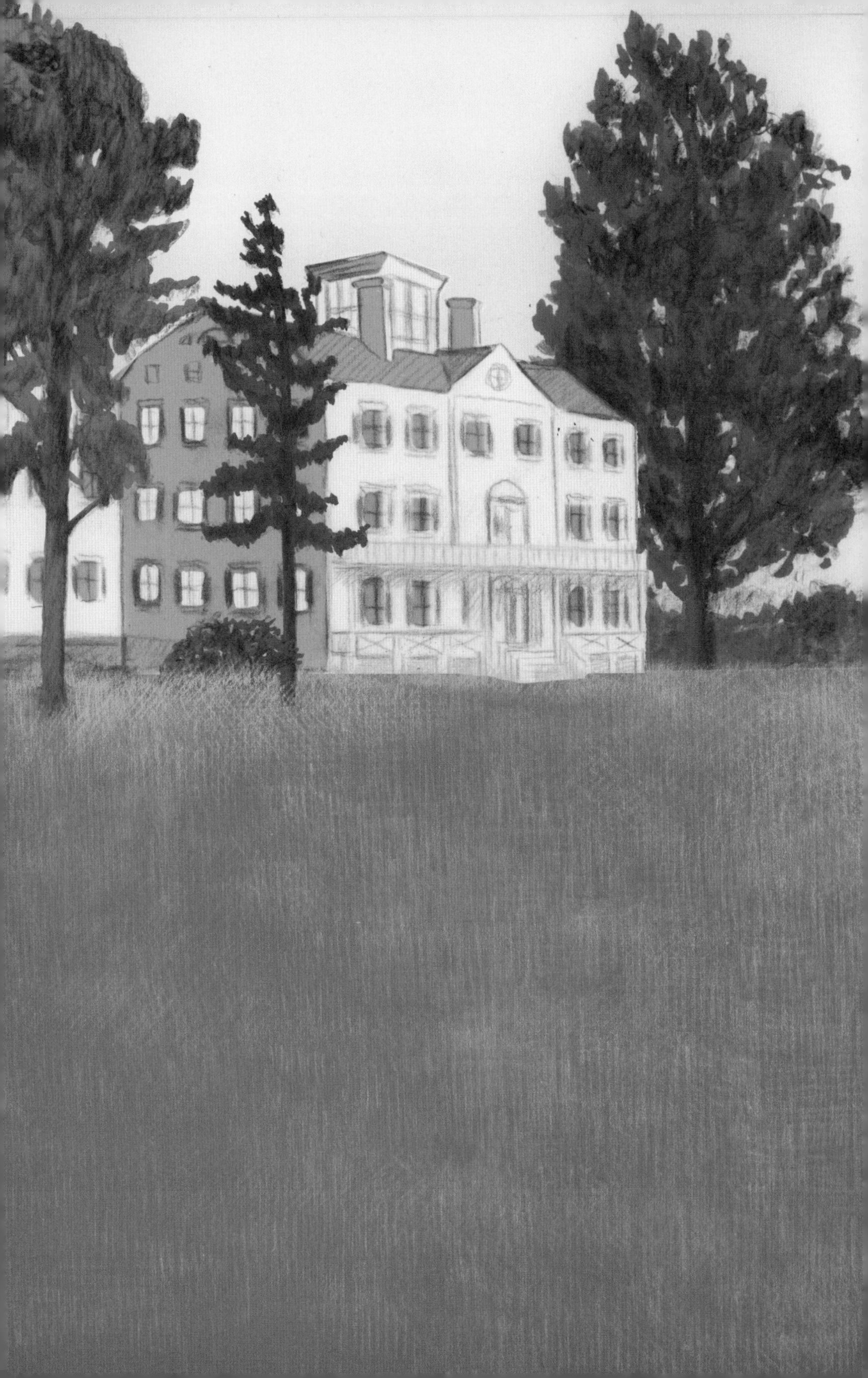

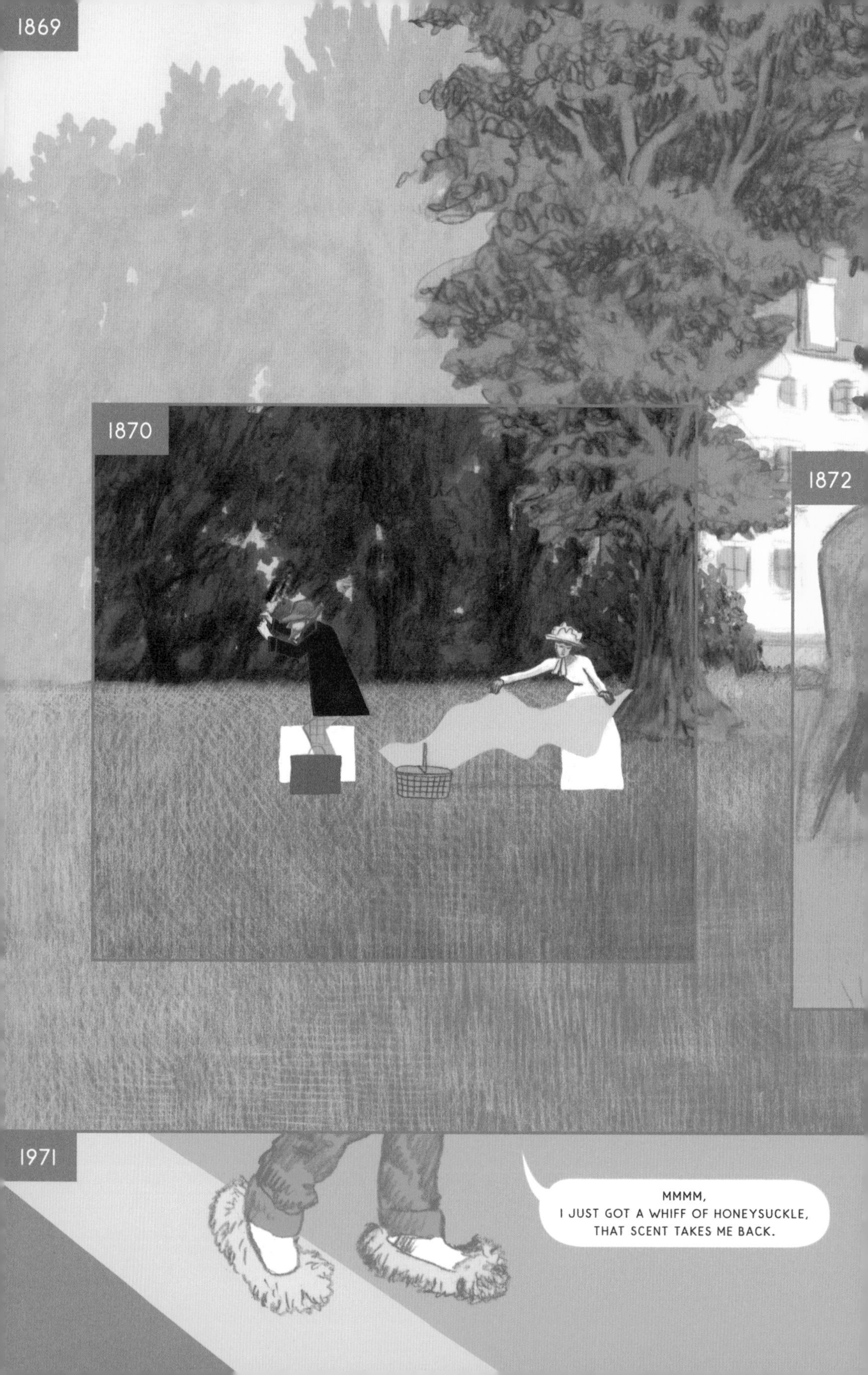
1869
1870
1872
1971
MMMM,
I JUST GOT A WHIFF OF HONEYSUCKLE,
THAT SCENT TAKES ME BACK.

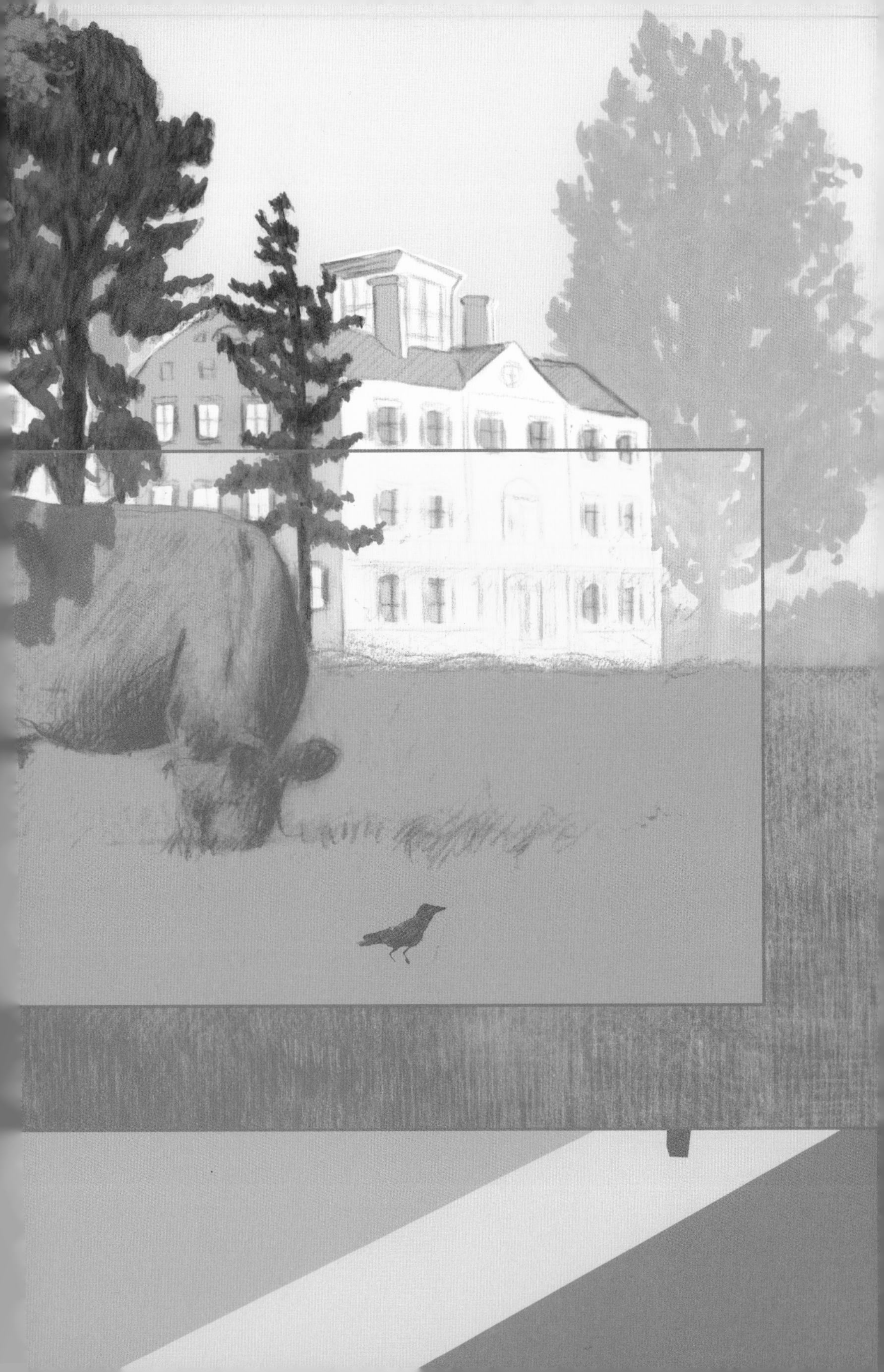

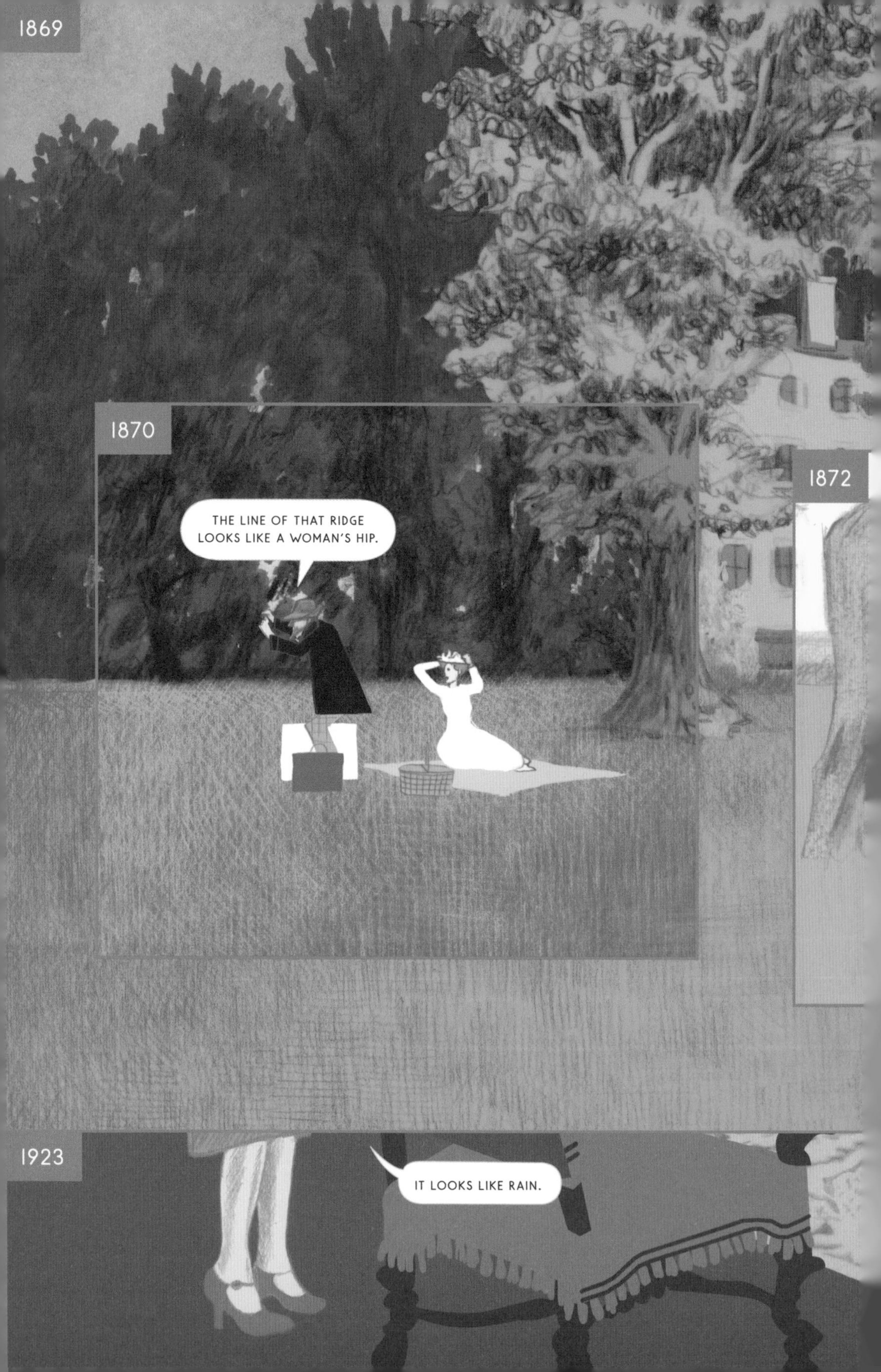
1869
1870
THE LINE OF THAT RIDGE LOOKS LIKE A WOMAN'S HIP.
1872
1923
IT LOOKS LIKE RAIN.

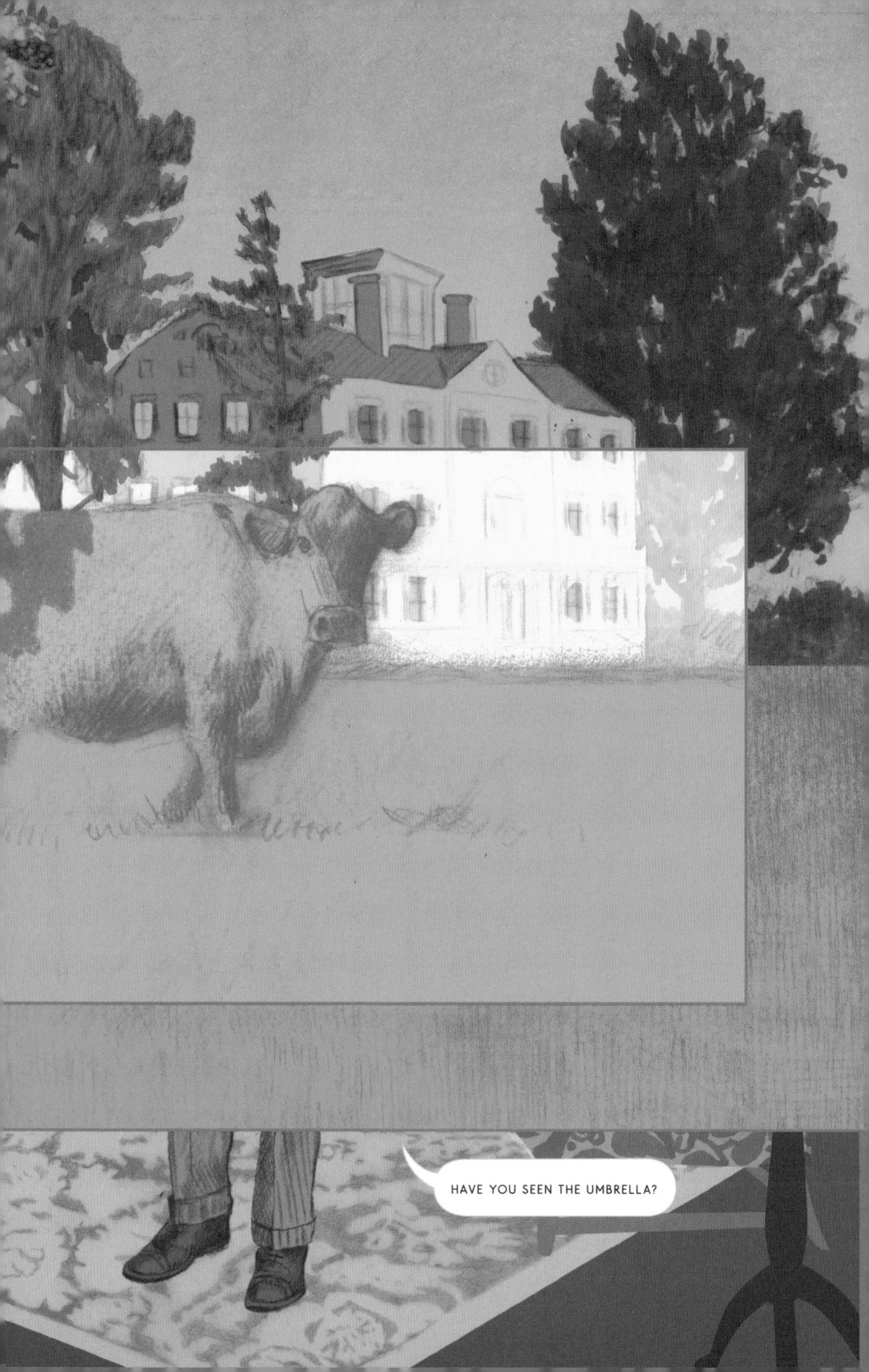
HAVE YOU SEEN THE UMBRELLA?

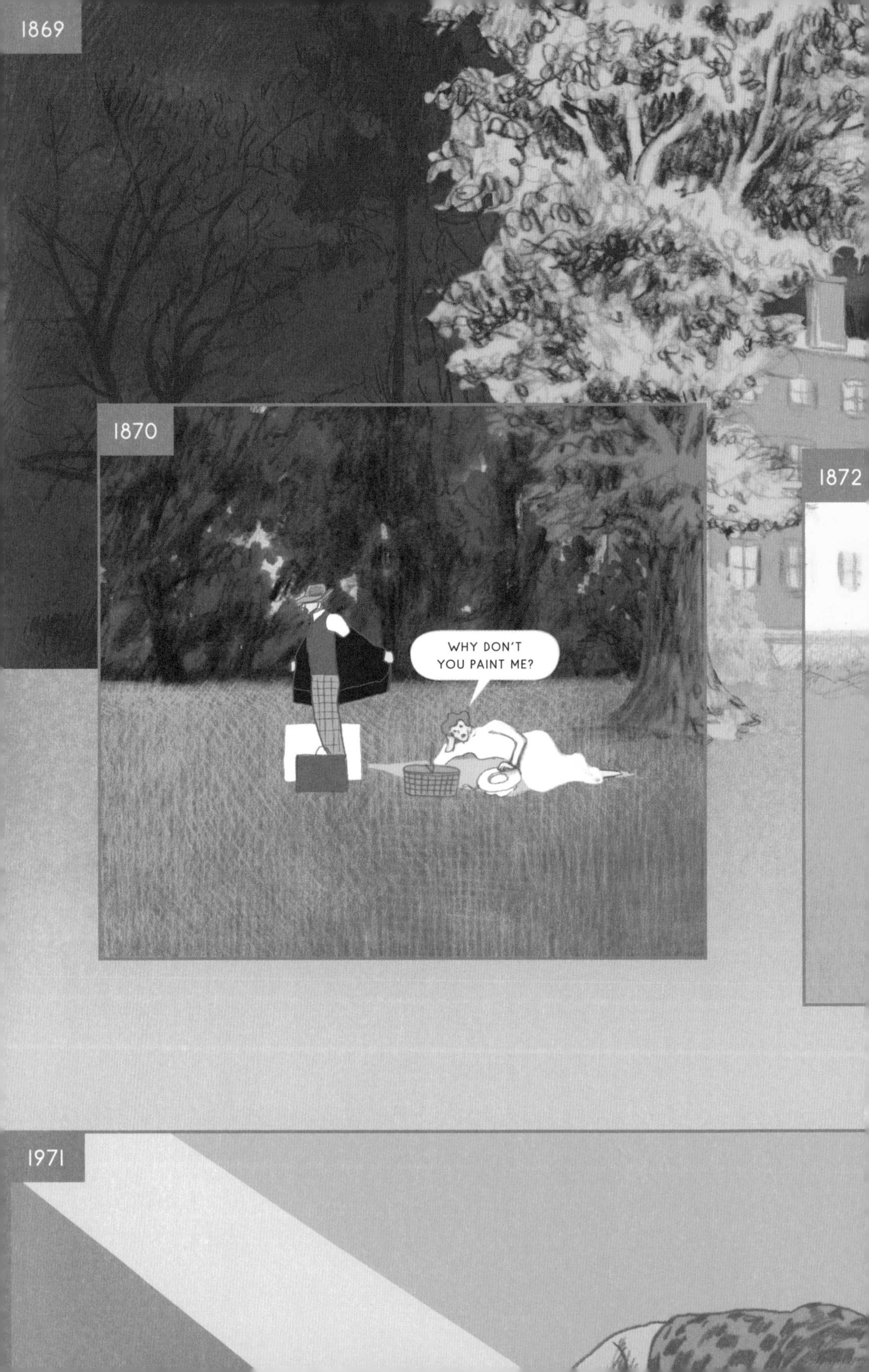
1869
1870
WHY DON'T
YOU PAINT ME?
1872
1971

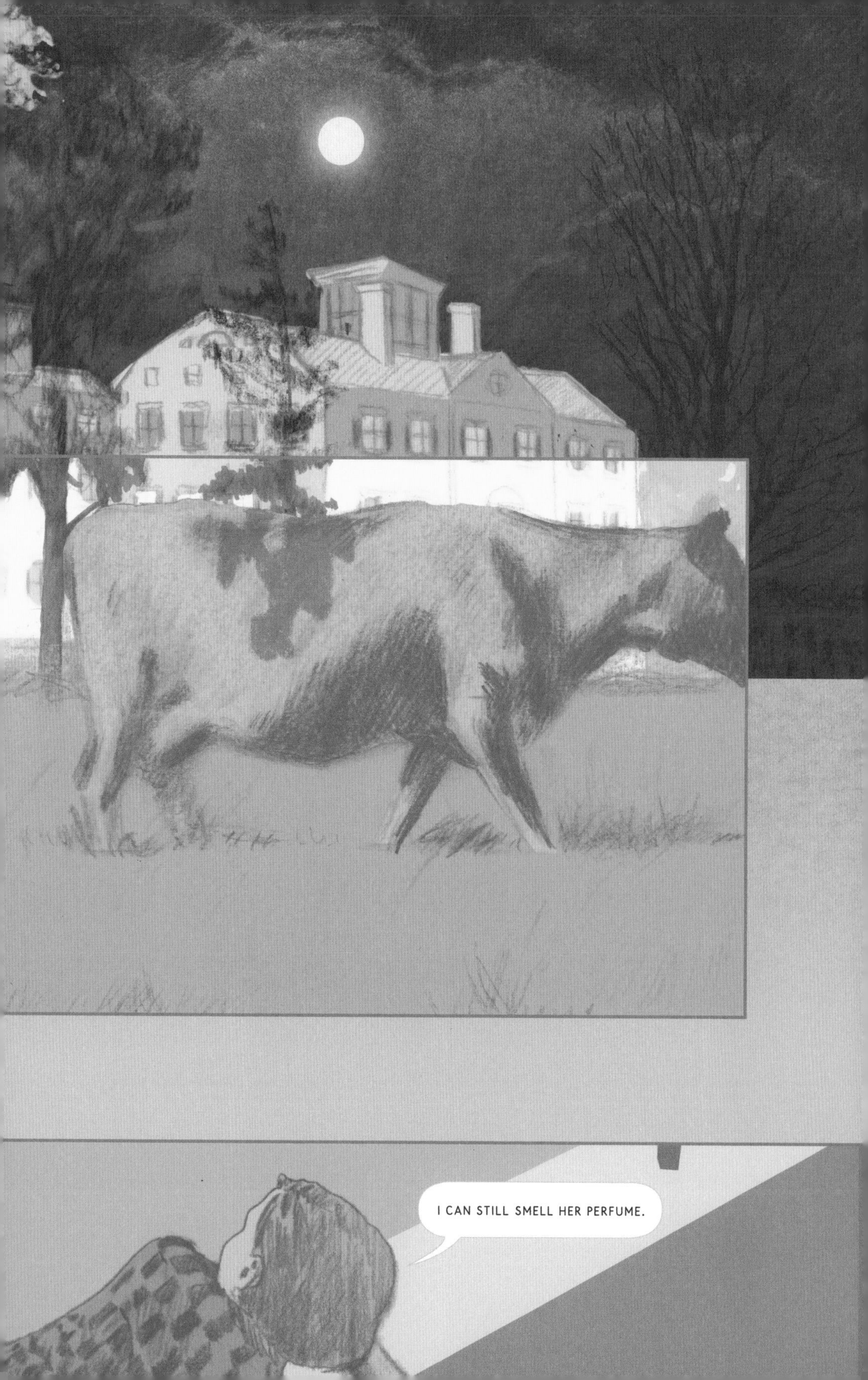
I CAN STILL SMELL HER PERFUME.

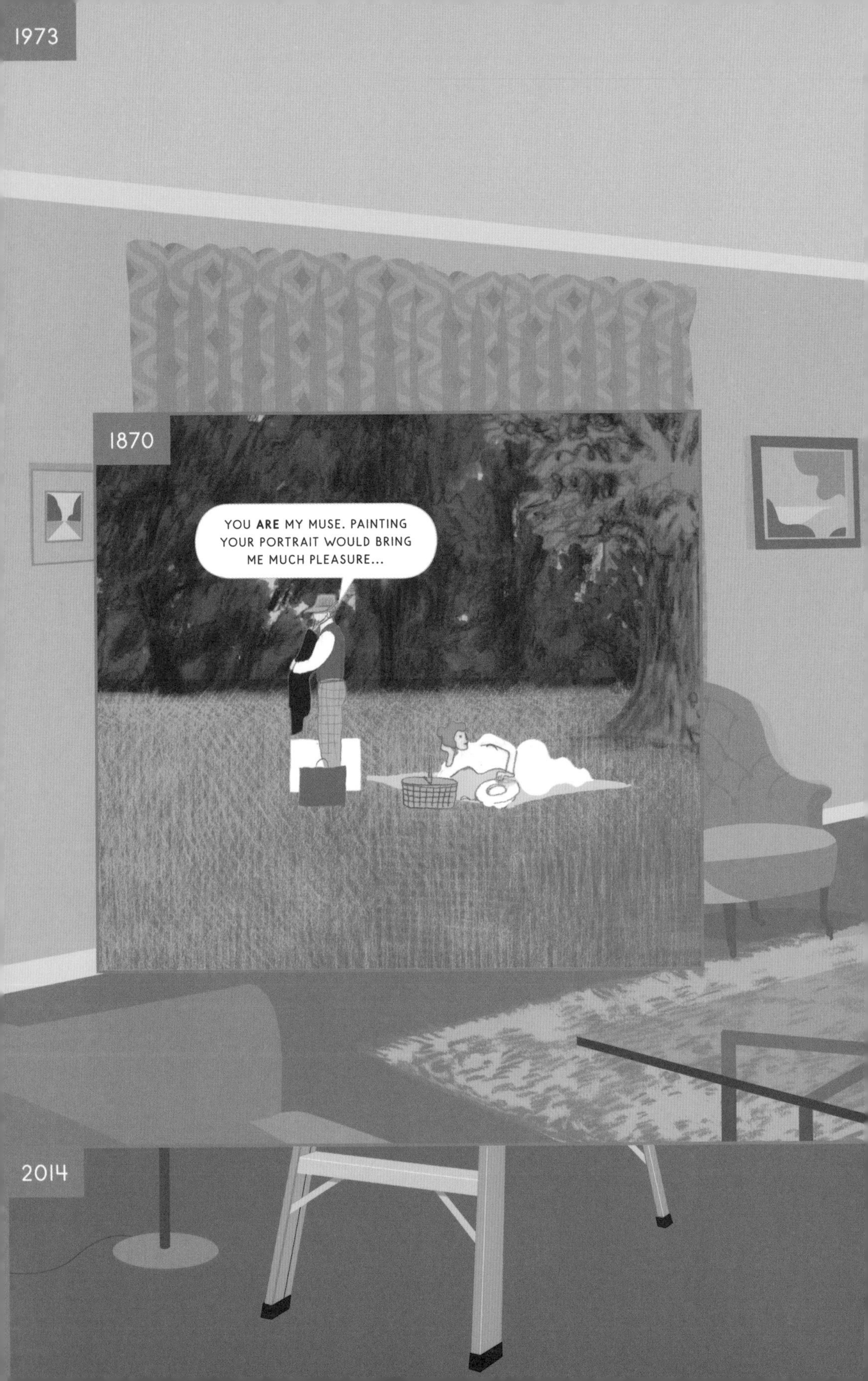
1973
1870
YOU **ARE** MY MUSE. PAINTING YOUR PORTRAIT WOULD BRING ME MUCH PLEASURE...
2014

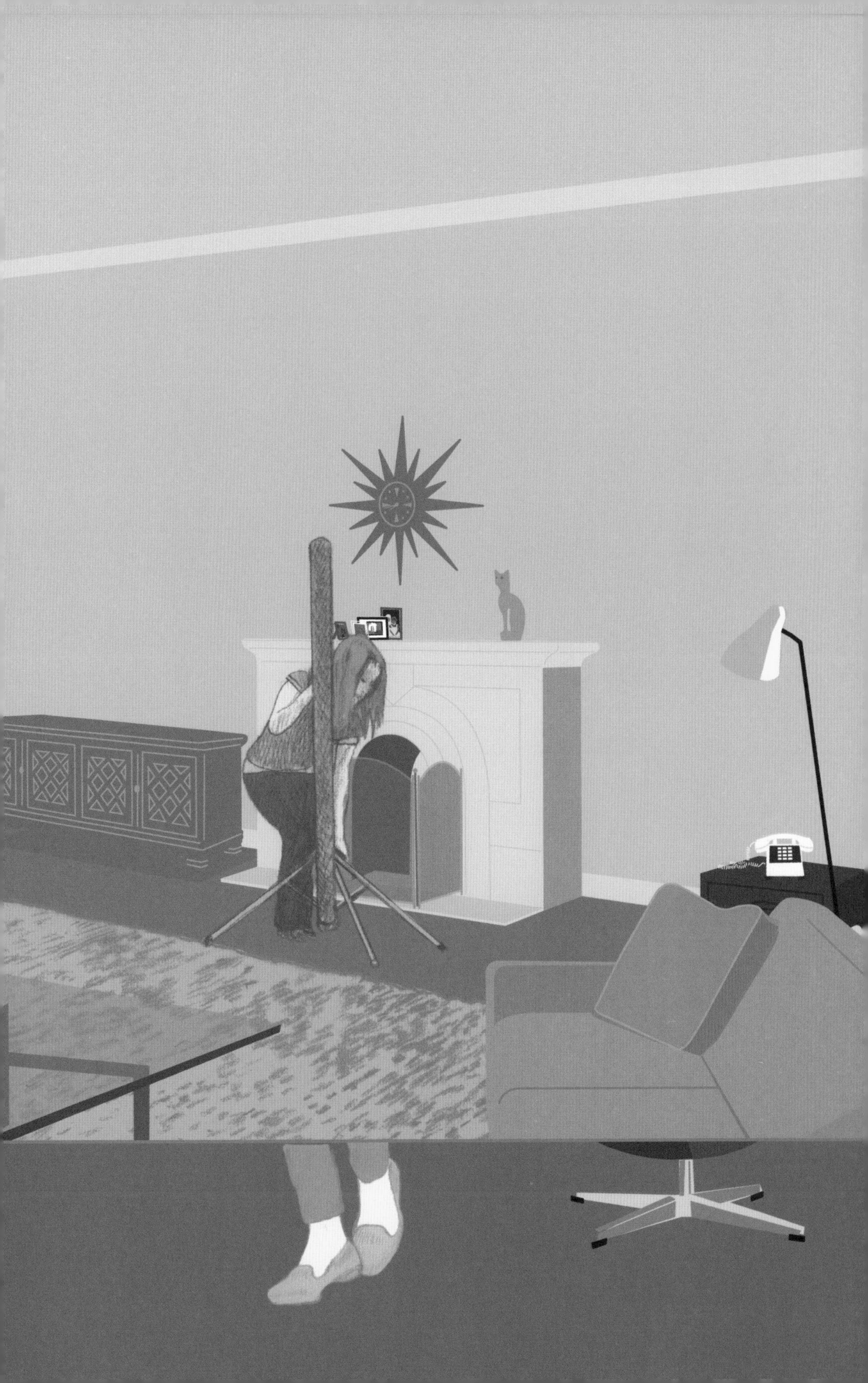

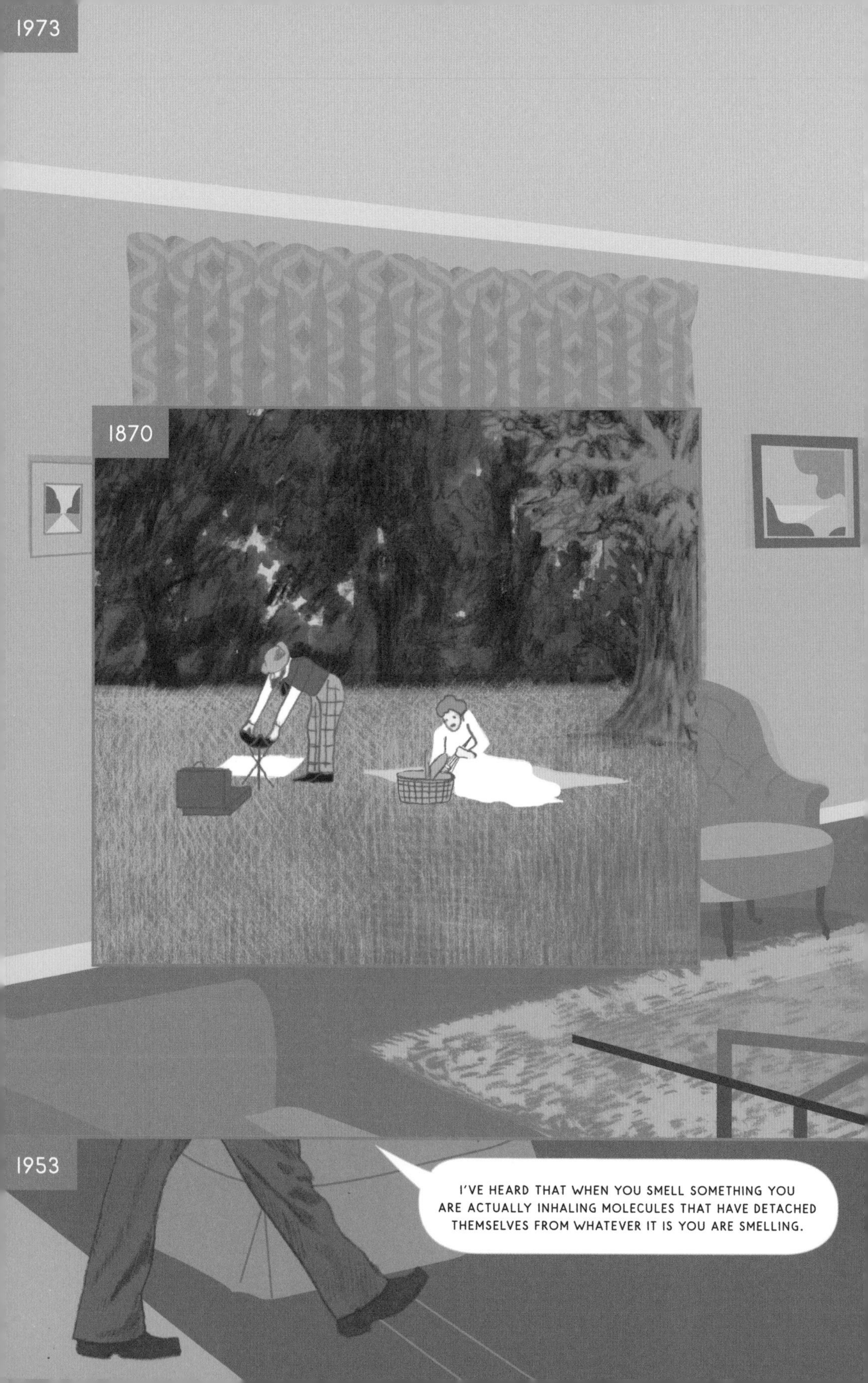
1973
1870
1953
I'VE HEARD THAT WHEN YOU SMELL SOMETHING YOU ARE ACTUALLY INHALING MOLECULES THAT HAVE DETACHED THEMSELVES FROM WHATEVER IT IS YOU ARE SMELLING.

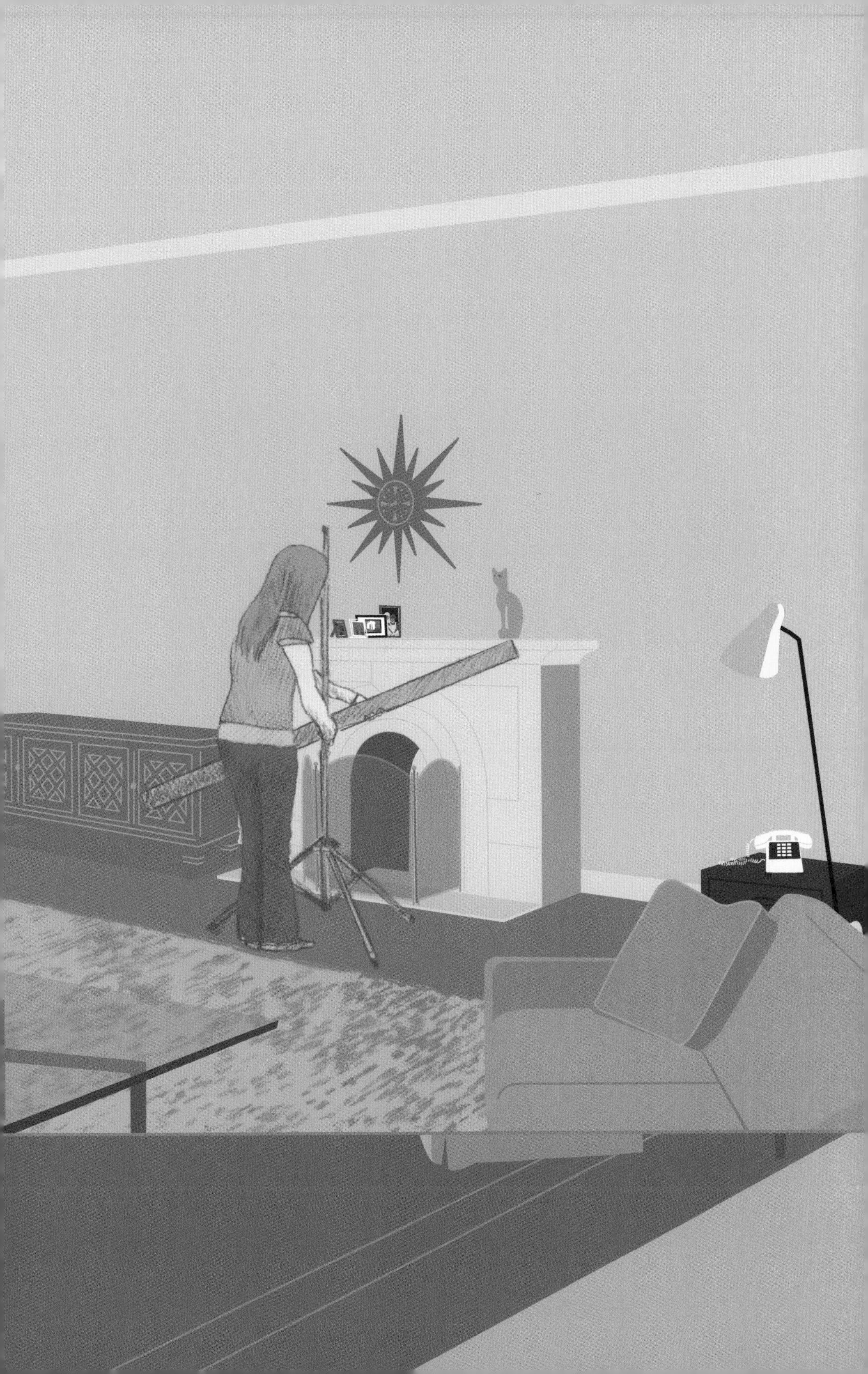

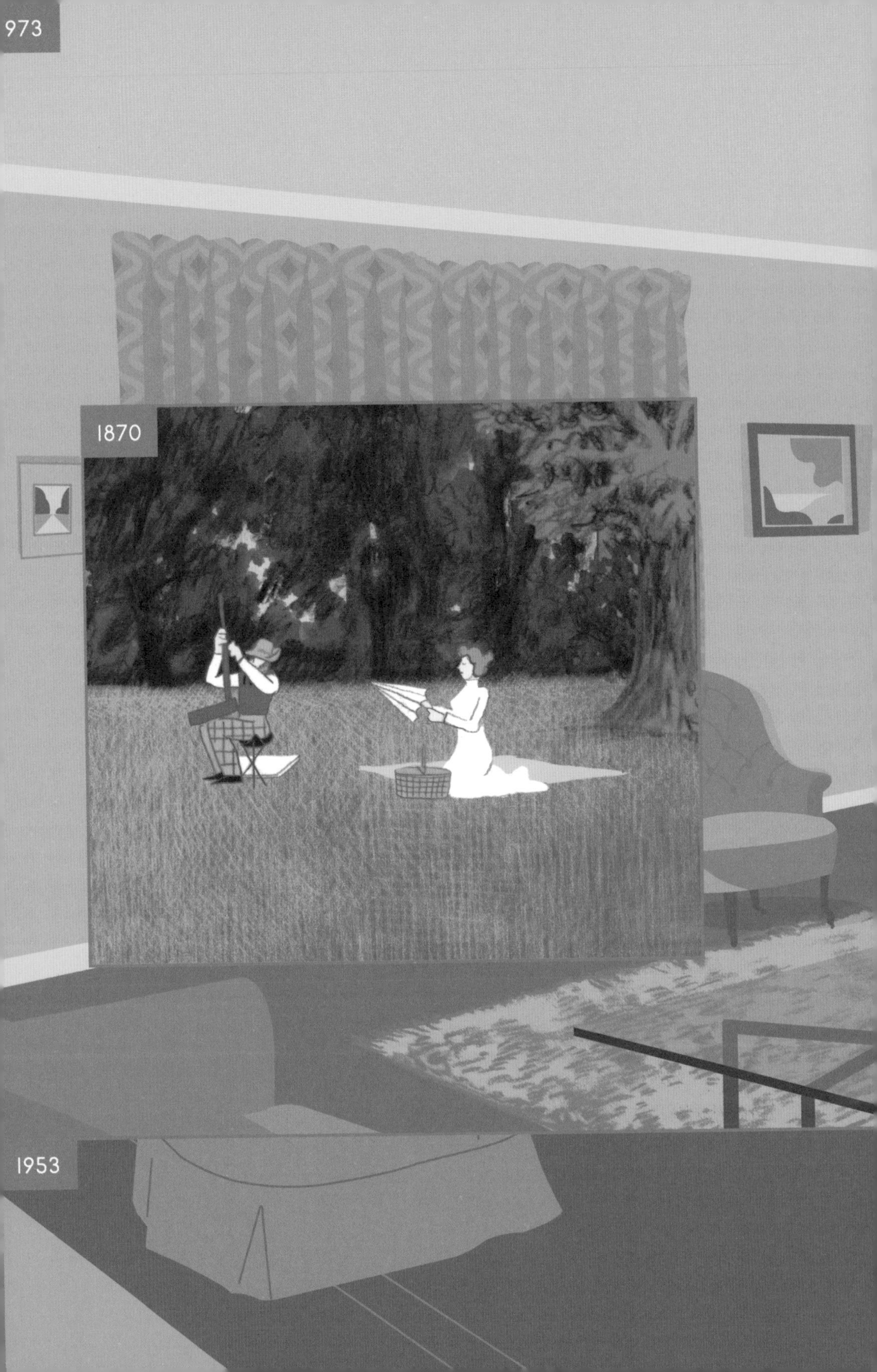
973
1870
1953

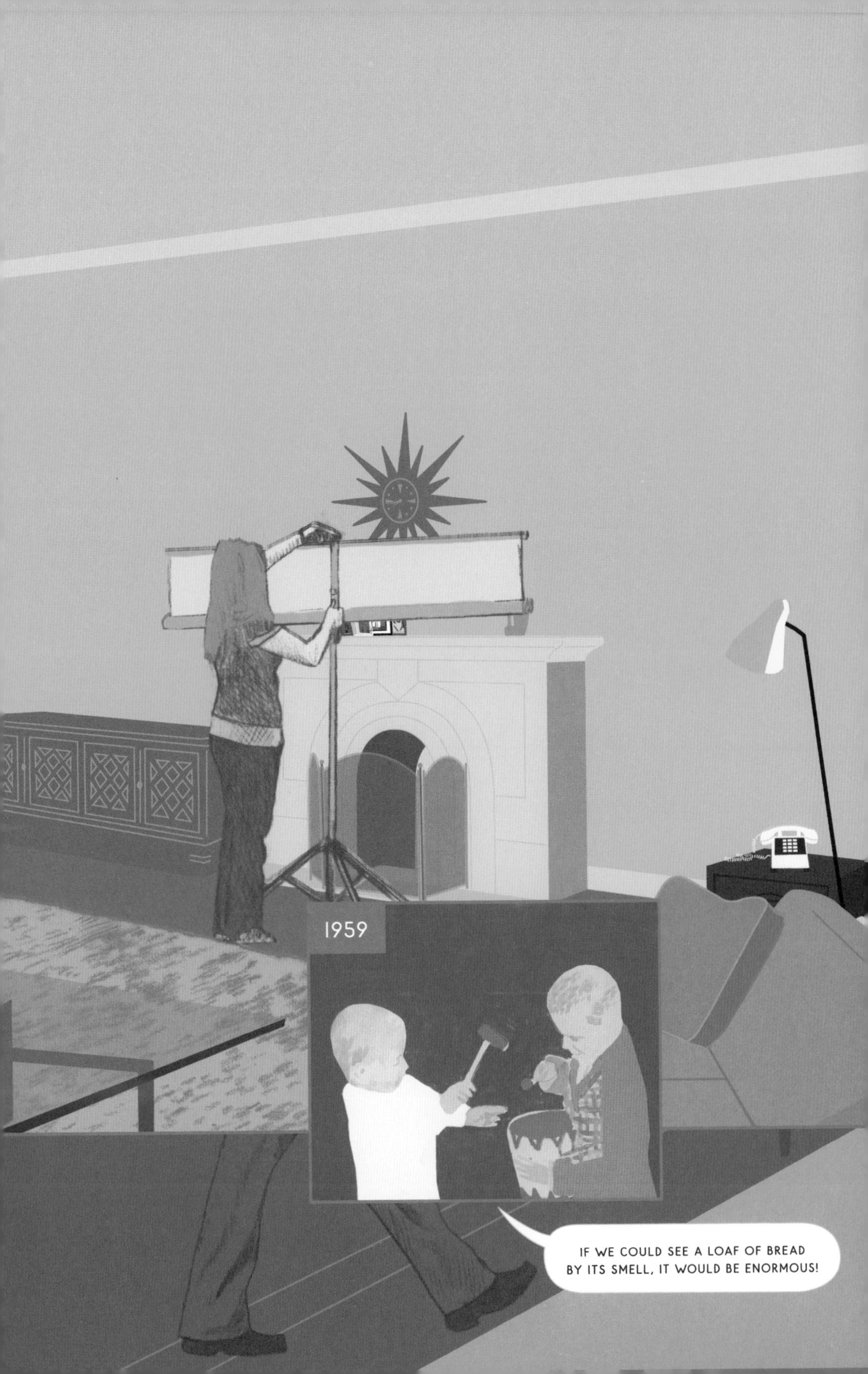
1959
IF WE COULD SEE A LOAF OF BREAD BY ITS SMELL, IT WOULD BE ENORMOUS!

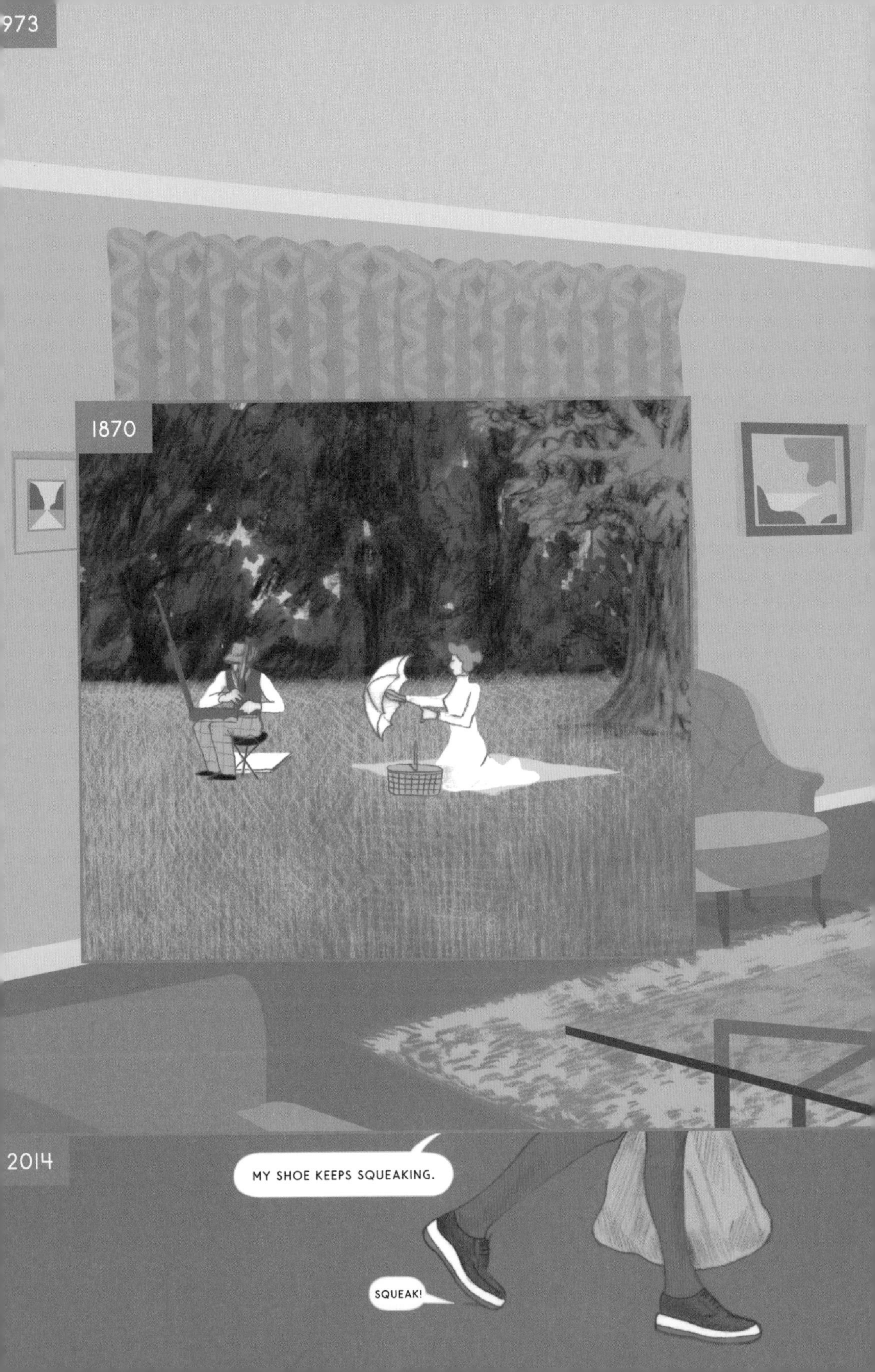
973
1870
2014
MY SHOE KEEPS SQUEAKING.
SQUEAK!

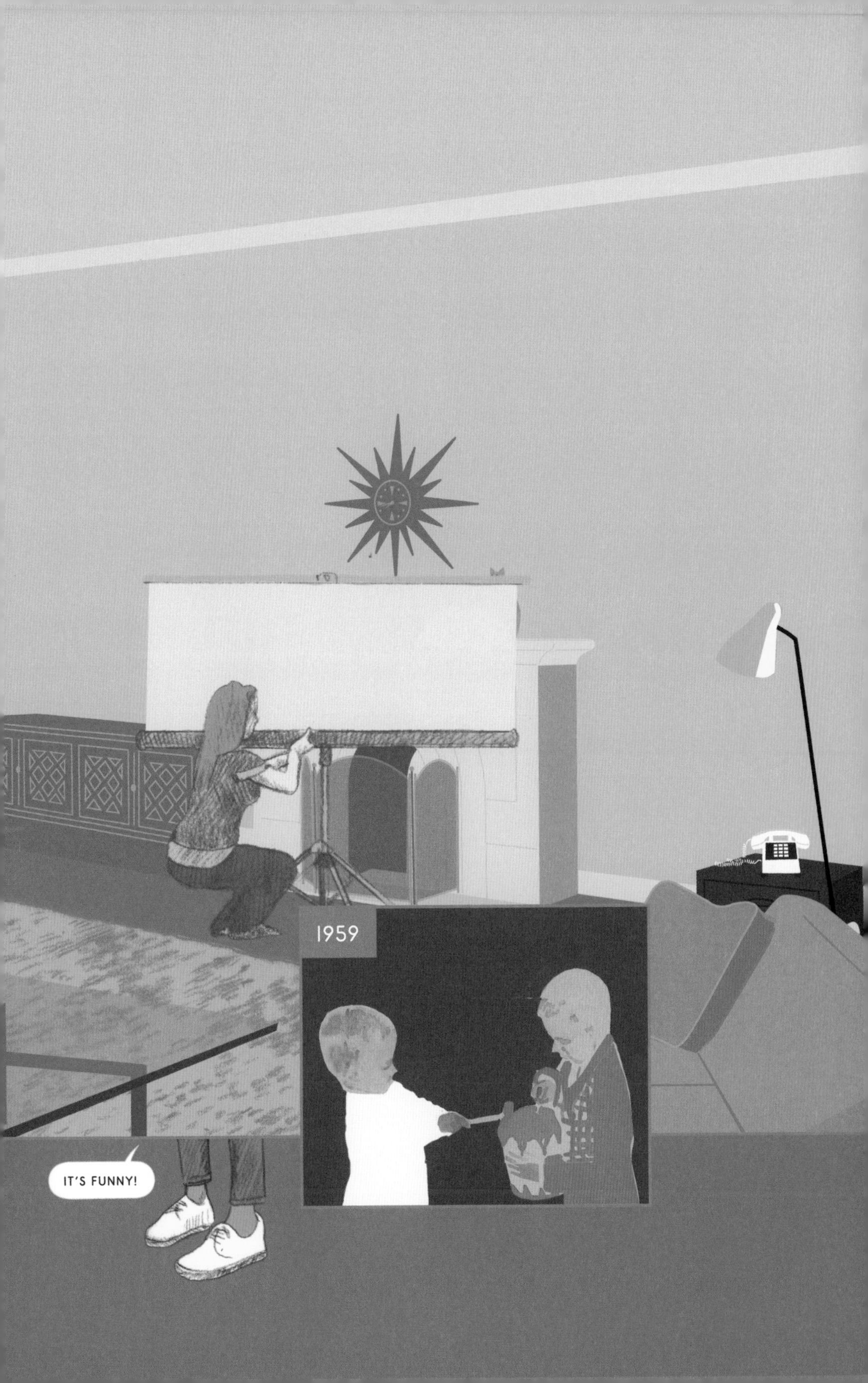
1959
IT'S FUNNY!

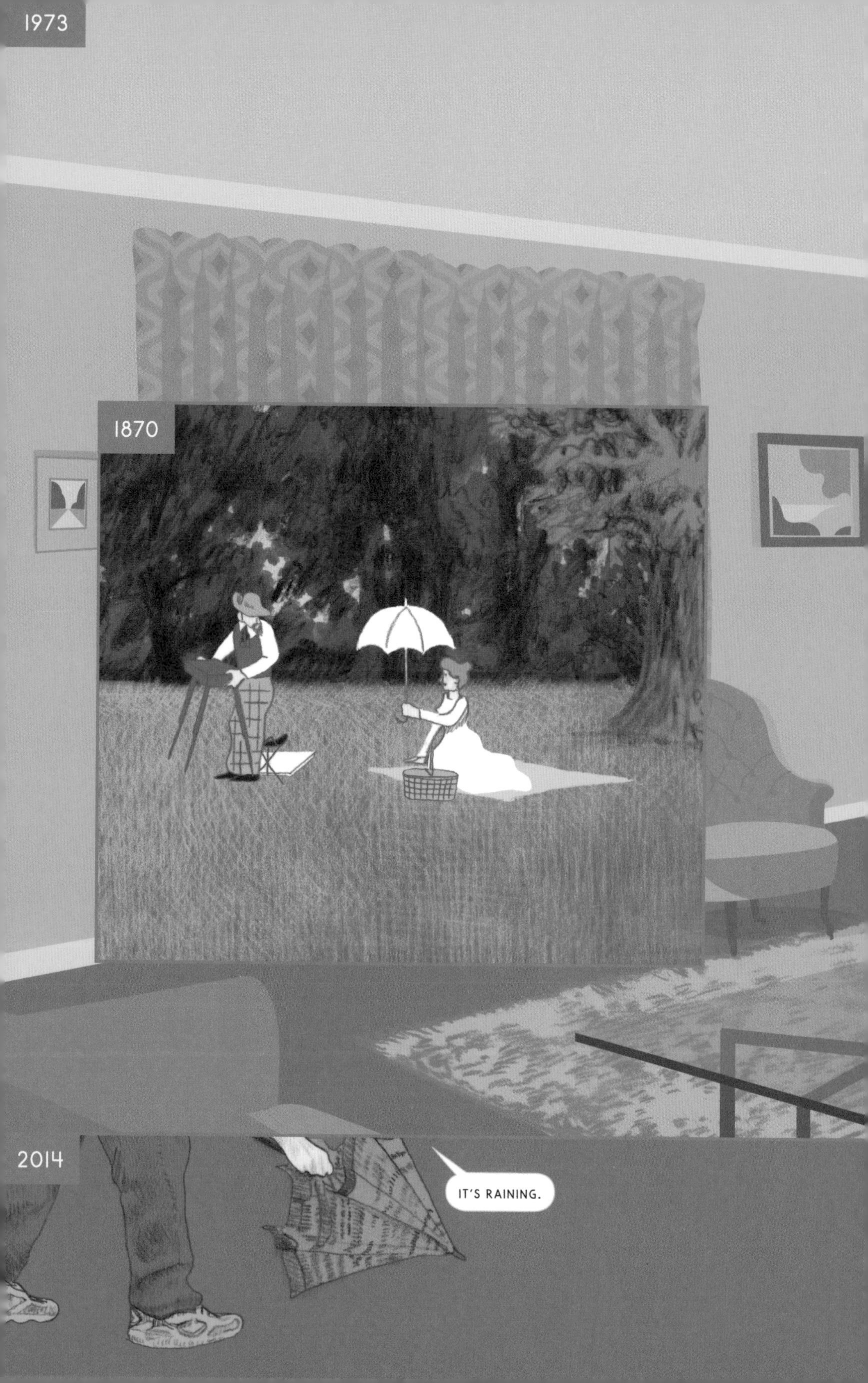
1973
1870
2014
IT'S RAINING.

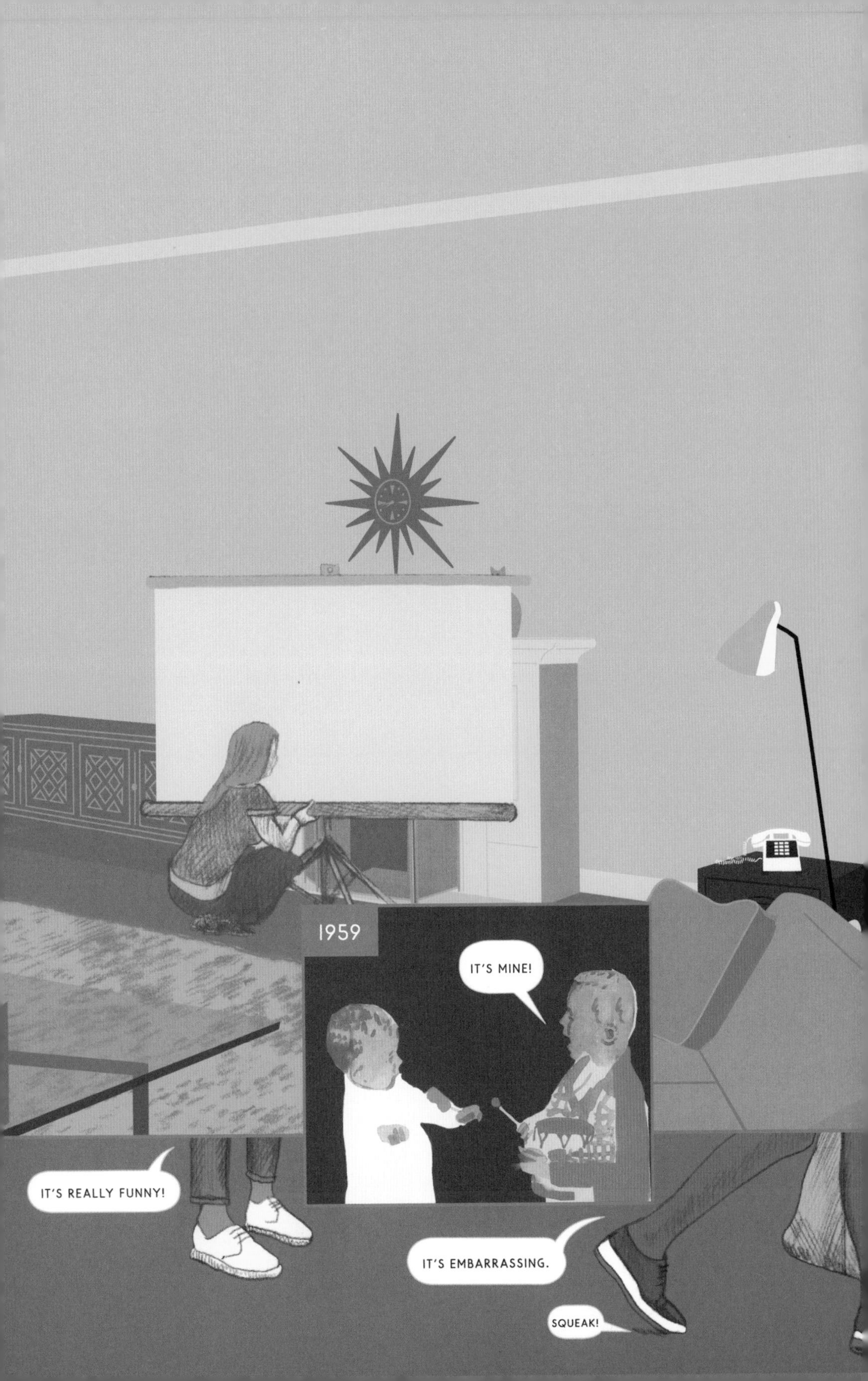
1959
IT'S MINE!
IT'S REALLY FUNNY!
IT'S EMBARRASSING.
SQUEAK!

973

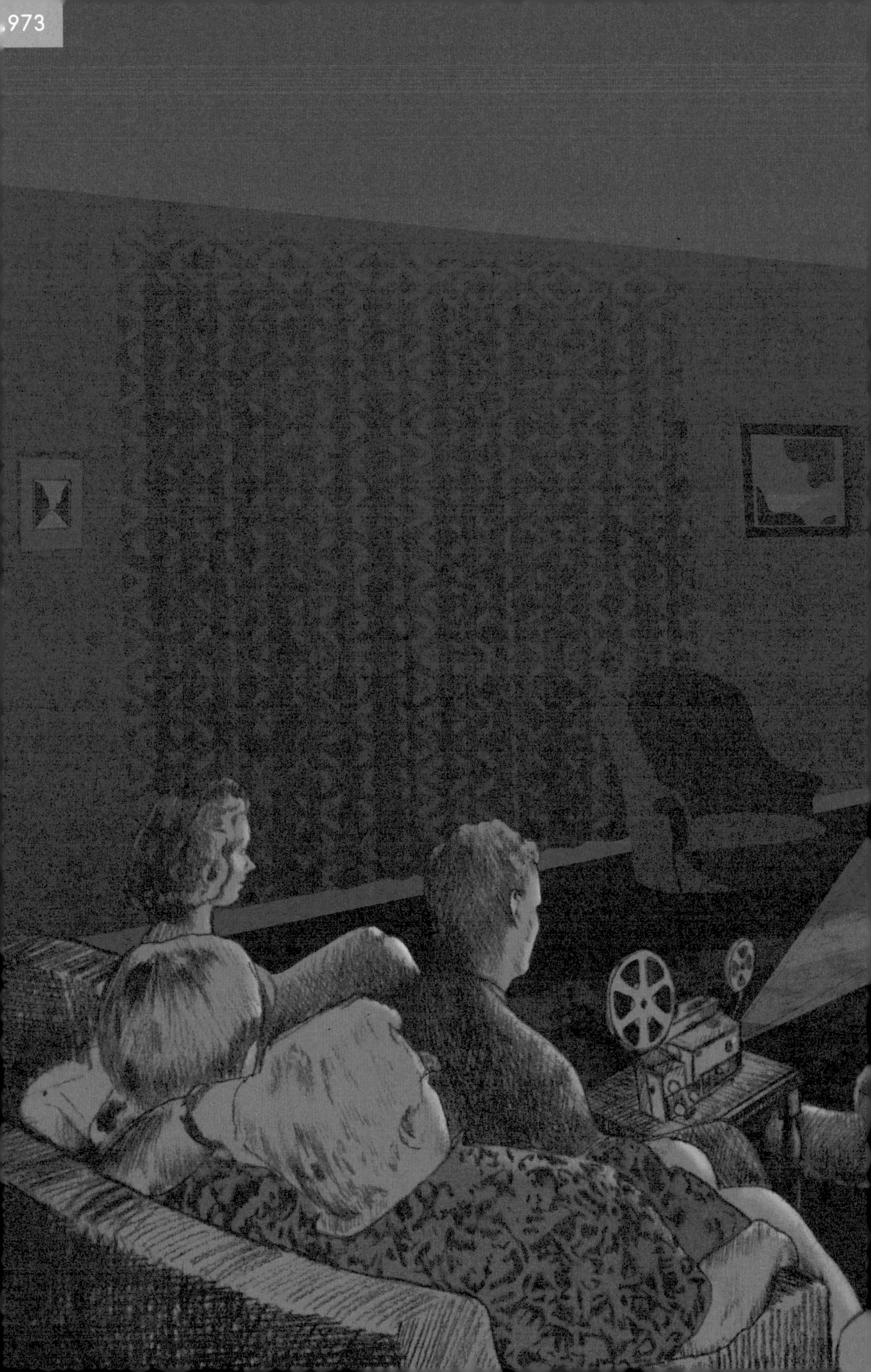

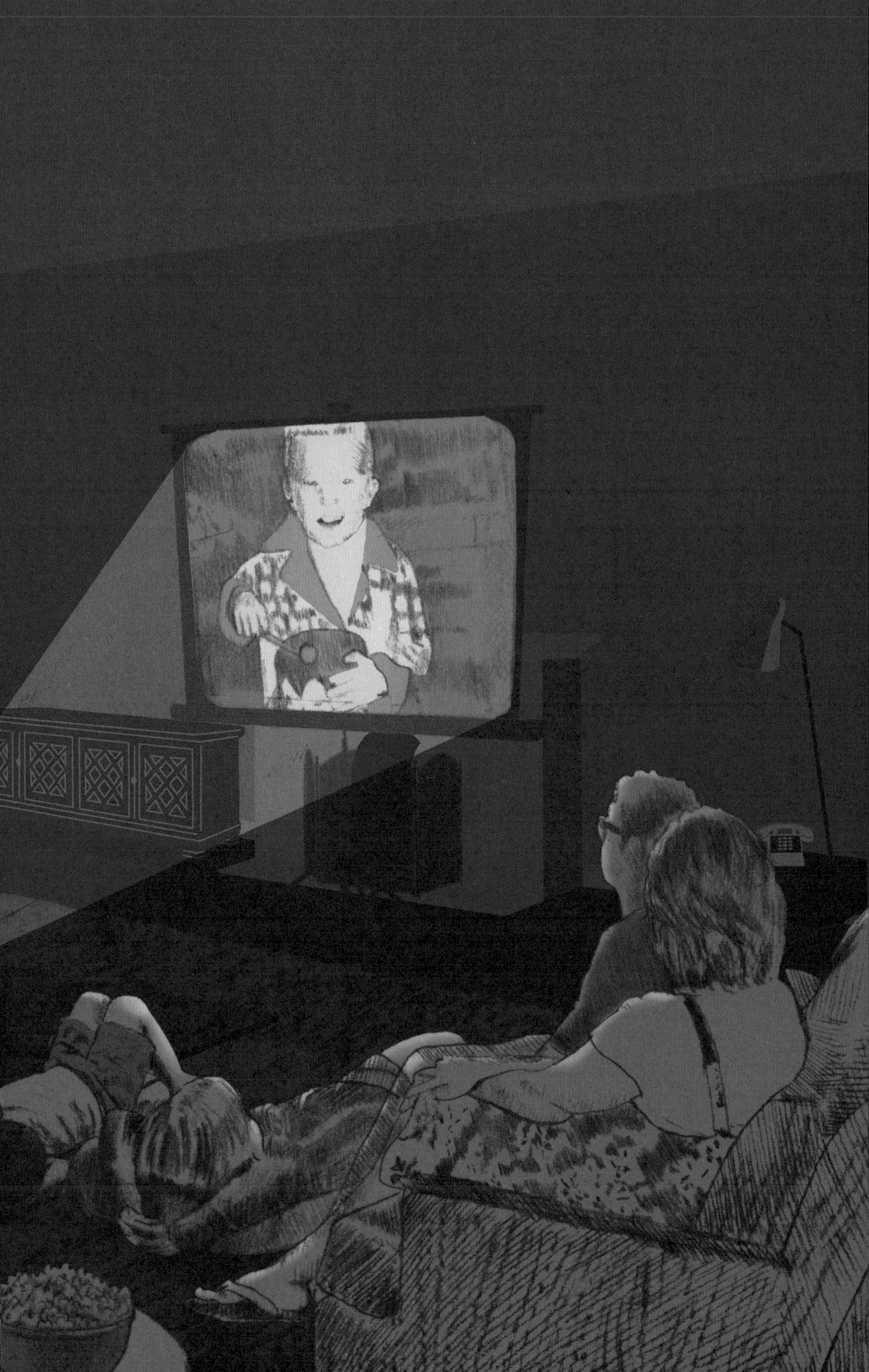

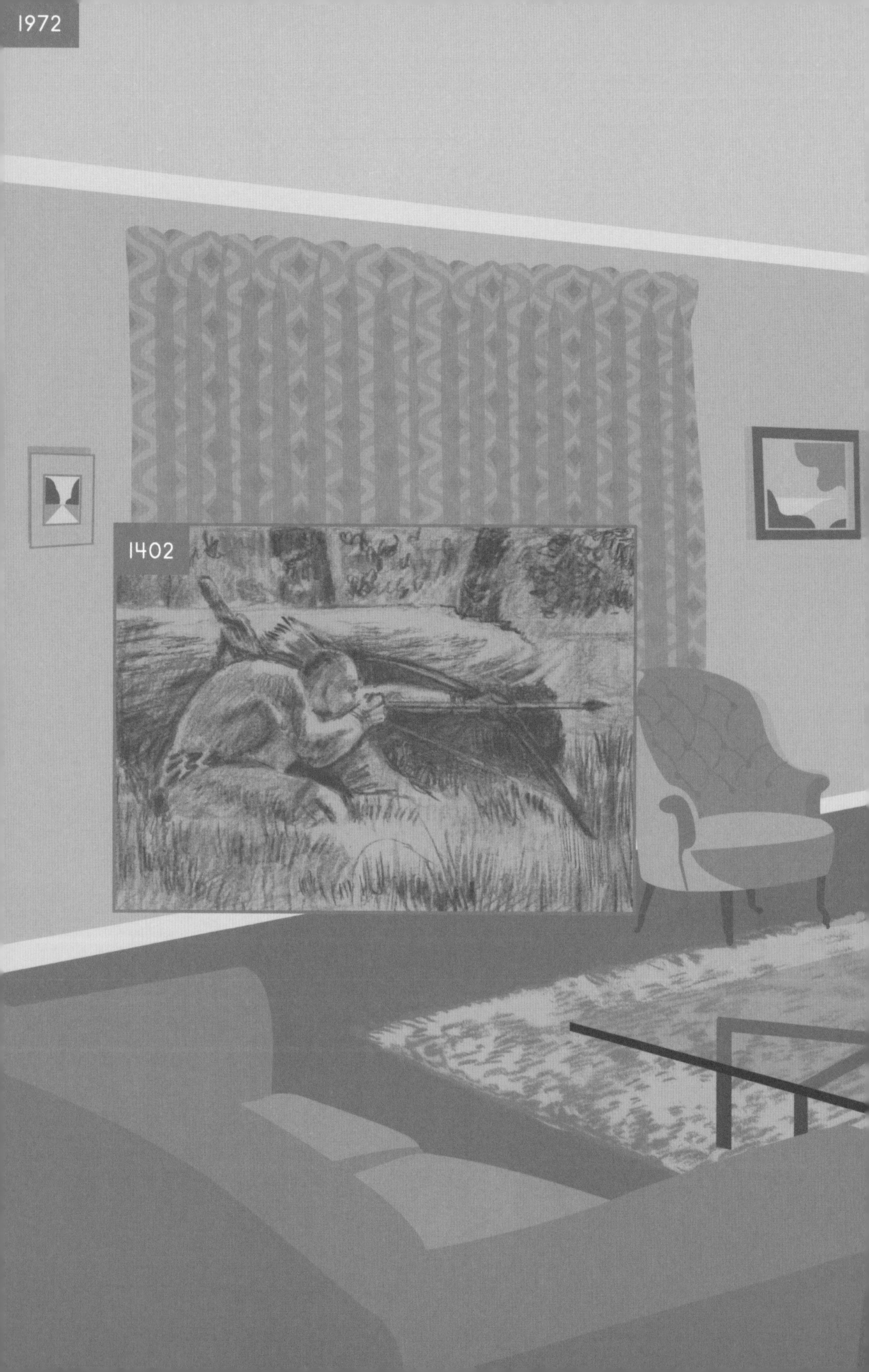
1972
1402

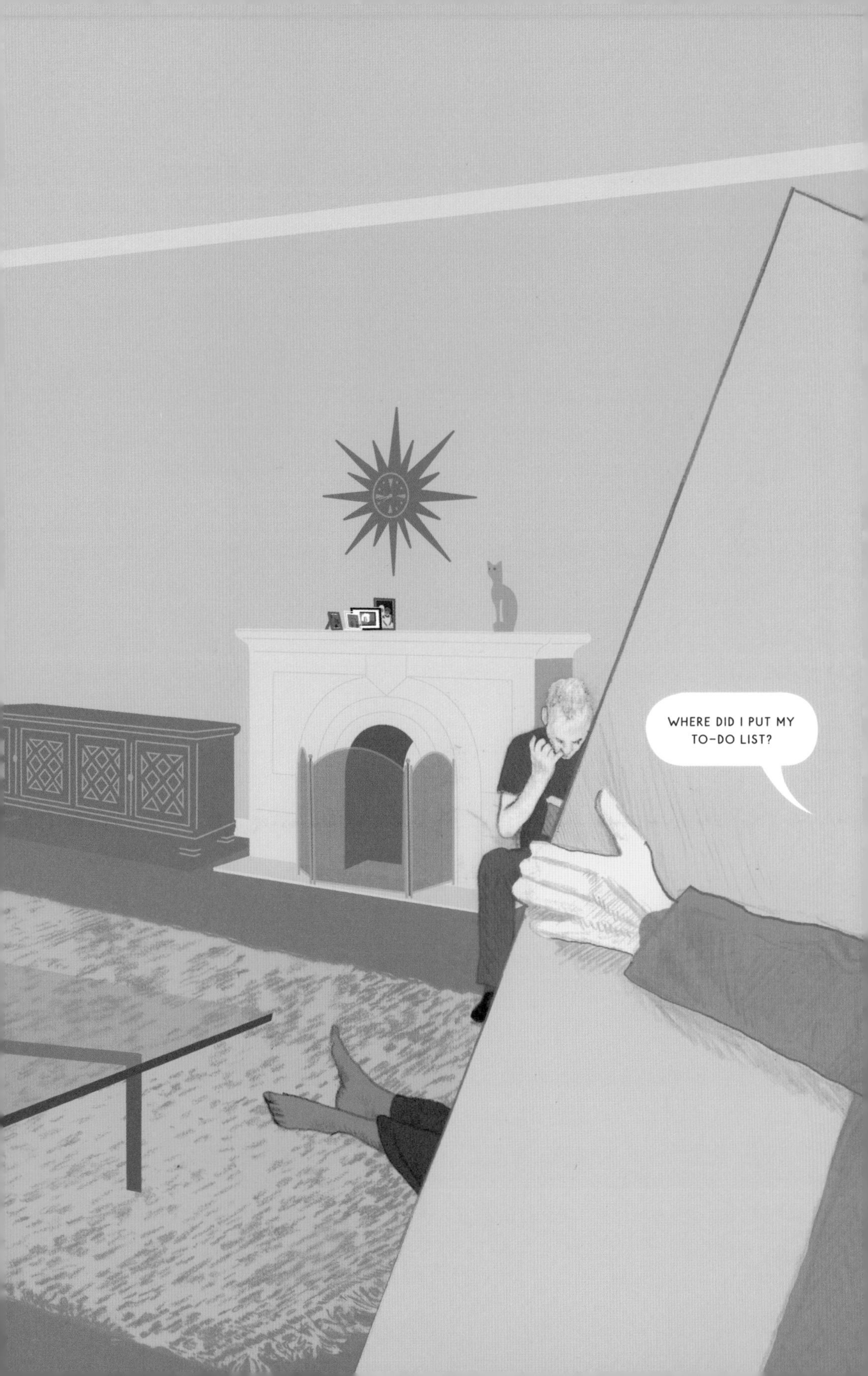
WHERE DID I PUT MY TO-DO LIST?

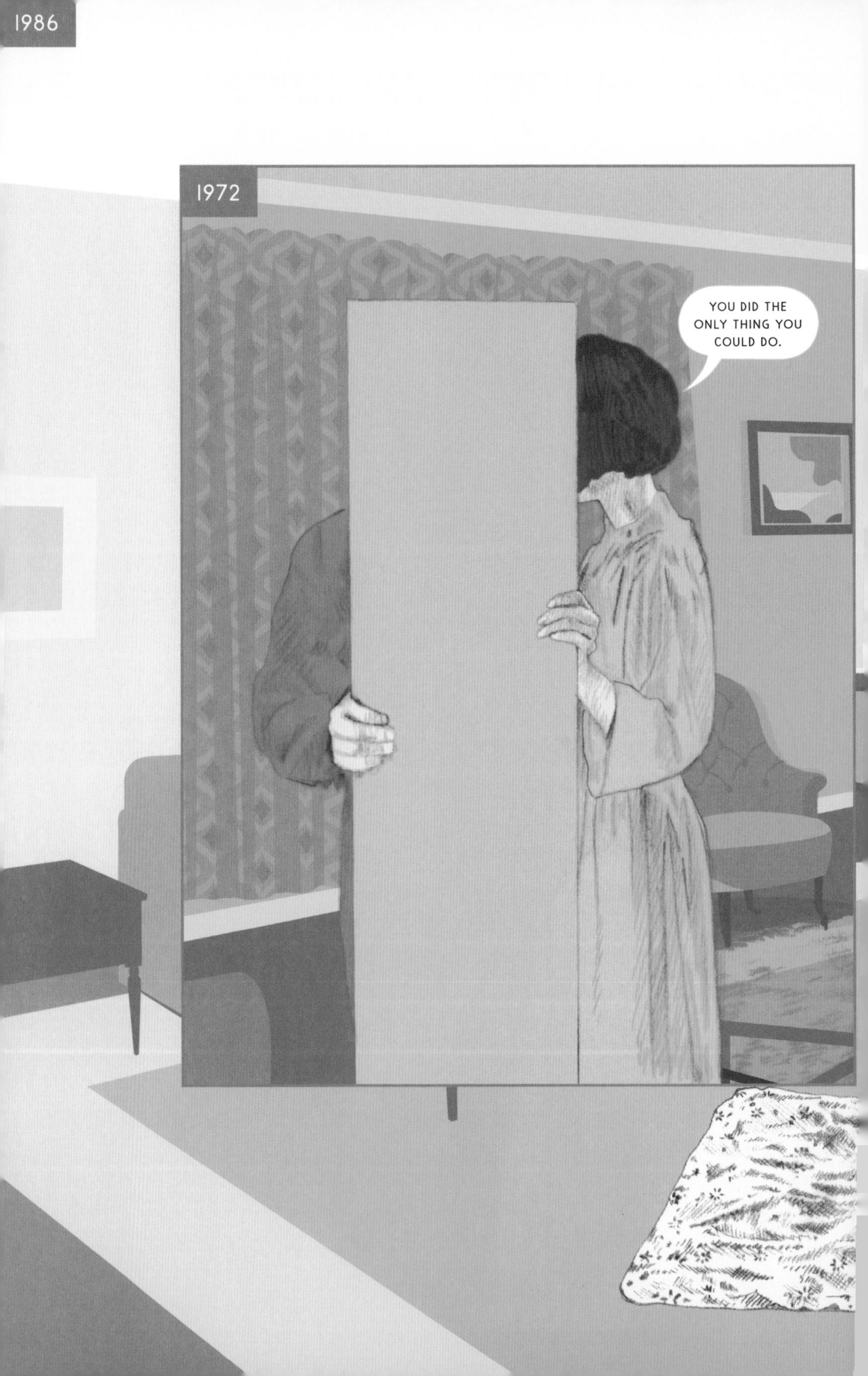
1986
1972
YOU DID THE ONLY THING YOU COULD DO.

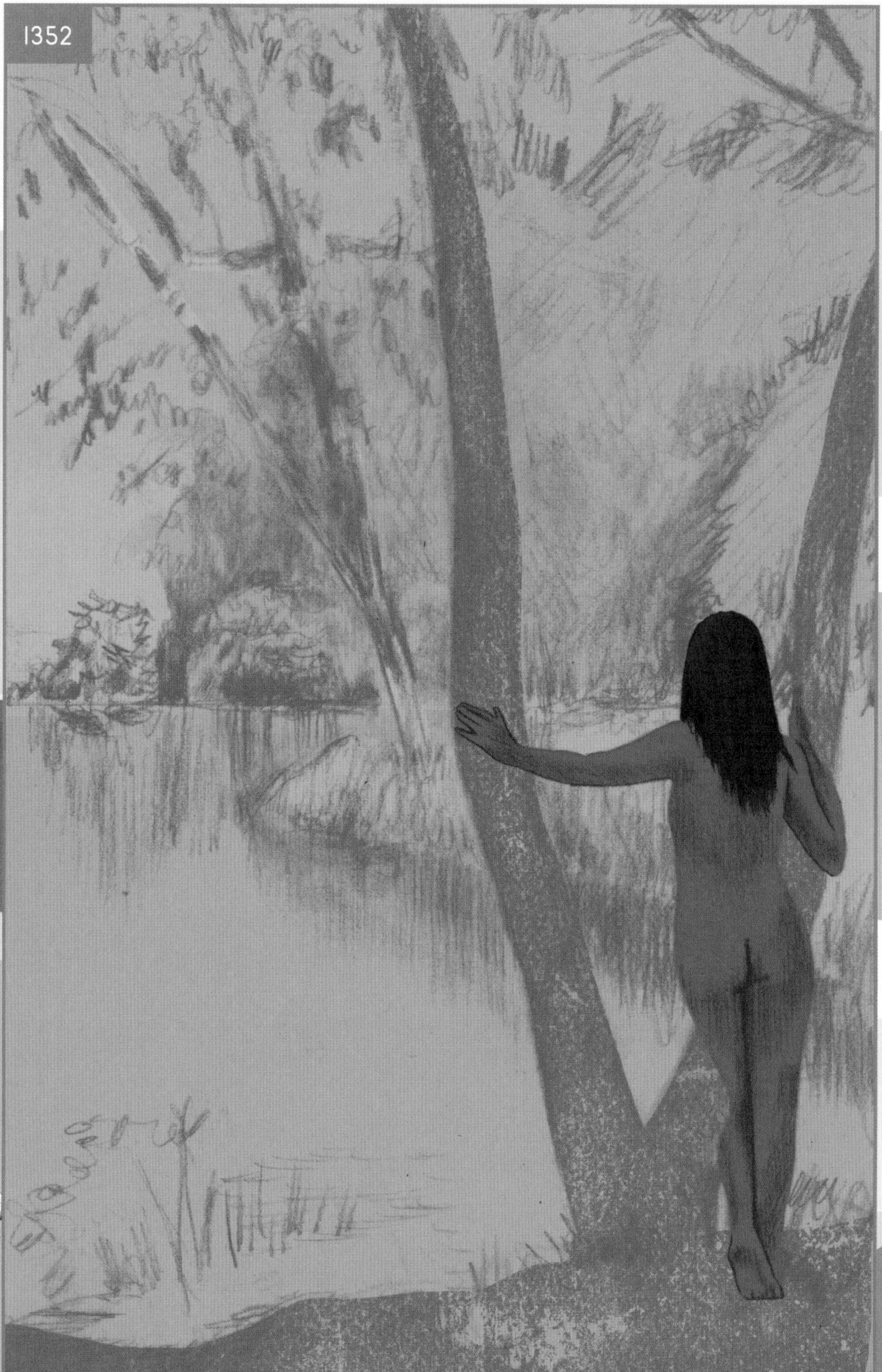
1352

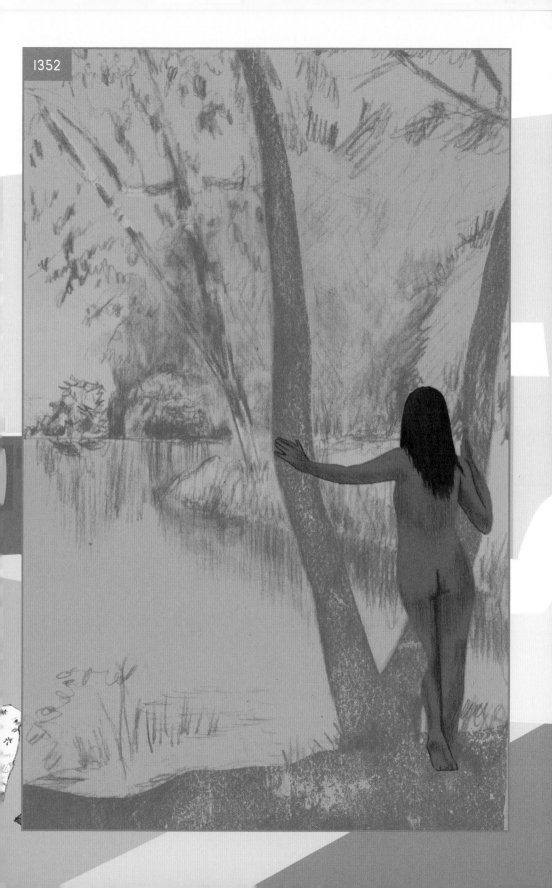

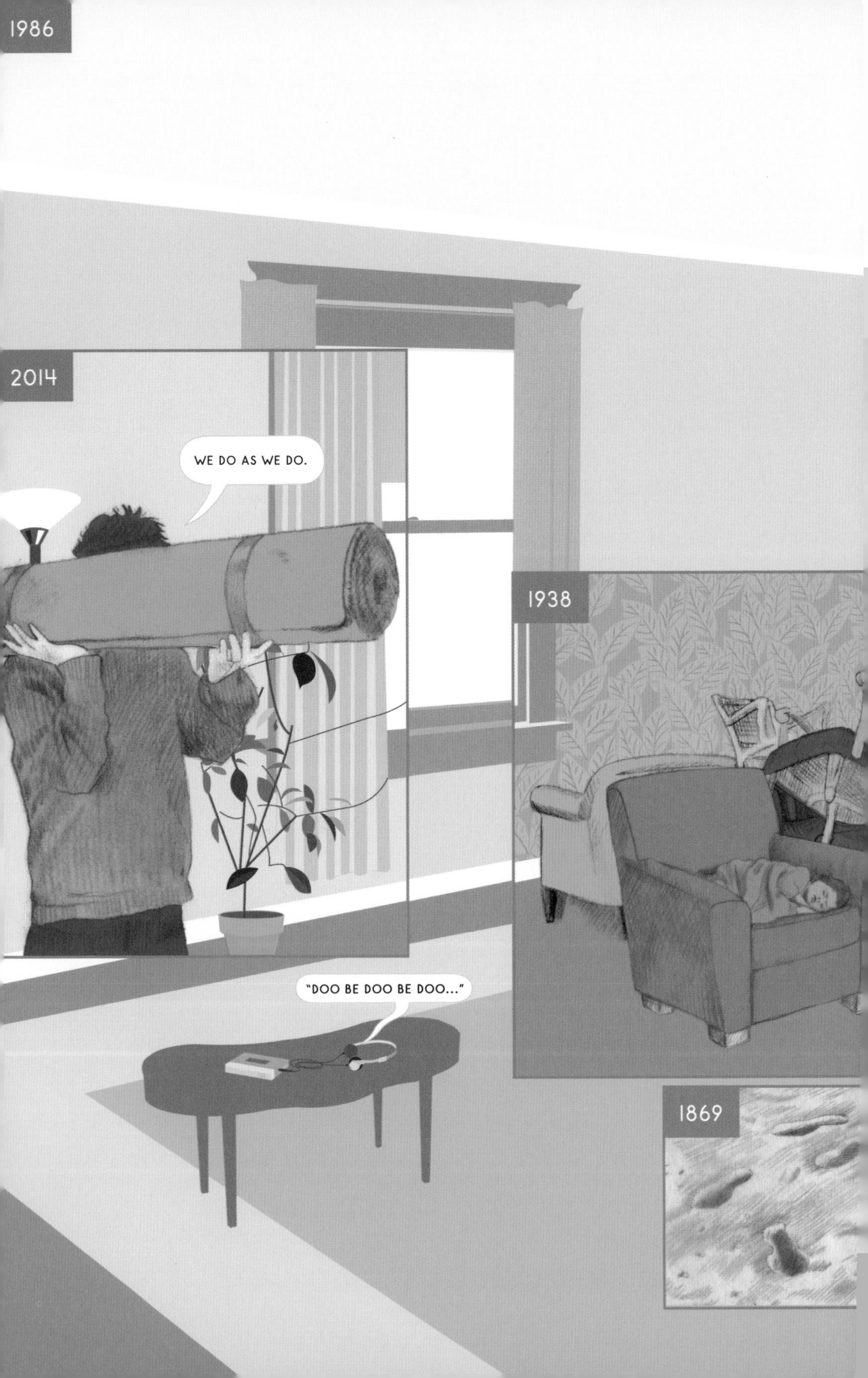
1986
2014
WE DO AS WE DO.
1938
"DOO BE DOO BE DOO..."
1869

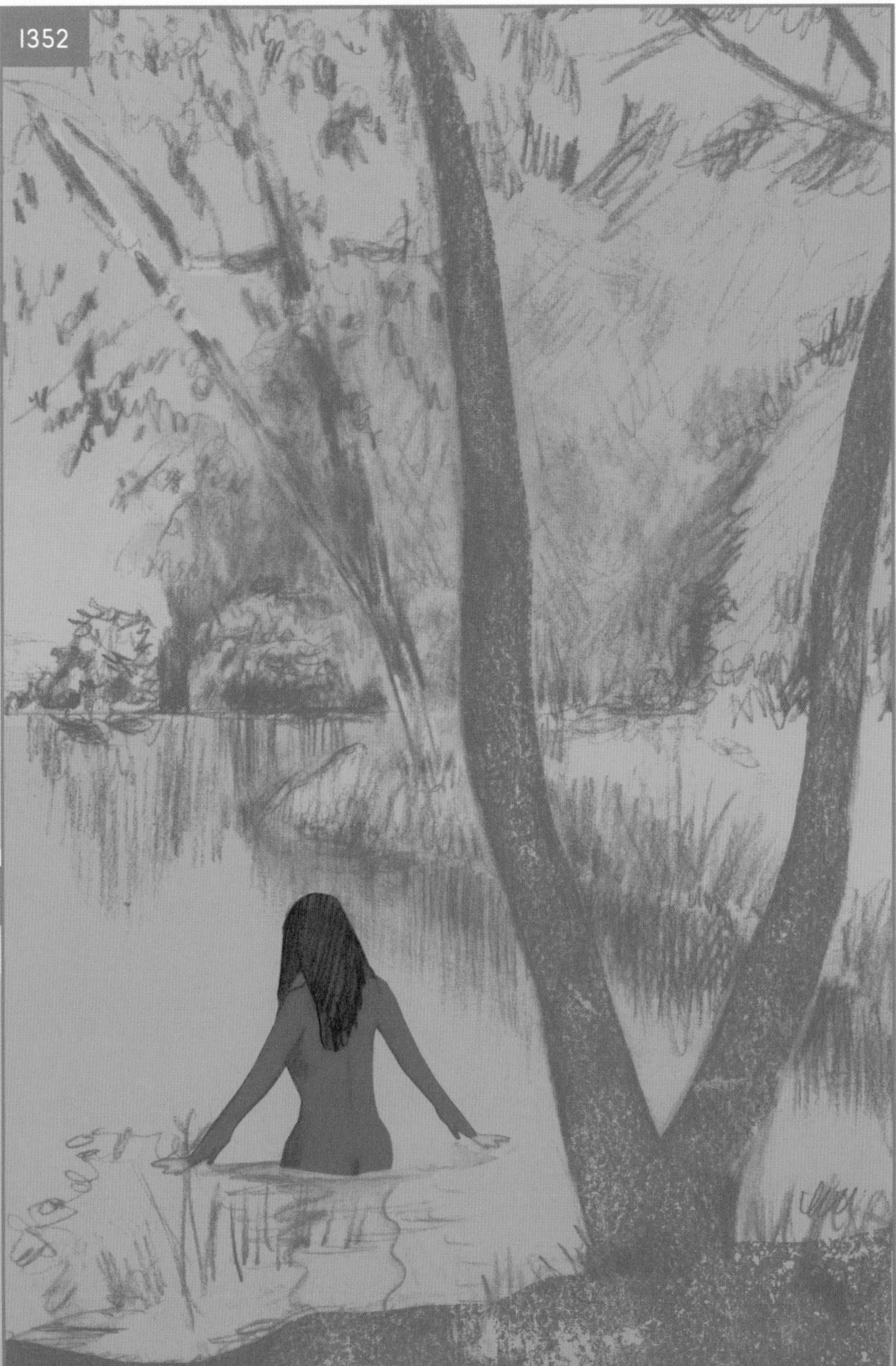
1352

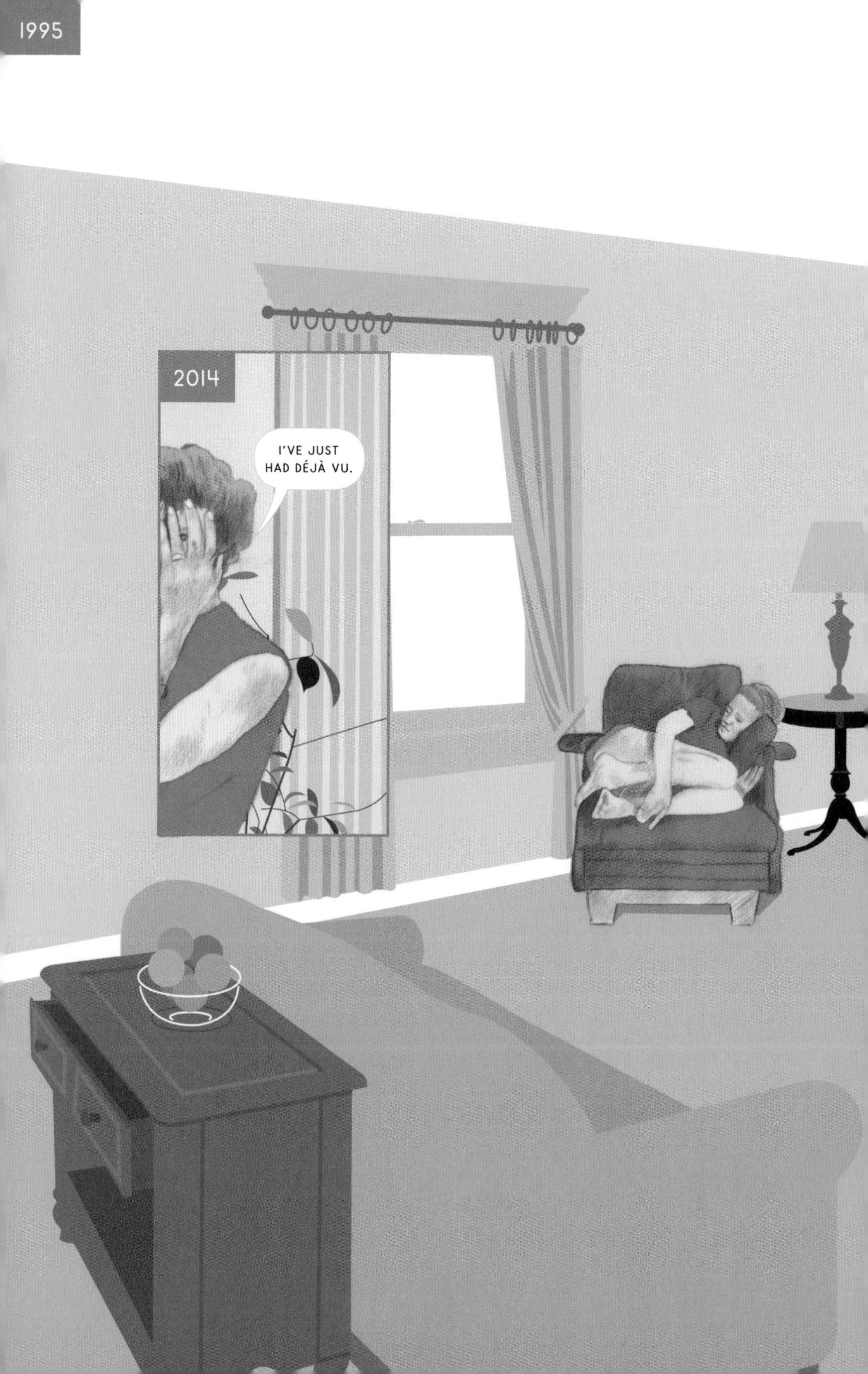
1995
2014
I'VE JUST HAD DÉJÀ VU.

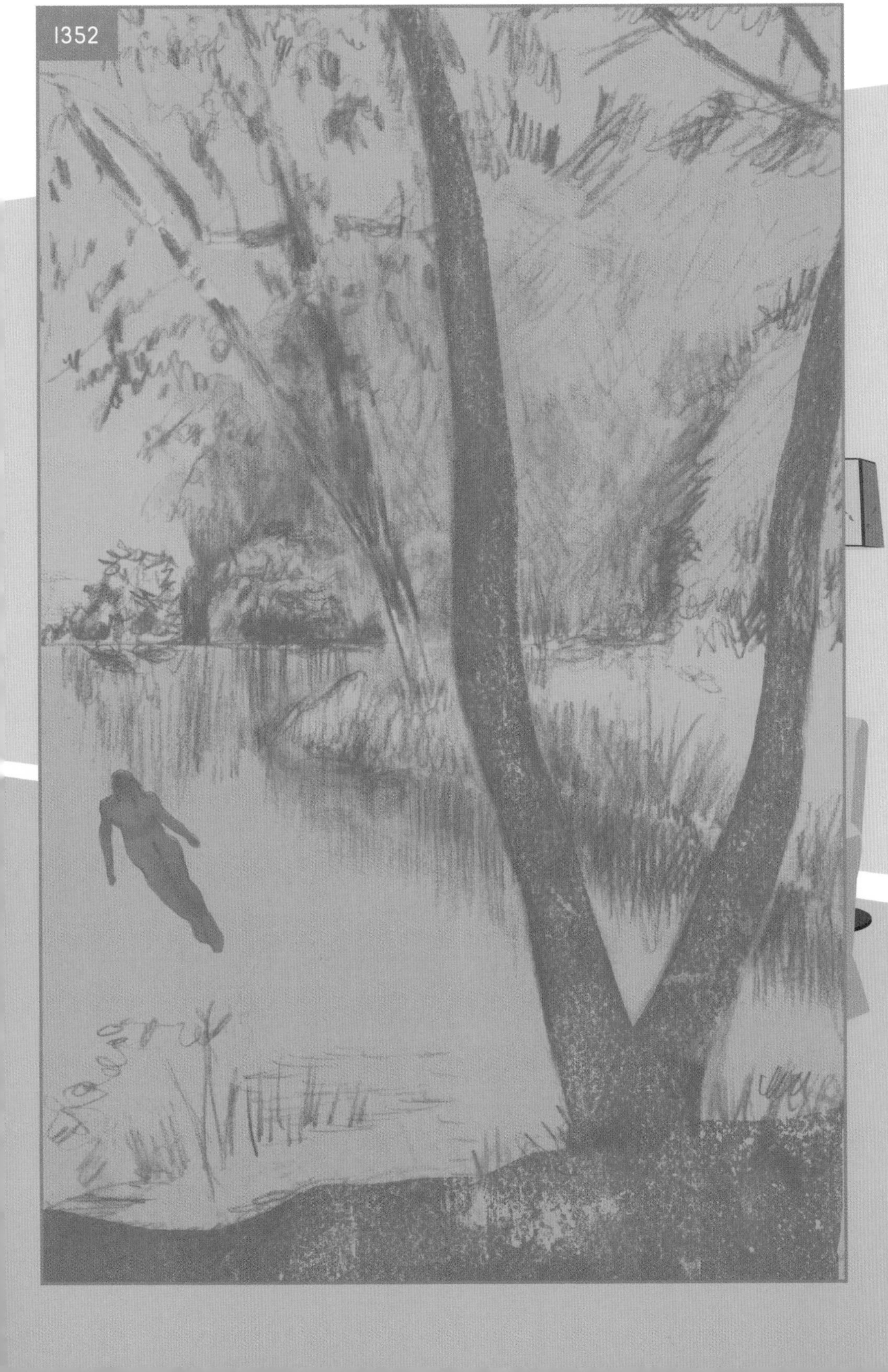

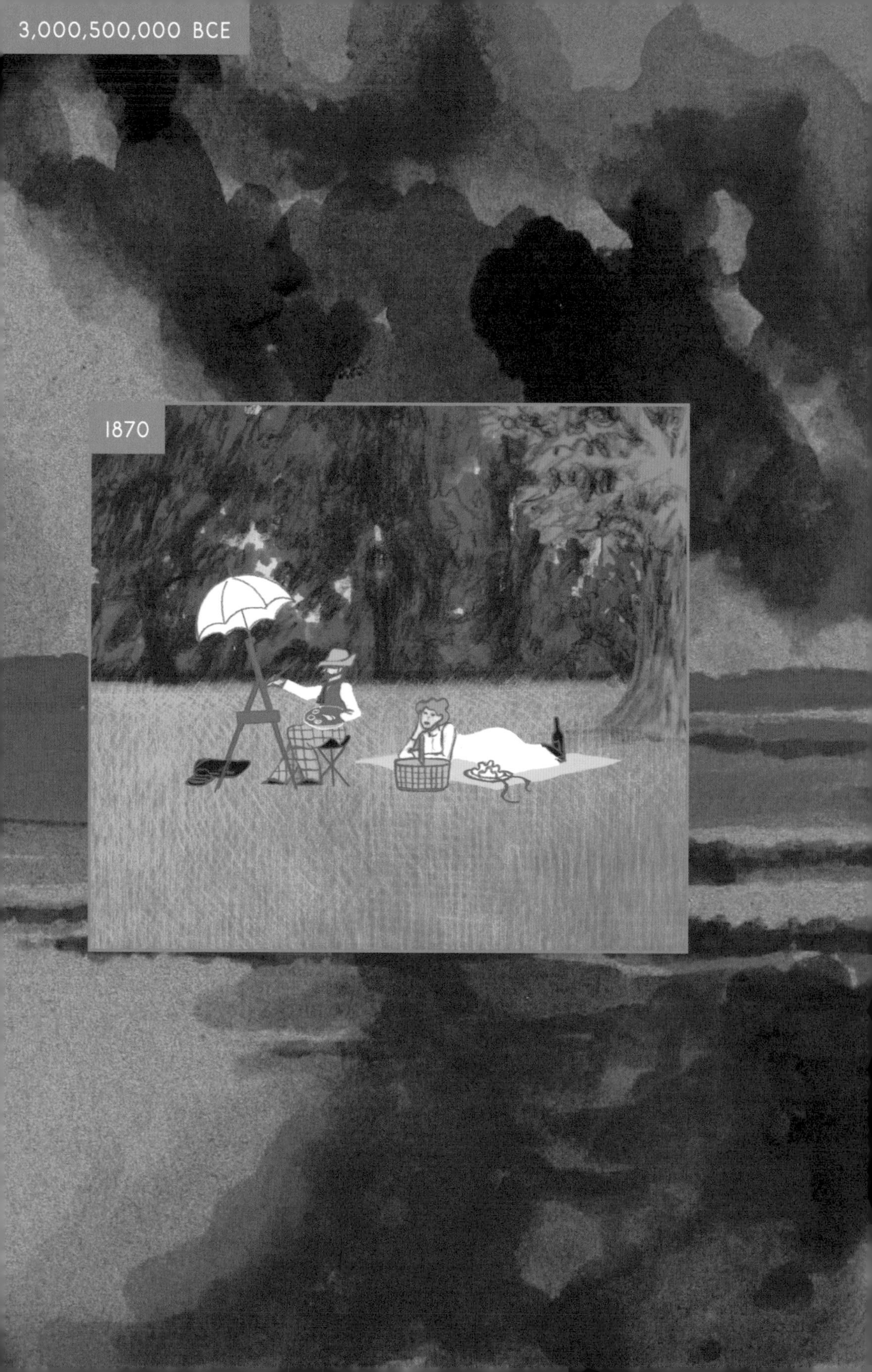
3,000,500,000 BCE
1870

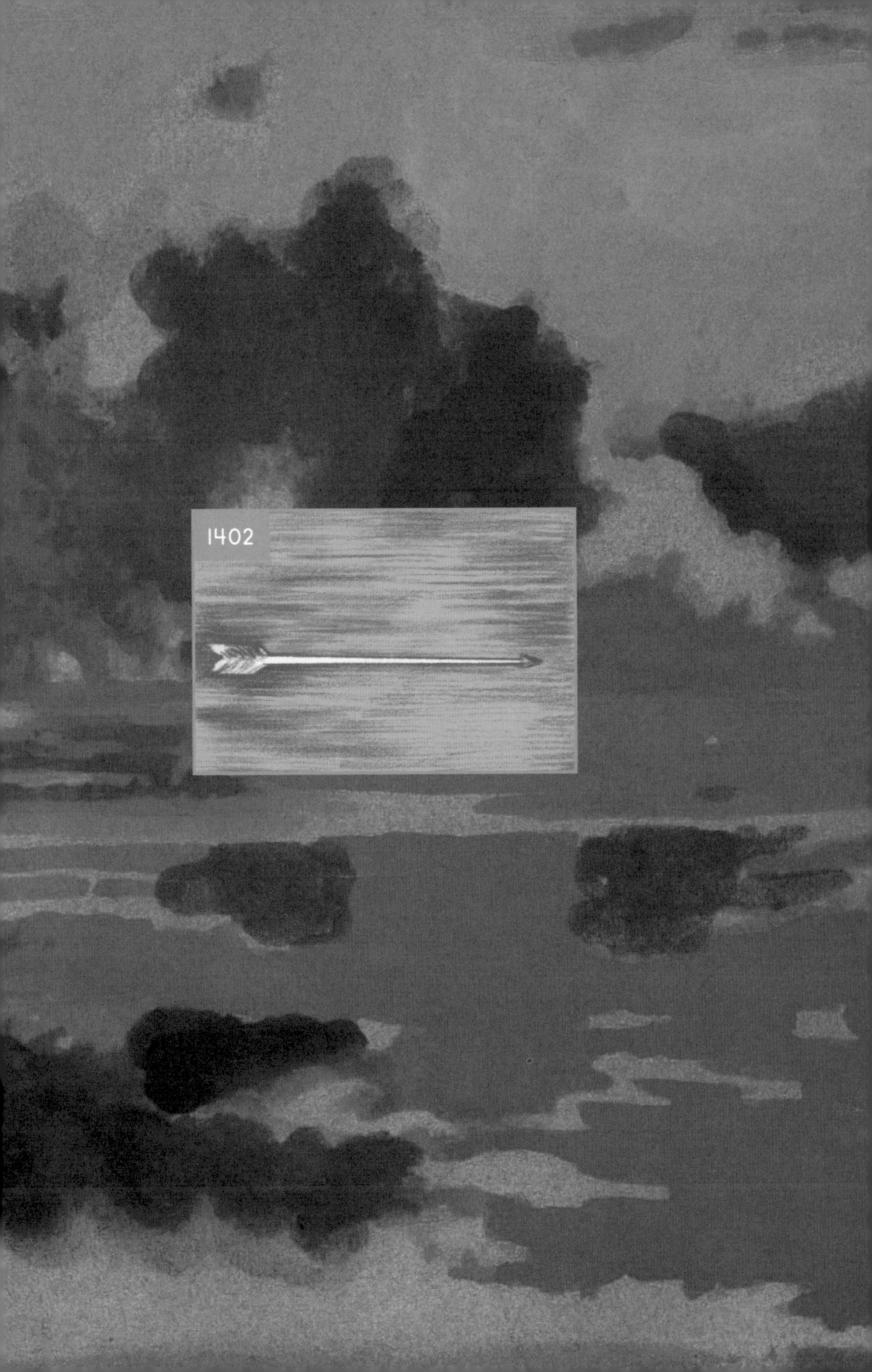
1402

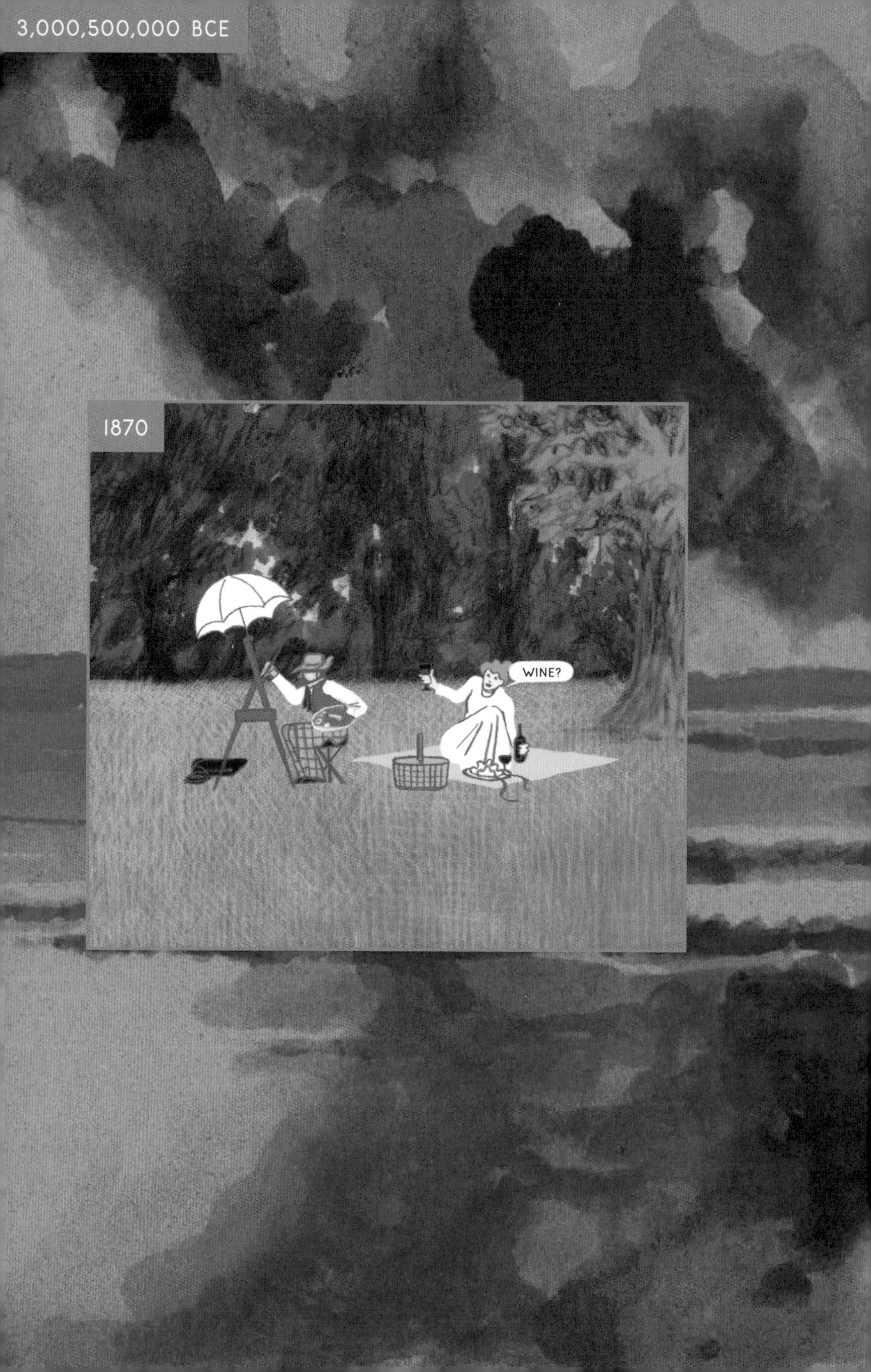
3,000,500,000 BCE
1870
WINE?

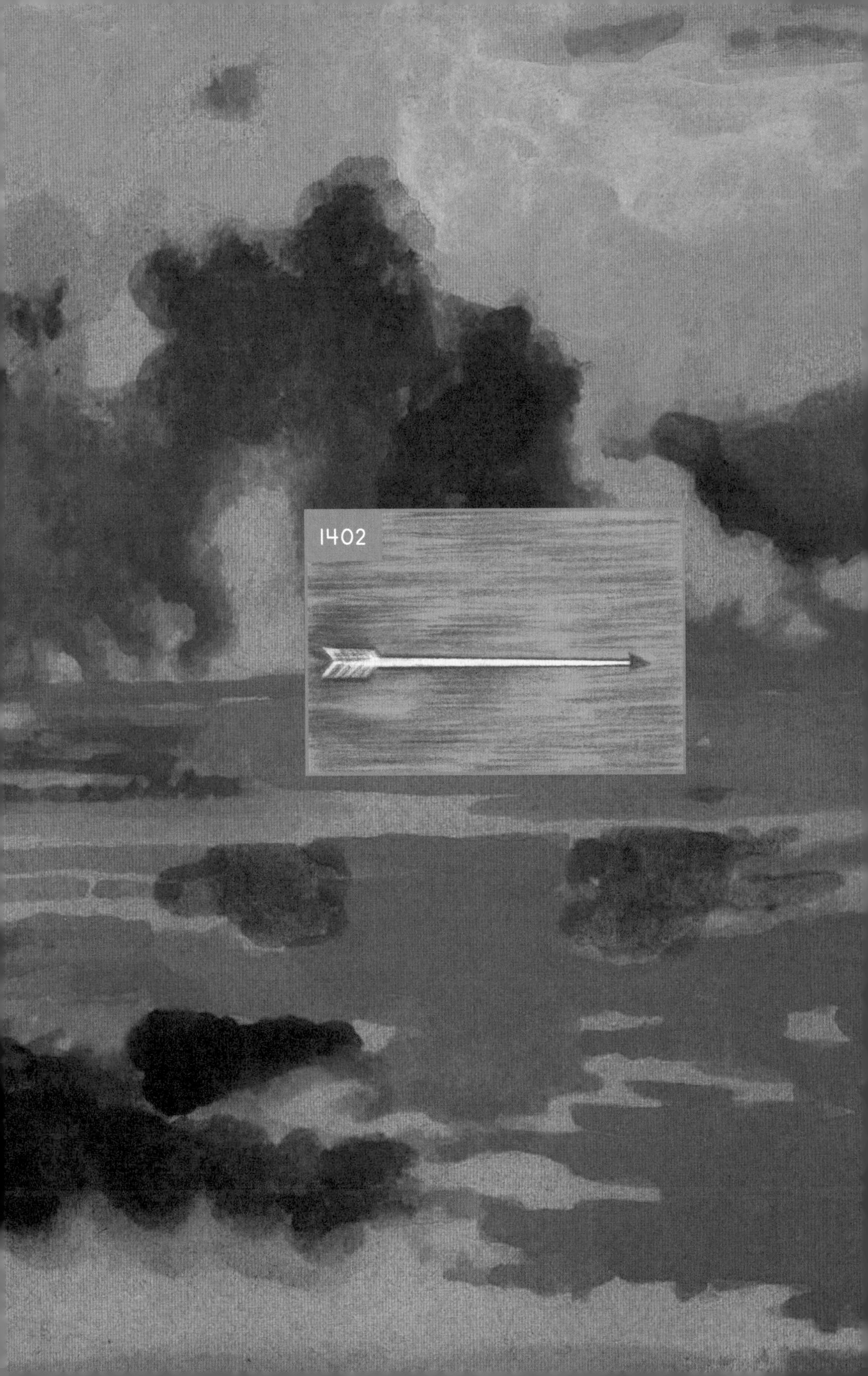
1402

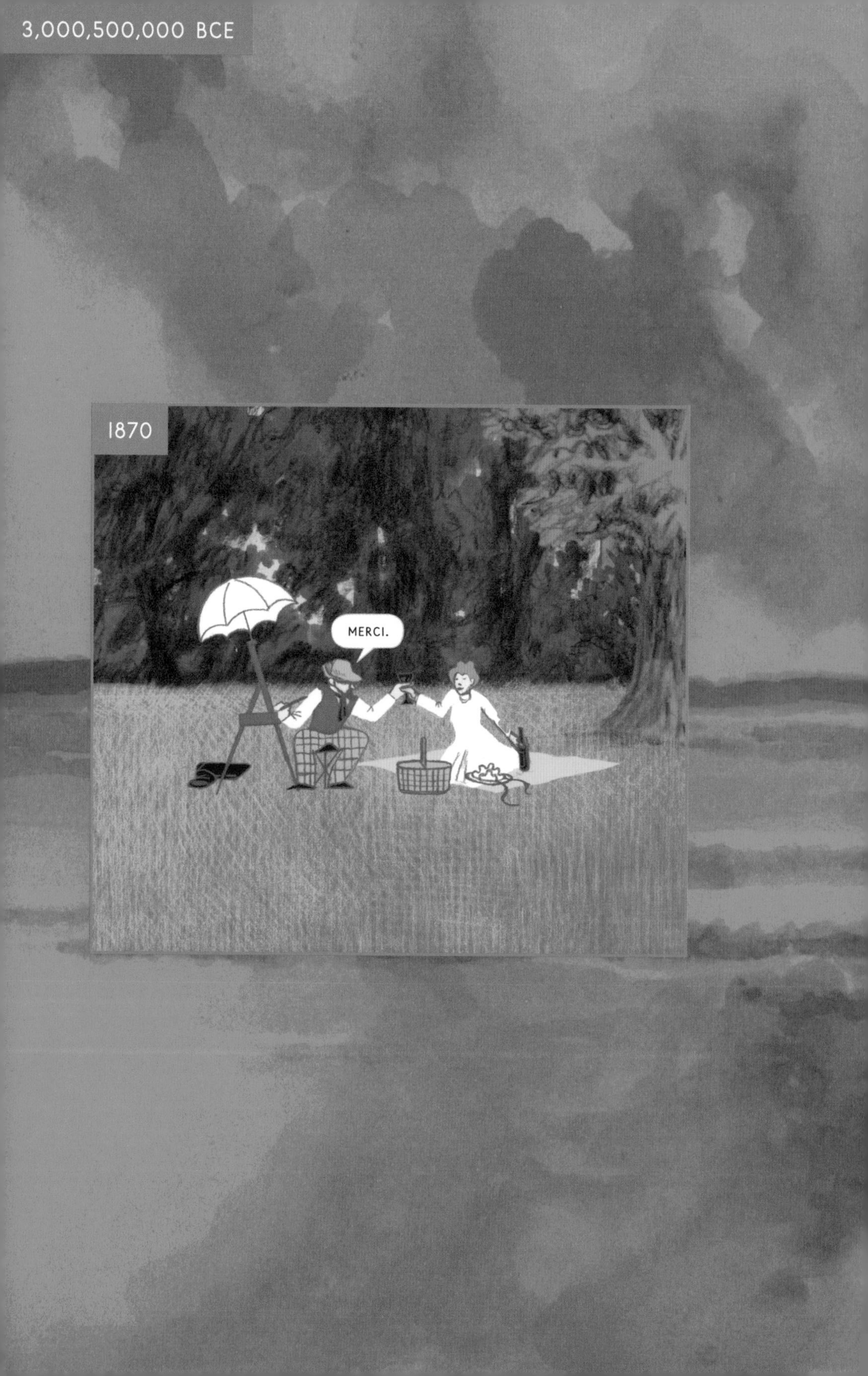
3,000,500,000 BCE
1870
MERCI.

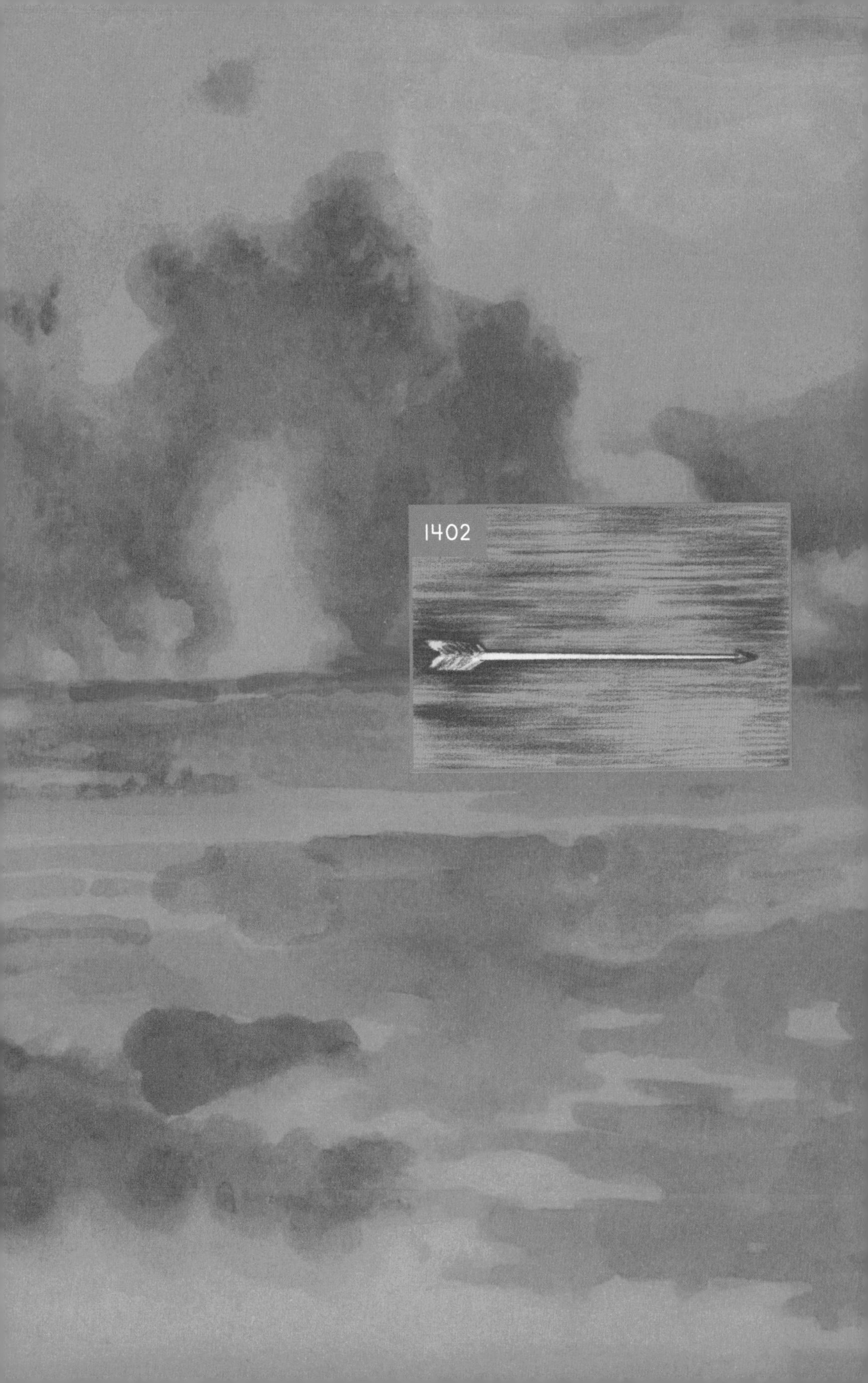
1402

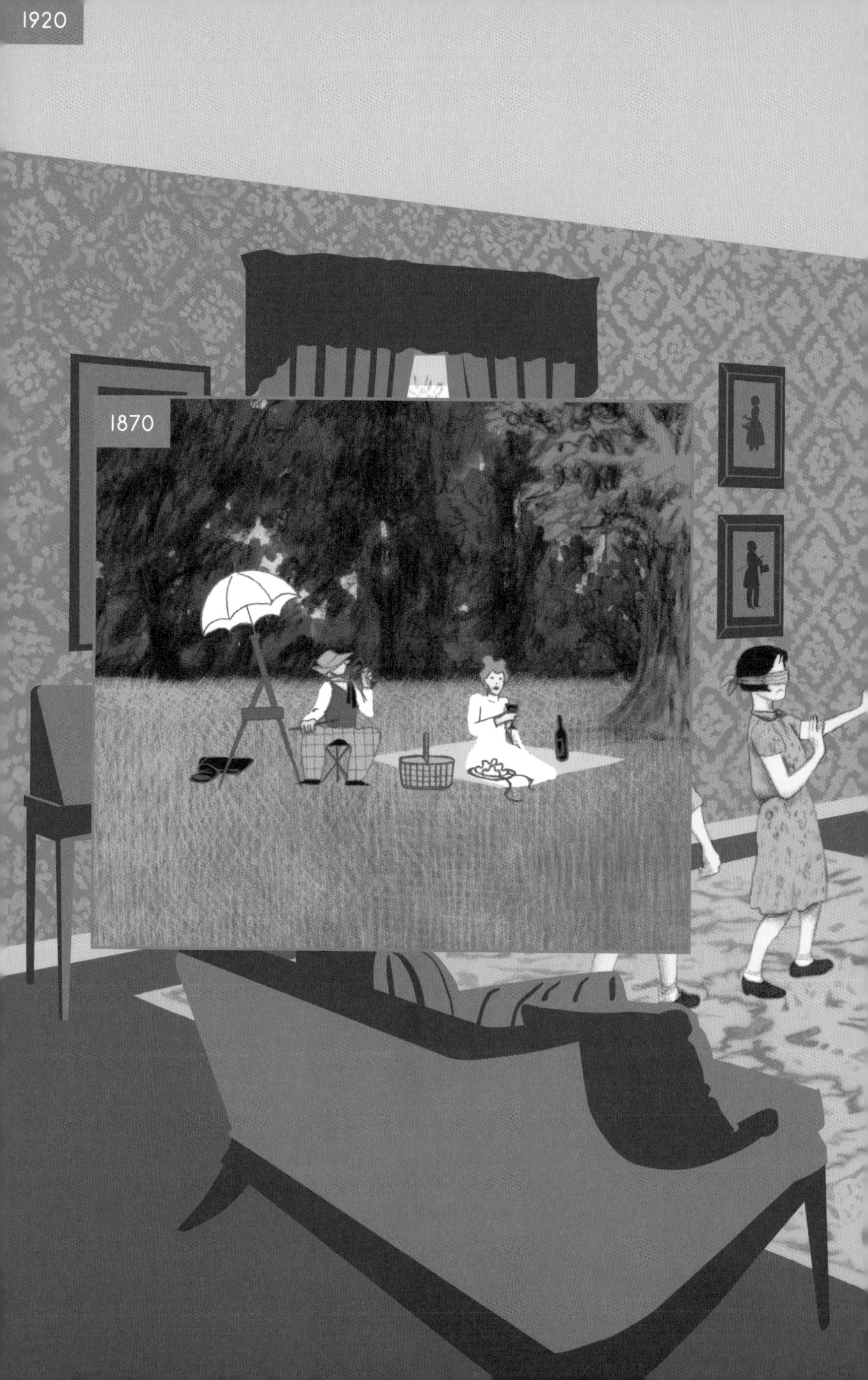
1920
1870

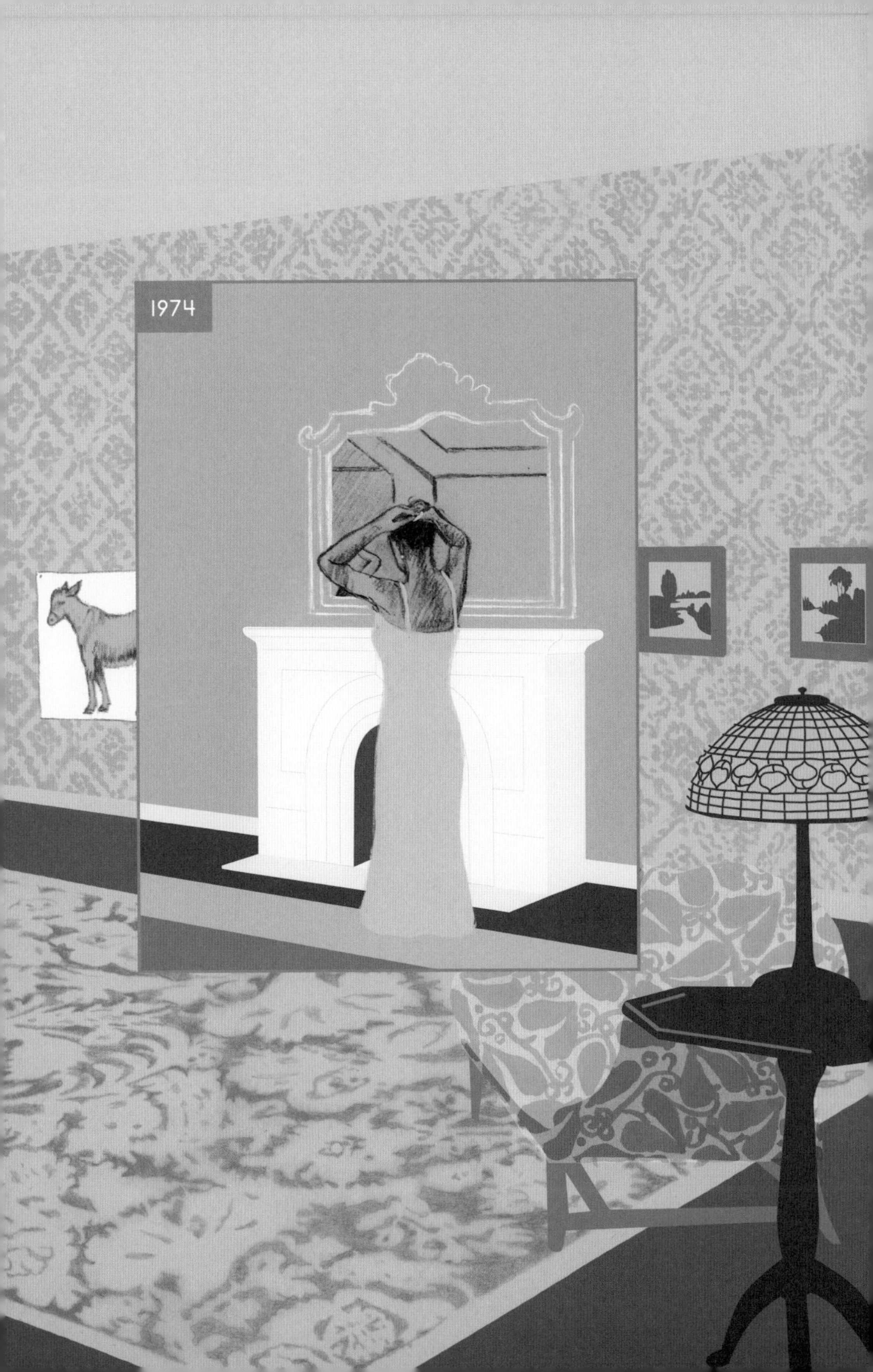
1974

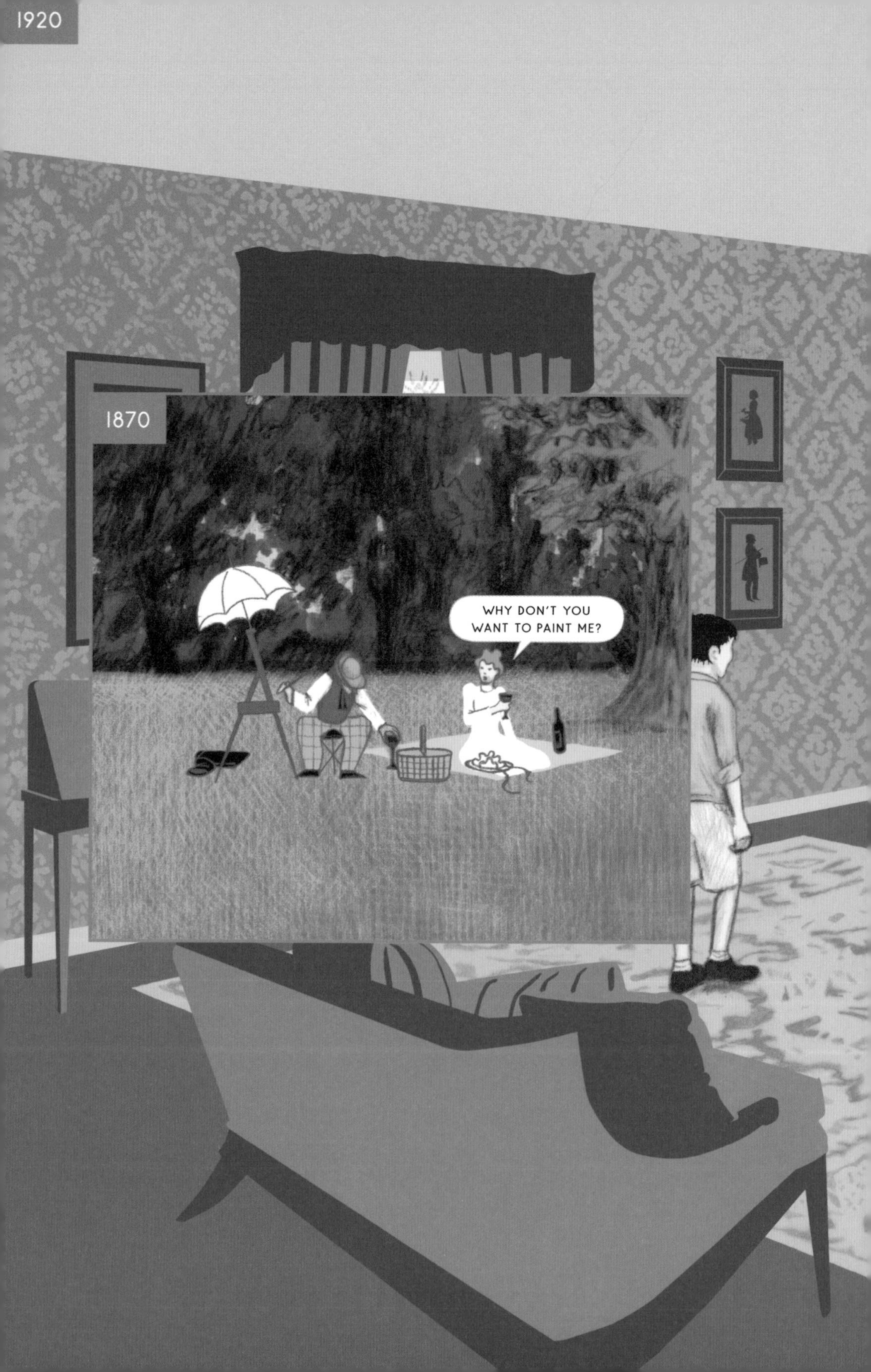
1920
1870
WHY DON'T YOU WANT TO PAINT ME?

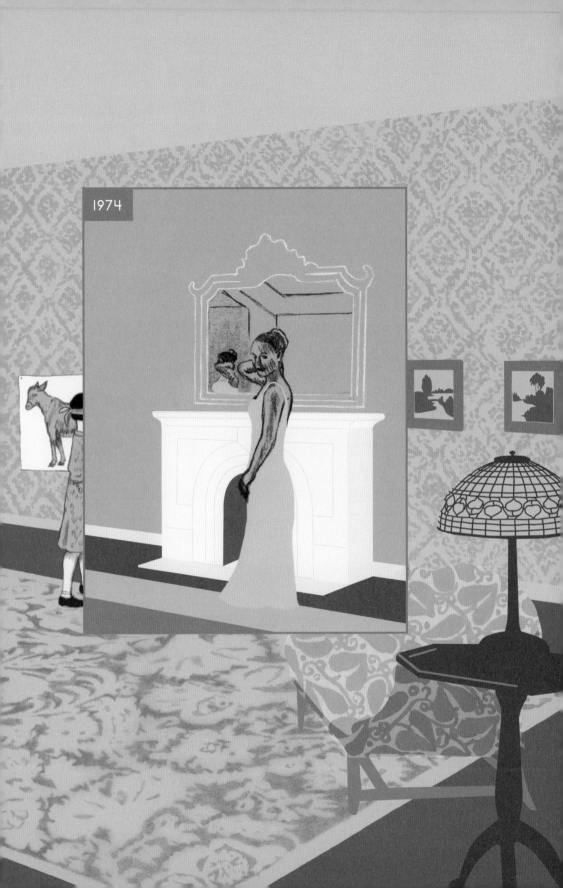

1974

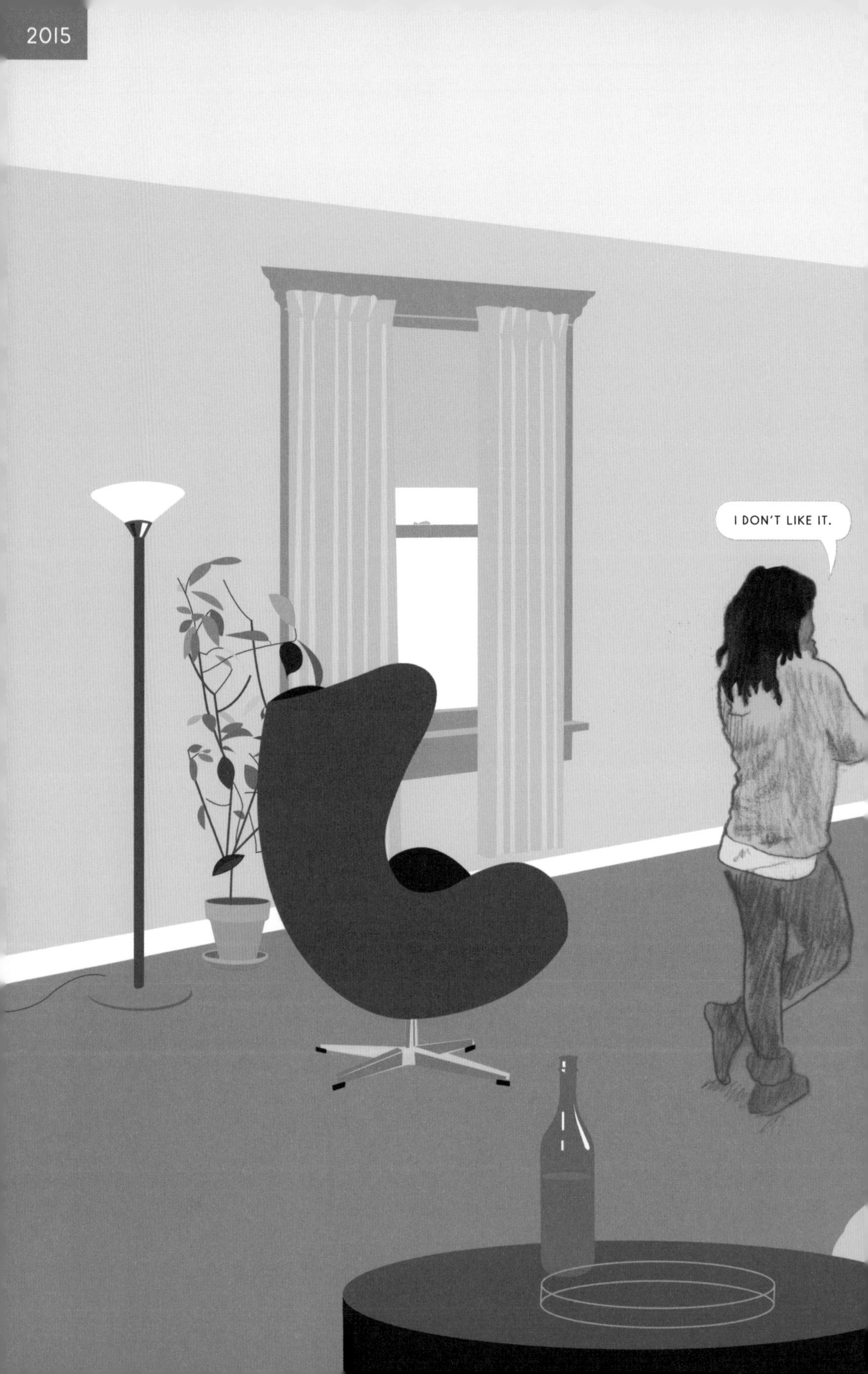
2015
I DON'T LIKE IT.

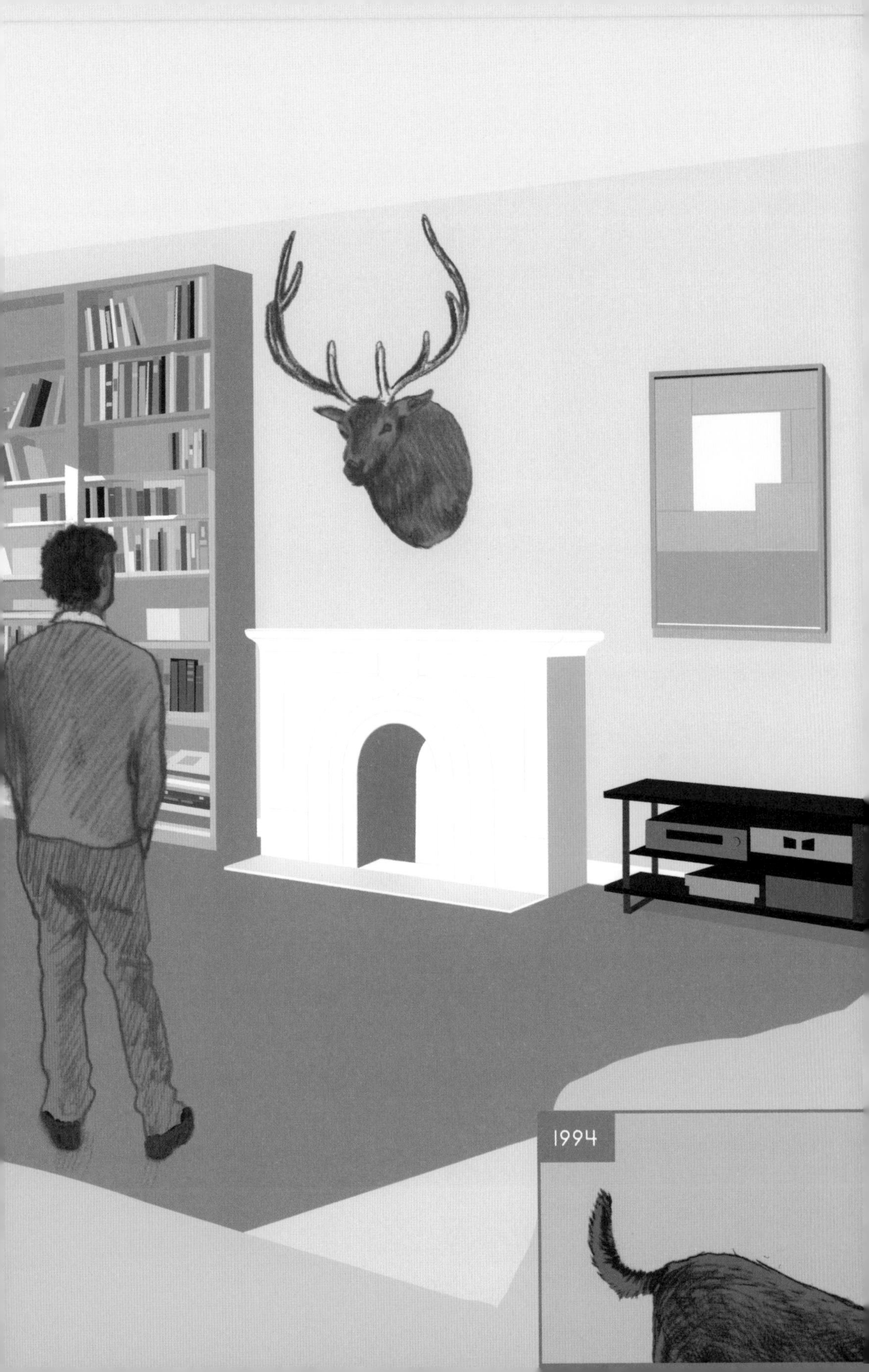
1994

1984
WHAT'S THE STORY WITH THAT BUILDING ACROSS THE STREET?
1929

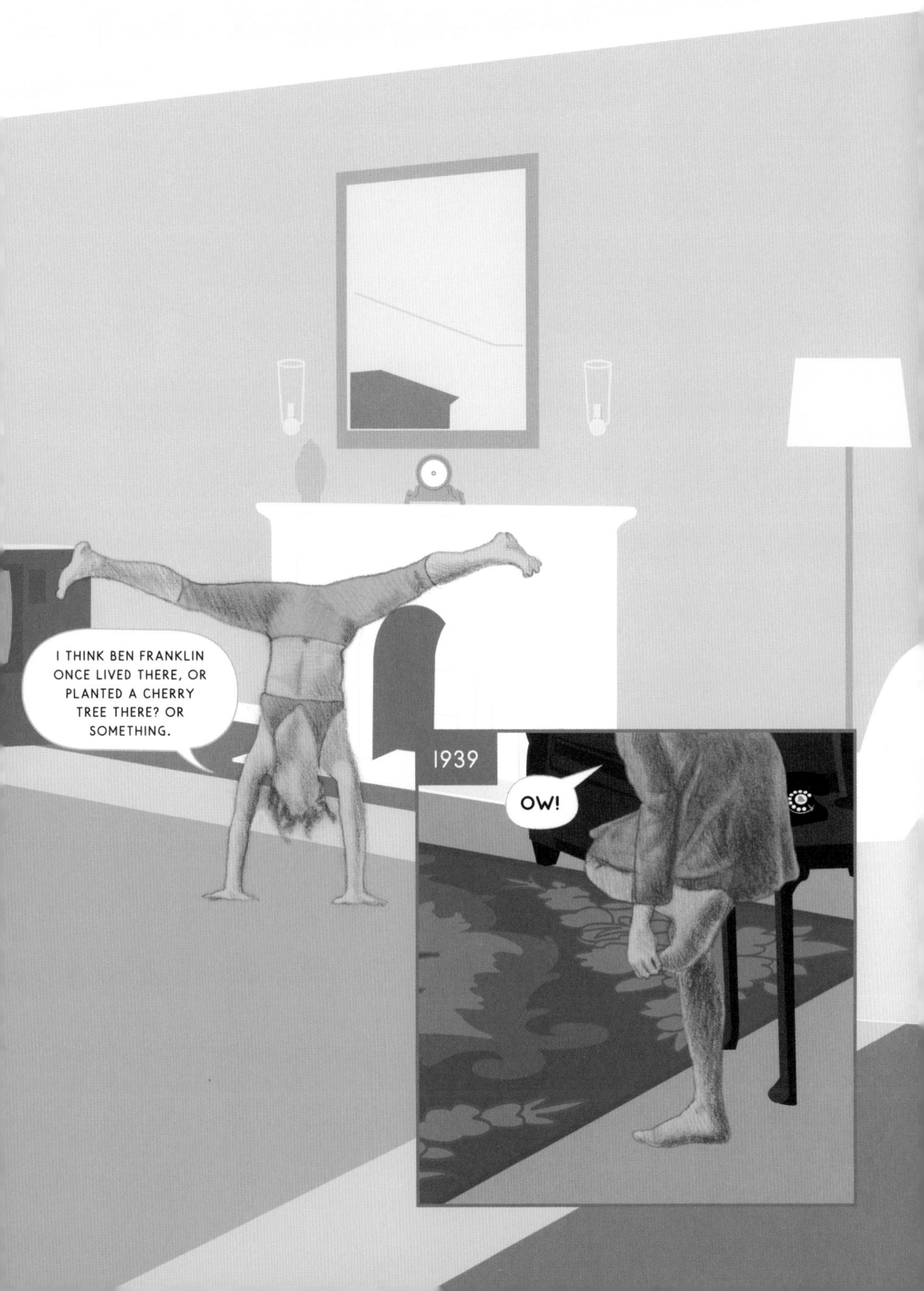
I THINK BEN FRANKLIN ONCE LIVED THERE, OR PLANTED A CHERRY TREE THERE? OR SOMETHING.
1939
OW!

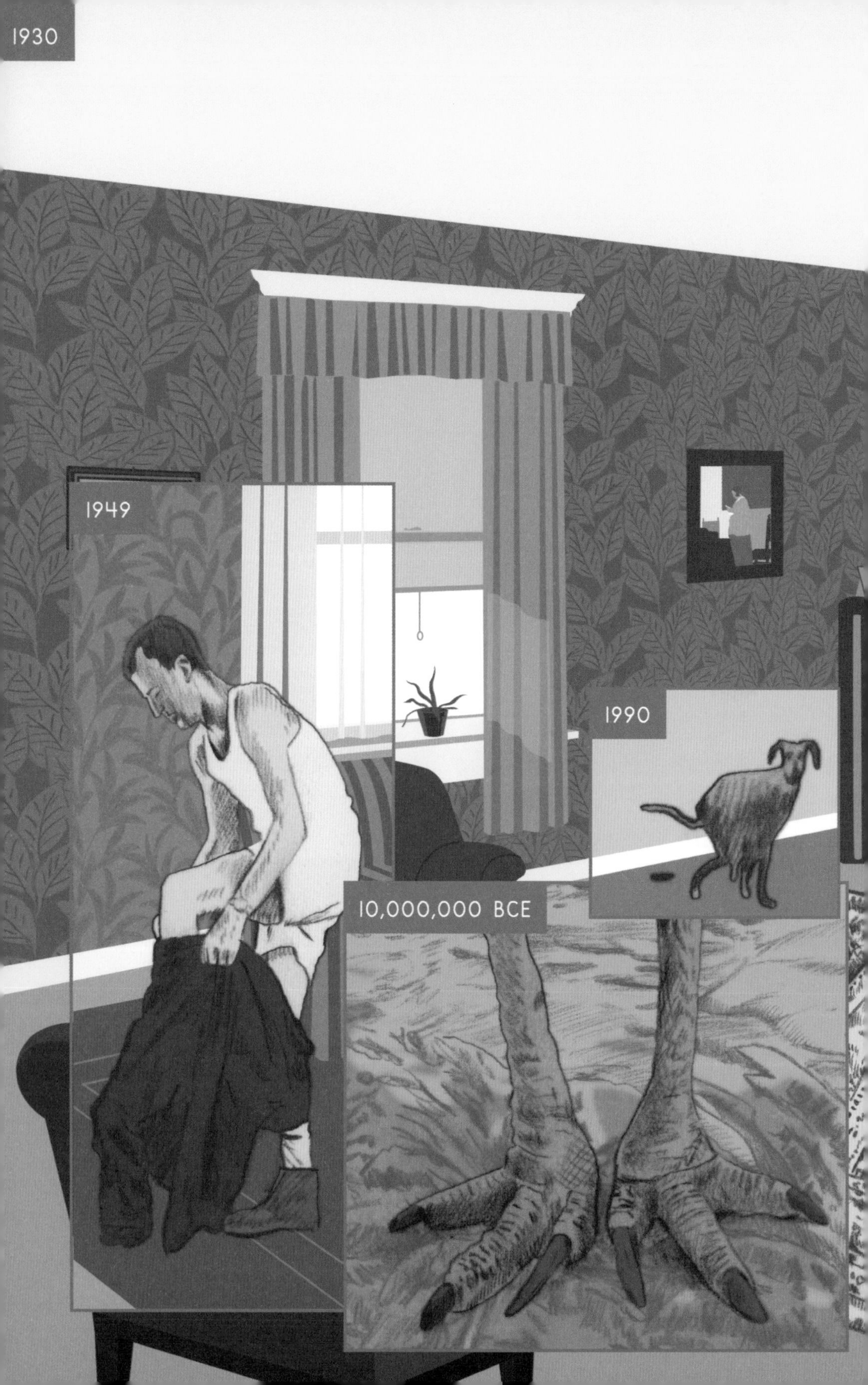
1930
1949
1990
10,000,000 BCE

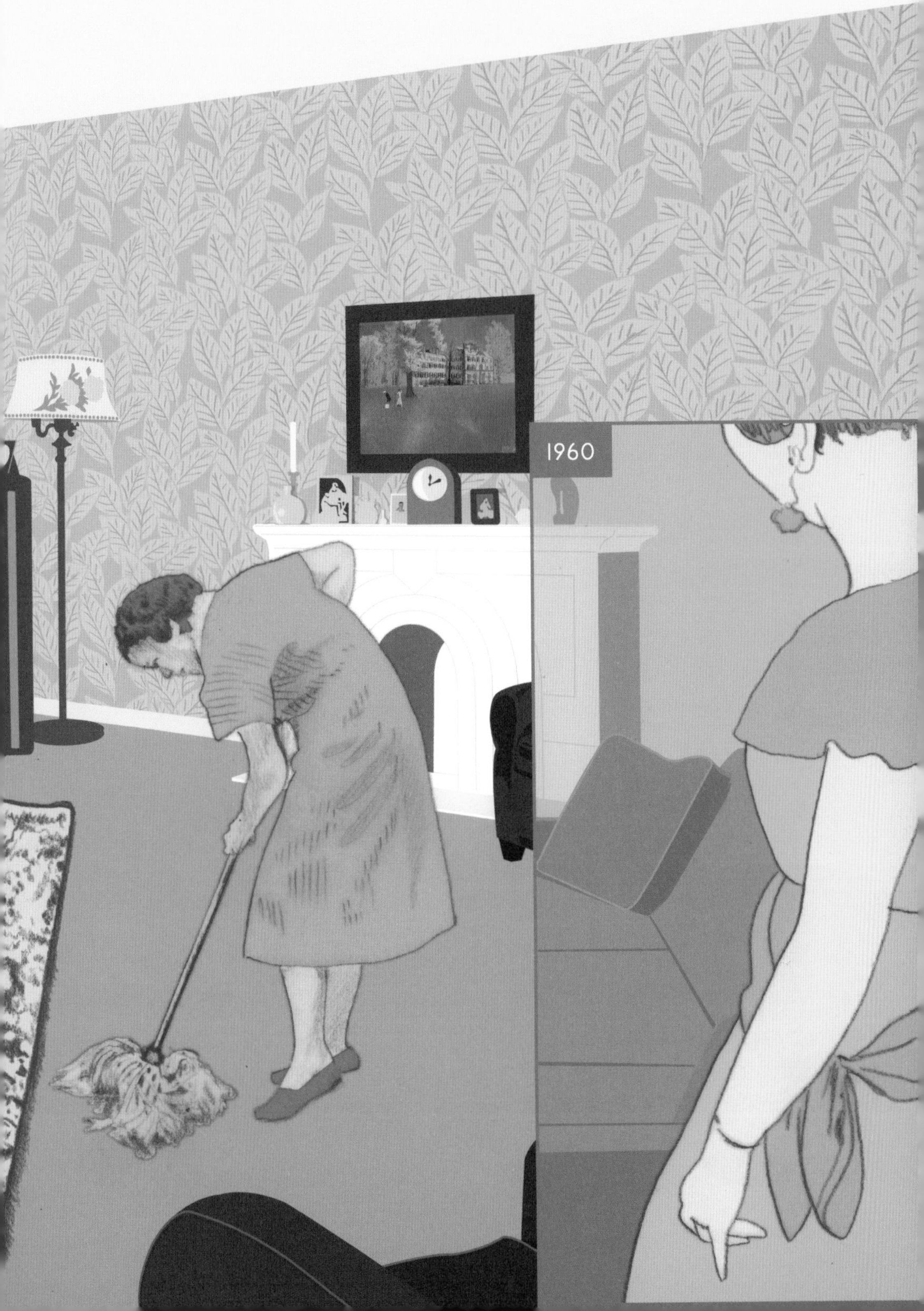
1960

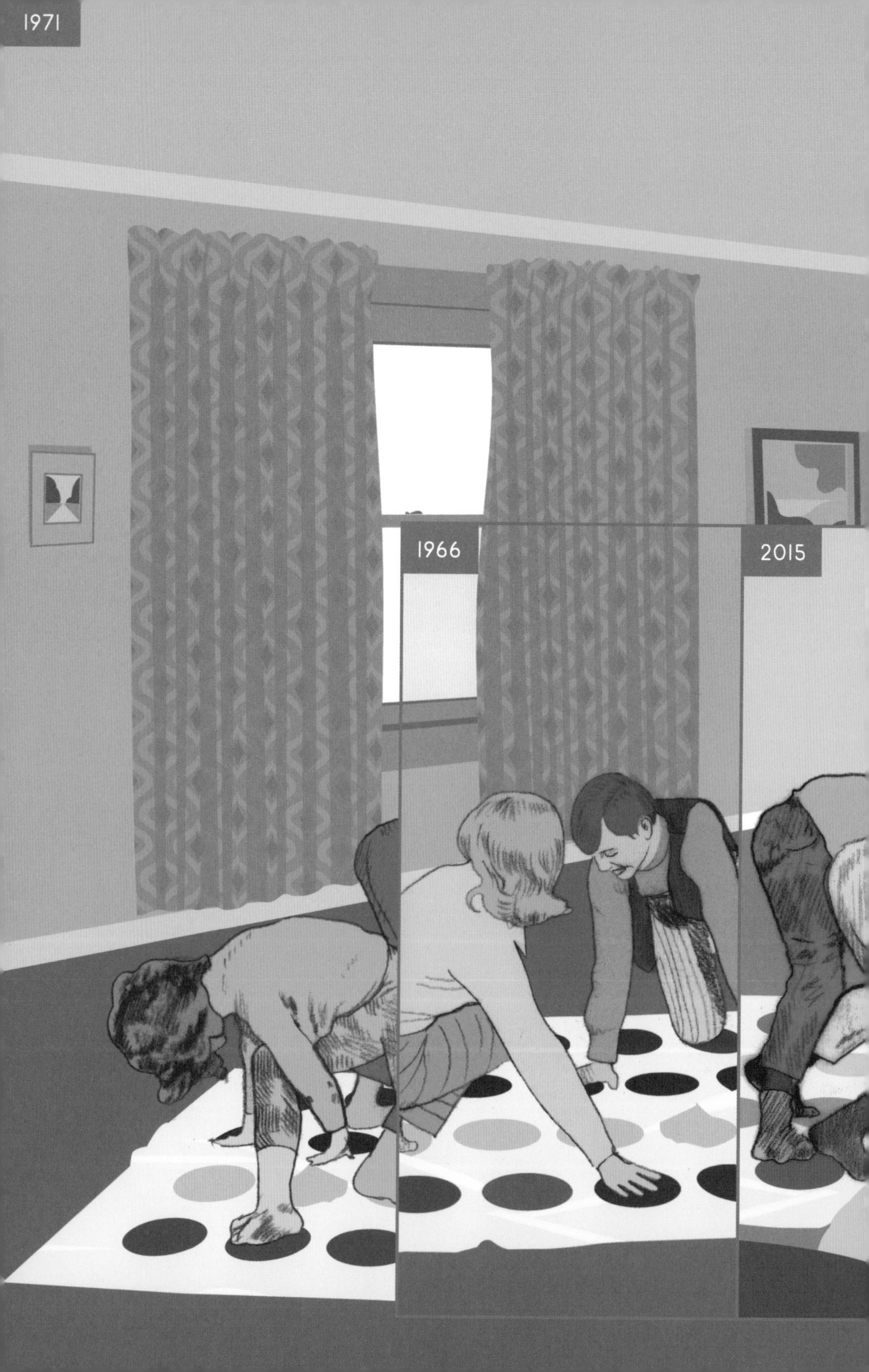
1971
1966
2015

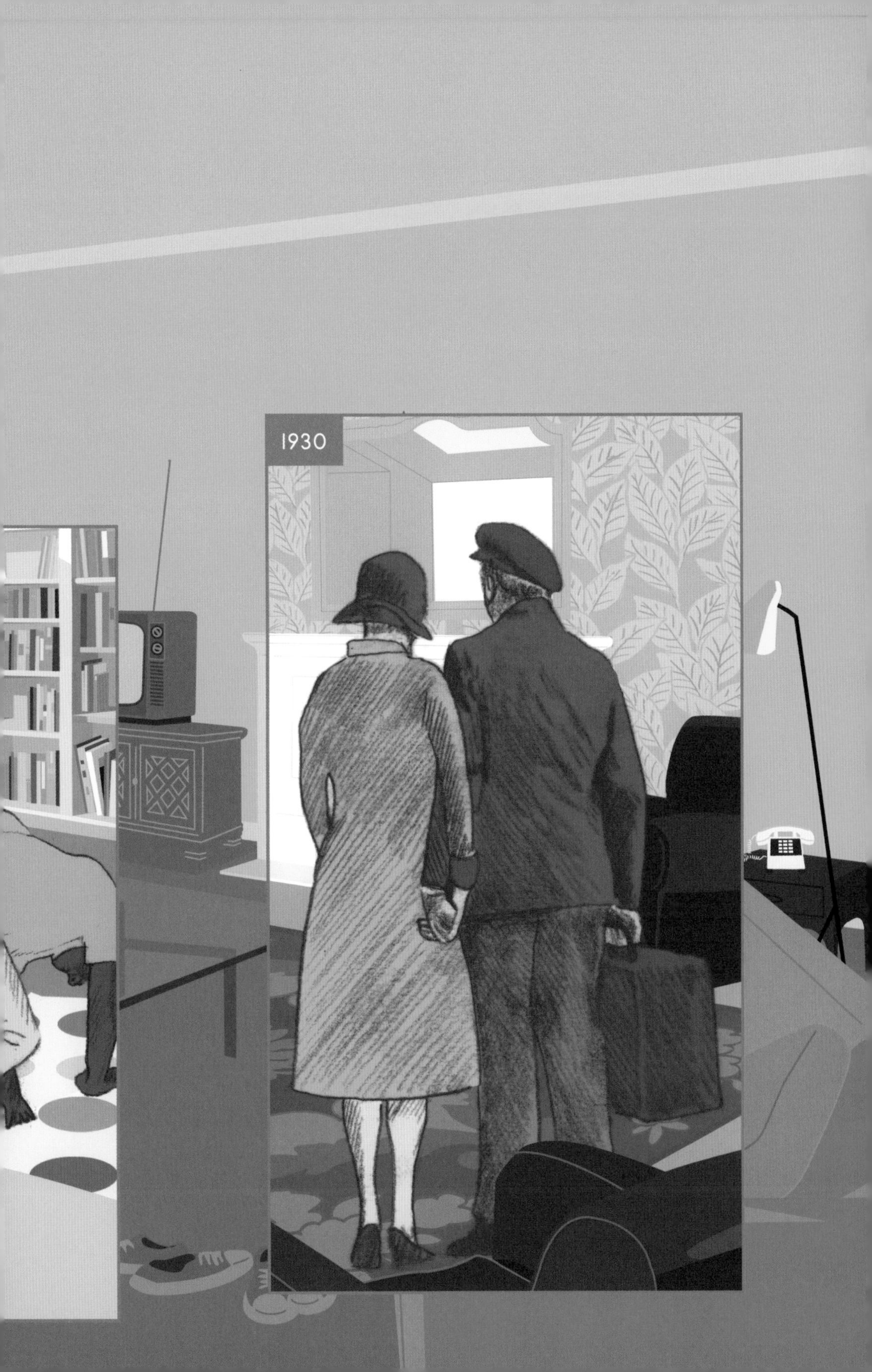
1930

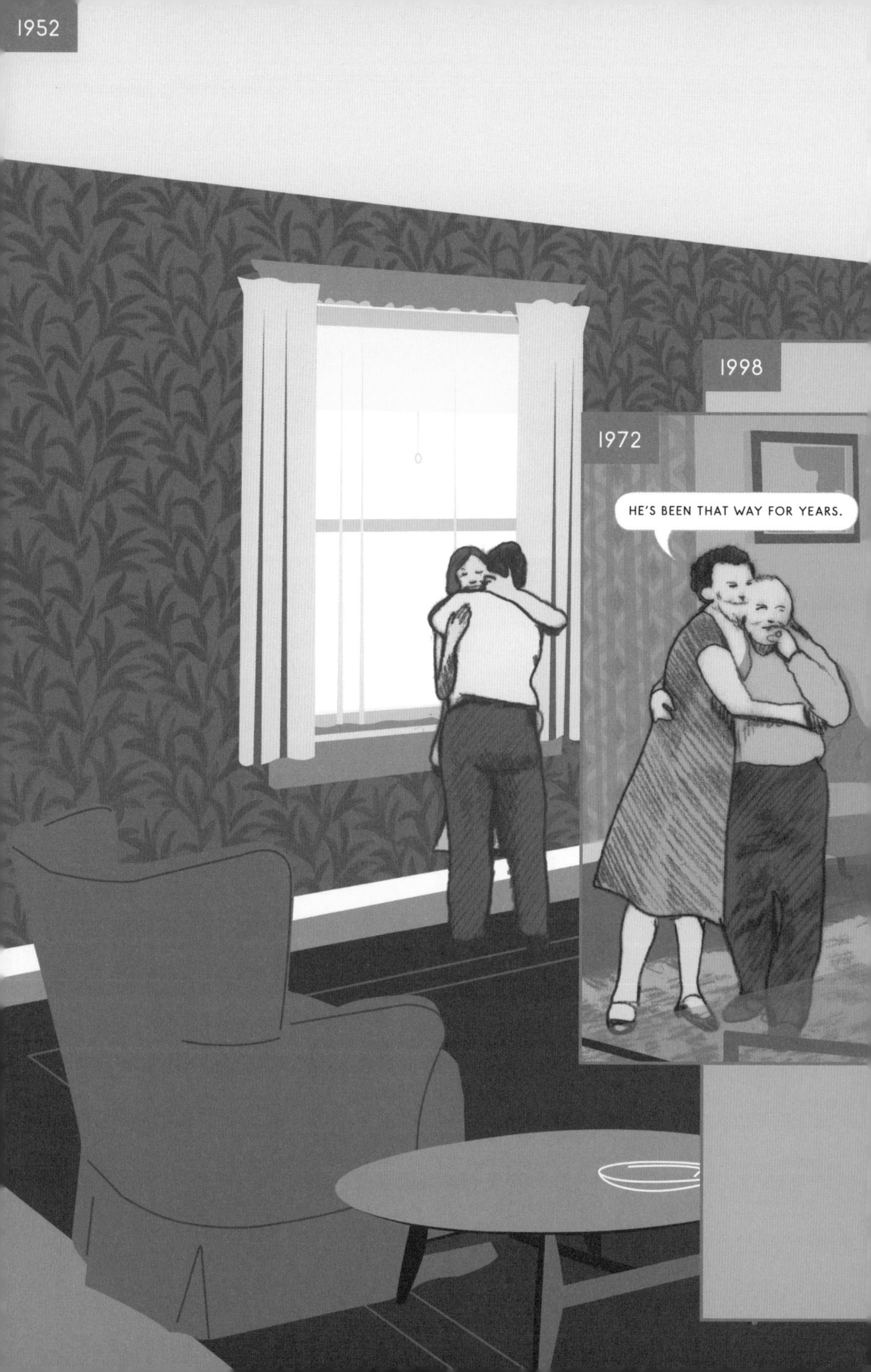
1952
1998
1972
HE'S BEEN THAT WAY FOR YEARS.

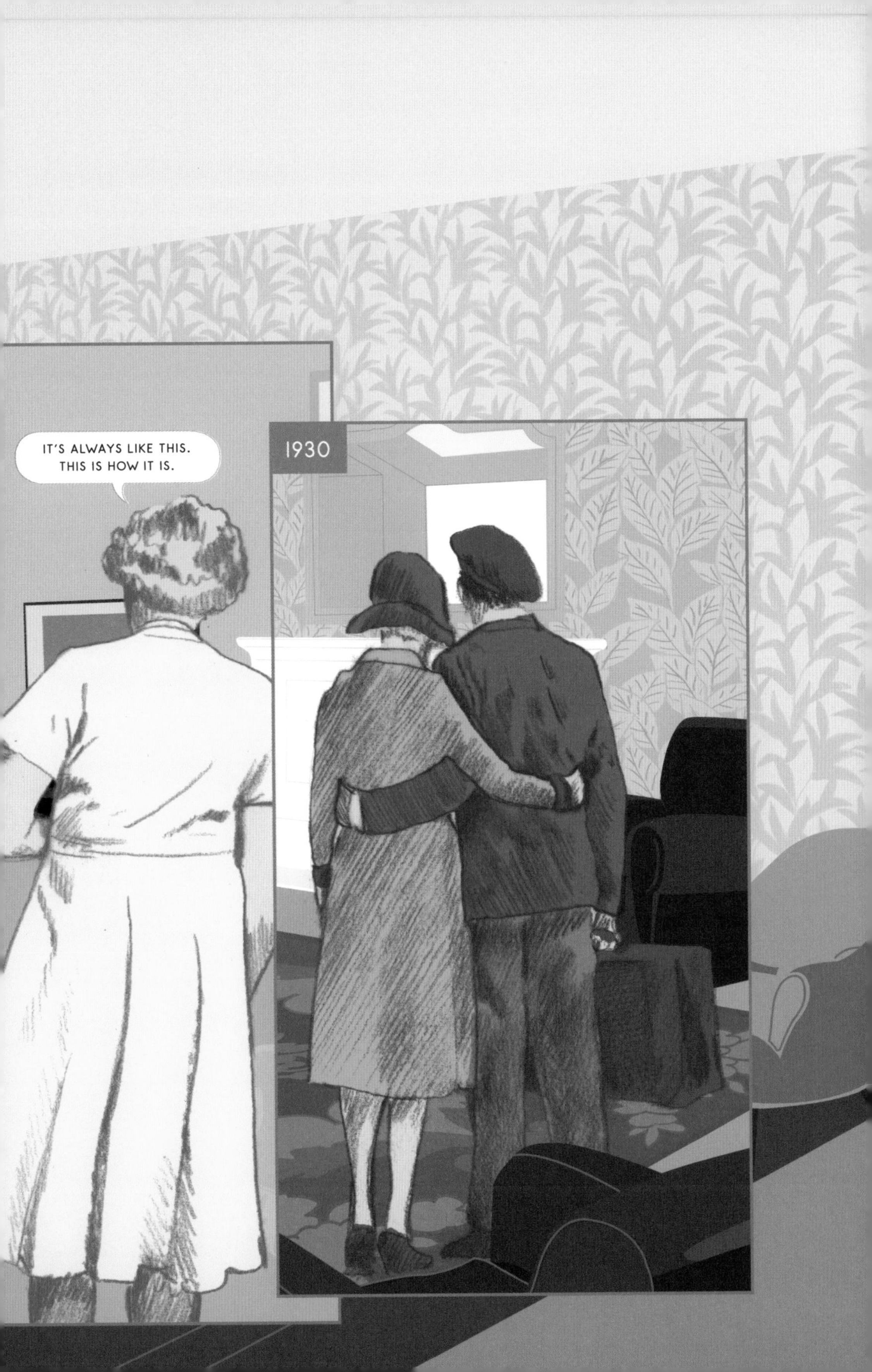
IT'S ALWAYS LIKE THIS. THIS IS HOW IT IS.
1930

1973
WHAT ARE YOU TWO DOING?
THIS IS OUR **FORT!**
YOU HAVE TO KNOW THE PASSWORD TO COME IN!

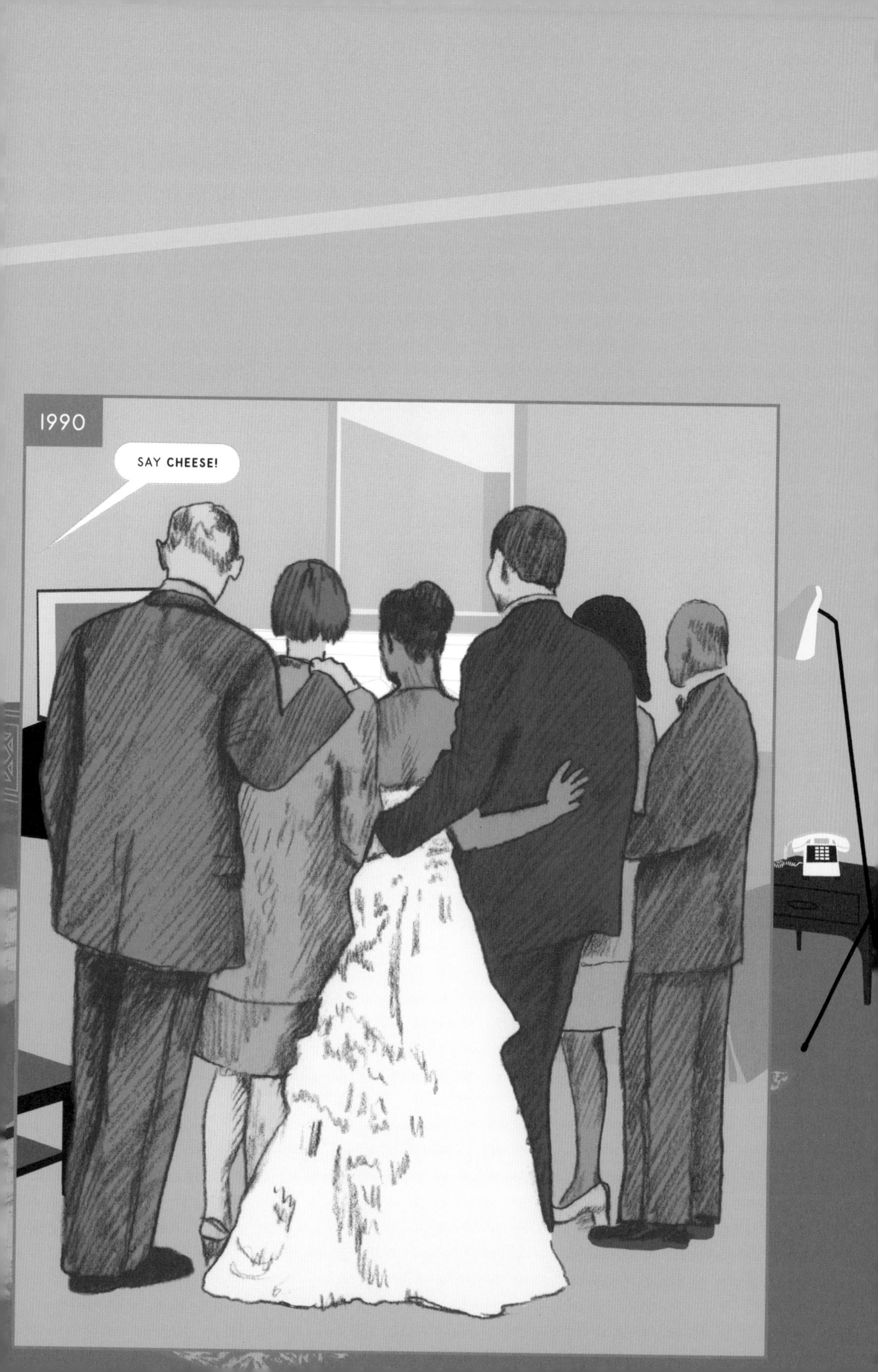
1990
SAY CHEESE!

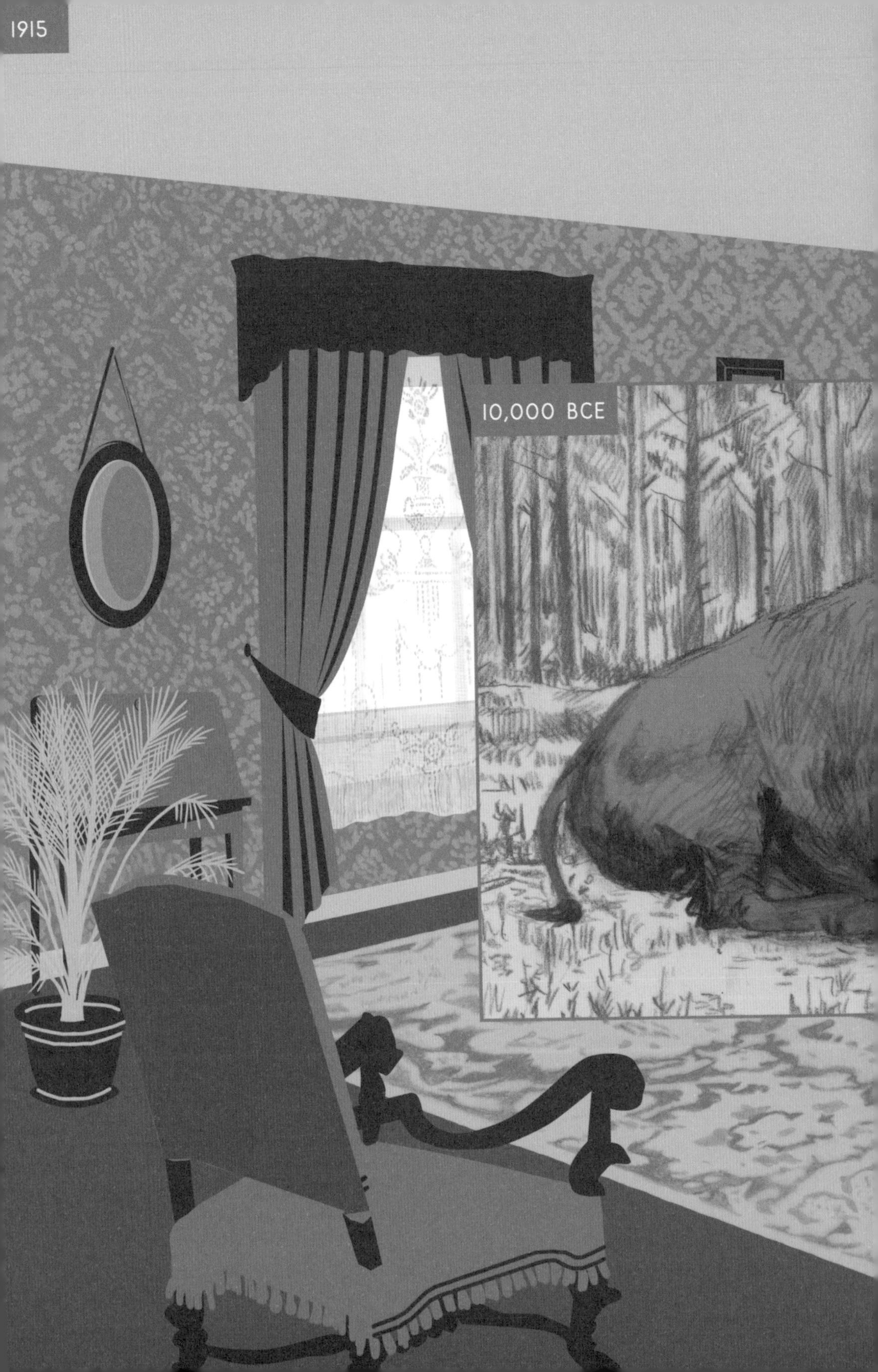
1915
10,000 BCE

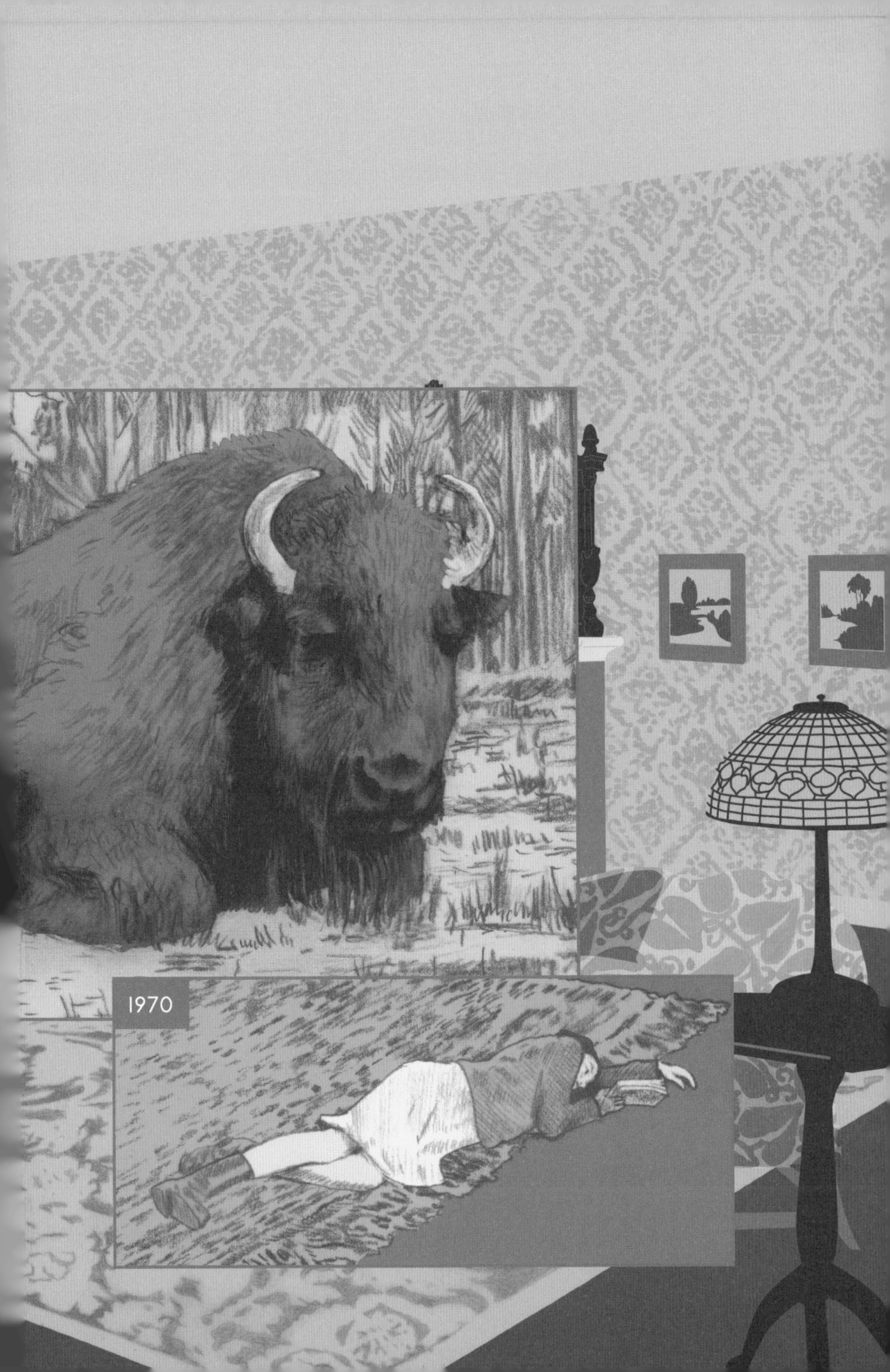
1970

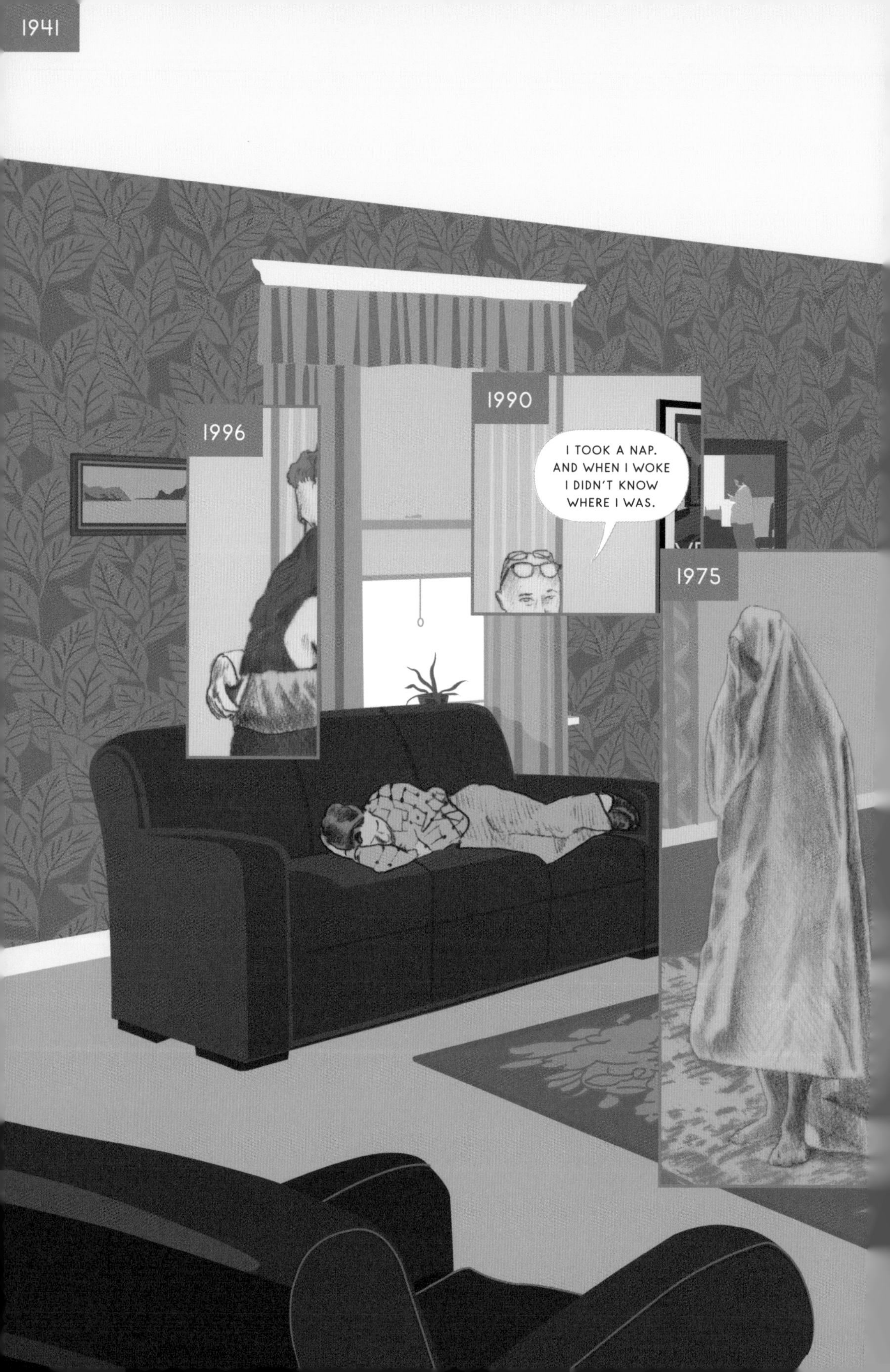
1941
1996
1990
I TOOK A NAP.
AND WHEN I WOKE
I DIDN'T KNOW
WHERE I WAS.
1975

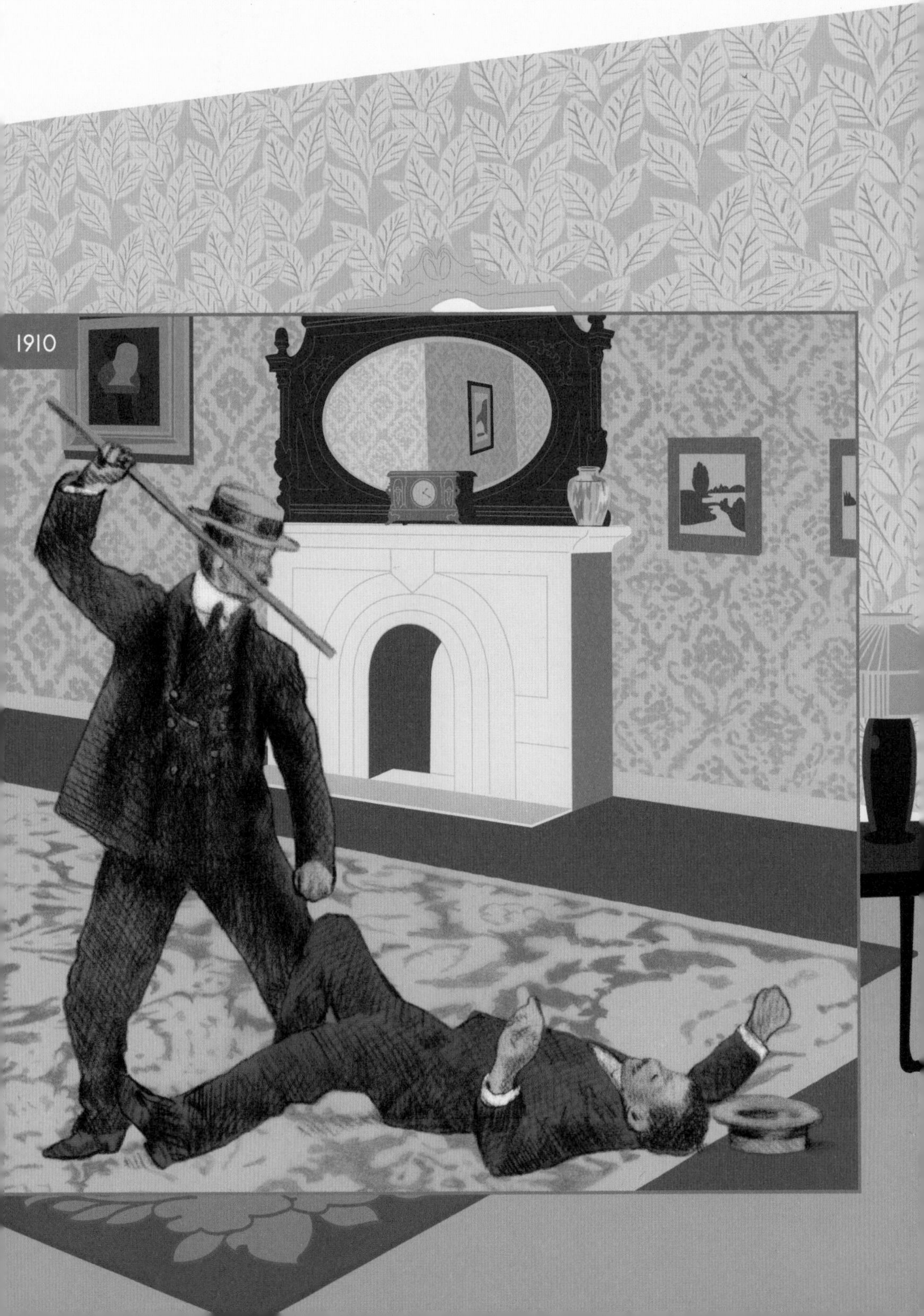
1910

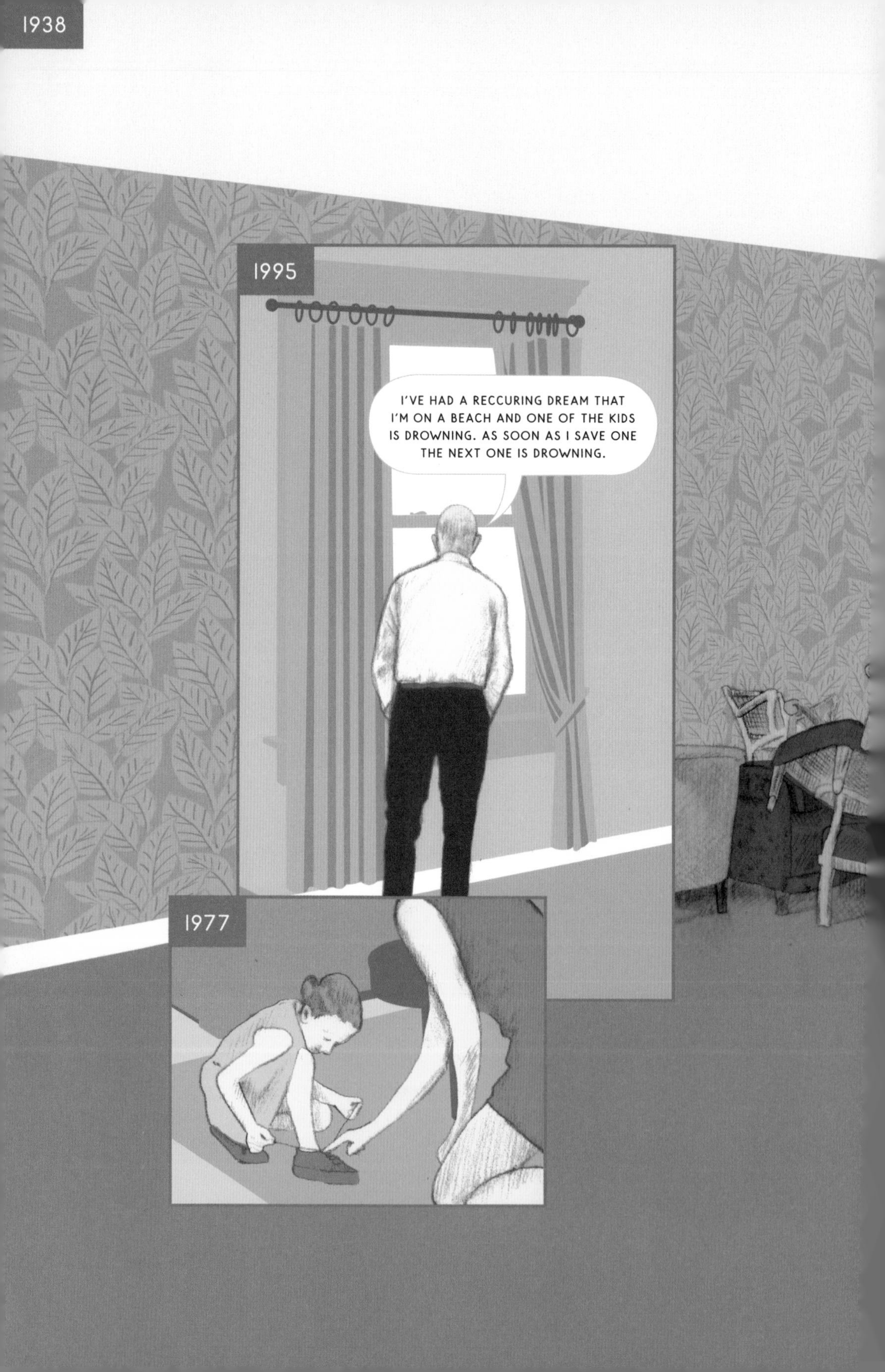
1938
1995
I'VE HAD A RECCURING DREAM THAT I'M ON A BEACH AND ONE OF THE KIDS IS DROWNING. AS SOON AS I SAVE ONE THE NEXT ONE IS DROWNING.
1977

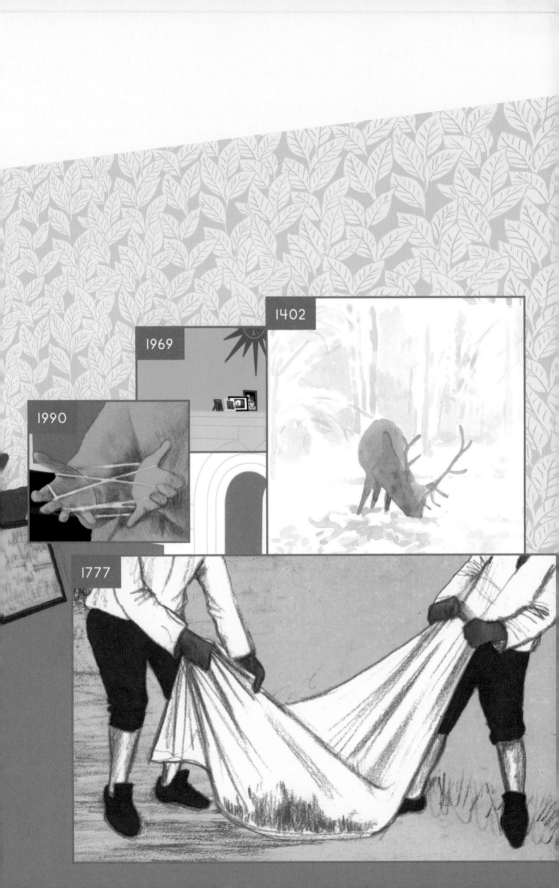

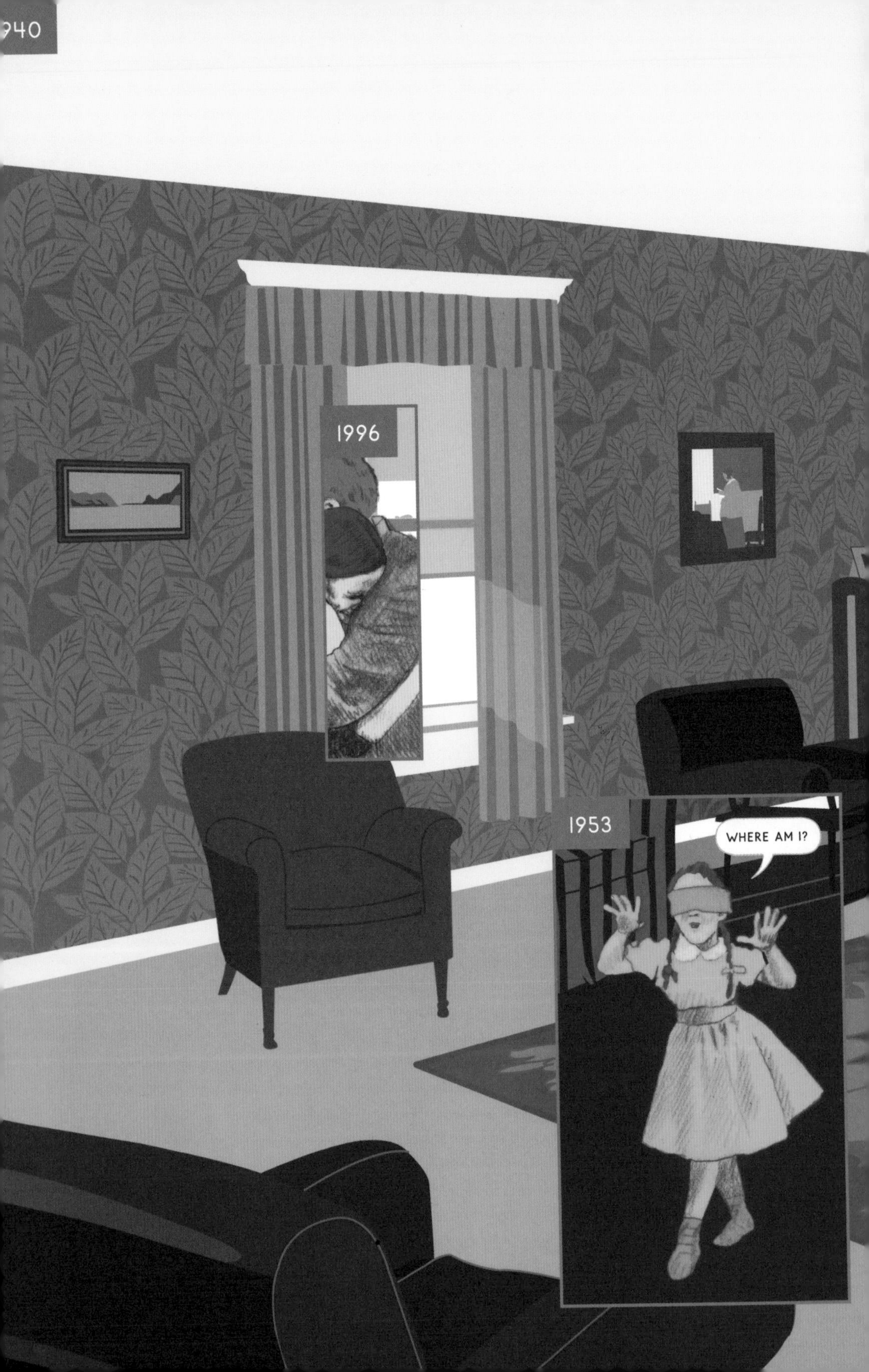

940
1996
1953
WHERE AM I?

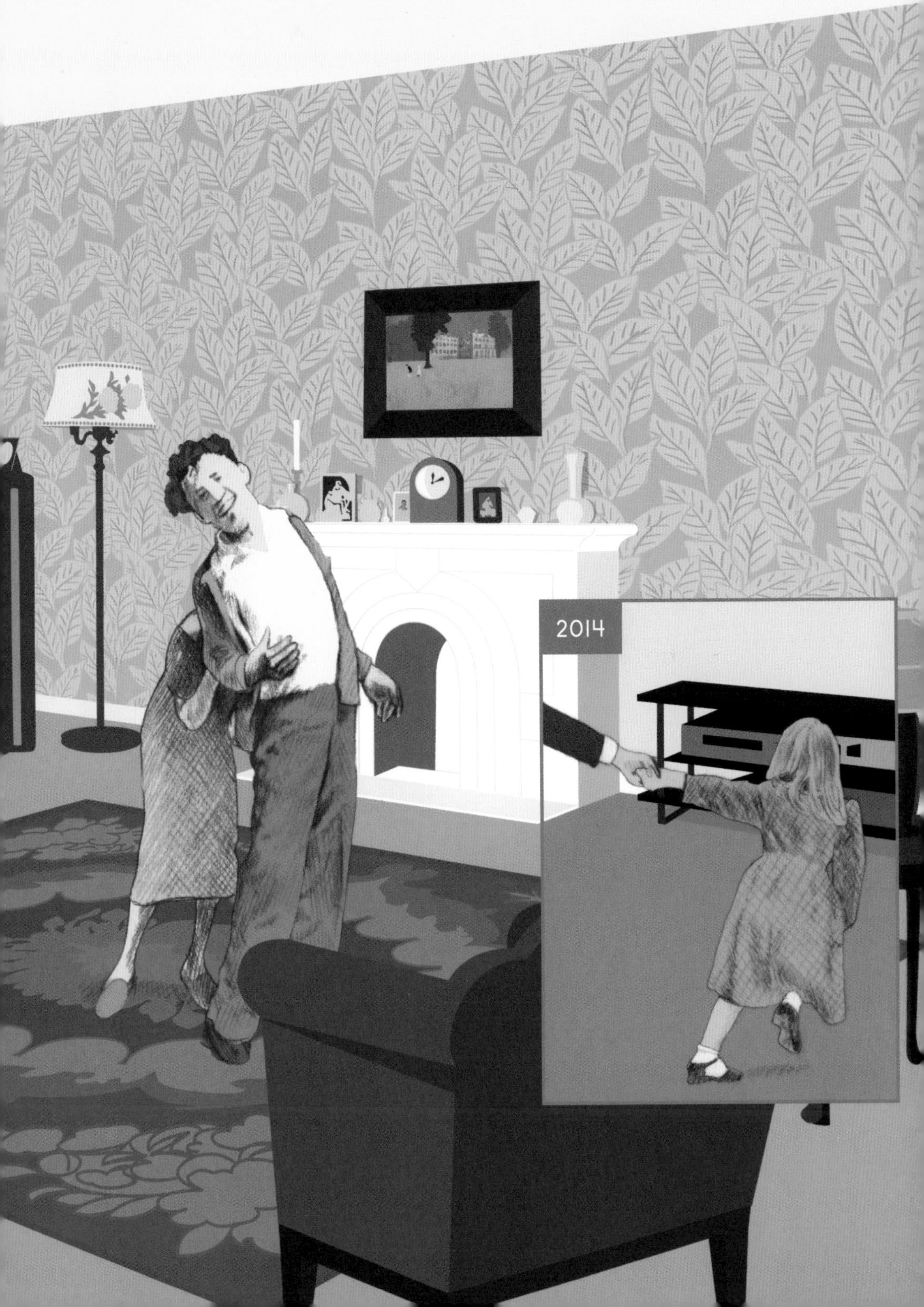
2014

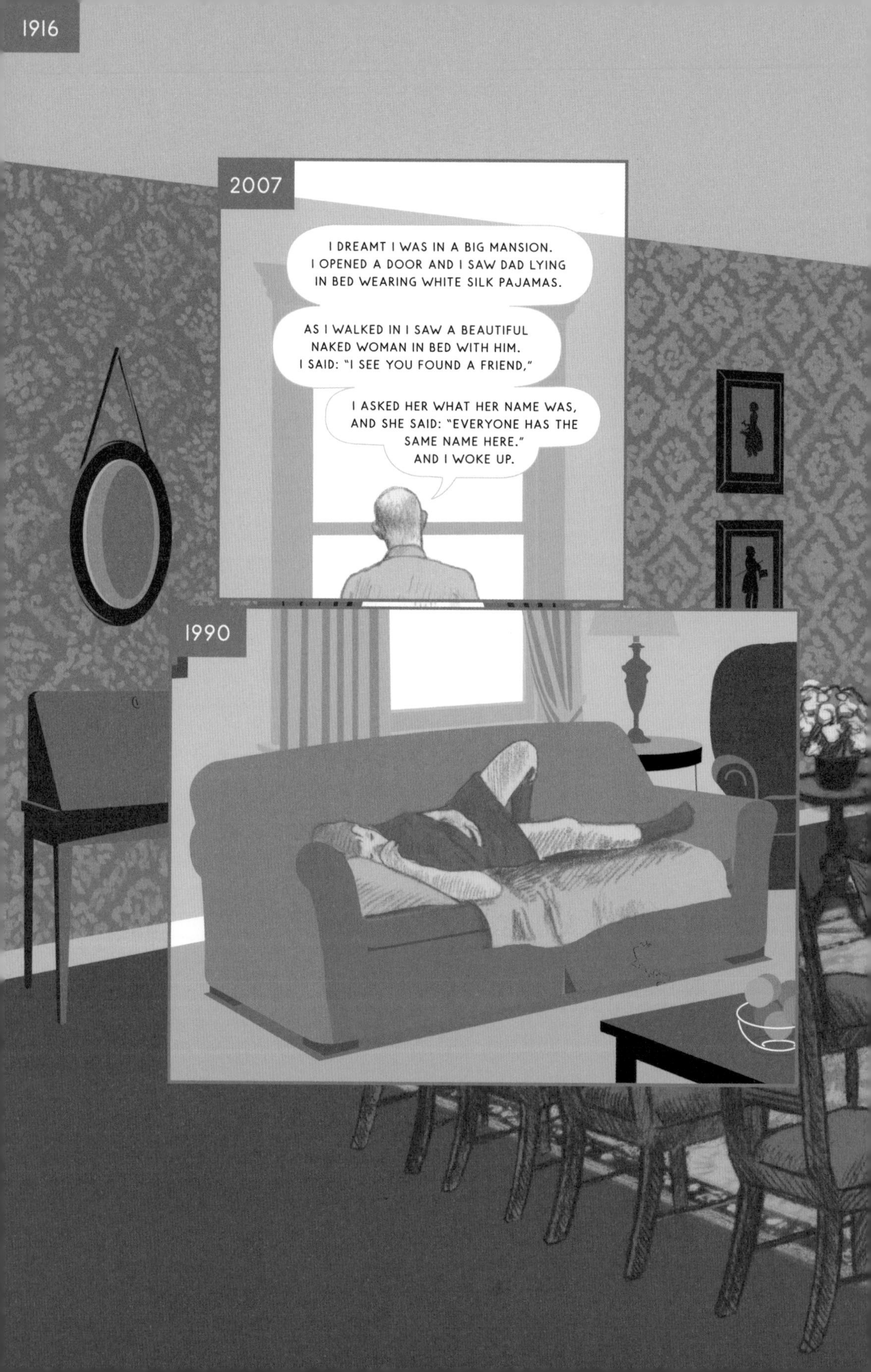
1916
2007
I DREAMT I WAS IN A BIG MANSION. I OPENED A DOOR AND I SAW DAD LYING IN BED WEARING WHITE SILK PAJAMAS.
AS I WALKED IN I SAW A BEAUTIFUL NAKED WOMAN IN BED WITH HIM. I SAID: "I SEE YOU FOUND A FRIEND,"
I ASKED HER WHAT HER NAME WAS, AND SHE SAID: "EVERYONE HAS THE SAME NAME HERE." AND I WOKE UP.
1990

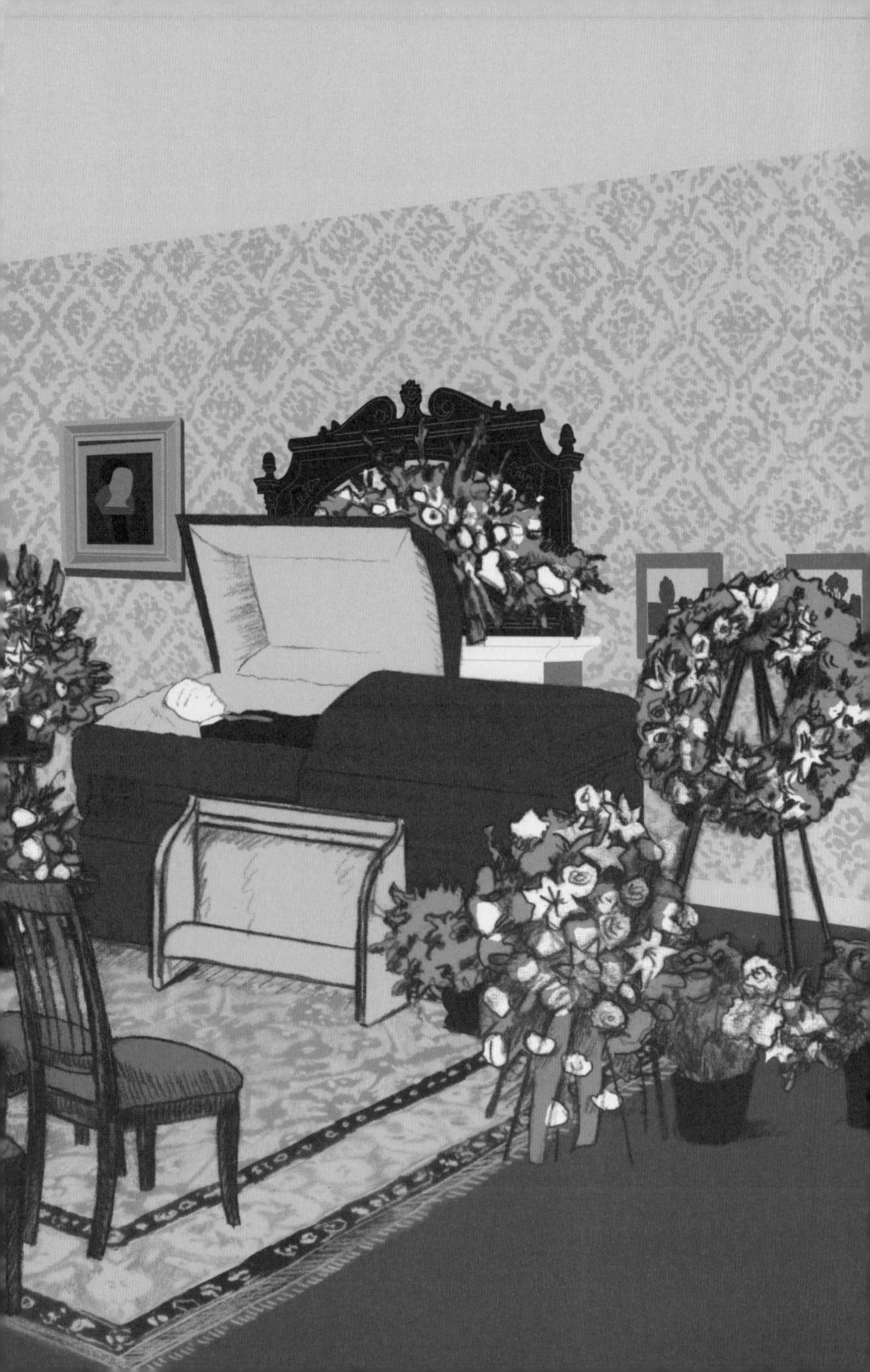

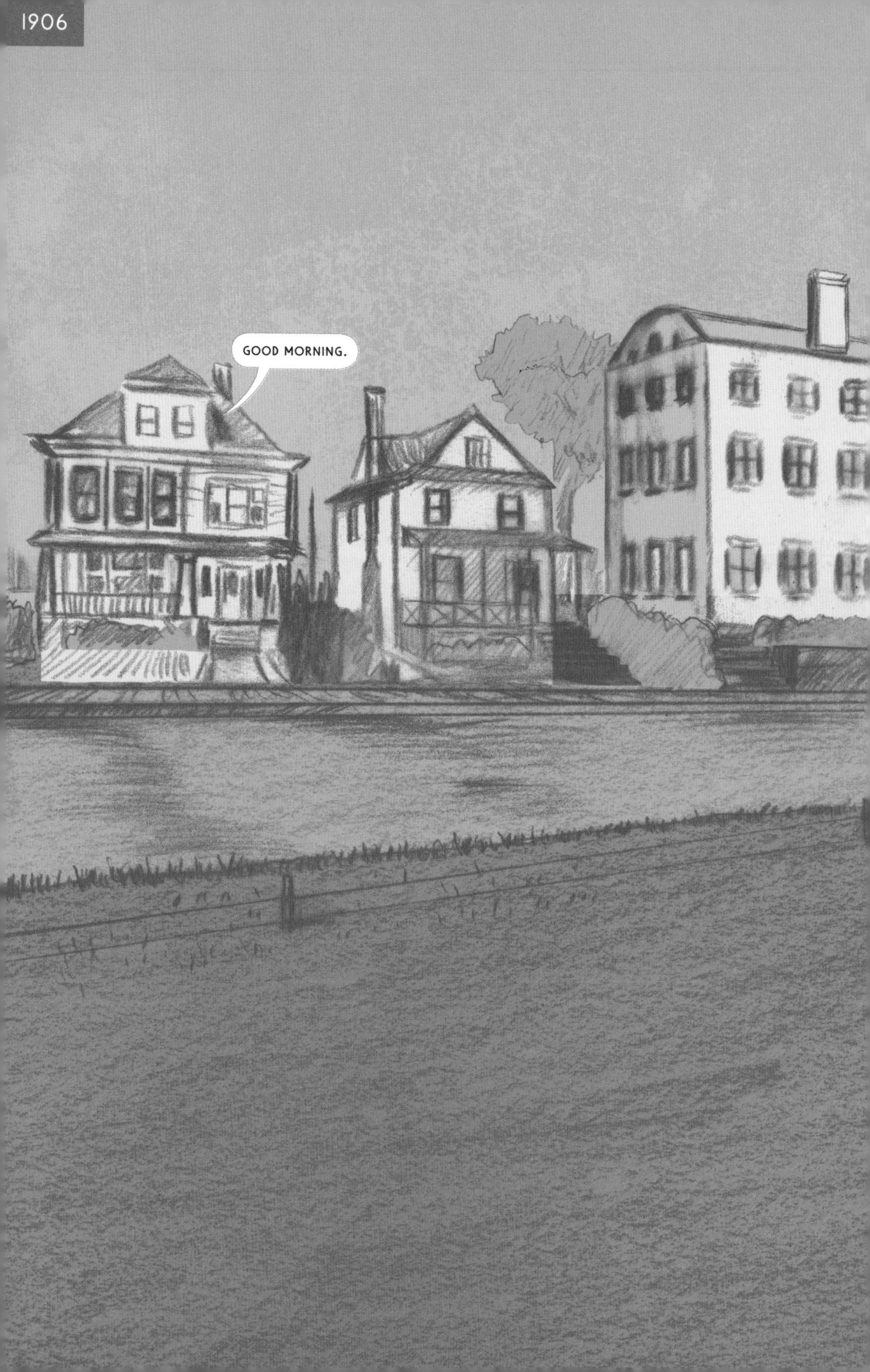
1906
GOOD MORNING.

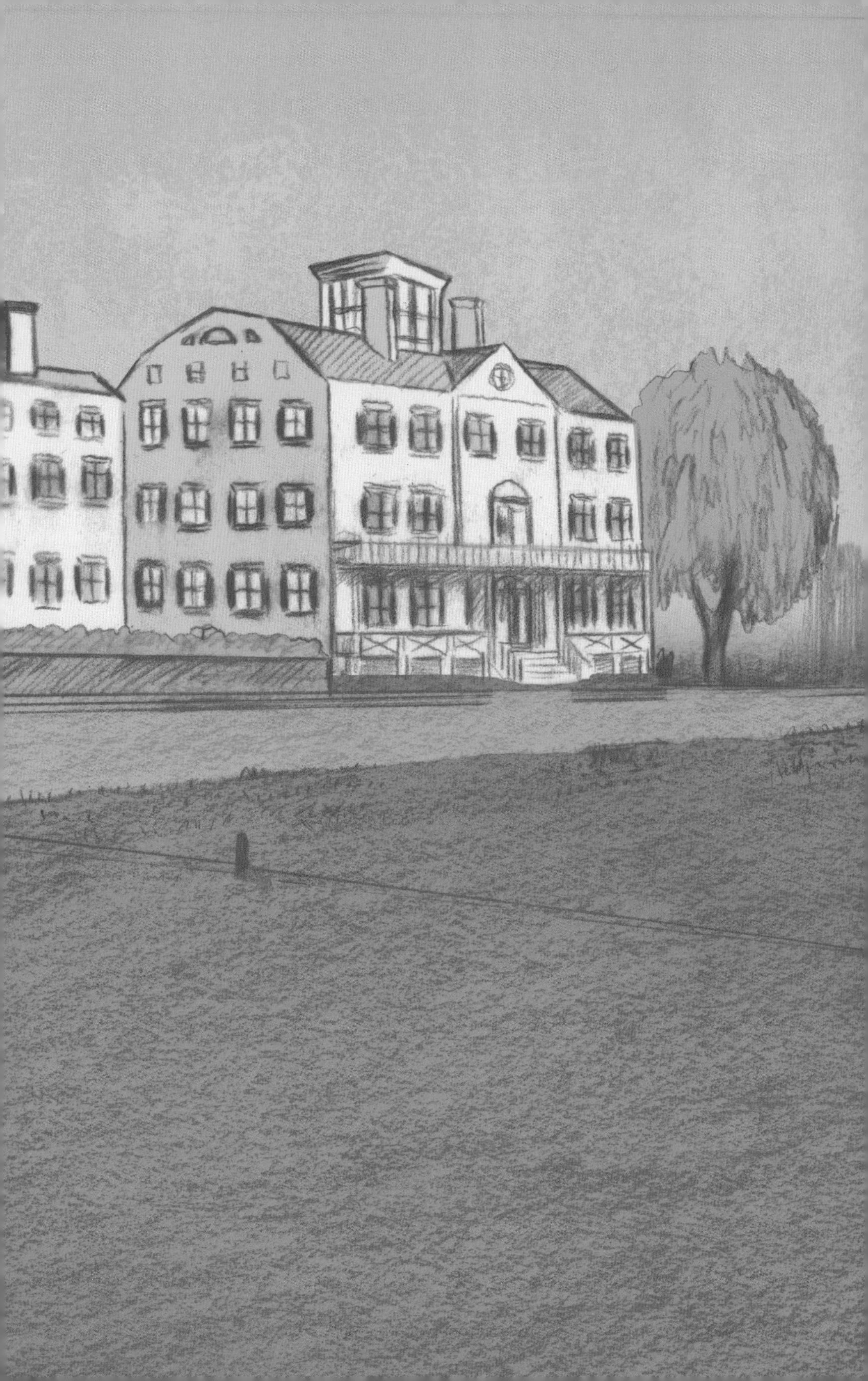

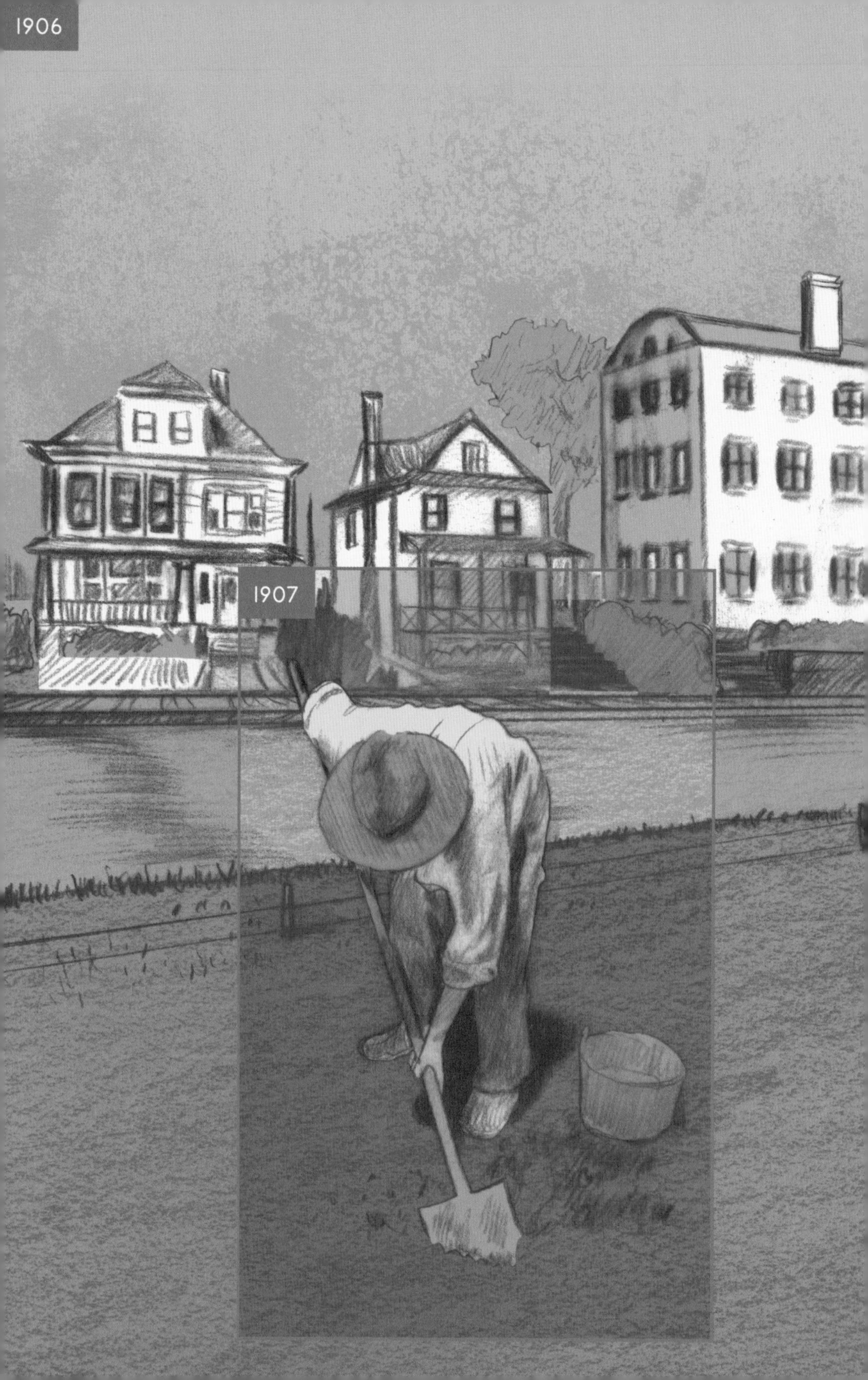
1906
1907

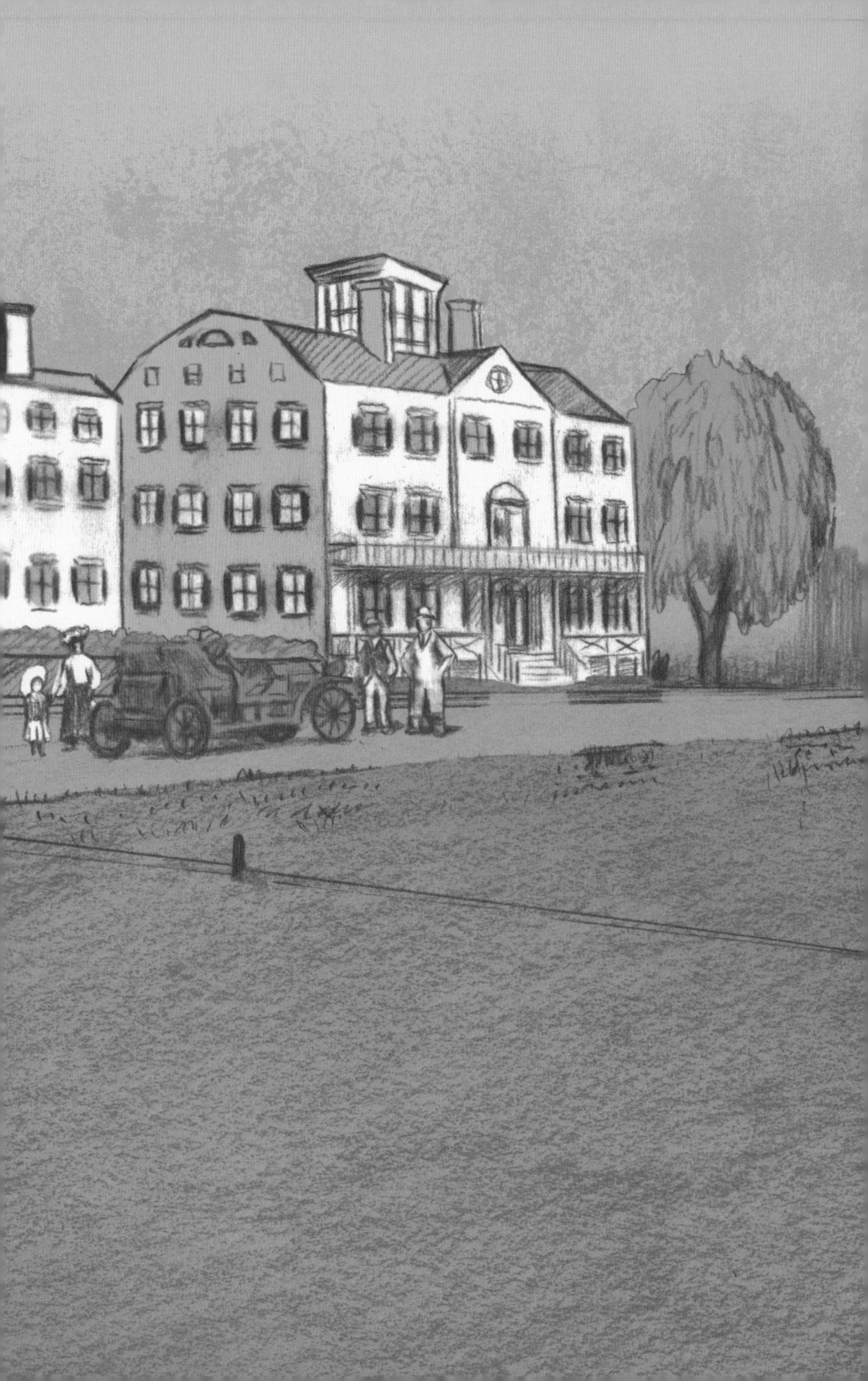

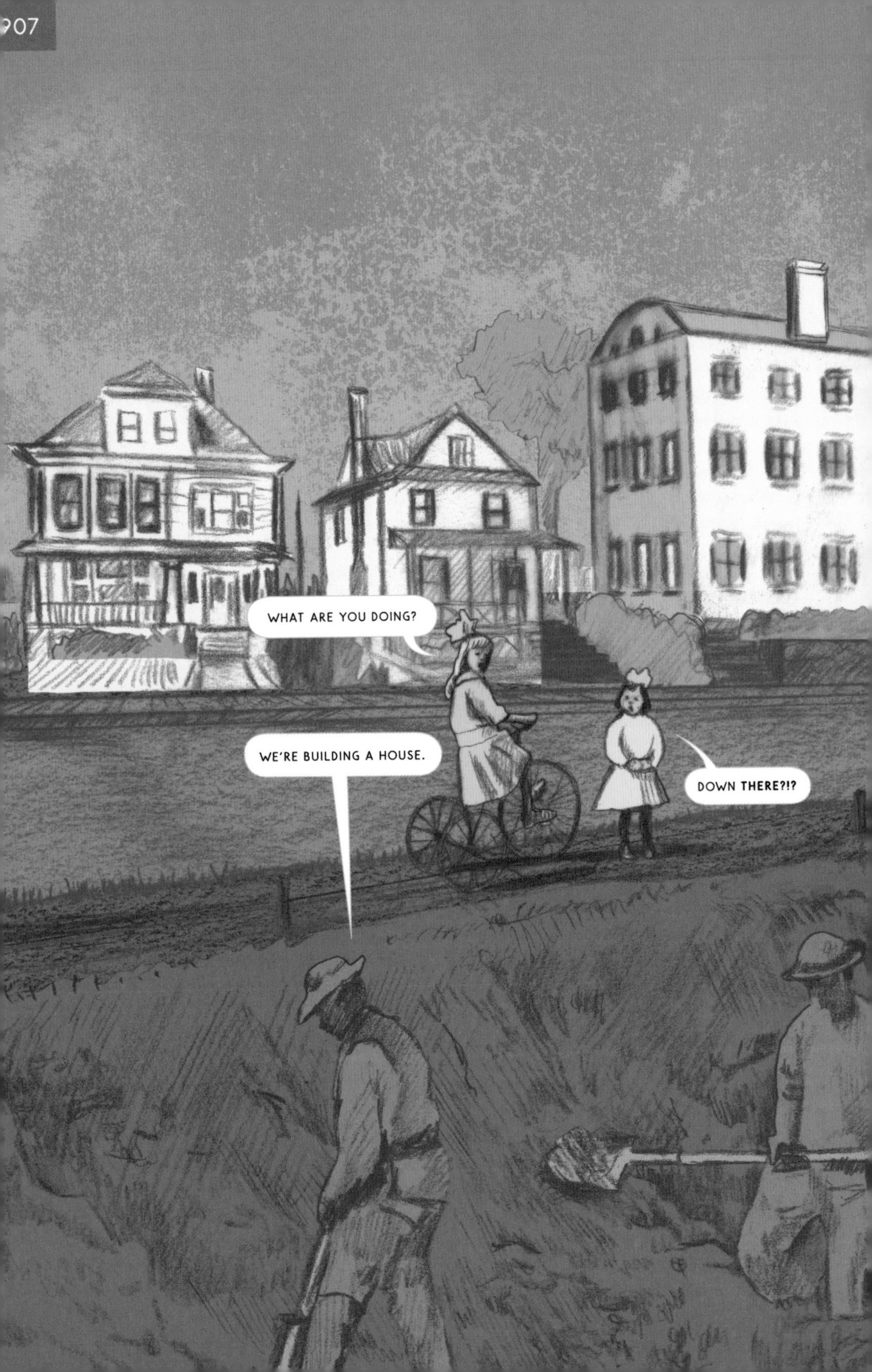
WHAT ARE YOU DOING?
WE'RE BUILDING A HOUSE.
DOWN THERE?!?

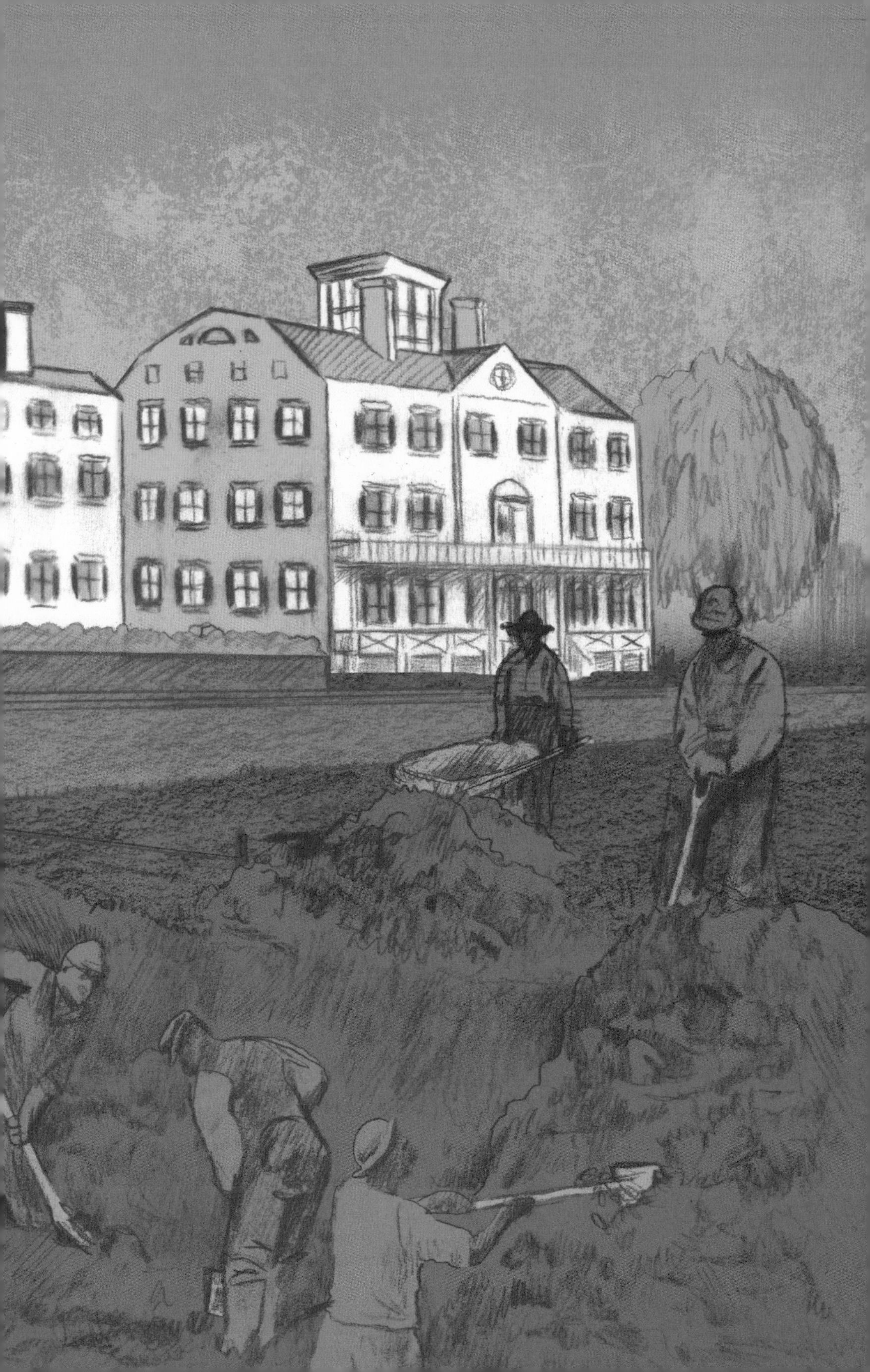

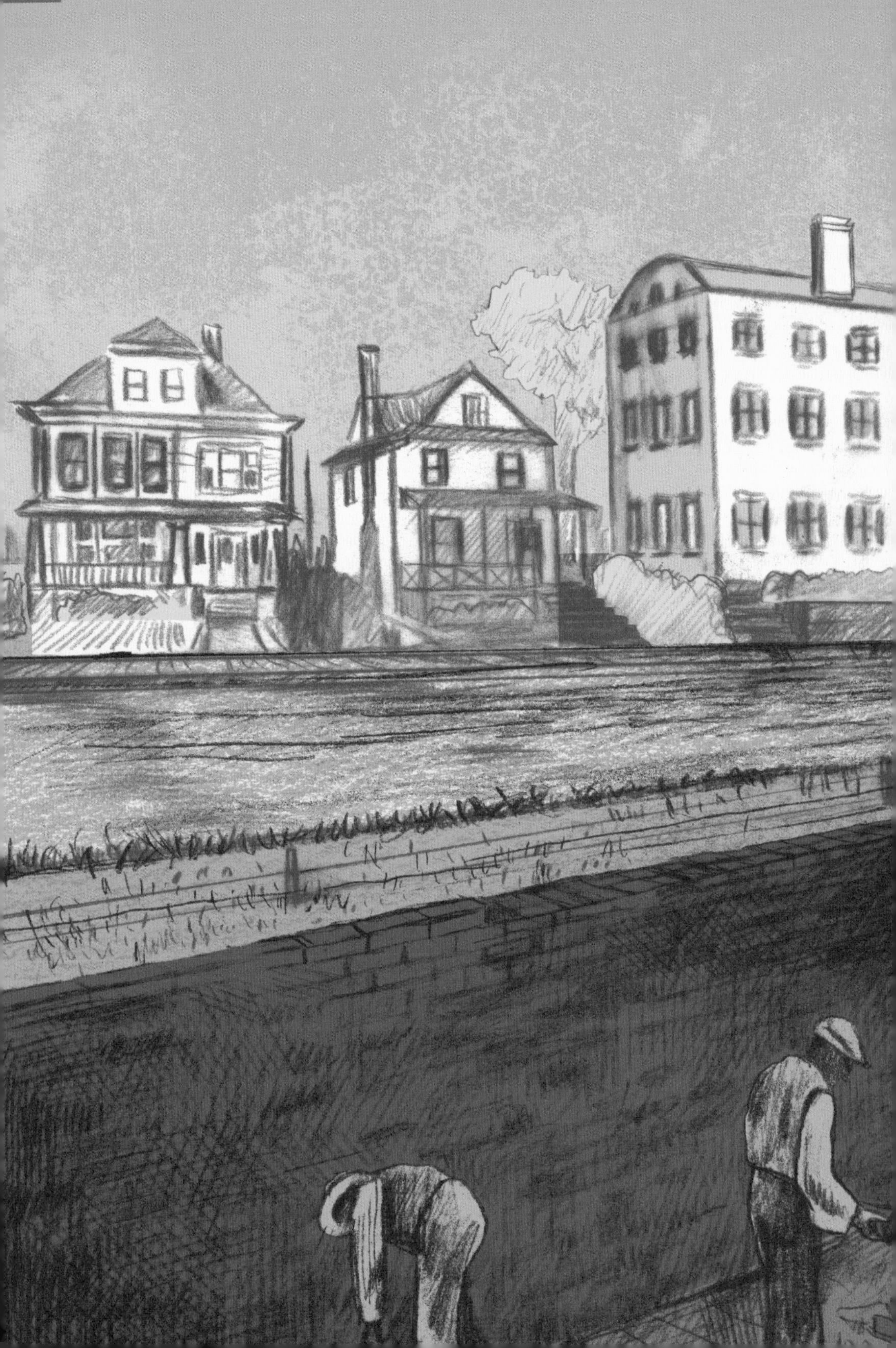

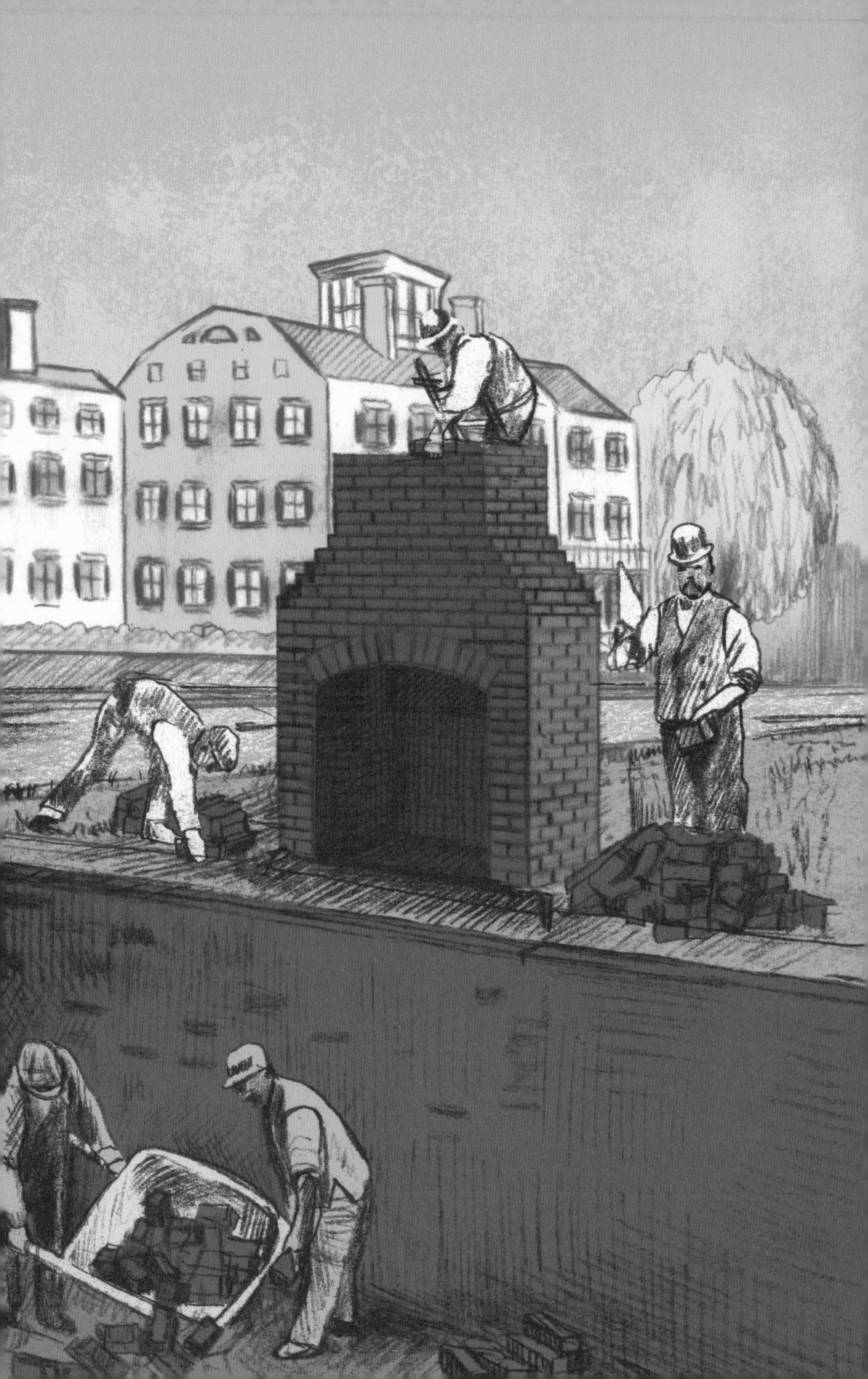

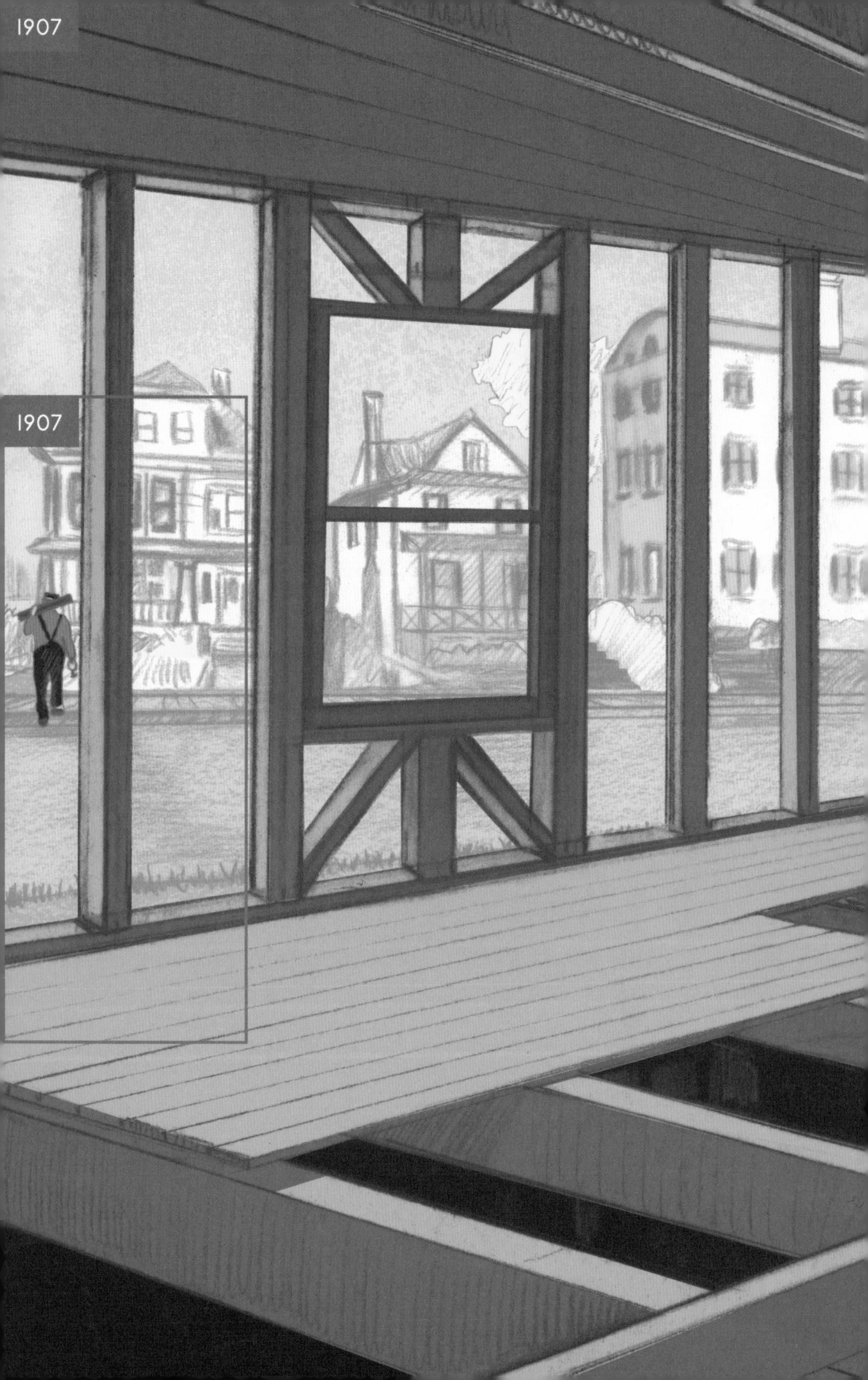
1907
1907

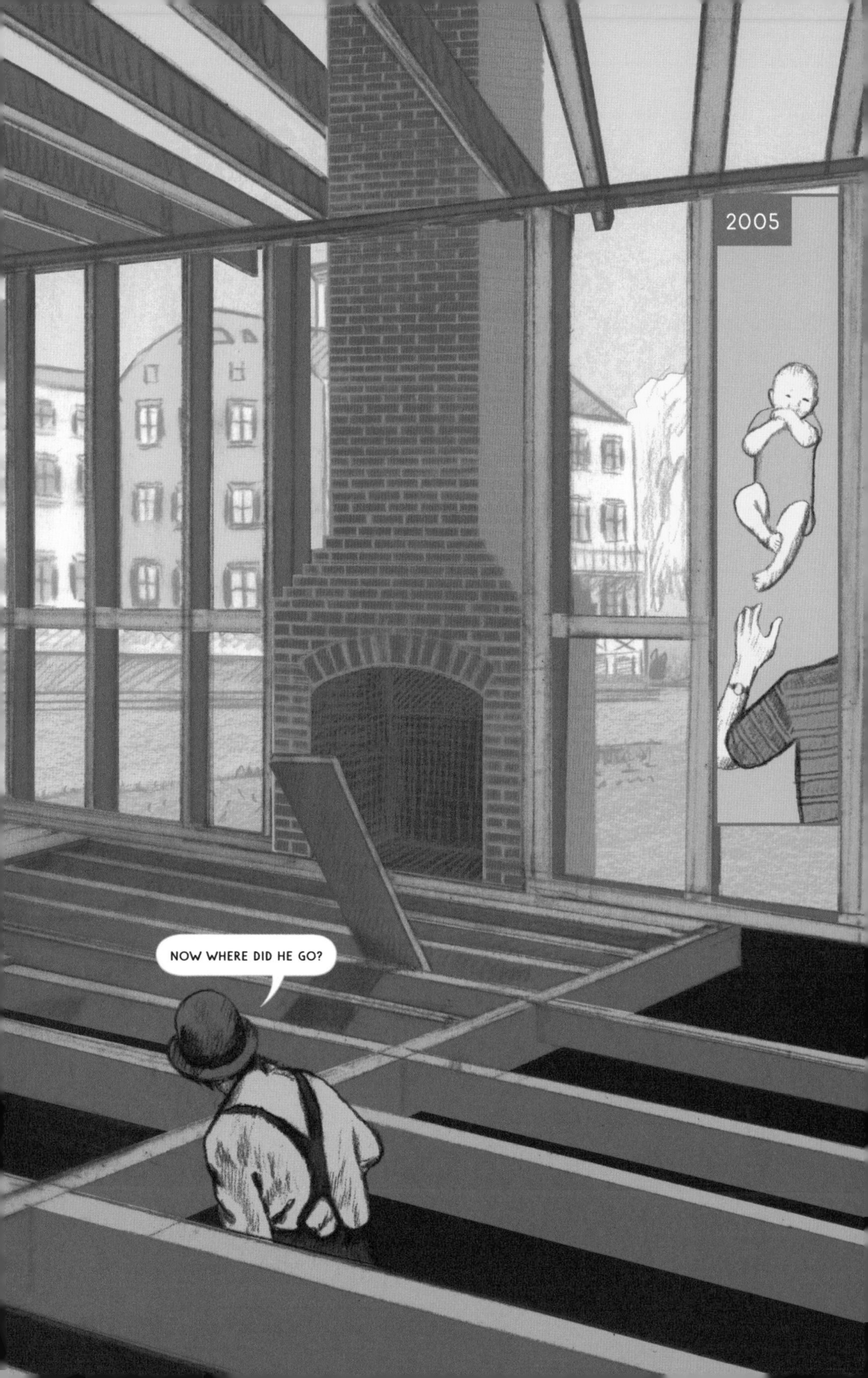
2005
NOW WHERE DID HE GO?

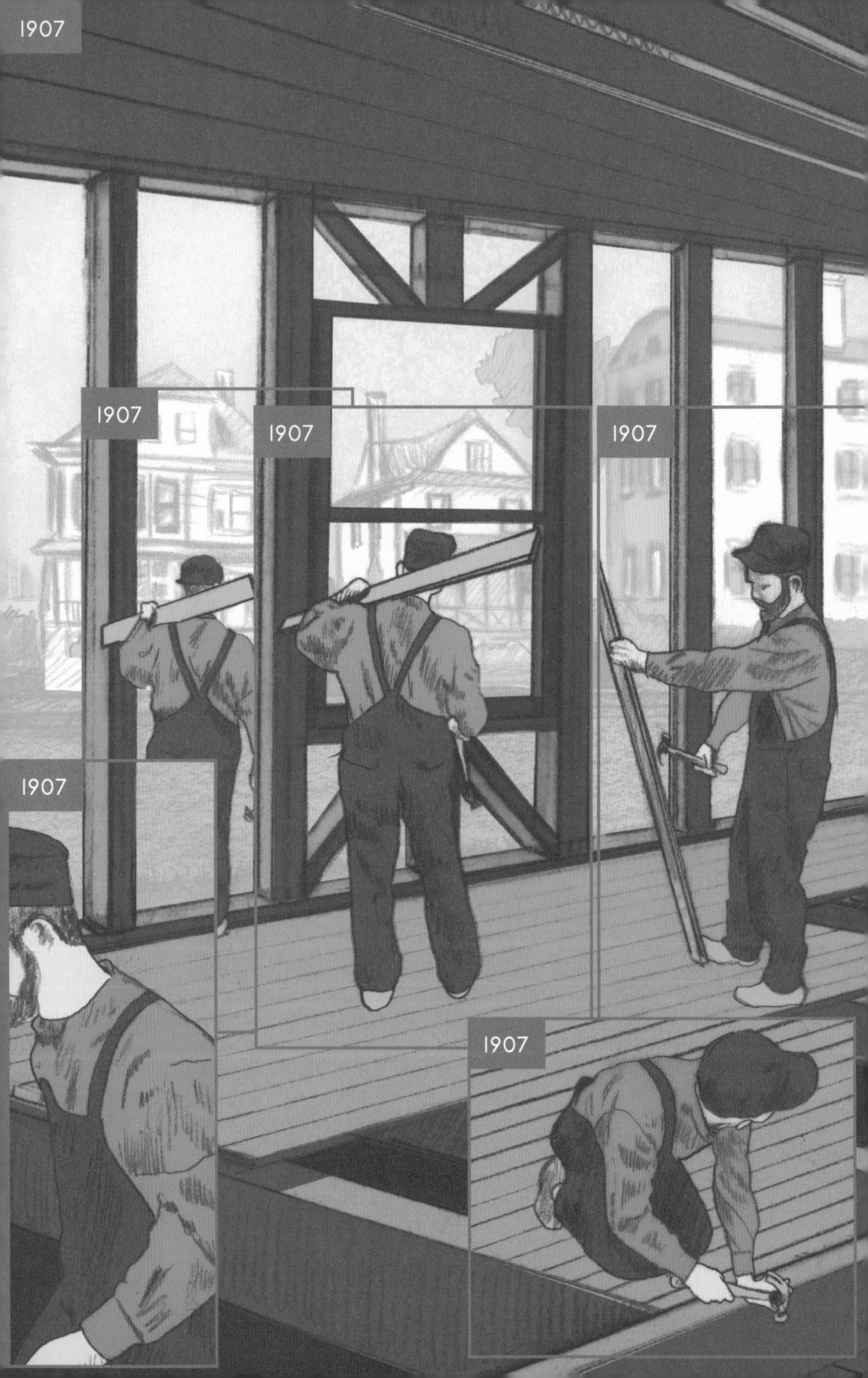
1907
1907
1907
1907
1907
1907

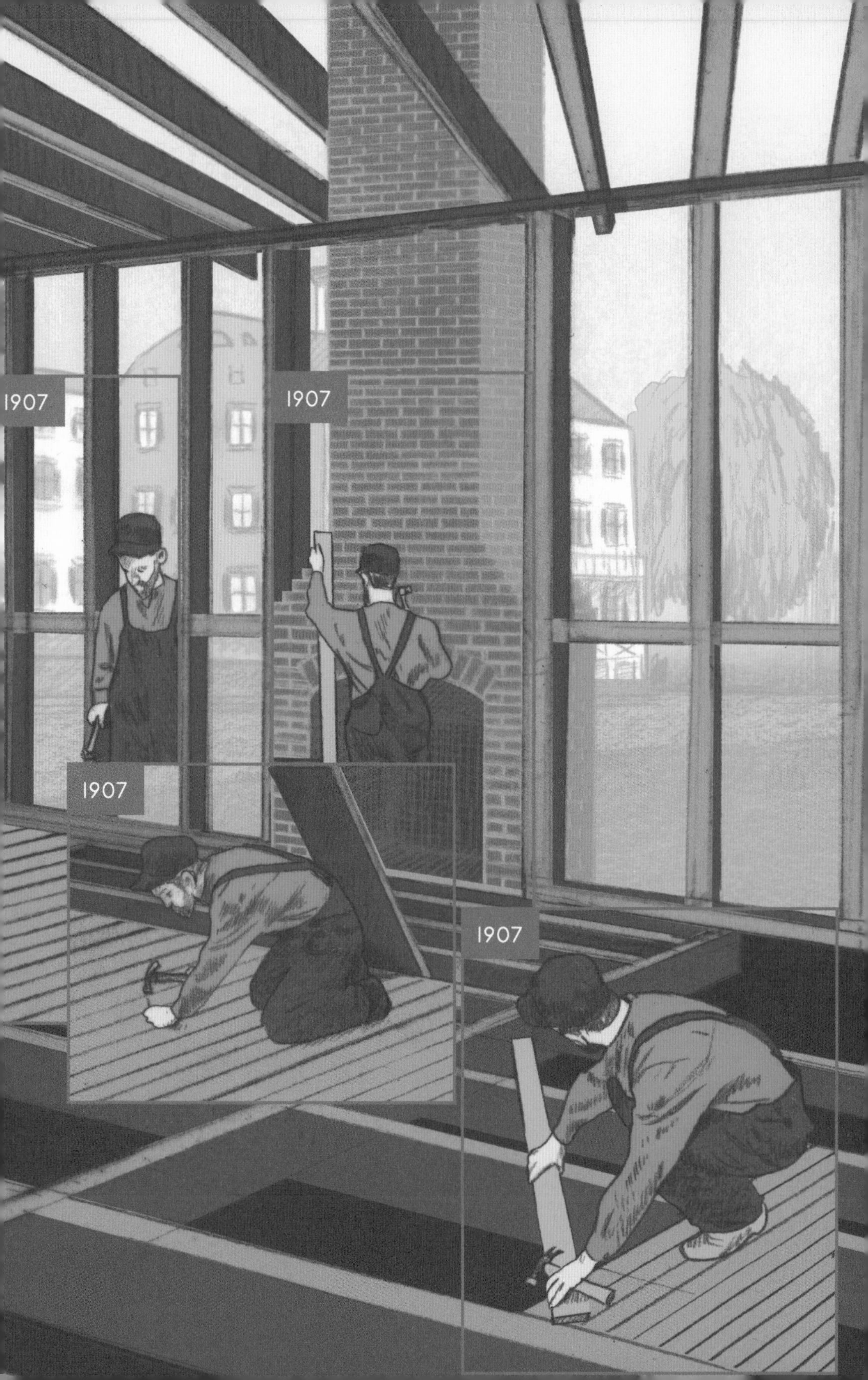
1907
1907
1907
1907

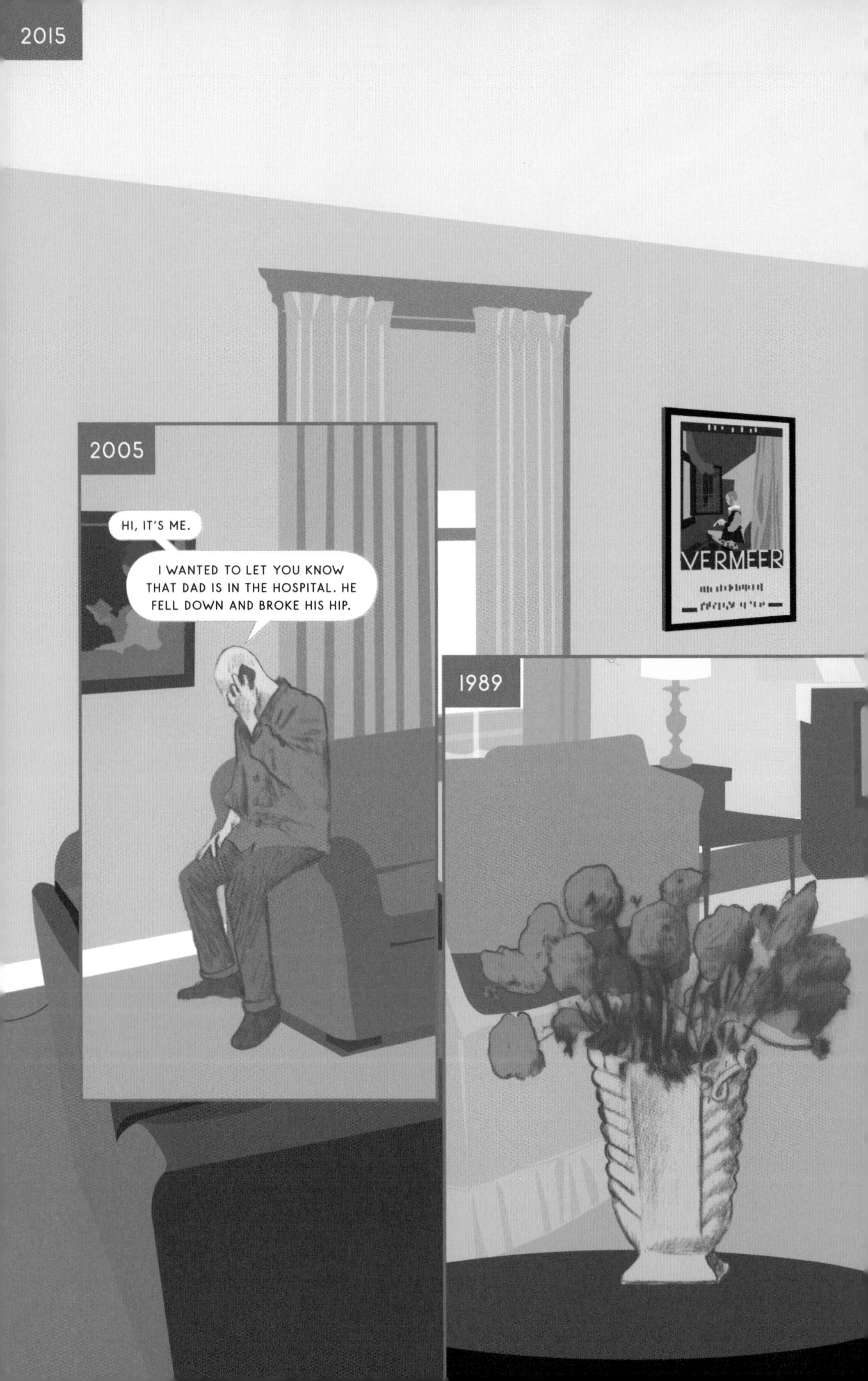
2015
2005
HI, IT'S ME.
I WANTED TO LET YOU KNOW THAT DAD IS IN THE HOSPITAL. HE FELL DOWN AND BROKE HIS HIP.
VERMEER
1989

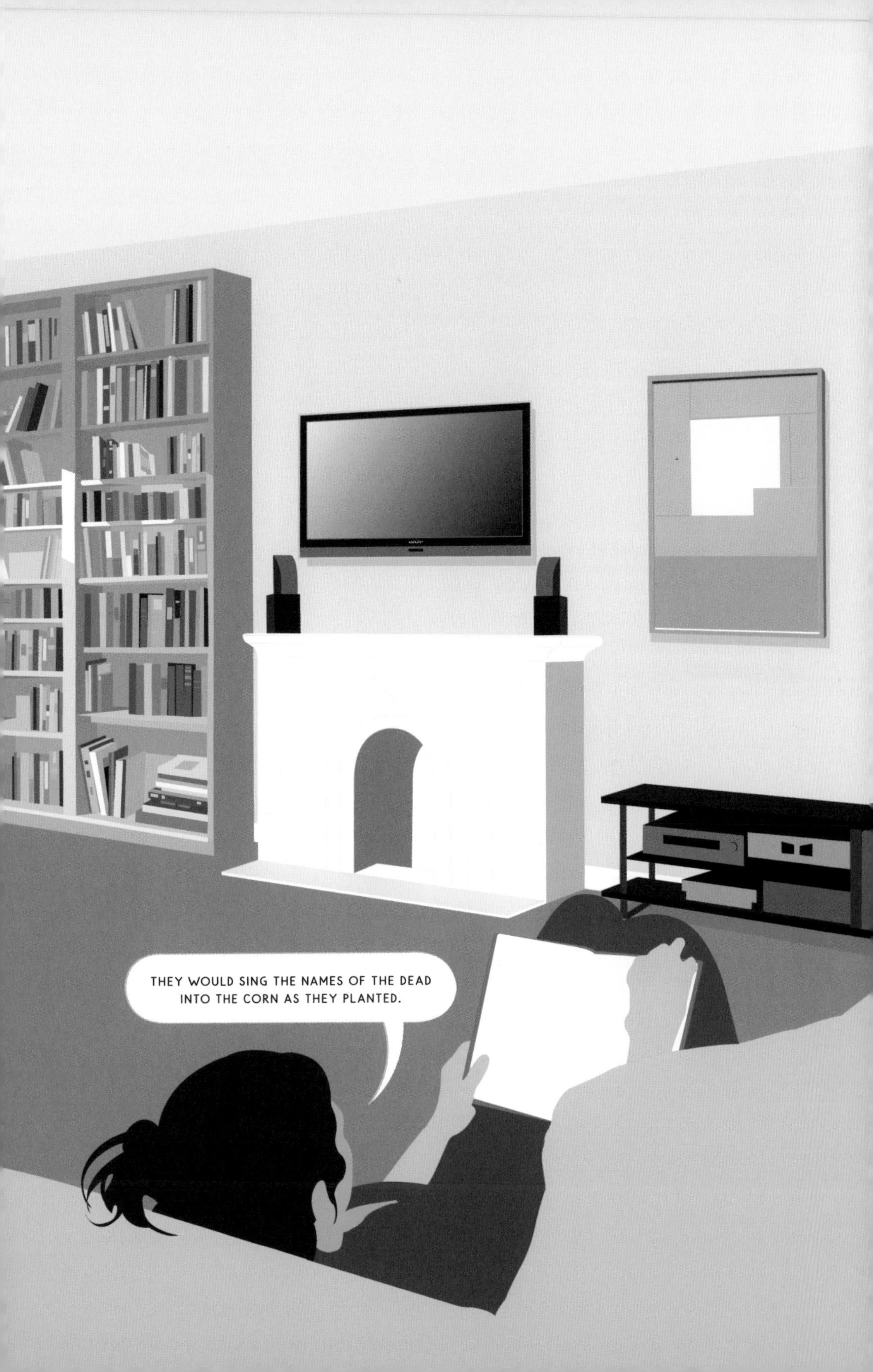
THEY WOULD SING THE NAMES OF THE DEAD INTO THE CORN AS THEY PLANTED.

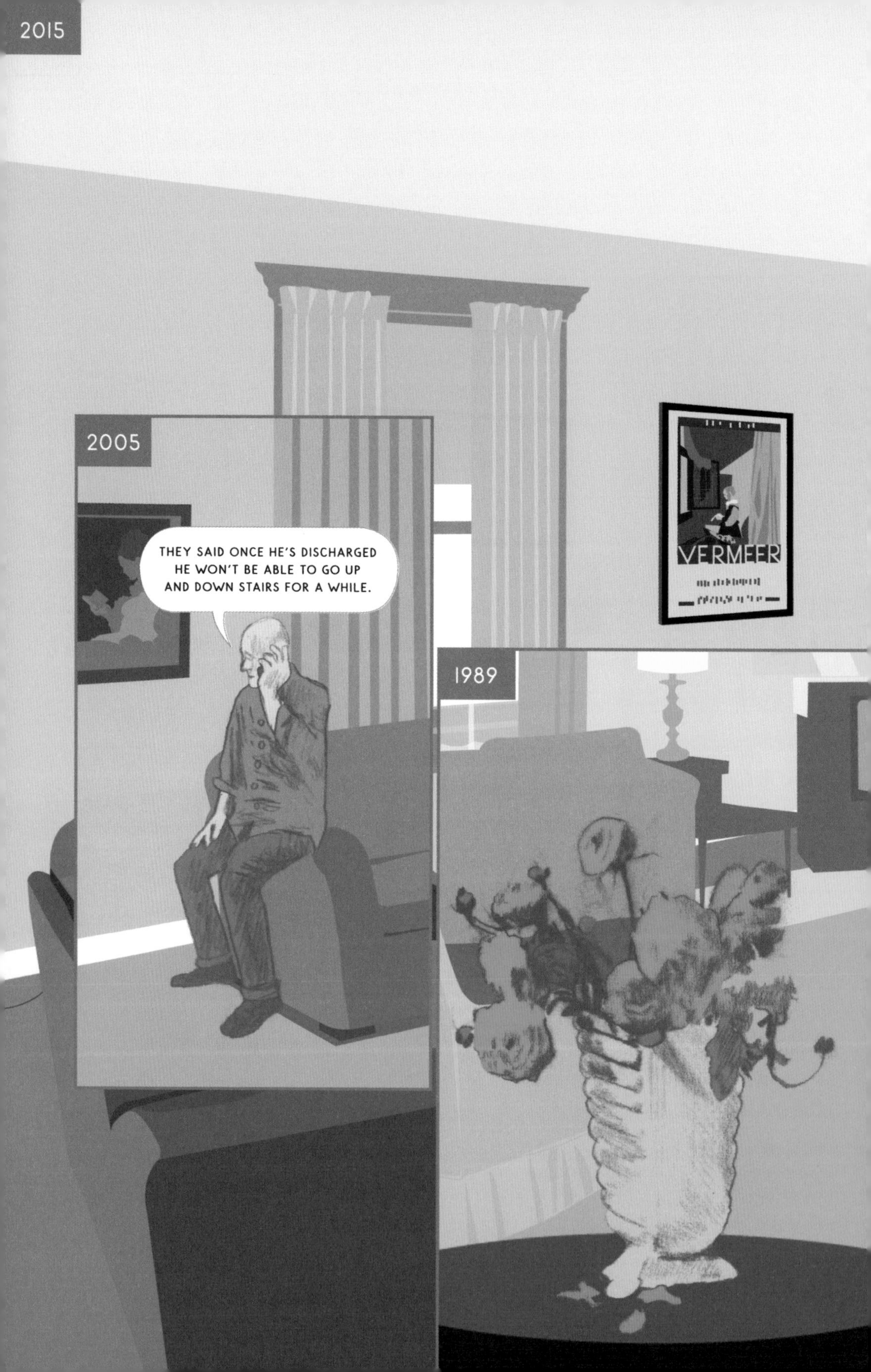
2015
2005
THEY SAID ONCE HE'S DISCHARGED HE WON'T BE ABLE TO GO UP AND DOWN STAIRS FOR A WHILE.
VERMEER
1989

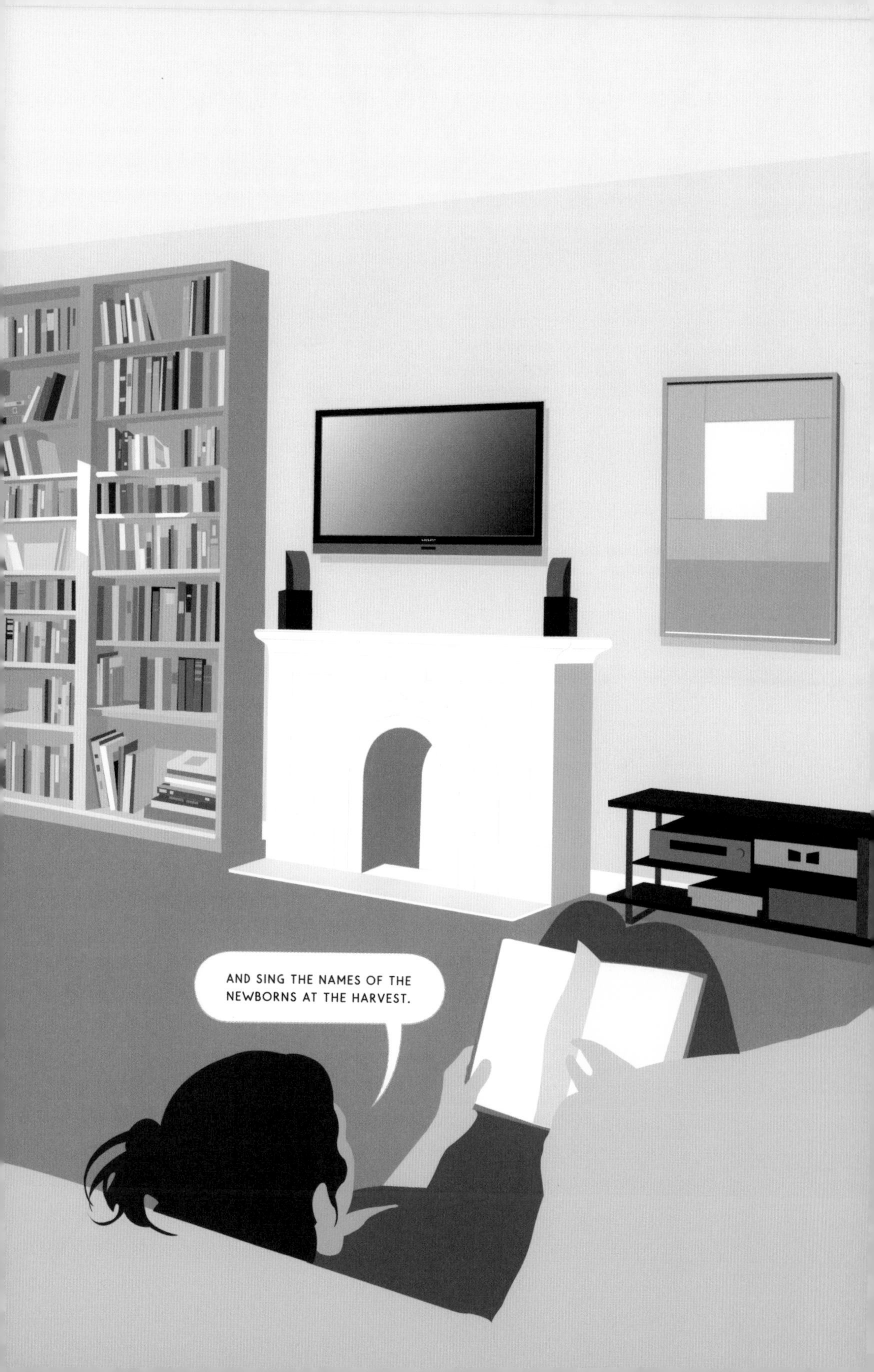
AND SING THE NAMES OF THE NEWBORNS AT THE HARVEST.

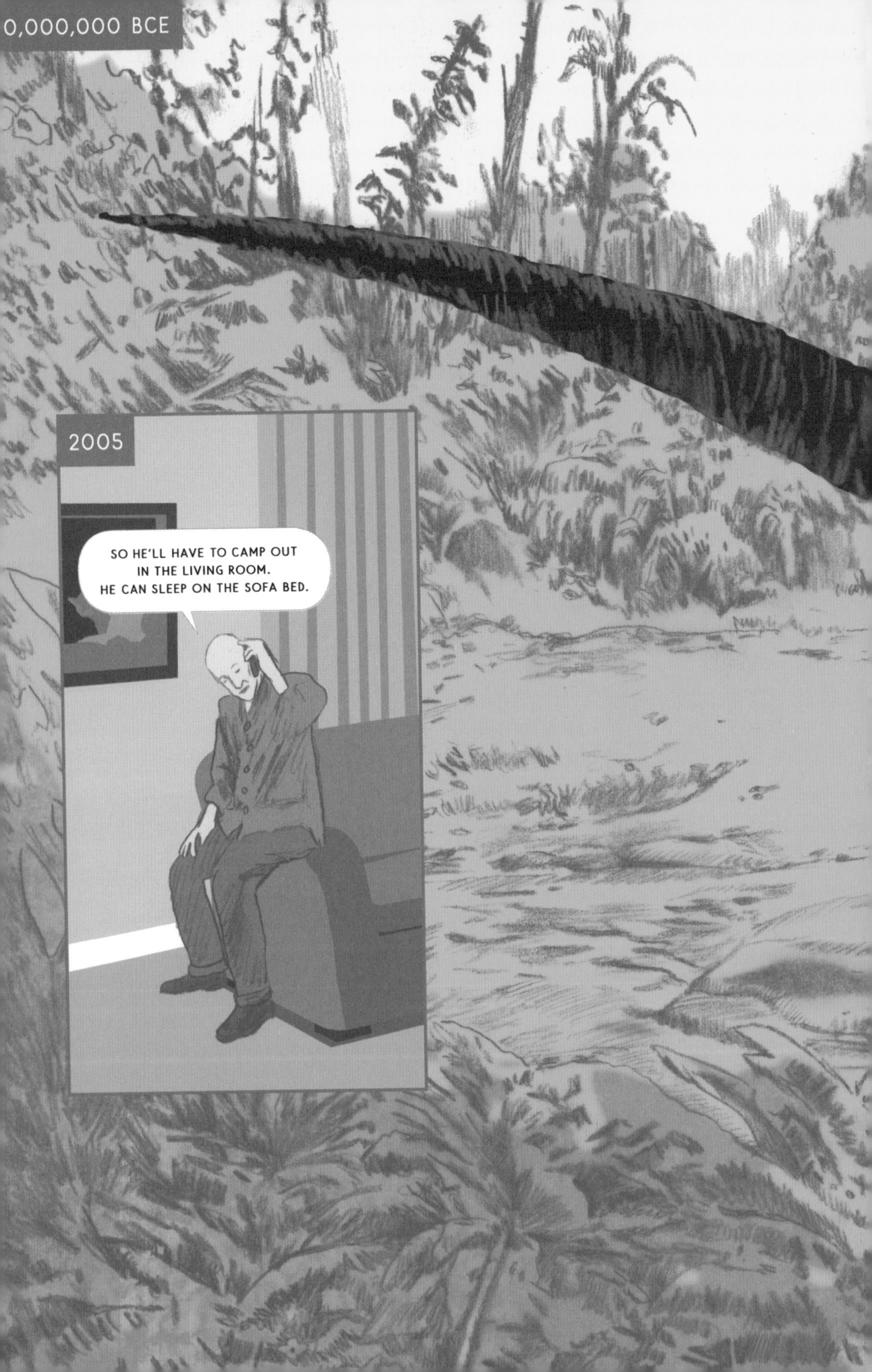
0,000,000 BCE
2005
SO HE'LL HAVE TO CAMP OUT
IN THE LIVING ROOM.
HE CAN SLEEP ON THE SOFA BED.

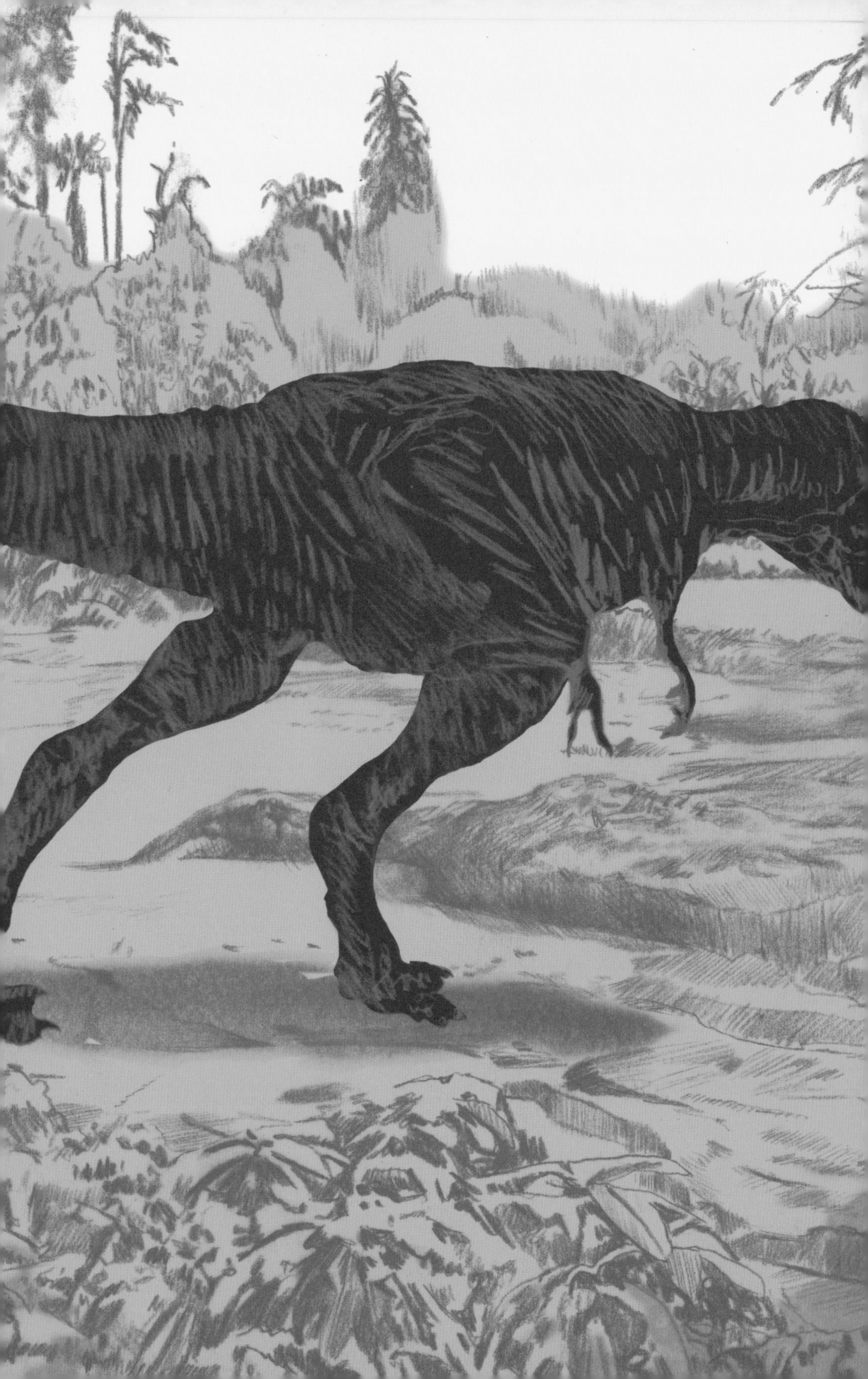

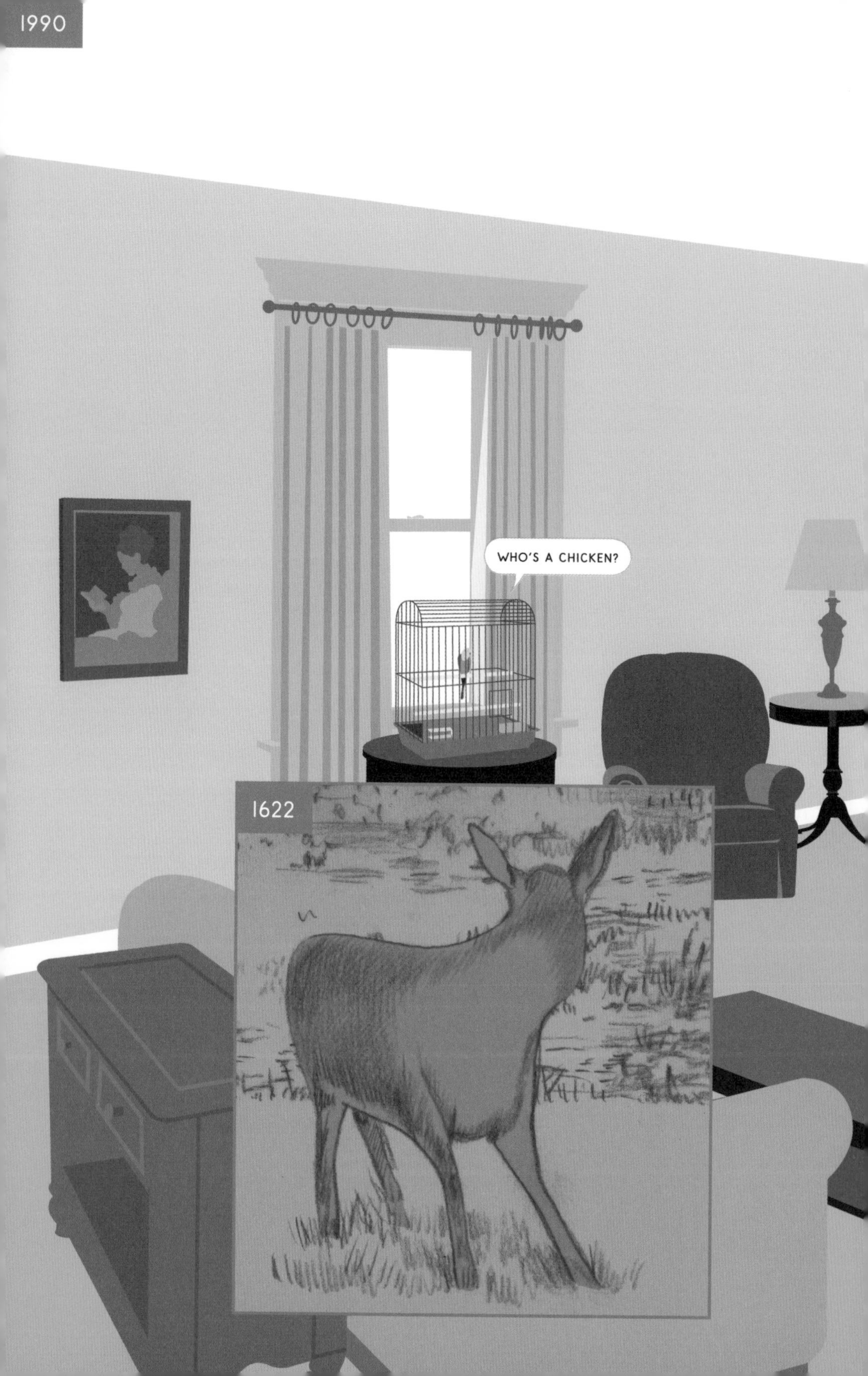
1990
WHO'S A CHICKEN?
1622

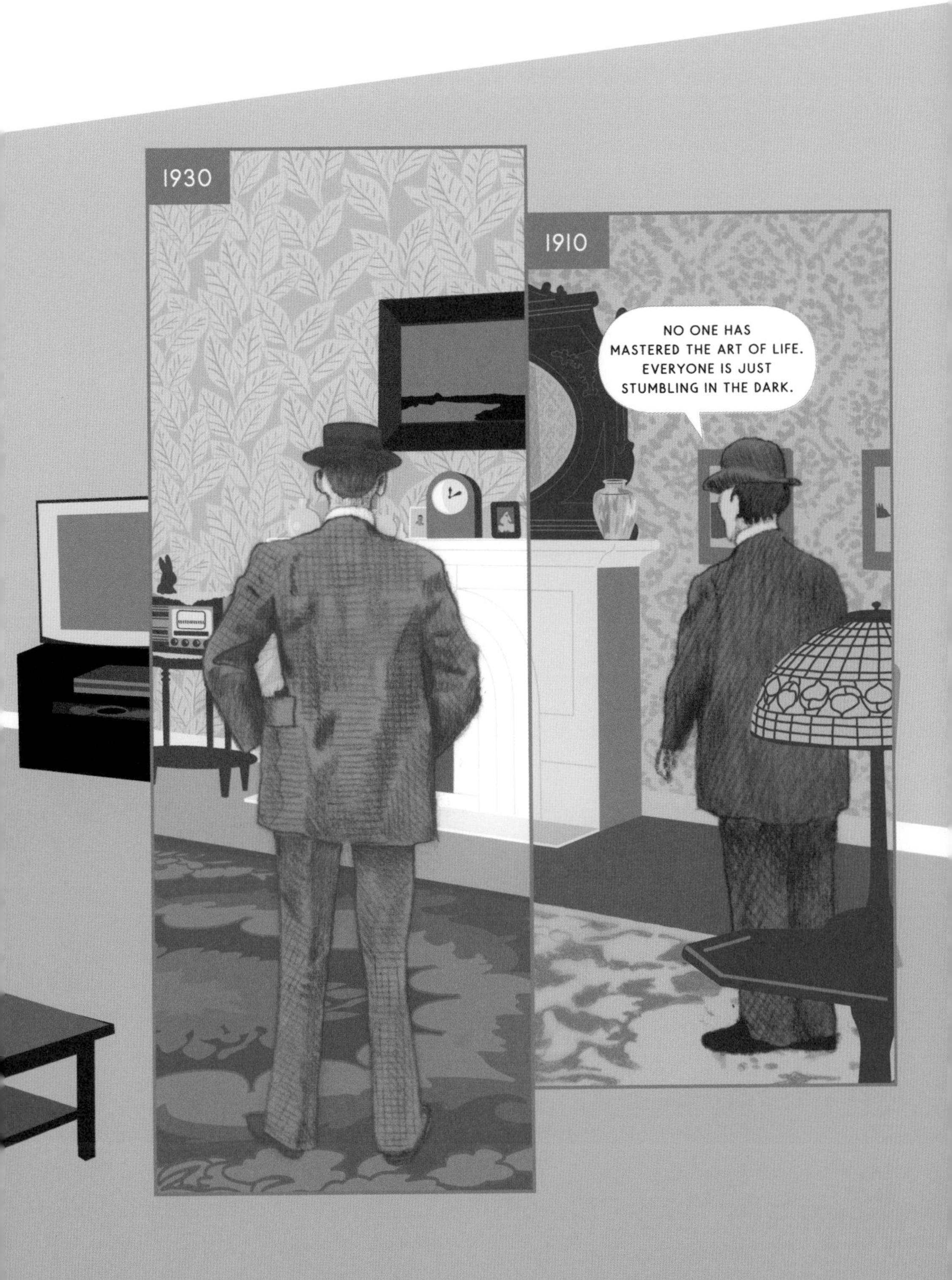
1930
1910
NO ONE HAS MASTERED THE ART OF LIFE. EVERYONE IS JUST STUMBLING IN THE DARK.

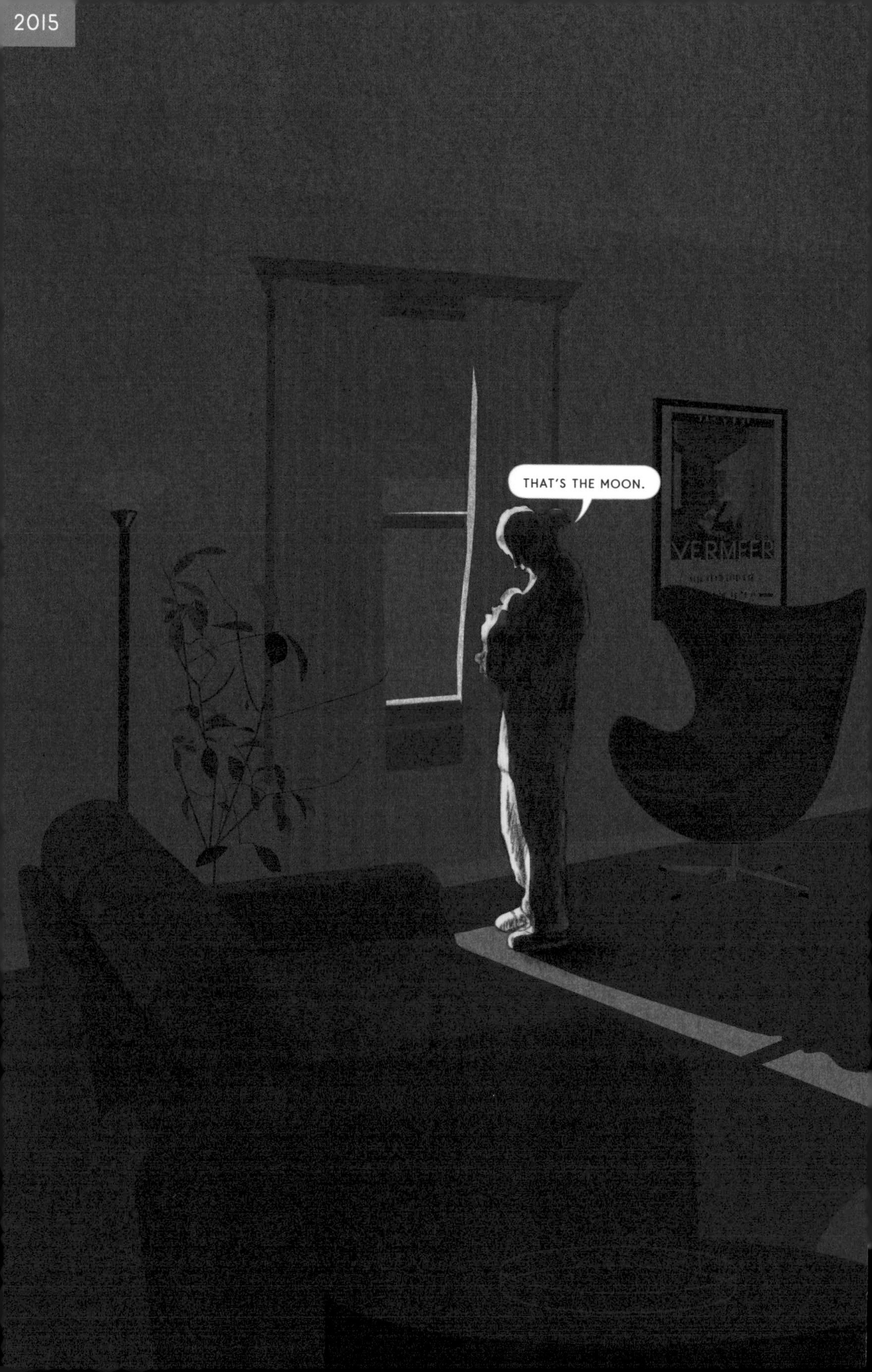
2015
THAT'S THE MOON.
VERMEER

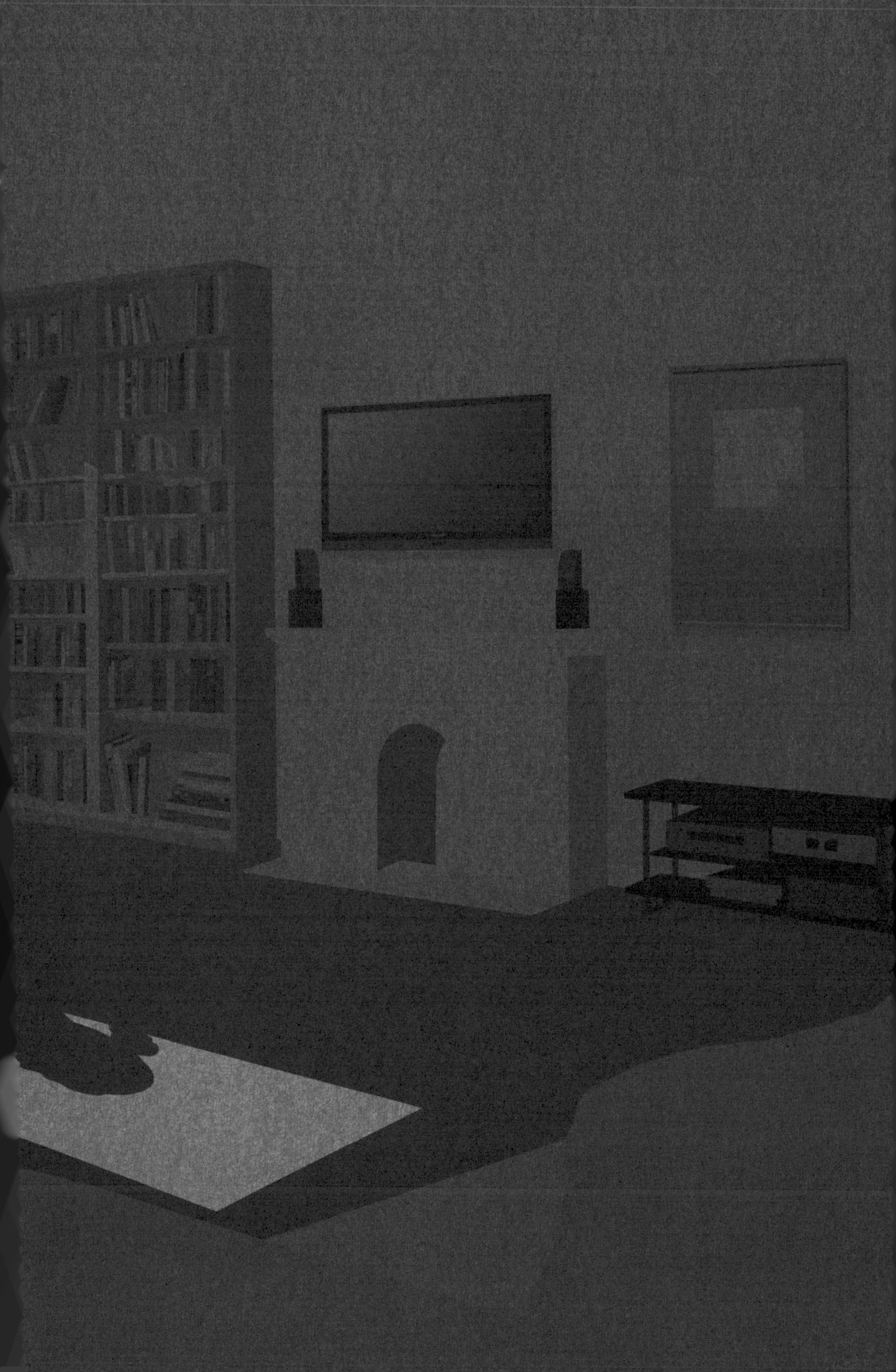

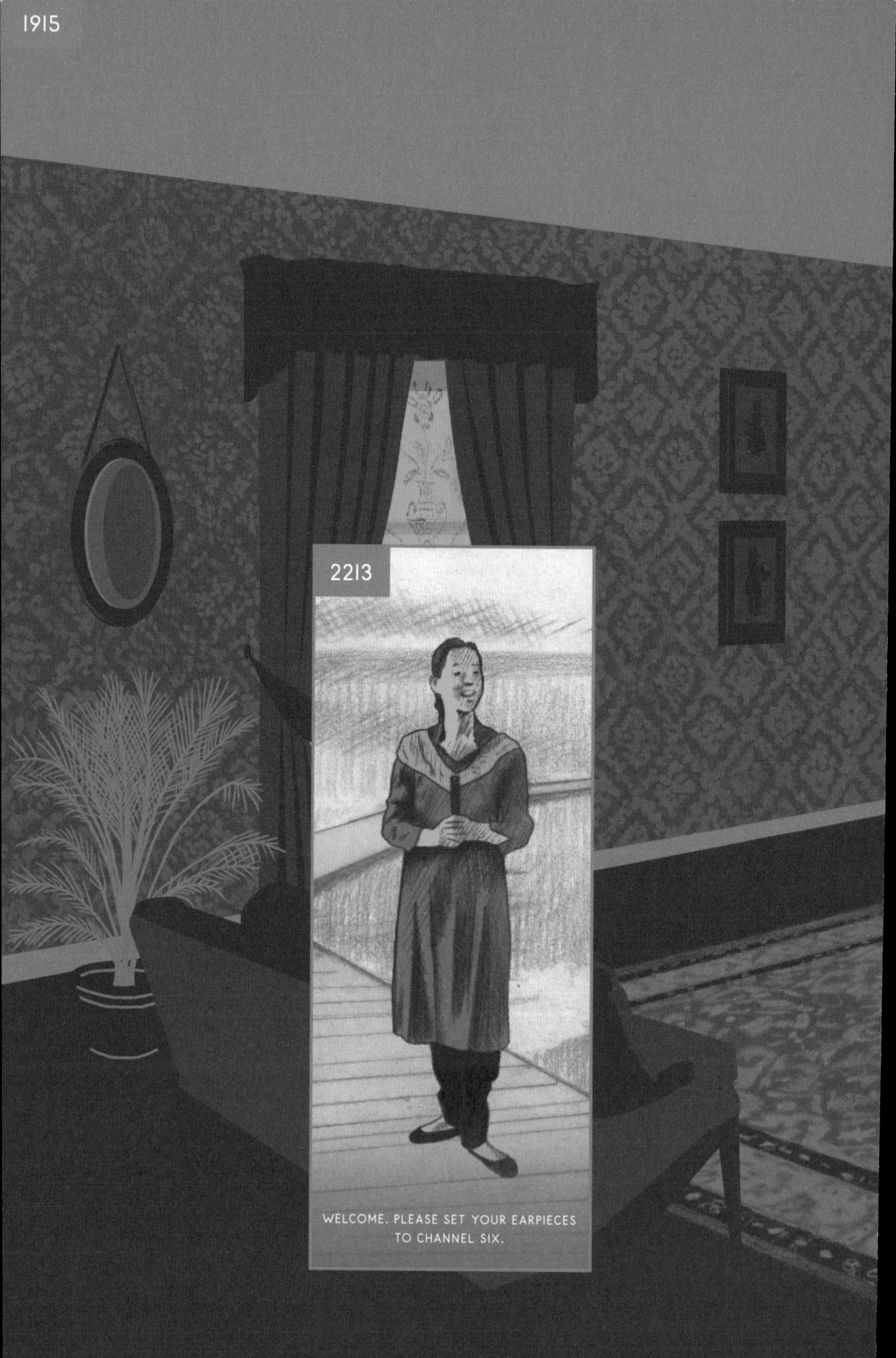
1915
2213
WELCOME. PLEASE SET YOUR EARPIECES
TO CHANNEL SIX.

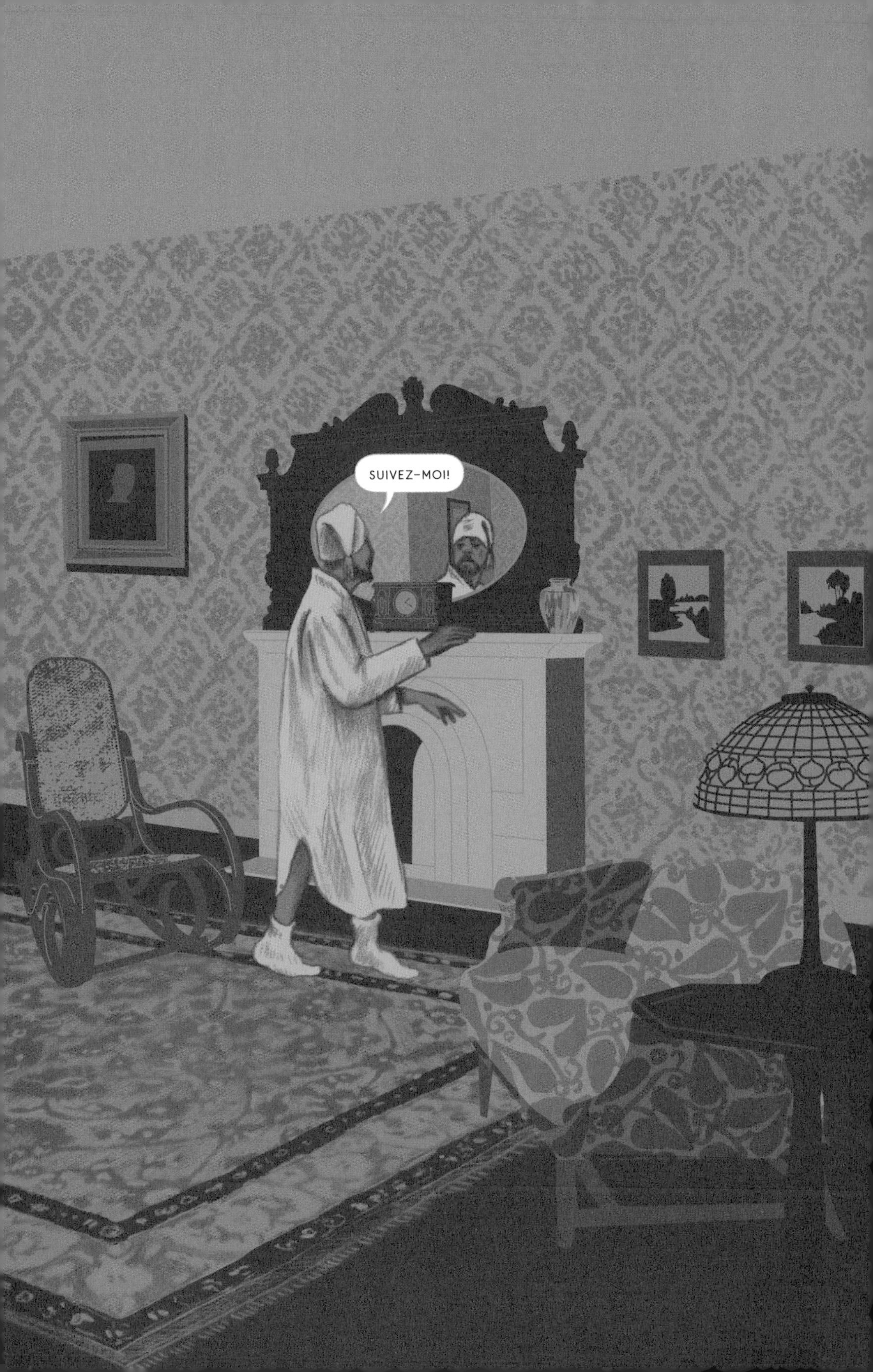
SUIVEZ-MOI!

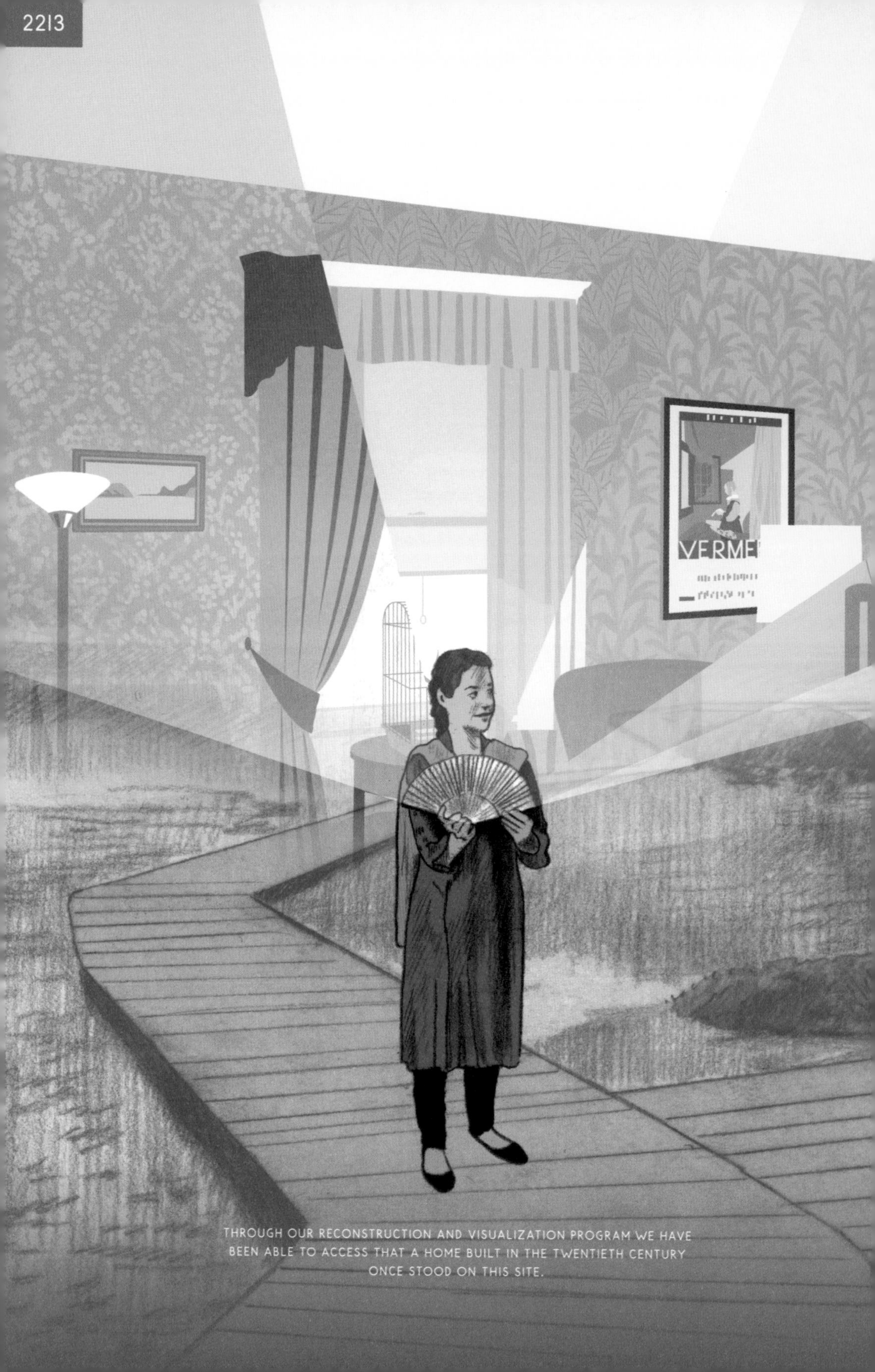
2213
THROUGH OUR RECONSTRUCTION AND VISUALIZATION PROGRAM WE HAVE BEEN ABLE TO ACCESS THAT A HOME BUILT IN THE TWENTIETH CENTURY ONCE STOOD ON THIS SITE.

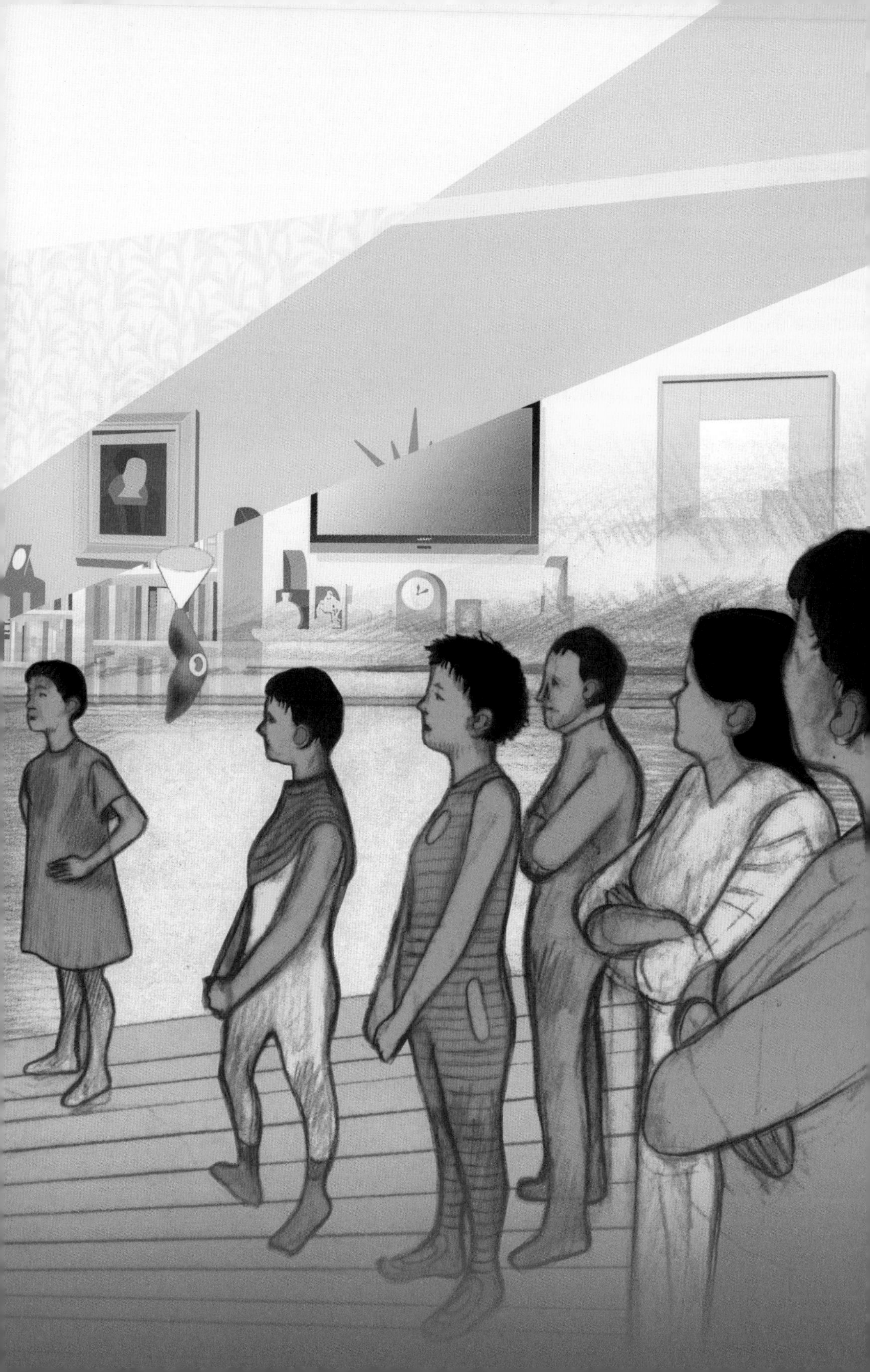

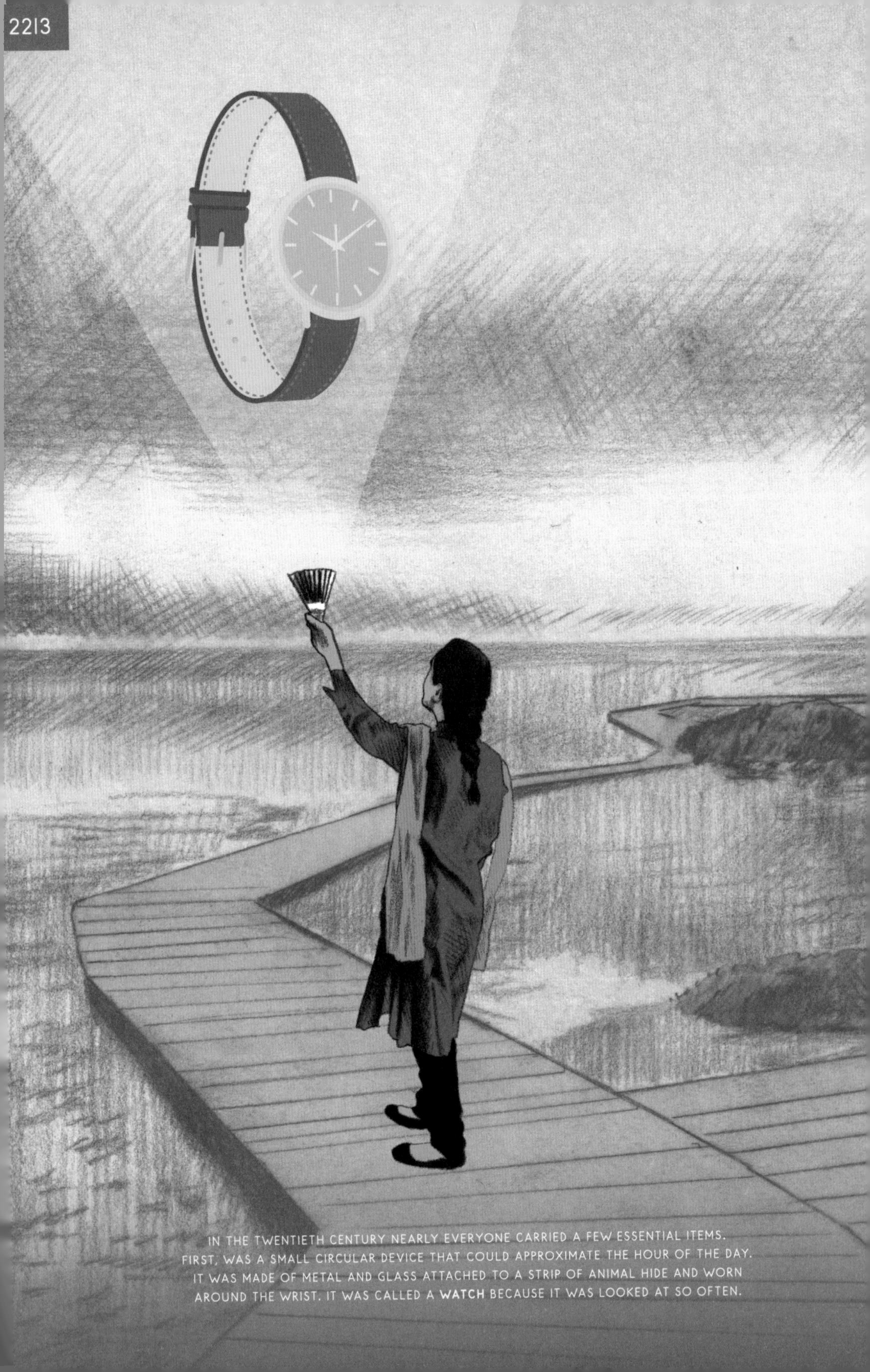
2213
IN THE TWENTIETH CENTURY NEARLY EVERYONE CARRIED A FEW ESSENTIAL ITEMS.
FIRST, WAS A SMALL CIRCULAR DEVICE THAT COULD APPROXIMATE THE HOUR OF THE DAY.
IT WAS MADE OF METAL AND GLASS ATTACHED TO A STRIP OF ANIMAL HIDE AND WORN
AROUND THE WRIST. IT WAS CALLED A **WATCH** BECAUSE IT WAS LOOKED AT SO OFTEN.

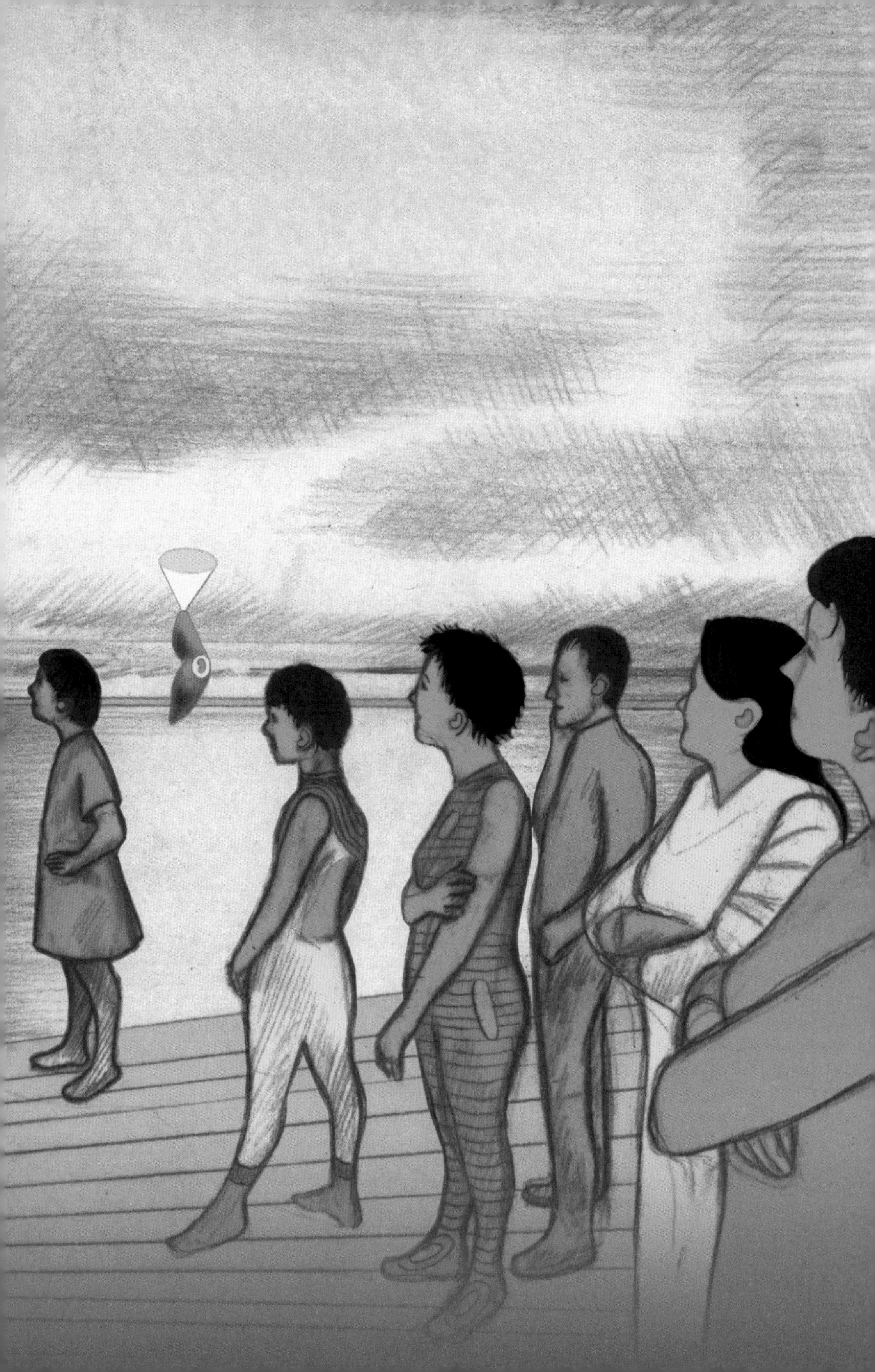

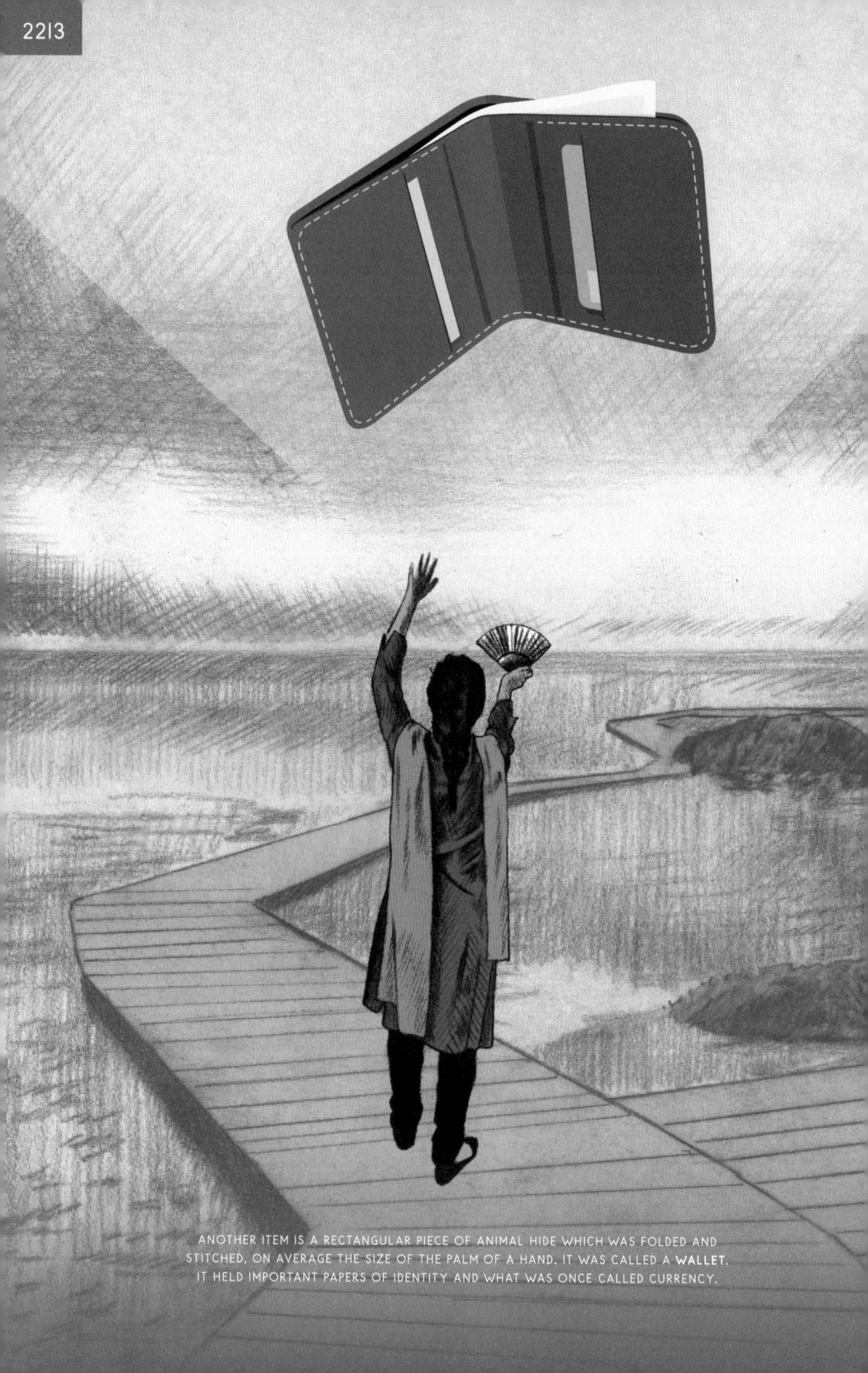
2213
ANOTHER ITEM IS A RECTANGULAR PIECE OF ANIMAL HIDE WHICH WAS FOLDED AND STITCHED, ON AVERAGE THE SIZE OF THE PALM OF A HAND. IT WAS CALLED A **WALLET**. IT HELD IMPORTANT PAPERS OF IDENTITY AND WHAT WAS ONCE CALLED CURRENCY.

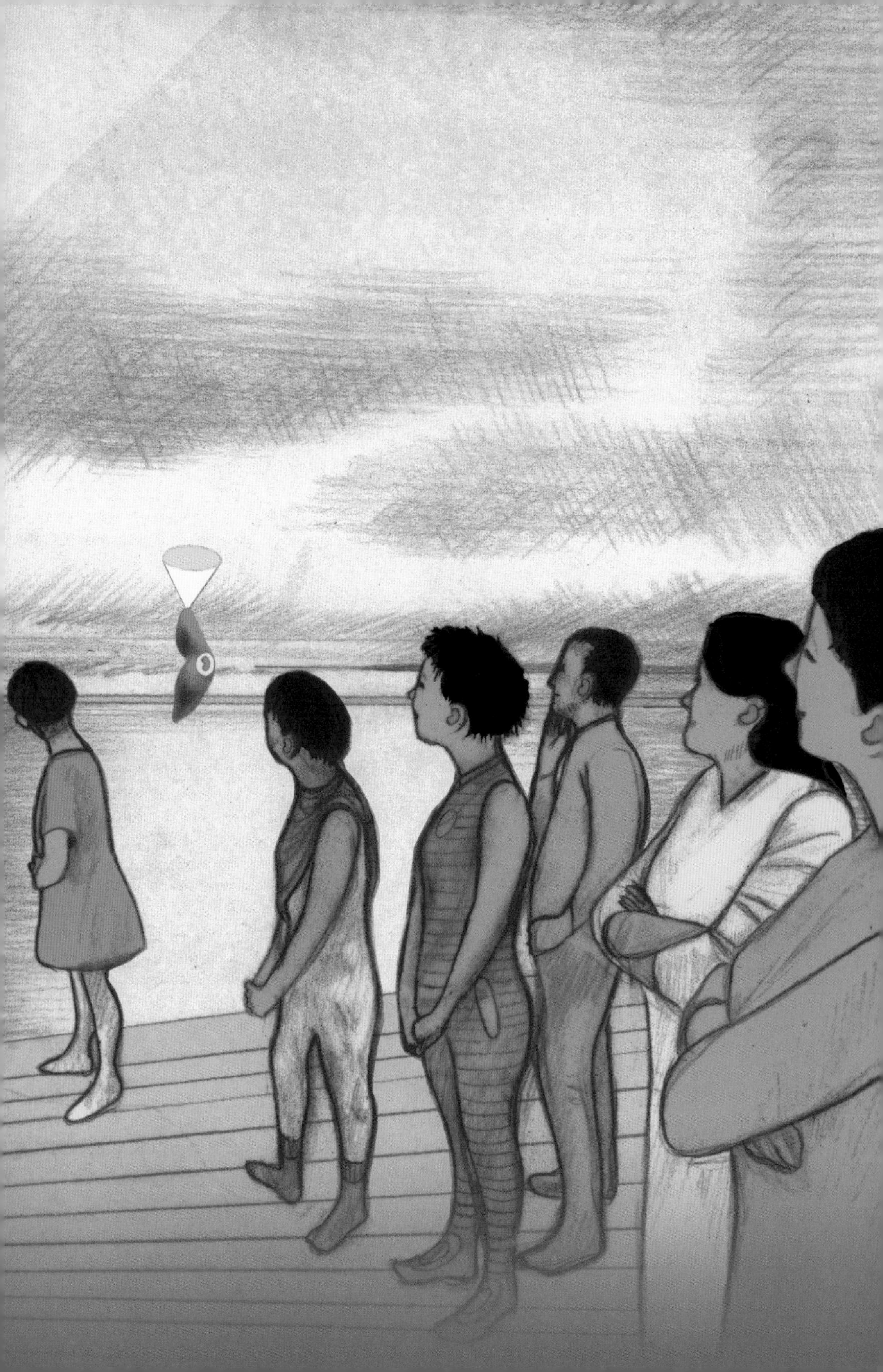

2213

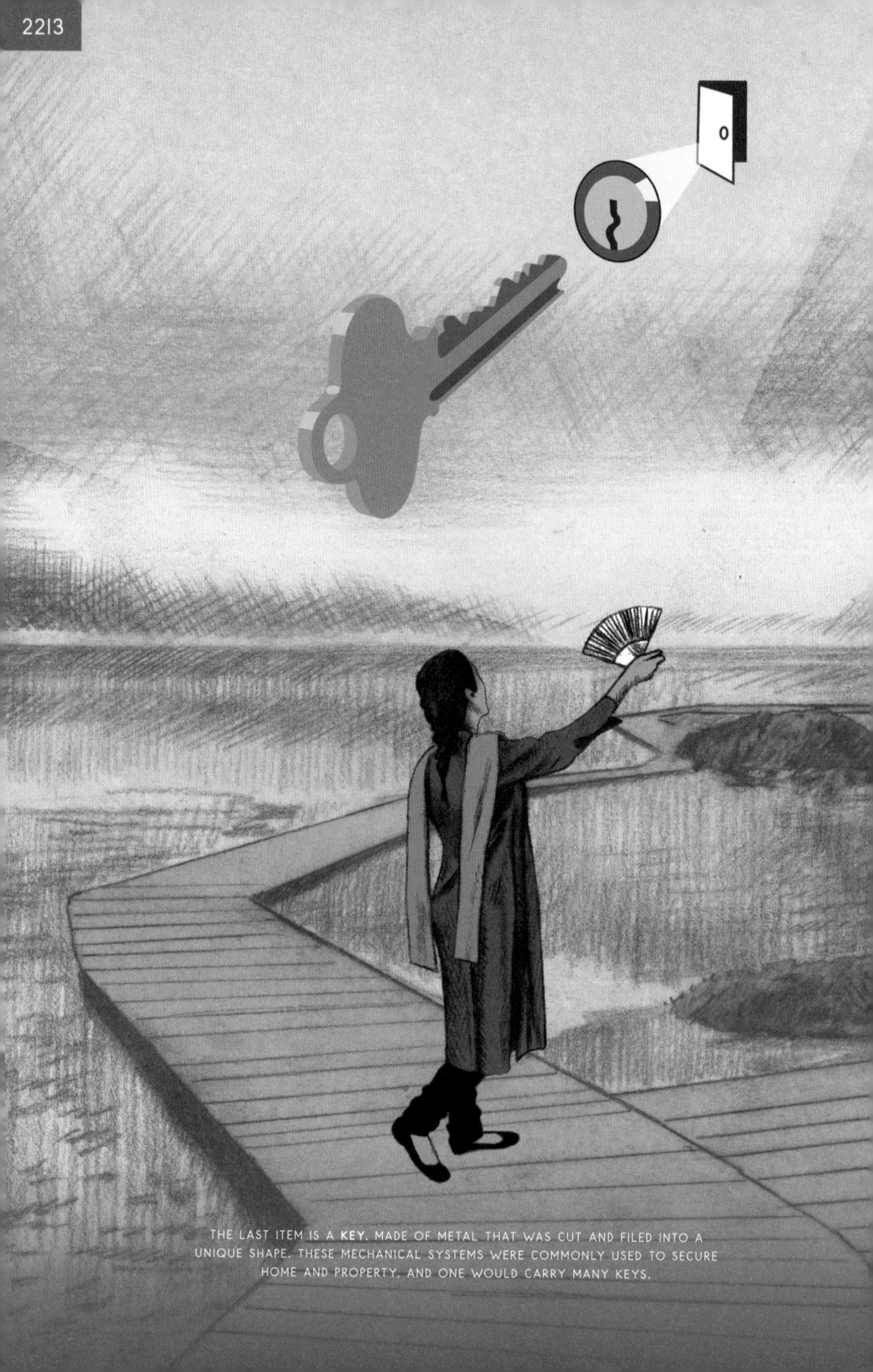

THE LAST ITEM IS A **KEY**. MADE OF METAL THAT WAS CUT AND FILED INTO A UNIQUE SHAPE. THESE MECHANICAL SYSTEMS WERE COMMONLY USED TO SECURE HOME AND PROPERTY, AND ONE WOULD CARRY MANY KEYS.

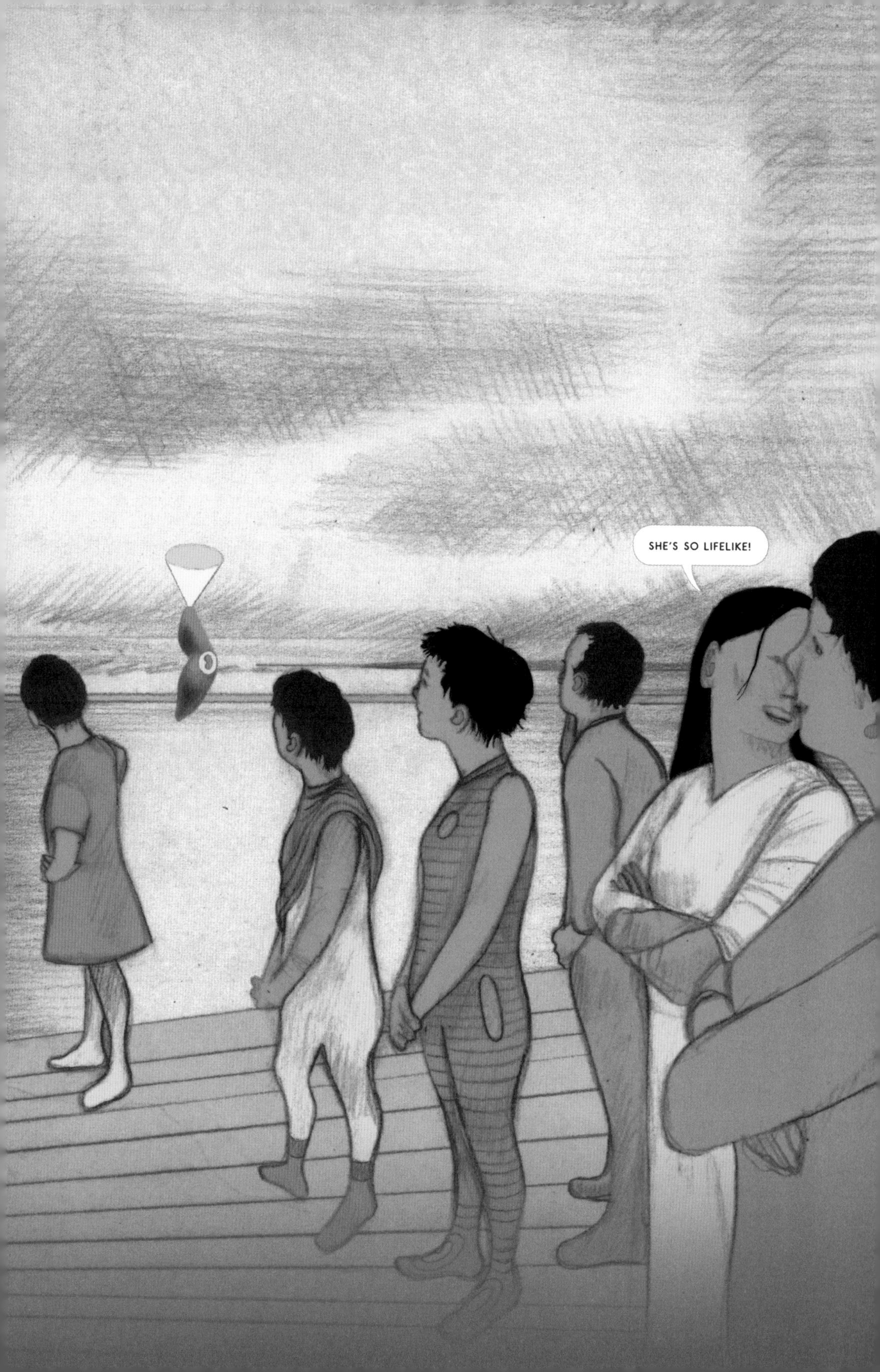
SHE'S SO LIFELIKE!

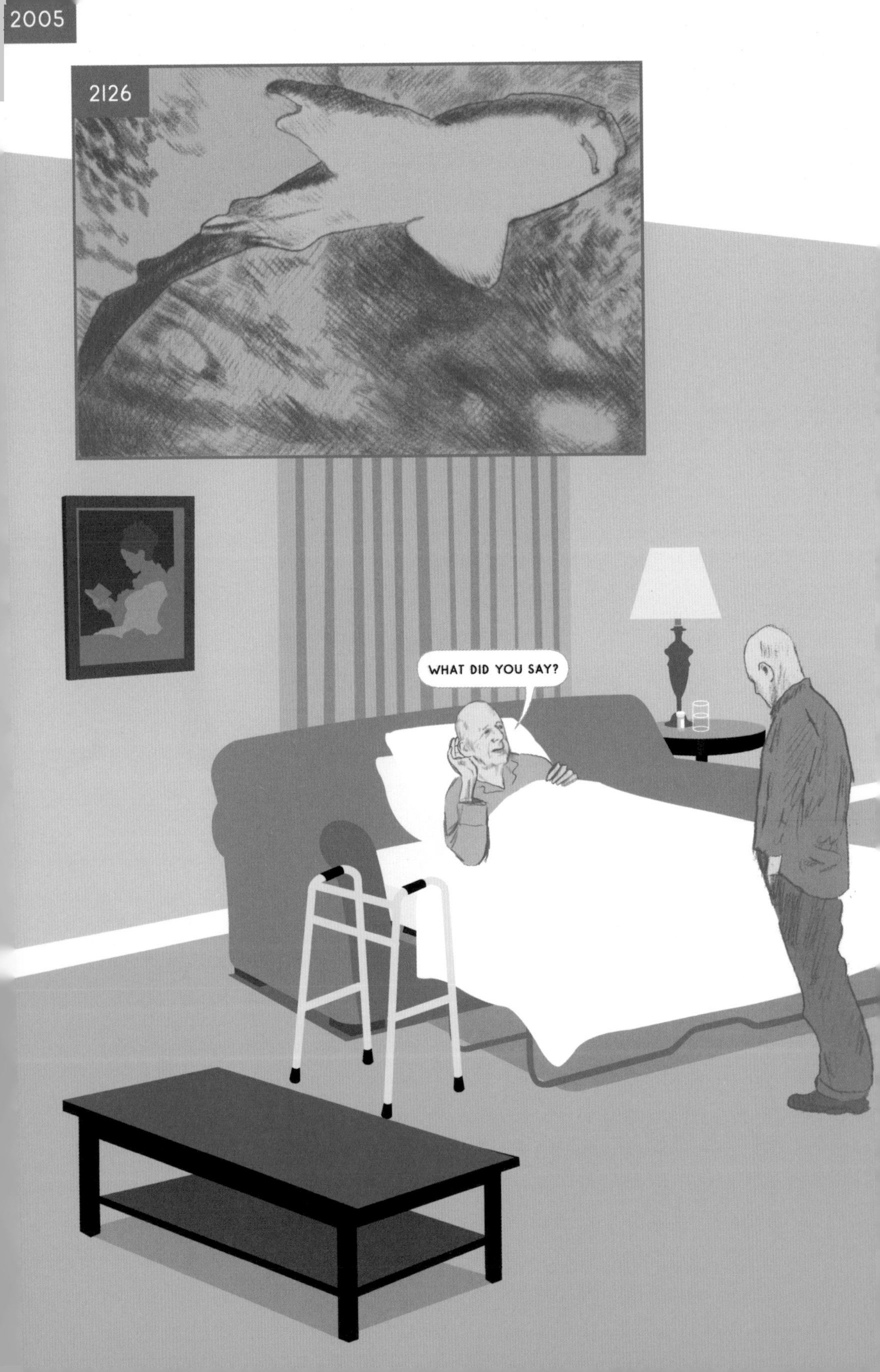
2005
2126
WHAT DID YOU SAY?

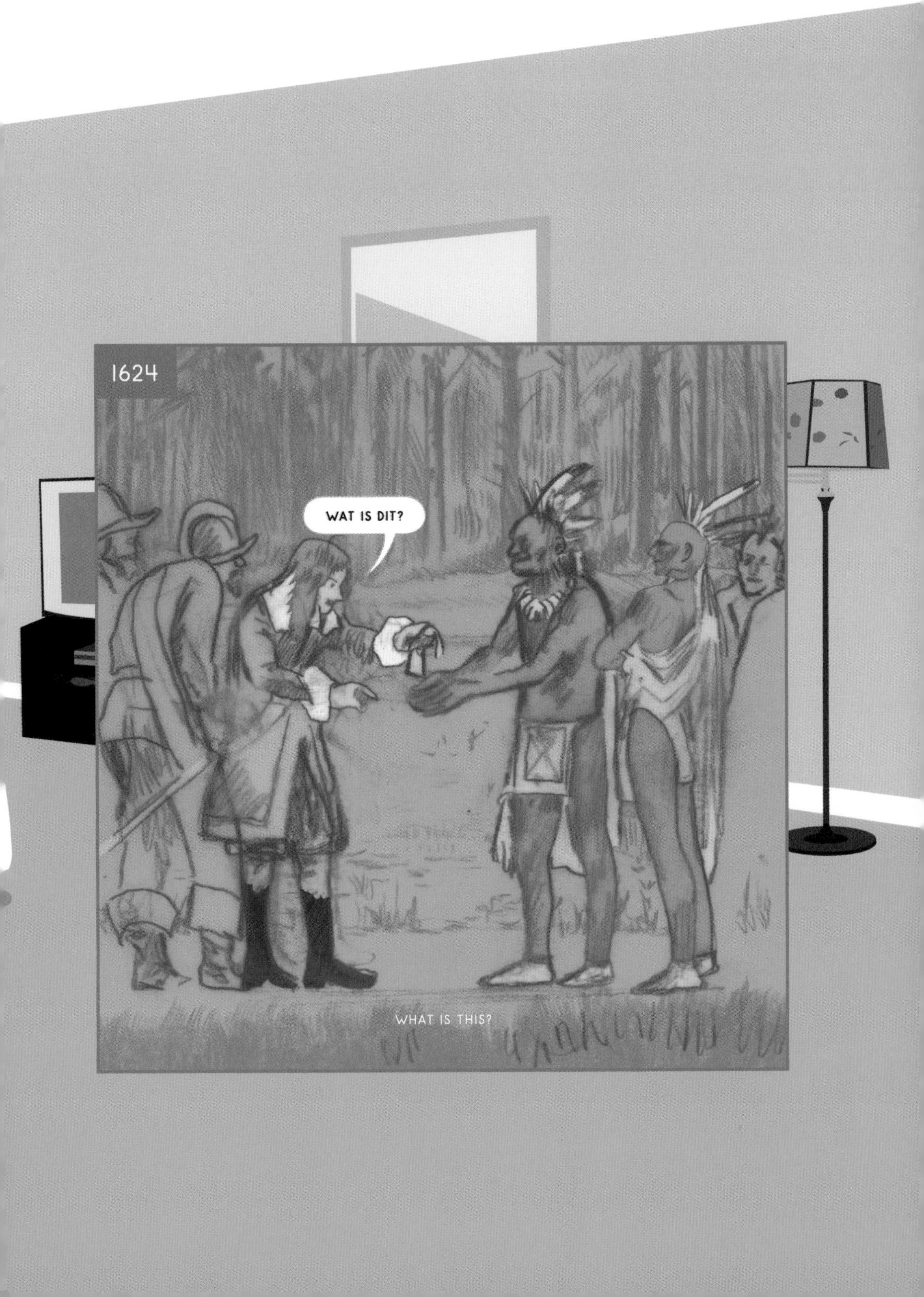
1624
WAT IS DIT?
WHAT IS THIS?

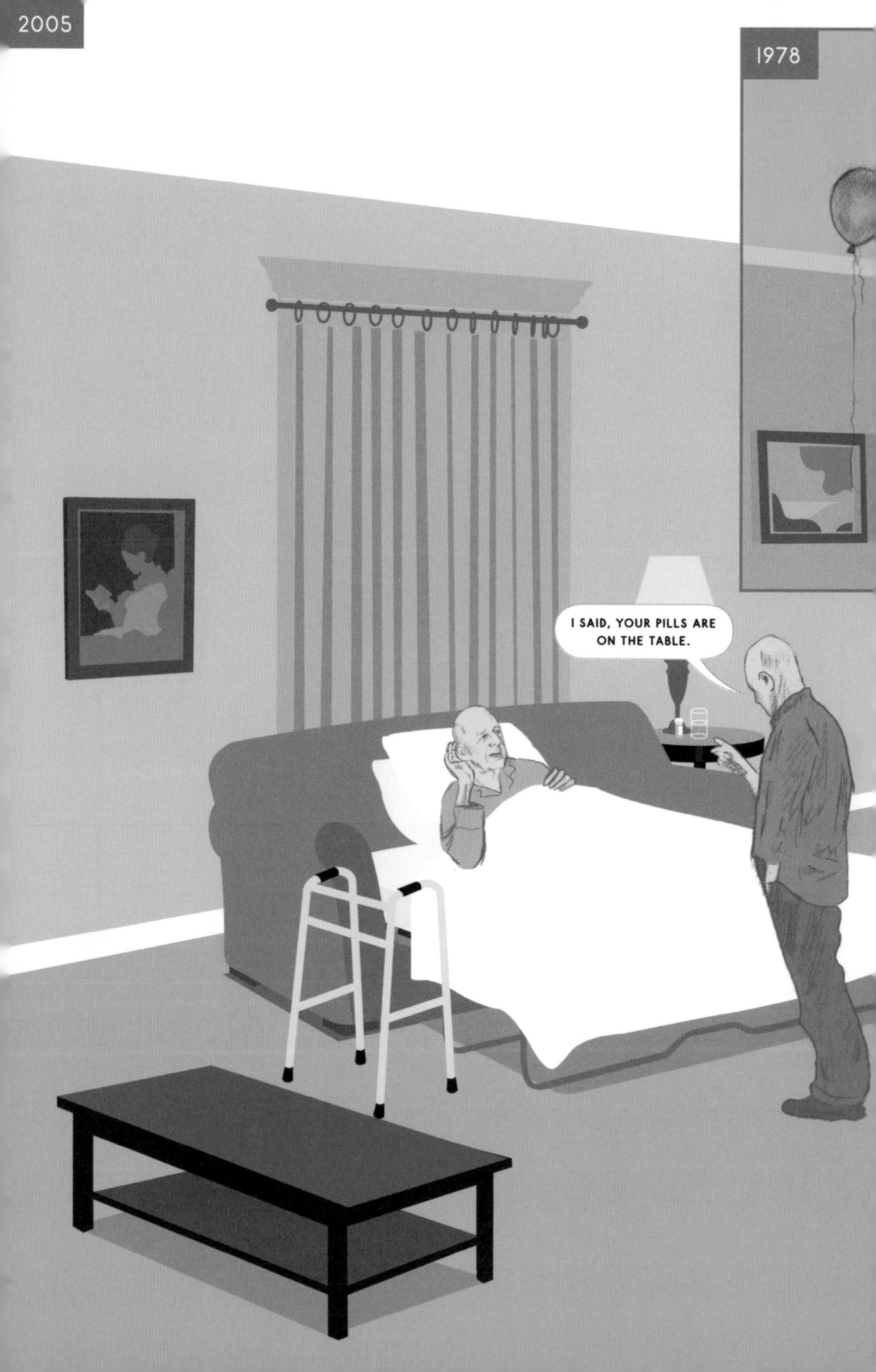
2005
1978
I SAID, YOUR PILLS ARE ON THE TABLE.

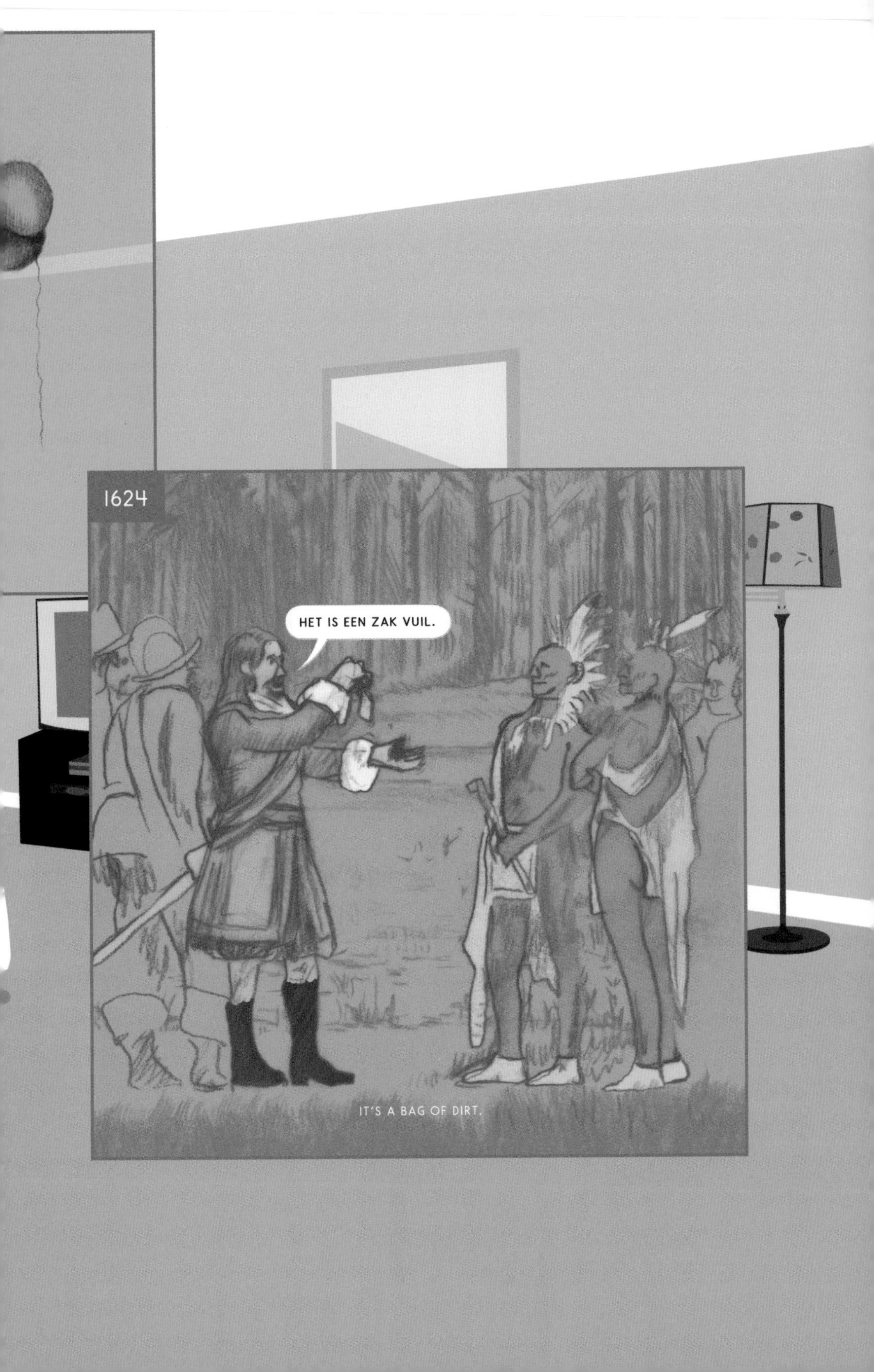
1624
HET IS EEN ZAK VUIL.
IT'S A BAG OF DIRT.

2005

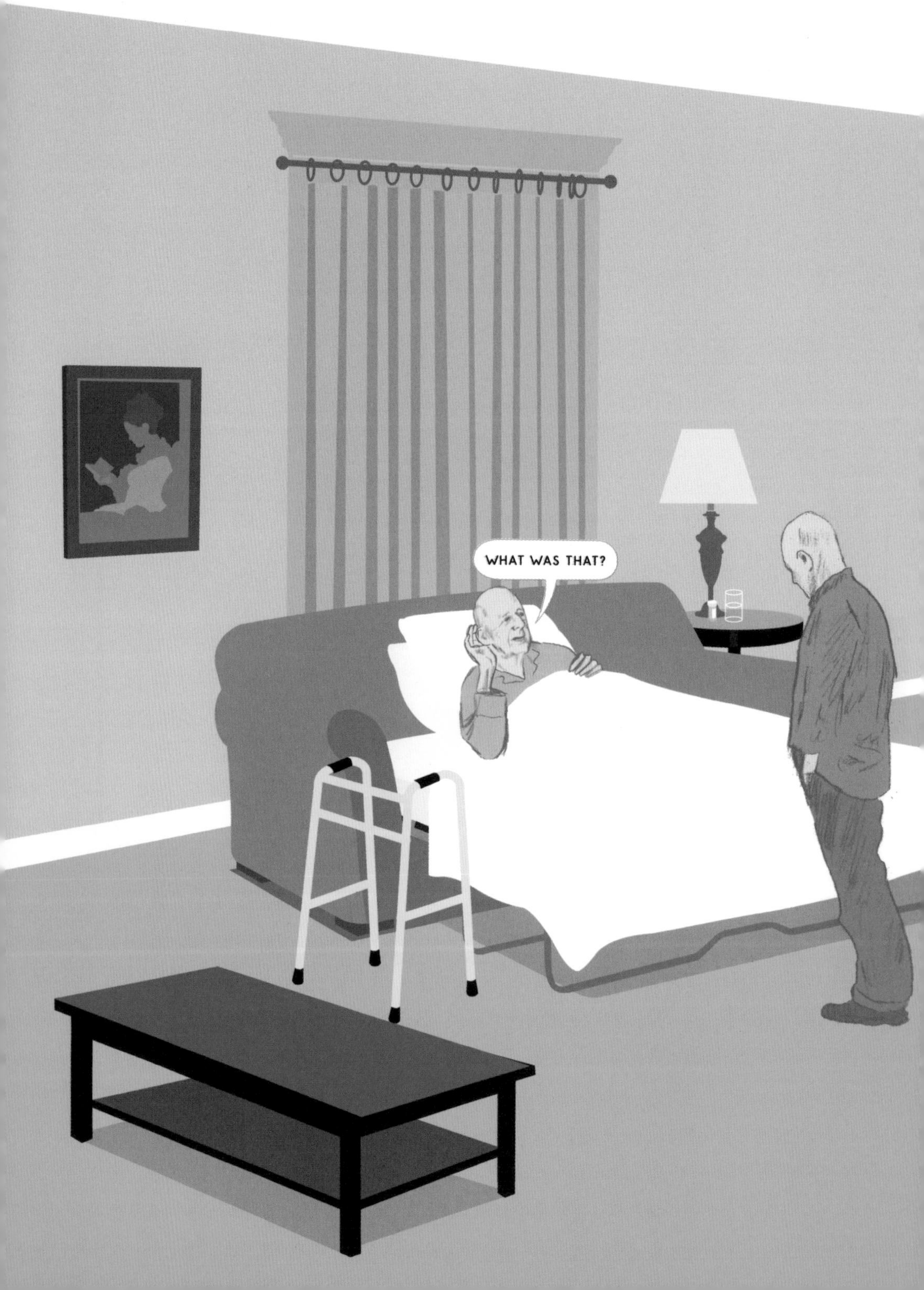
WHAT WAS THAT?

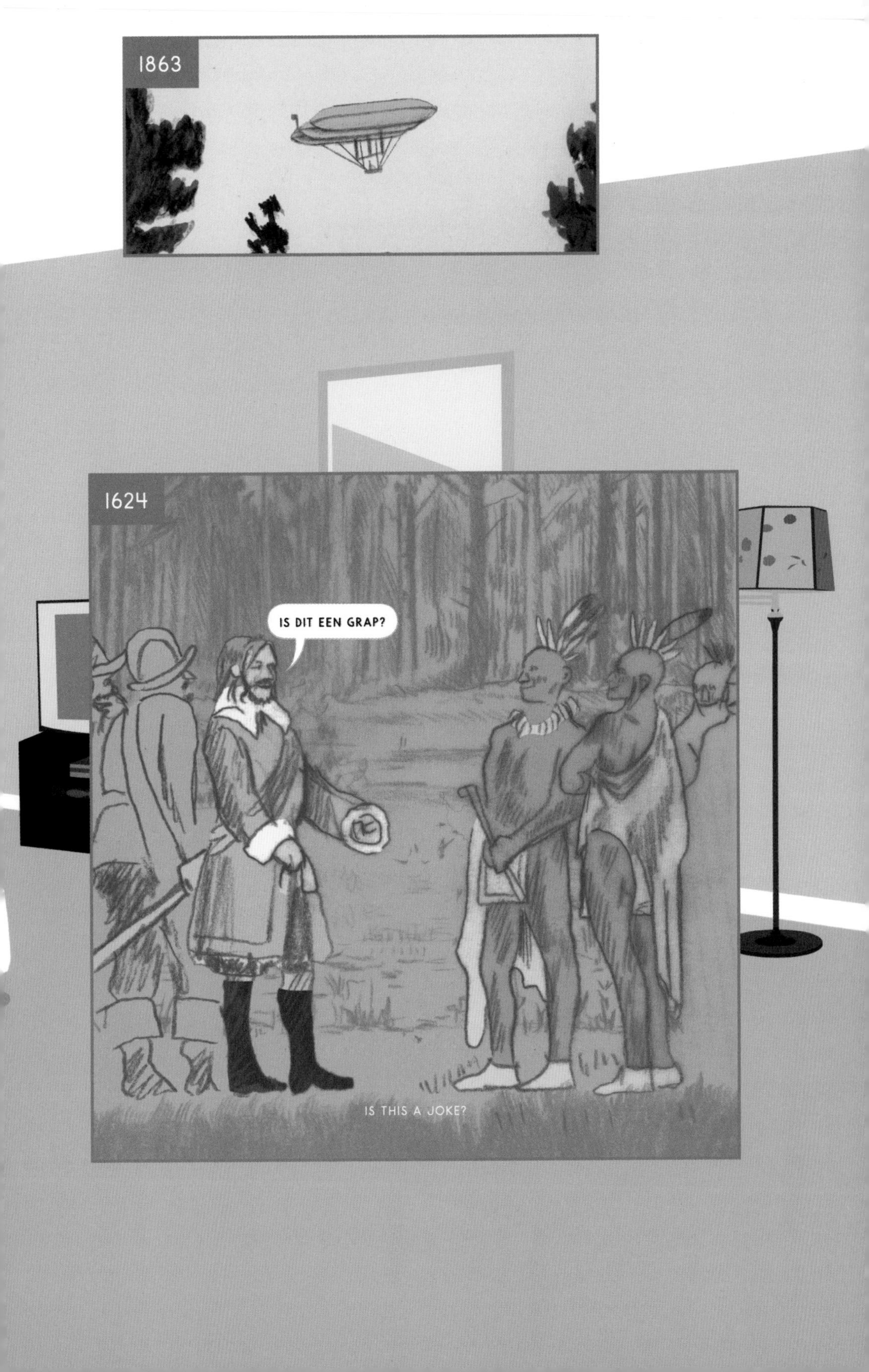
1863
1624
IS DIT EEN GRAP?
IS THIS A JOKE?

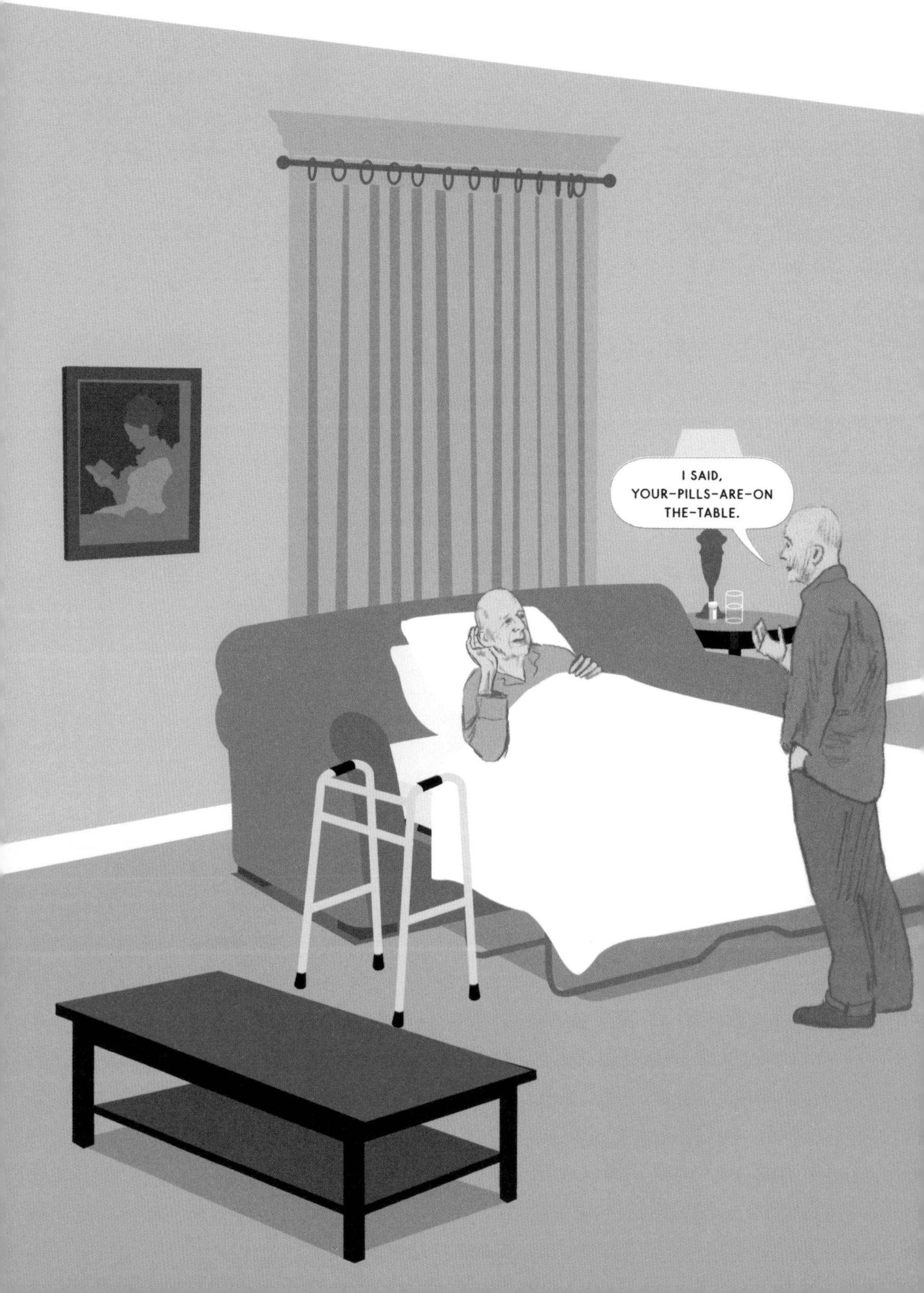
I SAID,
YOUR-PILLS-ARE-ON
THE-TABLE.

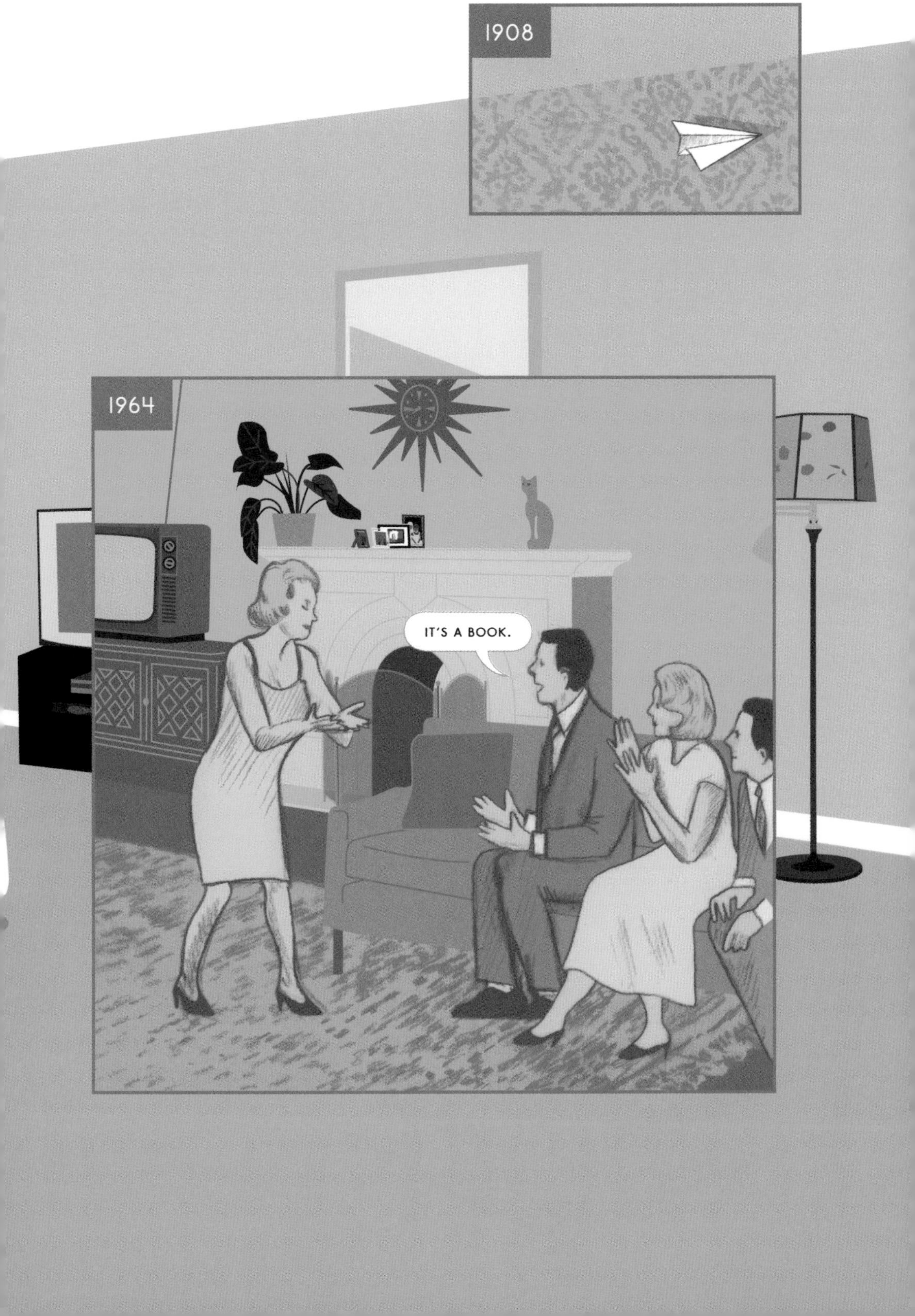
1908
1964
IT'S A BOOK.

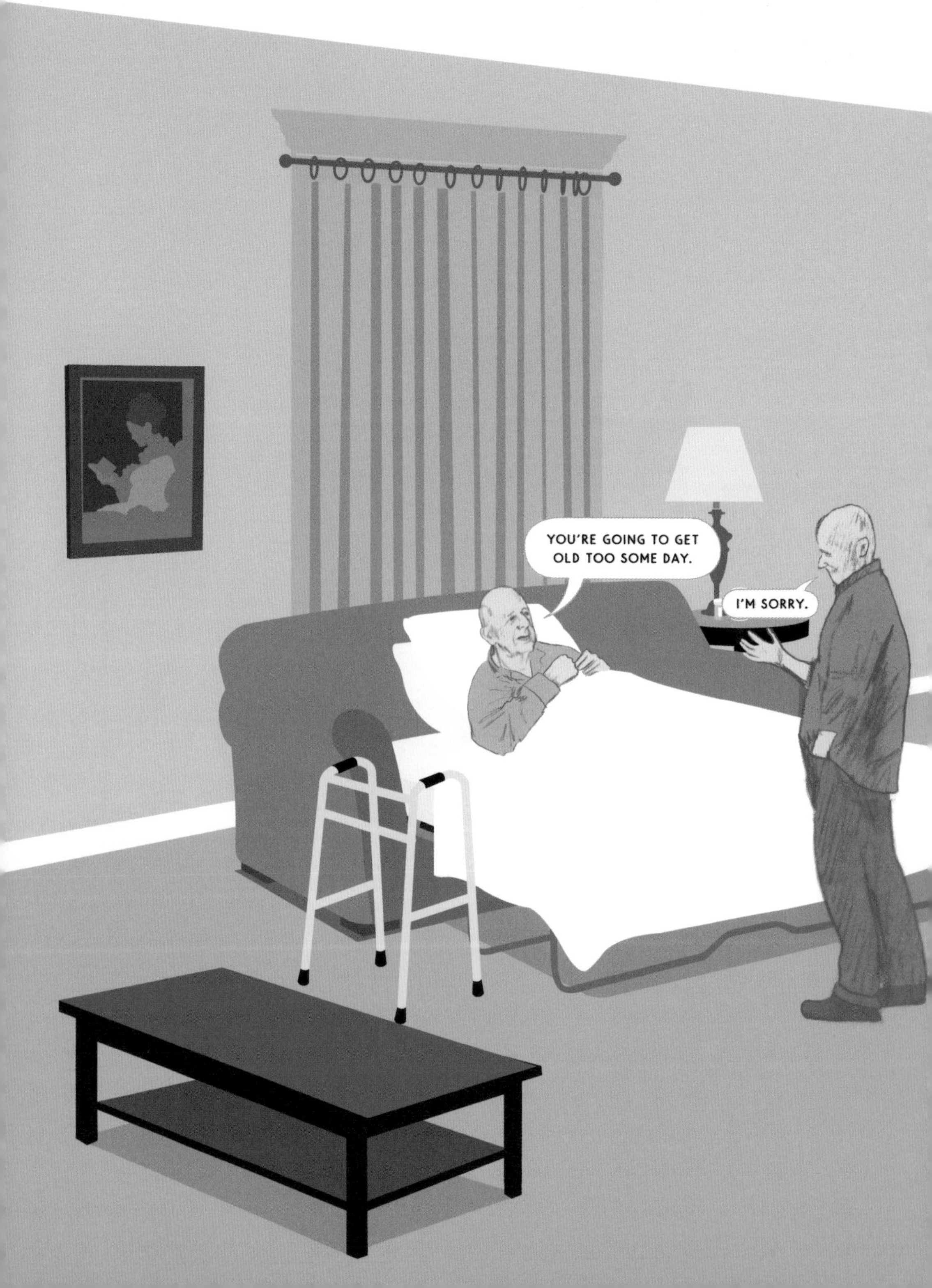
YOU'RE GOING TO GET OLD TOO SOME DAY.
I'M SORRY.

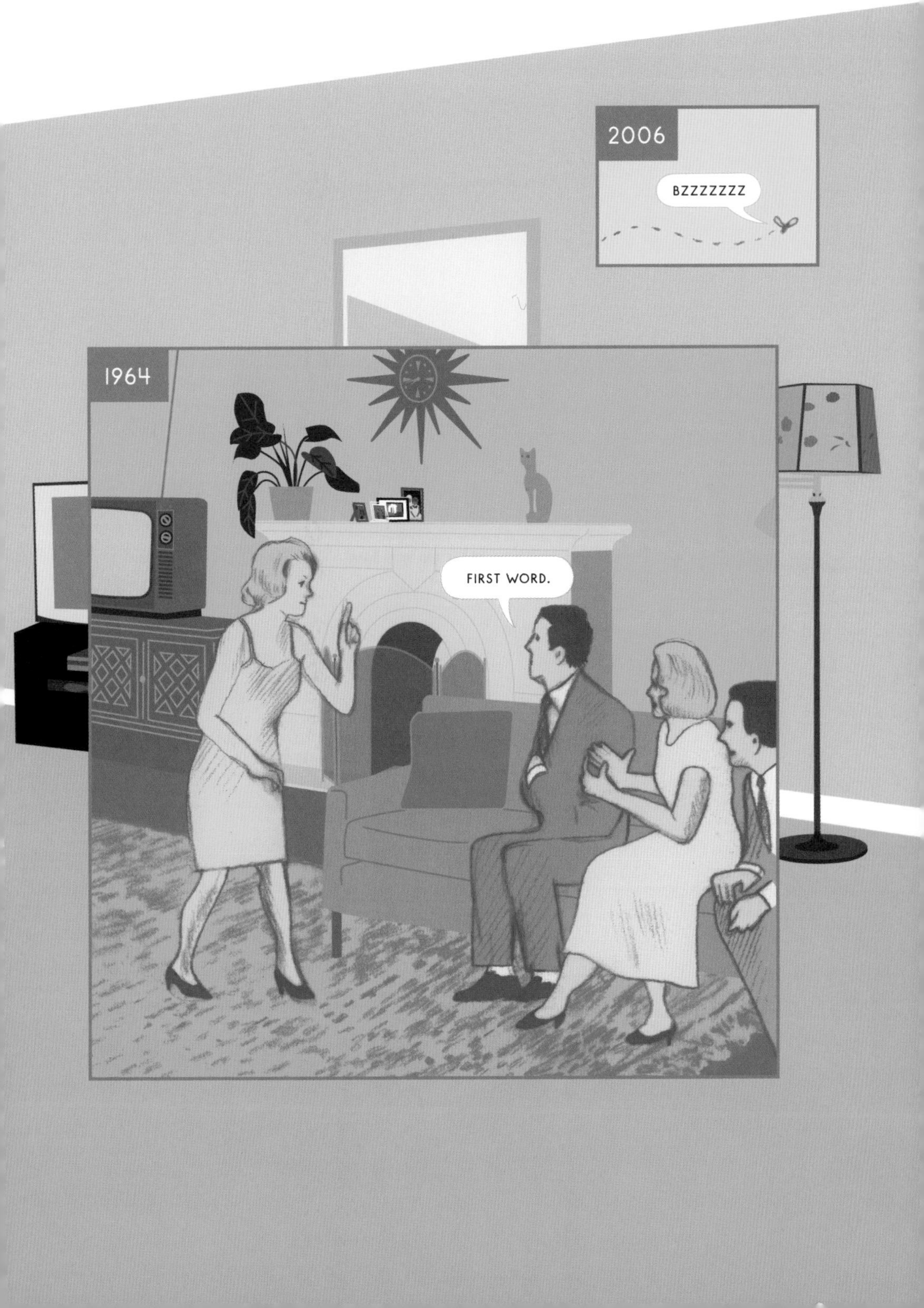
2006
BZZZZZZZ
1964
FIRST WORD.

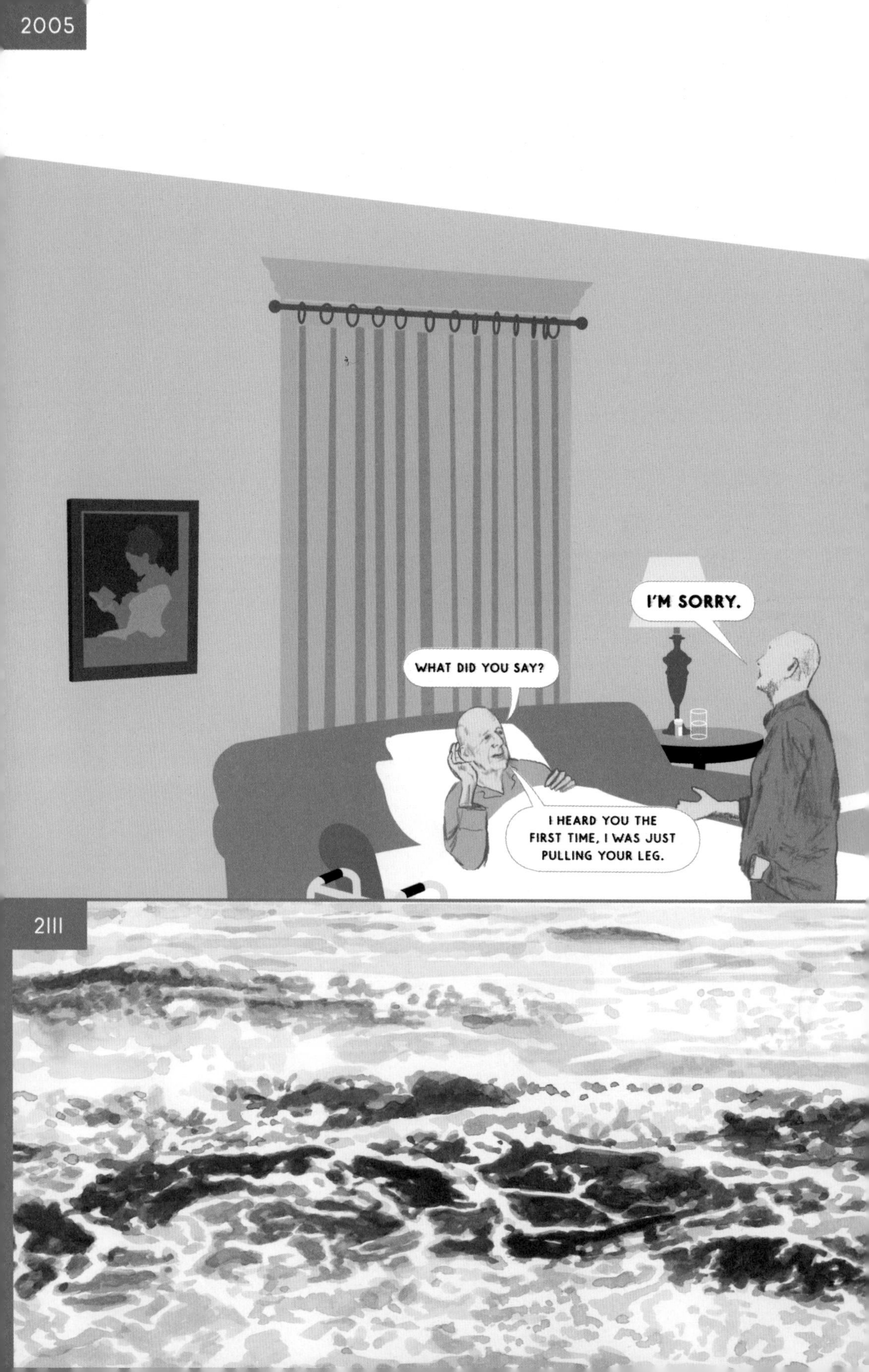
2005
I'M SORRY.
WHAT DID YOU SAY?
I HEARD YOU THE FIRST TIME, I WAS JUST PULLING YOUR LEG.
2111

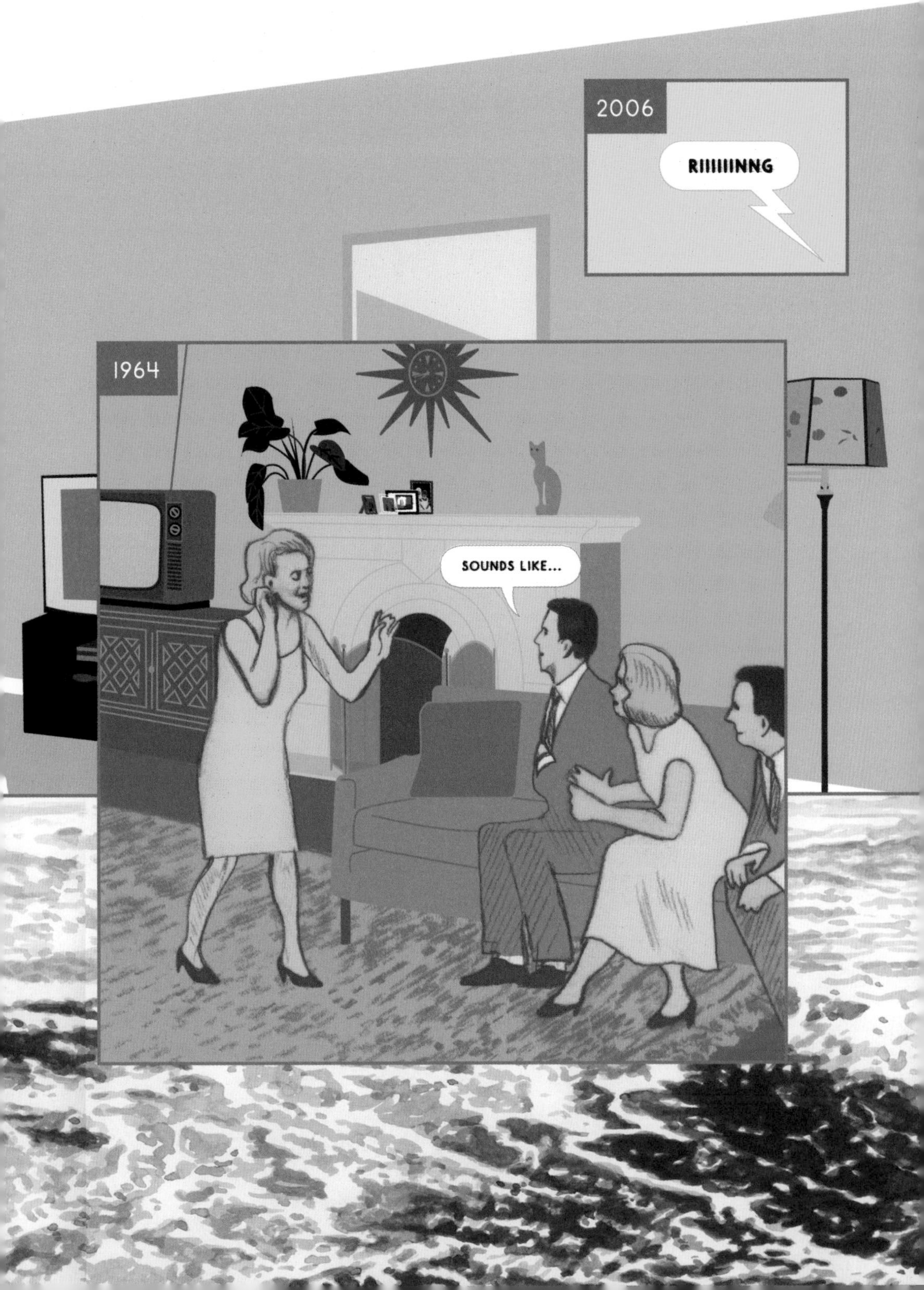
2006
RIIIIIINNG
1964
SOUNDS LIKE...

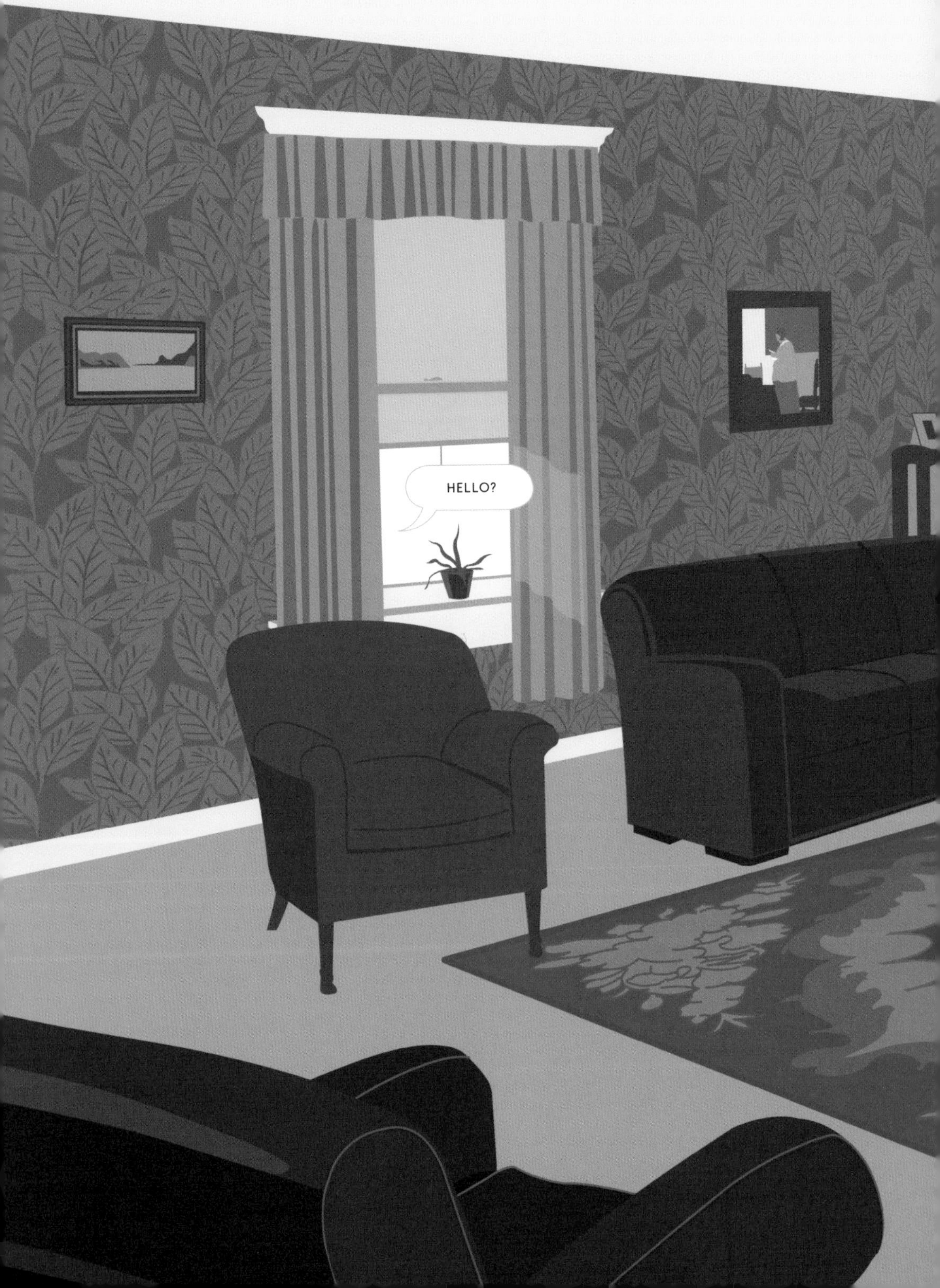
HELLO?

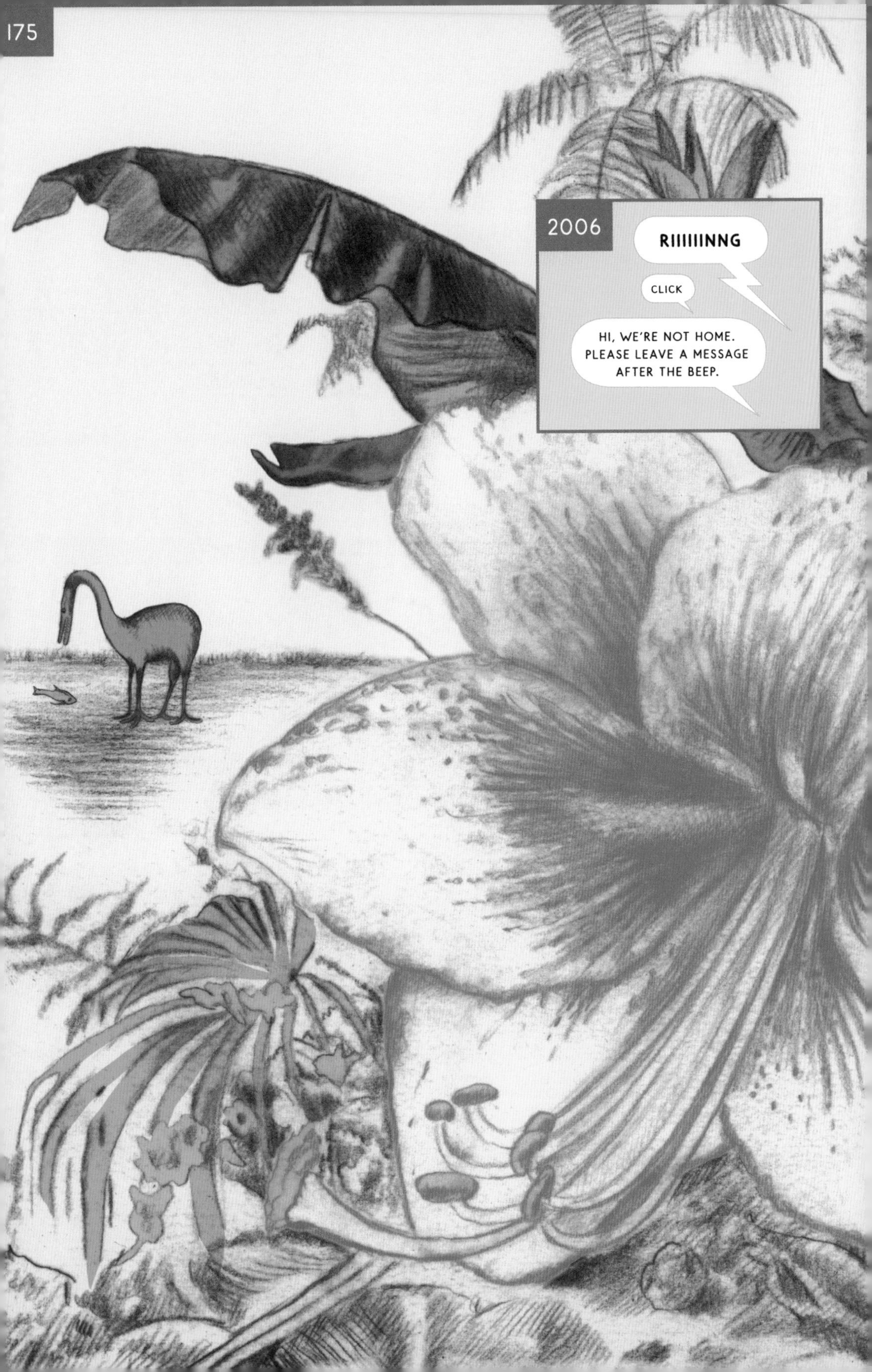
2006
RIIIIIINNG
CLICK
HI, WE'RE NOT HOME. PLEASE LEAVE A MESSAGE AFTER THE BEEP.

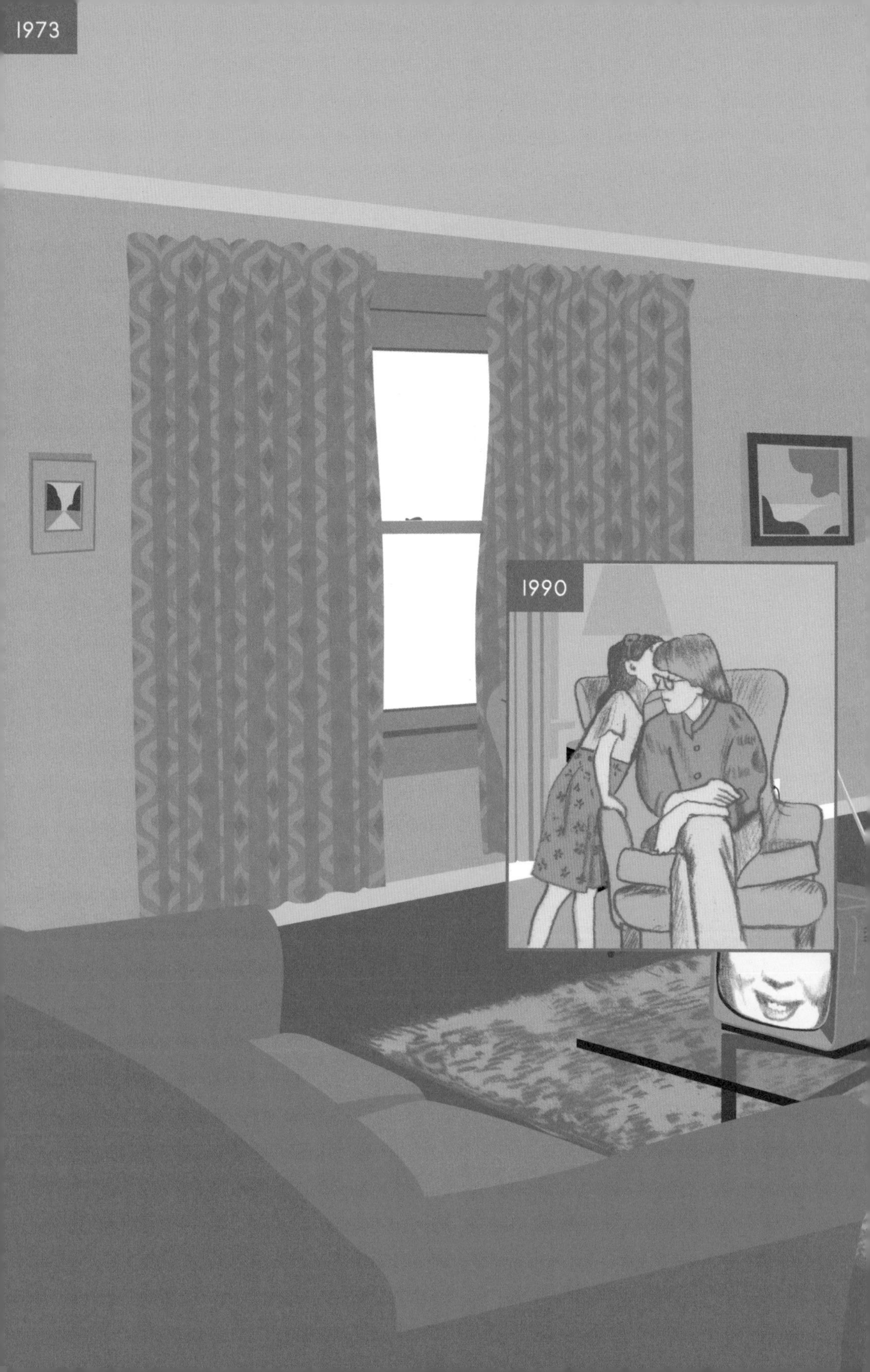
1973
1990

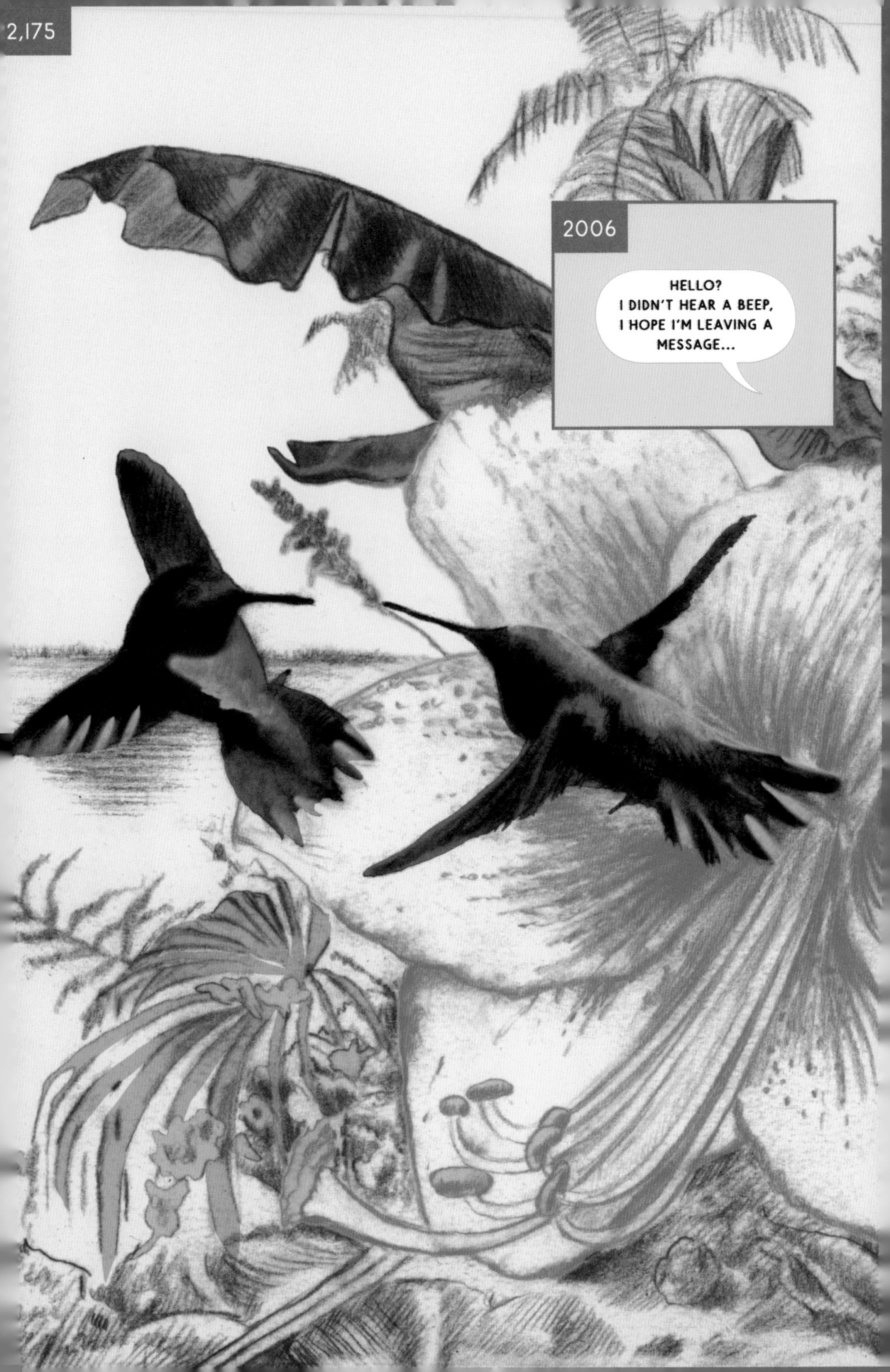
2006
HELLO?
I DIDN'T HEAR A BEEP,
I HOPE I'M LEAVING A
MESSAGE...

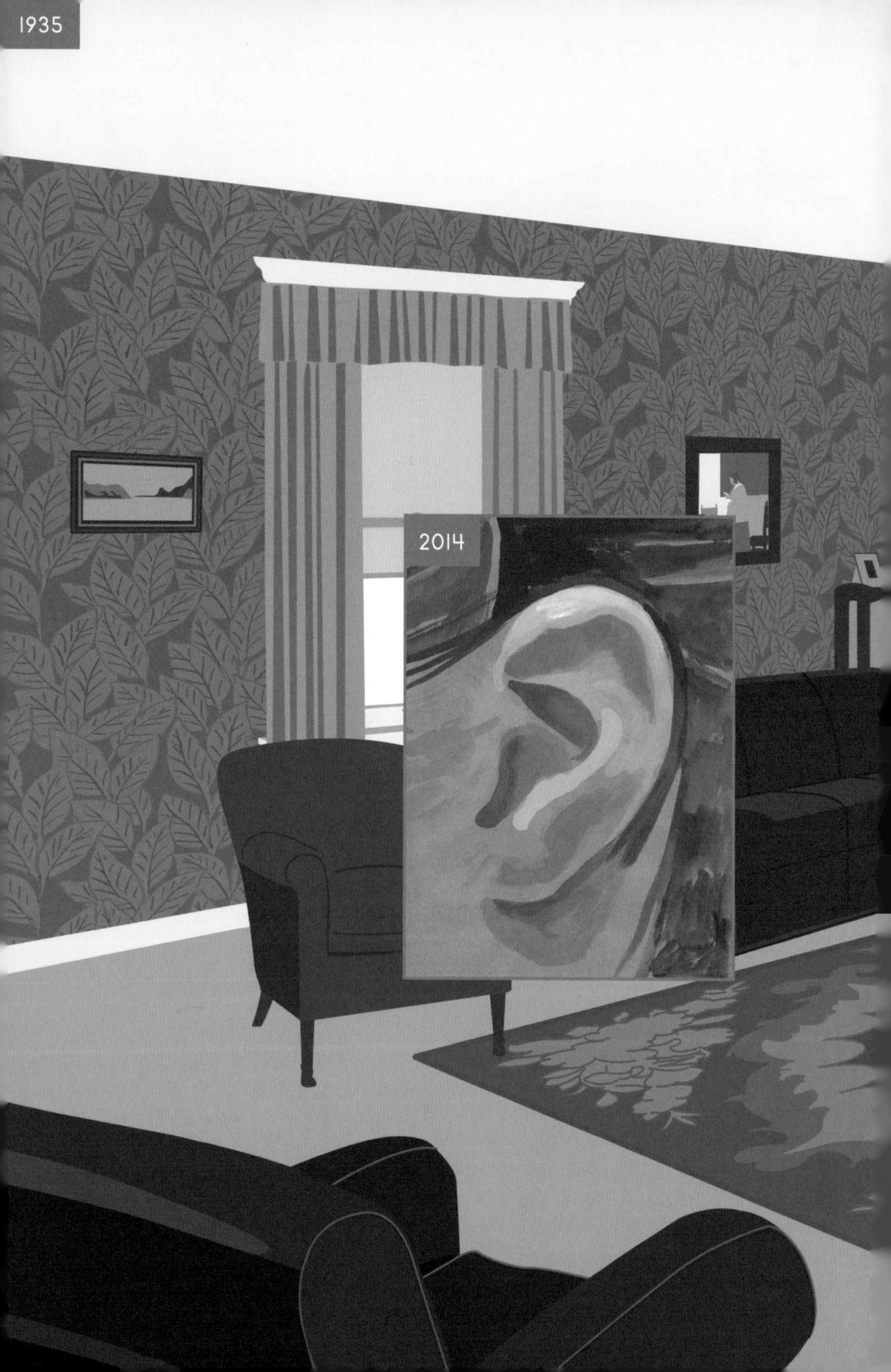
1935
2014

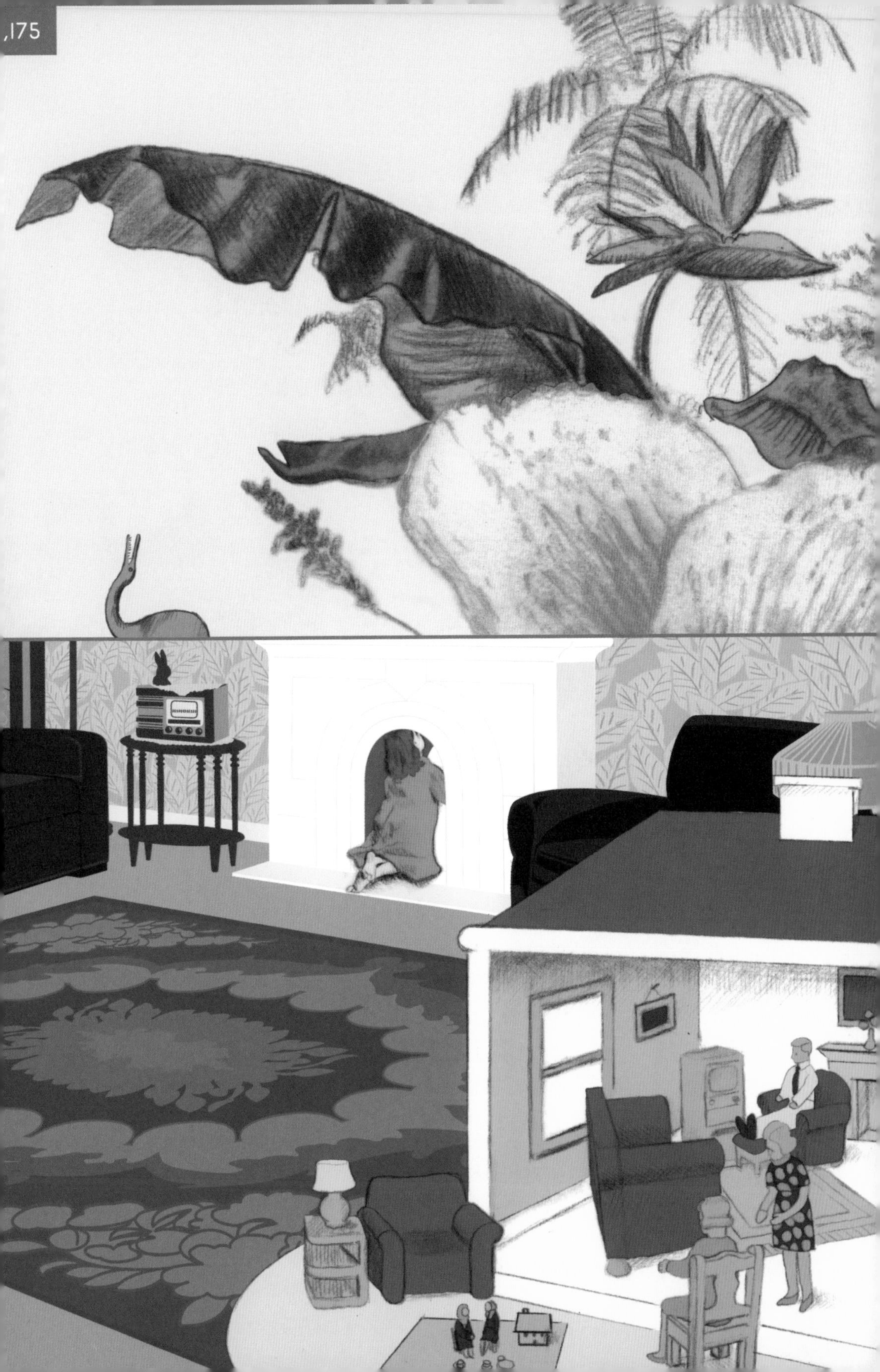

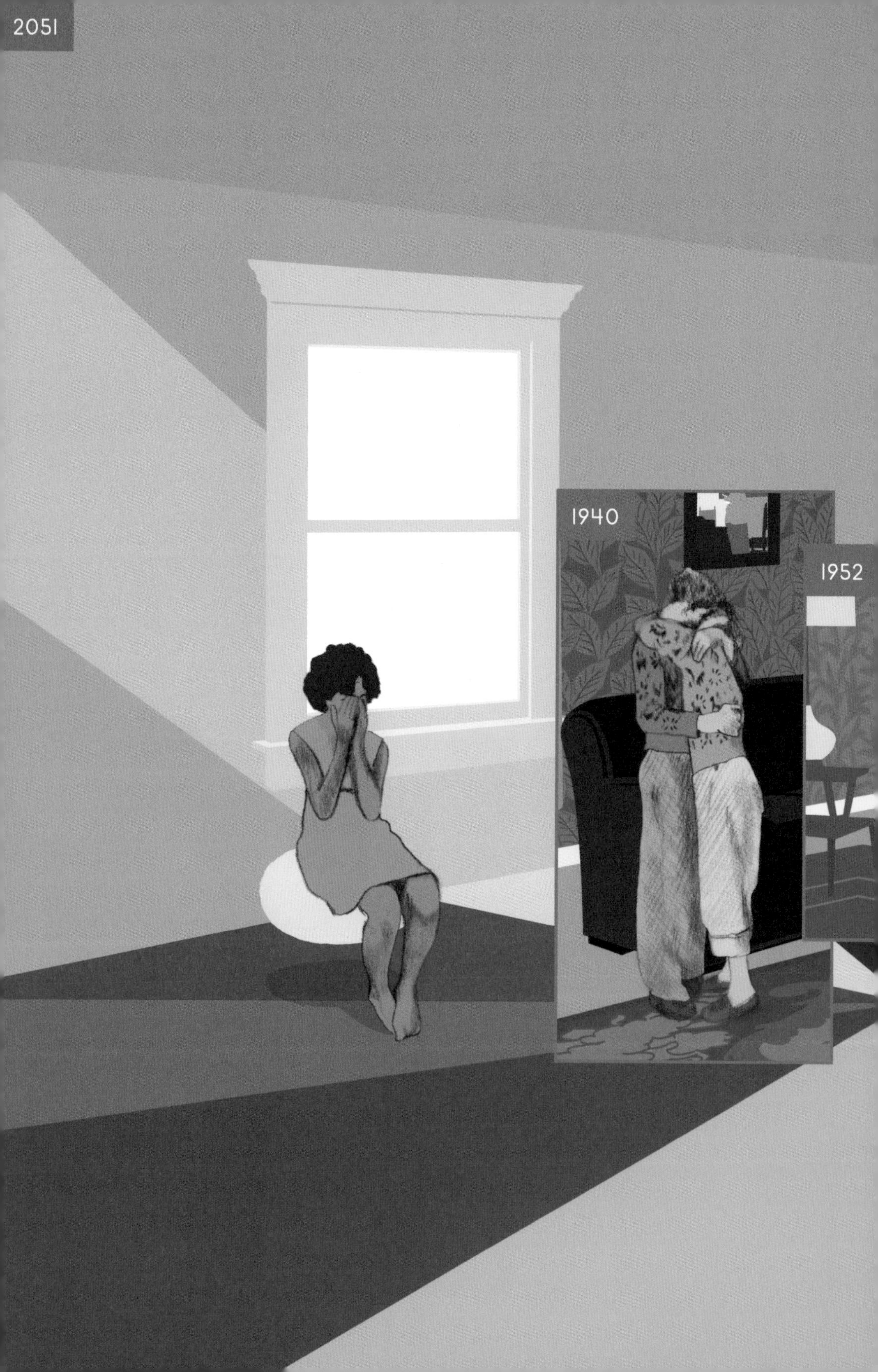
2051
1940
1952

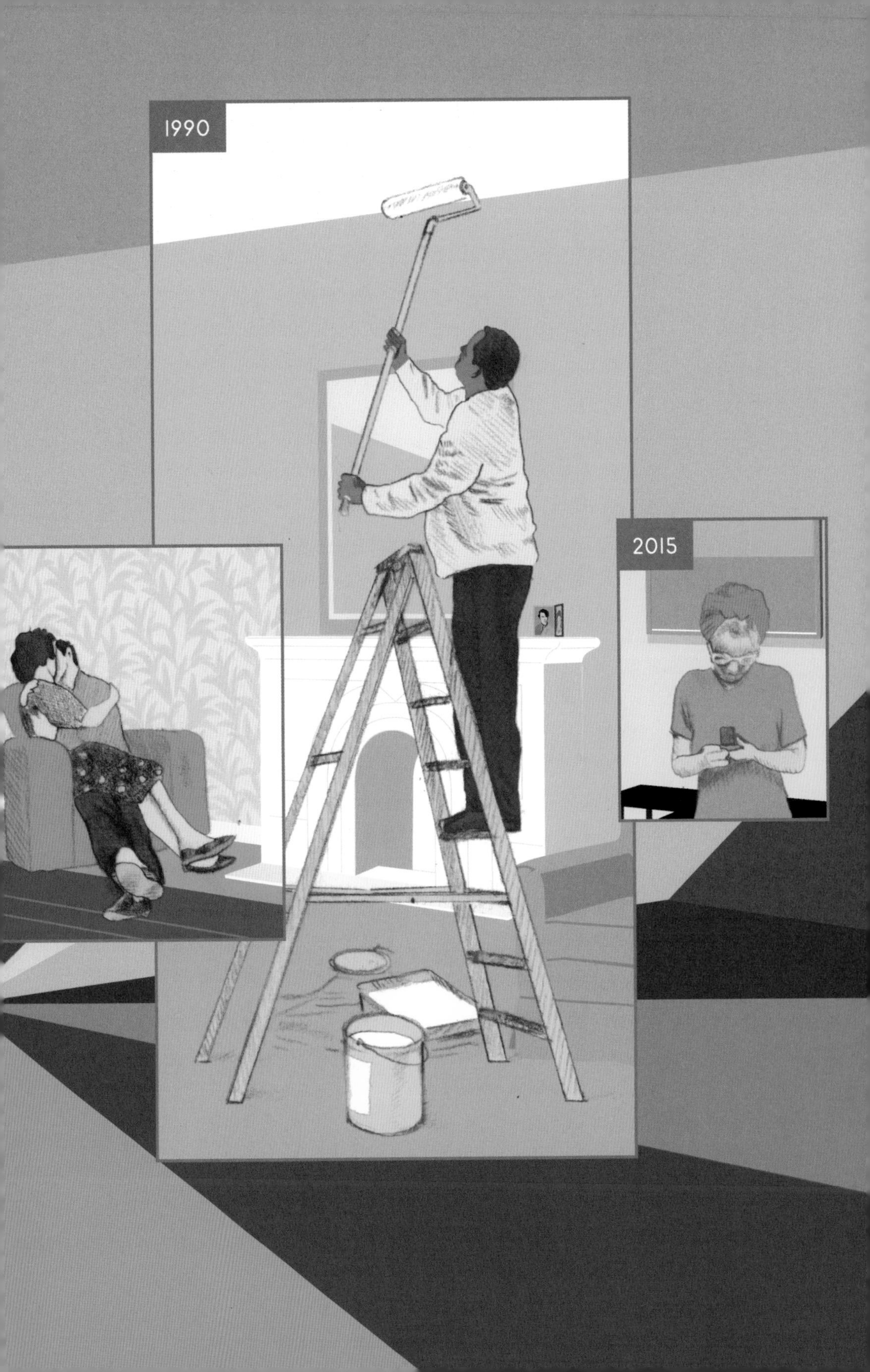
1990
2015

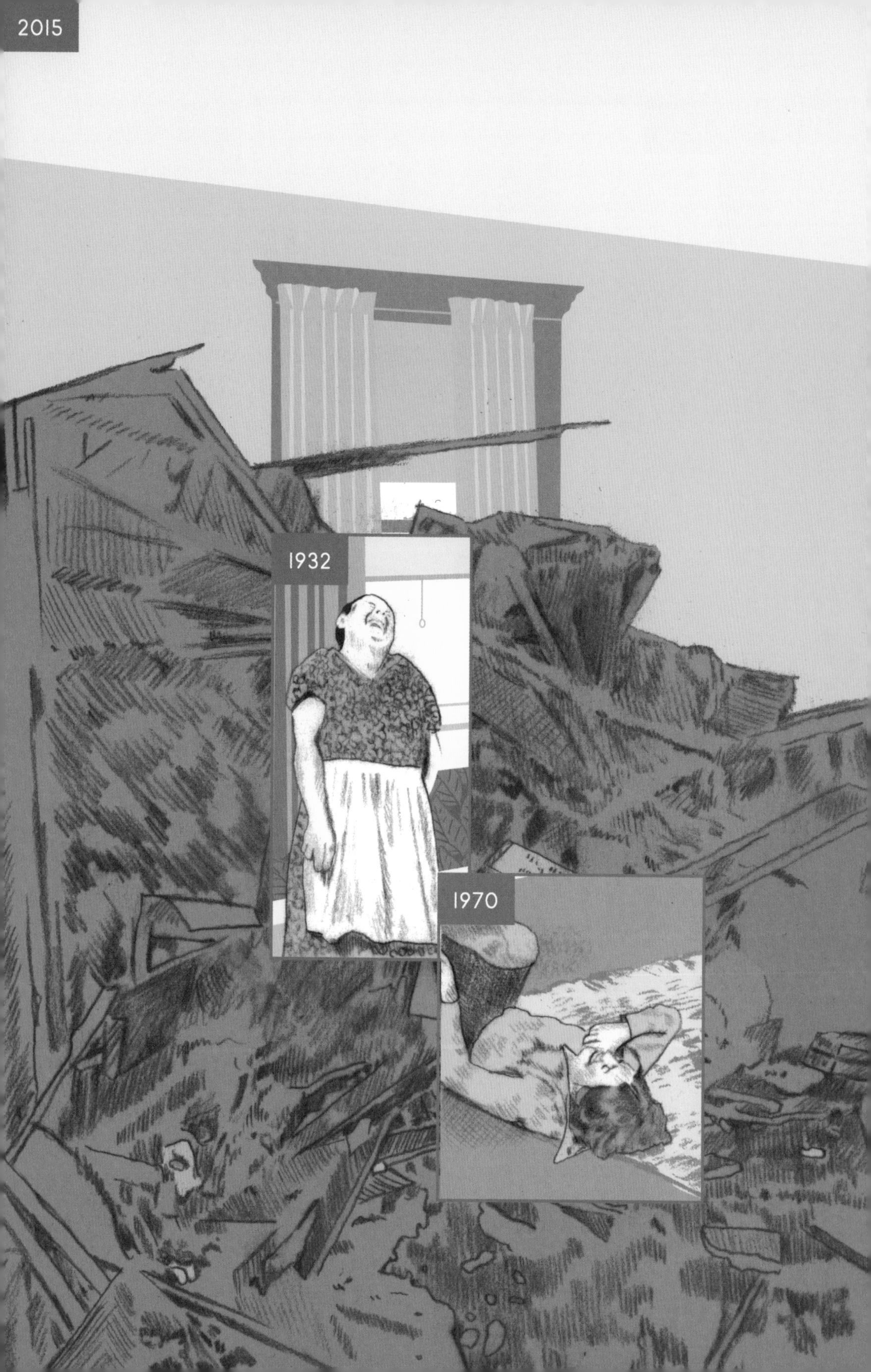
2015
1932
1970

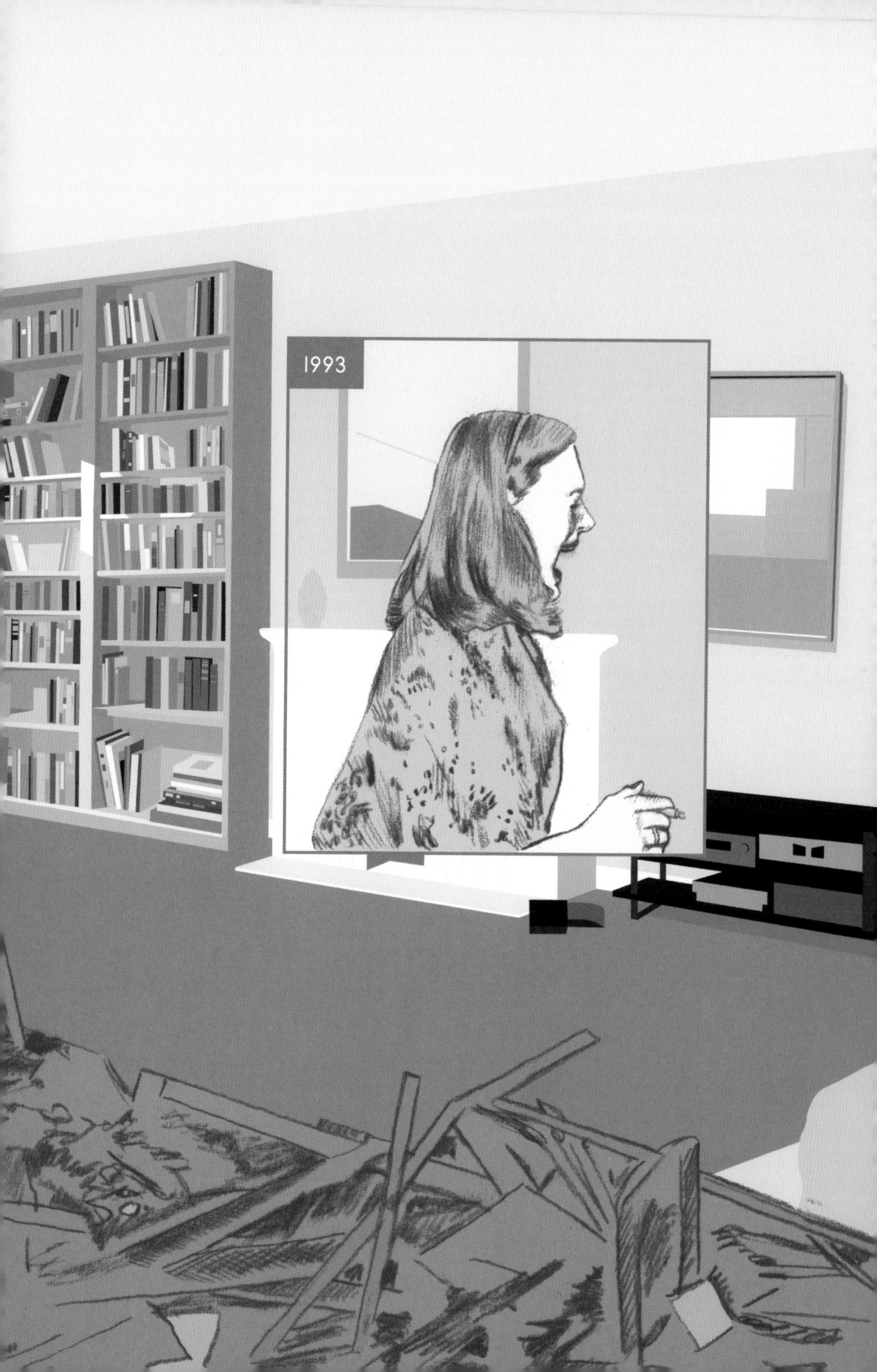
1993

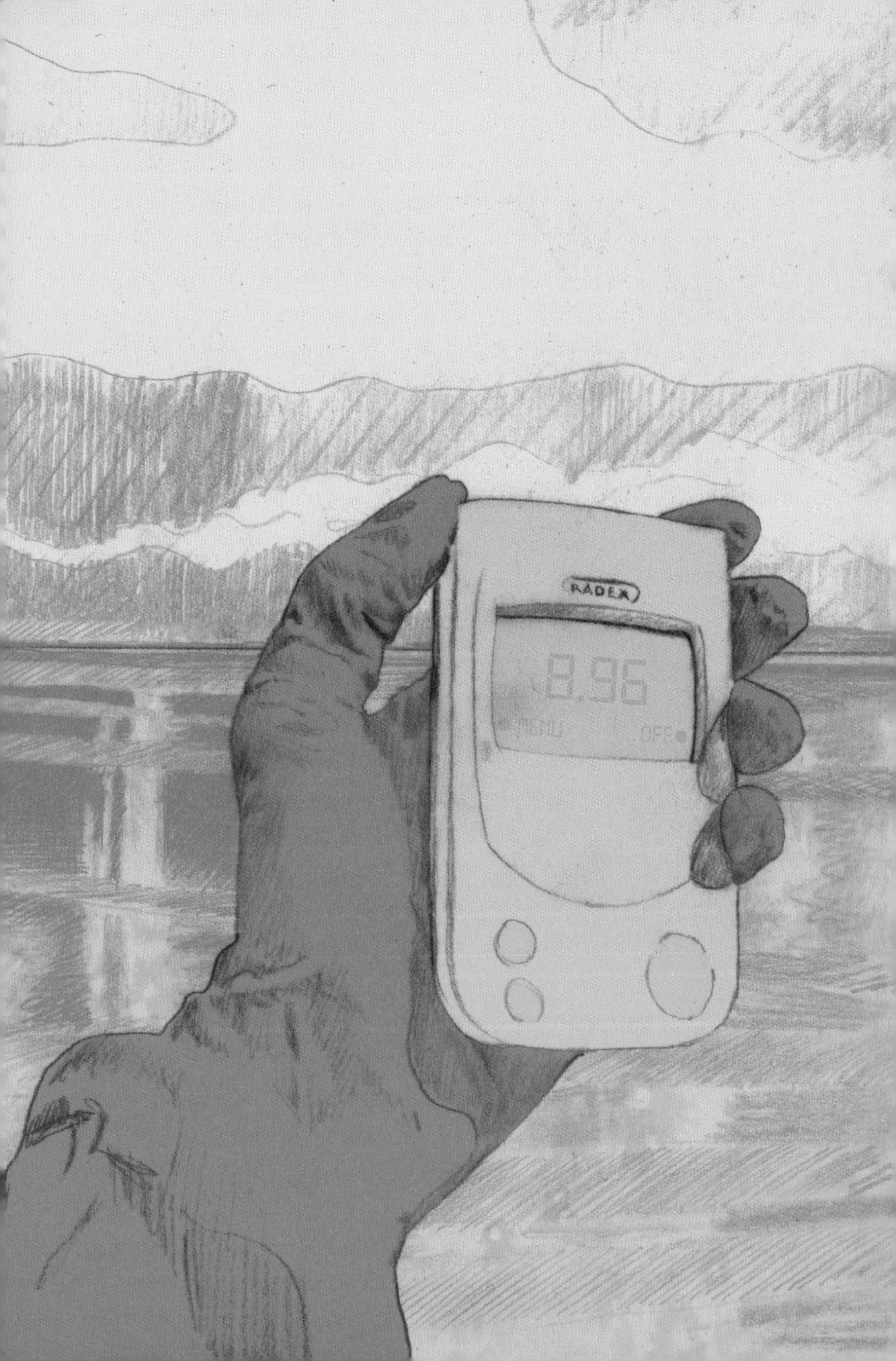
RADEX
8.96
MENU
OFF

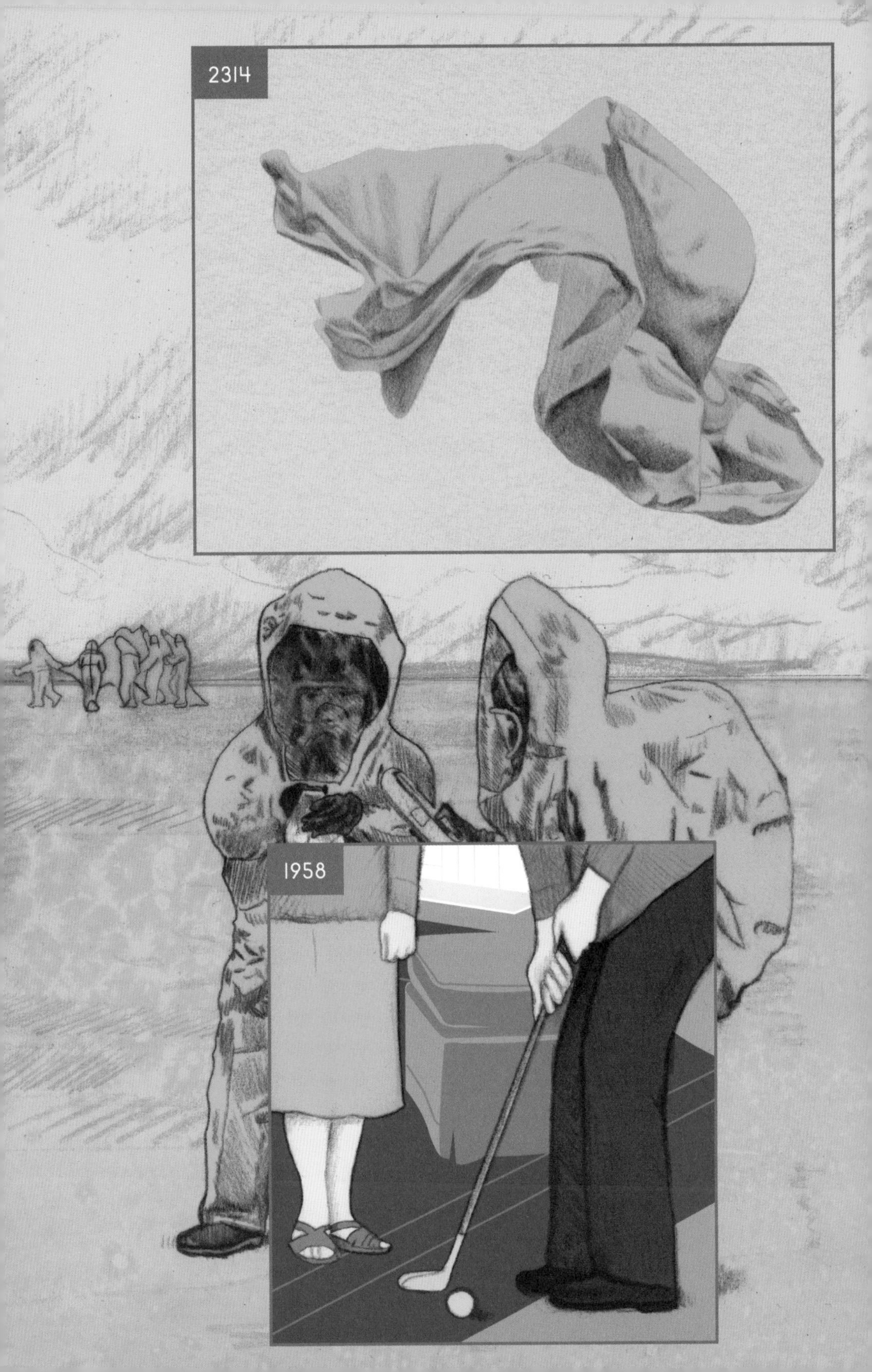

2314
1958

1960
1957
1972
"IT'S STILL THE SAME OLD STORY,
A FIGHT FOR LOVE AND GLORY,"
1870

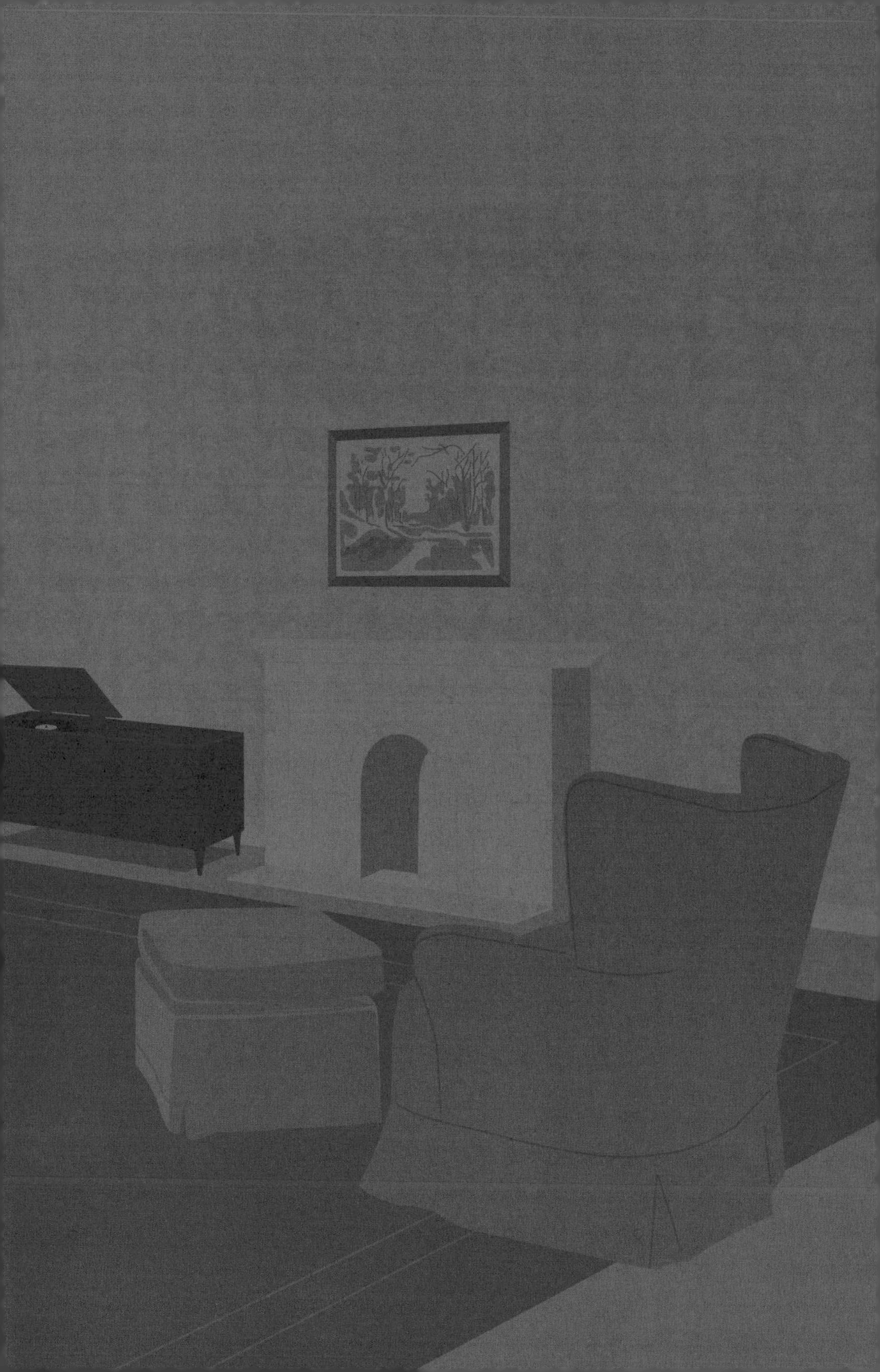

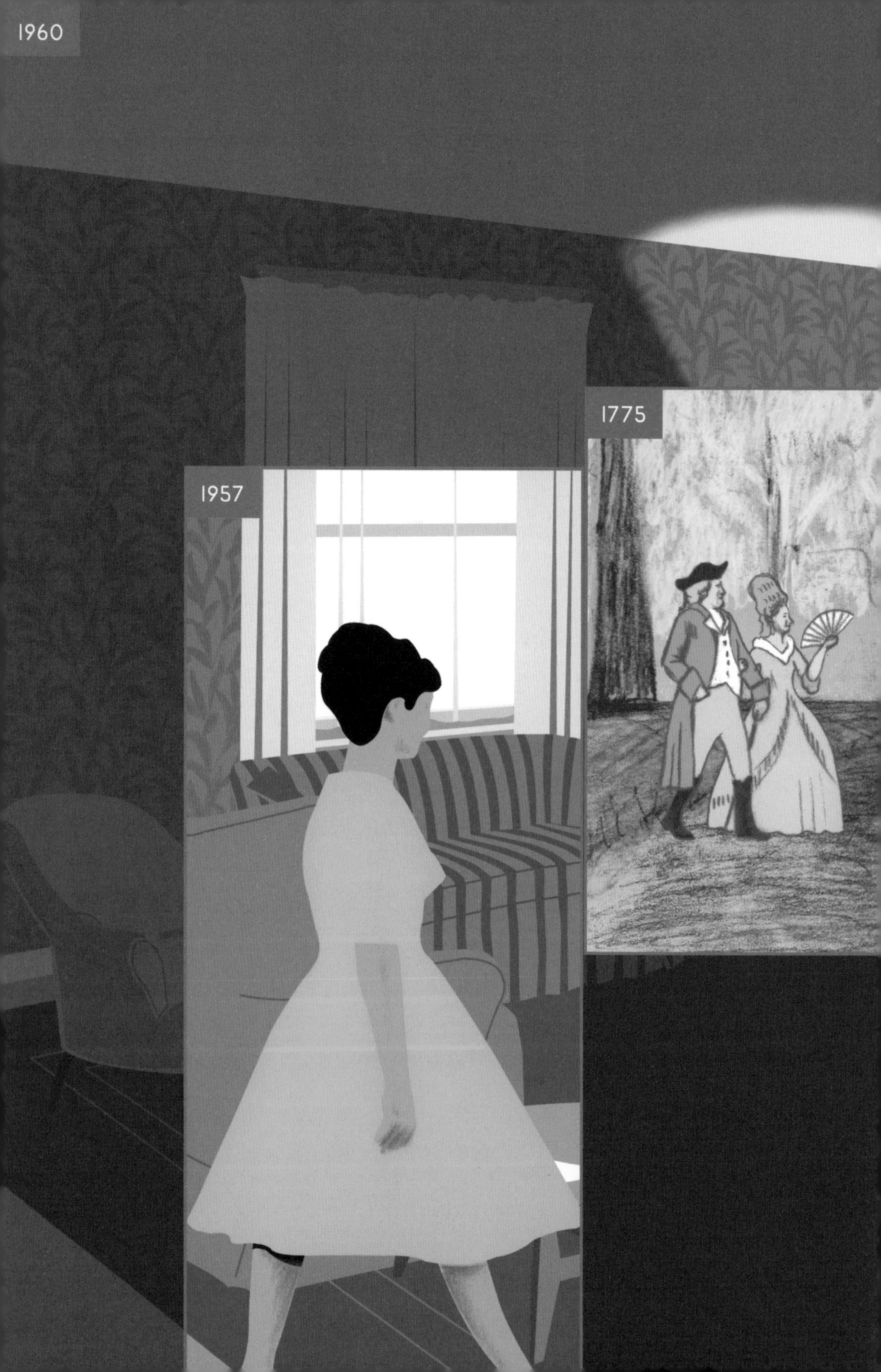
1960
1775
1957

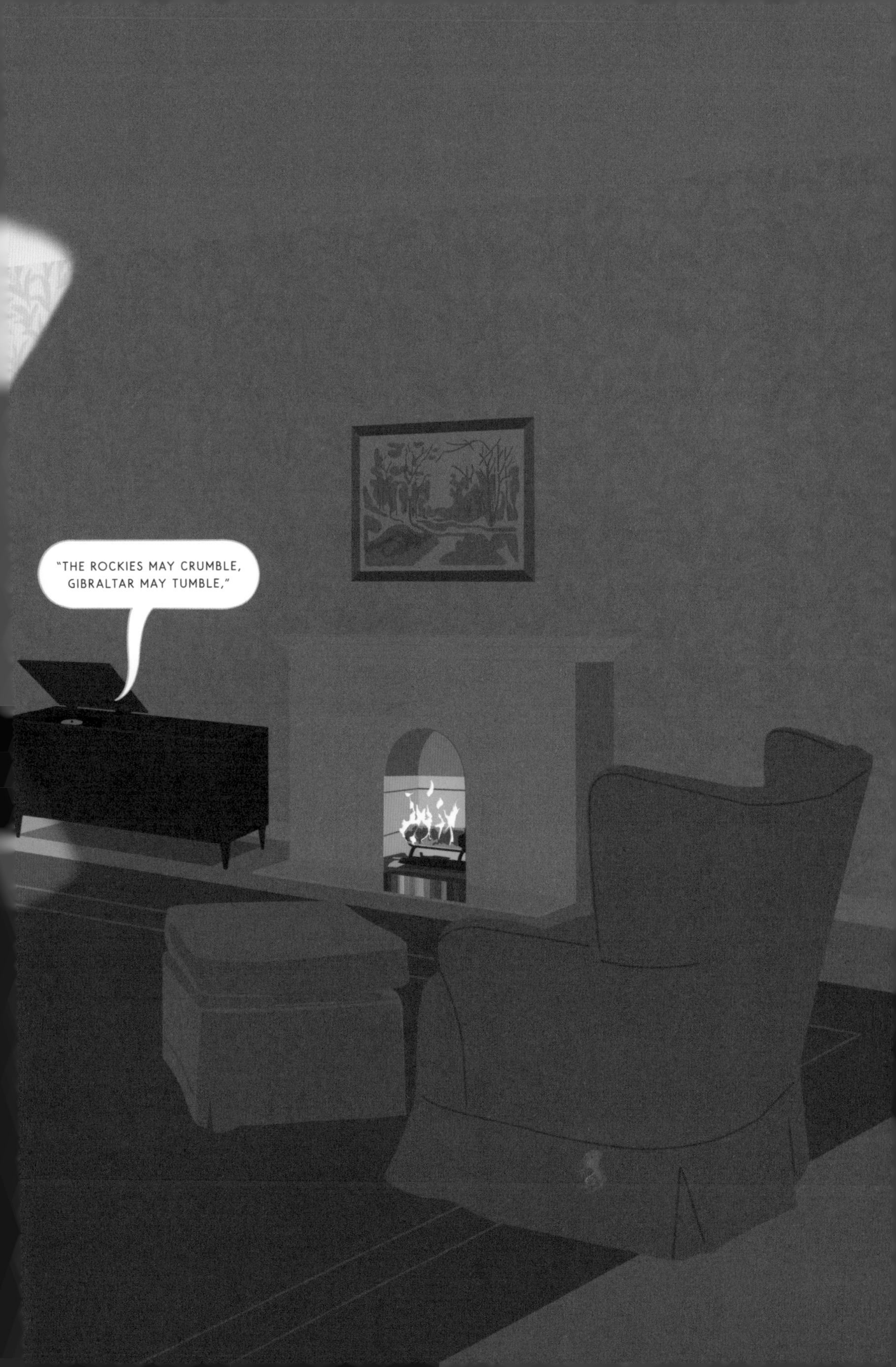
"THE ROCKIES MAY CRUMBLE, GIBRALTAR MAY TUMBLE,"

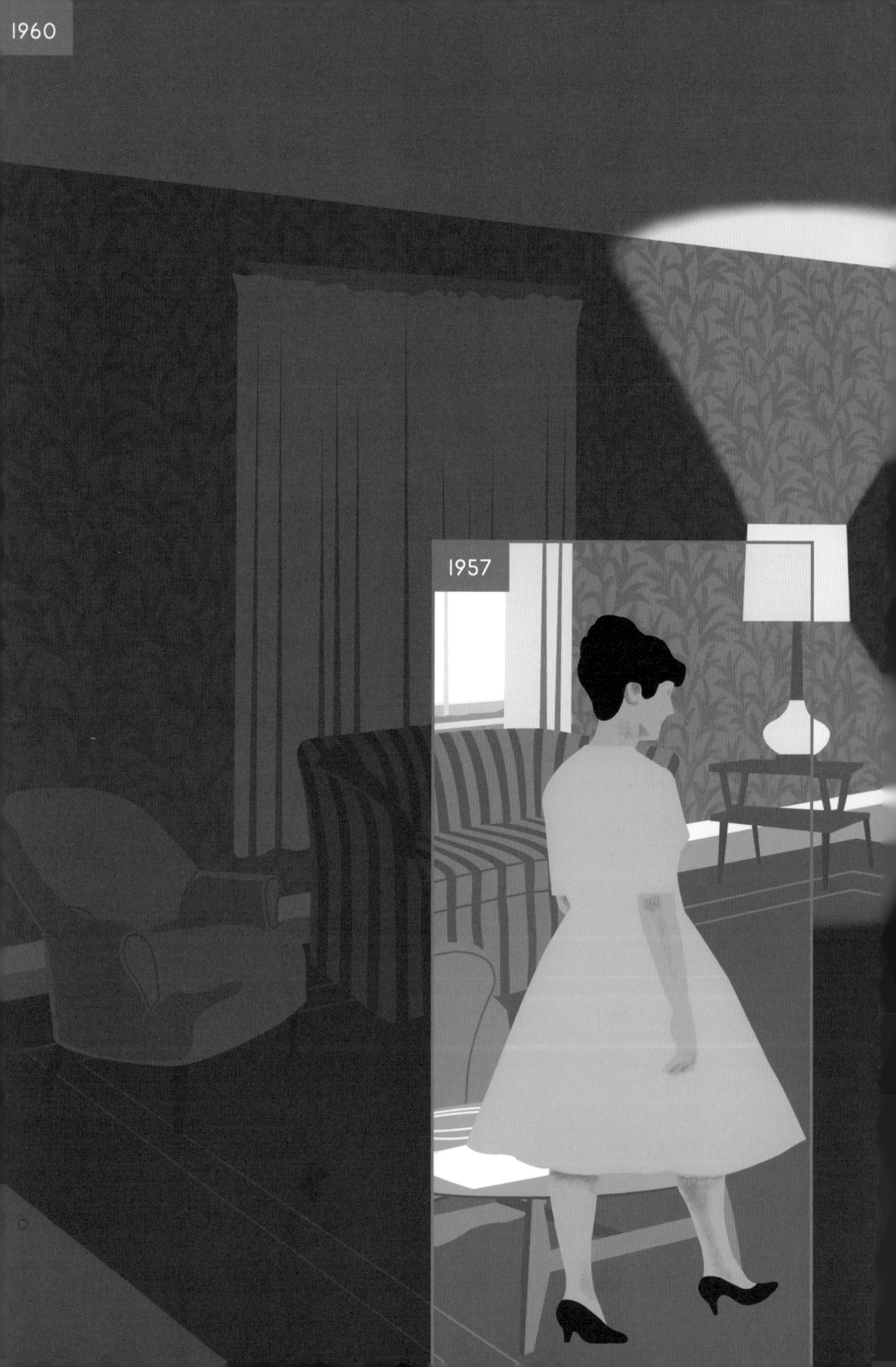
1960
1957

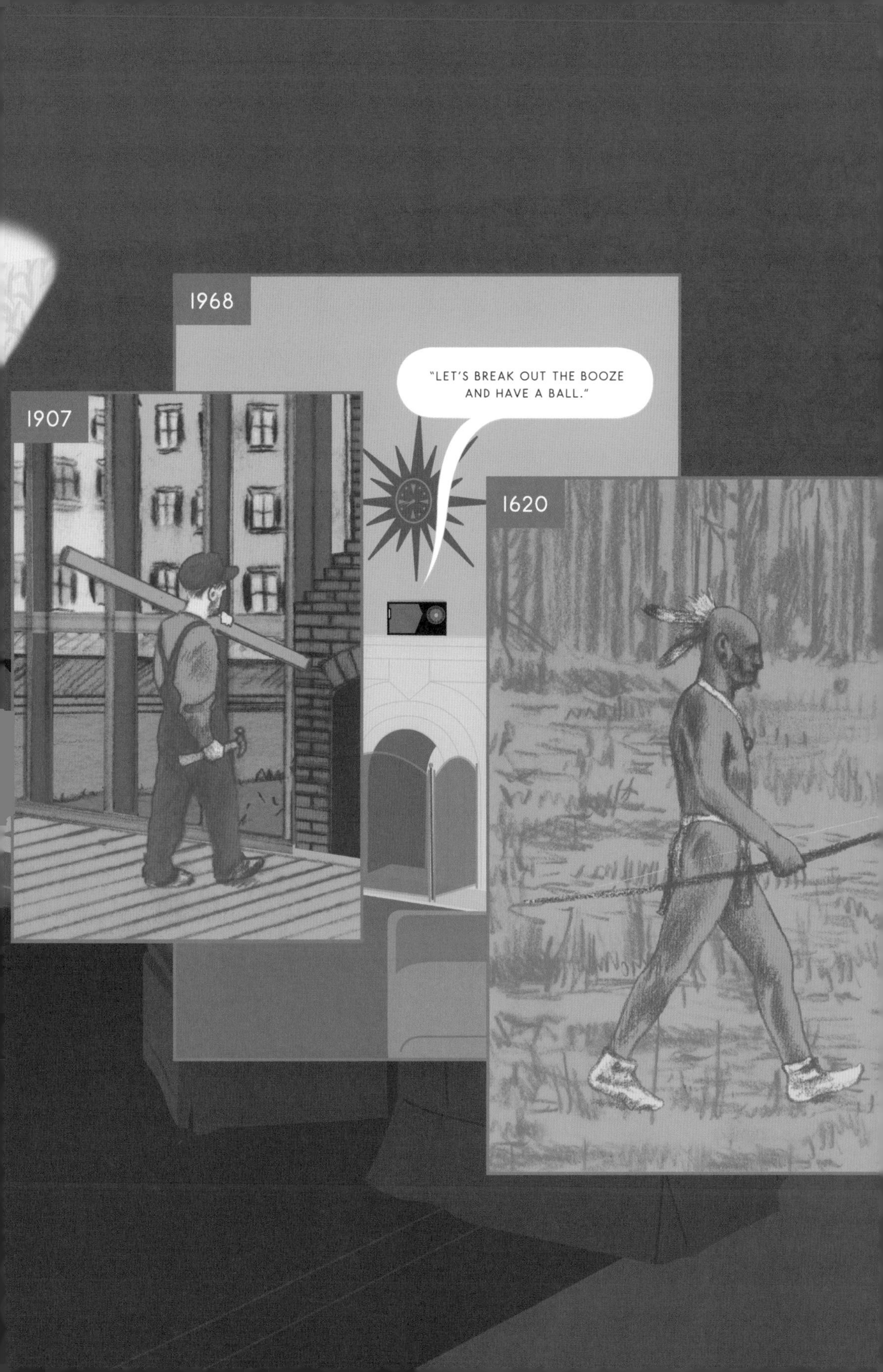
1968
"LET'S BREAK OUT THE BOOZE AND HAVE A BALL."
1907
1620

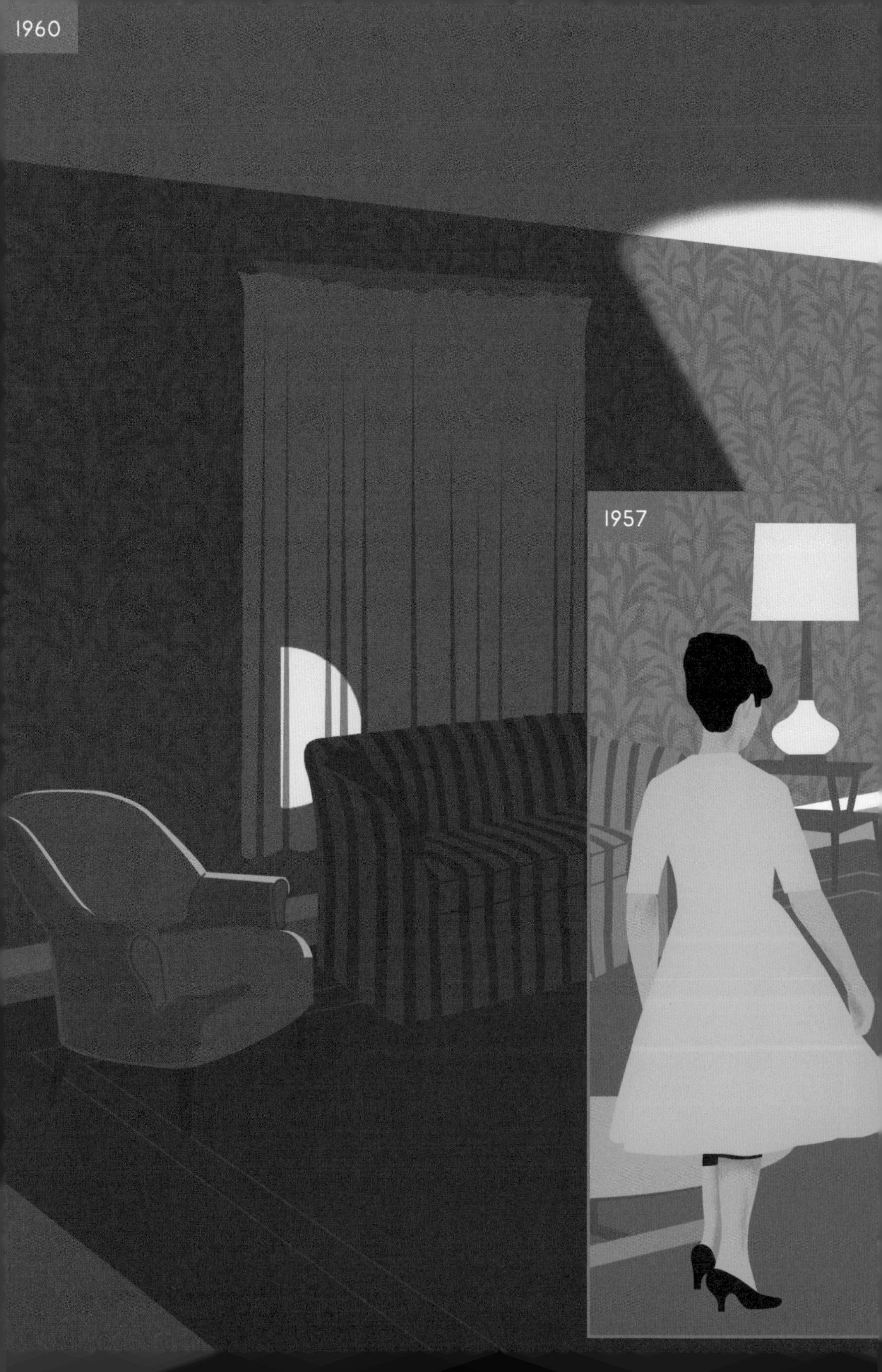
1960
1957

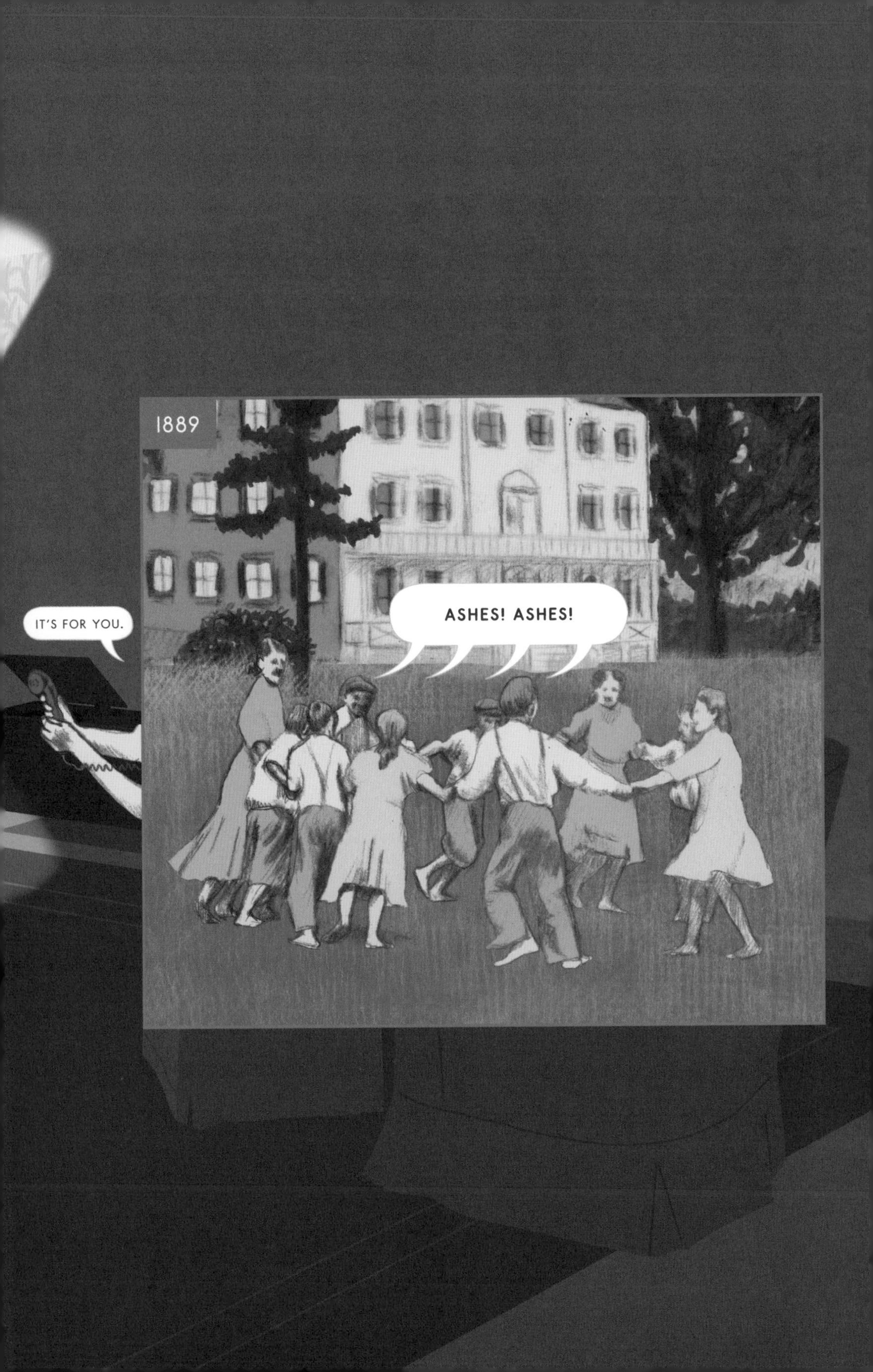

IT'S FOR YOU.
1889
ASHES! ASHES!

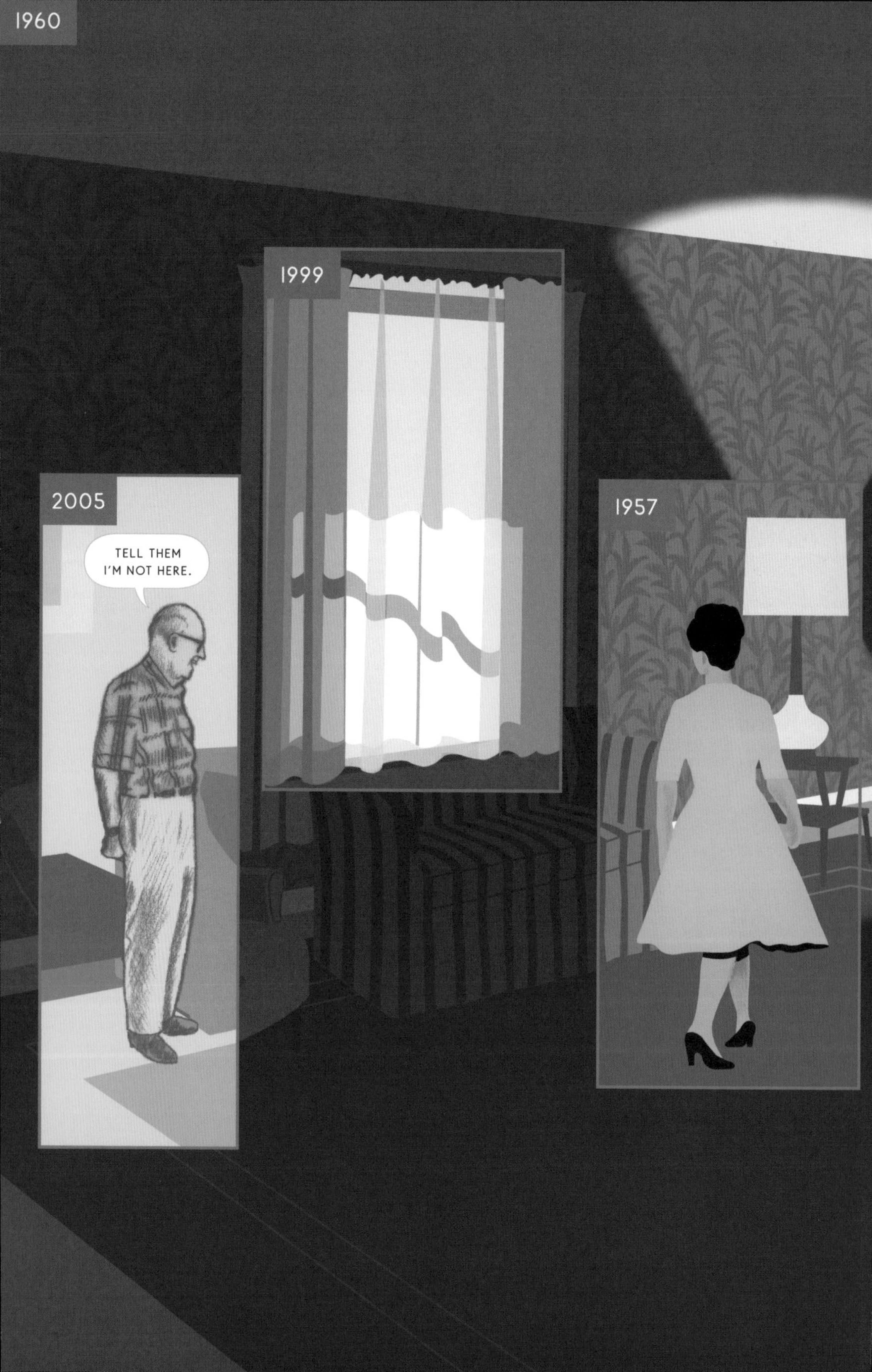
1960
1999
2005
TELL THEM
I'M NOT HERE.
1957

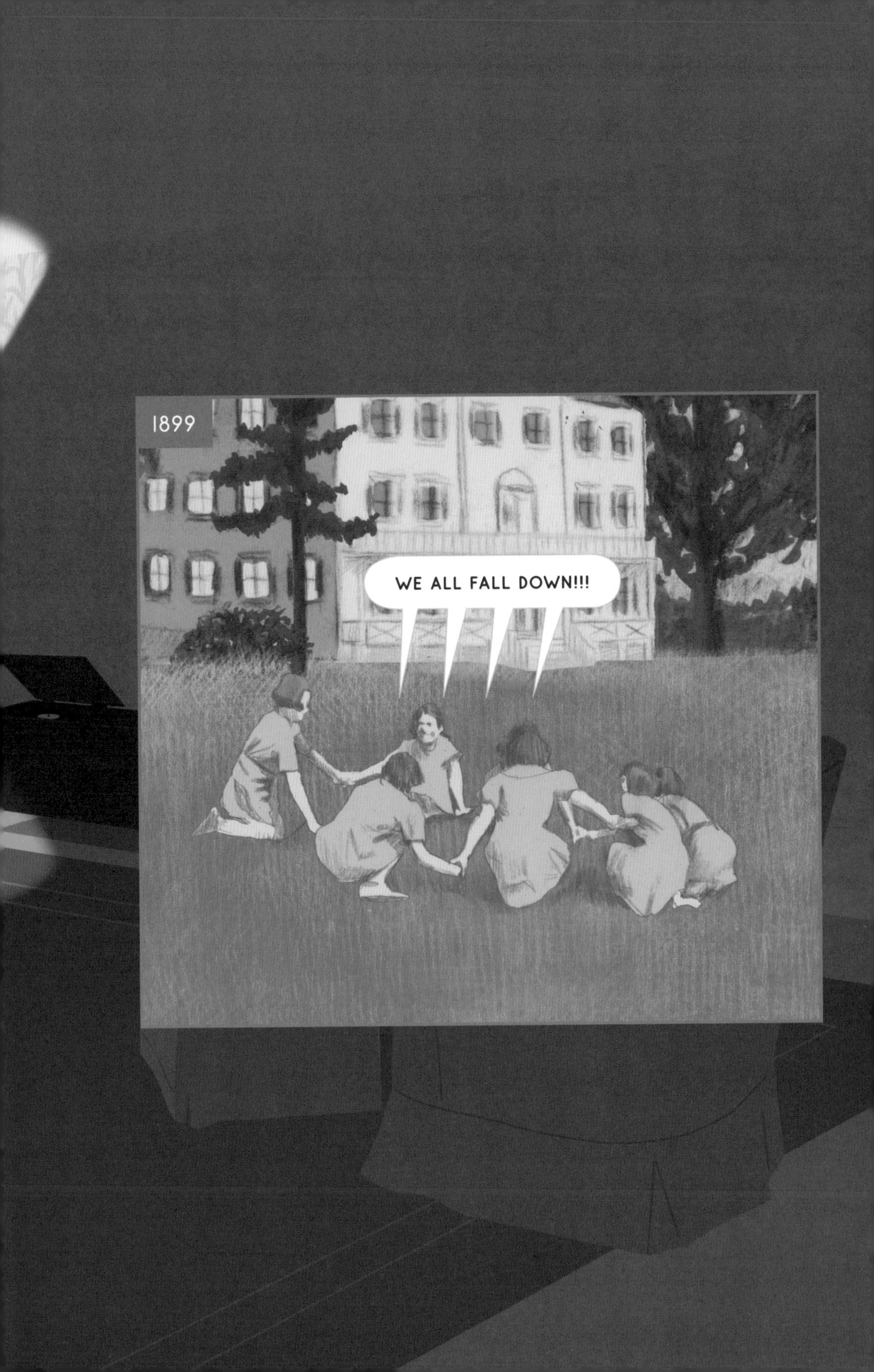
1899
WE ALL FALL DOWN!!!

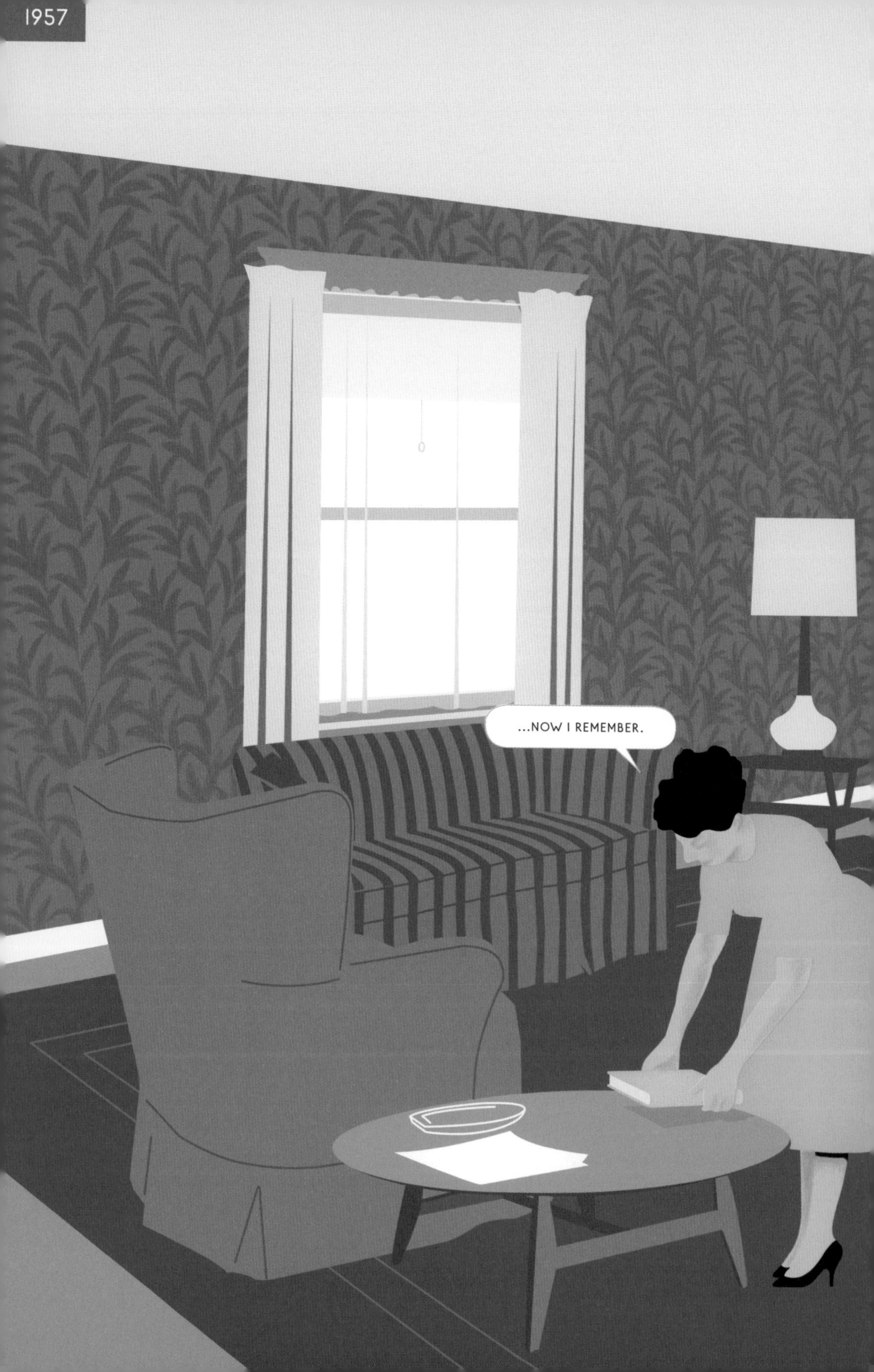
1957
...NOW I REMEMBER.

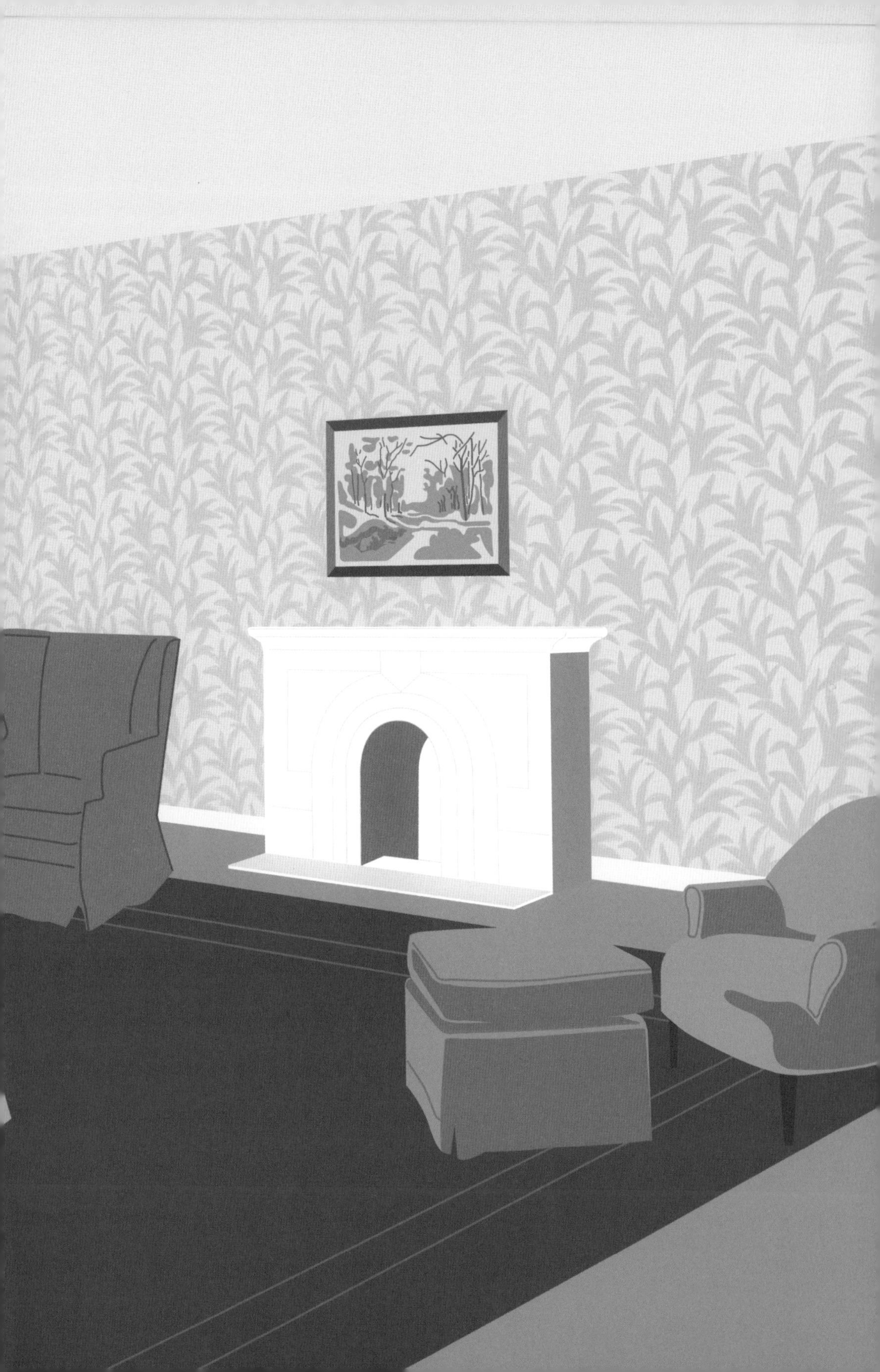

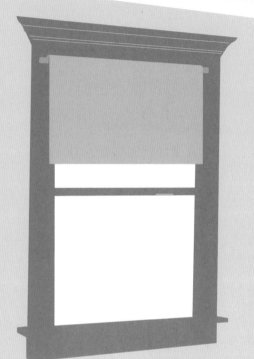

Team HERE:
Min Choi: Production Designer
Maëlle Doliveux: Colorist
Keren Katz: Development Artist / Flatter

Acknowledgements

Many thanks to Leanne Shapton, Joel Smith,
David Sandlin, Gabrielle Bell, Chris Ware,
Françoise Mouly, Art Spiegelman, Jean Strouse,
Marie d'Origny, The Cullman Center, Ben Katchor,
Mark Newgarden, Paul Karisik, Bill Kartalopoulos,
Bob Sikoryak, Ken Calderia, Lauren Redniss,
Bernard Granger, Stephen Betts, Ellen Linder,
Chris Gelles, Simon Prosser, Prithi Gowda,
Peter Mendelsund, Tony Cenicola, Saul Leiter,
Peter Cohen, Patrick Smith, Kjersti Skomsvold,
Sam Alden, Alexander Rothman, Andrea Tsurumi,
Andrew Dubrov, Li-Or Zaltzman, Duncan Tonatiuh,
N.C. Christopher Couch, Altie Karper, Dan Frank,
Andy Hughes, Kathleen Fridella, Chip Kidd,
Andrew Wylie, Rebecca Nagel, Luke Ingram,
to my family, Robert & Eleanor McGuire,
Mary Andresini, Bob McGuire, Bill McGuire,
Sue Wells, The Andresini Family and the Czapiga Family.

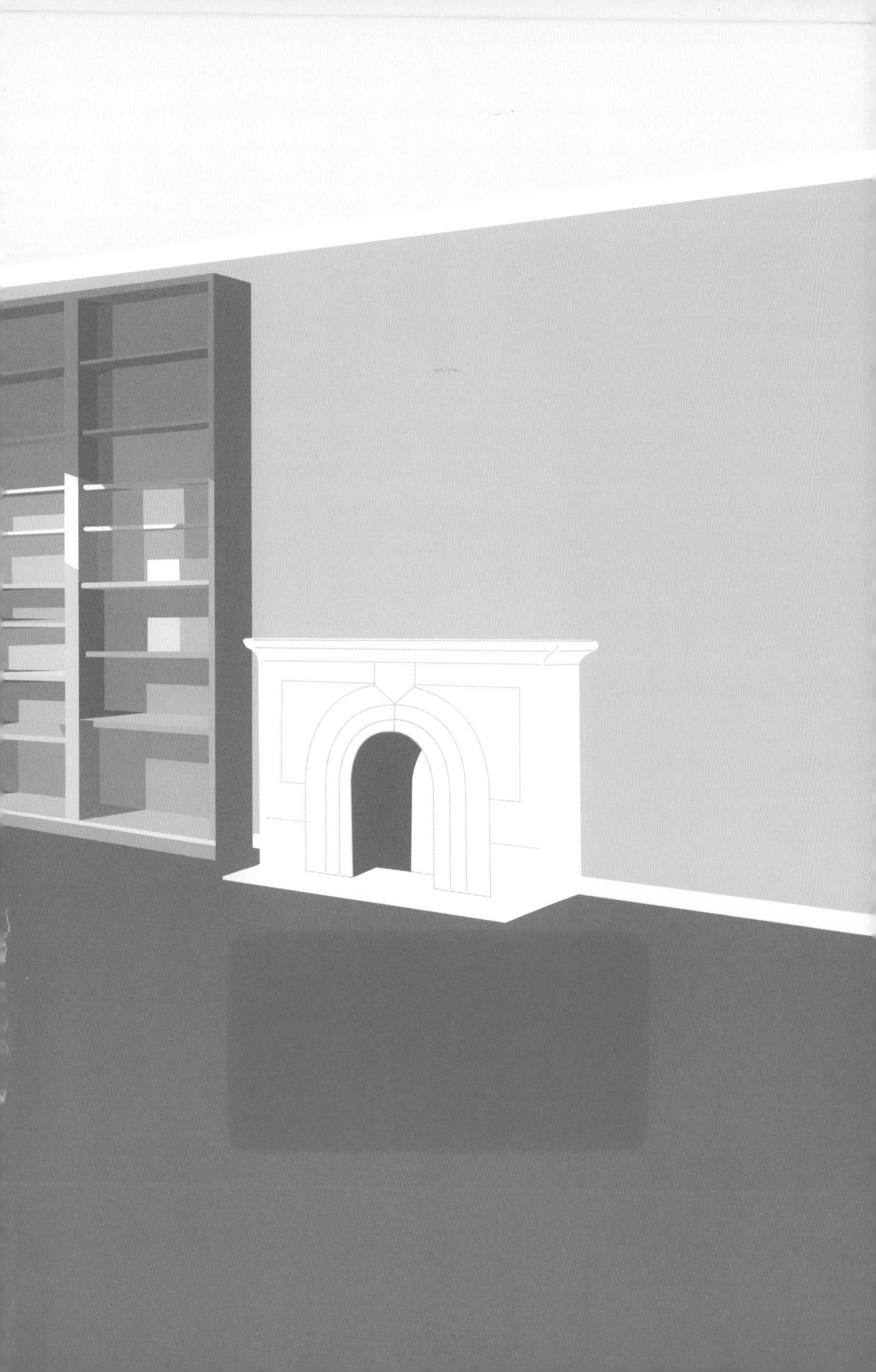

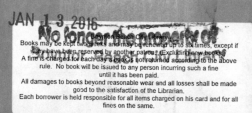